EXPERIMENTAL PSYCHOLOGY
AN INFORMATION
PROCESSING APPROACH

EXPERIMENTAL PSYCHOLOGY
AN INFORMATION
PROCESSING APPROACH

Dominic W. Massaro
University of California, Santa Cruz

Harcourt Brace Jovanovich, Publishers
San Diego   New York   Chicago   Austin   Washington, D.C.
London   Sydney   Tokyo   Toronto

a mia madre
til min kone
to my children

Preface

It is an important time for students of psychological inquiry in that it is no longer possible to insulate oneself from the products of psychological science. Education, communication, the workplace, and leisure time all reflect influences of the psychologist's state of the art understanding of human behavior. The goal of *Experimental Psychology* is to engage the student in this worthwhile enterprise. This endeavor is not an easy one. Of the many questions psychologists pose, seldom do they ask why mental activity is so inherently rewarding. Solving a puzzle is fun, but discovering or uncovering something about how we work is both thrilling and productive. I hope that my enthusiasm for human experimental psychology is contagious. Informed students will necessarily contribute to the advance of our discipline.

The main objective of this book is to integrate the methods of experimental psychology with content. The argument is that methods cannot be learned independently of content. The methods are explained in the context of fundamental questions about human behavior. In addition, the first two chapters in Part One provide a philosophical and historical foundation for our study while the last four chapters 3 through 6 describe and illustrate the methods of inquiry. Chapter 5 explores the nature of the psychological investigator in addition to the methods of investigation.

Part Two covers the major lines of inquiry of experimental psychology since its founding. Psychologists are limited in what they are able to measure. Reaction time, the time taken for mental processing, and psychophysics, the relationship between the environment and behavior, are the fundamental measurements available in experimental psychology. The chapters in Part Two provide the groundwork for the experimental study of perception and cognition. Part Three is a state of the art, but not exhaustive, coverage of the topics defining human information processing and cognitive psychology.

Experimental Psychology does *not* have to be read in a front-to-back order or in an exhaustive fashion. Rather, parts, and even chapters, can be read independently. The book can be adapted to most courses in experimental psychology or cognitive psychology without significantly altering the instructor's syllabus.

The chapter opening outlines should be used as an organizational framework for reading and studying the material. Similarly, the subject and name indices should be used to retrieve material relevant to a given topic. In many cases, the student will be able to find related material in other chapters. For example, there are several uses of factorial designs throughout the book, and relating them to one another should prove a valuable tool in mastering their use in experimental psychology. The suggested readings provide sources for students who wish to explore a topic in greater depth.

Acknowledgments

This book evolved from teaching courses in experimental and cognitive psychology at the University of California, Santa Cruz. Few students, staff, or colleagues have escaped some degree of involvement in this project. I thank them all for their contributions. The feedback I received from my students helped shape the book. Pat Sanders, Melessa Hemler, Carole Degan, Nicoletta Bolas, Sylvia Holmes, and Rosie Biggs typed various chapters over the years. Jan Robinson copyedited several early versions. Jennifer Hearst helped with the references and index. Michael Cohen mastered DITROFF to produce each of the following pages of text and generated many of the illustrations on the computer. My appreciation to Uli Frauenfelder for the elephant graph information; to Laura Thompson for her comments on the development of categorization; to Susan Aiken, who commented on several chapters; to Ray Gibbs, who gave helpful feedback at various stages; to Melanie Mayer and Kristina Hooper, who were valuable colleagues in the development of our introductory course in human experimental psychology; and to Alan Kawamoto, Jennifer Gille, and John Artim, who used various chapters in teaching the course. Special thanks to Marcus Boggs, acquisitions editor at Harcourt Brace Jovanovich, who remained supportive and involved throughout the project.

Dominic W. Massaro

Contents

Preface   v

PART ONE   Methods and Processes of Inquiry
1   Studying Mental Processes   4
2   A Brief History of Theory and Methods   24
3   Four Methods of Psychological Inquiry   44
4   Experimental Method   58
5   The Scientific Process   76
6   Reading and Writing Research Reports   92

PART TWO   Reaction Time and Psychophysics
7   Duration of Mental Processes   128
8   Operations of Mental Processes   140
9   Reaction Times and Performance   156
10   Psychophysical Methods   180
11   Sensory and Decision Processes   196
12   Theory of Signal Detectability   210
13   Scaling Psychological Processes   230

PART THREE   Perception and Cognition
14   Visual Perception   254
15   Testing Theories of Attention   290
16   Recognition and Categorization   312
17   Memory   340
18   Learning and Thinking   370
19   Understanding Speech   398
20   Reading   430

Suggested Readings   454
References   459
Figure Credits   490
Name Index   491
Subject Index   501

EXPERIMENTAL PSYCHOLOGY
AN INFORMATION
PROCESSING APPROACH

Do a little plowing each day; otherwise, you're a goner.

Red Barber on his 80th birthday

Research is what I'm doing when I don't know what I'm doing.

Wernher von Braun

Quite simply, to be taken seriously, it (the theory) must engage the data; it must verify results, it must give coherent explanations, it must be testable, and it must open experimental doors.

Paul Churchland

Whatever trouble life holds for you, that part of your lives you spend finding out about things, things you can tell others about, and that you will learn from them, that part will be essentially a gay, a sunny, a happy life.

J. Robert Oppenheimer

There is something fascinating about science. One gets such wholesale returns of conjecture out of such a trifling investment of fact.

Mark Twain

PART ONE

Methods and Processes of Inquiry

1

Studying Mental Processes

Mind-Body Problem

    Interactionism
    Parallelism
    Materialism
    Epiphenomenalism
    Idealism

Best Choice

    Hypnosis
    Placebo Effects
    Biofeedback Training
    Monism
    Summary

Mental Operations

    Creativity
    Computers

Three Levels of Inquiry

    Arguments against Lower and Upper Levels
    Arguments for a Middle Level

Information Processing

    Properties of Information Processing
    Information-Processing Model
    Information
    Prospective

William James
Consciousness

Psychology is the Science of Mental Life,
both of its phenomena and their conditions.
William James (1890)

Our study of psychology follows in the tradition of William James who, in 1890, defined psychology as the science of mental life. What James meant by a science of mental life was nothing more or less than understanding the psychological processes of perception, imagination, memory, thinking, and decision making. These processes seem to be fundamental to our conscious experience and behavior. For example, one important problem in perception is how the reader derives meaning from a page of text. How is he or she able to imagine the theme of Beethoven's Ninth Symphony? How do you remember what you were doing one year ago today? Think of a four-letter word that ends in *eny.* Should you continue reading or consider some of the thoughts generated by these questions?

James' definition of the content of psychology appears reasonable and provides a fascinating challenge to the experimental psychologist. Before accepting this challenge, however, we need to explore the assumptions that are implicit in James' definition about the nature of a person as the subject of science. The assumptions are first, that mental phenomena exist, and, second, that these phenomena can be subjected to the scrutiny of scientific endeavor. These assumptions have rival assumptions, and although the issue among them cannot be decided with the certainty of science, they can be subjected to rational, critical examination.

MIND-BODY PROBLEM

Early in the history of philosophy the mind was isolated and identified as distinct from the body. Immediately the relationship between mind and body became a central problem of human thought. The ingenuity of generations of philosophers provided various models of a person, all starting from the dualism of mind and body. One of the first great thinkers to reflect on this problem was Plato. He observed that whereas the body follows laws embedded in physical events and circumstances, the mind appears to be free from these events. Building on the mind as the agent of our incorporeal acts—perceiving, thinking, decision making, and so on—and on the vague cultural concept of spirit, Plato conceived the soul. Immortal and incorporeal, the soul in this life is imprisoned by the body. Its escape is death, when it breaks free of the body's limitations and exists as pure thought. Plato's notion that the soul or mind is free from the demands and laws to which the body is subject permeated Western culture. This dualism still determines the framework in which most of us think about ourselves: we tend to dissociate biological and psychological functions.

Plato's formulation—called Platonic dualism—immediately raised a problem that has exercised philosophers ever since: How can these two distinct entities, with their two distinct sets of functions, be related within one entity? The mind-body problem is a metaphysical one. No experimental paradigm can be set up to solve it, and no final answer is possible with currently available techniques. We can only analyze it carefully and review the answers that philosophers arrived at by using the methods of metaphysical speculation.

William James

William James is to experimental psychology what Aristotle is to philosophical inquiry. Just as almost every question in philosophy can be traced to Aristotle, some observation made by James sets the stage for most inquiries in experimental psychology. In his two-volume treatise, *The Principles of Psychology*, finally published in 1890 after about a dozen years in the writing, James surveys the range of psychological processes fundamental to human conduct. Born in New York in 1842, James was a philosopher and psychologist, teaching at Harvard from 1872 to 1907. James had an uncanny ability to integrate physiology, philosophy, and psychology in his eclectic coverage of human functioning.

One reason that James may have been so influential is that he wrote as a novelist. Some of you may be familiar with his brother Henry James who wrote novels as might a psychologist. Almost one hundred years later, the *Principles* continues to make fascinating reading, although a shorter version of the 1890 book, *Psychology: Briefer Course*, is recommended.

Interactionism

About twenty centuries after Plato, Descartes, a Catholic scientist, came up with a famous solution to the problem. As a good scientist, Descartes maintained that the human body, like all physical entities, could be described by mechanical laws. Accordingly, through mechanical laws, we would understand the functioning of the human body as human physical behavior. In this respect, the physical body was no different from other physical objects. As a good Catholic, however, Descartes also maintained that the human soul was not subject to the laws that governed the body. Being spiritual, immortal, and eternal, the soul was free of physical necessity and could not be understood by the laws of science.

Descartes' solution to Plato's problem was to accept that the mind and body must somehow meet, since their operations are in some ways interlinked. For this meeting place Descartes chose the pineal gland; he was drawn to it as the seat of the interaction between mind and body because this gland is not duplicated as are most of the brain structures (one hemisphere of the brain being a mirror image of the other). In the pineal gland, according to Descartes, spiritual fluids interacted with bodily fluids, so that some control of the body by the mind was possible.

Descartes illustrated the mind-body interaction in a diagram shown in Figure 1. Consider a person's reaction to some aspect of the visual world. Light is reflected from an object and imaged on the retinas of the eyes; optic nerves carry the message to the pineal body. The soul apprehends the message and initiates some action; the action is transmitted from the pineal body by way of motor nerves. The pineal body of Descartes antedated more contemporary views of a homunculus, literally translated as a little man and believed to be an agent within each of us responsible for our mental actions. Freud's id, ego, and superego might be thought of as homunculi.

Cartesian interactionism is represented graphically in Figure 2 (upper left), in which we have the human body interacting with the human mind. Cartesian interactionism maintains that a person is made up of two different things: mind and body. Two things ought to be capable of being thought about independently of each other. For example, this book and a table are separate entities, and one should be able to think about them separately. One can, indeed, think about the book without thinking of the table, and about the table independently of the book. But to attempt to do the same with the two entities of interactionism causes some difficulty. When thinking of the body, thoughts of the mind arise. Thoughts of the mind also give rise to those of the body. Our thinking, therefore, poses a problem for Descartes' theory. Our argument is somewhat weakened by Descartes' thinking, however. In establishing a metaphysics based on certainty, Descartes argued for one truth only: Cognito, ergo sum (I think, therefore I am). However, for Descartes, the *I* whose

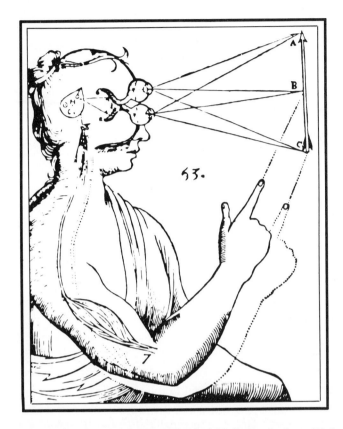

Figure 1. Descartes' diagram illustrating the mind-body interaction. Light reflected from an object (ABC) is imaged on the retinas of the eyes. The image is then conducted by the optic nerves to the brain, where it is apprehended by the soul at the pear-shaped pineal body, which Descartes regarded as the site of interaction of mind and body. Movement is initiated at the pineal and is effected by "animal spirits" which travel down motor nerves to the arm muscle, which the spirits inflate.

existence could not be doubted was spiritual and not material. Such is the discipline of metaphysics. The nature of scholarly inquiry in metaphysics contrasts with experimental inquiry, the topic of this book.

Parallelism

As in most philosophical and psychological endeavors, one viewpoint usually stimulates development of another. Only a few generations after Descartes, a German philosopher, Leibniz, proposed that mind and body are independent. Although there is a natural correlation between the mental and physical worlds, their coincidence reflects only the harmony established by God. Leibniz saw that a correlation between two events does not convey information about causality. A correlation or systematic relationship between two things does not imply that one thing is causing the other (see Chapter 3). Given the correlation between our mental and physical worlds, either could be the causal agent or some third agent such as God could be responsible. For Leibniz, our physical and mental activities are perfectly parallel events, each varying with variation of the other, and both with a common cause. Figure 2 (lower right) provides a graphic representation of the parallelism solution to the mind-body problem.

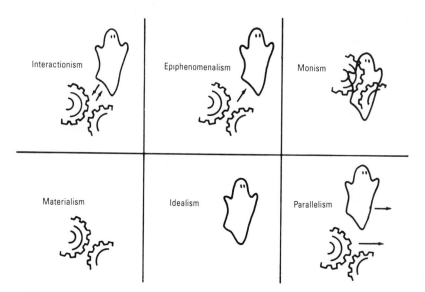

Figure 2. Six solutions to the mind-body problem.

Materialism

For both Descartes and Leibniz, mind and body play equally important roles in our worldly existence. Unhappy with the basic proposition of the separation of these two events, philosophers have evolved alternative theories. One of the most influential of these is materialism, shown in graphic form at the lower left in Figure 2. Materialism simply denies the existence of the mind. If the mind does not exist, then to understand people we need understand only their behavior. A materialist rejects James' definition of psychology as the study of mental life. For the materialist, there is no mental life and no need to study it. The proper subject of psychology is observable behavior; materialism is the metaphysical foundation of behaviorism.

Epiphenomenalism

Another solution to the mind-body problem depicted in Figure 2 is epiphenomenalism, which holds that consciousness—or mental life—is nothing more than the by-product of material life, an epiphenomenon with no consequence of its own. The mind can be compared to the glow around a lightbulb that in no way influences the behavior of the bulb itself. Epiphenomenalism, then, rejects both Descartes' conviction that the mind interacts with the body and the independent parallelism of Leibniz. Instead, the body controls the functions of the mind without being influenced by it. For a complete understanding of our experience, therefore, it is not necessary to study our mental life.

Idealism

Do you deny mind? I'll deny matter. Thus said Bishop Berkeley, some time after the age of Descartes, and in so doing formulated the theory of idealism (lower middle panel of Figure 2). For Berkeley, the body, as matter, does not exist. Therefore, only the mind need be studied; physical events may be ignored. Samuel Johnson put Berkeley's solution to an uncommon test; maintaining that there was a material reality, he kicked a stone, thereby hurting his toe and proving, to his own satisfaction at least, the existence of matter. (In truth, Berkeley wasn't denying the existence of matter. Berkeley was able to restore mind to an independent existence by making it responsible for the existence of matter. To Johnson, Berkeley would have replied, "the stone is real only because you do feel the pain." Berkeley's viewpoint antedated contemporary science, in which the observer and the measuring instrument are important aspects of our knowledge of any phenomena.)

BEST CHOICE

We now have discussed five different theories of the respective roles of mind and body in human life. Today the three most influential theories among scientists are Cartesian interactionism, epiphenomenalism, and materialism. Each of these deserves careful thought, given the consequences of accepting a particular theory. Consider the implications of epiphenomenalism and materialism. If mental phenomena do not influence our behavior or do not even exist, then we need not understand mental life to understand behavior. Upon introspection, however, we find it difficult to believe that our mental life has no influence on bodily processes. Methods of controlling bodily processes by the mind are now widely used and have become an important part of psychological study. We discuss three methods of control which may shed light on the mind-body problem. The phenomena of hypnosis, placebo effects, and biofeedback training are good examples of the important role mental events play in the control of our observable behavior.

Hypnosis

The induction process for hypnosis usually involves some form of relaxation, concentration, and focusing of attention. As an example, the hypnotist asks the subject to stare at a target for an extended period of time. The subject is told to concentrate on certain aspects of the target and to allow the eyes to close when they become strained and tired. A hypnotized person can distinguish the uniqueness of the hypnotic experience. The subject is able to report the degree of hypnotic depth or involvement. In addition to increased suggestibility, hypnotized subjects lack the desire to initiate their own actions. People under hypnosis, however, can be encouraged to perform feats requiring great strength, tolerance of "painful" events, and recall of forgotten events in the distant past. Hypnotic behavior is a good illustration of the important role mental events play in the control of our observable behavior. (There is much to be said for the skeptical point of view about the uniqueness of the hypnotic state. In many instances, people can be encouraged to perform impressive feats without being hypnotized. For example, a person can be a "human plank" by supporting the rigid body with head on one chair and ankles on another (Barber, 1972). These feats usually require much mental encouragement and only strengthen the argument of mind over matter.)

Placebo Effects

People can also influence "involuntary" physiological functions. If a patient is told that the application of an ineffective treatment (a placebo) is effective, this is sometimes sufficient for a cure. In one instance, warts were cured by the application of colored water when the patient was told that it was an effective medicine. More recently, it has been shown that cures by placebos sometimes produce the same physiological changes as those produced by a physiologically effective medicine.

Biofeedback Training

By employing electronic devices, psychologists are able to record several physiological responses, such as heart rate, brain waves, and galvanic skin potentials of human subjects. Electrodes can be attached to a subject's head so that the electrical changes in brain activity can be monitored. The electrodes pick up these brain waves, take their electrical potential, and put it through an amplifier (analogous to the amplifier of your record player). The amplified signal is then fed into an oscilloscope which, in essence, renders a graphical analysis of the electrical changes in the subject's brain. With an oscilloscope, time is represented along the horizontal axis, and the intensity of the electrical current along the vertical axis. Figure 3 presents an oscilloscopic display of two prominent brain waves: the alpha wave and alpha blocking.

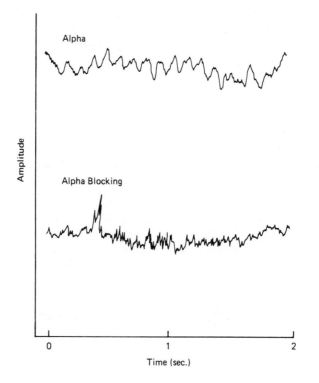

Figure 3. The alpha wave shown at the top oscillates regularly at about 9 cycles per sec. The wave produced by alpha blocking shown at the bottom oscillates at a much higher frequency in a highly irregular fashion.

A subject with attached electrodes can be seated at the oscilloscope so that she can observe her own brain waves. This touches on the question of whether a mind can look upon itself. Experimental studies indicate that subjects *can* control the nature of their brain waves. Indeed, as you may already know, yoga has provided a system of mental exercises allowing the yogi to control his body with his mind. By thinking the right thoughts, the yogi can change his heart rate and the wave shape of his brain activity. This has great implications for our metaphysical problem, implications that are fortified by data gathered from subjects controlling their brain waves in the laboratory.

Different types of brain waves can be distinguished by the intensity (the height of the wave) and the number of repetitions of the wave per second. The alpha wave is regular, has a high intensity, and usually cycles between eight and fourteen times per second. A second wave, alpha blocking, is more irregular, has a smaller intensity, and repeats at a much higher frequency than the alpha wave. With a little training, a subject finds that these two brain waves can be produced at will. Alpha blocking is produced by attending to an interesting scene, or by forming a visual image if the eyes are closed, or merely by attending to the changes in the brain waves that are appearing on the oscilloscope. The alpha wave state is a meditation state; to produce it, one maintains a relaxed alertness, thinking about nothing at all, or alternatively, one concentrates on something mundane, like a regular bodily process. A subject concentrating on the steady beating of heart rate to the exclusion of everything else produces alpha waves.

What do the phenomena of hypnosis, placebo effects and biofeedback training imply for theories of the relationship between mind and body? The mental states of the hypnotized subject and the placebo-cured patient are capable of affecting certain bodily processes. Consider an understanding of the student in biofeedback training: The direct and immediate influence of mental processing on bodily functions exposes the weakness of the important assumption in the parallelism solution proposed by Leibniz. The brain pattern constitutes a physical behavior of man; the epiphenomenalist, or behaviorist, should be able to predict it. On the contrary, however, it is the subject alone who can predict which wave shape will come next. The student controls the phenomenon, and may choose, from the point of view of the behaviorist, quite arbitrarily. This creates difficulties for both materialism and epiphenomenalism. Mental processes, say epiphenomenalists, play no part in controlling the body. But here we have an experimental situation in which a mental event does control a behavioral event. Materialists tell us that mental events do not exist. But here they are, controlling the body. In this experiment we can, and must, grasp the real existence of something we call mental processing.

So the mind exists and influences the body. That the body affects the mind is also known. Recalling one's last trip to the dentist should remove any doubt of that; pain hurts. Hurt is a perception, a phenomenon of mind. We seem to have been led back to interactionism, to the theory, originally espoused by Descartes, that mind affects body and body affects mind. Unfortunately the problems in this theory remain. *How* do body and mind interact? If a spiritual entity can affect a physical one and vice versa, this seems to imply that anything can cause anything. Here are two things, mind and body, which can neither be related to one another satisfactorily, nor thought of separately.

At this point it is necessary to retrospect and ask why mind and body have been postulated as separate and distinct in the first place. The philosophers from whom we inherit this distinction were unable to conceive that a physical entity could be conscious, that is, lead a mental life. They experienced consciousness as altogether other than a corporeal function. Consciousness, they believed, was free of all but its own dictates, whereas the body was subject to the accidents of time and place, the random influence of exterior events, the laws of nature, and death. It was not logical that thought, an incorporeal function, could be caused by, produced by, and dependent on a mortal body. Plato had the only possible solution. There must be a second entity, a spiritual being, to do the thinking.

Attributing mental processing to an incorporeal entity does not, however, resolve the problem. The operations of consciousness are not in any sense easier to understand if they are assumed to be independent of the body. Conversely, in the age of computers and other nonhuman information-processing systems, it is much easier to accept the fact that physical things have memories, perform intelligent actions, and make difficult decisions. Computers, to whose absolute corporeality humans can attest since they made them, do perform incorporeal operations with incorporeal results. We ourselves have designed their operations and can usually understand the rules by which they occur. Many of the internal operations of computers seem to be analogous to the mental operations of man. So it is simply not unreasonable or illogical that some physical things are conscious and can lead a mental life. Nor is it inconceivable any longer that certain physical organisms can perceive, imagine, and remember. Our task is to describe how these physical entities—ourselves—perform these internal operations.

Monism

These observations lead us to a distinctly different alternative solution to the mind-body problem, which is called monism (upper right panel of Figure 2). The term monism is used to describe this solution because the mind and body are not considered to be separate entities whose interaction must be explained. Rather, it is assumed that human beings are highly complex organisms with several complex attributes such as a complex brain and nervous system. One property of this complex being is that it leads a mental life. To understand it, we must understand these mental processes. This solution is also referred to as "embodying" because the physical being embodies or contains mental processes.

One critical attribute or dimension of this physical entity is consciousness. Throughout history, consciousness has been attributed to a nonphysical entity, the mind or soul. However, it is more logical to conceptualize consciousness as a dimension of human beings in the same way that the thumb and forefinger arrangement represents one of their characteristics. Mental life is the distinguishing feature of the subject of psychological study. When we say that the contribution of the mind is critical to understanding, we are not positing another entity; we are referring to a dimension or attribute. In studying the processes that William James laid down in 1890, we shall be studying neither mind nor body alone, but the internal mental operations of the whole person.

Summary

We have defined psychology as the science of mental life. To build our metaphysical foundation, it was necessary to determine how our mental life related to our behavioral life: how the mind related to the body. Popular solutions to the mind-body problem were discussed. Materialism and epiphenomenalism were rejected because mental events or processes exist, and these affect our behavioral life. We were left with the monistic solution, which posits that the physical nature of a person possesses the attributes that allow him to lead a mental life. Monism has its roots in both parallelism and interactionism, without assuming the separable worlds of the spiritual and the physical. Mental and physical functioning are attributes of a single entity; they differ significantly enough, so it is reasonable to differentiate them. They also share properties, primarily as a result of being functions of the same entity. The competitive athlete profits from both mental alertness and good physical shape. Does a golfer sink a 50-foot putt for the winning shot on the eighteenth hole because of the complex mental processing involved or because of the physiological control of the putter? The golfer will attest to the critical role played by both mental and physical control.

Mental processes are tied to physical systems but cannot be reduced to physical processes. We are organized with a conscious awareness that is integrated with the different sense modalities. Visual perception is an example. Input for vision comes by way of our eyes; but they are not sufficient for perceiving. We actively construct and synthesize our view of the world. As an example, we make several false alarms or misidentifications looking for a friend in a crowd. How our expectations interact with the sensory impressions to produce some recognition is what is referred to as a mental process. Another mental process exists when, with no visual input, we can reconstruct what we saw earlier and form a mental image of the scene. Mental events exist and must be studied to understand human behavior. Accordingly, the subject of psychology as seen here is the study of mental processes.

MENTAL OPERATIONS

Earlier researchers assumed that mental processes could be ignored because the stimulus alone would be enough to predict the response. This expectation has not turned out to be the case. For instance, it would have been nice to predict the simple detection response (in which the subject reports whether or not a stimulus was presented), based on the intensity of the stimulus. Indeed, it was long assumed that there existed a threshold of intensity above which the subject would detect a stimulus and below which he would not. On investigation, what actually happens is that, although subjects grow increasingly more likely to detect (experience) a stimulus as its intensity is increased, their response on any given trial is also a function of a decision or a response rule. The response rule governs how often the subject will say "yes" or "no" to a given experience and is influenced by the attitudes and motivations of the subject. For example, some subjects might want to give the "right" answer and others might want to outsmart the experimenter. Subjects, therefore, may claim to hear a sound that is well below any possible threshold; later they may ignore one that is surely above it. In these experiments the subject has acted on the information derived from the stimulus before the response is produced. The subject does not constitute a passive reactor but is an agent that influences the response. The response cannot be understood without understanding how the subject acts on the information made available by the stimulus.

Some might object that no reliable method exists for studying the mental processes of the subject. This is no longer true. The information-processing approach described later in this chapter provides us with a framework which has proved extremely fruitful in generating experimental designs for studying the sequence of operations between stimulus and response. Each mental process is considered as an operation on the information made available to it by an earlier operation or by the stimulus itself. What this means can be illustrated by an analysis of the creative process in human invention and discovery and also by the sequence of operations performed by a general purpose computer.

Creativity

The creative process is a large, ill-defined process at present and as such has not been adequately studied by experimental methods, but the data received from introspection can be analyzed in the framework of information processing. Most creative people report that they go through a series of operations or stages of processing from the inception of a project until its publication. The first of these is a preparation stage in which the problem takes shape as such, and relevant information in the person's storehouse of knowledge is called up and sensitized and made available for the solution. This information is now available for the next stage of the creative process, in which the individual stops consciously processing the information. We know nothing about this incubation stage, which is widely reported by creative people, except that the processing taking place here is accomplished at a subconscious level, and that when the problem emerges again into the creative person's consciousness, it has been transformed into a new conceptualization.

Under the new conceptualization the creative person might experience an insightful stage of processing. Campbell (1960) has suggested that this stage is analogous to Darwinian evolution.

Darwin solved the problem of adaptation by assuming a blind mechanism of mutation along with the reproductive advantage of good mutations. In an analogous fashion, problem solutions are generated by an unconscious process of randomly combining ideas in memory. The solutions best fitting the problem draw attention and become conscious. He or she may now see the theoretical revision that will permit a solution, or the link between this conception and other problems in the area, or the key piece of knowledge that will furnish a solution. Finally, the creative person must go through the final editing, or mopping-up, stage in which the insight must be validated. The implications of the solution must be worked out to verify its consistency. The creative person may refine it by mapping it into mathematical or logical terms, which are a further check on its validity. Whatever the tests, if the solution passes them it is now ready to be made public.

Computers

In each of the stages of creativity a certain amount of information is made available. The operation of a particular stage transforms the information and passes it into the next stage of processing. A computer's operations on a computer program follow the same pattern. Figure 4 illustrates the series of operations between the input of the program and the output of its solution. The series is initiated by an input; the first stage transforms the input into a language comprehensible to the computer. After this peripheral encoding, the central processor of the computer routes the information into the memory bank, where it remains available as needed for execution of the program. The central processor executes the program and produces an output which must pass through the peripheral decoding device before it can be communicated to the outside world.

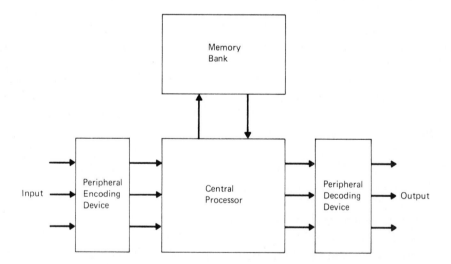

Figure 4. Computer behavior. A graphic representation of the sequence of component operations between the input of a program and the output of its solution.

A computer is usually equipped with devices to read magnetic disks or tape; information meant for ears and eyes is meaningless to it. (However, there are some computer devices and toys, even within the budget of the parents, which can recognize a limited vocabulary of human speech). Given the input, the central processor moves the information to memory, which is made up of a set of locations. Each location in memory has an address, and the information stored there is its content. Now the central processor can refer to the contents by their addresses only. The central processor can then begin to execute the program. The execution of the program involves performing the sequence of operations listed in the instructions of the program. The outcome of the program is the solution or information wanted by the computer user. To communicate the solution, the central processor must translate it into a form that is intelligible to the computer user.

In the experimental laboratory, we usually begin with some observable environmental event and end with some observable response by the subject. The goal of this book is to present methods of experimental psychology that will enable the experimenter to understand the sequence of operations (mental processes) that occur between stimulus and response. We have noted that to understand the creative process it is necessary to understand the sequence of events that occurred between the inception of the problem and its solution. Analogously, to understand a computer's behavior it is necessary to understand the internal set of operations and transformations of information between input and output. The study of people is fundamentally no different. To understand ourselves we must determine and understand the sequence of mental processes that occurs during the events of interest.

THREE LEVELS OF INQUIRY

There is considerable basis for assuming three different levels of explanation in psychological inquiry (Bieri, 1985). Although the three levels are represented discretely in Figure 5, the boundaries among the three different levels should be viewed as fuzzy rather than categorical. The three levels span the continuum from the molecular to the global levels of reductionism. At the most reductionist level, the properties of physics and neurophysiology are used to explain behavior. This level of analysis is most compatible with the scientist's concept of explanation. At the most molar level of explanation, behavior is rationalized in terms of conceptualizing a person as an intentional system with beliefs, desires, and goals. This top level of analysis is a description of our phenomenal experience. This level of analysis is valued by the layperson and the psychotherapist. At the middle level, referred to as the functional level, an information-processing system is used to explain observable behavior. There is some controversy over the value of this middle level of analysis and several papers have reviewed arguments for and against the middle level of description (Massaro, 1986; see also Mehler, Morton, & Jusczyk, 1984). Although one can argue forcefully that there is a fundamental need for this level of description, the true test will be the success of research strategies, such as the information-processing approach, aimed at a functional description of mind and behavior.

Arguments against Lower and Upper Levels

The physiological or neural level is the most natural level of explanation because the brain is necessary for mind, and because we can expect brain functioning to underlie mental functioning. In fact, there has been a recent fascination with models that supposedly resemble neural processing rather than the functional level addressed by information processing models. What we sometimes forget, however, is that neural models are also metaphoric; that is, they are models, they are not the real thing. As noted by Gentner and Grudin (1985), neural models are less detectable as metaphors and less subject to the analytical scrutiny that leads to greater precision and systematization. Neural models also seem to convey greater face validity because of our value of reductionism in scientific inquiry (Krech, 1955). However, Nelson Goodman (1984) argues that there is no logical priority of one level over any other level. Recent progress in the natural sciences illustrates that much can be gained from relatively molar levels of analysis.

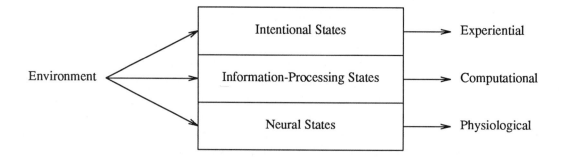

Figure 5. Three levels of inquiry. The top level corresponds to our phenomenal experience, the middle level represents functional mental processes, and the bottom level corresponds to physiological brain states (after Bieri, 1985).

Consciousness

My dictionary defines consciousness as "The faculty of knowing what affects or what goes on in one's own mind, such as is given in sensation and perception." Our conscious experience represents both the product of certain mental operations and some awareness of other mental operations. The introspectionists (see Chapter 2) implicitly defined psychological phenomena with those that were consciously available. Freud, on the other hand, gave great weight to processes that were usually out of grasp of the immediate awareness of the participants. The mental operations studied today span the continuum from the workings of tacit knowledge and unconscious processing to the phenomena of conscious knowledge and judgment. To date, understanding the operations of mental phenomena has not been advanced by defining the degree to which they are conscious.

The degree to which a particular mental operation is conscious has not been a central issue in experimental psychology. It appears that consciousness is involved at only the most general level of our thinking and action. Read a few sentences with the book turned upside down. What did you do differently? Our awareness had little influence on reading the upside-down text, and introspective inquiry is of little help. We were aware of reading slightly more slowly from right to left and from bottom to top, but little else seemed to be different from normal.

Although not apparent in today's research, the fundamental question that psychological inquiry may resolve lies at the heart of the mind-body problem and other philosophical issues. How do our sensory systems and mental processes provide such a large window to the outside world? Magritte addressed this mystery in his painting *False Mirror*, an attempted synthesis of our inner and outer visual worlds. The person on the street, whom we might call a naive realist, is not baffled about the experience of the world out there since that's where it is. Others, less accepting, find it a mystery that *internal* mental operations are sufficient to give an experience of a world out there. Without being intrigued by some aspect of this mystery, few would enter the arena of psychological science.

At the other end of the continuum of levels, the phenomenological level is limited in uncovering satisfactory explanations of our actions. The phenomenological level is grounded in introspective explanations of our behavior, and will see in Chapter 2 that introspection failed as a school of inquiry in psychology. As an example, Stefanski's research (cited in Lewicki, 1986) reveals how little of everyday activity is open to conscious introspective analysis. Consider the judgment of people and personalities on the basis of sketches of their faces. Subjects, faced with schematic sketches varying along many different dimensions, rated various dimensions of personalities. They were influenced systematically by various properties of the faces, such as the spread of eyes and width of nose, but could not articulate this influence. In fact, the subjects consistently denied that they were influenced by properties of the face that were influential. Although it cannot be denied that both the neural and phenomenological levels offer essential insights into our functioning, the emphasis in this book is on the middle functional level of inquiry. The methods of inquiry that are developed and the domains that are studied are best attacked at the middle level. We now proceed with arguments for this middle level.

Arguments for a Middle Level

The existence of hidden psychological operations requires that students of human behavior provide a theoretical description at the psychological level, in addition to whatever descriptions may be available at the intentional or physiological level. One analogy that argues for a psychological description, in addition to a purely physiological description, is to a computer. If a scientist wants to understand how a computer works, certain levels of inquiry are possible and necessary. Following one line of inquiry, an electronics engineer could tear the computer apart and describe the physical makeup of the computer. This description provides information about the physical components such as whether the memory in the computer is composed of magnetic core or semiconductor chips. Even given a complete physical description of the hardware, however, a curious person would still not be satisfied with respect to how the computer works. Little would be known about the software. The scientist would not know what programs the computer uses, how those programs work, whether the computer learns, forgets, or can do two things at the same time. The distinction between the hardware and software levels of a computer is emphasized by many computer languages that disguise the hardware of the machine. The same program can run on a variety of computers fundamentally different in their hardware makeup. The issues raised with respect to the programs of a computer are similar to the questions that we ask about people. To study the software of the computer, we would want to observe the computer in operation. We would manipulate the environment in certain ways and see how the computer reacts to those manipulations. This is how we study psychological functioning in humans. We manipulate the environment in an orderly manner, and we see what effect it has on the subject. From the relationships between the changes in the environment and changes in behavior, we hope to learn something about the hidden psychological operations involved.

The distinction between physiological and psychological levels of description is analogous to a similar distinction made in artificial intelligence, a field of computer science aimed at creating intelligent machines. Designing machines to resemble human intelligence might follow one of two principles. In the first instance, the hardware of the machine is made to imitate the brain as much as possible. The binary or on-off logic of a computer might be viewed as analogous to the all-or-none behavior of brain cells. An example of the approach is the neural-net approach of perceptrons (Rosenblatt, 1958; Minsky & Papert, 1969). In the second approach, intelligence is modeled by the manipulation of symbols, as on a digital computer. In this information-processing view, the computer's ability to process information is viewed as analogous to a human's ability to process information. In this case, the programs or software of the machine might be designed to mimic human thought processes (Newell & Simon, 1956, 1972; Simon, 1969). Contemporary thought and research in artificial intelligence appears to have adopted the information-processing over the brain-imitation approach (Raphael, 1976; Winston, 1977). Intriguing and challenging realizations of artificial intelligences have materialized within the information-processing model. More recently, the neural-net approach has been revived and is being applied to a number of problem domains (Feldman, 1985; Hinton & Anderson, 1981).

The idea of the necessity of a psychological level of explanation is similar to the functionalist philosophy of Cummins (1975, 1977) and Fodor (1968, 1975, 1981). These philosophers develop a solid foundation for the idea that a physical/physiological level of description is not sufficient for an understanding of mind/philosophy. To return to our computer example, both an electronic computer and an abacus can perform addition; i.e., they are adding machines. Although these machines are both physical, they do not share any properties that are not also shared with machines that do not add. That is, there is nothing unique about the physical properties of adding machines that identifies them as adding machines. The machines share a function and this function is most clearly explained at a non-physical level.

INFORMATION PROCESSING

A psychological framework that follows in the experimental tradition of scientific inquiry has come to be known as the information-processing approach (Palmer & Kimchi, 1986; Sternberg, 1969b). The central thesis is that complex behavior is the result of a myriad of simpler behaviors or processes. These component processes are assumed to be fairly modular; that is, the functions of one component are relatively independent of the functions of other processes. Given this autonomous functioning, there is the possibility that the nature of a component process can be studied and described independently of the other component processes making up complex behavior.

The human agent, often described as a black box between environment and behavior, is now decomposed into several smaller black boxes that communicate with one another. Each black box is referred to as a stage of processing, and each stage has a memory component and a process component. The memory component holds information and the process component transforms this information from one store into another. As illustrated in Figure 6, the storage component is represented by a box and the process component by a circle. Each stage of processing takes time, and it is this time-consuming property that is fundamental to the information-processing approach. The modularity of stages and their temporal occurrence allow the curious to tap into a particular stage of processing, or at least isolate it from other processes.

The information and information processing that occurs along this communication channel is responsible for the complex behavior that is observed. Within the information-processing framework, the goal is to determine how many boxes there are, how each of the boxes works, and how the boxes talk to one another. This science of boxology has proven fairly productive in several domains of complex human performance, such as in an analysis of reading, learning to read, and reading assessment and instruction (Carr, 1986; Stanovich, 1986). We have learned about the necessary processes involved in skilled reading and how these differences in processes contribute to differences in reading ability (Perfetti, 1985).

The information processing approach has illuminated linguistic performance; for example, some observed language deficit might be due to production, perception, or both behaviors. The child, who pronounces *rabbit* as *wabbit*, might perceive the difference between /r/ and /w/. This same child will correct a mischievous adult who imitates the child by saying *wabbit*. The child reacts to the imitation by correcting the adult with the reply, "not *wabbit*, *wabbit*." An information-processing analysis distinguishes between perception and production and also decomposes each of these processes into several component processes. Progress involves a series of decompositions that allow finer and finer distinctions among the contributions to the observed behavior. Analogous to Winston Churchill's view of democracy, information processing is not perfect but it's the best that's currently available.

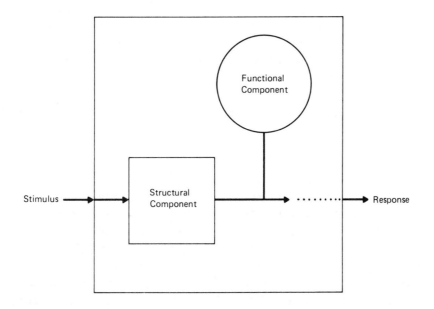

Figure 6. Information-processing model. A graphic representation of the structural and functional components between stimulus and response.

Properties of Information Processing

There are several important properties or characteristics of an information-processing approach to psychological inquiry. First, behavior can be described in terms of the interaction of a set of component processes. Although each process functions independently of the other processes, some processes can communicate to other processes. Each process can be conceptualized as informational mapping between some input to the process and some output from the process. The process transforms the input information into the output information. Each process can be decomposed into a set of component processes in a recursive manner, depending on the level of analysis that is being formulated. Finally, each process consumes some significant amount of time when it occurs.

These properties are reasonable and correspond to the scientific approach in other domains. The explanation that is sought by the information-processing approach is similar to the standard types of explanation given other phenomena. To take an example from Dawkins (1987), the workings of a steam engine would be explained in terms of how parts of the engine interact with each other to transform wood or coal into power. At a fairly molar level of description, the interacting parts would be things like the fire-box, boiler, cylinder, piston, and steam regulator. Each part would be described in terms of its function and how its action influences the action of other parts. All of the parts interacting together explain the emergence of the global behavior of the steam engine. Explanation has no logical stopping point. Each of the component parts can now be explained in terms of its component parts, and so on in a recursive fashion. The boiler of our steam engine, for example, might be further described in terms of the interplay of the tank and the pump.

Information-Processing Model

The information-processing approach is usually formalized in terms of a stage model of some specific behavioral performance. A stage model operates on the assumption of relative independence in that some stages are hypothesized to be influenced by only some variables, and other stages by other variables. Evidence consistent with this hypothesis allows a more parsimonious description of behavior than highly interactive or nonindependence models. In addition, this independence is what makes a theoretical description possible in that the functioning of some stages can be described relatively independently of others. The model is a useful heuristic and is presented in the spirit of falsification and strong inference strategies of scientific inquiry (Massaro, 1987b). Specific alternatives or contrasts, not otherwise transparent, can be formulated within the context of an information-processing model.

The prototypical information-processing model is serial, as illustrated in Figure 6. In nonserial models, stages are assumed to be somewhat autonomous processes, each with a unique starting time and a unique finishing time. Although the processes can overlap in time, they each contribute to or affect performance time. A serial model is assumed here because it is the most parsimonious and, in many instances, mathematically identical to the nonserial models (Townsend & Ashby, 1983). In both instances, performance can be broken down into its component parts and a theory must describe the parts and how each part is influenced by the multiplicity of variables available to nature and the experimenter (Theios & Amrhein, 1985).

The main purpose of the information-processing model is to formally represent the psychological processes that are important in a given experiment. By delineating the psychological processes, an understanding is obtained that not only clarifies the stimulus-response relationship but also illuminates the processes themselves. Our goal is to understand what the psychological processes do and how they do it. The model functions as a formal representation of our knowledge of these processes and forces us to be consistent in our psychological research. It enables us to study methodological, logical, and theoretical issues in a consistent and coherent manner. The model also provides a tool we can use to summarize our findings, predict the results of new experiments, and describe real-life scenarios. Remember that a model is used to represent the phenomena under study as simply as possible; it is not meant to correspond to the phenomena exactly. If it did, it would no longer be a model but would be identical to the phenomena.

Information

The use of information in information-processing research is relatively casual, but it can be defined as the increase of certainty or reduction of uncertainty. If I tell you that the display to be exposed in a tachistoscope is going to be a letter in the English alphabet, this information has increased your certainty about the nature of the forthcoming display. Note that the message is only informative if you are literate and know the structure of written English. Accordingly, information is defined in terms of the person in the processing tasks rather than in terms of the environmental events themselves. The environmental events might be referred to as data, which become informative only when they are processed by an information-processing system.

A specific measure of information was proposed by Shannon in 1948. If we return to our example of telling the subject that the display will be a letter of the English alphabet, we have limited the number of possible displays to 26. This is less information than if we told the subject that the display would contain either the letters A or B. Now if we flash the display in the tachistoscope and ask the subject to report what she saw, a correct answer would be more informative in one case than in the other. Given that the subject was more uncertain with 26 than with two alternatives, a correct report is more informative with the larger set size. We are more impressed with correct performance given a larger set size. If the message ensemble is limited to a single alternative, our subject would not have to look at the display and a correct answer is completely uninformative.

The amount of information in a given message is a measure of how much it reduces the number of possible outcomes. The amount of information is not linear with the number of alternatives. If a person hears a message that reduces the number of alternatives from 100 to 99, this seems to be less helpful than a message that reduces the number of alternatives from two to one. It seems intuitively more attractive to make information a function of the fraction of the alternatives that are eliminated. Here, the 100 alternatives would have to be reduced to 50 to provide the same amount of information as the reduction from two to one.

In information theory, the basic unit of information is the *bit*, which is an abbreviation of *binary digit*. A bit of information is the amount of information gained when a subject reduces the potential message set in half. If a person flips a coin, guessing which side will turn up gives one bit of information. If the coin is flipped three times, predicting exactly the sequence of heads and tails gives three bits of information. There are eight equally likely outcomes for three coin flips, HHH, HHT, and so on, and the message set of the eight alternatives must be divided in half three times to arrive at the correct sequence. Table 1 illustrates three questions used to find the correct sequence.

Table 1. Predicting the correct sequence of three coin flips requires three binary questions and produces three bits of information.

Coin sequences	First toss	Second toss	Third toss
1.	H	H	H
2.	H	H	T
3.	H	T	H
4.	H	T	T
5.	T	H	H
6.	T	H	T
7.	T	T	H
8.	T	T	T

Question 1. Was there a head on the first toss?
Answer 1.   No (can eliminate sequences 1-4)

Question 2. Was there a head on the second toss?
Answer 2.   Yes (can eliminate sequences 7 and 8)

Question 3. Was there a head on the third toss?
Answer 3.   Yes (can eliminate sequence 6)

The answer must be sequence 5—THH.

A mathematical formula to compute the amount of information, H, is

$$H = \log_2 N \qquad\qquad 2^H = N \qquad\qquad\qquad (1)$$

where H is measured in bits of information and N is the number of equally likely outcomes. As will be noted in our discussion of logarithms in Chapter 12, H is the number of times 2 must be multiplied by itself to produce N.

An interesting psychological question has been to what extent information measured in bits can predict behavior. Much of behavior involves reacting to specific stimulus events in some situation with specific responses. One question is whether the time to make a response (the reaction time) is a function of the number of stimulus-response alternatives. Some investigators believed that the reaction time should increase with each doubling of stimulus response alternatives. After some initial support for this prediction (Hick, 1952), several studies reported a number of limiting conditions. Consider an experiment carried out by Longstreth, El-Zahhar, and Alcorn (1985). Subjects were visually presented with any one of a number of digits. In a typical study, each digit was paired with a unique response key. The task was simply to press the appropriate key indicated by the digit.

In one condition, there were two possible test digits. In the other condition, there were four possible test digits. The reaction time was about a tenth of a second longer in the case with four than with two alternatives. This result is consistent with information measured in bits because increasing the number of bits in the task increases the reaction time. A second task carried out by the authors, however, reveals a limitation of bits or any similar information measure. Test digits were presented as in the first task, but now subjects were required to simply hit a single key and hold it for a duration given by the value of the test digit. The digit 2, for example, would require the duration of the key press to be two time units (usually about 30 msec per time unit), and so on for other test digits. Subjects learn to be fairly accurate in this task very easily. The result of interest was that their reaction time did not increase much with increases in the number of test alternatives. This second task produced results very different from the first task. There was very little increase in reaction time when there were four alternatives relative to just two. Figure 7 gives the mean reaction time as a function of the number of alternatives in the two tasks.

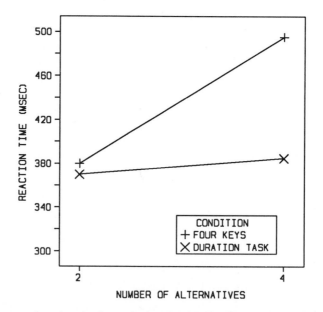

Figure 7. Mean reaction time in the typical task with four keys and the duration task with a single key as a function of the number of alternatives in the task (adapted from Longstreth et al., 1985).

These results indicate that a definition of information is not sufficient to explain human performance. In addition to the stimulus events and the responses of the subject, it is necessary to know the information processing that is required by the task. In the first task, the subject has to keep each stimulus-response pairing (digit-key pairing) in mind to do the task accurately. With few alternatives, subjects can hold these translations in memory and access them fairly quickly. Increasing the number of alternatives will make this process more difficult and, accordingly, lead to an increase in the reaction time. In contrast, just a single stimulus-response code can be used by the subjects in the duration task: press the key for the duration specified by the test digit. The recognition of the test digit provides the numerical code needed for the duration task. The differences between the two tasks illustrate that a measure of information will not be successful in predicting behavior without also accounting for the processing required by each task.

In our study we do not limit ourselves to a single formal definition of information, such as the one given by Equation 1. It is important to realize that information must be defined in terms of the knowledge and procedures of the subject. Strictly speaking, stimulus events are not information until their processing of the sensory system provides data that are meaningful to the subject. For example, knowledge of the octal number system can improve the processing and memory of long sequences of 1's and 0's in random order. The information available to a person with knowledge of octal counting is different from that available to a person with a knowledge of just decimal counting. The data given by the 0's and 1's provide different information to the two people. Our concern is with the nature of the information at a particular stage of processing and the operations carried out on that information.

Prospective

Our psychological model of information processing is built by a method of successive approximations to demonstrate how knowledge is accumulated in science. Chapter 2 begins our study with a short discussion of the history of theory and scientific method in psychology. One of our goals there and throughout the book is to show how the method of experimentation follows from psychological theory, even if it is not explicitly articulated by the experimenter.

2

A Brief History of Theory and Methods

British Empiricism

Structuralism

    Act Psychology
    Introspective Method
    Critique

Associationism

    Verbal Learning and Memory
    Critique

Behaviorism

    Operant Conditioning
    Classical Conditioning
    Critique

Freudian Psychology

    Psychoanalysis
    Critique

Gestalt Psychology

    Perceptual Reports
    Critique

Functionalism and Information Processing

Wilhelm Wundt
Knowledge and Perception
John B. Watson
Students in History

... The best ... take-off point is to ask how psychologists
conceived the fundamental task of psychology as a science.
Gardner Murphy and Joseph Kovach (1972)

Given that psychological phenomena exist, how do we go about understanding them? No single set of methods is correct for psychological study in the same way that no single set of rules is followed for proposing marriage. The method used in both cases is critically dependent upon one's perception of the situation and what one wants to know. In most cases, a "yes" or "no" answer is not sufficient; there is concern for other aspects, such as the rationale for the answer. In psychology, the methods we use to study psychological processes can only follow, not precede, the questions we wish to ask. Scientists with different questions or conceptions of the topic to be studied develop different experimental methods. They then use the results of the experiments to argue for the importance of asking just these questions in their particular experimental manner. We will discover throughout this book a wide range of experimental methods as varied as the content areas of psychological inquiry.

Consider the change from the Aristotelean to the Galilean view of motion. Aristotle saw a falling stone as a change of state rather than a process. Aristotle's conceptualization of the problem highlighted an object starting in one place and ending in another. From this point of view, the important facts were the initial position and starting time of the falling stone and the destination and arrival time at the end of the fall. The relevant measures of motion were the total distance covered and the amount of time elapsed. From these two observations the Aristotelean could compute the average speed or the average distance covered per unit of time. In contrast, Galileo, like some of the scientists before him, saw the falling of a stone as a process; therefore, it was reasonable to speculate on the operations of this process. What caught Galileo's attention was the method of travel rather than the starting point and destination. One hypothesis put forward was that stones fall with a uniformly accelerated motion. This idea led to new methods of experimentation and data analysis which were unlikely in the conceptual framework of Aristotle's view of motion.

Research in psychology has also been dictated by the theories and conceptual ideas of the investigator. A brief review of some different psychological theories will indicate how the methods of research followed directly from these theories. The goal of this chapter is to evaluate several schools of psychology during its century-old history. We hope to learn something about the history of psychology as well as to see how theoretical questions influence research method. That is, there is no ideal method of inquiry that is independent of theory. Even B. F. Skinner, who has argued forcefully against theory, has a very strong theory that has enforced acceptable methods in Skinnerian research. We also study history because we do not want to repeat it blindly. Finally, as much as we would like to believe otherwise, most progress in science is cumulative and gradual: we have little to offer today that does not build on the work of our psychological ancestors.

BRITISH EMPIRICISM

The British empiricists (John Locke, George Berkeley, and David Hume) of the seventeenth and eighteenth centuries provided a model of human psychology that stimulated the beginning of its systematic study in the nineteenth century. The empiricists rejected the venerable philosophical notion of innate ideas as the working material for thought to take place. Instead, they postulated that all knowledge is acquired through experience. According to Locke, experience consists of sensation and reflection. Sensation is what we see, hear, feel, or touch. Reflection is a process of the mind and involves building directly on our sense experiences. Accordingly, phenomena such as knowing are a direct consequence of the reflective process operating on our sense experiences. Thus sensation—a phenomenon with observable tangible properties—becomes the basic unit of human psychology.

Thomas Reid, an eighteenth-century empiricist, was the first to further refine empirical psychology by distinguishing sensation from perception. Sensation, according to Reid, is the impression that an object makes on the mind; it constitutes the bare content, the raw materials, of the mind. Perception, on the other hand, includes a further step or operation by which that content is supplied with meaning. Perception is the apprehension or recognition of an object; it contains not the sensation of the object, but a concept of it.

Reid answered the question of how the mind applies meaning to bare sensation and transforms it into perception by appealing to the Supreme Being. We need not look so far. The source of the meaning by which the observer transforms the sensed or detected object into the recognized one is his storehouse of knowledge, his memory. William James made this point by stating: "We perceive only that which we preperceive." For example, we hear, or detect, a foreign language as well as we do our native tongue, but very little if any meaning can be attached to the message. Certain syllables may be recognized as corresponding to some that we know in English, but even these do not have the same meaning. The words of the foreign language are not making contact with our semantic memory that continuously provides meaning to the words of our own language.

STRUCTURALISM

The empiricist theory of knowledge emphasized sensation as a process that could be observed and measured; and in the nineteenth century people who had been influenced by the empiricists began to think of doing so systematically. Wilhelm Wundt set up the first laboratory dedicated to experimental psychology in 1879. Wundt was, at least functionally, a dualist; he believed that the study and description of mental phenomena should differ from that of physical phenomena. Fixed laws could be developed to describe physical phenomena, he believed, but mental phenomena could be characterized only by psychological causality involving purpose, value and anticipation. For example, Wundt utilized different methods of study for sensory motor events and cognitive mental events. To study the former, he employed the empiricist concepts of association and contiguity of events. In studying the latter he relied on developments of Kant and his followers. As an example, he formalized and tested the concept of a control process called "apperception" to describe the focus of attention in which the observer selects and structures his conscious experience.

Given his belief in conscious experience, Wundt proposed to analyze this experience into its elements. In order to do this, he developed an approach to psychological inquiry called *structuralism*. Using the method of introspection, the goal was to identify the elements and describe how they are combined to produce thought and affect. In this method observers were trained to report the elements of their conscious experience. Carefully collecting and systematically analyzing their own and others' reports of mental processes, the introspectionists defined some of the most important areas of psychological investigation, such as attention and the analysis of consciousness. In his best-known finding, Wundt claimed that conscious feeling could be described by values on three basic dimensions: pleasant-unpleasant, excitement-calm, and strain-relaxation. Titchener and his students also utilized Wundt's methods but found slightly different results. They argued that there were only two basic dimensions to feeling since Wundt's excitement-calm and strain-relaxation dimensions measure the same psychological experience. Unfortunately, this disagreement grew into a controversy which could not be resolved by the introspective method itself. Accordingly, no advancement in knowledge could occur until psychologists agreed on a new method of analysis or until a new method was developed.

Wilhelm Wundt

Wilhelm Wundt is known to most students as having founded the first experimental laboratory in psychology. However, little else seems to be understood concerning this extremely prodigious scholar. Wundt's solution to the mind-body problem appeared to follow the parallelism view of Leibniz discussed in Chapter 1. He was also highly influenced by the great German philosopher Schopenhauer, who understood will and volition as central to human function. Blumenthal (1979) states that Wundt saw himself as the first empirical voluntarist. Wundt's important psychological process was called apperception, which might be considered to be the control process of generating experience. In some ways similar to the Gestalt psychologists years later, Wundt saw that experience could not be reduced to the stimulus elements surrounding the perceiver.

Blumenthal (1979) points out that most American psychologists have learned about Wundt through Boring, who used Titchener, his mentor, as his guide to Wundt. Titchener, after falling out with Wundt, appears to have distorted some of his views. Wundt saw psychology as process oriented and opposed the structuralism promulgated by Titchener. Although Wundt utilized the introspective methods at the initial stages of hypothesis construction, he always sought objective measures in actual experimental tests. For example, Wundt's tridimensional theory of emotion was tested by analyzing the physiological responses of the participants. It was Titchener, not Wundt, who relied solely on the introspective method for sufficient tests of hypothesis.

Act Psychology

Rather than accepting Wundt's definition of psychology, Franz Brentano argued against focusing the study of psychology on the *contents* of consciousness; instead, psychologists should be concerned with the *acts* of consciousness. In this sense, Brentano saw the importance of mental processes, or psychological operations carried out over time. Freud, a student in Brentano's psychology courses, developed the first systematic psychological theory that emphasized dynamic processes (Rancurello, 1968). The critical weakness in Brentano's contribution was that his theoretical development did not include a new method or paradigm for research. Thus, although Wundt emphasized the contents or structure of consciousness while Brentano attended to the acts or function of consciousness, both thought in terms of the introspective method.

Knowledge and Perception

Philosophers and psychologists have been concerned with how the mind applies meaning to bare sensation or how knowledge influences perception. It is always fun to demonstrate how prior knowledge influences our perceptual experience. The top half of Figure 1 presents a view of a scene familiar to all of us, but from an unusual and therefore ambiguous perspective. Very few people can make sense of this picture until they are given some additional information. When told that the nonsense actually represents a view of a cow, some people see it. Others cannot impose the appropriate organization until more specific information is given. In this case, the relatively unambiguous picture in the bottom half of Figure 1 might help you get the appropriate perspective for understanding the top picture. The bottom picture is a cow looking at the viewer and the top picture is a near view of the cow's head. Once you have experienced the cow, it will be difficult not to see the cow, even if viewed again in this ambiguous format in the distant future.

Figure 1. See the text for disambiguating these pictures.

Introspective Method

Although the introspective method sometimes proves valuable as an adjunct to the experimental method, it does not, by itself, lead to precise and quantitative knowledge. We have all been dissatisfied with someone else's subjective report of some psychological experience. Consider St. Theresa's description of a mystical experience known as the Ecstasy of St. Theresa.

> Beside me on the left hand appeared an angel in bodily form, such as I am not in the habit of seeing except very rarely. Though I often have visions of angels, I do not see them ... He was not tall but short, and very beautiful.... In his hands I saw a great golden spear, and at the iron tip there appeared to be a point of fire. This he plunged into my heart several times so that it penetrated to my entrails. When he pulled it out, I felt that he took them with it, and left me utterly consumed by the great love of God. The pain was so severe that it made me utter several moans. The sweetness caused by this intense pain is so extreme that one cannot possibly wish it to cease. (Hibbard, *Bernini*, 1965)

The famous Baroque sculpture representing this hallucinatory event was created by Bernini who was inspired by this description (see Figure 2).

Critique

In Chapter 1, we distinguished among three levels of phenomena: phenomenological, functional, and physiological. It appears that introspection can reflect the phenomenological level, but the other two levels are not open to, or are impenetrable to, introspection. Recently, psychologists have documented the limitations of the introspective method by showing how the causes of our behavior remain opaque to us. One well-documented phenomenon in social psychology is that helping behavior is influenced by the presence of others. Before reading on, you might speculate on the direction of the influence. Anecdotes abound such as the deaf woman Virginia being stabbed repeatedly with 20 people looking on, and none of them coming to her aid. People become less likely to help others in need as the number of bystanders or witnesses increases (Latane & Darley, 1970). Experimentally, the phenomenon is demonstrated by having a naive subject sitting in a waiting room with a number of other individuals who are actually in cahoots with the experimenter. A person in an adjacent room feigns an epileptic seizure and the question is the likelihood of the subject going to his aid, and how this varies with the number of other persons in the waiting room. Subjects are less likely to help as the number of individuals increases. Although this is an engaging result, our focus is on the subject's introspective report about their behavior. Although many different reasons are given for giving or not giving help, subjects never mention the number of people as an influencing factor (Latane & Darley, 1970). Thus, there is a functional relationship (see Chapter 3) between the number of onlookers and helping that is outside the purview of our introspective analysis.

One result must be bolstered by others for a convincing thesis. We will mention two supporting results. Subjects were asked to memorize word pairs, such as ocean-moon (Nisbett & Wilson, 1977). After this task, they were asked to name a detergent. Studying ocean-moon increased the likelihood of giving Tide as an answer but, when asked, subjects almost never mentioned the words in the memorization test as an influencing factor. In another task, subjects choose an article of clothing of the best quality from several arranged in a row (Nisbett & Wilson, 1977). After choosing among four nightgowns, for example, the subject is asked why that

Figure 2. *The Ecstasy of St. Theresa* as represented by Bernini.
Art Resource, New York.

particular one was preferred. Subjects revealed a strong position effect in that there was a strong bias to pick the nightgown that was on the right. Subjects were four times as likely to choose the one on the right regardless of the actual nightgown in that position. These same subjects never mentioned position as an influencing factor in their decision and virtually all the subjects adamantly denied the experimenter's proposition that position had an influence. Clearly, then, the introspective method falls short of providing an understanding of behavior in these domains.

Notwithstanding these limitations, one should not relegate out of order all introspective analyses. To see the positive contribution of introspection, consider the question: "In the house that you lived in two houses ago, was the front doorknob on the right side or the left side of the door?" How do you retrieve this memory? Most likely you will first fix on the house in which you live at present, go back one step to the house before that, and then to the house before that one. In other words, you trace back your history until you have arrived at the correct house, then you gradually recall details that build a picture of the front door. At some point it becomes clear on which side the door opened. In the final step, one person might be picturing herself coming home in the evening after a hard day's work; another might see himself leaving. One might remember the position of his own body as he went through the door; another might remember the door itself as it opened.

The introspective method can tell us a great deal about the psychological processes involved in answering this question. The task is a difficult one and involves a sequence of processing operations or stages between question and answer. Employing the experimental method to study this task would not be informative, due to the complexity of the task. The performance of this task, however, involves the performance of myriad smaller tasks, such as those involved in the perception of a message or in the retrieval of a single item in memory. Some of these processes do not lend themselves to introspection at all, but each of these processes can be studied and evaluated by the experimental methods articulated in this book.

Ericsson and Simon (1984) defend the use of the introspective method, but remind us that the verbal reports elicited by this method are data. Previous uses of the introspective method did not determine which psychological processes were responsible for the reports and how these processes might change with instructions and tasks. Understanding the results goes hand in hand with understanding the measuring instrument (how the results were obtained); in this case, understanding the processes responsible for an introspective report will help account for the actual outcomes of that report. On the basis of a review of many studies, the authors claim that subjects are capable of giving reliable verbal reports of conscious experience. However, observers cannot be expected to give reliable accounts of processes outside of consciousness or of events no longer available in memory. Verbal reports have proved to be particularly illuminating in understanding the processes involved in complex tasks such as the anagram task discussed in Chapter 18.

ASSOCIATIONISM

The British empiricists were also responsible for the concept of association, the linking together of sensation, perception, and thought by the temporal contiguity of experience. The concept of association has had a major influence on the study of verbal learning. In 1885, Hermann Ebbinghaus published the first experimental study of verbal learning. He was committed to the experimental method as the appropriate framework for the study of mind. His major contribution involved applying the techniques of one area to another; in this case, Ebbinghaus extended the methods of psychophysical measurement to study learning and retention of verbal material. His theoretical approach was rooted in the tenets of British associationism in which frequency of experience of events played a central role (Postman, 1968). Following the ideas of the British empiricists, he hypothesized that associations between different events are learned by contiguity. Two events that are experienced together become associated (related) to one another. The presentation of one event will tend to lead to the experience of an associated event. His goal was to assess the learning and retention of verbal material. Rather than using real words, he made up a new vocabulary of consonant-vowel-consonant nonsense syllables, which have claimed a role in psychology ever since. Ebbinghaus realized that people would already have many associations to the words in their vocabulary and, therefore, any study of learning and retention of words would not be free of previous knowledge. Using only himself as subject, Ebbinghaus carried out a highly systematic series of experiments involving the learning and retention of nonsense syllables.

Verbal Learning and Memory

Ebbinghaus' established laws of learning and memory that still stand today, 100 years later. The first law is that learning increases with the time spent on the memorization task. This law, called the total time function, can be summarized by the aphorism, "you get what you pay for." Beginning with a number of lists, each containing 16 nonsense syllables, a new list that had not been learned before would be selected on a given day. The list would be recited at 2 1/2 syllables per second for a given number of repetitions of the list. On the next day, memory for the list would be measured by determining the number of additional trials required to relearn the list by heart. The idea is that the more that is learned on day 1, the less study time is needed on day 2 to relearn the list. Figure 3 plots the amount of time to relearn the items on day 2 as a function of the number of repetitions on day 1. As can be seen, Ebbinghaus found a simple linear relation between the study time and the amount learned.

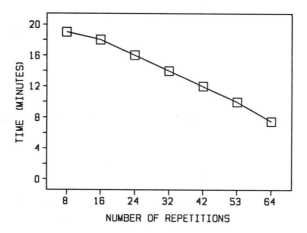

Figure 3. Time taken to relearn the nonsense syllables on day 2 as a function of the number of repetitions on day 1.

A classic study of forgetting involved an even more heroic effort. Ebbinghaus taught himself 169 separate lists of 13 nonsense syllables each. A given list was relearned after an interval as short as 20 minutes to as long as 31 days. Figure 4 shows that memory for the nonsense syllables decreases systematically with increases in the time between original learning and test. The second law is that forgetting increases with increases in the time intervening between learning and test. Forgetting is not linear, however, but is negatively decelerated in that the amount forgotten per unit time decreases with time. The absolute amount forgotten per unit of time decreases with increases in the retention interval.

Critique

We are indebted to Ebbinghaus for bringing the study of memory into the laboratory. Following the tenets of experimental design, he controlled all variables except the one of interest. For this reason, his results are still valid today. However, current memory researchers are somewhat wiser about two characteristics of his work. We have learned that even nonsense syllables differ with respect to how much meaning they bring to the mind of the participant (Underwood & Schulz, 1960). The nonsense syllable is not really nonsense, but is meaningful. What Ebbinghaus failed to realize was that people abhor nonsense. As an example, the syllable

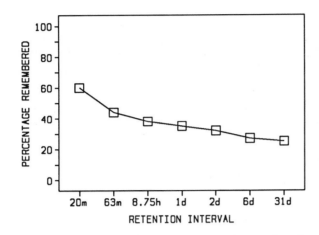

Figure 4. Percentage of nonsense syllables remembered as a function of the retention interval between study and test (m = minutes, h = hours, and d = days).

JAL might be associated with *jail*, *jello*, or *jolly*, and a subject might actively use this association to encode and remember the test syllable. The nonsense syllable might actually have given the experimenter less control over previous associations than actual words would have. We might expect larger individual differences when subjects are given syllables rather than words because a nonsense syllable has less definite information than does a word. Our associations to the test word ROBIN would probably have more in common than our associations to JAL. Rather than trying to eliminate meaning, one goal of memory research should be how meaning influences memory.

An important limitation in Ebbinghaus' research program was that he ignored the psychological processes involved in recognition and memory. Thus, he tried to make sense of many functional relationships between independent and dependent variables without addressing how those variables influence psychological processing. We will see in Chapter 14 that coherent laws of memory and forgetting are possible only if the intervening psychological processes are accounted for. There are acquisition, retention, and retrieval processes involved in the simpliest task and each of these contributes to the final outcome. Without isolating the contribution of each of these processes, the functional relationships that Ebbinghaus observed are meaningless.

BEHAVIORISM

John B. Watson (1913), primed with the findings and methods of Pavlov and Thorndike in the study of animal behavior, rejected the methods of Wundt and Brentano. Watson proposed, instead, an entirely objective psychology in which public observable behavior was the focus of study. In his favor, Watson cited the current controversies that grew out of defining psychology as the study of consciousness and the use of the introspective method. He concluded that introspection was an invalid scientific method; hence, because he believed that mental processes were not discoverable in any other way, they were not a proper study for psychology at all. Only behavior, observable, measurable, and controllable, could be studied scientifically.

Watson correctly realized that advancement in any scientific discipline requires methods of study the results of which can be agreed upon by the scientific community. Since our phenomenal experience was not directly observable, introspective reports were open to alternative interpretations. On the other hand, all scientists would agree on some observable behavior, such as whether a rat turned left or right in a maze. In this respect, Watson was entirely correct and was following in the methodological development in the physical sciences. However, Watson went beyond arguing for observable behavior as the basic phenomena to be explained and denied that any theoretical references to consciousness or other mental processes could increase our understanding of behavior. Watson's argument reached its logical consequence with B. F. Skinner's (1950) proposal that psychologists should develop a stimulus-response psychology with no reference to any psychological processes between stimulus and response. Given this framework, proponents of the paradigm set about attempting to define functional stimulus-response relationships without reference to intervening psychological processes.

John B. Watson

Although this author rejects behaviorism, it is important to acknowledge the scholarship and important contributions of its founder. Watson did not take the idea of behaviorism lightly; nine years and a nervous breakdown intervened between the idea and its first formal presentation (Cohen, 1979). Watson investigated a broad range of psychological phenomena ranging from animal psychophysics and ethology to educational psychology. He was also a strong advocate of the study of human sexuality, child rearing, and marriage. His greatest contribution may have been his firm belief in applied psychology, the utilization of psychological knowledge in all aspects of society. Most students learn that Watson was forced to give up his teaching career for having an affair with a student. Most of us do not learn that the student eventually became his wife and primary collaborator. Faced with the challenge of a nonacademic career, Watson implemented his own philosophy in a highly successful career in the field of advertising.

The empirical basis for a stimulus-response psychology has centered around the phenomena of classical and operant conditioning. There has been a large body of research on conditioning and considerable knowledge has been gained. In addition, the concepts and principles of conditioning have been extended to more complex aspects of human learning and memory. The principles and concepts of conditioning discovered in the psychological laboratory have also been applied successfully to real-world problems. We begin our discussion with classical conditioning.

Classical Conditioning

Classical conditioning refers to a set of procedures used to train an animal to respond in a unique way to the presentation of a particular stimulus. The procedure is called classical because of the historical priority of its development by the Russian physiologist Ivan Pavlov (1927). At the turn of this century, Pavlov performed the following experiment. A dog was first given a minor operation to make a small opening in his cheek so that saliva could be collected and measured. The dog was then adapted to a loose harness to keep him relatively restrained in the experimental situation. The experimenter, situated in another room, was able to present sounds (such as a bell) and food powder to the animal. Initially the food powder but not the sound would elicit salivation. After pairing the sound followed by food powder for a relatively small number of trials (five or ten) the animal began to salivate before the presentation of the food powder. Presenting just the sound after this experience would be sufficient to elicit the response of salivation.

Figure 5 illustrates the basic procedure and the terminology of the classical conditioning experiment. The food powder is called the unconditioned stimulus (UCS) since it has the capacity to produce a response at the beginning of the experiment. The salivation response to the UCS is called the unconditioned response (UCR). The sound is called the conditioned stimulus (CS) and the salivation to the sound alone is called the conditioned response (CR). In a sentence, classical conditioning represents an animal's acquisition of a CR to a CS because of prior pairing of the CS with a UCS.

1.	UCS (food)	$\rightarrow$	UCR (salivation)
2.	CS - UCS (tone - food)	$\rightarrow$	UCR (salivation)
3.	CS (tone)	$\rightarrow$	CR (salivation)

Figure 5. Schematic diagram of the sequence of events in the classical conditioning procedure.

The most studied classical conditioning with humans has been eyelid conditioning. A puff of air delivered to the eye elicits a blink. In this case, the puff of air is the UCS and the blink is the UCR. If the UCS follows a tone CS for a series of presentations, the CS will now elicit the blink, which is now a CR. Classical conditioning has been used to eliminate undesirable behaviors. In this case, usually an aversive stimulus such as a loud bell or electric shock is used. Classical conditioning might work for people who want to eliminate or reduce their consumption of fattening foods such as sweets. Pairing the food (CS) with an aversive stimulus such as a small electric shock (UCS) might reduce eating. The negative emotional response (UCR) to the shock will eventually be elicited by the food. This CR should compete with a natural positive reaction to the food and might reduce the likelihood of eating the food or, at least, the amount eaten.

Operant Conditioning

Operant conditioning is most often represented by a rat in a chamber called a Skinner box, developed by B. F. Skinner. There is a small lever in the box and food is delivered when the lever is pressed. A rat, placed in the box, explores the interior and eventually stumbles onto the lever. Some amount of food deprivation helps the exploration and the learning process. When food follows each lever press, the animal learns to press the bar and will do so until satiated. The learning process can be speeded up by selectively rewarding the animal's initial exploration to encourage movement near the bar. The guiding rule of thumb is to reward successive approximations to the behavior to be learned. In this case, the animal is first rewarded for going near the lever, then for raising his paws near the lever, and so on until the lever press response is obtained. The theoretical rule describing operant conditioning is that an animal will tend to repeat a response that has been previously rewarded (reinforced).

Operant conditioning with a negative reinforcer will tend to extinguish the response. If the rat were shocked every time he pressed the lever, there's no way the experimenter could convince him to press the lever after a few presses. This kind of conditioning has been used with autistic children who have self-destructive behavior. Some of these children will bang their heads against sharp corners or bite off pieces of their skin. If these behaviors are followed with electric shock, the behavior is usually eliminated. The use of conditioning techniques in the treatment of behavior disorders is called behavior therapy.

Critique

Watson's and Skinner's elimination of any reference to mental processes in psychological study is not a logical consequence of demanding observable behavioral measures. Although two psychologists might agree on *when* a rat turned right or left in a maze, they might not agree on *why* the rat turned in a particular direction. In order to explain and to predict the direction of turning, it might be necessary to propose intervening processes which cannot be directly observed. To return to our physical example of motion, Aristotle and Galileo would agree on Aristotle's observation of the relationship between the distance that an object moves and the time taken for the movement. In addition, Galileo proposed an unobservable intervening process—uniformly accelerated motion— that predicted the relationship and allowed him to predict results in other experimental situations. Although it may be argued that, with present techniques, a uniformly accelerated motion can be observed directly, it could not at the time of Galileo's proposal. In the physical sciences today, the idea of an unobservable process is not bothersome and is considered essential to theory and accurate prediction.

FREUDIAN PSYCHOLOGY

Sigmund Freud has probably influenced the development of psychology more than any other single individual. Freud (1900) viewed psychological behavior as resulting from a set of component systems. Like the Donders stage model (discussed in Chapter 7), excitation would pass from one system to another in a unique temporal sequence. The mental apparatus is bounded by sensory and motor events. All psychological activity begins with external or internal stimuli which influence the sensory apparatus. The perceptions produced by these sensations leave memory traces which are relatively permanent. This conceptualization was illustrated in diagrammatic form as can be seen in Figure 6.

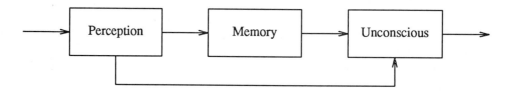

Figure 6. Freud's flow diagram of the processing of an external stimulus (after Freud, 1900).

Freud's view can be considered a version of a stage model of psychological functioning. The different stages have different properties; as an example, perception makes sensory qualities available to consciousness and to the memory system. The memory system can retain a record of this experience, whereas the perceptual system does not. For the most part, the memory record is unconscious. Our "character" is based on the memory traces of our perceptual and cognitive impressions, and these seldom become conscious. In the waking state, all psychical activity starts from some external or internal stimuli. Excitation, therefore, flows from left to right in the model. In dreaming, the excitation moves in a backward direction.

Psychoanalysis

Freud believed that dreams provide a window into psychological functioning and the role of the unconscious. His interpretation of dreams makes fascinating reading. In one case, a father had been watching a sick son who succumbs to his illness. The exhausted father finally goes to bed leaving the dead son to be watched by an old man. The father has a vivid dream of his son standing beside his bed and saying, "Father, don't you see that I am burning?" At this point, the father wakes up and finds that the old man had dozed off, the candle had been knocked over, and there is a burn on his dead child's arm. This dream, according to Freud, was overdetermined or fully caused by the father's recent experience and his overwhelming loss. The child's saying "I am burning" reflects his fever during his illness, whereas his speaking at all reflects the desire of the father to keep him alive. Another contribution to the dream unmentioned by Freud might have been the incorporation into the dreaming process of the light and the burning candle. These external stimuli probably had some sensory impact during sleeping and could have been incorporated into the dream along with events from memory.

Reports of dreams are problematic in the same way as introspective reports. Freud was clearly aware of the various contributions to the actual reports of a person's dreams. He realized that people may distort what actually occurred in their account of dreams. These distortions could be revealing, and the forgetting of certain aspects of the dream was related by Freud to psychical censorship in which unacceptable conscious drives are kept from conscious awareness. In summary, Freud believed that dreams are important acts which can reveal not only underlying psychological processes but also the wish-seeking motive forces of the participant. In his words, "the interpretation of dreams is the royal road to a knowledge of the unconscious activities of the mind."

Critique

Freud developed the method of psychoanalysis to determine the significant determinants of a person's particular behavior. One interesting case is his psychoanalytical study of Leonardo da Vinci (Freud, 1947). Freud used Leonardo's painting of the Virgin and her mother St. Anne as a window to understanding Leonardo's personality. He made great issue of the fact that Leonardo portrayed the two women as very much the same age. Freud saw a causal relationship between this and the fact that Leonardo, being an illegitimate child, had a close relationship with both his natural mother and his father's wife. In Freudian theory, the painting reflects a subconscious recollection of this situation. The major limitation of this type of study is that one interpretation does not eliminate others. Evidence consistent with one hypothesis is not necessarily inconsistent with other hypotheses (see Chapter 5). As observed by Shapiro (1956), portraying St. Anne as relatively young was conventional in painting at the time. The convention followed current Catholic beliefs and can be seen in paintings long before those of Leonardo da Vinci (Shapiro, 1956; Goldstein & Goldstein, 1978).

As is well-known, the neurotic symptoms noticed by Freud were assumed to be symbolic reactions to emotional traumas and these are repressed by the mind to defend itself from anxiety. The trauma becomes consciously registered only under special circumstances, such as in dreams and slips of the tongue. Freud was both wrong and right about slips of the tongue. He was wrong about slips being the window into the repressed traumas of our past, but he was right about unconscious mental processes causing slips of the tongue. There is now a burgeoning literature on slips of the tongue (Fromkin, 1973, 1980; Norman, 1981). What the slips reveal is a highly efficient speech production system that allows thought to be mapped into words. Most of this action goes on unconsciously, as captured by the common introduction to a talk, "I can't wait to hear what I have to say on the subject."

Consider the student asking for a postponement of an exam because "last night, my grandmother lied—I mean died." Perhaps the student is lying and the guilt prompted the error. Or perhaps she was aware of how much it sounded like a lie, or even more engaging is the possibility that she used to lie to her grandmother. On the other hand, the initial /l/ shares several properties with the initial /d/ and it is not uncommon for these to be substituted for one another in this way. Many slips of the tongue can be described more simply by the functioning of linguistic memory and speech production than by a Freudian analysis. Although it is not easy to disprove one account in favor of the other, parsimony or the value of simplicity in scientific explanation has favored the linguistic explanation. In turn, linguistic explanations have encouraged researchers to look at slips with renewed interest in terms of revealing fundamental properties of language production.

One thing is clear: multiple sources of information influence our linguistic productions. Consider an experiment carried out by Motley (1987). Men read aloud a series of fill-in-the blank sentences in either a sexually-aroused situation with an attractive experimenter or in a dull situation with a male experimenter. The experimenter influenced the choices that were made. In one sentence, "The hillbilly kept his moonshine in big ...," "jugs" was the most frequent answer of the aroused subjects, whereas the nonaroused men tended to answer "vats," "barrels," or "jars." Similarly, "Tension mounted at the end, when the symphony reached its ...," produced "climax" responses for the aroused men in place of "finale," "conclusion," or "peak" for the unaroused. The choice and production of the missing words was sensitive to the context of the utterance in a rather subtle way.

GESTALT PSYCHOLOGY

Another paradigm of psychology is Gestalt, developed by Max Wertheimer and his students (Koffka, 1935; Kohler, 1929). Wertheimer and his followers objected to the introspective methods of Wundt and Titchener and to Watson's behavioristic approach. Against Watson they maintained that immediate conscious experience is an essential subject for psychology. Against Wundt and Titchener they asserted that experience could not be reduced to the elements of sensation, that indeed the experience cannot be understood through analysis of any of its parts.

The research by the Gestalt psychologists led to the development of a set of principles of perceptual organization. These principles followed from the law of Pragnanz which holds that the percept will be as good and simple as possible. (An example of Pragnanz can be seen in Figure 12 of Chapter 14). The best-known principles are grouping by proximity and grouping by similarity.

According to the proximity principle, we organize the world by grouping neighboring elements together. We do not perceive a face in terms of separate elements of nose, eyes, and so on, but as a whole person (Gestalt is a German word that can be translated as whole). The similarity principle states that similar objects or elements tend to be grouped together. The proximity principle can be considered as a special instance of the similarity principle if by proximity we mean similarity in space. Grouping by similarity is also apparent in melody perception. Melody contains a series of pitch changes, and we organize these into a coherent whole. However, if the pitch changes are too large the notes are difficult to group into a coherent organization. This method of grouping was exploited by Baroque musicians in what is called counterpoint. Listen to some examples of counterpoint. Two melodies played in different pitch ranges could be interleaved with one another. Grouping by similarity in pitch enables the listener to follow one of the melodies without interference from the other.

Gestalt psychologists assumed that the physical universe contains organized information and that we preserve this organization in our perception. Accordingly, the study of psychology should focus on the description of this organization. A series of dots arranged to form a circle appears as a circle, not as an unrelated series of dots. Given this framework, psychology should develop methods and theories that delineate the rules of our perceptual organization.

Perceptual Reports

A series of experiments carried out by Erich Goldmeier (1936/1972) illustrates the theoretical and methodological approach taken by the Gestalt psychologists. This scientist was interested in the perceived similarity among objects and hoped to discover the rules accounting for our experience of similarity. As the author acknowledged, people see similarity but can not adequately explain the basis for their experience. His imaginative and innovative experiments involved the presentation of a test object along with two or more other comparison objects. Subjects were simply asked to rank the comparison objects in terms of degree of similarity to the test object. This measure of the relative degree of similarity could then be used to derive testable hypotheses about the bases for the impression of similarity.

Figure 7 presents an example of the test and comparison objects used in one of many experiments that were carried out. The test object 7A is a small circle of dots. The comparison objects were also circles of dots, but now significantly larger in diameter. In 7B, the dots were kept at the same size and distance as in 7A. In 7C, the test figure was simply made proportionately larger. Therefore, 7C has the same number of dots as 7A, and the dots are larger. In 7D, the number and size of the dots are equivalent to those in the test object 7A. All observers saw 7B as most similar to 7A. This result and other similar studies revealed that the appearance of an object is best preserved by keeping the density of the outline configuration constant. Figure 8 shows a similar result for straight lines. Object 8B is seen as most similar to object 8A. Once again, similarity in appearance is greater when the size and density of the elements are preserved. Goldmeier's experiments are convincing because it is easy to see the results directly. One can be his or her own subject in the experiment and no complex data analysis or statistics are necessary to verify the significance of the result. Although current studies of similarity are much more sophisticated in method and data analysis, the logic of this type of inquiry has not changed.

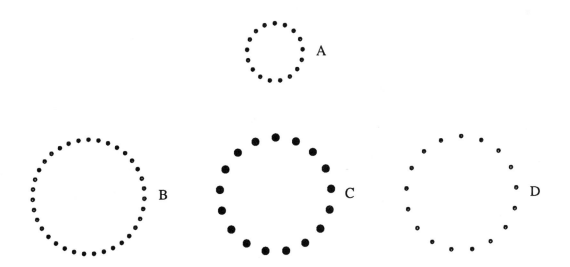

Figure 7. Test object A and comparison objects B, C, and D similar to the ones used by Goldmeier (1936/1972).

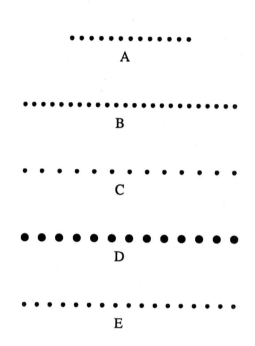

Figure 8. Test object A and comparison objects B, C, D, and E used by Goldmeier (1936/1972).

Students in History

Students of psychology (and even faculty) seldom acknowledge that they are contributing to its history. Scientists are human, and contrasting views of psychological science are handled in a variety of ingenious exchanges. Consider an experience of a graduate student at the University of Wisconsin in 1927 (Gengerelli, 1976). At that time both Clark Hull and Kurt Koffka were professors and served on Gengerelli's committee for the oral examination required for a master's degree. Hull was just beginning a highly productive and influential career in which he developed a formal behavioristic theory of learning and motivation. Koffka was already well-known as one of the three founders of Gestalt psychology and the promulgation of this view as an alternative to Wundt and Titchener's elements of sensation and Watson's behaviorism.

Gengerelli recalls how unsettling it was to go from one class to the other and to experience these two antithetical views of psychology. Of course, these gentlemen also did not shy away from more direct interactions, one of which was at Gengerelli's expense during his oral examinations for his master's thesis. After Koffka asked a number of questions on perception, he said, "Mr. Gengerelli, would you give us a behavioristic explanation of the figure-ground phenomenon?" Of course, this is hard to do within the framework of behaviorism. When Hull's turn came, he posed the following question, "Gengerelli, would you mind explaining the conditioned reflex in Gestalt terms?" Gengerelli comments that Hull then looked at Koffka with a quizzical smile on his face; how Koffka returned this move, we are not told.

Critique

Although the Gestalt psychologists argued against both the structuralist and behavioristic approaches, they shared with them some critical assumptions about the content and method of psychological study. In agreement with the structuralists, they viewed consciousness as a structure rather than a process, even though they differed in their conceptualization of this structure. Accordingly, they mainly were concerned with rules that describe the structure of perceptual experience rather than with processes that led up to it. In many of their studies, they relied on simple reports of perceptual experience similar to the introspective reports utilized by Wundt and his followers. In a manner similar to the behaviorists, they refused to postulate intervening psychological processes to account for observed behavior. Rather, their primary assumption was that our nervous system was wired in a certain way to perceive particular configural stimulus situations in the real world. Gibson (1950, 1966, 1979) ignores intervening psychological processes given his assumption that perceptual systems respond directly (resonate) to invariant aspects of the stimulus environment.

Perceptual reports do not mirror exactly the processes that led to the experience underlying the report. The perceptual report is only one source of evidence among many that the experimenter must use to gain an understanding of mind. Consider the continuum of letters ranging between e and c shown in Figure 9. One of these letters is chosen randomly and flashed on a computer screen for a very short duration followed immediately by a second masking stimulus composed of bits and

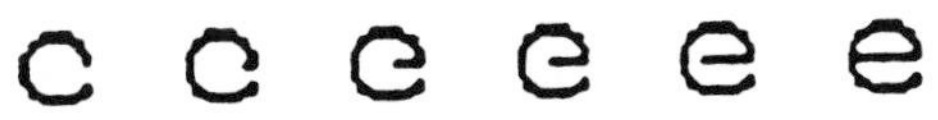

Figure 9. A continuum of letters between c and e.

pieces of letters. In a binary-choice task, the subject is asked to indicate whether an e or a c was presented. The results shown in the right panel of Figure 10 show that some letters were consistently classified as e and other letters were consistently classified as c. From these perceptual reports, it might (and in fact has been) concluded that subjects perceived some of the letters as equivalent to one another. However, this conclusion would be in error because the task does not permit the subject to give a direct index of what he or she saw. Another task is to ask subjects to rate the point at which the letter falls on a continuous scale between c and e. These judgments are shown in the left panel of Figure 10. Subjects rated adjacent letters on the continuum as different from one another, even though they were identified equivalently in the binary-choice task. Given that the nature of the judgment should not have influenced how the letter was processed, we can conclude that subjects saw differences in the binary-choice task even though they did not report them. The experimenter must tap into perceptual processing in different ways and at different times to overcome the limitation in just a single type of perceptual report.

FUNCTIONALISM AND INFORMATION PROCESSING

The information-processing approach appears to have its roots in the functional psychology of William James, James Baldwin, James Angell, and others. As noted by Hilgard (1987), American temper was better prepared for a psychology of activity than a psychology of the structure of consciousness. Angell summarized two properties of functionalism. First, functionalism is concerned with mental operations rather than simply the contents or elements of mind. Second, it

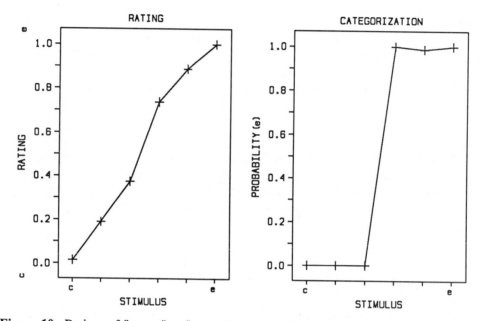

Figure 10. Ratings of "c-ness" to "e-ness" as a function of stimulus level (left panel) and proportion of "e" judgments as a function of stimulus (right panel).

acknowledges that mental operations mediate between the environment and behavior. A central component of functionalism involved the organism's adaptive behavior and learning. A natural outcome of this latter emphasis was stimulus-response psychology as, for example, in the research programs of Cattell and Thorndike. Cattell built on the developments of Donders (Chapter 7) to study the mental operations involved in word recognition and reading. Thorndike studied the learning processes involved in the organism's adaptation to its environment. Perhaps the most direct link is the connection between information processing and Robert Woodworth's dynamic psychology, if it can be interpreted as the analysis of behavior over time. Woodworth's book *Experimental Psychology* (1938) served as the bible for Columbia graduate students a couple of decades before its publication. A sobering experience is to read a chapter or two, such as the ones on reading and reaction times. Although the metaphors for psychological inquiry may have changed, the problems to be solved have not.

A central assumption of the development of theory and method in this book is that psychological phenomena are conceptualized as processes, not as stimulus-response relationships. In this case we are primarily interested in what psychological events do, even though we may be somewhat foggy about what they are. We address ourselves to the psychological processes that intervene between some stimulus and some response for two central reasons. First, explanation and prediction of stimulus-response relationships fail without prior understanding of the intervening sequence of mental processes. Second, we are interested in developing a psychological explanation of exactly those processes that lead to the response. Our inquiry into psychology is primarily directed at understanding the form of psychological behavior, not at merely predicting simple cause and effect relationships between stimulus and response.

The goal of this book is to illuminate the proper methods of psychological study. However, the illustration of these methods is completely interwoven with the study of the psychological processes themselves. As illustrated above and throughout this book, the methods of psychology cannot be discussed independently of the theory and content of psychology. Also, the knowledge of the proper methods of psychology is best acquired by doing science rather than by learning a set of abstract rules for doing it. After defining a given scientific method, it is illustrated in the context of specific experiments and theories rather than in isolation. In the next chapter, we consider alternative methods of psychological inquiry.

3

Four Methods of Psychological Inquiry

Naturalistic Observation
  Astrology
  Performance Slips
  Critique

Correlational Relationship
  Reading and Knowledge of Spelling
  Spelling Test
  Method
  Results
  Critique

Functional Relationship
  Seeing Light under Optimal Conditions
  Dark Adaptation and other Influences
  Method
  Results

Hypothesis Testing
  Bat Navigation
  Importance of Control Manipulations
  Publication and Acceptance

Correlation and Causation

*The kind of inference a great scientist employs in his creative moments
is comparable to the kind of inference the master at chess employs; it
involves an ability to keep a lot of variables in mind at once, to be
sensitive to feedback ..., to perceive the relevance of one fact to
another, or of a hypothesis to facts.*
Peter Caws (1969)

Psychological inquiry can be implemented in a variety of ways and our goal in this chapter is to present the important characteristics of four different methods. We distinguish between four methods, although a number of finer distinctions could be made that would easily increase this number. In addition, the boundaries between the four methods are not exact and classification is accordingly somewhat arbitrary. However, distinguishing among these four methods captures the significant aspects of psychological inquiry and the classification of the methods into these four categories should facilitate learning, memory, and utilization of the principles of psychological inquiry. The four methods are naturalistic observation, correlational relationship, functional relationship, and hypothesis testing. The methods can be distinguished from one another on the basis of a number of characteristics, as illustrated in Figure 1.

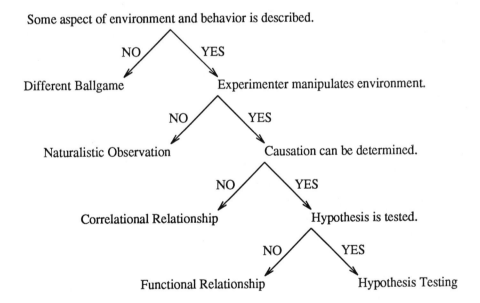

Figure 1. Binary tree illustrating binary oppositions central to defining the method of psychological inquiry. The diagram should be read from the top down.

NATURALISTIC OBSERVATION

Naturalistic observation in psychology involves the systematic recording of some aspect of environment and behavior. It is a scientific method since the observations are meant to be objective and can be repeated by other members of the scientific community. In the domain of physics,

Aristotle used naturalistic observation to present evidence for the roundness of the earth. One source of evidence easily observed by adherents and skeptics alike was the round shadow cast on the moon during a lunar eclipse. If the shape of the earth was other than round, the shadow cast on the moon would have been different. Other scientists might disagree with the interpretation of this observation, but there would probably be little disagreement about the observation itself.

Astrology

A particularly good example of naturalistic observation was used by St. Augustine to bury astrology, the pseudoscience which relates behavior to the position of the stars. Students of this belief at the time of Augustine were highly attentive to the exact time of births, since this was believed to completely determine the person's horoscope. It so happened that a noble son and a slave boy in the same house were born at the same time and, therefore, their horoscopes should have been identical. But as most of us would have predicted, the slave boy acquired great wealth and honors whereas the noble boy spent his life in hard slavery (I hope you did a double take since actually the opposite occurred).

Augustine's observation provides striking contradiction of astrological theory, but we shouldn't be surprised if persons dedicated to this practice do not waiver because of it. In many cases, although probably not in this one, a scientist is wise not to abandon a theory on the basis of one piece of evidence. As an example, John Snow did not abandon his theory that cholera was a communicable disease when a man, who unknowingly digested some of the poison, did not get the disease. Allowing for other influences, both the germ-theorist and the astrologer are equally justified in living with a few cases that do not fit their mold. What is important, though, is that naturalistic observation allows for repeated observations of certain conditions to build a large data base for classification of the phenomena of interest.

Performance Slips

More recently, naturalistic observation has been used in psychology to study errors in performance. Speech errors, called slips of the tongue (Fromkin, 1973, 1980; MacKay, 1973b), were made famous by Professor Spooner at Oxford. His memorable statements include such pronouncements as, "You tasted the whole worm," instead of "You wasted the whole term." Slips of the mind are also common experiences for all of us (Norman, 1981; Reason, 1979). In the kitchen, we put some material in the wrong container. Preparing breakfast, we pour juice in our coffee cup or put sugar and cream in our juice.

Ellis (1979) analyzed a corpus of his own slips of the pen, collected over a period of approximately a year and one-half. He recorded every writing error that he noticed and included the intended (appropriate) form together with the relevant context within which the error occurred. Ellis was able to provide a detailed classification of about 75 percent of the corpus of 766 errors. The author justifies the method of classifying his own errors on the basis of the writer having the best information about his intentions. The current study of slips of the tongue, mind, or pen might be viewed as analogous to the study of physical and biological phenomena before the time of Linnaeus and before the development of the Periodic Table in Chemistry. Before Linnaeus, classification was the method of investigation in the biological sciences. The discovery of the Periodic Table allowed experiments to be carried out.

In his analysis of slips of the pen, Ellis was able to distinguish slips at the level of words, letters, and strokes. Table 1 gives some actual examples of a selection of these errors. Word substitutions sometimes included homophonic confusions such as writing *their* for *there* or *week* for *weak*. Homophones are words which sound the same but have different meanings. Homographs are words which are spelled the same but have different meanings. Letter errors included repetitions, transposing two letters, omitting letters, and substituting letters. Stroke errors were additional strokes made in writing a letter. The value of this research seems to be in the development of testable hypotheses about writing. Writing errors might provide some insight into the various ways information is recalled and utilized in writing performance.

Table 1. Different types of slips of the pen as intended, written, observed, and classified by Ellis (1979).

Type of error	Intended	Written
1. lexical substitution	piece speaking last week	peace reading next week
2. letter repetition	looks inaccurate these	looks inna these
3. letter transposition	council	conu
4. letter omission	than when short-term dependence	than wen shor-term depence
5. letter substitution	and lapse from	ang lapse trom
6. stroke repetition	show	show
7. homophonic substitution	there weak	their week

Critique

Natural(istic observation) scientists might face some formidable obstacles in their view of the events of interest. It is not only difficult to record what exactly took place during a particular error situation, but needless to say, errors can be recorded only if the scientist is present when they are made. One scientist studying speech errors records slips of the tongue during the oral papers presented at professional meetings. Of course, she attends only those talks she's interested in, not because these speakers make good slips but because of her other research interests. Her colleagues are also becoming aware of her recordings and whether they will be more careful in what they say remains to be seen. There may also be some difficulty in estimating the relative frequency of occurrence of errors, unless a highly systematic observational study is carried out. In the area of motor control and performance, naturalistic observation and classification offers a viable method of study and offers the potential of understanding certain performance skills not easily studied in the experimental laboratory. Since it is possible to induce some errors experimentally in the laboratory, the experimental methods that follow might be used profitably to test certain questions that cannot be answered using naturalistic observation.

CORRELATIONAL RELATIONSHIP

The second category of inquiry involves the systematic analysis of repeated observations of co-occurring events. To return to our astrology example, an enthusiastic investigator could perform a longitudinal study of correlating time of birth and some index or indices of living conditions, such as happiness. According to astrological belief, persons born at the same time should experience similar circumstances whereas persons born at different times should experience different circumstances. The more complicated belief that the position of the stars at the time of observation is also important could be evaluated using correlational analysis. Correlational relationships depend upon systematic and repeated observations of two or more variables, and evaluating the degree to which the variables co-vary. In the astrological example, two variables could be time of birth (for example, which of the twelve signs of the zodiac) and some measure of psychological and physical well-being at a given time. The correlational analysis will provide a measure of the relationship between the two variables, although there are considerable restrictions on the inferences which can be made from the results.

Correlation and Causation

In a correlational design the scientist attempts to find a relationship between two variables. For example, he or she may collect data on the relationship between affection and juvenile delinquency. A measure of each variable is defined, such as number of hugs received and number of hubcaps stolen. A survey is made of a neighborhood and the two variables are correlated. A negative correlation is obtained; increase in hugs means a decrease in hubcaps for these children. One appealing conclusion to make is that delinquency is due to lack of affection. The conclusion is not justified, however, because causality can not be determined from correlation alone. Delinquents on the streets stealing hubcaps may have less time at home receiving hugs. The relationship might also be due to a third variable: there may be fewer cars in affectionate neighborhoods. The correlational design indicates that A and B are related but A may cause B. B may cause A, or C may cause A and B.

Reading and Knowledge of Spelling

A correlational relationship is nicely illustrated in a study of reading carried out by Massaro and Hestand (1983). Readers comprehend print by the active process of deriving meaning from it. A knowledge of spelling regularities in the written language provides one important source of information that readers use to derive such meaning. Readers utilize the regularities of spelling along with other sources of information and knowledge in their efforts at finding meaning. Earlier work has documented that expert readers use their knowledge of spelling letter and word recognition (see Chapter 20). The goal of this correlational study was to relate the beginning reader's knowledge of spelling to reading ability.

Spelling Test

To assess knowledge of spelling among young readers, the authors asked first, second, and third graders to pick the item that "looks more like a word" from a pair of letter strings. This assessment method was based on previous research. Rosinski and Wheeler (1972) asked children in these grades to choose which of two groups of letters "was more like a real word." The test items were nonsense words which could or could not be pronounced (Gibson, Pick, Osser, & Hammond, 1962; Gibson, Osser, & Pick, 1963). First graders could not discriminate pronounceable from unpronounceable items whereas both third and fifth graders could do so over 80 percent of the time. Each pair of items in the Massaro and Hestand (1983) study had one regular and one irregular item. Irregular items violated certain rules of spelling as illustrated in Table 2. There were a total of 60 pairs of six-letter items. Chance performance is 50 percent correct, or 30 of the 60 items, since the children were required to choose one item for each pair.

Table 2. Examples of the regular and irregular test items used in the Massaro and Hestand (1983) study. The numbers in parentheses indicate the number of spelling irregularities.

regular	irregular
movule	plaged (1)
morebs	ydlaes (2)
hemort	cdrtei (3)

The rules for determining the irregularity count are given in Massaro, Taylor, Venezky, Jastrzembski, and Lucas (1980). One item of each pair of items on the test had no violations of spelling. The other item had either 1, 2, or 3 violations. Both members of a pair were typed on the same line and the irregular item was equally likely to be on the right or left. The items were given on the test in order of roughly increasing difficulty with respect to the number of violations of the irregular member of the pair. This format was used to discourage an early "giving up" on the part of students who found the task difficult and to compensate for learning during the task itself. The students were asked to play a game of picking possible words over nonwords. The children had the written instructions in front of them and they were also read aloud by the experimenter. Examples of the test items are given in Table 2 along with the number of violations of each of the irregular items.

Method

One of the authors administered the test in the classroom with the teacher present. The students were told that they would be asked to play a game which would help us understand how children learn to read. The test was handed out and the students followed along as the experimenter read the instructions. When the first example question was reached, the students were asked to put their finger on it. After checking to see that all children had found the question, the experimenter spelled each item and asked which item looked more like a word. Given the appropriate response, the students were asked to circle the correct item. The experimenter repeated this for each of the remaining three examples. Students were then told to start the test and work until it was completed. Testing time never exceeded 20 minutes. The number of correct items on this test was taken as a child's knowledge of spelling.

The relationship of interest was between knowledge of spelling and reading ability. Reading ability of these same children was measured by the California Achievement Tests (1978), which had just been taken a few weeks before the experiment. This reading test consists of reading vocabulary and comprehension questions in addition to an assessment of phonics, expression, spelling, and language skills. A grade equivalent reading ability score was derived for each student's combined performance on the reading vocabulary and comprehension portions of the reading test.

The performance of each student on the spelling test was correlated with his or her reading ability score. A correlation between two variables can be assessed in two ways: visually and numerically. The visual analysis is in terms of a scatterplot in which one variable is plotted on the x axis and the other variable is plotted on the y axis. By observing the relationship among the points, one can obtain some idea of the correlation between the two variables. Figure 2 shows the scatterplot of the spelling test performance as a function of reading grade level as measured by the achievement tests. As can be seen in Figure 2, there is a reasonably consistent positive relationship between performance on the spelling test and reading grade level.

The visual analysis of a relationship provides only a rough index of the correlation between two variables. Luckily, the numeric analysis is much more precise and provides a descriptive statistic called a correlation coefficient. The correlation coefficient is simply a number between +1.0 and -1.0. The sign indicates whether the relationship is positive or negative and the magnitude of the relationship is given by the degree to which the number differs from zero. A perfect relationship would give 1.0 for a positive relationship and -1.0 for a negative relationship. A respectable correlation coefficient is .5. Given that respect isn't enough, a statistical test is necessary to determine if the correlation is statistically significant, i.e., not due to chance.

Results

The correlation of this measure of reading ability with performance on the spelling test was .663. Although this correlation was statistically significant, it is also informative to assess the magnitude of this correlation. One strategy is to compare this correlation with some other less interesting correlation. We would expect that grade level in school would also correlate with performance on the spelling test, but not as highly as reading ability if knowledge of spelling is related to reading ability. Grade level in school correlated .504 with performance on the spelling test. This correlation is significantly smaller than the correlation with reading ability, which makes it safe to conclude that knowledge of spelling is related to reading ability and not simply to year in school. Reading achievement as measured by comprehension and vocabulary is more highly related to knowledge of spelling than is grade level.

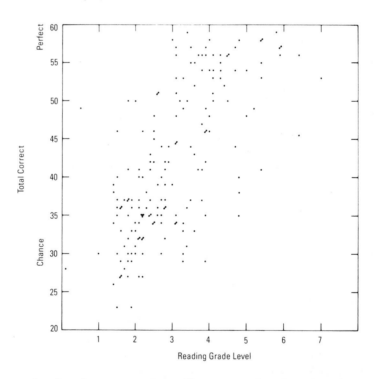

Figure 2. Scatterplot of performance on the spelling test as a function of reading grade level as measured by comprehension and vocabulary achievement tests.

Critique

The reading research demonstrates that knowing and using spelling regularities is correlated with reading ability among young readers. Given a correlational result, however, no conclusion can be made about causation. It remains to be determined whether differences in this skill are partially responsible for differences in reading ability. Early reading instruction seldom teaches spelling regularities structure directly. Hence it is difficult to assess whether knowledge of this structure plays a causal role in learning to read or whether it is only a concomitant outcome of learning to read. Varying instructional offerings on spelling regularities would permit an experimental assessment of the role knowledge of spelling may play in learning to read.

FUNCTIONAL RELATIONSHIP

The third method of inquiry involves the experimental study of some relationship between environment and behavior. Some aspect of the environment is manipulated and the consequences of this manipulation on behavior are observed. The manipulation is called the independent variable and the behavior is called the dependent variable. This method allows the investigator to make some conclusions about causation. If the dependent variable changes systematically with changes in the independent variable, it seems reasonable to conclude that changes in the independent variable were responsible for the changes in the dependent variable. To insure that the conclusion is correct, the investigator must control and account for all other variables that might also be contributing to the relationship.

Seeing Light under Optimal Conditions

The concept of functional relationship will be discussed within the context of our visual experience of light. That is, we will examine functional relationships addressing how our visual experience of light is dependent on many environmental variables. The functional relationships will be made apparent in the consideration of the question, "What is the minimal amount of light that is visible to the human observer under optimal conditions of seeing?" This experimental question was asked by Hecht, Shlaer, and Pirenne in 1942. Hecht et al. found that the answer to their question was dependent on the answer to a number of related questions. First it was necessary to analyze the results from a number of previous experiments that were relevant to these related questions.

Finding optimal conditions for the visual system was the significant aspect of the experimental question. To optimize visual detection it is necessary to consider a number of variables that affect how well an observer can detect a light. For example, the adaptation state of the observer could be very important. Visual detectability will be poorer if the observer has been exposed to a bright light recently than if the observer has been in the dark for a while. A second variable that must be dealt with is the location of the test stimulus in the visual field. Whether the observer is looking directly at the stimulus or whether it is off to one side could make a difference. The size of a visual stimulus of constant intensity is also an important stimulus variable. As the area of a fixed amount of light becomes larger, there would be less light in any given area. Perhaps we would not see the flash as well when it is spread across a large area relative to being concentrated in a small area. Another important variable is the duration of the light flash. Visual detectability should be dependent upon whether the light is presented for a brief moment, or whether this same light intensity is spread out over time. And finally, the hue of the test flash should make a difference for optimal detection. Visible light is only a small portion of the electromagnetic spectrum. It seems reasonable that we would be less sensitive to colors presented at the extremes than in the middle range of the visible spectrum.

Dark Adaptation and other Influences

Entering a movie theater, it is difficult to find one's way, but after a few minutes many features of the theater and the people inside it become visible. This is an example of dark adaptation; we become more sensitive to light with increased time in the dark. To define this relationship exactly, it is necessary to measure experimentally the sensitivity of an observer to a flash of light after different periods of dark adaptation. Such an experiment had been done many times and some typical results are shown in Figure 3. This functional relationship shows that the amount of light necessary for its detection decreases with increases in the time in the dark. The intensity necessary for detection before dark adaptation is 4 log units more intense than that needed after 30 minutes in the dark. Four log units indicates that one light is 10,000 times as intense as the other.

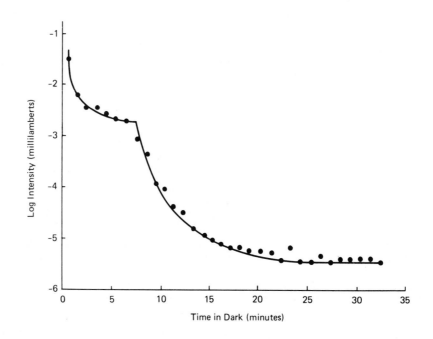

Figure 3. The minimum intensity of light necessary for visual detection as a function of the duration of dark adaptation, after a preliminary light adaptation to a high-intensity field of light (after Hecht, 1934).

These results can also be plotted with relative sensitivity as the dependent measure. In this case, an increase in sensitivity reflects a decrease in the amount of light needed for detection. Figure 4 shows that these results are the mirror image of the results in Figure 3.

The dark-adaptation curve is actually the combination of two curves. There is a discontinuity in the function around 7 or 8 minutes of dark adaptation. The two parts of the function reflect the contributions of two different visual systems, photopic and scotopic vision. In photopic vision, light detection in the light-adapted subject is due to central (foveal) vision. In scotopic vision, peripheral vision is responsible for dark-adapted light detection. More light is required to see in foveal than in peripheral vision and that is why a star at night might be seen only out of the corner of your eye. This differential sensitivity as a function of the location of the light gives a clue for the optimal location of the test flash. In fact, systematic measurement of sensitivity as a function of location has shown that the optimal location is 20 degrees to the nasal side of the fixation point.

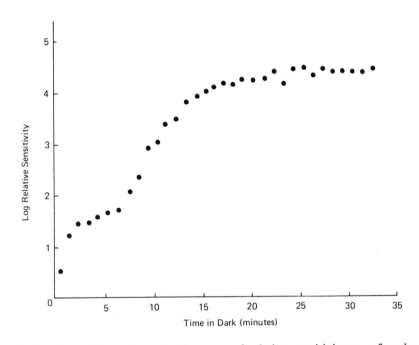

Figure 4. Results in Figure 3 plotted in terms of relative sensitivity as a function of the duration of dark adaptation.

Similar experiments had been done to determine the optimal size, duration, and wavelength of the test flash. As might be expected, maximum sensitivity occurs for a relatively small and a relatively short test stimulus. This allows the light to be concentrated in a small region over a short period of time. Finally, our optimal sensitivity has been shown to be for wavelengths in the middle of the visible spectrum—the blue-greens or about 510 nanometers (nm).

Method

After determining the optimal visual condition for each of these five variables, these conditions could then be employed to determine the minimal intensity of light at which the observer could reliably report, "I see some light out there." The experimental apparatus was designed so that the stimulus variables could be precisely controlled. Figure 5 illustrates the optical system and the experimental situation used in the study. The duration, location, size, wavelength, and intensity of the light could be controlled by Hecht et al. Given the results of previous experiments, the subject could now be tested under optimal conditions of detecting light in the real world. The subject was dark adapted before the experiment. A flash of 10 minutes (′) of visual angle was used and it was presented 20 degrees off the point of fixation. (One degree contains 60 minutes.) Ten minutes of arc represents the approximate size of a thumbtack at a distance of 10 ft. The duration of the flash was 1 msec. The energy in the flash was concentrated at a wavelength of 510 nanometers (nm).

Hecht et al. determined the observer's sensitivity by employing the method of constant stimuli (see Chapter 10). The experimenters chose randomly one of 6 intensities for presentation on a given trial. The subject sat at the apparatus, had a fixation point, and on each trial pressed a button which initiated presentation of the visual target. He then reported whether or not he saw a test flash. Hecht et al. were interested in the relationship between number of quanta in the test flash and the probability of the observer saying, "Yes, I detect it."

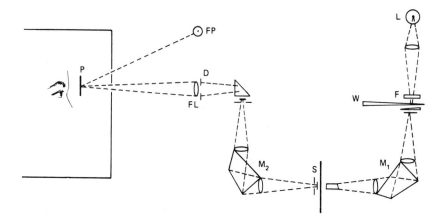

Figure 5. An illustration of the Hecht et al. experimental situation. The subject sits in a dark room; his head is held in a fixed position by keeping his teeth in a "bite" rest—a hard impression of the upper jaw. His left eye is next to the artificial pupil P and by fixating on the red fixation point FP, he sees the field lens FL. The light source is a ribbon filament lamp L focused on the slit of a double monochromator $M_1 M_2$ which controls the wavelength of the light sent on to the field lens FL. The light intensity is controlled by the filters F and neutral wedge and balancer W. The size of the test field is controlled by the diaphragm D. The shutter S controls the exposure (after Hecht et al., 1942).

Results

The results for three subjects from the Hecht et al. experiment are shown in Figure 6. Detection is positively related to the intensity of the test flash and this relationship can be described roughly by an ogive curve. The shape of the function agrees with most functions obtained using the method of constant stimuli (see Chapter 10). The three subjects in Figure 6 were actually the three experimenters and authors of the report. Being very practiced and very well trained, their attitudes probably had very little influence on the results.

Hecht and his associates detected the light about 50 percent of the time when the light stimulus contained only about 90 quanta. Upon examining the anatomy and physiology of the ocular system, Hecht et al. discovered that the system is even more sensitive than their result first indicated. First of all, as the test flash comes into the eye, about 3 percent of the 90 quanta are reflected back out into the world. In other words, these quanta never get to the receptor system. Then, 50 percent of the remaining light is absorbed in the eye itself before it reaches the light-sensitive area. Our eyes are built backwards. The light-sensitive area lies behind the optic nerve fibers and other neural tissue. Light has to get through this other pigment before it reaches the retina. Therefore, about 50 percent of the 97 percent of light that enters the eye is absorbed, and about 48 percent hits the light-sensitive part of the dark-adapted retina, the rods. There is also pigment between the rods that does not function as a receptor; this pigment, therefore, cannot signal light or no light. When the light absorbed by this pigment is accounted for, only about 9 or 10 quanta are found to be captured by the rods. Hecht et al. knew that there were about 300 rods covered by the test flash. Therefore, it was very unlikely that 2 of the 9 or 10 quanta would hit the same rod. Hence, we need about 9 or 10 rods catching a quanta each in order to detect, under optimal conditions, that a light stimulus is present.

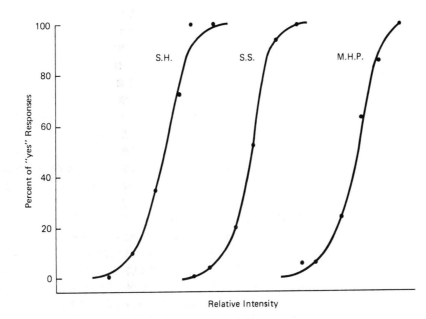

Figure 6. Percent "yes" responses for each of the three subjects as a function of the relative intensity of the test flash (after Hecht, Shlaer, & Pirenne, 1942).

When the experimenters analyzed the physics of their light stimulus, their interpretation of the results could be made even more precise. The stimulus was an electrical filament that emitted quanta of light. A quantum is the smallest nondivisible unit of energy making up light. But the experimenters found that the number of quanta coming from the filament varied from trial to trial, even though the intensity of the light was experimentally held constant. When they thought they were putting out 90 quanta, on some trials they were putting out even less quanta and on other trials they were putting out more quanta. Light behaves according to a Poisson process, such that at any point in time the probability that a quantum will be emitted is described by some probability value. Since the number of quanta emitted per unit of time varies, Hecht et al. had variability in their stimulus. This variability in the stimulus could, therefore, account for some of the variability in the response to a given stimulus.

In any task we also have variability due to the subject. By variability due to the subject we mean that sometimes one of the rods fires without a light quantum hitting it. So we have background activity in our receptor system. The background activity of the rods is one example of noise in the sensory system postulated by the theory of signal detectability (see Chapter 11). The number of rods firing per unit of time varies and this variation could conceivably follow a normal distribution. Accordingly, the subject's task is actually one of determining when the activity outputted by the sensory system is from background activity alone or background activity plus activity due to the test flash. Taking into account this variability of the physiological receptor, we see that the eye is indeed a very sensitive apparatus, in the sense that you have to add only about 9 or 10 quanta to its background activity for the light to be seen.

What is the minimal amount of light that is visible to the human observer under optimal conditions? This question involved the method of determining functional relationships between the visual environment and the detection of light. The question led to a series of experiments that required precise stimulus and experimental control and measurement in a psychophysical situation. The answer indicated that under optimal conditions for seeing, an observer was essentially as sensitive as he or she could possibly be.

HYPOTHESIS TESTING

The fourth method of psychological inquiry involves the actual test of some hypothesis (prediction) about some aspect of behavior. In 1909, Francesco Redi refuted the dogma that insects arose spontaneously from decaying carcasses. Careful observation revealed that a given insect originates only from eggs of insects of the same kind. Redi's observations qualify as experimental because the scientist intervened, at least, somewhat with nature. For example, Redi would take the dead flesh of horses and in one case add wasp eggs and in another add nothing. When wasps were observed only in the flesh with eggs, he refuted the hypothesis held by Greek philosophers who believed that wasps arose directly from dead flesh of horses. Redi's observations could be repeated by any skeptic or extended by himself or other interested parties. Scientific study has the important feature of repeatability, which allows the systematic accumulation of knowledge and understanding. An even nicer example of how experimentation proceeds and involves a series of artistic maneuvers is Lazzaro Spallanzani's study of bat navigation.

Bat Navigation

People didn't know much about how bats navigated their environment when, in 1793, a curious priest, Lazzaro Spallanzani, was seduced by the problem. What first captured his curiosity was his pet owl. One night, the owl snuffed out the candle and proceeded to fly into objects and walls in the darkened room. Spallanzani was surprised at the difficulty the owl had navigating because at that time owls were reputed to be night animals who could see relatively well in minimal light (Stevens & Warshofsky, 1965).

Having learned that owls do not see all that well in the dark, he asked, what about other animals? Bats were reputed to see well in the dark. When tested under similar circumstances, bats had no problem zipping around the dark room. One might conclude that bats see in the dark, but Spallanzani wondered, "it appears dark to me but there must be enough light for the bat." The bat could have a much more sensitive visual system than humans. To test this hypothesis, it was necessary to eliminate all light. If the bat would stumble about, it would support the idea that bats see with less light than required by priests. He covered the bat's head with an opaque hood and set him loose in the room. The outcome confirmed the hypothesis because the bat failed to navigate accurately with the hood on.

Importance of Control Manipulations

Spallanzani was, for a time anyhow, satisfied with the demonstration that bats must have some light to navigate accurately. Myth would have it that he woke up in the middle of one night unhappy with his experiment. Putting the hood over the bat's head blocked out the light but may also have done something else. An experimental manipulation usually needs a control manipulation. It cannot be assumed that the hood did nothing but eliminate light. He needed a control condition to evaluate the effect of putting on a hood. To accomplish this, Spallanzani covered the bat's head with a transparent hood made of similar material as the opaque hood. According to his logic, if the hood was doing nothing but eliminating the light, the bat should have no problem navigating with the transparent hood. In fact, the opposite occurred; the bat flew equally poorly with both hoods. The hood was doing something in addition to changing the amount of light and whatever it was doing interfered with how the bat navigated.

Some thought about the problem led to the observation that the hood was also blocking the bat's ears. Bats obviously do not see with their ears; however, Mother Nature sometimes works in strange ways and Father Spallanzani was encouraged to study what role the ears play in the navigation of the bats. After Spallanzani's findings were known, Louis Jurine, a contemporary of Spallanzani, repeated the original study and also filled the ears of bats with wax and observed the consequences. When Jurine did this, the bats stumbled about in the environment. Having been caught earlier without the appropriate control, Spallanzani was aware of the fact that the wax in Jurine's bats could be having some other effect in addition to influencing the hearing system. The vestibular system is intertwined with the auditory system and the wax could have interfered with its functioning. The vestibular system controls balance and could be responsible for the bat's poor navigation. He needed some way to block the hearing without messing up the vestibular system. He developed a funnel that he could put in the bat's ears and the outside of the funnel could be left clear or filled with wax. The wax would not be in the inner ear; if the hearing was responsible then the bat should have problems when the funnel is filled with wax but not when the funnel is clear. In fact, this was the result of his experiment. To check again on the contribution of the eyes, he simply blinded the bats and found no impairment in navigation skills.

Publication and Acceptance

Although Spallanzani was able to publish his findings, they were ignored and forgotten for 150 years (see Chapter 5). It wasn't until 1939 that the scientific community was able to understand how bats could see with their ears. A sonic detector was developed that could measure sound vibrations in the environment. Sound is communicated by changes in pressure through the atmosphere. One property of pressure changes is the frequency of vibration. The sonic detector takes higher frequencies and changes them so they can now be heard at lower frequencies. The discovery of sonar and its use to detect German submarines was an important factor in World War II. Sound sent through the water would pick up the reflection of a submarine.

When you put a sonic detector in a room with a bat, it records sound. The bat emits short bursts of sound, sometimes lasting only 2 msec (1/500 of a second) and the frequency of these sounds is around 50,000 Hz, much higher than the range of human hearing. Humans are limited with respect to the frequencies that they can hear. The frequency range of humans is roughly 20 Hz to 20,000 Hz. Bats can hear at much higher frequencies. A bat sends out high-frequency sounds in the environment and listens for the echoes from these sounds. The frequency 50,000 Hz is a very nice frequency to send out because the wavelength of the sound is only about one-quarter inch. This is a perfect size to bounce off a mosquito. A mosquito will bounce back the sound in the same way that the sound of a lecturer bounces off the walls of the room. Bats interpret the echoes to see their environment and we enlightened people know that bats navigate using echo location. Not only bats but also porpoises and possibly whales use sonar to navigate. The blind are also able to navigate somewhat using echo location. Hard shoes can produce high frequency sounds which will bounce off obstacles in the environment.

This ends our example of hypothesis testing. Some of the problems are unique to the particular area being studied; however, there are certain rules of thumb that are fairly general. For example, when you make a manipulation to produce a certain effect, you have to be careful that it is not doing something else. You need a control condition to evaluate whether your manipulation is having an effect other than the desired one. For Spallanzani, an important control was a transparent hood to evaluate extraneous effects of the opaque hood.

4

Experimental Method

Experimental Psychology

Experimental Design and Control
  Properties of Dependent Variables
  Properties of Independent Variables
  Confounding Variables

Perceiving Letters
  Controlling Variables
  Interpolation and Extrapolation

Seeing, Spatial Location, and Age
  Eye Movements
  Memory and Report Limitations
  Developmental Issues
  Experimental Solutions

Infant Perception
  Preferential Looking
  Operant Conditioning

  Confounding Processes
  Statistics
  Within-Subject and Between-Subject Designs

Above all an experiment enables us to photograph the transient
phenomena and subject them to objective explanation and measurement.
James McKeen Cattell (1888)

How does one proceed when faced with the challenge of explaining how people behave and experience the world. Science progresses by manipulating the world of interest. Complex phenomena are broken into simpler components and these components are examined in the laboratory. Most laws of the universe are not apparent in the natural world (Manicas & Secord, 1983). Complexity of the natural setting far exceeds what any scientific theory could hope to accommodate. Theories will have the most predictive power in the laboratory in which the complexity of everyday life can be simplified, measured, and controlled.

Natural observation might even distort the appearance of these laws in action; for example, the sun appears to rise and set on our flat world. Laws of the universe must be revealed in highly artificial, controlled, and manipulated laboratory environments. Along with these contrived demonstrations, very precise (fine-grained) measurements are necessary. Examples of experimental manipulations and precise measurements are well-known in the physical sciences. Currently, there are plans to build a superconducting super collider under the heartland of California. This giant underground atom smasher would be a 52-mile racetrack that promises insights into the origins of the universe and the basic building blocks of matter. Paraphrasing Minsky (1985, p. 20), we will try to imitate Galileo and Newton. They learned a phenomenal amount by studying the simplest types of problems. A profitable assumption in science has been that one can learn the most by studying what seems the least. Our point of departure is even more pessimistic in that the complexity of poorly designed psychology experiments might exceed any theory's predictive power. Following the dictum that "data without theory are meaningless" (Coombs, 1969), laboratory experiments must be closely linked with some well-defined model or theory in order to advance our knowledge.

The experiment is the ideal domain to implement the study of functional relationships and the testing of alternative hypotheses. We discussed the properties of these two types of inquiry in the previous chapter. Additional examples of these types of inquiry will be presented in this chapter to provide a better understanding of the experimental method. The goal is to illustrate some general principles within the context of specific examples of research. It will become apparent that the methods are aimed at the study of individuals; methods for the study of differences among groups of individuals must follow directly from these methods. The reason is the belief that group differences in a task are relatively uninformative without understanding how an individual functions in the task. Thus, I am unwilling to endorse methods that can be used to show that two groups of individuals differ from one another without addressing how they differ. Several examples in the present chapter and in Chapter 8 describe how group differences might be assessed within the present framework.

EXPERIMENTAL PSYCHOLOGY

Experimental psychology can be regarded as a set of general methods for attacking certain problems (Hearst, 1979). The methods are analogous to those used in other sciences. This discipline has been criticized by Neisser (1976) and others for utilizing highly artificial experimental situations to explore psychological processes. It has been claimed that experimental psychology often lacks *ecological validity*. In this context, ecological validity is taken to mean how well our experiment resembles the real world. The ecological validity of the research framework must be assessed, not in terms of the ecological validity of the experiments, but in terms of whether it leads to the development of ecologically-valid theories. Our experiments do not have to be like the real world; they only have to inform us about it.

Simplification is true in all scientific endeavors and, therefore, experimental psychology is not unique among scientific disciplines. Psychological inquiry is in its infancy, and we should not be overwhelmed by the complexity of the issues to be resolved. We are confident in the need for controlled observation and the systematic manipulation of independent variables. It is true that many of the laws discovered in the laboratory might be highly specific to the experimental situation; the belief is that the correct laws will generalize not only to a variety of experimental situations but also to real-world events.

Today, most people acknowledge the positive contributions of experimental psychology and its potential for understanding much of human nature. Experimental psychology can be a profitable experience for experimenter and subject alike. Subjects in perception experiments become sensitized to the subtleties of perceptual experience and might become more attentive observers. A laboratory problem-solving task might encourage subjects to become more creative in their thinking and contact with real-life challenges. Mnemonic aids used in a memory experiment might profitably be applied to school, work, or recreation. At least we have learned enough to know that previous objections to experimental psychology are unfounded. In Wundt's day, critics opposed his experimental work because they believed that extensive study of the mind could lead to insanity. Even Cambridge University, a symbol of enlightenment in the nineteenth century, prohibited psychophysical experiments because measuring the human soul would insult religion (Hearst, 1979). When faced with a choice between study of the human mind and any of the variety of prohibitions against this study, people, by their very nature, will take the path of inquiry. Science has proven to be the best method of travel and the experimental method the best agenda.

EXPERIMENTAL DESIGN AND CONTROL

Throughout this book, we discuss how the experimental method is used to study the psychological processes that intervene between stimulus and response. Before beginning these experimental approaches, it is necessary to discuss the experimental method itself. In this method the experimenter manipulates nature, in the form of an *independent variable*, and looks for the effect of the changes in the independent variable upon changes in a *dependent variable*. The dependent variable is the indicator of the psychological event of interest.

Properties of Dependent Variables

How does the experimenter find a good dependent variable? Most experimental psychologists agree that a dependent measure should be valid, reliable, and sensitive. Validity refers to how accurately the dependent variable measures the psychological process of interest. If a psychologist is interested in how well an observer detected (experienced) a stimulus, the proportion of times he said he detected it may not be a valid measure. In this case, the psychologist is interested in a psychological process (detection), and the subject's observed behavior may not be a true (valid) index of that process. The validity of dependent measures in psychological experimentation is one of the central themes of this book.

The second criterion, reliability, refers to the desire to have as little random variability in our measure as possible. For example, distance might be measured by counting the number of steps one takes between two points or by utilizing a yardstick. The first measure would have more variability than the second, and although both measures would increase our knowledge about the distance between the points, we use the least variable measure possible in the experiment. A perfectly reliable dependent measure gives us exactly the same result with repeated observations.

The third criterion, sensitivity, is bound up with validity. Most experimental design books tell us to find a dependent measure which is sensitive to changes in our independent variable. Those that vary most with variations in the independent variable are preferred. However, here our interest is in a dependent variable that reflects the operation of a psychological process. So we look for variables that are sensitive to changes in the psychological process itself. Accordingly, in our approach we look for dependent variables that are (1) valid, reflecting accurately the operations of a psychological process, (2) reliable, fluctuating or changing very little for other reasons, and (3) sensitive, changing with changes in the psychological process they measure.

Properties of Independent Variables

Independent variables come in many different guises. Each level of an independent variable represents an unique experimental condition. The levels might might differ from one another quantitatively or qualitatively. A quantitative difference would correspond to the different intensities of a test tone in a psychophysical task, for example. A qualitative difference would correspond to whether or not a hood was placed over a bat's head in Spallanzani's experiment (Chapter 3). Although most independent variables are easily classified as quantitative or qualitative, some reflection will make apparent a somewhat fuzzy distinction between quantitative and qualitative.

A single-factor design involves the manipulation of only one independent variable, although the number of levels of the independent variable can be two or more. A factorial design involves the independent manipulation of two or more independent variables. A two-factor design would have two independent variables. By independent manipulation we mean that each level of one independent variable is paired with each level of the other independent variable. The number of unique experimental conditions, thus, is equal to a multiplicative combination of the number of levels of each of the independent variables. A three-factor design whose independent variables have 3, 2, and 5 levels, respectively, would have 3 x 2 x 5 = 30 experimental conditions.

Confounding Variables

The experimental design permits various forms of control by the experimenter. These controls are used to prevent other variables besides the independent variable from influencing or confounding the observed relationship between stimulus and response. A second variable is confounded with the independent variable if it is possible that changes in the second variable are partially responsible for the observed relationship between stimulus and response. Some methods of control are (1) eliminate the variables, (2) hold them constant, (3) counterbalance or randomize their effects in the experimental task.

PERCEIVING LETTERS

An experimenter might be interested in discovering how many letters a subject can perceive in a single eye fixation as a function of the number of items in the visual display (Sperling, 1960). Using a tachistoscope or a computer-controlled monitor, a visual display of letters can be presented for a very short time. Given the time required to make an eye movement, the duration can be made short enough so that it does not exceed a single eye fixation. The independent variable, under the experimenter's control and manipulation, is the number of letters presented on each trial. The dependent variable is the number of letters reported correctly on each trial. The experimenter presents the subject with a variety of trials containing anywhere from one to nine letters per trial. On each type of trial, the experimenter records the number of letters correctly reported. From these data a functional relationship between the number of letters reported and the number of letters in the display can be determined.

In an experimental design, the experimenter seeks to establish a functional relationship between an independent variable and a dependent variable. In order to assure that this relationship is reliable, all other variables must be accounted for in the experimental task. If they are, the experimenter is safe in assuming that changes in the dependent variable were caused by changes in the independent variable. This is only the first step—but a critical one—in defining the experimental task. The experimenter must also account for the sequence of mental processes or processing stages that the task requires before it is possible to understand the functional relationship between stimulus and response. The central theme of this book is the presentation of experimental methods for understanding the processing stages between stimulus and response. Before discussing these methods, however, it will be worthwhile to discuss many of the important features of an experimental design. These features will be illustrated in the context of a couple of specific examples of investigation.

The experimental question in the sample experiment presented above concerned how many items an observer could recognize in a single glance. This question was answered by varying the number of items in a display and recording the number that the observer recalled correctly. The answer to the question is seen in a functional relationship between the independent variable and the dependent variable. A number of other variables, however, could affect this relationship. These variables must be controlled so that the relationship will reflect the direct influence of the independent variable on the dependent variable.

Controlling Variables

Some of the variables that can influence the experimental results are given in Table 1. They are (1) how long the observer looks at the display, (2) the nature of the test items, (3) the size of the test field, (4) the acuity of the subject, (5) the figure-ground contrast of the items in the display, (6) the amount of practice, and (7) the opportunity that the subject has for chance guessing. Controlling for these variables should provide the desired functional relationship between the independent and dependent variables, supplying an answer for the experimental question.

Our experimental question requires that subjects get only a single glance at the visual display for recognition. Therefore, the effective duration of display must be controlled to eliminate additional glances. Evidence that will be presented later shows that we cannot take discrete looks at the world faster than about five times per second. To give the subject only one look, then, it is necessary that the display be presented for a duration of less than 200 msec. A msec (millisecond) is one-thousandth of a second. Presenting the display for 50 msec at each experimental condition will not only give a clear look at the display, it will hold display duration constant and will also eliminate additional looks at the visual display.

The test items chosen must be items that can be recognized; in other words, they must be meaningful to the observer. The letters of the alphabet provide a good population of items for our experiment; since we operationally define test items as letters, it is necessary to prevent the subject from employing other test items in his recognition strategy. For example, if the letters in the

Confounding Processes

The experimental psychologist has traditionally been interested in the effects of one variable, called his independent variable, on the dependent variable. The goal, in this case, is to eliminate the influence of other irrelevant variables on the dependent measure. When the experiment has failed to adequately control for the effects of an irrelevant variable on his dependent variable, we say the experimenter has confounded their effects and the results are invalid. Confounding variables are not always spotted by the experimenter or his or her colleagues. Scientific progress carries with it the revelation of previous confounds in the literature.

The problem of experimental psychology examined in this book is the confounding of psychological processes in an experiment. This confounding invalidates the experiment in the same way as a confounding of variables. Consider the question of the effects of the size of the display on perception as measured by the number of items correctly reported from a visual display. The memory process is a critical one in this task and its effects must be accounted for before any conclusions about perception can be reached. That is to say, increasing the number of items in the display not only affects the perceptual process, but also influences memory so that the results reflect some combination of both of these processes. The experimenter must design his study so that he can isolate the effects of each of these processes before conclusions can be reached. If he fails to pull apart their effects, his dependent measure gives no information about the functioning of psychological processes in this task. Our goal is to discuss designs and analytic methods that can be used to study one psychological process without the confoundings of other processes. We shall find that the traditional experiment which manipulates only one independent variable is usually insufficient to accomplish this.

display spell words, the subject could possibly treat the whole word as a single item. Accordingly, the experimenter would overestimate the number of items an observer could recognize, since the experimenter counts each letter as a test item. The experimenter can eliminate this possible confounding by making sure that the letters in the display do not spell words or wordlike items.

Table 1. The important variables and how they are controlled with respect to the question, "How many items can an observer recognize in a single glance?"

Variable	Control
1. Display duration	short enough for only a single glance
2. Test items	meaningful items that cannot be grouped together
3. Size of the visual display	hold constant with changes in the numbered items in the display
4. Acuity of the subject	test subject under all conditions
5. Figure/ground contrast	make items legible
6. Practice	give initial practice and control with respect to different levels of the independent variable
7. Guessing	reduce as much as possible

When the experimenter increases the number of letters in the visual display it would be only natural to increase the overall size of the visual display. In this case, the size of the display is completely confounded with the number of items in the display. This confounding creates a particular problem since the visual acuity of the observer decreases as letters are moved from the center of the visual display. It is necessary, therefore, to control for the visual display size as the number of letters in the display presentation increases. One way to do this is to define a given display size, for example, a 4 x 4 matrix of cells. Figure 1 gives two sample displays. The subject is instructed to fixate at the center of the matrix. Now, on each trial, the experimenter can choose the cells randomly for presentation of the test letters. In this case, even single-letter displays would lie off the center of the display. This procedure randomizes the location of the letters in the visual field to eliminate a confounding of display location with the independent variable (the number of letters in the display).

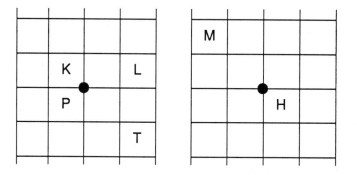

Figure 1. Two sample displays in the experiment testing how many items can be seen in a given glance. The dot is the subject's fixation point. The lines in the matrix are not actually presented but simply serve to illustrate the 16 possible locations.

Visual acuity of the subject is an important variable. We can hold this variable constant by testing the same subject under all the experimental conditions. If we tested different subjects under different experimental conditions, the results might differ simply because the subjects differed in acuity (or some other ability), not because of differences in our independent variable. Another solution to this problem would be to test a very large number of subjects at each of the levels of our independent variables in order to average out any differences in the different subjects. Although there are times when such a design is appropriate, we shall see that the best control for individual subject differences is to test each subject at all of the experimental conditions.

Figure-ground contrast (legibility) of the display is also an important variable that can affect performance. Performance would be positively correlated with the figure-ground contrast of the display. To control for this variable, the experimenter should print the display letters so as to optimize legibility and to maintain the same legibility at all levels of the independent variable. We noted earlier that a 50 msec display presentation was adequate for a legible display.

The amount of practice an observer gets in this task will affect his performance. Observers show some rapid improvement over the first few trials in almost any experimental task. To eliminate this large practice effect, some general practice should be given before the experiment proper is carried out. Also, the experimenter must not confound the order of presentation during the experiment with the levels of the independent variable. The order of presentation in the experiment can be randomized to insure that all conditions in the experiment are tested at the same average level of practice in the task. Assume that there are five levels of the independent variable in the experiment: test displays of 1, 3, 5, 7, and 9 items. The experimenter can, therefore, perform one replication of the experiment every five trials. Each of the five levels must be presented once within the five trials. To do this, the experimenter can have five cards, each of which represents one of the five experimental conditions. He mixes the cards randomly, in a hat, for example, and draws one card for the condition to be presented on each trial. Since he wants to present all five trial types once before he repeats a given trial type, he does not replace the cards into the hat until the hat is empty. This is called sampling without replacement. Sampling with replacement involves replacing the cards into the hat after each draw.

The opportunity that the subject has for chance guessing must also be controlled with changes in display sizes. If subjects were simply required to recall the letters that had been presented on a given trial, they would be more likely to correctly guess an item with large display sizes, since they would feel free to name more items during the test. One control is to have the subject also indicate the location of the letter in the display. In this case, the subject would write the letters in the appropriate cells in a 4 x 4 response sheet on each trial. A reported letter would be scored as correct only if it were written in the appropriate cell. The experimental question is now in terms of how many items an observer can recognize and locate correctly in a single glance. As a learning exercise, try to develop a design that would allow an independent assessment of the accuracy of recognition and location perception. Table 1 summarizes the controls for the important variables for the experimental question of how many items an observer can recognize in a single glance.

Our hypothetical experiment was modeled after a seminal study carried out by Sperling (1960) as part of his dissertation research at Harvard. Results of his experiment are plotted as a functional relationship in Figure 2. The number of correct letters is plotted on the ordinate (y axis) as a function of the number of letters in the display plotted on the abscissa (x axis). As can be seen in the figure, a surprisingly flat function is found. Subjects report correctly all of the letters from

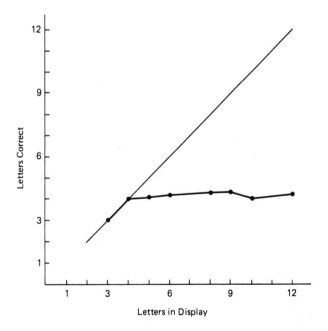

Figure 2. The number of letters correctly reported as a function of the number of letters in the display (after Sperling, 1960). The 45 degree diagonal represents what would be expected from perfect performance.

visual displays containing 3 and 4 letters. With more than 4 letters in the display, however, the number of letters reported correctly fell dramatically below what would be expected from perfect performance. Subjects averaged only about 4.5 letters correct with 5 or more letters in the display. One conclusion reached by Sperling is that subjects cannot report more than 4 or 5 letters, regardless of display size.

Interpolation and Extrapolation

Sperling's results give us the opportunity to discuss interpolation and extrapolation of functional relationships. Interpolation between two points is illustrated by the line drawn between the observed points at 6 and 8 letters in the display. In this case, we believe that a seven-letter display would have given roughly equivalent performance roughly halfway between the performance observed for the six- and eight-letter displays. Extrapolation from a functional relationship would involve making conclusions for displays containing less than 3 and greater than 12 letters. Thus, Sperling extrapolated from the results when he concluded that the maximum correct report is about 4.5 letters. This extrapolation was reasonable because it is hard to imagine how performance would improve with even greater than 12 letters in the display.

Extrapolation and interpolation are necessary because an experimenter cannot test all possible conditions of interest (even for a dissertation). Of course, generalizing from the observed conditions to untested conditions can be dangerous. For example, if Sperling had used only three- and nine-letter displays, interpolating linearly between the results between these two points would have been incorrect. Similarly, no matter how unlikely, it might be wrong to conclude from Sperling's results that subjects would report both letters correctly from a two-letter display. In all cases, both the experimenter and the scientific community provide the checks and balances to keep extrapolation and interpolation honest.

SEEING, SPATIAL LOCATION, AND AGE

A second example of experimental inquiry also concerns seeing in terms of how well we see as a function of where the information is in the visual field. Superimposed on this direct experimental question is a developmental question: we ask how well we see in the visual field as a function of age. There is no simple logical order to solving this problem. We will discover also that when you ask one question about how something works it helps to know the answer to other questions about it.

It may be necessary to convince you that this is a problem since the visual world seems to be perfectly clear. In addition to making head movements to look where you want, you can make eye movements. For example, reading a page of text, the reader has the impression that her eyes are moving gradually over the page of text. Secondly, the page of text appears legible as a whole.

Eye Movements

Eye movements in reading are called saccadic. The eye knows where it wants to go before the movement begins, and once the movement begins you can't change your mind about where the eye is going to go. In reading, we make about 3 or 4 saccadic eye movements per second. The movements are very fast, and we pause between these movements for about a quarter of a second. If the eyes could rotate completely in the head, 360 degrees, we could perform one rotation in one second. Small eye movements, as in reading, might take 10 or 15 msec.

This experiment asks how well the reader sees as a function of where the information is relative to fixation. To carry out the experiment, we need to know where the eye is and we want to prevent eye movements. Since we don't have an eye movement camera to keep track of where the

Statistics

We give very little weight in this volume to the statistical test of significance in evaluating our results. Statistical tools were developed in order to estimate the extent to which any observed effects in an experiment are due to chance rather than to changes in the independent variable itself. If the investigator can eliminate chance as the contributing factor, he is safe in attributing the observed effect to changes in his independent variable. The psychologist usually performs his statistical tests as a matter of habit and because they are usually required by the psychological journals. However, it is a truism that one can lie with statistics. Whether or not the effects of an independent variable are statistically significant—not due to chance—transmits very little information. There are many uninteresting reasons for a significant effect of the independent variable, and the knowledgeable investigator carries out his experiment or finds a statistical test in ways that will give the significance so desired. For example, increasing the number of observations at each level of the independent variable increases the likelihood of getting statistical significance, and so on.

In order to safeguard against the statistical significance problem, we evaluate the *magnitude* of the effect of our independent variable, rather than whether it is statistically significant. Second, and more important, we are interested in the variable in terms of what it tells us about a psychological process, not simply in terms of whether the observed behavior differs under different levels of the independent variable. Consider the case in which we postulate a variable, say, processing time, as being critical for the psychological process of recognition. If we carry out an experiment that shows performance is at chance with very little processing time, and gradually improves to perfect accuracy with increases in processing time, there is no need to ask whether this variable is statistically significant. We have shown the variable to be psychologically significant by the way it illuminates the rules of a psychological operation or process. The discussion of experiment and theory in this book illustrates with many examples how research without statistical tests can increase our knowledge of psychological phenomena.

eye is, we have to give the subject a fixation point. Most people can do this very well. To prevent the subject from changing his eye fixation, we present the stimulus for a very short duration. It takes subjects on the order of 150 to 250 msec to program their eyes to move. The subject will look at a screen at a fixation point, a short duration stimulus will be presented somewhere in the visual field, and the subject reports what was presented.

Memory and Report Limitations

For many years psychologists did the following kind of experiment. They would present a sequence of letters for a short period and ask the subjects to report what they saw. Accuracy of report of the letters was the index of how well the subject saw the letters in the display. If we were to follow this tradition, we would present a random list of letters and ask the subject to report what was present. The dependent variable would be the spatial location of the letters. For example, a row of eight letters centered around the fixation point could be presented and the dependent variable would be the accuracy of report as a function of spatial location. On every trial the subject would look at the fixation point, the experimenter would flash 8 letters for a short duration, the subject would report back what he saw, and the experimenter would score his responses with respect to their accuracy. This trial sequence would be carried out a number of times using different letter sequences. This experiment asks how well we see letters at 8 locations with respect to fixation point, so it is mainly concerned with acuity along this horizontal dimension.

When this experiment is done the results resemble those in Figure 3. The subject is most accurate for the letters at the left side of the display and the accuracy falls as we go from left to

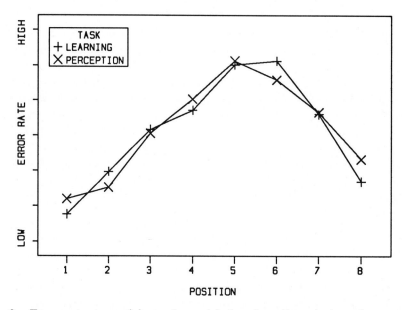

Figure 3. Error rate to anticipate in serial learning (Learning) and error rate in tachistoscopic letter-recognition (Perception) (from Harcum, 1967).

right. There is also some advantage for the two right-most letters. Are the results a direct reflection of the acuity of the subject with respect to spatial location of the visual field? These results may not reflect only how well the subject saw but also how well the subject remembered what was seen and the order in which the letters were reported. Evidence supporting this interpretation is also given in Figure 3. The serial learning of a list of eight letters gives a similar error pattern. Given that each letter was accurately perceived in the serial-learning task, perceptual differences can not be responsible for the pattern of errors.

This free-report task appears to have memory components and report components that contribute to the results, and we cannot analyze results in a way that will allow us to eliminate the contributions of memory and report in order to get a true assessment of the perceptual capabilities. If this experiment is repeated using Hebrew characters and Hebrew readers who will read from right to left, the best performance will occur for the right-most letters. This confirms the impression that the order of report is critical in this kind of task, so we have to eliminate any effect of the order of report. Similarly, memory and forgetting play a role, so that subjects may be biased to remember items in some locations rather than others. We have to change this experimental situation to eliminate as much as possible the contribution of memory and order of report. One possibility would be to flash one letter on at a time. In this case, on each trial, the subject fixates on the fixation point and the test letter can occur anywhere in the display. Now the subjects report simply what the letter was. This task appears to eliminate tendencies to report from left to right.

Developmental Issues

If we think about the developmental question, young children may not know the alphabet. The use of alphabetic materials is not optimal; young readers have trouble identifying all the letters and make some confusions between b and d or p and q and so on. What is needed is some non-linguistic stimulus, such as just a vertical line. The subject would simply indicate whether or not a vertical line was presented. The results would be the percentage of correct recognitions as a function of where the vertical line was presented. Having solved the problem of eliminating linguistic material, we created another. If we present a vertical line on every trial, some subjects may realize this and tend to lie to the experimenter, saying that they saw the line when in fact they didn't. We need some way to check up on the subject's honesty. The easiest way is to have a vertical line and a horizontal line as our two stimuli and present one of these on each trial. The subject simply indicates which line was presented. For the kids we could paint the lines on their response buttons so they would not have to describe them. We don't accept "I don't know" as an answer. Although subjects may insist that they don't know what they saw, they will be correct more often than expected from chance guessing. You can't trust the subject to evaluate whether or not he knows; this is true in all experimental situations.

Within-Subject and Between-Subject Designs

The most frequently used method in experimental psychology is a within-subject study. The distinguishing characteristic of this method is that a subject is tested under all conditions of interest. Individual differences are acknowledged and considered to be mostly irrelevant to the question of interest. What is of interest is how some variable or set of variables influences behavior with all other things held constant. People differ from one another in a variety of interesting and uninteresting ways; and the within-subject experiment mostly bypasses these differences. The justification is that once orderly behavior is observed for a given individual, differences across individuals become more informative.

Between-subject studies are used in two instances; first, when a given experimental manipulation is not feasible to implement in a within-subject study. In social psychology, for example, many manipulations cannot be repeated for a given subject because the subject "catches on" to the purpose of the experiment after being tested in just one of the experimental conditions. The second use is when the differences between groups of individuals are of direct interest. Thus, developmental, social, and clinical psychology make heavy use of between-subject designs. Children are compared to adults, selfish individuals are compared to altruistic, and "normals" are compared to "neurotics." We will learn that the between-subject comparison is most fruitful when combined with a within-subject experiment. The within-subject results provide information about the psychological process of interest and the between-subject comparison reveals how it varies across individuals.

Experimental Solutions

Schaller and Dziadosz (1975) were aware of the controls necessary to provide a true assessment of how well we see as a function of location in the visual field. To eliminate memory and forgetting contributions, only one item in the display had to be reported. Also, the item to be reported would be obvious from the display itself. The visual stimulus and response were nonverbal. Fixation was controlled as much as possible. The visual display was a 5 row x 7 column array of white outline circles on a dark background. One of the 35 circles contained a white bar, which was either vertical or horizontal. The task of the subject was simply to indicate the direction of orientation of the bar. Subjects made their responses by hitting one of two push panels. One panel was marked with a vertical line and one with a horizontal line. Figure 4 illustrates the stimulus presentation sequence in the experiment.

Pretesting was carried out to instruct the subjects and accommodate them to the task. In addition, this pretesting allowed the experimenter to determine an exposure duration that would

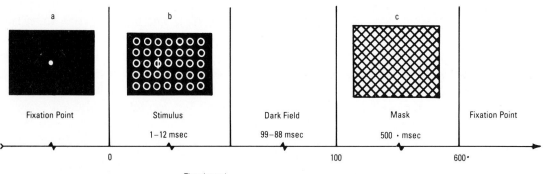

Time (msec) →

Figure 4. Stimulus presentation sequence. (A red fixation point appeared at the beginning of each trial. The stimulus array appeared for 1-12 msec. Following a blank field interval for the remainder of 100 msec, the mask appeared and remained for a minimum of 500 msec or until a response was made.)

avoid *ceiling* and *floor* effects. A ceiling effect occurs when performance is as good as it can possibly be. A floor effect is the case when performance is as poor as it can be. In both of these cases the dependent variable is no longer sensitive to potential influences of an independent variable. To maximize the sensitivity of the independent variable, an exposure duration was chosen individually for each subject. The goal was to choose a duration that would be most likely to give an average of 75% correct for that subject. Even with these precautions, some subjects performed close to chance and some near perfect. These subjects were eliminated from the final analysis since their results are uninformative with respect to the experimental question of interest.

In one experiment, the authors analyzed the results of 32 introductory psychology students. Performance was a systematic function of location in the visual field. Overall performance decreased with increases in distance from the fixation point. One way to plot performance in this situation is in terms of contour maps projected into the visual field. Figure 5 gives such a contour map. Each contour represents a drop of 2% in accuracy. There was a slight asymmetry in that performance was slightly better for circles in the top half than in the bottom half of the display. Although there was no main effect of left versus right, a second analysis revealed that some subjects showed superior performance on the left and the other subjects on the right. Statistical tests revealed that these two types of superior performance were not due to chance variation. A test-retest would provide a better evaluation of this conclusion, however. Figure 5 gives the contour map for the subjects who showed a right superiority. The subjects showing a left superiority gave a similar contour map but with the maximum sensitivity to the left rather than the right.

Given the success of their paradigm, Schaller and Dziadosz (1975) tested preschool children and third-grade subjects. The first group of children averaged about 4 1/2 years old and the second group about 9 years. One question was to what extent learning to read would change sensitivity across the visual field. The experiment was carried out in a similar manner to the adult study. Recall that the exposure duration was adjusted to give an overall average of 75% correct in the task. Developmentally, younger children need a longer duration for the same performance accuracy. However, it is necessary to allow this confounding because it is safest to compare different groups of subjects at the same overall level of performance. In this case, differences in the effects of the independent variables are more meaningful (Loftus, 1978). Preschool children show very little

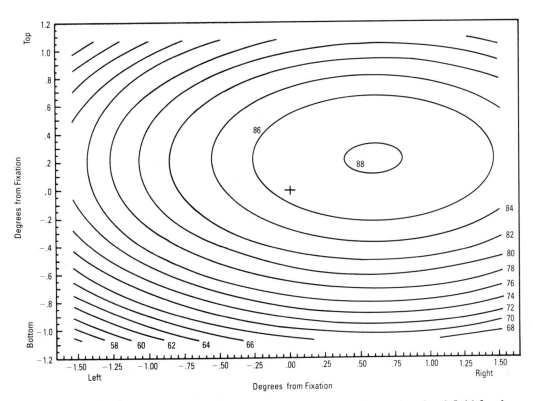

Figure 5. Equal-accuracy (percent correct) contours projected onto the visual field for the significant effects shown by the right-superior subjects. (Each contour represents a drop in accuracy of 2% of perfect. The fixation point, marked by the cross, was at 0 degrees horizontal and 0 degrees vertical. Measurements on each axis are in terms of degrees from fixation.)

asymmetry in either direction. The third-graders, on the other hand, show a top and right superiority. Although Schaller and Dziadosz consider a number of possible reasons for these differences, no firm conclusions could be reached about the individual differences. The experimental procedure not only provides a direct assessment of visual acuity as a function of location in the visual field, it offers a promising methodology to study developmental changes.

INFANT PERCEPTION

One of the most fundamental and yet most challenging areas of psychological study is the perceptual capabilities of infants. Any casual observer of infants is intrigued by their energy, enthusiasm, and curiosity. They seem to have all of the appropriate programs for perception and action; the psychologist would like to gain some insights into these programs. The challenge, of course, is how do we test the infant. They cannot be told what to do as can college students, they become more easily bored, and their forms of communication are much more subtle.

How well do infants see and how does this ability change with development? Concern with this question goes back, at least, to the time of Bishop Berkeley who believed in a central role of learning by experience. According to Berkeley, an infant learns to judge the depth of objects accurately by associating sight with touch. Within the last two decades, investigators have developed ingenious psychophysical techniques for the study of infant perception. We will review a few of these along with some representative experiments.

Preferential Looking

It is immediately obvious to the observer that young infants will stare at bold edges, objects, and patterns. They will also track these patterns with head and eye movements if the patterns are moved slowly enough. The "preferential looking" technique was formalized by Fantz (1965, 1967). An infant is presented with a pair of stimuli on a screen. An experimenter sits behind the screen, looking at the infant through a peephole. If the infant has a preference for one of the two patterns, he or she should spend more time looking at it. The experimenter's task is to judge the direction of the infant's fixation and the time spent looking at each of the two stimuli.

In a further elaboration and quantification of this technique, Teller (1979) and her colleagues have developed a new psychophysical technique called forced-choice preferential looking. This technique has been used primarily to study visual acuity (the ability to see fine lines) in infants a couple of months old. The infant is held facing a gray screen with two stimuli. One stimulus is the same gray as the background screen whereas the other contains a set of black and white stripes. The assumption is that infants will prefer to look at the stimulus with black and white stripes rather than at the homogeneous gray. If these stripes are invisible to the infant, the stripes will be mixed, resulting in a gray equivalent to the background gray of the screen. In this case, no preferential looking will be observed. The question of interest, then, is to what extent infants discriminate the black and white stripes as opposed to seeing a homogeneous gray.

The experimenter, looking through the peephole between the two stimuli, also serves as a psychophysical subject. His or her task is to guess the location of the striped stimulus. A diagram of the experimental display is shown in Figure 6. To insure that the situation is completely objective, this experimenter does not know the actual location of the striped stimulus. The situation is called a double-blind experiment because neither the subject nor the experimenter knows the actual position of the correct stimulus. The experimenter makes the choice on the basis of the infant's eye and head movements and particular staring patterns. The experimenter's response is scored as right or wrong and a series of trials is carried out in this way. The experimenter's

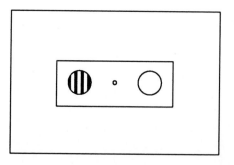

Figure 6. A diagram of the experimental display used to test an infant's ability to discriminate striped patterns. The small hole between the two displays is the experimenter's peephole to view the infant (after Teller, 1979).

performance reflects the infant's ability to discriminate the striped pattern from the surrounding gray field. To the extent that the infant is capable of discriminating the striped pattern and the experimenter observes the resulting differences in the infant's behavior, the experimenter is above chance guessing. Chance performance means either that the infant could not discriminate the striped pattern or that the infant's discrimination was not communicated to the experimenter.

As in standard tests of acuity, a series of test stimuli varying in stripe width are used. The infant is tested on the series of stimuli to produce a psychometric function (see Chapter 9). Results of tests with one infant are shown in Figure 7. As can be seen in the figure, performance is at chance for the narrowest stripes and improves with increases in stripe width. As in traditional adult psychophysics, the stripe width needed for 75% can be used as an estimate of the visual acuity of the infant.

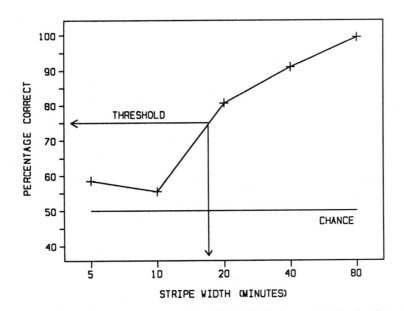

Figure 7. Psychometric function for an 8-week-old infant tested with the forced-choice preferential looking procedure. The observer's percentage correct is plotted as a function of the five stripe widths on which the infant was tested. Conversions to Snellen equivalents (using the convention that 1′ per stripe equals 20/20 Snellen) are given on the abscissa. The infant performed near 100% for an 80′ pattern but near chance for 10′ and 5′ patterns, with an estimated "threshold" (75%) at about 16′ or 20/320 acuity (after Teller, 1979).

As you might expect, this experiment requires time, dedication, and patience. The trial to trial sequence has to be highly flexible and tuned to the infant's state of alertness. Only about 50 trials per day are given and the infant is usually tested for about 10 days. Most importantly, randomization and counterbalancing of stimulus conditions is critical since the infant's state can fluctuate so drastically across time. In addition, only a few difficult stimuli can be tested in a row since the infant will lose interest in the game. One has to mix easy with difficult stimuli throughout the experiment. Therefore, it is necessary to keep track of the infant's performance during the actual experiment and to modify presentation of the stimulus conditions accordingly. This technique has proven successful not only with human infants but with Macaque monkey infants and clinical assessment of the infant's vision. Teller (1979) provides a detailed description of the technique and its uses in experimental and clinical settings.

Operant Conditioning

An operant conditioning procedure has also been used with some success in the study of infant perception. Infants are taught to respond to a particular stimulus by rewarding responses to that stimulus. As an example, Schaller (1975) was interested in whether three-month-old infants could discriminate hue. The infants were trained to look at either a red or a green stimulus. During training, one red and green stimulus was presented and the parent or experimenter prompted the infant to look at the correct color. After a couple of days of training, the prompts were eliminated. A blind experimenter recorded the cumulative looking time to each side and turned both colors off when the cumulative time reached two seconds to either stimulus. If the child was correct, a reinforcement was given. The correct stimulus reappeared and flashed, a ding-dong door bell was rung, and the parent or experimenter looked at the infant, smiled, talked, patted, or rubbed the infant and at times presented a pacifier dipped in honey. Given all of these rewards, and extreme patience, the experimenters were able to train eight infants in the task.

One additional problem that the investigator faced was to make sure that the infants were responding to hue and not to brightness. Our sensitivity to red and green colors differs so that equally intense reds and greens are not necessarily seen as equally bright. Given the difficulty of controlling exactly for these sensitivity differences, Schaller devised an ingenious solution to the problem. Rather than attempting to match the red and green stimuli in perceived brightness, he systematically varied their intensities over a range of 200 to 1. Therefore, on some trials, the infant was sure to see the red as brighter than the green stimulus whereas on other trials green would be seen as brighter than red. Accordingly, if the infant were responding to brightness and not hue, performance would be near chance. Only by attending to hue independently of brightness would the infant be able to solve the problem. Randomly varying the brightness probably made the problem much more difficult. Because two dimensions are varying, the infant has to discover that hue and not brightness is the relevant dimension.

Figure 8 presents the results of the Schaller study. The dependent measure was average looking time per trial. To the extent that the infant looks at the reinforced hue and not at the incorrect hue, there is evidence that the infant sees hue. The results show clear discrimination of hue in that red was looked at longer when it was reinforced, and green was looked at longer when it was reinforced. Much to the infant's credit, the results also show that infants spent more time looking at the brighter stimuli. Infants are attracted to sharp contours and the brighter stimuli would be more attractive. The color stimuli were not homogeneous patterns. The experiment was successful in answering an old question: infants appear to discriminate red from green and we might expect that this will be true for other hues also.

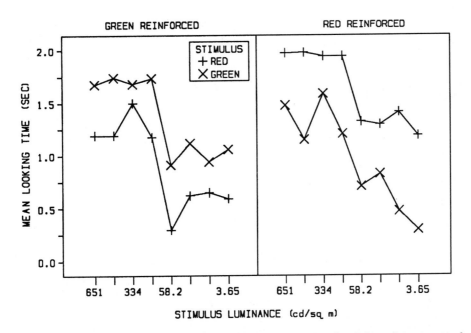

Figure 8. Mean times (seconds) looking per trial to each stimulus. Mean times were taken across all three subjects in each condition on their final testing sessions, right panel is for the "red"-correct infants; left panel is for the "green"-correct infants (after Schaller , 1975).

5

The Scientific Process

Scientific Investigation

  Hypothesis Generation
  Scientific Frameworks
  Hypothesis Testing
  Analogy in Science
  Psychology of Science

People as Scientists

  Confirmation Bias
  Competition in Science

Scientists Are People

  Potential Pitfalls in Research
  Dimensions of Science
  Style in Science
  Moral Responsibility

Hypotheses, Models, and Theories
Intuitive Scientists

The fundamental question is ... how science is possible
because it includes the aberrant (features of human behavior)
as well as the rational.
Ian I. Mitroff (1974)

The endeavor of psychological inquiry is unique among all sciences in one important respect. The scientist hopes to understand phenomena which themselves are critically involved in the process of understanding. Ultimately, the subject matter of the psychologist is the psychologist. This observation is not meant to return us to the metaphysical turmoil encountered in Chapter 1, but is made to remind ourselves of this possible conundrum. M. C. Escher's *Drawing Hands* (Figure 1) sums up our dilemma more exactly than might any verbal statement. In this chapter, we study how people investigate the world around them. By doing so, we gain insights not only into the processes involved in psychological inquiry but also into the appropriate framework for the scientific study of mind and behavior.

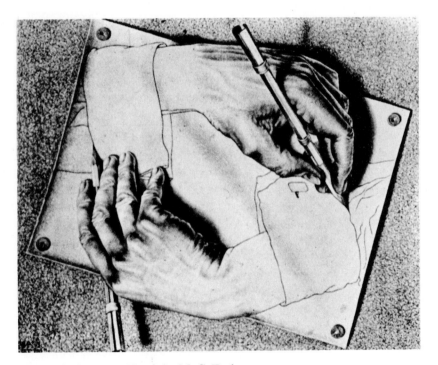

Figure 1. *Drawing Hands* by M. C. Escher.
© 1989, c/o Cordon Art, Baarn, Holland.

SCIENTIFIC INVESTIGATION

A rough characterization of scientific investigation includes a number of distinguishing attributes or features. The domain of the investigation centers around some form of systematic or controlled observations. The phenomenon under study is measured or quantified in a relatively precise manner. These observations are used to accumulate evidence, measure relationships, or to test one or more hypotheses (see Chapter 3). The nature of the scientific process is most easily illustrated in the context of hypothesis testing, that is, determining whether or not an explanation is correct. Any hypothesis must be testable, which means that the observations are capable of disconfirming it. Usually, certain assumptions are necessary in order to apply the hypothesis to the observations under study. Finally, a law of parsimony (simplicity) pervades the domain of scientific investigation. Given two equally good hypotheses, the most parsimonious one is preferred. A more complicated hypothesis includes more assumptions and the greater the number of assumptions, the easier it is to predict or describe some phenomenon.

Hypothesis Generation

Where do hypotheses come from? Given some preliminary observations, a person hits upon some explanation of the phenomenon of interest. Applied to a new situation, this explanation is referred to as a hypothesis. Figure 2 illustrates the ideal sequence of events in scientific endeavor. Needless to say, actual science does not always proceed in such a systematic fashion. A scientist has available a set of observations which consists of the research literature, current theory, and direct experience and hunches of his or her own. These phenomena are organized and interpreted in the framework of an explanatory system. This explanation should imply the outcomes of additional observations. These implications lead to specific hypotheses and tests of the hypotheses. The outcome of the test may falsify a hypothesis, requiring some revision of the explanatory system. If the outcome of the test is positive, the scientist continues to work within the same explanatory system, generating additional hypotheses and tests.

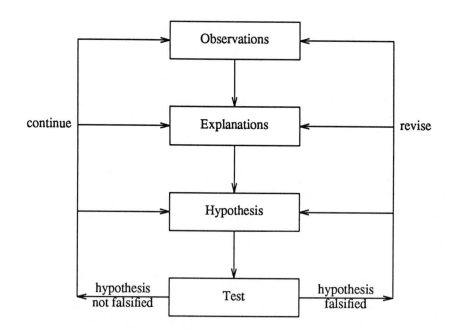

Figure 2. Ideal model of the scientific process.

Scientific Frameworks

Experiments are usually developed and conducted within general scientific frameworks, whether these frameworks are explicitly defined or only implicitly assumed by the experimenter. One framework for scientific endeavor has been expressed most succinctly by Popper (1959). The central assumption is that hypothesis testing must follow deductive rather that inductive methods.

Deductive reasoning is a process in which a conclusion follows logically from given assumptions, hypotheses, or premises. The conclusion contains no more information than that which is contained in the given assumptions. All humans are animals; I am a human; therefore, I am an animal. As can be seen from this example, the conclusion that "I am an animal" was directly deduced from the given information that all humans are animals, and I am a human. No new information is presupposed, for instance, by concluding that humans are a unique type of animal. Everything follows from what is given. On the other hand, inductive reasoning is a logical process in which the conclusion contains more information than that which is contained in the observations and experience on which it is based. Additional information is assumed in the conclusion. Every cat I have ever seen has hated being given a bath; therefore, all cats hate being given baths. From my experience it seems as though all cats do hate being given baths, but since it is impossible to give baths to every cat on planet earth, we are assuming that they all hate it. There is no certainty that tomorrow a dirty cat will not come to my door begging for a bath.

Following Hume, Popper claims that we are not justified in inferring universal or general statements from specific ones. Any conclusion drawn inductively might always turn out to be false. Although we may have many instances of white geese, this does not justify the conclusion that all geese are white. Therefore, the scientist should not try to verify a particular hypothesis, generalizing that it is universally true, by demonstrating that it works in specific instances. Since new instances can always falsify a given statement, no experimental observation can verify a hypothesis.

Hypothesis Testing

Popper proposes that hypotheses once constructed must be subjected to the following analyses. The investigator begins by comparing the conclusions derived from the hypothesis in order to determine whether they are internally consistent (that is, do not contradict one another). An analysis of the conclusions will also indicate whether or not the hypothesis is testable. By contrasting this hypothesis with other hypotheses, the investigator then determines whether the theory is unique and whether it would constitute a scientific advance should it survive experimental tests. Finally, if the conclusions drawn from the hypothesis meet these requirements, then it is worthwhile to subject its conclusions to experimental tests.

Experimental tests will decide how well a hypothesis or theory survives. If a theory survives the experimental tests, we should not discard it. On the other hand, if the experimental tests falsify conclusions drawn from the theory, then the theory should be rejected or modified accordingly. A critical feature of Popper's scientific framework is that verifiability and falsifiability do not have a symmetrical relationship. Although theories can be falsified, they cannot be truly verified. Positive results do not necessarily mean that the theory is true; they simply mean that the theory was not falsified. Popper proposes that it is best to conclude that positive results only corroborate a particular theory; they do not verify it.

Table 1 illustrates the falsification strategy of hypothesis testing. A hypothesis H predicts some observation O. Two outcomes of the experiment are possible. If the predicted observation O is not obtained ($\neg$O), the hypothesis is rejected. If the observation is obtained, the hypothesis is not rejected but neither is it verified. The bottom half of Table 1 acknowledges the fact that any experimental test of a hypothesis usually requires auxiliary assumptions relevant to the specific experimental situation. It could be the case that certain observations do not disprove a hypothesis if the assumptions involved in testing the hypothesis are not appropriate.

Table 1. Illustration of the strategy of falsification in hypothesis testing.

	falsification	
prediction	$H \Rightarrow O$	
observation	$\neg O$	O
conclusion	$\neg H$	none
prediction	$H + A \Rightarrow O$	
observation	$\neg O$	O
conclusion	$\neg(H + A)$	none

H = hypothesis, O = observation, A = assumptions, $\neg X$ = the negation of X, $\Rightarrow$ = implies

In a more recent contribution, Popper (1976) acknowledged that models could be modified indefinitely to incorporate inconsistent results. This prolongation of falsification is called immunization. Successive modification of a model keeps it alive and holds off its eventual death. In this case, a better contribution is an alternative model rather than another inconsistent experimental result. As observed by Conant (1947, p. 36): "A theory is only overthrown by a better theory, never merely by contradictory facts." Surviving a particular experimental test only temporarily supports a theory since another investigator may soon provide a test that overthrows it.

In a slightly different approach to scientific endeavor, Platt (1964) encourages scientists to employ a strong inference strategy of testing hypotheses. In contrast to generating a single hypothesis, Platt would have the scientist generate multiple hypotheses relevant to a particular phenomenon of interest. The experimental test would be designed to eliminate (or in Popper's words, falsify) as many of these hypotheses as possible. The results of the experimentation would allow the generation of new hypotheses which could be subjected to further tests. Table 2 illustrates the testing of two hypotheses. One hypothesis predicts one observation (O_1) and the other predicts (O_2) If O_1 and $\neg O_2$ results from the experiment, H_2 is rejected, and analogously for H_1.

Table 2. Illustration of the strategy of strong inference in hypothesis testing.

	strong inference	
prediction	$H_1 \Rightarrow O_1, H_2 \Rightarrow O_2$	
observation	O_1 and $\neg O_2$	$\neg O_1$ and O_2
conclusion	$\neg H_2$	$\neg H_1$
prediction	$H_1 + A \Rightarrow O_1, H_2 + A \Rightarrow O_2$	
observation	O_1 and $\neg O_2$	$\neg O_1$ and O_2
conclusion	$\neg(H_2 + A)$	$\neg(H_1 + A)$

H = hypothesis, O = observation, A = assumptions, $\neg X$ = the negation of X, $\Rightarrow$ = implies

Both Platt and Popper adhere to Hume's axiom prohibiting inductive arguments. The message is that the scientist should not attempt to confirm a single pet hypothesis. However, Platt's solution seems more productive in that at least one of the multiple hypotheses under test should fail and can, therefore, be rejected. Strong inference has the potential of providing more information than falsification. If an experiment can be designed to falsify one hypothesis with one outcome and another hypothesis with another outcome, then there is a greater likelihood of rejecting a hypothesis. By making H_1 and H_2 mutually exclusive, then the experiment should be able to falsify one of the hypotheses. However, other outcomes might be possible; for example, neither or both of the outcomes may be obtained.

Hypotheses, Models, and Theories

A hypothesis is a conjecture to account for some phenomenon or set of phenomena not yet understood. In this regard, hypotheses, models, and theories are all defined similarly. Models and theories usually consist of a set of hypotheses or allow specific hypotheses to be derived from them. For our purposes, the terms will be used interchangeably, although they usually can be considered to be on a continuum of specific to general accounts of phenomena. A specific instance of a model and its role in scientific study is a computer program of memory search and comparison.

A good theory is 1) verifiable or testable, 2) parsimonious or relatively simple compared to the phenomena being explained, 3) comprehensive or reasonably complete and general, and 4) heuristic or a useful framework for generating predictions, analyzing results, and explaining them. A good theory provides an integrative framework for a set of hypotheses. It allows one to organize knowledge about the world. An important advance occurs when a theory is developed to integrate hypotheses and empirical findings that were previously believed to be unrelated. This integration makes available a larger domain for application of the theory. The theory becomes useful both in directing future research and in facilitating communication among scientists. To the extent that the theory applies to a large domain of phenomena, we can be increasingly confident that the theory will not be easily falsified.

Analogy in Science

Popper's and Platt's framework may be most appropriate for a relatively mature scientific discipline. In an early stage of model development, an empirical scientist might have to be content with a relatively facile acceptance of models or systems from other domains. As an example, Descartes used the machine as an analog of overt behavior of people; the behavior of a person was viewed as following the same principles as those for machines. Models derived from analogs can be tested to some extent in that conclusions drawn from the analog can be tested in the system of interest. Using the pump as an analog for a model of the circulatory system, it is possible to derive certain relationships between pressure and output flow in pumps and test whether this relationship holds in the circulatory system.

A familiar example in cognitive psychology is that of the digital computing device as a model for certain aspects of the human's mental functioning. The computing device can be described in terms of a number of stages beginning with input to the computer, operations on this input with respect to information stored in the memory of the computer, and finally output of the outcomes of the operations. In order to test whether the computer provides a good analog to mental functioning, a more specific analog is necessary to generate testable hypotheses. As an example, one could develop computer programs that carry out specific types of memory search and test if any describe how humans carry out memory search.

In some situations, an analog can be shown to produce the same outcome as a human, but with an entirely different set of processes. If this is the case, the analog is a poor model even though it makes correct predictions. Work in artificial intelligence has encouraged psychologists to adopt working systems in this area as models of psychological processing. For example, computing machines have been programmed to play games such as Chess, Master Mind, and Othello. One problem with this artificial system as a model for psychological functioning is that the computing capacity and speed can compensate for the deficiency of certain intelligent processes by sheer processing power and time. Although an artificial system may be shown to perform some task such as playing chess, the critical question is whether the artificial system performs the task in the same way as humans. This question requires the investigator to compare the nature and time course of the internal processes in humans to those of the artificial system. Only if the internal processes are similar can we say that the artificial system is a good model of the human system.

As students of psychological processes, we are interested in not only whether a model holds up to its experimental tests, but also whether or not practical applications can be derived from the model. Although the model helps us understand human conduct, we also want it to help us modify it. An obvious example is whether a model of the act of reading written language proves useful in assessment of reading skills and development of reading instruction. A model's adequacy in providing assessment and guiding instruction provides additional tests of the model. If a model assumes that a reader must have some knowledge of spelling constraints (orthographic structure) in order to recognize words for rapid reading, then readers without this knowledge should reveal reading problems. Acquiring this knowledge should lead to rapid reading if no other deficits exist.

J. Robert Oppenheimer, one of the best-known physical scientists of this century, rallied for greater scientific literacy. Scientific inquiry bears a strong resemblance to art, music, and sports and he believed that science could engage both the amateur and professional. Sheer joy would be the primary motivator. Our goal is captured by the cartoon in Figure 3; we inquire about inquiry but stop at this first level of regress.

Psychology of Science

Scientific endeavor can be viewed as a natural but formal extension of human perception, memory, thinking, and problem solving. Within this light, we might expect to find many of the properties of these basic psychological processes to be reflected in scientific inquiry. This framework offers a productive exchange between the science of psychology and the psychology of science. We begin by reviewing some important attributes of psychological processes that play an important role in scientific investigation.

Campbell (1977) reviews evidence for the "idols" or "false images" that are characteristic of human thought. These less than optimal characteristics were provided by Francis Bacon, a famous philosopher of the early seventeenth century. Bacon believed that humans tend to suppose "a greater degree of order" than is really present. That is, our interpretation of an environmental situation is too orderly, too simple, ignores details, and essentially contains too few variables (parameters) of importance. There are several examples of this kind of behavior that have been observed in the psychological laboratory. If a hungry pigeon is placed in a box in which a small amount of grain is given randomly every 20 seconds or so, an orderly sequence of responses will develop. This "superstitious" behavior reflects the pigeon's "belief" that the food is contingent on his behavior and is not simply random.

A second proposition of Bacon's is that people tend to interpret new experiences as fresh evidence for strongly-held beliefs. In the more recent literature, this is called a confirmation bias in the evaluation of new evidence. A related proposition is that we tend to give more weight to positive than to negative evidence. These propositions capture the idea that the interpretation of

"GRANTED, WE HAVE TO DO THE RESEARCH. AND WE CAN DO SOME RESEARCH ON THE RESEARCH. BUT I DON'T THINK WE SHOULD GET INVOLVED IN RESEARCH ON RESEARCH ON RESEARCH."

Figure 3. Potential levels of research inquiry.

evidence is heavily influenced by the eye and mind of the beholder. Consider an experiment in which subjects were shown a slide at various degrees of focus and were asked to guess the content. Subjects who were shown an out-of-focus slide and made a premature guess had more difficulty in seeing the slide correctly on successive trials as it was brought into focus. The subject required a less fuzzy slide to identify the content correctly when the slides were shown in a sequence of fuzzy to clear than when the slides were shown in isolation and, therefore, without premature guesses (Bruner & Potter, 1964).

One aspect of a confirmation bias is obvious in scientific practice. Scientists (or their research assistants) tend to check their method, procedure, and data analysis when the unexpected outcome obtains but not necessarily when the expected outcome materializes. However, if errors are found when unexpected outcomes are obtained, we might expect as many errors when expected outcomes are obtained.

Given these prescriptive frameworks of scientific endeavor, it is important to evaluate our natural disposition in the scientific process. Can scientists be expected to conform to some philosophers' ideal code of scientific inquiry? As psychologists, we can also ask whether this mode of scientific inquiry is compatible with our nature in addition to being optimal for the generation of knowledge.

PEOPLE AS SCIENTISTS

How do you evaluate your hypotheses of the phenomena surrounding you? Are you completely objective in your analysis of some situation? How do you react to negative evidence which does not support your hypothesis? Experiments have provided some answers to these questions.

Persons attempt to verify rather than falsify their ideas about the nature of their environment. Assume that there is a rule that generates a sequence of three numbers. For example, given the sequence 2 4 6, your task is to guess the rule governing the sequence (Wason, 1960). The rule can be tested by generating a new sequence of numbers, and asking whether the sequence follows the rule. Subjects are asked to test their hypothesized rule until they are fairly confident that it is correct. Given the sequence 2 4 6, most subjects test the rule with sequences that increase by 2, such as 6 8 10, 10 12 14, or 9 11 13. Subjects report that the sequences are being generated to test the rule that the three numbers must increase by two. This simple example illustrates the powerful verification (confirmation) bias found in most people. The subjects show a confirmation bias because they test the hypothesized rule with sequences that are consistent with the rule rather than with sequences that are inconsistent with the rule. A subject who believes that the rule is increasing by two will test it with sequences that increase by two rather than with sequences that do *not* increase by two. We will see this bias in even the most weathered scientists. Subjects generated many of these positive instances for test rather than negative instances such as 10 11 13. Finding that other sequences that increase by two are also consistent with the rule leads most subjects to believe that the correct rule is, in fact, a sequence that increases by two. In this example, however, the rule was any increasing sequence of three numbers. Accordingly, the conclusion that increases by 2 is the correct rule would be premature because other rules are equally consistent with the observations.

Another experimental task, somewhat more involved, further illuminates the hypothesis-testing processes (Johnson-Laird, 1983). Consider a situation involving 4 cards, each with a number on one side and a letter on the other. The cards are showing 4, K, E, and 7, as illustrated in Figure 4. How would you go about testing the rule, "if a card has a vowel on one side, then it has an even number on the other side"? Which cards are absolutely necessary to turn over to test the rule? It costs fifty dollars to turn over each card so it is desirable to turn over only the cards absolutely necessary to test the rule. The cost of research should not be ignored. Jot down your answers and let's proceed with another rule to test. Four new cards have a city on one side and a means of transport on the other (see Figure 5). Given the cards showing (Leeds, train, Manchester, car), test the rule, "if I go to Manchester, then I travel by train"? Again, it costs fifty dollars to turn over each card. What cards are necessary to turn over to test the rule?

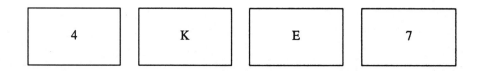

Figure 4. Each card has a number on one side and a letter on the other. Which cards must be turned over to test the hypothesis, "If a card has a vowel on one side, then it has an even number on the other side"?

Figure 5. Each card has a city on one side and a means of transport on the other. Which cards must be turned over to test the hypothesis, "If I go to Manchester, then I travel by train"?

If you performed as most of the subjects did, you turned E and 4 over to test the first rule and Manchester and car to test the second rule (Wason & Johnson-Laird, 1972; Wason & Shapiro, 1971). Table 3 gives the implications of the possible outcomes of the situation illustrated in Figure 4. As can be seen in the figure, 4 does not test the first rule since the rule is not bidirectional. An even number can occur without a vowel but not the reverse. Even if a vowel is found on the other side of 4, this result does not prove the rule since negative instances may still be found. The card with 7 can disconfirm the rule since it might have a vowel on the other side. Therefore, E and 7 are the appropriate tests for the first rule as are Manchester and car for the second rule.

Table 3. The implications of the possible alternative outcomes for the situation illustrated in Figure 3. Only E and 7 can lead to inconsistent outcomes, and therefore, test the rule.

Card	Outcome	Implication
4	vowel	consistent with hypothesis
	consonant	not inconsistent with hypothesis
K	even number	not inconsistent with hypothesis
	odd number	not inconsistent with hypothesis
E	even number	consistent with hypothesis
	odd number	inconsistent with hypothesis
7	vowel	inconsistent with hypothesis
	consonant	not inconsistent with hypothesis

These experiments and many others (Johnson-Laird, 1983, Rips & Marcus, 1977) reveal certain weaknesses in human deduction. First, people tend to interpret conditional statements of the form, If P, then Q, as bidirectional. Accordingly, they believe that the statement, If Q, then P, follows from the conditional statement, If P, then Q. In fact, the bidirectional is given by the statement, If and only if P, then Q. About half of the people believe that 4 tests the rule in Figure 3. Second, people fail to use the rule of inference called *modus tollens* in logic. This rule states the following with respect to the proposition, If P, then Q; if Q is false, then P is also false. In our example, *modus tollens* means that if Q does not occur, P can not occur. Therefore, if the digit is not even, then the letter can not be a vowel. According to *modus tollens*, 7 can disconfirm the rule in Figure 3 and yet only about one person in ten chose 7 to test the rule.

People do better in testing conditional statements in the concrete world of travel than in the abstract world of letters and digits. This result illustrates the important interaction of problem solving and natural experience. The game with vowels and even numbers is extremely abstract whereas traveling is part of our every day experience. Errors of assuming that a statement is bidirectional are decreased when that statement is expressed in concrete, real life experiences rather than in abstract notions. In the former we have past knowledge and experience to help us picture the conditions in our mind. We can picture a situation in which the only means of transportation to a city called Manchester is by train. We know by experience or prior learning that this city of Manchester would not be the only place that a train traveled to. On the other hand, the letters and numbers are simply symbols that are related in an arbitrary way. We have no prior experience or knowledge to help us picture the test situation. In psychological science, an experienced investigator may see alternative tests which have gone unnoticed by an equally logical but less experienced colleague. One is the "better" scientist because he or she has more experience available for taking appropriate action.

The reasoning task studied by Wason and Johnson-Laird sheds some light on confirmation bias in hypothesis testing. A rule or hypothesis mentions some events explicitly and ignores others. As an example, one hypothesis might be that poor readers read poorly because they are easily distracted. In terms of the material implication statement, this hypothesis is: If a person is a poor reader, he will be easily distracted. The person testing a rule concentrates on the events mentioned in the hypothesis. Therefore, the obvious test of the example hypothesis is to evaluate whether poor readers are easily distracted. Another necessary test, however, is to ask whether good readers are easily distracted. Therefore, a general rule of thumb is to go beyond the events in the hypothesis to test its validity.

Confirmation Bias

Mynatt, Doherty, and Tweney (1977) initiated a systematic series of studies of the psychology of scientific inquiry. These researchers created an artificial research environment and allowed college subjects to make preliminary alterations in the environment. After observing the environment, the participants were instructed to formulate a hypothesis to account for the behavior of objects in the environment. The subjects were then given the opportunity to test their hypotheses. One group of subjects was instructed that the job of the scientist was to confirm hypotheses. Another group was told that the job was to disconfirm hypotheses. A third group was given neutral instructions in terms of simply testing hypotheses. Subjects were shown hypothetical environments that would allow tests of their hypotheses. Given a pair of environments, a subject was asked to choose one member of the pair to test the hypothesis. By evaluating these choices against the subject's original hypothesis, the authors determined whether the subjects chose situations to confirm or to disconfirm their hypotheses.

Subjects chose a situation to confirm their hypothesis about 7 times out of 10 regardless of how they were instructed. These results and other evidence adduced by the authors revealed a strong confirmation bias in this simulated research inquiry. People chose hypothetical situations to confirm their hypothesis and avoided consideration and testing of alternative hypotheses. A second result revealed that subjects, when faced with disconfirming evidence, changed to a new hypothesis. Negative results were usually effective in changing the participant's opinion of the truth of the hypothesis. Although subjects may not seek disconfirmatory evidence, they use it correctly when it is available.

In a second study by the same authors (Mynatt, Doherty, & Tweney, 1978), subjects were faced with a much more complex research environment. Subjects attempted to determine how 27 fixed objects influenced the direction of a moving particle in a two-dimensional display. The objects differed in size, shape, and brightness and their influence on the particle varied as a function of these dimensions. A confirmation bias was again observed and could not be modified with highly explicit training in strong inference. In contrast to the previous study, however, subjects often kept or returned to their disconfirmed hypotheses. The more complex environment seemed to limit the generation of new hypotheses and, therefore, subjects kept alive those few ideas that they had. This is reminiscent of the compulsive gambler's dilemma, "I know the game is crooked, but it is the only one in town." A final result indicated that complete abandonment of a disconfirmed hypothesis also proved unproductive. For example, a general hypothesis of how the objects influence particle direction was abandoned when it failed experimental test. The principle itself was correct but only for some of the objects. Accordingly, it can be worthwhile to modify disconfirmed hypotheses based on the previous results rather than rejecting all aspects of the disconfirmed hypothesis.

Continuing their research, Doherty, Mynatt, Tweney, and Schiavo (1979) had subjects decide from which of two islands an archaeological find had come. Subjects usually asked for information relevant only to their preferred island rather than for information relevant to both islands. The requested information was useless since knowing that a characteristic of the found object is representative of one island does not provide information about whether the characteristic is also representative of the other island. This confirmation bias led to an inappropriate confidence in the subject's hypothesis. If the subject believes that the pot with a curved handle came from one island and then finds out that 80% of the pots from that island have curved handles, he or she becomes even more convinced that the pot is from that island. What the subject fails to realize is that pots from the other island may be as likely or even more likely to have curved handles.

The behavior of college students in a simulated research environment might not be typical of professional scientists. However, observational and historical accounts of scientific endeavor argue just the opposite. Mitroff (1974) carried out an intensive study of 40 scientists participating in the Apollo lunar missions. These scientists had devoted much of their life to studying the nature of the universe and the missions offered a unique observation of that nature. The observation centered around the moon rocks that the astronauts carried back to earth. The majority of these scientists revealed a strong commitment to their scientific beliefs; in addition, these beliefs could be considered to be outright biases since they did not have sufficient supporting evidence. These scientists were aware of their biases and commitments and saw them as perfectly natural in the pursuit of knowledge. These commitments and biases were not completely disfunctional; scientists learn to cope with disconfirming data and usually modify their ideas accordingly. What is obvious is that the storybook picture of the completely objective, unbiased, and disinterested scientist requires modification.

Confirmation bias also reveals itself in terms of a reluctance to accept findings that do not fit into the current mold of thinking. Spallanzani's discovery of bat navigation (Chapter 3) met with this fate. Being a good scientist and possibly hoping that publications count as much as prayers for tenure in heaven, he rushed off his findings to the scientific community and described how bats navigate with their ears. He didn't know how but bats seem to get around not in terms of seeing but by way of hearing. As you might expect, he was ridiculed by the scientific community. At that time there was just no way that one could understand how bats could navigate with their ears. If bats see with their ears, does that mean they hear with their eyes? Not on your life: eyes are for seeing and ears are for hearing. The research done by Spallanzani was correct but it took at least 150 years for the scientific community to accept it. Given his difficulties, scientists, faced with a rejected paper, can take heart.

Competition in Science

Most of the theoretically driven research aims at supporting rather than falsifying theories. A scientist tends to view the world in terms of his or her theory; he or she may be the least equipped person to invent a critical test of the theory. Empirical tests usually turn out to provide results consistent with the theory without really providing a critical test of the theory. Given a natural predisposition for the scientist to verify rather than falsify his or her theory, it is important that scientific endeavor remain competitive. The competitive dimension is probably as fundamental to the game of scientific endeavor as it is in most games (McCain & Segal, 1973). Scientists are much more willing to falsify other theories while seeking support for their own. If one accepts the ideal of falsifying models, the scientist is usually making most progress when he or she is testing someone else's theory rather than his or her own. A model is a good model to the extent that its conclusions are easily tested by other scientists, just as a good scientific test is one that can be repeated by other scientists. Experimental tests should allow not only falsification of the model but should provide clues to building new models if falsification occurs. Of course, the new models must also be easily testable.

SCIENTISTS ARE PEOPLE

The defining characteristics of scientists are not any more obvious than those of other fuzzy concepts such as ethics, games, and happiness. At some level, scientists enjoy various aspects of the process of psychological inquiry and this reason alone may sustain a scientist's career. When challenged, scientists may also attempt to justify their life's work with more socially acceptable goals; however, our cognitive explanations of our behavior usually fall short of the actual motivational precursors (Nisbett & Wilson, 1977). As might be expected, scientists differ in their talents and styles of scientific inquiry (Mitroff & Kilmann, 1978; Wachtel, 1980). One person might be particularly adept at creative theorizing, but has difficulty mapping these ideas into an experimental framework. Another might be a concise and thorough experimentalist, but cannot advance beyond the current theoretical framework. Some scientists do both with similar competence. On the enjoyment side, some scientists delight in the stage of formulating and testing ideas, but dread the process of *writing up* their research. Others love writing, but find the mechanics of equipment design, testing subjects, and data analysis relatively boring.

Most young scientists are required to carry out all stages of psychological inquiry. As an example, few graduate programs in psychology permit a purely theoretical study to qualify as a dissertation and young faculty qualifying for tenure are expected to do both empirical and theoretical work. Wachtel (1980) has illuminated some of the limitations of this model of psychological research and suggests that the field accept and support a broader range of research styles. An alternative solution would involve teams of research scientists whose interests and skills are complementary rather than requiring the individual scientist to perform all stages of research enterprise. Some collaborations of this sort have been reasonably profitable and current scientific endeavor seems to be moving more in this direction. Programs in cognitive science have brought together scientists from a wide range of disciplines to collaborate on issues in cognitive science. Linguists, anthropologists, computer scientists, philosophers, and psychologists have uniquely different skills and styles of inquiry and their collaboration on an important problem such as reading offers a promising research strategy (Gardner, 1985).

Scientists learn and adopt not only intellectual frameworks for research, but also psychological and sociological frameworks. All scientists might be expected to be competitive, ambitious, narrow-minded, idealistic, practical, and emotional, but in fact they differ widely on these psychological characteristics. On the sociological dimension, scientists can usually be classified into one of two types. Some scientists are committed to their favorite hypotheses and take strong stands on most issues. Other scientists avoid this kind of polarization and see, at least, two sides to every issue.

It is apparent that the actual practice of the scientist does not follow an ideal set of procedures dictated by philosophers and logicians. Scientific inquiry is not performed by objective and unbiased humans but involves the participation of involved and committed observers. It is important to acknowledge that there are no unbiased facts; we are simply not equipped to interpret data passively. As Churchman (1971) observed, theories are not tested by observations arrived at independently of theory. Facts and interpretations are inseparable and both are human products. Although science is subjective, it is not completely arbitrary. The scientific community must assess the emotion and bias in the same way that it assesses the facts and theory.

One of the goals of this book is to teach the appropriate methods for psychological inquiry. The irony is that some of this kind of knowledge might be tacit knowledge (Weimer, 1979). Polanyi (1966) refers to tacit knowledge as information not directly available to conscious awareness and not capable of being directly communicated. In this regard, scientific methodology can be considered to be analogous to other skills such as riding a bicycle or playing good tennis. Instructors insist that a comprehensive description of these skills cannot be given explicitly. The coach teaches some things by example and the student must learn by observing and doing. In this book, we also ask the participant to learn from examples of scientific practice. Although there is no concrete set of rules for doing science, there are examples of good, mediocre, and poor research enterprises. The perceptive student will learn the rules of the science game by observing, participating, and practicing.

Intuitive Scientists

We might be led to believe that psychologists are a unique group among humans whose aim is to understand and predict psychological behavior. According to one view, however, all people are intuitive scientists and the scientific process can serve as a model for human action (Kelley, 1967; Weimer, 1979). People attempt to make sense out of the world around them and test their ideas with every new encounter. As an example, a person believes that a new acquaintance is insincere and future encounters with this person are used to confirm or disconfirm this belief. If this view approximates some of our behavior, we can see certain interpersonal conflicts materializing if intuitive scientists also have a confirmation bias. According to Kelley, proper resolution of a person's predictions takes on greater psychological significance than the material rewards usually claimed to motivate behavior.

If all people are intuitive scientists, psychological researchers might begin to explore the possibility of a more collaborative relationship with their subjects. Even if a collaboration is not possible, an experimenter might ask subjects to predict and explain the outcome of their study. The experimenter should be able to assess how the subject may have influenced the results in seeking to confirm certain beliefs about the experimental situation. As noted elsewhere in this book, people as the subject matter of scientific endeavor offer unique challenges to the scientist. Progress might depend on the degree to which intuitive scientists can be outwitted to reveal their mental functioning.

Potential Pitfalls in Research

The human element in the scientific process can distort the procedures, methods, results, and interpretations of experimentation. Scientists have not been unaware of this fact, and a good number of investigators have studied the problem intensively (Barber, 1976; Rosenthal, 1966, 1976). Rosenthal and Fode (1963) evaluated the influence of experimenter expectancy on the outcome of experimental tests. Here it is worthwhile to distinguish between the investigator and the experimenter. The investigator initiates the research, and the experimenter does the actual testing of the subjects. In many cases, the investigator serves as experimenter and sometimes even as subject. The investigators, Rosenthal and Fode, had 30 student experimenters test hundreds of subjects in a photo rating task. Subjects were asked to rate the people on a scale from -10 (extreme failure) through 0 (neutral) to +10 (extreme success). The photos were human faces cut from newsmagazines. The faces were selected to be relatively neutral in terms of whether or not they would be rated as being successful. There were two groups of experimenters. The investigators told one group of experimenters that they would obtain positive ratings of about +5, whereas the other group was told that they would obtain negative ratings of around -5.

The instructions to the subjects were identical for both groups of experimenters, and the same faces were shown. The results indicated higher ratings for subjects tested by experimenters who were told to expect higher ratings. There were many potential reasons why this result was obtained, and many later experiments were directed at assessing what accounted for the findings. Cheating by the experimenters and feedback from the experimenters did not seem to be responsible. Rosenthal (1976) concluded that nonverbal communication is responsible, although he has not delineated the nature of this communication. Careful observation of the testing procedure was unproductive in discovering the communicator cues that are used if, in fact, nonverbal communication is the culprit.

Rosenthal's research has been criticized for a wide variety of reasons (Barber, 1976). Much of the criticism centers around the use of inappropriate statistical methods for testing the significance of the results. We all know that it is easy to be misled with statistics, and Rosenthal seems to be guilty of this behavior. In many cases, the standard comparison was not significant, and either eliminating subjects from the analysis or performing a large number of additional statistical tests was needed to achieve statistical significance. In our framework, a between group difference is not psychologically significant if it doesn't reveal anything about the psychological processes responsible for the difference. There are probably many subtle ways the experimenter might cue the subject to adopt a slightly more positive criterion for rating the faces; however, the questions addressed in most research require a much more complex pattern of results to be of interest. The experimenter in these situations would have a difficult time communicating the exact pattern that is expected or desired. Also, the face-rating task is an ambiguous one since there is no well-established method for rating success or failure of people on the basis of pictures of their faces. It is not surprising that subjects in this situation will look to the experimenter for whatever hint they can get for performing the task. When considering these factors, one wonders why it isn't even easier to show experimenter-expectancy effects. For our purposes, it does not hurt to insure that the results of a particular study cannot be influenced by expectancies of the experimenter.

The use of computers can allow complete control over experimenter-expectancy influences. In this case, the experimenter can be blind as to the experimental condition given to the subject. The computer can be programmed to choose the specific condition for each subject and then present the experimental test without any human intervention. Here we might say that the subject was untouched by human hands. The human experimenter would welcome the subject, introduce her to the laboratory and computer, and then put her in the hands of the program. The program would choose the conditions randomly and test the subject. The human experimenter would return at the completion of the experiment and retrieve the results from the computer. Both the investigator and the experimenter will feel more comfortable with this procedure. In addition, the scientific community reading the results would not have to worry about experimenter-expectancy effects.

Dimensions of Science

There are many psychological and sociological dimensions to the scientific enterprise (Platt, 1970). Humans seek more than the simple fulfillment of needs as a naive behavioristic or sociobiological view might indicate. Harry Harlow (Harlow , 1953), an early critic of behaviorism, demonstrated that monkeys would learn and work to see novel situations, such as the picture of a colleague. Many of the early learning studies of rats in mazes were plagued with the rats' curiosity seeking behavior. Rather than turning to the arm of the maze that had a food reward earlier, the rat would venture down another arm. Later testing revealed that the rat "knew" were the food was. One of the biggest problems in human infant research is keeping them interested in the experimental task; they are easily bored and must be continuously challenged with new problems. Science is novelty seeking at its most challenging; it is exciting and provides a range of rewards for a wide number of participants. The rewards range from the most basic, such as earning a living, to the most abstract, such as a fulfilling and competent interaction with some aspect of nature or obtaining admiration from respected colleagues.

Style in Science

The style of the successful scientist is as varied as human nature itself. However, a critical ingredient is the willingness to participate in intellectual work. Platt suggests that struggling scientists structure their formal thinking by putting their reasoning into bound notebooks. The notebook serves as a diary and provides the needed continuity for any kind of intellectual inquiry. Our problem-solving skills are critically dependent on the information available. Most memories are not capable of providing the information when needed. The notebook holds the scientist's representation of the problem and frees the processing capacity to question and modify the representation. Knowledge is a natural extension of the mind in the same way that a tool is an extension of the hand.

Moral Responsibility

As in all human endeavors, scientific practice entails moral responsibility. Science and technology have placed our survival and destiny in our own hands. Scientific knowledge is not good or bad, but represents the closest approximation to objective truth. To the extent that scientific knowledge reduces uncertainty about many of the important issues facing society today, much of the debate will stop and we can get on with the business of making decisions and implementing those decisions. Scientists have little control over the nature of phenomena but all humans have the power to decide and act. Science only provides knowledge of the operations and consequences of these actions.

Ethical principles for research with human participants have been published (*American Psychologist*, 1981). The investigator assumes the responsibility for the ethical acceptability of the research. Before the study, the investigator describes to the participants the important aspects of the research that might influence their willingness to respond. Each participant's are respected and subjects are free to withdraw from the study at any time. After participating, subjects are informed about the nature of the study and any misconceptions that they might have had are addressed.

6

Reading and Writing Research Reports

Writing as Problem Solving

Manuscript Format
  Title
  Author's Name and Institutional Affiliation
  Abstract
  Introduction
  Method
  Results
  Discussion
  References

Writing Style

Figures

APA Editorial Style
  Headings
  Abbreviations and Symbols
  Numbers
  Seriation
  Tables and Figures
  Reference Citations in Text
  Reference Lists
  Footnotes
  Typing Format

Sample Research Paper

_____

  Sexist Language
  Common Glitches

_____

*Vigorous writing is concise. A sentence should contain no
unnecessary words, a a paragraph no unnecessary sentences.*
William Strunk, Jr. & E. B. White (1972)

Why do most people, even students and scholars, view writing as a difficult and unpleasant task? It seems that seldom is a promised paper delivered on time and the delays and excuses of writers exceed even those of politicians. Only recently has writing and composition attracted the interest and study of many researchers (Gregg & Steinberg, 1980). The insights we gain into the skill should not only illuminate fundamental psychological functioning, but should also lead to a better understanding of the writing process and serve as a basis for instruction on writing.

WRITING AS PROBLEM SOLVING

How does one tackle the study of writing research? One method that has proved successful in other domains of complex behavior is that of protocol analysis. Subjects are asked to write an essay on a topic and to "think aloud" while writing (Hayes & Flower, 1980). The subject's comments are transcribed and analyzed together with the essay. Hayes and Flower (1980) discuss their research on this topic and offer a model of writing as problem solving. Since it became apparent that not all writers write in the same way, their model was formulated to describe specific individuals rather than the average writer. The hope is that the number of types of writers is relatively small and that, therefore, understanding one individual writer will illuminate the processing involved with all writers of that type.

The authors divide the writer's task into three parts:

A. The writer's long-term memory
B. The writing processes
C. The task environment

These three parts are apparent in the overall structure of the model illustrated in Figure 1. The authors have been able to delineate a number of conclusions about the writing process, simply on the basis of their protocol analysis. It should be possible to subject the conclusions to more direct experimental tests.

Writing is goal directed. This conclusion is not too surprising and is seen in the writer's setting of goals early in the writing session. In writing a laboratory report for class, for example, the student wants to convince the teaching assistant that she understands the methodological and theoretical issues, has read the relevant literature, and knows the APA format.

Writing is hierarchically organized. Given some major goals, writers identify subgoals which might be hierarchically arranged. Some writers might develop an outline of the paper before beginning. With an outline, the hierarchical arrangement becomes more apparent to the writer and the writing task at hand.

While writing, primitive editing functions can interrupt higher-order organization and planning processes. In writing this sentence, for example, I scribbled the word planning and therefore crossed it out and rewrote it. The monitor plays an important role in the editing process. We must have some mechanism monitoring everything being written and interrupting the writing process at the appropriate times. We have all observed something similar to this in typewriting. We interrupt typing when the wrong key is typed. Of course, sometimes the monitor misses an error and it is not noticed until sometime later, if at all.

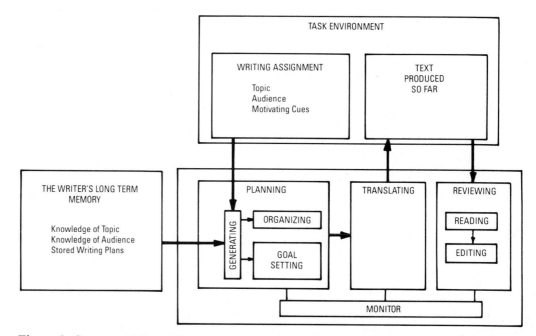

Figure 1. Structure of the writing model (after Hayes & Flower, 1980).

As in all problem solving situations, the actor must continually modify goals. As described by one researcher, planning is replanning. In the model, goal setting processes must be continually evaluating the match between the current goals and progress being made and modify the goals when appropriate.

An integral part of a psychologist's research is communicating the results to the scientific community. The knowledge gained through a study is of no scientific worth until it is made public. The primary medium for the communication of research results is the scientific journals. The standardized format for presentation of a research report is described in a manual published by the American Psychological Association, (APA), titled *Publication Manual of the American Psychological Association* (American Psychological Association, 1983). This specific style must be used in articles submitted to journals published by the APA as well as dozens of other journals which have adopted APA style. The most important criterion determining whether a study has been clearly and explicitly reported is the criterion of replication. If your study could be precisely replicated by another researcher after reading your report, then you have most probably satisfied this criterion. Becoming familiar with APA format is important not only to enable you to write a research report in the proper format, but also to become a more intelligent consumer of psychological research.

MANUSCRIPT FORMAT

The research manuscript is made up of eight sections: (1) title, (2) author's name and institutional affiliation, (3) abstract, (4) introduction, (5) method, (6) results, (7) discussion, and (8) references. An appendix, although rarely included, may be attached if necessary. A copy of a research article is reprinted at the end of this chapter. It will be helpful to refer to the article during the discussion of the sections of a research paper.

Title

The title should summarize the main concept of the study in a recommended maximum of 15 words. It should state concisely the relationship between the independent and dependent variables or the theoretical issues being studied. A good title is explanatory when standing alone. It supplies the reader with the general nature of the study without having to read any portion of the report itself. A concise title is also important for indexing and retrieval purposes in publications such as *Psychological Abstracts*. It is often helpful to leave the title until last even though it is the first part of the manuscript.

Empty phrases such as "A Study of" or "An Experiment on" should not be used, nor should abbreviations. Direct references to methods or results should not be made. A title should not be posed as a question.

In addition to the title of the manuscript, a shortened title of no more than 60 spaces, called a running head, should be included on the cover page along with the title and the author's name and institutional affiliation.

Author's Name and Institutional Affiliation

The by-line consists of two parts: the author's name and the institution at which the investigation took place. The words *by* and *from* should not be included.

The APA manual states that "Authorship encompasses ... not only those who do the actual writing but also those who have made substantial scientific contributions to a study" (1983, p. 20). Authors' names should appear as they are customarily written, and without titles or degrees. Individuals contributing relatively minor assistance are recognized in a footnote.

Institutional affiliations can be used by students as well as faculty members. The formal name of the institution should be cited, not an abbreviation.

Abstract

The abstract is a 100–150 word summary of the content and purpose of the article. Like the title, it should be self-contained. Also, like the title, it is often easiest to write it last, enabling you to paraphrase your own words in the article.

An abstract should contain brief information about the problem investigated, methods, results, and conclusions. The number, type, age, and sex of the subject population should be described. The research design, test instruments, apparatus, and data-gathering techniques should be summarized in enough detail to reflect their importance in the experiment.

Introduction

The introduction specifies the problem under investigation and describes the research strategy. It informs the reader as to why the study was done, and why a specific research design was chosen. The theoretical implications of the study should be covered, as well as its relationship to related work in the field. The introduction is not labeled since its purpose is obvious.

Think of the introduction as a camera panning the landscape and then zeroing in on a specific feature. It begins with a broad conception of the problem, then narrows to the origin of the problem and the theoretical hypotheses tested. Related theories and research are then discussed. Describe related previous research, but do not give a complete literature review. Summarize precisely the present state of knowledge on the subject. Then demonstrate how the present study evolved from previous work. Finally, a formal statement of your hypotheses should be made. Independent and dependent variables can be discussed. Expected results and the reasons behind these expectations may be stated.

Method

The primary purpose of the method section is to tell the reader, step-by-step, how the study was conducted. It should be in sufficient detail to allow an experienced investigator to replicate the study, or to evaluate the adequacy of your research.

The method section is typically divided into subsections: a description of the subjects; the apparatus or the materials; the procedure; and if many independent and dependent variables are involved, a design subsection. Include only enough information to understand and replicate the study.

Subjects. The subjects subsection tells who the research participants were, how many there were, and how they were selected. Major demographic information, including sex, age, and other relevant characteristics should be given. The total number of subjects as well as the number assigned to each experimental condition should be cited. Subject loss should be explained. The number of participants who did not complete the experiment and reasons should be included. Selection of subjects and the procedure for assignment to experimental conditions is very important. Were the participants volunteers? Were they paid for their participation? If so, how much? Were they members of an introductory psychology class? These details may have a bearing on your results, and any investigator wishing to replicate your experiment would need to test similar subjects. If animals were used in the study, report their sex, age, physiological condition, genus, species, and strain number.

Apparatus. This subsection describes the apparatus or materials employed and their function in the experiment. All pertinent information should be presented, including supplier's name and model number. Drawings and photographs should only be used in the case of unusual or custom-made equipment.

Procedure. This subsection is a chronological description of the step-by-step procedure in the experiment from beginning to end. Typically, this section is written from the viewpoint of the subject. Instructions to the participants, stimulus conditions, and control features, such as randomization and counterbalancing, should be included. Report the debriefing procedure used, if human subjects were the participants.

Design. This optional subsection is included for the sake of clarity when a large number of variables could lead to confusion. Otherwise this information is included in other subsections of the manuscript, usually the procedure subsection. It provides an overview of the independent and dependent variables, and the levels for each variable. The design of the experiment should be described (i.e., within subjects, between subjects, random groups, or matched groups).

Results

The results section describes the data obtained in an experiment, and the statistical treatment of them. Begin by briefly discussing the main idea of the results in terms of the experimental hypotheses. Then go on to report the data, including main effects and interactions. All relevant results should be revealed including those that are contrary to your hypotheses. Do not include individual scores, unless a single-subject study was conducted, or unless the performance of each subject is relevant to the experimental question. Do not present statistical formulas unless they are unusual, new, or not standard statistical tests. Finally, this is not the place to discuss implications of the data.

Results should be presented in the medium which most clearly and economically communicates them. Tables and figures should only be used when the data are too complex to describe in the text. Do not repeat the same data in numerous places; do not present data in tables that can be clearly described in a few lines of text. Do make sure to refer to the table or figure in the text of the manuscript. For example, "Sound intensity influenced speed (see Table 1)..." or "Figure 1 illustrates the significant Age x Sex interaction." Tables best express main effects; figures best express trends and interactions.

At the textual location where you want the table or figure to appear, type the following phrase set off by lines and centered:

```
-----------------------------
     Insert Table 1 about here
-----------------------------
```

To present statistics in the text, state the name, degrees of freedom, value, probability level, and direction of the effect.

```
The analysis of variance revealed a significant main effect of
   age, F (1, 52) = 8.39, p< .005.
```

It is also preferable to give the results in terms of the psychological result, rather than simply the statistical result.

```
The older subjects averaged 3 seconds longer than the younger
   subjects, F (1, 52) = 8.39, p< .005.
```

Do not use abbreviations for statistical terms in the narrative; use the terms themselves (e.g., "the means were," not "the Ms were").

Discussion

The purpose of the discussion section is to interpret and evaluate the results of the experiment emphasizing their relationships to the original hypotheses of the study. Were your original hypotheses supported; were alternative or conflicting theories discussed in the introduction supported? Discuss any similarities or differences between your results and those of others. Use speculation cautiously, and only when is identified as such, is related closely to data or logically follows from theory, and is concise. Include the limits and flaws of your study without dwelling on them. Practical implications for further theorizing and research can be stated. Brief suggestions for improvements on your research may be discussed, but do not get carried away. Remember that the major function of your study is to add to the knowledge of a particular subject area, and the discussion section explains in what way your study has made this contribution.

References

All references cited in the text must be listed in the reference list, and each entry in the reference list must be cited in the text. This is not a bibliography in which background information sources are included. Make sure that all information is complete and correct.

WRITING STYLE

Good scientific writing is concise, clear and unambiguous, orderly, economical, and smooth-flowing. It is important that every word you use means precisely what it is intended to mean. Use words correctly, don't use colloquial expressions, and avoid coined terms. Make sure that all referents (i.e., this, that, those) for each term are clear. Experimental groups should be labelled with a key word rather than a number or letter to avoid ambiguity. Present words and paragraphs in

Sexist Language

"When a scientist performs an experiment, (?) must make a number of decisions concerning the appropriate design and data analysis." Did you insert the pronoun *he* or *she* for the missing word in the previous sentence? Form an image of who the pronoun referred to. Is it masculine or feminine? It is possible that you have noticed something unusual about the use of generic pronouns in this book. Rather than always using *he* to refer to *he* or *she*, as has been prescribed by acceptable grammar, we try to use he and she equally. Although most grammarians would want to believe that the generic use of a pronoun is unbiased with regard to sex, recent experiments have shown just the opposite.

In one experiment (MacKay, 1980), subjects were asked to read textbook paragraphs containing the *he* pronoun referring to neutral antecedents such as person. A comprehension test revealed that subjects "understood" the generic *he* to refer to *a male* 50% of the time and to *a male or female* the other 50% of the time. The generic pronoun *he* was never interpreted as *a female*. These results show that the generic pronoun *he* is not understood to be neutral with respect to sex, even though it stands for a neutral noun such as person (other subjects had rated the antecedents of the generic pronoun *he* as neutral). It appears that the use of the male meaning of *he* is so powerful that the context-restricted meaning of the generic usage is subverted. MacKay (1980) also points out that the generic meaning of *he* is intended to include women and, therefore, contradicts the male meaning of *he*. This semantic incompatibility could tend to override the "he or she" meaning of generic *he*.

As an alternative to the generic *he*, MacKay (1980) offers *E*. Subjects were consistent in pronouncing it as the vowel in *he* and *she* and were able to interpret the neologism as meaning "he" or "she." It is too early to know whether *E* is the best possible neologism and in this book we divide up our time between he and she when referring to experimenters, subjects, and people in general.

an orderly fashion. Use simple, concise words whenever possible over long, technical words which are harder to comprehend. Wordiness, evasiveness, and redundancy are signs of unprofessional writing. Do not introduce subjects abruptly or abandon them suddenly. Avoid sudden shifts in tense. Use past tense for a literature review or an experimental procedure. Use present tense to describe the experimental results, or with statements which have a continuing or general applicability such as definitions, statements from well defined theory, and hypotheses. Avoid literary devices such as poetic expressions, alliteration, and cliches which draw attention to words rather than ideas. Traditionally, third person and passive voice have been insisted on in scientific writing, but the trend is toward more personal writing. Use restraint though. The purpose behind impersonal writing is to draw attention to the research, not the researcher. Keeping this in mind will help you to write more personally while still emphasizing the research. Finally, avoid the general use of male nouns and pronouns when referring to both sexes (see Sexist Language).

FIGURES

An important part of scientific communication is visual in the form of graphs of theories and data. (Visual thinking has also been shown to make an important contribution to scientific discovery, Miller, 1986.) Graphs become valuable and even necessary when the relationship between two variables is of interest. As you may have already experienced in this book and elsewhere, graphs are central to illustrating theories, interpretating the results of experiments, and evaluating relationships. The most common relationship in psychology is the one between an independent variable and a dependent variable. A graphical plot of the relationship puts the independent variable on the horizontal or x axis (abscissa) and the dependent variable on the vertical or y axis (ordinate).

Common Glitches

A glitch is a small mistake and experimental psychology students should be warned of several common glitches in this field. One important distinction that is often missed is the difference in meanings between the verbs *affect* and *effect*. To affect something is to influence it such as the independent variable of visual quality affecting the time it takes to name a written word. To effect something is to cause or initiate it, such as an agent effecting an action. The noun forms of *affect* and *effect* usually mean expressed emotion and consequence, respectively. The experimenter's affect was one of depression, therefore, her subjects believed that they had given the wrong responses. The word *data* is plural and its singular name is *datum*. The results are reflected in the data which are interpreted with respect to the experimental hypothesis.

Another writing ghost is distinguishing among the various uses of the homophone principal-principle. Principal means first or foremost in importance; chief. A principle is a basic truth, law, or assumption. A scientist who leads a research project is called the principal investigator. We are concerned with the important principles of experimental design and the principal attributes of good method.

Another pair of misunderstood words of interest to the budding experimenter is *disinterested-uninterested*. Disinterested means impartial, while uninterested means not interested in. It would be ideal for an experimenter to be disinterested in his own experiments but not uninterested in results that disconfirm his hypotheses.

Other irregular words commonly misused in writing are the following:

singular	plural
analysis	analyses
apparatus	apparatuses
criterion	criteria
phenomenon	phenomena
stimulus	stimuli

The abbreviation *cf.* means *compare*, not *see*. When referring to a table or figure, use *see*, not *cf.*

Some terminology is necessary to discuss graphs. A graph is referred to as a figure. Each figure has a figure caption that gives a comprehensive description of the contents of the graph. The axes of the graph are labeled with figure legends. The figure legend also gives the scale that is being used. For example, the ordinate might read "Reaction Times (msec)." The scale values are placed at ticks along the axis.

There are two main categories of graphs: bar graphs or histograms and line drawings. Examples of histograms are Figures 1 and 2 in Chapter 11. The relative frequence of occurrence is plotted on the ordinate and the outcome on the abscissa. Histograms can be thought of as the discrete version of the plot of probability distributions. Examples of probability distributions are Figure 4 in Chapter 9 and Figure 4 in Chapter 11.

Line drawings are similar to histograms, but can be more easily extended to plot the relationship between two independent variables and a dependent variable. Given the value of factorial designs with two or more independent variables, most of the graphs in experimental psychology are of this type. Given a one-factor design, the dependent variable is plotted on the ordinate and the independent variable on the abscissa. The points are usually connected by a line, such as Figure 10 in Chapter 2. In other cases, a theoretical function is plotted. Figure 6 in Chapter 3 is an example of a theoretical function plotted along with the observed data points. With two-factor designs, the second independent variable is a parameter of the graph. Figure 3 of Chapter 4 is a graph of this type.

Although most of us read and produce graphs every day, the psychology of graphing data and theory is in its infancy. The American Psychological Association devotes only about five percent of the *Publication Manual* to the use of figures. It is probably fair to say that our writing in psychology is better than the average quality of graphs published in our journals. This discrepancy is not limited to psychology. Cleveland (1985) found that 30 percent of the graphs in one volume of *Science Magazine* had at least one of four types of problems: incomplete explanation of the components, difficulty in discrimination of the components, construction mistakes, and degraded image due to poor reproduction. We need ideals for graphical communication as we have ideals for verbal communication.

Cleveland (1985) presents some valuable principles of graph construction which include: 1) the use of reference lines to facilitate seeing a scale value across the entire graph; 2) avoid *chartjunk*—or superfluous elements on a graph; 3) use visually prominent graphical elements to show the data; 4) avoid clutter in graphs; 5) plotting symbols corresponding to superposed data sets must be easily discriminated; 6) make legends informative and comprehensive; 7) the scale label should correspond to the tick mark labels as, for example, when logarithms of a variable are graphed; 8) choose corresponding scales as much as possible when graphs are compared; and 9) use a scale break only when necessary; use a full scale break and do not connect values on two sides of a break.

Good construction and aesthetics are inseparable components of graphs. For example, one choice is whether to put the tick marks on a scale outside the data region rather than within the data region. One person's aesthetic judgment may differ with another's. Of course, with the tick mark inside the graph, one has to guard against placing data points on a tick mark, a common occurrence in our journals. Data points should not fall on the scale lines either, so tick marks outside the data region do not eliminate this problem. Generally, the data region should be offset from the scale lines (see Figure 5). Similarly, one must decide to place the figure legends (the parameter of the graph) outside or inside the graphing area. In this book and in psychology generally, the legends are usually placed inside the graphing area, as illustrated in Figure 5.

In his popular book, *How to Lie with Statistics*, Huff (1954) warns us that the scale can be expanded or shrunk to produce a large or small apparent effect. Huff's solution is that zero should always be included on the scale. Including zero on the scale, however, can produce poor resolution. Cleveland's rebuttal is that the viewers will be misled only if they do not look at the scale labels and apply the most trivial of quantitative reasoning. Thus, in graphical style as in writing style, there are tradeoffs that must be considered by the creator.

Cleveland (1985) offers several novel graphical methods that psychologists will find of value. The dot chart shown in Figure 2 represents an appealing alternative to our traditional histogram. The fine dotted line combined with the dot substitutes for the clumsy box we were weaned on. Strictly speaking, a bar chart would be incorrect since the bar length would be meaningless given that it represents the data minus some arbitrary number. There is also good reason to violate the principle of plotting the dependent variable on the y axis. In this case, the different languages can be printed in standard orientation directly on the graph.

Several of the proposals have been inspired by John Tukey (1984). A box graph shown in Figure 3 is a novel method of showing selected percentiles of the data. A graphical method of this form might encourage some of us to communicate the distribution rather than just the average of a set of data.

The four-dimensional scatterplot in Figure 4 isn't comprehended in a glance but provides in one graph what would otherwise require at least four separate graphs.

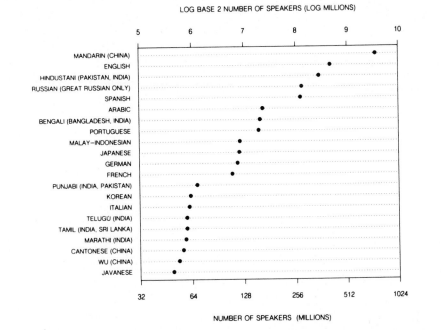

Figure 2. Graphical methods. The figure shows a graphical method called a dot chart, which can be used to show data where each value has a label. The data are the number of speakers for the world's 21 most spoken languages. The data are graphed on a log base 2 scale, so values double in moving left to right from one tick mark to the next.

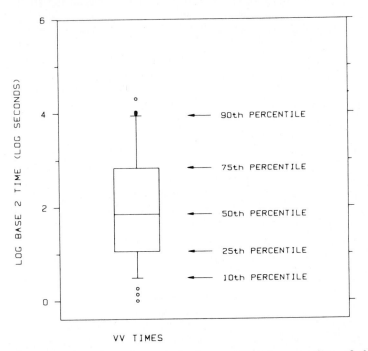

Figure 3. Tukey box graph. A box graph shows selected percentiles of the data, as illustrated in this figure. All values beyond the 10th and 90th percentiles are graphed individually as on a point graph.

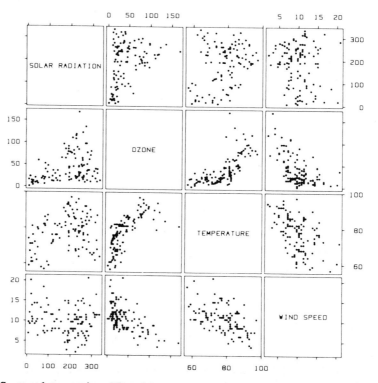

Figure 4. Scatterplot matrix. The data are measurements of solar radiation, ozone, temperature, and wind speed on 111 days. Thus, the measurements are 111 points in a four-dimensional space. The graphical method in this figure is a scatterplot matrix: all pairwise scatterplots of the variables are aligned into a matrix with shared scales.

As the word processors have freed us from the constraints imposed on having multiple revisions of the text, computer graphics now make it possible to experiment with and iterate our graphing of data. We are no longer at the mercy of having our graphs drawn by the local artist but are free to develop and draw them ourselves.

Figure 5 shows a common graph in experimental psychology in which the dependent variable is plotted as a function of two independent variables. One common question central to the evaluation of the results is whether the lines can be considered to be parallel or nonparallel (see Chapter 8). For most viewers, the graphs on the left look parallel, whereas the graphs on the right appear to be closer together in the middle of the *x* axis than at the extremes. However, in fact, the opposite is the case. The curves on the right are exactly parallel to one another, whereas the curves on the left are 100% further apart in the middle than at the extremes of the abscissa. Usually graphical perception involves determining horizontal or vertical extent between points or lines. Given our limitation in selective attention, we find that one of these dimensions can influence judgments of the other. When presenting data of this form, it might be worthwhile to warn the reader of this perceptual bias. The problem is that when we compare the distance between the two lines we tend to travel in the shortest distance possible, thus not maintaining the strict vertical direction that is required in determining the distance between the two lines. One strategy that can overcome this illusion is to rotate the graph 90° and to attend to the relative distance along the dependent-variable axis between the curves (Leon & Anderson, 1974).

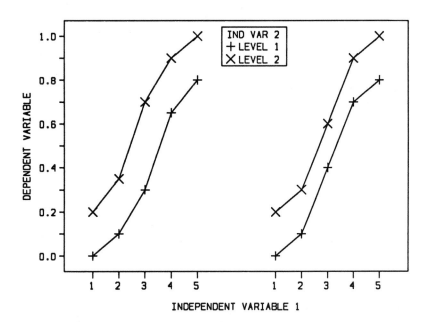

Figure 5. Hypothetical results showing apparently parallel lines in the left panel and lines apparently converging in the middle range of the *x* axis in the right panel. In fact, the distance between the lines at level 3 is twice the distance at levels 1 and 5 in the left panel. The lines are parallel in the right panel.

APA EDITORIAL STYLE

Most journals and books in psychology follow the guidelines of the APA. The purpose behind a standard editorial style is to ensure uniform presentation and clear communication.

Headings

Headings organize an article and indicate the importance of each topic. A heading is not used for the introduction. Main headings are centered and underlined with the initial letters of the main words capitalized. Side headings are flush with the left margin, underlined, and the initial letters of the main words are also capitalized. Text begins with a paragraph indentation on the next double-spaced line. Paragraph headings are indented as a new paragraph. Only the initial letter of the first word is capitalized, and the heading is underlined. Include a period at the end of the heading, skip two spaces, and begin the text on the same line.

If four levels of headings are required, for example, when an article is reporting a series of related experiments each with their own sections, use a centered heading in all capital letters to subordinate the other three levels. Do not underline this heading.

Abbreviations and Symbols

Abbreviations are used sparingly in APA journals, and only when they help communication with the reader, not hinder it. If a term which has a standard abbreviation appears frequently in a paper, generally the abbreviation is used, throughout the paper, except the first time the term is used when it is spelled out completely and immediately followed by the abbreviation in parentheses.

```
"The reaction time (RT) measure..."
"Subjects were administered the Minnesota
Multiphasic Personality Inventory (MMPI)..."
```

Use abbreviations for standard Latin terms,

e.g.,	for example
i.e.,	that is
et al.	and others (note that the period only follows al, and not et)

Use abbreviations for reference terms. Do not abbreviate titles of journals.

chap.	chapter
ed.	edition
rev. ed.	revised edition
Ed. (Eds.)	Editor(s)
Vol.	Volume (as in Vol. 3)
vols.	volumes (as in 3 vols.)
p. (pp.)	page(s)

Use abbreviations for metric units. But do not use a period with metric measurement abbreviations. (Metric units should be used in all reports.)

Abbreviations should also be used for statistical terms, except when they appear in the narrative, as previously mentioned. Letters used as symbols for statistical terms, and also for conventional test scores are underlined to indicate italics. Do not underline Greek letters.

The abbreviations *S*, *E*, and *O* for subject, experimenter, and observer are no longer appropriate for articles in APA journals. If a more descriptive term, such as freshman students or rats, better describes the experimental sample, use that term rather than a less descriptive term, such as subjects.

The percent sign (%) is used after numbers to indicate percentage quantity. The word *percentage* is used when no number is given.

```
"It was found that 32% of the students..."
"The percentage of students who..."
```

Numbers

The numbers zero through nine are ordinarily spelled out. Use words to express any number that begins a sentence. Numbers of two or more digits not beginning a sentence are expressed in numeric figures. Use figures to express *any* numbers that indicate: page numbers, ages, or dates; scores or percentages; ratios or arithmetic manipulation; fractional or decimal quantities; exact sums of money or actual numerals; series of four or more numbers such as 3, 6, 9, 12; numbers grouped within a sentence or related sentences in which one of the numbers is 10 or more; or numbers which precede a unit of measurement such as 10 mg, 24 hours, or 9 point scale.

Ordinal numbers are treated as you would cardinal numbers with the exception that percentiles and quartiles are always expressed in numeric figures. Use arabic numerals over roman numerals whenever possible. In sentences in which numeric figures and words appear together it is usually better to recast the sentence. "The first day 28 males and 32 females were tested," is better than, "Twenty-eight males and 32 females were tested on the first day."

Seriation

Greater clarity can be obtained by using a series of phrases, sentences, or paragraphs to organize information. Seriation within a paragraph or sentence is shown by lowercase letters in parentheses: (a)..., (b)..., and (c).... To show seriation of paragraphs, number each paragraph with an arabic numeral followed by a period.

1. First start with a paragraph indentation. Then type the second and succeeding lines flush with the left margin.

2. The second entry starts a new paragraph.

Tables and Figures

Tables and figures should be numbered in the order in which they are first mentioned in the text. Each should have a brief but clearly explanatory title.

A table classifies and compares related items by arranging data in labeled rows and columns. The number and title of the table are centered above it. The left-hand column usually displays the independent variables, and always has a heading. Headings at the top of the table identify the items in the vertical columns. At times the need will arise for another set of vertical headings. These headings span the entire width of the table, providing further divisions. Each column and row must be labeled.

The term "figure" refers to all graphs (e.g., line graphs, bar graphs, frequency polygons), charts, illustrations, and photographs. Figures do not have titles above them; rather, figure numbers and informative, concise captions appear below them. In a graph, the two axes must be labeled. Labeling should include the unit of measurement (e.g., "RT in msec" instead of simply "RT"). Remember that the independent variable is plotted on the abscissa, or x axis; the dependent variable is plotted on the ordinate, or y axis.

Reference Citations in Text

Instead of footnotes, APA journals use the author-date method of citation in which the surname of the author and the year of publication are introduced into the text at the appropriate point. If there is no author, use the first words of the title and the year.

```
"Smith (1980) investigated typing speed..."
"In a recent study of typing speed (Smith, 1980)"
"In 1980, Smith investigated typing speed..."
"(Random House Dictionary, 1969)"
```

In further discussion, the name of the study may be mentioned again without the parenthetical citation of the year, providing that ambiguity does not result.

If a work has two authors, always cite both authors. If a work has more than two authors, cite all of them the first time the reference appears; cite only the surname of the first author followed by "et al." and the year in all further occurrences of the same reference. The exceptions to this are when different references in the same year shorten to the same reference, and in footnotes, tables, and figures.

Multiple-author citations occurring in running text are connected by "and," while in parenthetical and tabular material, the names are joined by an ampersand (&). If the reference list includes publications by two or more authors with the same surname, include their initials in the text in order to avoid confusion.

Multiple citations in parentheses follow the order of the reference list (i.e., chronological order for citations by the same author, alphabetical order for citations by different authors).

Semicolons separate references to works by different authors while commas separate references to different works by the same author; the author's name is not repeated for each work.

```
"Recent studies (Smith, 1969, 1976, 1979, 1980a,
1980b, in press) have demonstrated..."

"Recent studies (Brown, 1976; Brown & Smith,
1978; Williams, 1981) have demonstrated..."
```

Reference Lists

All entries are arranged alphabetically by the author's surname or in the case of multiple authorship, by the surname of of the first-named author.

When several works by the same first author occur in the reference list, always begin the entry by repeating the author's name. Single-author references precede multiple author references beginning with the same name. Entries with the same first author but different second or third authors are arranged alphabetically by the name of the second or third author. References to the same author published in the same year are alphabetically arranged by the title (excluding *a* or *the*); lowercase letters in parentheses, (a), (b), (c) are included after the final period of each entry.

```
Harlow, H. F. (1962).  Fundamental principles for preparing
psychology journal articles.  Journal of Comparative and
Physiological Psychology, 55, 893-896.

Atkinson, R. C., & Shiffrin, R. M. (1971).  The control of
short-term memory.  Scientific American, 255(2), 89-90.
```

The elements in a reference entry should begin with the authors. Each surname is followed by initials. The publication year; the title of the article, chapter, or book; and the facts of publication follow. For journals, publication information includes the complete journal name, the volume number, and inclusive pages. For books, publication information includes the city of publication, the publisher's name, and the inclusive pages.

Periods are used to differentiate the three major parts of a reference citation: author, title, and publication facts. Commas are used within the different parts (e.g., between the volume and page numbers in a journal entry). Colons are used between the publication location and the book publisher. Parentheses are used for extensions or qualifications of a part of an entry or the entire entry itself (e.g., (2nd ed.), (Vol. 2), (Abstract)).

In journal titles, capitalize the initial letter of all major words. In article, chapter, or book titles, capitalize the initial letter of the first word only, except in certain cases such as proper names and the first word after a colon or dash.

Book and journal titles and journal volume numbers are underlined to indicate italics. Do not use quotation marks with article and chapter titles.

```
Strunk, W., Jr., & White, E. B. (1972).  The elements of style
(2nd ed.).  New York: Macmillan.
```

For material that is not widely available, give as much data about the information source as is available, including the address from which the material may be obtained and any official number.

Sheperd, J. C. (1973). An evaluation of group and individual models of career counseling (Doctoral dissertation, University of Utah, 1973). *Dissertation Abstracts International, 34,* 3071A-3072A. (University Microfilms No. 73-29, 395)

Footnotes

Footnotes of acknowledgment and author identification are a standard part of every manuscript and therefore are not numbered, and always appear first. All other text footnotes are numbered consecutively with arabic superscript throughout the text.

Typing Format

The manuscript should be typed on heavy, standard size bond paper. Double space *everything*! Leave margins of 1½ inches (4 cm) on all four sides of the page. Indent five spaces at the beginning of each paragraph, except for the abstract, which is typed as a solid block. References are typed with every line of the citation indented except the first.

Each of the following parts of the manuscript begins on a new page, and in the order presented.

Cover page   (title, author's name and affiliation, running head)
Abstract
Text
Reference notes
References
Footnotes
Tables   (each on a separate page)
Figure captions
Figures   (each on a separate page)

Pages are numbered consecutively, beginning with the abstract page; only the cover sheet and figures are not numbered.

Each page of the manuscript is identified with the first two or three words from the title in the upper right-hand corner above the page number.

SAMPLE RESEARCH PAPER

The following section reproduces the manuscript version of a research paper. The goal is to illustrate the principles of writing, manuscript format, and APA editorial style discussed in this chapter. The student should find it valuable to refer to this manuscript for specific implementations of these principles.

Visible Language in Speech Perception:
Lipreading and Reading

Dominic W. Massaro, Michael M. Cohen, and Laura A. Thompson

Program in Experimental Psychology

University of California, Santa Cruz

Santa Cruz, CA 95064

Send Correspondence to:

Dominic W. Massaro

Program in Experimental Psychology

University of California, Santa Cruz

Santa Cruz, CA 95064

Massaro et al.: Speech Perception   2

Abstract

Watching a speaker in face-to-face communication can influence what the perceiver hears the speaker saying. Faced with this influence of visible language on the perception of audible language, an interesting question is whether written language would also influence audible speech perception. To test this possibility, subjects identified spoken syllables either while viewing the speaker's face or while reading a written syllable. In both conditions, subjects identified what they heard the speaker saying. Replicating previous studies, lipreading had a large influence on the identification. In contrast, reading a written syllable had a much smaller, but statistically significant effect. Although lipreading appears to be much more influential than reading, it remains a possibility that written language can contribute to our auditory experience of speech.

Massaro et al.: Speech Perception   3

Acknowledgment

The writing of this paper and the research reported in the paper were supported, in part, by NINCDS Grant 20314 from the Public Health Service and Grant BNS-83-15192 from the National Science Foundation.

   Although speech perception is usually thought of as an auditory

process, it appears to be visual as well. As exemplified by this special

volume of Visible Language, visible speech in the form of the lip movements

of the speaker influences what we hear the speaker to be saying. Viewing

the speaker can enhance understanding, especially when the auditory signal

is degraded by masking noise.   Three decades ago, Sumby and Pollack (1954)

demonstrated that perceiving the face of a speaker was equivalent to

increasing the signal-to-noise ratio of the auditory signal by 20 dB. The

visual influence is not limited to situations with degraded auditory

inputs. As reported by McGurk and MacDonald (1976), the visual input from

the speaker can change the perceptual experience of an auditory speech

event. Using videotape, these investigations dubbed a labial speech sound

/ba-ba/ onto the visual articulation of a velar stop consonant /ga-ga/.

Subjects viewing and listening to the dubbed videotape often heard /da-da/.

   Massaro and Cohen (1983) extended the McGurk and MacDonald (1976)

demonstration by independently varying auditory and visual information in a

factorial design. Subjects identified as /ba/ or /da/ speech events

consisting of high-quality synthetic syllables ranging from /ba/ to /da/

combined with a videotaped /ba/ or /da/ or no articulation. Although

subjects were instructed specifically to report what they heard, viewing

the visual articulation made a large contribution to identification. There

were effects of both visual and auditory information and an interaction

between these variables. The contribution of one source was larger to the extent the other source of information was ambiguous.

Given the impact of visible speech in the form of a speaker's articulations, it appeared possible that visible language in the form of writing might also influence how speech is heard. In this case, seeing a written segment, such as BA, would bias the auditory perception of a spoken syllable towards /ba/. To test for this possibility, the present experiment directly compared the contribution of lipread to written information in speech perception. Subjects were asked to watch a monitor and to listen to a speech sound. They were told to report whether they heard the sound /ba/ or /da/. The speech sound was chosen from nine synthetic speech sounds along a /ba/ to /da/ continuum. Simultaneous with the speech sound, a visual event could also be presented. In the lipreading condition, the person on the TV monitor was sometimes seen articulating the syllable /ba/ or the syllable /da/. On some trials, no articulation was produced. In the reading condition, the two asterisks on the monitor were sometimes changed to the letters BA or DA during the audible presentation of the syllable. On other trials, no change in the asterisks was made. In both conditions, subjects identified whether or not a visual event occurred, in addition to identifying the speech syllable that was heard. This dual task provided a check on whether the subject was actually looking at the visual event when it occurred.

There is some historical precedence that is of interest. In 1667, Baron Franciscus Mercurius ab Helmont proposed that the letter symbols of

Massaro et al.: Speech Perception   6

the Hebrew alphabet were not arbitrary but actually represented the tongue positions of the corresponding speech segments. Figure 1 gives one of Helmont's illustrations for M, the 13th letter of the Hebrew alphabet. The letter is pronounced /mɛm/ as indicated in Hebrew writing (right to left) in the bottom panel of the figure. The headband consists of other forms for the letter M as found on ancient coins, for example. Not unlike some extant ideas, Helmont's position was not airtight; it would have been enjoyable to watch him justify the small appendage at the tip of the tongue. Actually, it would not be unreasonable to interpret this element as corresponding to the teeth and alveolar ridge. Helmont's study was followed by a series of studies culminating in Alexander Melville Bell's (1867) visible speech symbols. These symbols illustrated the vocal action in producing the sounds. It is interesting, however, that the symbols adopted and still used by the International Phonetic Association to represent all speech sounds have no speech-production connotations. This might be due, in part, to the fact that a unique speech gesture is not necessary to produce a given sound category.

There is some basis for expecting that printed language might influence the perception of spoken language. Ehri (1984) makes a strong case for the influence of orthography on a child's spoken language processing. As an example, a pre-reader has difficulty recognizing spoken function words (such as might, could, or from) as single words. A novice reader, on the other hand, performs the same task quite easily. Learning to read also enables children to segment spoken words into their constituent phonemes more easily. Written language also influences the processing of spoken language for literate adults. In one task, subjects are asked to indicate as quickly as possible whether or not two spoken words rhyme (Seidenberg & Tanenhaus, 1979). They are faster in detecting that two orthographically-similar words rhyme compared to two dissimilar words. As an example, subjects respond yes more quickly to the spoken words name-blame than to the words name-claim. Other encouraging evidence comes from Campbell (in press) who used written pseudo-homophones (wunn, tooe, threa) in the suffix memory task. Recency effects were observed and this advantage for the last few items in the list was eliminated by an auditory suffix (the spoken word go). Ehri (1984) reviews other positive evidence for the influence of spelling on the perceptual processing of spoken language. For our purposes, the evidence encourages asking whether an orthographic stimulus could influence speech perception in the same manner as a visible spoken articulation.

Method

Subjects --Seventeen adult subjects were recruited from the university community. Three subjects were eliminated for failing to follow instructions and two because of an error in recording the results, giving a total of twelve subjects contributing to the results.

Massaro et al.: Speech Perception   8

  <u>Stimuli</u> --For the lipreading condition, the speech events were recorded
on a videotape. The author was seated in front of a wood panel background,
illuminated with ordinary fluorescent fixtures in the ceiling. The
speaker's head was centered in the video field and filled about two thirds
of the frame in both the horizontal and vertical directions. On each trial
the speaker said either /ba/ or /da/ or nothing, as cued by a video
terminal under computer control.

  The original audio track was replaced with synthetic speech. The
speaker's /ba/'s and /da/'s were analyzed using linear prediction to derive
a set of parameters for driving a software formant serial resonator speech
synthesizer (Klatt, 1980). By altering the parametric information
regarding the first 80 msec of the CV, a set of nine 400 msec CVs covering
the range from /ba/ to /da/ was created. During the first 80 msec, F1 went
from 300 Hz to 700 Hz following a negatively accelerated path. The F2
followed a negatively accelerated path to 1199 Hz from one of nine values
equally spaced between 1000 and 2000 Hz from most /ba/-like to most /da/-
like, respectively. The F3 followed a linear transition to 2729 Hz from
one of nine values equally spaced between 2200 and 3200 Hz. All other
characteristics of synthetic CVs were identical for the nine test stimuli.
Additional details of the video recording and the speech synthesis are
given in Massaro and Cohen (1983).

  An experimental tape was made by copying the original tape and
replacing the original sound track with the synthetic speech. The

presentation of the synthetic speech was synchronized with the original
audio track on the videotape and gave the strong illusion that the
synthetic speech was coming from the mouth of the speaker. To accomplish
this synchronization, the audio signal was monitored by a schmidt trigger
circuit. When the original audio channel on the videotape exceeded a
preset threshold, one of the 400 msec CV syllables was played.

On each trial of the lipreading condition, one of the nine auditory
stimuli on the continuum from /ba/ to /da/ was paired with one of the two
possible visual articulations, /ba/ or /da/, or with no articulation. The
stimuli were presented in 11 blocks of the 27 possible combinations,
sampled randomly without replacement. A practice block of 10 trials
preceded the 297 experimental trials. The subjects had about three seconds
to make their response before the next trial.

The reading condition was designed to duplicate the lipreading
condition except for the nature of the visual information. Subjects viewed
a TV monitor and fixated on a row of two asterisks centered on the monitor.
On two thirds of the trials, the asterisks could be replaced by the letters
strings BA or DA during the 400 msec presentation of the speech sound. On
the other one third of the trials, the asterisks remained in view during
the presentation of the speech sound. The sequence, number, and timing of
speech and visual events were identical to those in the lipreading
condition. In both the lipreading and reading conditions, subjects
listened to the speech stimuli over headphones (Koss Pro 4AA) at a
comfortable listening intensity (71 dB-A).

Massaro et al.: Speech Perception   10

On each trial, subjects were instructed to hit one of four buttons, indicating the outcome of two events: first, whether they heard the sound /ba/ or /da/ and second, whether or not there was a change in the visual domain. A visual change represented the speaker moving his lips to say /ba/ or /da/ in the lipreading condition and the occurrence of the letter strings BA or DA in the reading condition. The buttons were arranged in a two-by-two configuration with the ba and da alternatives corresponding to the top and bottom rows, and the yes and no alternatives corresponding to the left and right columns. For example, hitting the top right button indicated that the subject heard a /ba/ and that there was no visual change during the speech sound.

With an open-ended set of response alternatives in the task, subjects have reported a variety of percepts: /tha/, /va/, /bda/, and /ga/ (Massaro & Cohen, 1983). We limited the choices to two alternatives for practical reasons because subjects also had to report whether there was a change in the visual domain. Importantly, the two-alternative task provides an assessment of perception based on the evidence that subjects have continuous information indicating the degree of support for each alternative and choose an alternative from the permissible set of alternatives (Massaro & Cohen, 1983). Given this evidence, two choice alternatives in the present task provide an appropriate measure of the influence of visual information on speech perception.

All subjects were tested in both the lipreading and reading conditions in two consecutive sessions on a given day. The order of the two conditions was counterbalanced across subjects with six of the subjects receiving the lipreading condition first and six receiving the reading condition first. Each subject was tested for 594 experimental trials, giving a total of up to 11 observations for each subject at each of the 54 experimental conditions.

Results

One important requirement in the present test is that the subjects look at the visual event during the speech sound. To encourage the subjects to monitor the visual information and to evaluate whether they were looking at it, they were required to indicate whether or not a visual event occurred during the speech sound. Subjects were extremely accurate in this task, averaging 96% and 97% correct in the lipreading and reading conditions, respectively. In both conditions, subjects were about 2% or 3% more accurate in determining the presence, rather than the absence, of a change in the visual event.

Given that the subjects were looking at the visual event in both the lipreading and reading conditions, it is meaningful to analyze the identification results. The proportion of /da/ identifications was computed for each subject at each of the 27 stimulus conditions for both the lipreading and reading conditions. A preliminary analysis revealed no effect of the order of presentation of the lipreading and reading conditions and this variable is ignored in the analysis presented here.

Massaro et al.: Speech Perception   12

The left and right panels of Figure 2 give the average results for the
lipreading and reading conditions, respectively. The proportion of /da/
responses as a function of the nine levels along the auditory speech
continuum is shown with the visual ba, da, or none as the curve parameter.
The average proportion of /da/ responses increased significantly as the
level of the auditory syllable went from the most /ba/-like to the most
/da/-like level, F (8, 80) = 311, p < .001. There was also a large effect
on the proportion of /da/ responses as a function of the visual stimulus,
with fewer /da/ responses for a visual "ba" than for a visual "da", F (2,
20) = 26, p < .001. The interaction of these two variables was also
significant, F (16, 160) = 11.2, p < .001, since the effect of the visual
variable is smaller at the less ambiguous regions of the auditory
dimension.

The result of central interest is the difference between the lipreading
and reading conditions given in the two panels in Figure 2. What is most
apparent is the much larger effect of the visual information in the
lipreading relative to the reading condition. The visual variable was
about 9 times more effective in the lipreading than in the reading
condition. Figure 3 gives a graphical representation of the visual effect
for each subject in the lipreading and reading conditions. Every subject
showed a larger effect of lipreading relative to reading. Only two
subjects showed lipreading effects of about the same size as the reading
effect. The lipreading/reading comparison interacted with the auditory
variable, F (8, 80) = 2.68, p < .025, the visual variable, F (2, 20) =

p 4.11, < .05 and the auditory/visual interaction, F (16, 160) = 5.5, p <
.001. Although the magnitude of the visual variable was much less in the
reading condition, it was still statistically significant, F (2, 22) =
14.3, p < .001, as was the interaction between the auditory and visual
variables, F (16, 176) = 2.73, p < .005. Thus, although the magnitude of
the visual variable differed greatly between the lipreading and reading
conditions, the form of its interaction with the auditory variable was very
similar in the two conditions. The visual influence was always largest at
the most ambiguous levels of the auditory variable.

Discussion

The results of the present study are difficult to evaluate primarily
because of the finding of a small reading effect. Without a doubt,
lipreading a face has a substantial influence on auditory speech
recognition. Reading print, on the other hand, had a comparatively smaller
effect.

Future research should be aimed at inducing a larger effect of reading
to allow a better test of the contrasting models. Perhaps some other form
of presentation would enhance the contribution of a written input. For
example, a word rather than a meaningless syllable might induce a larger
effect of reading. Based on previous findings, a printed multisyllabic
word should influence auditory perception of the latter syllables of the
spoken form of the word. Marslen-Wilson and Welsh (1978) had their

subjects shadow (repeat back) a spoken message that contained
mispronunciations of some of the words (the word confusion might be
pronounced as gunfusion). Of interest was the extent to which subjects
would be swayed by the linguistic context to miss these errors in
pronunciation. If subjects fail to notice the mispronunciations, they
should not include them in their shadowing of the message; that is, they
should restore the mispronounced words to their correct form. In fact,
subjects restored many of the mispronunciations and were more likely to
restore mispronunciations in the third syllable than in the first syllable
of a three-syllable word. A reasonable explanation is that recognition of
the word occurred before the third syllable was heard and this information
influenced how the latter part of the word was heard.

A similar result might occur if a printed word is paired with a spoken
word. Because the printed word might be recognized before hearing the
third syllable of the spoken word, a positive result would still not
necessarily mean that print influenced auditory speech perception directly.
The effect could have been mediated by word meaning. Printed and spoken
nonwords could be used to assess whether word meaning is necessary to
obtain the influence of print on auditory speech perception.

                              References

Bell, A. M. (1867). Visible speech: The science of universal alphabetics.

    London: Simpkin, Marshall & Co.

Ehri, L. C. (1984). How orthography alters spoken language competencies in

    children learning to read and spell. In J. Downing & R. Valtin (Eds.),

    Language awareness and learning to read (pp. 119-147). New York:

    Springer-Verlag.

Helmont, B. F. M. ab. (1667). Alphabeti vere naturalis Hebraici

    Brevissima Delineatio.

Klatt, D. H. (1980). Software for a cascade/parallel formant synthesizer.

    Journal of the Acoustical Society of America, 67, 971-995.

Marslen-Wilson, W., & Welsh, A. (1978). Processing interactions and lexical

    access during word recognition in continuous speech. Cognitive

    Psychology, 10, 29-63.

Massaro, D. W., & Cohen, M. M. (1983). Evaluation and integration of

    visual and auditory information in speech perception. Journal of

    Experimental Psychology: Human Perception and Performance, 9, 753-771.

McGurk, H. (1981). Listening with eye and ear (paper discussion). In T.

    Myers, J. Laver, & J. Anderson (Eds.), The cognitive representation of

    speech. Amsterdam: North-Holland.

Seidenberg, M. S., & Tanenhaus, M. K. (1979). Orthographic effects on rhyme

    monitoring. Journal of Experimental Psychology: Human Learning and

    Memory, 5, 546-554.

Massaro et al.: Speech Perception   16

List of Figures

1. Hebrew letter M as a tongue position according to Helmont. The lower panel gives the Hebrew (to be read from right to left) pronunciation of the letter /mɛm/.

2. Observed (points) and predicted lines proportion of /da/ identifications as a function of the auditory and visual levels of the speech event. The left panel gives the results for the lipreading condition and the right panel for the reading condition. The predictions are for the fuzzy logical model of perception.

3. The proportion of /da/ identifications for the 12 individual subjects as a function of the visual level in the lipreading and reading conditions.

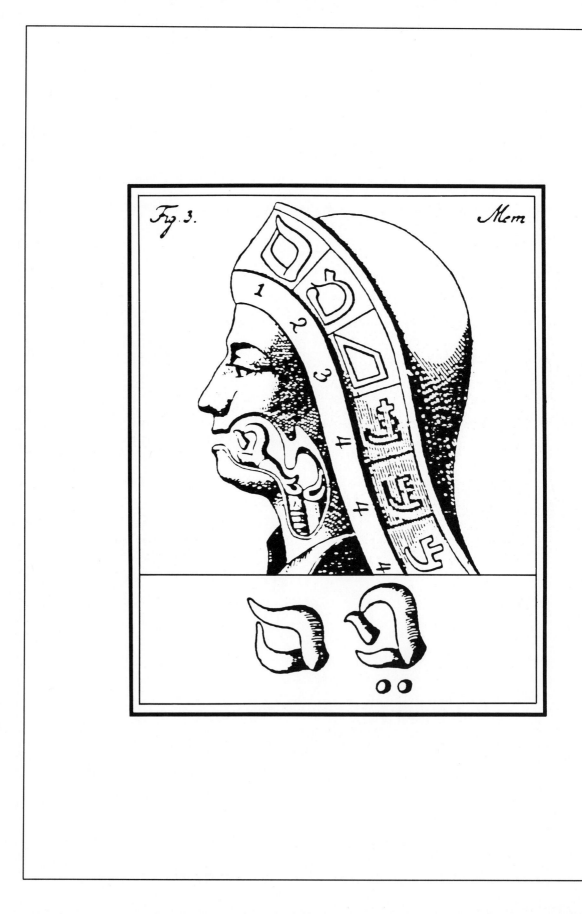

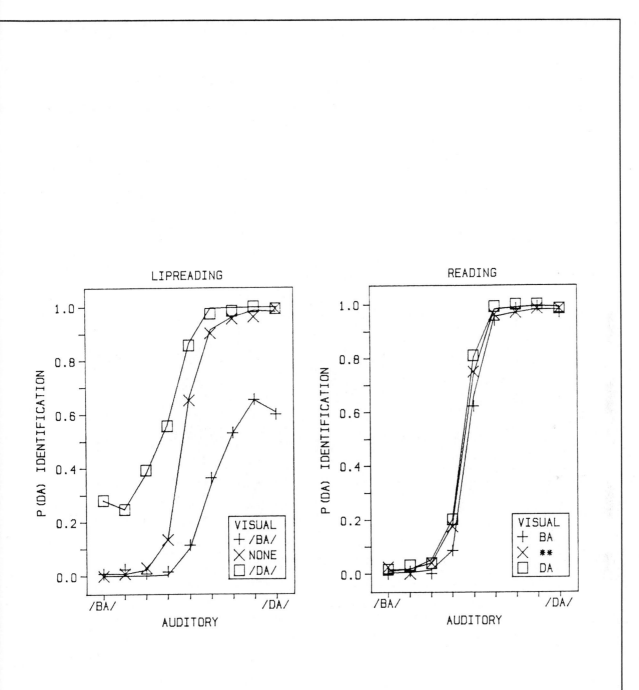

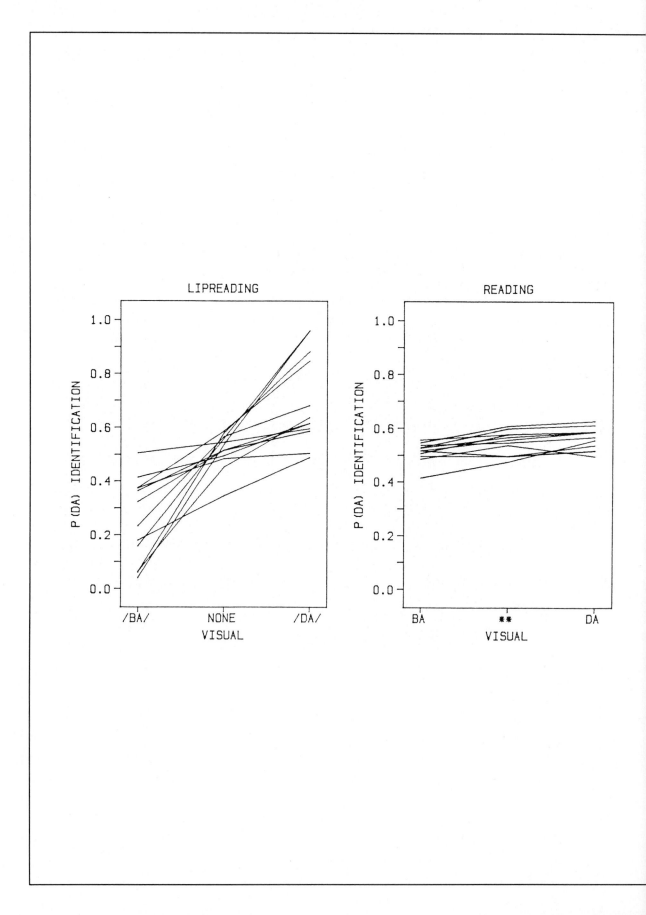

PART TWO

Reaction Time and Psychophysics

7

Duration of Mental Processes

Isolating Stages
   Detection, Recognition, and Response Selection

Reaction Time
   Eyes and Ears in Astronomy
   Pointers and Bells
   Donders and Helmholtz

Subtractive Method
   Intensity of Stimulus
   Simple versus Choice RT Tasks
   Anticipation Errors
   Visual Presentation
   Auditory Presentation
   Recognition Time
   Response-Selection Time
   A, B, and C Tasks
   Criticism of Donders' Methods

   Stages of Information Processing
   Questioning Assumptions

Would it not be possible to determine the time required
for shaping a concept or expressing one's will?
For years this question intrigued me.
Franciscus C. Donders (1869)

An experimental psychologist studying human information processing is concerned with the psychological processes that intervene between stimulus and response. This chapter discusses a technique for studying these processes. The logic of the experimental approach tells us that in order to interpret performance properly, we must ask how many processes occur between a stimulus and a response in an experimental task. How do these processes work? What rules describe the operations of each process? How long does each operation last? What variables influence each of the mental processes?

For example, suppose a student is sitting in a classroom and a fire alarm goes off. The appropriate response would be to leave the room. The siren functions as the stimulus, and walking out of the room would usually be an appropriate response. The amount of time that elapses between the onset of the siren and the onset of walking out of the room is referred to as reaction time (RT) or latency.

ISOLATING STAGES

Our interest lies in the processes that occur internally between the onset of the stimulus and the onset of the response. We can identify the probable stages of mental processing hypothetically by a logical analysis of the fire alarm scenario. First the observer must certainly become aware that some new stimulus has occurred. This reminds us of the British empiricists' concept of sensation—the imprinting, as they thought of it, of the stimulus upon the sensory system. Sensation, or detection, is the process that initiates the flow of information through the human processing system. This takes an amount of time which we can call T_d.

Second, before he or she can act appropriately, the observer must recognize the siren and identify it as a symbol indicating that a fire, hence danger, may be in the building. Recognition and identification are used interchangeably for describing this stage of processing. The stimulus has now been given a meaning by making contact with some knowledge in memory. If this process does not take place, if the observer experiences the alarm simply as an extraneous event without meaning, then it provides no reason to leave the building. Recognition is similar to the concept of perception used by the British empiricists—the point at which mere sensation has acquired meaning. It also takes a certain amount of time which we will call T_r.

After the observer has recognized the stimulus, he must select a response. He might stand on his head, or jump out the window, or do one of any number of things; we may assume he will pick the response most appropriate to the situation. The choice may be more or less difficult. For instance, if the observer has experienced a number of false fire alarms in the same building and, moreover, is engaged in important work with a deadline to meet, she may hesitate to leave. In any case, selection of the appropriate response also takes some time, which we will abbreviate as T_{rs}.

Finally, the response must be executed after it is selected. In our fire alarm scenario, however, we are not interested in response-execution time per se, but rather in the processing that led up to the execution of the response. Therefore, we measure RT from the onset of the stimulus to the onset of the response, so that response-execution time contributes very little to the overall RT. Response-execution time is of interest in the study of motor skills such as typing, speech production, and writing.

Stages of Information Processing

The processes we have identified between stimulus and response in the fire alarm scenario can be clarified in terms of our information-processing analysis. Each process has some information available to it and transforms this information, making the transformed information available to the next processing stage. The information available to the detection process is the stimulus. The detection process transduces the physical signal into a neurological code which provides information about the presence or absence of an external stimulus. The operations of this process are usually studied employing psychophysical methods (see Chapters 8 through 11). At this point in the processing chain, the observer has enough information to report that something has occurred. He cannot, however, say what it is.

The detection process makes available the neurological code to the recognition process. The recognition process must transform this preperceptual information into a perceptual form. There are actually two stages to the recognition of a fire alarm. First, the recognition process must resolve the sound quality so that it can be distinguished from other possible sounds, such as the bell that signals the end of the class period. Second, the observer must know that this particular sound means "fire alarm." Having never heard a fire alarm before, an observer may recognize the sound as one of a certain quality but it would have no meaning. In order to recognize its meaning, he must first perceive the sound of the alarm and, second, know that this sound signifies a fire alarm.

The recognition process, therefore, must translate the neurological code given by the detection process into a code that is meaningful to the response-selection process. The knowledge that a fire alarm is ringing is the outcome of a successful recognition. This information or symbolic encoding of the sound of the fire alarm is meaningful to the response-selection process. The response-selection process, therefore, receives the information from the recognition stage that the fire alarm is ringing. The response-selection process could have received this information in other ways; a deaf person, for example, could see someone ringing the alarm. The response-selection process must answer the question: Given that there is a fire alarm, what response should be executed?

The response-selection process is similar to the decision process discussed in detail in Chapters 8, 9, and 10. It is influenced by the subject's knowledge of the likelihood that, given a fire alarm, a fire did indeed occur. For example, there may have been a number of false alarms recently, which could lead the response-selection process to wait rather than to execute a "leave the room" command to the response-execution process. Payoffs for different responses also are important for response selection. The situation might be one in which a person could be arrested and fined if he does not leave the building during a fire alarm. In this case, the response-selection process might be biased to leave the room even though a fire is unlikely.

Detection, Recognition, Response Selection

Detection, recognition, and response selection, then, can be identified as three mental processes that would be expected to occur between stimulus and response. We expect also that each of these processes consumes a certain amount of time and the duration of each of these three processes contributes to the total RT. The average RT of leaving, given a fire alarm in a classroom, might lie between 2 and 10 seconds, with most of the time taken up by response selection. Detection and recognition of the meaning of the alarm would probably occur in less than 1/2 sec.

These mental processes are referred to here as sequential stages in the overall process. Think of a stage as one step in the progression toward the final outcome. Figure 1 presents a flow diagram representation of these stages in the task. Thus, in this example, there are at least three stages between stimulus and response. Of course the observed RT will be longer than the sum of these three times since other events, such as nerve conduction time, will contribute to the overall RT.

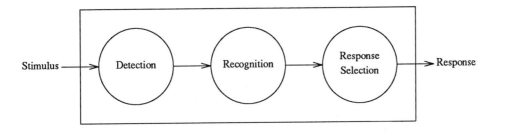

Figure 1. Three psychological operations or stages of information processing that occur between stimulus and response.

REACTION TIME

Early in the history of psychology, investigators used reaction time, the time it takes to perform a certain task, as an index of psychological function. The idea was that by measuring the time to perform a given task and analyzing the results in a certain way, one could discover the time that it took for certain mental processes. Quantifying the time for certain mental processes would illuminate those mental processes. One of the first uses of time in science, long before Wundt established his experimental laboratory, was in astronomy. In 1795 some astronomers, interested in physical phenomena, were faced with the problem of psychological functioning. At that time, astronomers were measuring the time at which stars would cross a point in space, the meridian. Then, most of the activity was at Greenwich, England, and we continue to refer to Greenwich mean time. A short boat ride up the Thames from London and a visit to the astronomy museum in Greenwich is a must on an English holiday.

Eyes and Ears in Astronomy

The astronomer's telescope had a vertical line representing the meridian. Viewing a star moving across the telescope, the task was to measure exactly when the star passed the meridian. The method used was called the eye and ear method. First viewing a clock that ticked off seconds, the astronomer would find out what time it was, to the accuracy of seconds, and then count the ticks as he viewed the star moving across the telescope. By counting the ticks, it was possible to see where the star was at each second. To get the exact time that the star crossed the meridian, it was necessary to interpolate between the two of the ticks of the clock encompassing the crossing. For example, if a star was three inches east of the meridian at 56 seconds after 10:30 and one inch west of the meridian at one second later, then by interpolation, the star crossed the meridian at 10:30:56.75. The time would then be recorded in the log book and so on for all of the stars.

Reaction time became a problem for these astronomers. It all started when Maskelyne, an astronomer, not the drug, fired his assistant, Kinnebrook, because Kinnebrook was recording different times than Maskelyne. According to Maskelyne, Kinnebrook was usually one-half a second too late. These astronomers knew that some stars should cross the meridian at the same time on different days. What Maskelyne observed was that Kinnebrook would be reporting his time about one-half second later than his mentor, Maskelyne. Since one of the two must have been in error, Maskelyne fired Kinnebrook.

Bessel thought about this problem and went through the log books to evaluate the recordings of different astronomers. In fact, most astronomers did not agree with each other with respect to when a given star crossed the meridian. Some astronomers always saw the stars later than others. Bessel was able to bring all the data into agreement by developing a personal equation, which corrected each astronomer's time by subtracting or adding a constant. If a given astronomer was early, he was usually early for all the stars, and his time could be corrected and brought into agreement with another astronomer's time by adding a constant. All of these data were brought into relatively good agreement by simply adding or subtracting a constant to each astronomer's time. Bessel also carried out experiments under controlled conditions to verify his observations. Two astronomers would not see a light cross a boundary at the same time; one would be consistently slower than the other.

Bessel's contribution made apparent that our phenomenal experience of the world does not agree exactly with the physical changes in the world. Previously, most scientists, at least implicitly, held a view of perception now called direct realism. According to this view, our experience of the environment is a direct and faithful mirror of it. Our experience of an event was believed to occur at the exact time of the event (possibly allowing for time for light and sound waves to travel). An alternative view assumes that there is some lag between the presentation of the events in the environment and our phenomenal experience of that event. We don't respond immediately to any change in the environment, and what Bessel's personal equation told us was that the time to react to a change differs for different people.

Pointers and Bells

One of the nicest early experiments demonstrating that it takes time to see was carried out by von Tschisch (cited in James, 1890, vol. 1). An observer monitored a clock with a pointer moving rapidly around the clock. The task was to indicate the position of the pointer when he or she heard a bell sound. In one situation, the bell rang when the pointer was at 6. The concern was where the subject reported seeing the pointer when the bell rang. Most of us would think the subject saw the pointer at 6 or 7. But the subject reported 5. This could have been the beginning of the study of extrasensory perception (ESP). Von Tschisch's conclusion was that the subject could anticipate the bell and actually hear it before it occurred. If you disagree with this conclusion, you might propose the following interpretation. The subject might think that it takes some time to hear the bell and, therefore, report the location of the pointer earlier than when it was actually seen at the sound of the bell. This is a good interpretation, but even when von Tschisch tested himself in the situation, he would see the pointer at a number before the bell occurred. He experienced the pointer at 5 when he heard the bell, which actually rang at 6.

Von Tschisch didn't consider the possibility that it takes time to hear and to see. There is a lag between the time the physical event occurs and the time that we experience that event. How does this lag account for the fact that the subject reports a pointer at a place before the bell actually occurred? First, there is no reason why the time it takes to hear the bell is equivalent to the time it takes to see the pointer. It may have taken longer to see the pointer than to hear the bell. Assume that it takes two time units of the clock to see the pointer at a particular point and one unit of the clock to hear the bell sound. In this case, perception lags behind the physical event two units in visual perception and one unit in auditory perception. If the bell is rung at 6, the pointer is objectively at 7 when the subject hears the sound. However, it takes two units of time to see the pointer, and when the pointer is at 7, the subject sees the pointer at 5. The subject did not hear the bell before it rang; it took one unit of time to hear the bell and two units of time to see the pointer. Von Tschisch's study makes it clear that it takes time to experience light and sound and that this time is of interest.

Donders and Helmholtz

The first experimenter to study mental life in terms of stages of processing between stimulus and response was F. C. Donders, a Dutch scientist best known for his work in ophthalmology. Donders described his work in psychology in a paper (1869) entitled "On the Speed of Mental Processes." In this article Donders recalled the pronouncement of physiologist Johannes Müller, twenty-five years before, that the time required for a stimulated nerve to carry its message to the brain and for the brain to activate the muscles was "infinitely short," and that therefore the velocity of nerve conduction could never be measured. Donders pointed out, however, that by 1850, H. von Helmholtz, the famous German scientist, was doing exactly that. Helmholtz worked out a technique for measuring nerve condition velocity in frogs, and subsequently applied the same principles to a series of experiments with humans. The experiment measured the time between the presentation of a stimulus on the skin and an involuntary reflex to the stimulus. Helmholtz compared two conditions of RT. In one, the muscles of the ball of the thumb were stimulated at a point on the wrist (the subject's hand and arm were immobilized). Reaction time was measured between the onset of this stimulus and the onset of the muscle contraction reflex of the thumb. In the other condition, the same muscles were stimulated at a point just above the fold of the elbow. The RT required for muscle contraction to the stimulus at this point was also measured and was found to be more than in the first condition.

The logic of this experiment was founded on the belief that the two RTs should differ only with respect to how far the nerve impulses had to travel between the point of stimulation and the nerve-muscle junction. The basic task did not differ under the two conditions, and therefore the time for all other elements of processing between the stimulation and muscle reflex could be assumed to be constant. Thus, all Helmholtz had to do in order to arrive at the nerve conduction velocity was to determine the extra time required for the longer distance and divide this time by the difference between the two distances. In this way, Helmholtz was able to estimate human nerve conduction velocity at 100 ft/sec. This result was surprisingly accurate, given the speed of nerve conduction time and the short distance between the two points.

SUBTRACTIVE METHOD

Helmholtz also was able to employ this subtractive method paradigm with voluntary responses. He stimulated the skin at either of two different distances from the brain. The subject was instructed to respond to the stimulus as rapidly as possible with a movement of the hand. The two conditions, therefore, only differed with respect to how far the nerve impulses had to travel to the brain. All other components of the task were assumed to be constant in the two conditions. Thus the difference in the reaction times provided an estimate of the difference in nerve conduction times for the two distances.

Donders was stimulated by another set of experiments also, those of the French astronomer A. Hirsch. Hirsch measured the RTs of simple detection responses (moving a hand) to stimuli presented to the eye, ear, and skin, respectively. Hirsch found that stimuli to the eye produced slower RTs than stimuli to the ear, which produced slower RTs than stimuli to the skin. Donders replicated these conditions and found that a reaction to a visual stimulus took 1/5 sec; to an auditory stimulus 1/6 sec; and to a touch stimulus 1/7 sec. It should be noted that the sensory modality could have been confounded with the intensity of the stimulus in these experiments. Given this confounding, the differences that were observed could have been due to either modality, intensity, or both of these variables. In fact, the RT to a stimulus in any modality is affected by the intensity of the stimuli used, although the early investigators did not appear to be aware of this.

Intensity of Stimulus

Today a number of studies have shown that RTs to a stimulus decrease as the intensity of the stimulus increases. Thus, an observer instructed to press a lever as soon as he hears a tone will respond sooner, as the loudness of the tone is increased. Logically, this effect should probably influence the sensation stage, the process of becoming aware of the stimulus. This logical analysis is supported by physiological studies, which have actually shown that nerve conduction time across the synapses on the way to the brain is inversely related to stimulus intensity. Consequently, it appears that stimulus intensity affects the detection or sensation stage in a simple signal detection task. According to a sequential process model, stimulus intensity is unlikely to also affect response selection because response selection occurs after the stimulus is detected and should be relatively independent of stimulus variables.

Given Helmholtz's measure of nerve conduction velocity and Hirsch's and Donders' RTs of simple detection responses, Donders correctly reasoned that nerve conduction time could only account for a small portion of the total RT. What Donders wanted to know, however, was what process or processes took up the rest of the RT. Although Donders calculated that there was at least 1/10 sec consumed by mental processes, his analysis did not allow one to measure the time it took for each mental process.

Helmholtz's experiment had taken the activity of the nerves out of the realm of the unfathomable. Donders was inspired to hope that the same might be done for mental processes. "Would thought also not have the infinite speed usually associated with it?" he asked. Helmholtz's method gave Donders a clue, and in time he devised a method for studying the speed of mental activities, employing the Helmholtz principle of subtraction in his research.

Simple versus Choice RT Tasks

Donders devised several experimental situations based on this principle. In one paradigm, an electrode was placed on each of the subject's feet and hooked up so that Donders could stimulate either foot as he wished. There were two conditions. In the first, Donders told the subject that he was going to stimulate the left (or the right) foot, and asked the subject to make a response as rapidly as possible with the hand on the same side. Thus, in this condition, the subject knew which foot would be stimulated and was prepared to respond with the correct hand. His task, therefore, was simply to detect that a stimulus occurred and give the predetermined response as fast as possible.

In the second condition, the subject was told that the stimulus might be given to either foot and was instructed to respond with his left hand if his left foot was stimulated and with his right hand if his right foot was stimulated. Donders would stimulate one or the other foot randomly from trial to trial. In this situation the subject did not know in advance which foot would be stimulated and, therefore, which hand would be the correct one for his response. Thus, two additional operations in the mental processing that occurred between stimulus and response were required in the second task. The subject had to first identify which of his two feet were stimulated and then select the appropriate hand for the response. The first condition is referred to as a simple RT task; the second is called a choice RT task.

Consider at this point what your intuition would predict as the result of the experiment. This can be a helpful tool in analyzing both one's own experiments and those of others. In this case, one would certainly predict that choice RT would be larger than simple RT. This was indeed true of the data Donders obtained. On the average, choice RT took longer than simple RT by 1/15 sec. For such fast RTs, psychologists use the measure of milliseconds; one msec is .001 sec. The value of 1/15 sec is 67 msec.

Donders reasoned that since all other aspects of the experimental situation had been held constant in the two conditions, the additional time necessary for completion of the task in choice RT could only be explained by the presence of the two additional mental processes. He concluded, therefore, that 67 msec was "the time required for deciding which side had been stimulated and for establishing the action of the will on the right or left side." That is, by comparing two tasks, the second identical to the first except for the addition of a recognition and a response-selection stage, Donders could isolate and identify the duration of these two stages as 67 msec. He found from this experiment that it requires 67 msec for an observer to recognize one of two possible stimuli and to choose between two responses when only one response was possible. It also seems reasonable that a larger number of possible stimuli and responses to choose among would take even longer.

Anticipation Errors

Donders' experimental design was such that the subject in the simple RT task, knowing which foot would be stimulated and all prepared to respond, could possibly respond before he actually detected the stimulus. We all jump the gun now and then. The measured RT would be affected, of course. It would no longer accurately reflect the duration of the mental events. Psychologists are careful to remain aware of the possibility that the subject might start to respond before information is sensed or perceived; such responses are called anticipation errors.

Subjects are instructed to respond as rapidly as possible without error in the RT task. How could a psychologist check for anticipation? In the choice task, an anticipation error will lead to an error about half the time. Given two responses, a fast guess will be lucky only one time out of two. In the simple RT task, there is only one response; an error can be observed by the experimenter only if it occurs before the stimulus is actually presented. One way to guard against anticipation errors in a RT task is to present a warning signal on every trial. The warning signal occurs about 1/2 sec or so before the test stimulus. Anticipation errors can be monitored by not presenting the test stimulus on a small proportion (20 percent) of the trials. Responses on these "catch trials" provide an index of anticipation errors; this information can serve as feedback to both the subject and the experimenter. Subjects making too many anticipation errors will want to slow down and be more conservative in the task.

Visual Presentation

Donders repeated the same experimental design for the visual modality, using a red and a white light in place of stimulating the right and left feet. Again, the first condition required a predetermined response to one of the lights; the second required a choice between the right or left hand, depending on which of the two randomly varied stimuli was perceived. His results averaged over five subjects indicated that the extra time required for choice RT over simple RT was 154 msec. The difference between the simple and choice RT was over twice as long (154 vs. 67) when the stimulation was visual rather than tactile. Why would recognition and/or response selection be more difficult in the visual than in the tactile experiment?

In a third set of experiments, the nature of the response was changed. The stimuli now were two letters of the alphabet, and the response required was to pronounce aloud the name of the letter presented on each trial, again (as always) as fast as possible without error. Thus, if the subject saw an E, for example, his task was to say "E" as quickly as he could. Again RTs were observed under two conditions: in one, the subject knew which of the two alternative letters of the experiment would be presented on each trial and thus was ready with his response; in the other, one of the two letters was presented randomly from trial to trial and the subject was not told which letter, so that he could only choose between the two responses after the stimulus was presented and correctly recognized. The extra processing in the choice task required an average of 166 msec longer than the simple RT task.

Auditory Presentation

Donders' stage-process model implied that insertion of additional stages would increase reaction time for all the sensory modalities, and he therefore took care to demonstrate that the results of an experiment using one modality could also be replicated for another. Thus, the above visual experiment was also done with auditory stimuli. Subjects were presented with vowel sounds and asked to respond as soon as possible by repeating the sound presented. For example, the two-alternative experiment was done using two different vowel sounds. In the choice reaction condition either of the two vowel sounds could be presented on a given trial, and the subject had to distinguish the sound and repeat back the vowel. This condition was compared with the simple reaction condition in which the subject knew in advance which vowel sound would be presented and repeated the sound as quickly as possible.

Insertion of the recognition and response-selection stages also added to reaction time with auditory presentations, but the amount of additional time was greater in the visual task (166 msec) than in the auditory task (56 msec). Either recognition, or response selection, or both, were easier in the auditory task with spoken vowel stimuli, than in the visual task with printed symbols. Donders believed that the differences in the two tasks must be due to the recognition stage rather than the response-selection stage since response selection is the same in the two tasks. To account for the results, Donders actually presented a detailed description of how the auditory identification of a vowel sound was not as complex as the visual identification of a vowel symbol.

Recognition Time

Donders was aware that choice RT tasks differed from the simple detection task with respect to two processes: stimulus recognition and response selection. So he devised another series of experiments to isolate the contributions of each of these stages. To determine the time for the recognition stage, Donders set up two experimental conditions. In the first condition, a subject was be required to push a button as rapidly as possible when he saw a light go on. In another condition, the light could be one of two colors, and the subject was instructed to respond only when one of the lights came on. In this case, the subject had to identify the color of the light after he had detected it in order to insure that he would only respond to the indicated light. Thus, the second condition required a second stage, recognition, in addition to the detection stage required by both conditions. Donders considered that he had held the detection stage constant and that response selection did not occur in the two conditions. He believed that when only one response was required, the subject could select this response before the stimulus was presented. Thus, any difference in RTs would represent the time required for the recognition stage inserted in the second condition.

Response-Selection Time

To determine the time for response selection between two alternatives, Donders devised another experimental comparison. The subject would be required to recognize the stimulus in both conditions, but should have to select a response in only one. In the first condition, the subject could be presented with either of two signals but was required to respond to only one. In this case, the subject could conceivably select the response before the stimulus is presented. In the second condition, the subject is required to respond differentially to both stimuli; therefore, he could not select his response in advance. Hence, the second condition requires all the processing of the first, plus the time for response selection. It follows that the difference in RTs between the two conditions represents the time for response selection.

A, B, and C Tasks

In order to estimate the time for mental processes, Donders' classic comparisons involve three different experimental conditions, A, B, and C: the detection task, the detection-recognition-response selection task, and the detection-recognition task, respectively. Table 1 gives the stages assumed to be involved in each task. In task A, the subject is told that a certain stimulus, let us say the letter X, will appear on every trial, and he is instructed to pronounce the letter X as soon as he sees it. Once he has detected the presence of a stimulus, he can execute the appropriate response immediately. The stimulus does not have to be recognized, and a response does not have to be selected, since it has been chosen in advance.

Table 1. The stages of processing assumed in Donders' A, B, and C tasks.

Task	Stages
A	detection
B	detection, recognition, response selection
C	detection, recognition

In task B, the subject knows that the stimulus will be one of two letters, say X and O, and he must respond appropriately to both stimuli. Therefore, he must detect the presence of the stimulus, recognize it as either one or the other, and select his response. Although the subject knows the stimulus must be one of two alternatives, it must be recognized on every trial. Similarly, although he can narrow his response in advance to the two alternatives, he cannot select a response until recognition is complete. Therefore, in task B, the subject is required to recognize the stimulus and select the appropriate response after the stimulus is recognized. In this case, detection, recognition, and response selection contribute to the RT.

In task C, either X or O can be presented on any trial, but the subject has been told to respond only when one of them, say X, is present. Therefore, he must detect the presence of the stimulus, recognize it as either X or O, and, if it is X, respond by pronouncing "X." Donders believed that the response-selection stage in this task was equivalent to the same stage in the simple detection task; that is, there is only one correct response, which the subject can prepare in advance and have ready whenever the stimulus is presented. Accordingly, response-selection time should not contribute to the overall RT in task C.

If Donders' analysis is correct, we should be able to compute the time for a stage of processing by subtraction. The time for the recognition process should equal the difference in RT between tasks C and A. Similarly, the RT difference between tasks B and C estimates the time for response selection. Donders' original results employing these three tasks were very promising. The RTs were ordered as predicted by the stage analysis. In one study reported, with vowel sounds, Donders found reaction times of 201, 284, and 237 msec for tasks A, B, and C, respectively. Using the subtractive method, he was able to estimate the time for recognition or identification as 237 minus 201, or 36 msec, and the time for response selection as 284 minus 237, or 47 msec. Of course, the time for detection cannot be estimated, since other events contribute to the reaction time in the task. That is to say, the RT in the A task does not simply represent the time for detection.

Criticism of Donders' Methods

Donders believed that he could insert a stage of processing in an experimental task and estimate its time using the subtractive method. For example, the difference in reaction time between tasks B and C was assumed to represent the time for response selection. It is assumed that task B contains response selection, whereas task C does not. But we can look at task C in a slightly different manner; there are two stimuli, X and O, and there are two responses, "X" and silence. That is, after recognizing the stimulus as either X or O, the subject must decide whether the appropriate response is now to say "X" or not to say anything. Indeed, there is a sense in which the subject can be said always to have to select a response; that is, he must always decide whether to respond or not, even in a simple detection task. Accordingly, we cannot say that the response-selection stage was present in task B and not present in task C. Task C required the subject to select between responding and not responding, depending on the stimulus presented.

It appears, then, that rather than inserting or deleting a stage of processing in the task, the different tasks changed the nature of the response-selection process. Donders' assumption that the experimenter could devise two experimental tasks which differed only with respect to an additional stage of processing is, therefore, untenable, and without this assumption his results cannot be used to estimate the duration of a processing stage. Indeed, it is difficult to see what meaning his results would have even if the method of insertion were a valid one. Even if we knew the duration of each stage, we would still be in the dark about how these mental processes operate. Donders' work, having proved at least that perception and cognition were not instantaneous, failed to open further doors and lent itself to criticisms that undermined what little it had seemed to achieve.

At the turn of the century, O. Külpe and his co-workers criticized the central assumption of Donders' subtractive method: the additivity of the times for mental events. They asserted that stages cannot be added in a task without affecting the time to complete other stages. Their central argument was that the tasks compared in the subtractive method differ by more than one or two stages: rather, the overall quality or gestalt of the tasks differs. Accordingly, the subtractive method cannot indicate the duration of a particular stage of mental processing. Being introspectionists, they did not present any RT evidence supporting this criticism of the Donderian subtractive method. Rather, they relied on the introspective reports of the observers. After this criticism, investigators lost interest in Donders' insertion method as a tool for studying mental processes. In the next chapter, we will consider a modification of Donders' method, one that overcomes these particular criticisms.

Questioning Assumptions

Donders' assumption that there was no response selection in either task A or task C seems unreasonable. In task A, the subject has to initiate a response upon detection of a stimulus. In task C, the subject, upon detecting the stimulus and recognizing it, has to decide whether to respond or not to respond. More importantly, response-selection time for task C could be greater than for task A, and the subtraction of RTs from the two tasks would be inappropriate. The difference in time of the two tasks would reflect not just recognition time, as Donders had hoped, but would also contain some response-selection time. Rather than discarding the paradigm of the subtractive method, some scientists attempted to modify it in order to salvage it. This usually happens in the development of scientific method and theory. Mend the holes as much as possible until a completely new structure is necessary.

Wundt proposed another task to measure recognition time, and called it task D, which would eliminate the problem of different response-selection times in tasks A and C. Since Wundt wanted to keep the response-selection time in task D the same as in task A, the subject had to make the same kind of response in both tasks. Given that the subject had to respond to every stimulus in task A, the subject should also respond to every stimulus in task D. Since Wundt wanted to measure the time for recognition, he told the subjects in task D, "don't hit the button until you recognize it." In task A, the subject responds as soon as he detects something. In task D, the subject also responds to every stimulus but not until it is recognized. Task D would allow a direct comparison to task A since they both contain the same detection and response-selection processes. The subject is detecting and selecting the same response in both tasks A and D, but must wait in task D until the stimulus is recognized.

Although Wundt solved one problem, he created another. The problem is that it is hard to keep the subject honest. It doesn't have to be a conscious honesty; subjects can be very well intentioned about responding immediately upon recognizing the stimulus, but they just may not be able to do this. Berger made the same criticism in 1886. Well, Wundt's reaction was, you do it your way and I'll do it my way. Wundt's faith in task D was consistent with his acceptance of the introspective method. According to Wundt, all mental events are available to conscious introspection and reliable report. This disagreement serves as a lesson to be learned with regard to disagreements in science. Results might be objective, but interpretations are not. Two scientists looking at the same results might interpret them differently. In this dispute, we can certainly side with Berger. In many of the experiments that were done comparing task A and task D, people came out with unreasonably small recognition times and sometimes even negative recognition times. Cattell said that the task puts the subject into a quandary. If the subject is really conservative, he or she hangs back after recognition, and you will observe a huge time for recognition. If the subject is eager, one observes very short time or negative times for recognition. Task D doesn't solve anything in terms of improving upon Donders' subtraction method in his tasks A, B, and C.

The central criticism of the subtractive method is that one cannot find tasks that differ in terms of just one mental process. It is expecting too much to develop a task that contains all of the processes of another task plus one. When this second task is developed, it has probably changed some of the other processes. The pure subtraction method is not usually feasible.

8

Operations of Mental Processes

Sternberg's Modification

Additive-Factor Method
    Stimulus Loudness and Hand Dominance
    Additive Effects
    Interactive Effects

Subtractive and Additive-Factor Methods Compared
    Naming and Button-Pushing Tasks
    Population Comparisons

Critical Evaluation
    Overlapping Stages
    Experimental Test

Factorial Designs and Counterbalancing

*We may be able in the future to use "brain waves" as indicators
of the beginning and end of a mental process; but in general
it has seemed necessary to let the timed process start with a
sensory stimulus and terminate in a muscular response.*
Robert S. Woodworth (1938)

Donders' stage model of mental life remained dormant along with his techniques until the 1960s, when it was revived by Saul Sternberg (1969a, 1969b). Sternberg accepted as valid the conclusions of Donders' critics that one cannot insert one stage without affecting the operations of other stages and that the new reaction time will confound the duration of the new stage with changes in the duration of the original stages. The method he devised avoided this problem while capitalizing on the possibilities in the stage notion. Sternberg's idea was to introduce changes in the experimental situation that affected the amount of processing or the number of operations required within a single stage rather than the number of stages present in the task.

STERNBERG'S MODIFICATION

For instance, using Sternberg's principle we might set up an identification experiment in which the subject is asked to push a button to a red light. In one condition, we would randomly mix red light presentations with blue light presentations. In the other condition, we would randomize red light trials with pink light trials. Therefore, the task remains exactly the same in both conditions—respond only to red—but the colors are more similar to each other in the second condition than in the first. We can test whether this variable might affect the time needed to complete the recognition stage; it seems logical that the observer would find it harder to discriminate between very similar stimuli than between very dissimilar stimuli. The detection stage, however, in which the subject in either case notices that something is out there, should not be affected; nor would we expect the variable to affect the response-selection stage which, in both cases, given one of two identifications, requires deciding on one of two possible responses.

To test these expectations, the experimenter must choose other independent variables that would be expected to affect other processing stages of the task. Assuming that the color of the stimuli does not affect response-selection time, an independent variable is introduced to influence this stage of processing. The experimenter might vary response compatibility in the task, since this is expected to influence response-selection time, but not recognition time. In our task, for example, we can also have the subject respond verbally with the word "red" when it is presented under the red–pink and red–blue conditions. Hence, we have four experimental conditions and measure the RT in each condition.

We expect significant differences in RT as a function of both of our independent variables. Reaction time should be larger in the red-pink condition than in the red-blue condition, and button pushing might take longer than verbal reaction. More importantly, if the two variables affect two independent processes (stages) in the RT task, their effects on RT should be additive. That is to say, the effect of the red-pink variable would be the same under each response compatibility condition and, analogously, the effect of response compatibility should be the same under both color conditions.

Thus, if our results show that it takes 50 msec longer to respond when the alternative stimuli are red and pink than when they are red and blue under both response compatibility conditions, we have evidence that indicates it is more difficult to distinguish red from pink than red from blue. We still do not know the absolute identification times in either case. Rather, the 50 msec is a measure of the increased difficulty of the recognition stage in the red-pink relative to the red-blue condition. By choosing other stimulus pairs according to increasing or decreasing color similarity, we should be able to determine the psychophysical similarity of the colors, using reaction times as our dependent measure.

Donders assumed that it was possible to introduce an entire stage without affecting the difficulty of the other stages. Sternberg assumes that one can introduce a variable that will selectively increase or decrease the difficulty and, thus, the time to complete a single stage without affecting the others. He has formalized the additive-factor method to validate the assumption that a given variable selectively affects the processing of only one stage. With Sternberg's method we have indeed abandoned Donders' hope of obtaining the absolute time to complete mental stages of processing. Donders was searching for some sort of platonic ideal of each stage, even if it was only quantitative: he wanted to be able to state that recognition takes 100 msec, detection 50 msec, and so on. As the example just described demonstrates, however, recognition time fluctuates from one condition to another, making the platonic ideal of recognition time a meaningless concept. Rather, it is the fluctuation itself that will interest us, not only because it alone can be studied but also because it is far more useful information than the absolute time required for identification in any particular task. Sternberg's paradigm, by allowing us to understand how variables affect the duration of mental processes, informs us about the nature of those processes themselves, an accomplishment which lay beyond the hope of Donders.

ADDITIVE-FACTOR METHOD

In Sternberg's formalized method of study, called the additive-factor method, each experimental task can be analyzed logically to determine the number of stages involved in the task. The experimenter then chooses an independent variable that is expected to affect the processing or operation of a particular stage. For example, the experimenter could choose two levels of stimulus discriminability (red-blue, red-pink) as a variable that affects recognition time. By pairing each level of this variable with levels of another variable that is expected to affect another stage, the experimenter can provide a test of the experimental assumption that the two variables affect different stages of processing. In our example, we chose a second variable—response compatibility—that is believed to affect response-selection time. If the two variables affect two independent stages in the RT task, their effects on RT should be additive. If not, their effects would most likely combine in a non-additive fashion; that is, they would interact.

The method of studying mental processes, in which the effects of two or more independent variables are evaluated, is an important one. We shall, therefore, analyze yet another task, in which the subject has to respond to a stimulus as soon as he detects it, using the additive-factor method. In this task there are two stages; first, the subject must detect the stimulus, which will take up a certain amount of time. Then the subject must select a response; it is necessary to remember which of the innumerable actions possible at the moment is the correct one, given the information put out by the detection stage. This response selection also takes some finite time; the two times should contribute to the total RT of the task.

Stimulus Loudness and Hand Dominance

We choose two independent variables to study in this task, asking whether each one affects only one or both stages. Stimulus loudness, it would seem, is a variable that should affect only the detection stage. The louder the stimulus, the easier it is to detect; we shall be surprised, on the other hand, if the louder stimulus results in a shorter response-selection time. We might choose response compatibility as the second variable, requiring subjects to use their dominant hand in one condition and their nondominant hand in the other, pushing a button with the index finger in each case. People are able to respond much more easily and rapidly with their dominant hand than with their nondominant hand, and thus we can expect RT to be longer in the nondominant than in the dominant case. Response compatibility should affect the response-selection stage, but, again, we will be surprised if it affects the detection stage. Logically, it should not be easier to detect a signal simply because the appropriate response is easier to make.

The experiment will thus have four separate conditions:

1. A tone of the loudness of a whisper; subject required to respond with his dominant hand.

2. A louder tone, of normal speaking intensity; subject required to respond with his dominant hand.

3. The soft tone of condition 1; subject required to respond with his nondominant hand.

4. The loud tone of condition 2; subject required to respond with his nondominant hand.

This experiment can be represented by a 2 x 2 matrix, shown in Table 1.

Table 1. An experiment that independently varies two levels of two independent variables: stimulus loudness and response compatibility. The numbers refer to the experimental conditions described in the text; RT_i, where $i = 1, 2, 3,$ or 4, represents the RT for each condition.

Stimulus	Response Compatibility	
Loudness	dominant hand	nondominant hand
Soft	(1) RT_1	(3) RT_3
Loud	(2) RT_2	(4) RT_4

The experimenter runs many trials under each experimental condition and records the reaction time. The dependent variable in the experiment would be the mean RT under each experimental condition. This RT is assumed to be the sum of the duration of the two stages plus the time taken up by other internal events. It should be stressed that the time taken for the other internal events, called t_0, is assumed to be the same at each condition. If one variable only affects one stage, and the second affects the other stage, then the effects of two independent variables, each of which affects the duration of only one stage, should be additive. That is, there is a time required for detection of a soft tone and another time required for detection of a loud tone; there is a time for selecting a response with the dominant hand and a different time for selecting a response with the nondominant hand. In Condition (1) the total reaction time includes the time it takes to detect a soft tone, plus the time to respond with the dominant hand. In Condition (2) reaction time includes the time for detection of a loud tone, plus the time for selecting a response with the dominant hand. Reaction time in Conditions (3) and (4) contains the time required for detection of the soft and the loud tones, respectively, plus the time needed to respond with the nondominant hand.

Letting d_L and d_S equal the detection times for the loud and soft tones and r_D and r_N equal the response-selection times with the dominant and nondominant hands, the RTs for the four experimental conditions are given by

1. $RT_1 = t_0 + d_S + r_D$

2. $RT_2 = t_0 + d_L + r_D$

3. $RT_3 = t_0 + d_S + r_N$

4. $RT_4 = t_0 + d_L + r_N$

Additive Effects

As an example of additive effects, let d_S equal 100 msec and d_L equal 50 msec. Let r_D equal 100 msec and r_N equal 200 msec. Further assume that t_0 is constant at 100 msec. Accordingly, these additive results would give the times shown in Table 2 under the four experimental conditions. Since the independent variables affect different stages, the sum of the RTs of Conditions (2) and (3) will be equal to the sum of the RTs of Conditions (1) and (4).

$$RT_2 + RT_3 = RT_1 + RT_4 \tag{1}$$

Table 2. Typical reaction times in the four experimental conditions assuming that the effects of stimulus loudness and response compatibility are additive.

Stimulus	Response Compatibility	
Loudness	dominant hand	nondominant hand
Soft	300	400
Loud	250	350

Given additive effects, the RTs take on a definite form. If we plot RT as a function of stimulus intensity and response compatibility, the two curves will be parallel, as seen in Figure 1.

Interactive Effects

Assume, however, that stimulus loudness affects not only the time it takes to detect the stimulus, but also the time it takes to be parallel because a decrease in stimulus loudness will change both detection time and response-selection time. Since response compatibility affects response-selection time, both of our variables affect response-selection time, and it is unlikely that their effects would be additive since they are in some sense compounded. As an example of this case, assume that response-selection time takes 100 and 150 msec, respectively, for the dominant and nondominant responses with a loud tone. If the loudness of the tone also affects response-selection time, we can expect that it might have a larger effect with the nondominant than with the dominant hand. Therefore, the soft tone may slow down the dominant response by only 50 msec and the nondominant response by 100 msec. Accordingly, the results would not be additive but would interact. Table 3 gives the response-selection times under the four experimental conditions.

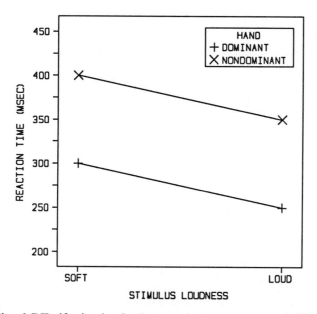

Figure 1. Predicted RTs if stimulus loudness and response compatibility affect only the detection and response-selection stages, respectively.

As can be seen in the table, the difference between the loud and soft conditions is not identical for the dominant and nondominant hands. Similarly, the difference between the dominant and nondominant hands is not identical for the loud and soft tones.

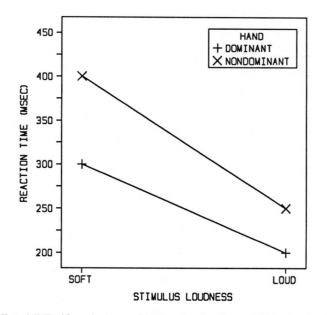

Figure 2. Predicted RTs if an increase in stimulus loudness influences both the detection and response-selection stages of processing.

Table 3. Typical response-selection times in the four experimental conditions assuming that both stimulus loudness and response compatibility influence the response-selection stage of processing.

Stimulus	Response Compatibility	
Loudness	dominant hand	nondominant hand
Soft	150	250
Loud	100	150

All other conditions are assumed to be equivalent to the example illustrating additive effects. Loudness affected detection so that detection time is 50 and 100 msec, respectively, for the loud and soft tones, The time for other processes is constant at 100 msec. The sum of the times of the three contributions would correspond to those given in Table 4. Plotting these results gives nonparallel curves as shown in Figure 2.

Table 4. Typical reaction times in the four experimental conditions assuming that stimulus loudness influences both detection and response-selection time.

Stimulus	Response Compatibility	
Loudness	dominant hand	nondominant hand
Soft	300	400
Loud	200	250

SUBTRACTIVE AND ADDITIVE-FACTOR METHODS COMPARED

To see how the additive-factor method improves on Donders' method of subtraction, let us consider an experiment by Donders and discuss its limitations. Then we can continue his study in the framework of the logic of the additive-factor method. Recall Donders' comparison of simple and choice RT tasks in naming visually presented letters. Donders found that the choice RT experiment took an average of 166 msec longer than the simple RT task.

To this experiment, Donders added one more condition, testing the effect of enlarging the number of alternative responses in the choice RT task. The subject was instructed as before to pronounce the name of the letter as rapidly as possible on each trial. This time, however, there were five possible test letters instead of only two. Donders expected that this task would be harder than the two-choice RT task since the five-choice task would require more time for identification and response selection.

Donders saw that the difference between the two- and five-choice RT tasks measured the processing time difference for at least two stages, identification and response selection. If Donders found that the five-choice RT was longer than the two-choice RT, he would not know whether the increased time was required because the subject must prepare himself for five possible responses instead of two, or because identification among five alternatives requires finer discrimination and therefore more time than between two. Where the response was to be one of a number of known alternatives, a subject could prepare these responses in advance and select among them when the time came. Obviously, it would be easier to select between two than among five. The subject could use an analogous strategy for identification as well. In the two-alternative case, a subject might determine that the stimulus on any trial has to be either X or O, and identify it by means of a single distinguishing characteristic or feature. In this case, a curved or straight line would be sufficient to discriminate between the two letters. To identify one of five alternatives, the subject would have to consider a larger number of distinguishing features. If the five alternatives were X, O, Y, Q, and M, for example, a single feature would no longer be sufficient to discriminate among the alternatives.

Naming and Button-Pushing Tasks

What Donders didn't realize, however, was that manipulation of the number of alternatives could be combined with a second independent variable. As was mentioned above, increasing the number of alternatives could conceivably affect stimulus recognition and/or response selection. However, logically, we should be able to find independent variables that affect only one of these stages. For example, Donders required his subject to respond by naming the letter symbol on each trial. Response selection in this case would involve determining the appropriate response and executing the necessary articulatory commands to name the stimulus. As a second condition, Donders could also have required his subjects to push a button for their response. In this case, the number of different button responses would increase with increases in the number of alternatives.

This manipulation of the nature of the response should affect response-selection time. Button pushing would probably take longer than naming, since naming a letter symbol is an overlearned response, whereas button pushing is not. The subject in the choice RT task would find it much more difficult to keep track of the appropriate stimulus-button pairings than the stimulus-name pairings. Moreover, the difficulty of the response-selection task would increase much more rapidly with increases in the number of alternatives in the button-pushing task relative to the naming task.

Whether the subject names or pushes the appropriate button to give a letter alternative, however, should not affect stimulus-recognition time. The stage model of the task is a sequential one. Stimulus recognition occurs before response selection and its duration should not be affected by the duration of mental events that follow it. Therefore, it is logical to assume that the type of response should not affect stimulus-identification time. In the fire alarm example, the time to identify the warning siren was independent of the difficulty of selecting the appropriate response.

Our experiment would accordingly manipulate the number of alternatives and the nature of the response. For example, we could choose 2-, 4-, 6-, or 8-letter alternatives and have the subject name or push the appropriate button to each stimulus. Reaction time would be measured from the onset of the stimulus to the onset of the response. This design gives eight experimental conditions. Each subject would go through all conditions with one condition per experimental session. The order of the conditions across different subjects could be counterbalanced to control for order effects in the task. In each of the eight sessions, the subject would be told the stimulus alternatives and the appropriate response to each alternative. Some practice should be given at each experimental condition before the experimenter records the results.

The results of the experiment could be presented graphically, plotting mean RT on the ordinate as a function of the number of alternatives on the abscissa. Two curves would be plotted; one for each response condition. Some hypothetical results of the experiment are presented in Figures 3 and 4.

Recall that the experimental question was whether the increase in RT with increases in the number of alternatives was due to stimulus-identification time, response-selection time, or both. If this increase was due only to stimulus-identification time, the increase should be independent of the

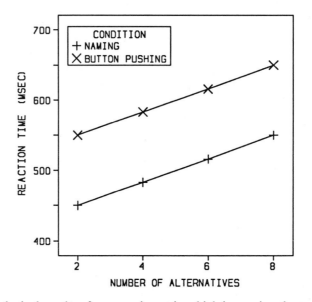

Figure 3. Hypothetical results of an experiment in which increasing the number of alternatives affects only the stimulus-recognition stage.

nature of the response. If the increase was due only to response-selection time, the increase should be directly related to the difficulty of the response. The hypothetical results in Figure 3 show that the increase in RT with increases in the number of alternatives is the same for the naming and button-pushing tasks. These results would indicate that increasing the number of alternatives does not appear to influence response-selection time. The logical alternative would be that the number of alternatives influences stimulus identification. Button pushing is more difficult than naming, but this difficulty does not interact (change) with changes in the number of alternatives.

Figure 4 plots another set of hypothetical results where the increase in RT with increases in the number of alternatives is flat between two and eight alternatives in the naming case, but increases sharply in the button-pushing task. What mental process accounts for the increase in RT with increases in the number of alternatives? Response-selection time can account for all of the increase in RT from two to eight alternatives. This follows from the fact that the naming function between two and eight alternatives is flat. If the response is an overlearned one, increasing the number of alternatives does not increase overall RT. Requiring a button-pushing task instead of naming should not change stimulus-identification time since the button-pushing condition simply changes the response-selection process, not the identification process. Accordingly, the increase in RT with increases in the number of alternatives in the button-pushing task cannot be accounted for by stimulus-identification time, but is due to response-selection time. When this experiment is carried out, the results shown in Figure 5 actually correspond to those predicted by the model in which the number of alternatives has its influence on only response selection (Theios, 1973).

The simple RT condition was not included in this experiment since this condition changes the overall nature of the task by eliminating the identification stage. Accordingly, we would expect RT to increase in both the naming and button-pushing tasks from a simple to a two-choice situation. If the subject is faced with two or more alternatives, stimulus identification is necessary for the response to be given. In the simple RT task, stimulus detection is sufficient for response selection to begin. We can see that the overall nature or quality of the task is changed in going from the choice to the simple task. Therefore, RT will be shorter in the simple than in the two-choice task for both the naming and the button-pushing conditions. This result indicates that stimulus-identification time must be different in the two cases. However, response-selection time also differs since the subject can prepare his response more exactly in one task than in the other. Therefore, the comparison between the one- and two-alternative conditions does not illuminate the operations of stimulus-identification and response-selection processes.

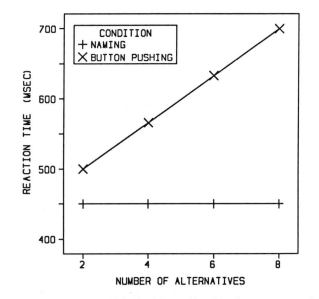

Figure 4. Hypothetical results in which response-selection time accounts for the increase in RT with increases in the number of alternatives in the button-pushing condition.

Adding the experimental factor of two to eight alternatives is an illuminating modification of Donders' experiment. If the alternatives are overlearned stimuli such as letters, it appears that stimulus-identification time is independent of the number of alternatives larger than two. Response-selection time is also independent of the number of alternatives larger than two if the responses are highly compatible and overlearned, as in the naming condition. If, however, the responses are not compatible and overlearned, response-selection time is a direct function of the number of alternatives in the experimental task.

In summary, varying two independent variables in a factorial design and using the additive-factor method can illuminate the nature of psychological processing. In this paradigm, the experimenter does not attempt to insert a stage of processing but simply to influence the amount of processing at a given stage. In the choice RT task with two or more alternatives, a stage of processing was not inserted when the number of alternatives was increased. Rather, the experiment tested whether the operations of each stage, as reflected in the time to complete each stage, differed with changes in the independent variables. This experiment makes transparent some of the operations of the recognition and response-selection processes, whereas the Donders method of insertion does not.

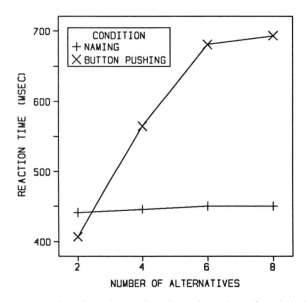

Figure 5. Mean response time (msec) as a function of number of equally likely stimulus alternatives for the verbal naming and button-pushing response conditions (from Theios, 1973).

Population Comparisons

It is well-known that individuals differ from one another, and a concern of much of developmental, personality, and abnormal psychology research is with these differences. Finding that one population differs from another is uninformative unless we learn about how it differs. A gross difference in performance in an experimental task does not provide information about the psychological process or processes responsible for the difference. The additive-factor method offers a good tool for studying population differences since its goal is to characterize the processes involved in the experimental task.

Sternberg (1966, 1969a) used the additive-factor method to design a series of experiments for studying memory-search processes. The experimental task is slightly more involved than the tasks Donders employed. The subject is told that the experimenter is going to present a list of digits of a certain size, say four digits. He will then present some sort of warning signal—a buzz perhaps—and finally one more digit, the test digit. The test digit is equal to one of the digits in the memory set on a random one half of the trials. On the other half, the digit is not in the memory set. The task of the observer is to respond "yes" by pushing one lever if the test digit was one of the digits in the preceding list and to respond "no" by pushing another lever if it was not. Thus, the subject hears 9, 2, 6, 7, buzz, 6. The correct response would be "yes," since the test digit was equal to a digit in the memory list. Had the test digit been "3," the correct response would be "no." Given this paradigm, Sternberg could vary the difficulty of the search task by varying the number of digits in the memory list. Thus, the independent variable in this task is the number of digits in the list; the dependent variable is the RT measured from the onset of the test digit to the onset of the subject's response.

Schizophrenics, alcoholics, and college students have been studied in Sternberg's memory-search task. One, two, or four items occurred in the memory set, and subjects responded whether or not a test item was a member of the memory set. Results with normal individuals show that

Factorial Designs and Counterbalancing

The design of the tone detection experiment is typical of experiments using the additive-factor method. It is called a factorial design because each level of one independent variable is crossed with every level of the other independent variable. The two independent variables are stimulus intensity and response compatibility, with two levels of each variable, which gives 2 x 2 = 4 experimental conditions. It will become apparent that the additive-factor method could not be used if the experiment was not a factorial one.

In this experiment, as in most of the experiments in this book, the subject goes through all of the experimental conditions. Accordingly, the experimenter must present the four different conditions (1), (2), (3), and (4) in such a way that the condition is not confounded with the temporal order of presentation. One way to do this is to first practice the subject sufficiently under all experimental conditions, say, for example, one hour. Then the subject is required to participate for four additional days. The conditions could be presented in the following order. On each day, we present all four conditions so that each experimental condition is presented once at each of the four possible temporal orders. This counterbalances for any possible learning or fatigue effects that may be present on each day. For a second subject, the experimental conditions can be presented in an entirely different sequence, but with the same counterbalancing constraints, and so on for the different subjects. This counterbalancing technique, although completely straightforward, is an important one in this kind of psychological experimentation.

Day	Order			
	1st	2nd	3rd	4th
2	(1)	(2)	(3)	(4)
3	(2)	(3)	(4)	(1)
4	(3)	(4)	(1)	(2)
5	(4)	(1)	(2)	(3)

Each condition is preceded with a number of practice trials under that condition. For example, we might have 25 practice trials before each condition, followed by 100 experimental trials. Also, the experimenter should not tell the subject which are practice trials, since the subject might be likely to treat these trials differently. The subject should be precisely instructed in the task and reminded to keep a constant motivation throughout the study.

reaction time is a linear function of memory-set size, supporting a serial model of the memory search and comparison process. Testing schizophrenics, alcoholics, and college students in this task should reveal the degree to which these populations differ in the process of memory search and comparison. The deviant subjects may have a qualitatively different memory-search process than normals do or deviant subjects may simply perform the same process at a much slower rate. In any event, the additive-factor method allows the investigator to provide a direct assessment of whether and/or how individuals differ with respect to a particular process.

Figure 6 gives the mean reaction times for the three populations of subjects as a function of memory-set size. Although the populations differ greatly with respect to overall speed in the task, the memory-search functions are nearly identical. All populations show a linear increase in reaction time with increases in memory-set size, and the search rates are within four msec of one another. This result is a strong one since we might expect deviant populations to be slower and less efficient in all aspects of information processing. The process of memory search and comparison seems to be relatively immune to the deviant behavior characteristics of schizophrenics and alcoholics (see also Russell, Consedine, & Knight, 1980, for converging evidence).

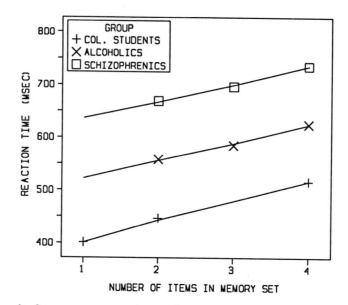

Figure 6. Results from memory-search experiments with three groups of subjects. Overall mean RTs as a function of the number of items in the memory set. Data for schizophrenics (average hospitalization, 15 months) and alcoholics (average hospitalization, 8 months) from an unpublished study by S. F. Checkosky. Data for college students from a similar study shown for comparison (after Sternberg, 1975).

The differences in intercept values for the three populations call for additional experiments to locate the process or processes responsible for the difference. There is some evidence that schizophrenics have deficits in processes involved in organizing complex events (Russell et al., 1980). A challenging exercise would be to design a series of experiments to locate the population differences in the stage model given in Figure 1 in Chapter 7. To evaluate whether these populations differ with respect to recognition, the quality of the test digit could be varied. Will the added processing time required for recognizing a degraded test digit be larger for the abnormal than for the normal subjects? If so, there would appear to be fundamental differences in the recognition process of the different groups of subjects.

CRITICAL EVALUATION

There have been important critical evaluations of the additive-factor method since the publication of it by Sternberg (1969b). Taylor (1976) has shown that additive effects do not necessarily imply that the two variables influenced different stages. It could be the case that the stages themselves overlapped in time and this overlap canceled the interaction effects that should have been observed. Analogously, additive effects do not necessarily mean that the two independent variables influenced different stages of processing. There is also the possibility that two factors influenced one stage but the nature of the influence was additive in nature. However, in both cases, the interpretation given by the additive-factor method is more parsimonious. Given two equally good interpretations, the simplest one is preferred.

Taylor proposes that the investigator should rely on interactions as informative results and verify and quantify these interactions. However, it seems equally important to demonstrate additivity among factors in the same experiments in which interactions are observed. This follows from the fact that an interaction alone is not an unambiguous indication that the stages in the task were discrete (nonoverlapping) and the two variables influenced one or more stages in common.

The discrete-stage model assumes that the successive processing stages do not overlap and that the output of one stage to the next does not change with the amount of time consumed by the previous stage. As an example in memory search, the output of the stimulus-identification stage was assumed to be the same for the intact and degraded stimulus conditions even though processing the degraded stimulus would take considerably longer than processing the intact stimulus. A failure of additivity of visual quality and memory-set size could be taken to reject this assumption and to support other interpretations.

Overlapping Stages

McClelland (1979) offers an alternative to the discrete-stage model underlying the subtractive- and additive-factor methods. He proposes a cascade model in which one stage begins before the preceding stage is complete. A stage can make its processing continuously available to the following stage. This assumption is not completely unprecedented and can be found in many experiments in which accuracy is the primary dependent variable. The assumption of successive but overlapping stages along with the assumption that the output of a stage may vary with different experimental conditions leads to a new framework for carrying out and interpreting RT experiments.

McClelland (1979) reanalyzes the implications of additive and interactive effects within the framework of the cascade model. In terms of the cascade model, there is a larger number of possible inferences given an interaction of two independent variables than from the discrete stage model. Table 5 gives the possible inferences from the discrete-stage model and from the cascade model. As can be seen in the table, there is considerably less certainty about the interpretation of

Table 5. Comparison of inferences derived from the discrete-stage model and the cascade model. Inferences from the cascade model assume a fixed criterion and very low error rates. The locus of an asymptote effect cannot be determined from the pattern of additivity and interaction.

Condition	Discrete-stage model	Cascade model
If factors interact	They affect the duration of the same process.	They affect the rate of the same process, *or* they both affect relative asymptotic activation, *or* one affects the rate of the rate-limiting process and the other affects the relative asymptotic activation.
If effects are additive	They affect the durations of different processes.	They affect the rates of different processes, *or* one affects the rate of a fast process and the other affects the asymptote.

an experimental outcome in the framework of the cascade model. McClelland illustrates the usefulness of the model by providing alternative interpretations of previous studies carried out in the discrete-stage framework.

Students of psychological science should not get discouraged and immediately conclude that Donders and Sternberg led us down the wrong path. Science can be viewed as a series of successive approximations to understanding the phenomena of interest. Theories in science usually go from simple to complex rather than the reverse. For example, Einstein's theory of relativity requires an incorporation of the properties of the measuring instrument whereas Newton's theory did not. It seems fair to say that McClelland's cascade model probably would not have been developed if Sternberg or someone else had not modified and extended the Donders subtractive method. We are taking the view of Toulmin (1972) that science and ideas develop gradually rather than in discrete jumps as proposed by Kuhn (1962). Many of the experiments carried out within the additive-factor method are now seen as open to additional interpretations. However, they have already eliminated some other interpretations and further knowledge can be gained with additional experimental and theoretical work. In point of fact, the most parsimonious interpretation given by the discrete-stage model holds up in a remarkable number of situations (Miller, 1982, 1988; Sanders, 1980; Sternberg, 1975). The field has simply enlarged the magnification level of our theoretical microscope used for studying hidden mental processes. The new possibilities that have become apparent not only offer immediate challenges to the researcher but also provide the methods to gain an even deeper insight into psychological processing.

Experimental Test

If stimulus identification and response selection can be considered two stages of processing, an important question is whether they can overlap in time. The additive-factor method is based on the idea that stages do not overlap in time, whereas the cascade model assumes that they do overlap in time. A test between these alternatives was carried out by Miller (1982). In Miller's terms, the question is whether response preparation can begin before stimulus identification is complete or whether the stimulus must be completely identified prior to any response preparation or activation. Miller's novel technique is to control the information available at various times during stimulus identification by making some relevant stimulus characteristics easy to discriminate and some difficult to discriminate. The question is whether the stimulus characteristics easy to discriminate could be used for response preparation before the stimulus was completely identified, i.e., before the stimulus characteristics difficult to discriminate were also resolved.

Consider an experiment with four letters created by independently varying the size and identity of the letters. Two stimulus sets were used; there were large and small S's and T's in one condition, and large and small I's and T's in the other condition. Pilot results indicated that letter discrimination could be made about 85 msec faster than the size discrimination in the first stimulus set (sStT), whereas the size discrimination could be made about 72 msec faster than the letter discrimination in the second stimulus set (iItT).

The utilization of partial information about the stimulus could be observed by the response requirements in the task. The usefulness of partial information was varied by manipulating the assignments of particular stimuli to responses. On each trial, subjects responded to one of the four stimuli with one of four fingers, two on each hand. Two responses made by the same hand can be prepared together more efficiently than two responses made by different hands. The preparation of two response fingers on the same hand has been shown to be more effective than preparation of two response fingers on different hands (Rosenbaum, 1980).

Subjects responded more quickly if the large and small versions of a given letter were assigned to the same hand for both stimulus sets. Subjects also responded more quickly if the two large letters were assigned to one hand and the two small letters were assigned to the other hand, but only when the size discrimination was very easy relative to the letter discrimination, that is, in the letter set (iItT). Thus, separate or discrete attributes of the stimulus could be encoded before the stimulus was completely identified, and this information could be passed on and influence response preparation. The idea is that determining that the letter is a large letter even though the letter has not yet been identified can tell the subject which hand is relevant and thus decrease RT relative to the case in which the two letters of the same size are not assigned to the same hand. Analogously, and much more intuitively, if the letter name is assigned to a given hand so that both the large and small versions of a given letter are responded to on the same hand, then determination of the letter name can aid response selection even though the size of the letter has not been completely determined to uniquely identify the alternative as one of four alternatives.

However, now consider the stimulus set with the capital letters M, N, U, and V. Information obtained early in processing can constrain the stimulus to be one of the two letters M or N versus one of two letters U or V. Thus, this information derived before the letter was completely identified could inform the subject about which pair of letters was present in the display. If subjects are able to utilize this information for response preparation, then the subjects should be faster to respond when the letters M and N are assigned to one hand and U and V are assigned to the other relative to the case in which these letters are assigned to different hands. This was not the case, however, in that no facilitation was observed. The explanation is that the information could not be encoded in terms of a discrete code to pass on to response preparation. In these simple information-processing tasks, information appears to be transmitted discretely from perception to action in terms of stimulus codes. Information that is not encoded discretely does not constrain response preparation.

Reaction Times and Performance

Memory Search

Stages of Processing
Serial Search: Self-Terminating
Serial Search: Exhaustive
Content Addressable Search
Size of the Memory Set
Quality of Test Stimulus
Variations in Memory Search

Visual Scanning

Differences between Sternberg and Neisser Tasks
Specific Practice

Accuracy and RT Methods Compared

Experimental Demonstration
Process Considerations

Speed-Accuracy Trade-off Method

Memory Search Revisited
Retrieval from Semantic Memory

Analysis of Variance
Within-Subject Design

*We know far more today about response times and their uses
than we did a decade ago, let alone in the early 1950s...*
R. Duncan Luce (1986)

Reaction times (RTs) can be used to study the operations of mental processes. One psychological process that can be studied very easily using RTs is memory search. To answer the question, where would you like to eat dinner? involves some form of memory search. We search in memory for restaurants we know about and test their qualities against our current appetite, budget, and whatever other considerations we deem important. The time it takes to search memory illuminates the nature of the memory-search process.

MEMORY SEARCH

As described in Chapter 8 (p. 150), Sternberg (1966, 1967) designed a memory-search task. A memory list of digits is presented followed by a test digit. The test digit is equal to one of the digits in the memory set on a random one half of the trials. The task of the observer is to respond "yes" by pushing one lever if the test digit was one of the digits in the preceding set, and to respond "no" by pushing another lever if it was not. The difficulty of the search task was changed by varying the number of digits in the memory set.

Stages of Processing

What stages of psychological processing does this task involve? First, it is clear that a good deal of processing goes on both before and after the test digit presentation. To respond correctly, the subject must first learn and remember the digits in the memory set. Accurate recognition and memory of the memory set is required. Recognition and storage of each memory item may take from 250 to 500 msec. In the typical memory-search task, in which the memory items are presented at 1/sec, we can assume that their processing is complete before the test item is presented. Therefore, the time it takes to perform this processing does not affect the RT to the test item.

Processing and responding appropriately to the test item determines RT in this task. First, the subject must detect and recognize the test item. To determine whether the test item was a member of the memory set, the subject must perform some sort of search and comparison of the test item with the memory items. The outcome of the search and comparison provides the necessary information for the response-selection process. We can discern, then, detection, recognition, memory search and comparison, and response selection as the processing stages in this task. Figure 1 presents a flow diagram of these stages of information processing in the memory-search task.

Which of these stages will be affected by the independent variable—changes in the number of items in the memory set? The detection stage clearly would not be, nor should recognition of the test digit be affected by the number of preceding memory items. Undoubtedly, however, a change in the number of items in the memory set is going to affect the difficulty of the memory search and comparison. Once the search is performed, on the other hand, and the observer knows whether or not the test item was present in the memory set, the nature of the response-selection task should still be the same: given that the item was or was not present in the set, is the appropriate response pushing the left or right lever?

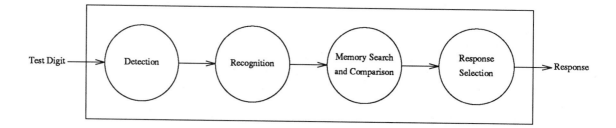

Figure 1. A flow diagram of the intervening stages of information processing between presentation of the test digit and execution of the appropriate response.

Analysis of the task, then, allows us to test the assumption that changes in the independent variable (number of items in the memory set) affect only the memory search and comparison stage. If this assumption is correct, if RTs change as memory-set size is increased, it can tell us a good deal about the nature of the memory-search process. For instance, we can hypothesize a particular search algorithm, a sequence of operations that might be used to perform the memory task. From this algorithm, we can determine the expected changes in RT as a function of increases in memory-set size. Two very different algorithms, or strategies, will be analyzed for their prediction of how RT will change as a function of change in the independent variable. The experiment, then, can provide a test of these two hypotheses. If the actual results match the function predicted by one of them, the results will support the assumptions about the processing stages in the task and provide evidence that a particular algorithm was used. If, however, the results match neither prediction, the results imply that either the assumptions about the processing stages were incorrect or that a different search algorithm was used.

Serial Search: Self-Terminating

The first strategy considered is a serial search. The memory set is maintained in memory. After the test digit is recognized, it is compared to an item in the memory set. Given no match, the test digit is compared to the next item on the memory set. If a match is found, the search stops. The search is self-terminating because no further comparisons are made once a match has been found.

Serial Search: Exhaustive

A serial exhaustive search proceeds in the same manner as a serial self-terminating search, except that all items on the memory set are searched independently of whether or not a match is found. It is important to note that the items in the memory set are not searched in any systematic order from trial to trial. In a self-terminating search, the number of items actually searched varies, ranging from all items on "no" trials and on trials in which the last digit in the set is equal to the test digit, through one item only on trials in which the first item is equal to the test digit. On the average, the search process would have to search $\frac{N+1}{2}$ items on "yes" trials, where N is the number of items in the memory set. In a serial-exhaustive search, it exhausts the set on "yes" and "no" trials alike.

To demonstrate whether either of these algorithms describes performance in Sternberg's task, we must analyze each one for its predictions regarding changes in RTs as a function of changes in memory-set size. Detection and recognition of the test digit and the response-selection stage should not be influenced by changes in the size of the memory set. The memory search and comparison stage, however, is affected by memory-set size: the more items to be searched, the longer the search should take. Each additional item in the memory set will add a constant increment to the RT. Thus, if detection plus recognition time equals x, memory search and comparison time per item equals y, and response-selection time equals z, then the total RT to say "no" will be equal to

$$RT = x + yN + z + o \qquad (1)$$

where N is the number of items in the memory set, and o is equal to the time for other necessary processes in the memory-search task.

Figure 2 plots "no" RT as a function of memory-set size according to Equation 1. With one item in the memory set, $RT = x + y + z + o$. With two items in the memory set, $N = 2$, $RT = x + 2y + z + o$. The results, when plotted, give a linear function, intercepting the ordinate at $x + z + o$, with a y msec increase in RT for every increase in memory-set size.

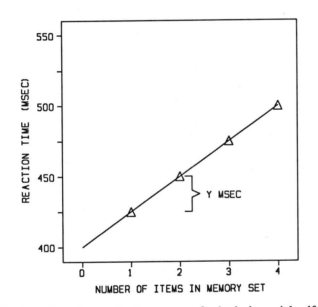

Figure 2. Predicted RT function for "no" responses for both the serial self-terminating and serial-exhaustive searches of the memory set.

Self-terminating and exhaustive searches make equivalent predictions for "yes" trials, but not for "no" trials. For an exhaustive search, the slope of the function will be the same for "yes" and "no" responses. The slope of the function will not be the same, however, for the self-terminating search. If the test digit is equally likely to occur at any serial position on "yes" trials, it will search $\frac{N+1}{2}$ items on the average, whereas on "no" trials it will search the entire set. If the strategy is a serial self-terminating search, therefore, we can expect the rate of increase in RT as a function of memory-set size to be one half that of "no" trials. The rate of increase is the slope, and is given in msec per item. Figure 3 presents the curves for "yes" and "no" responses under the assumption of a serial self-terminating memory search. If, on the other hand, the entire set is searched on both kinds of trials, it follows that the function will have the same rate of increase for both "yes" and "no" trials. Therefore, the "yes" and "no" curves will be parallel when the search algorithm is a serial-exhaustive one.

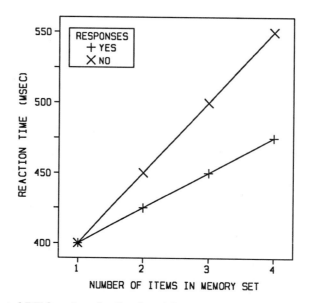

Figure 3. Predicted RT functions for "yes" and "no" responses for a serial self-terminating search of the memory set.

One of the first observations students usually make, when faced with the analysis of the memory-search task, is the critical role that should be played by the serial position of the test item on "yes" trials. Given the serial self-terminating search, for example, search time should be shorter for test digits that occur earlier in the list regardless of the size of the memory set. This observation is not only reasonable, it corresponds to what has been observed in a few instances (e.g., Klatzky, Juola, & Atkinson, 1971). Serial position should have no effect given a serial-exhaustive search, however, since every item in the memory set is searched. The initial findings of Sternberg were consistent with this prediction of the serial-exhaustive search model.

Content-Addressable Search

In a content-addressable search, the search process is parallel rather than serial. A parallel search means that all items in memory are searched at the same time. No matter how many digits are in memory, the test digit is compared simultaneously to all of them. The slope of the RT function with increases in memory-set size given this strategy would be zero; the function would be plotted as a horizontal line (see Figure 4). The horizontal function would be obtained for both "yes" and "no" responses.

Serial and parallel search are probably utilized at different times in normal cognitive functioning. If you are asked whether there is a given number—for example, "one"—in your telephone number, you will probably use a serial search. A content-addressable search seems unlikely since it is improbable that contents of your memory for "one" would have information whether or not it is contained in your telephone number. Rather, you must go to the location or address of your telephone number and inquire there whether a "one" is represented. In contrast, when asked if you keep your butter in the refrigerator, you do not search through all the foods you have stored in memory under refrigerator. Rather, your concept of butter is enough to tell you whether you store it in the refrigerator. Therefore, the time to answer this question should be independent of the number of foods kept in the house. (The use of serial and content-addressable search might be related to whether episodic or semantic memory is being searched, see Chapter 17.)

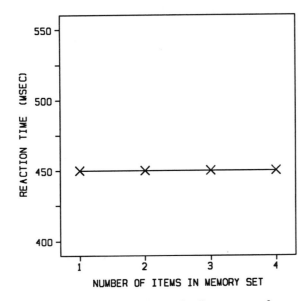
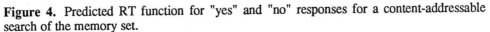

Figure 4. Predicted RT function for "yes" and "no" responses for a content-addressable search of the memory set.

Size of the Memory Set

Here, then, are two hypothetical strategies that generate two different RT functions across changes in memory-set size. These predicted functions can be compared to the function obtained in the actual experiment with humans. If the latter is a horizontal line, we have evidence that humans use something analogous to a content-addressable strategy in this task. If the results show a linearly increasing function, the serial-search algorithm is supported. In fact, Sternberg's results, plotted in Figure 5, showed a linear increase in RT as a function of memory-set size, supporting the hypothesis that humans perform this task by employing a serial-search strategy. Moreover, the function had the same slope for both "yes" and "no" responses, supporting the serial-exhaustive search algorithm.

It might be hypothesized that this search and comparison operation is performed during subvocal rehearsal that subjects employ in the task. Subjects report reciting the numbers to themselves in order to keep them fixed in memory. This hypothesis would predict that each additional item in the memory set would require at least an additional 160 msec for search and comparison, because the rate of implicit speech is about six items per second. Sternberg's results, however, show the increment of additional time for each additional item to be about 40 msec, demonstrating that the serial search and comparison cannot occur during subvocal speech.

The additive-factor method can be used to clarify further the operations of the search process in the search task. Simultaneously, this method can be used to substantiate the independence of the processing stages. Consider the three stages—recognition, memory search and comparison, and response selection—and independent variables that might affect each stage. The recognition process is dependent on the clarity of the test digit; if we present the test digit in degraded form, it should take the subject longer to recognize the test digit but should not necessarily affect the time to complete the following processing stages. We have seen how the number of items in the memory set appears to affect only the memory search and comparison stage. Finally, the response-selection stage might be affected by whether or not a match is found. The subject may find it more or less difficult to select a "yes" than a "no" response.

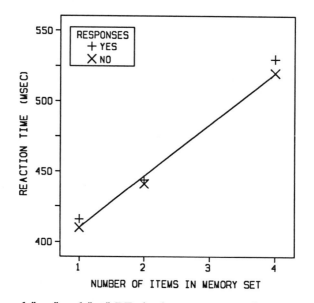

Figure 5. Observed "yes" and "no" RTs in the memory-search task as a function of the number of items in the memory set (after Sternberg, 1966).

Quality of Test Stimulus

This armchair analysis leads to further experiments which simultaneously vary these three independent variables. In one experiment, Sternberg (1967) manipulated the visual quality of the test digit, presenting it in degraded form on half the trials, and intact on the remaining trials. The stimulus was degraded by placing a masking screen of dots over the test digit. In this study, subjects were given a fixed memory set for a whole block of trials. For example, the subjects might be given a memory set containing the digits 4 and 7. Then each trial would be initiated with the onset of the test digit. After a series of trials, the subjects would be given a new memory set followed by a block of trials. The quality of the test digit was also varied between trial blocks. (To implement this study, it is necessary to work out a counterbalancing scheme for a factorial experiment of four levels of memory-set size times two levels of visual quality.)

In this study, Sternberg varied two independent variables in a factorial design: the quality of the test digit and the number of items in the memory set. The RT function under the intact condition was compared to the RT function in the degraded condition. Logically, one would predict that the case in which the test stimulus was embedded in noise would take longer than the intact stimulus case. In particular, one would expect that recognition of the test digit would be more difficult. Thus, the overall RT function would be higher than the typical function found with intact stimuli. One might expect, however, that the slope of the function would not change, that is, that the stimulus quality manipulation would not affect the difficulty of the memory search and comparison process. It seems reasonable to suppose that once the recognition stage has labeled the test digit, however easy or difficult it may have been to do so, the rate of memory search would be the same. If this is the case, the two functions will be parallel. If not, if changes in stimulus quality do affect the memory-search stage, the functions will diverge.

Thus, we can expect one of two alternative results, both of which would be informative. In Figure 6, the two independent variables have additive effects, the degraded function is parallel to the intact function, and the most likely conclusion is that the two variables affect different stages.

If the two variables interact, their effects should be compounded, resulting in the interaction presented in Figure 7. This result might imply that the subjects employ some direct visual representation of the test digit in the memory search and comparison so that the degraded digit not only increases recognition time but slows down the rate of memory search.

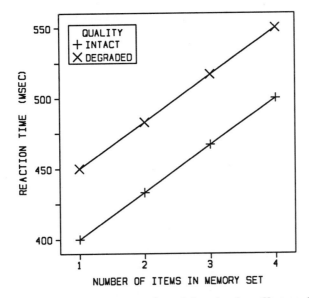

Figure 6. Predicted RT functions if the quality of the stimulus affects only the recognition stage of processing in the search task.

On the second day of the experiment, Sternberg found that the RT function in the degraded condition described a straight line above and parallel to the function of the intact condition, supporting the hypothesis that stimulus quality affected only the recognition stage. This result tells us something about the connections between the stage of recognition and the stage of memory search and comparison. If degrading the stimulus had affected the RT of the memory-search stage, then that would imply that the information in the recognition is handed over raw to the memory search and comparison stage. Sternberg's results, however, tell us that the recognition stage transforms the degraded information to produce an unequivocal digit value for the memory-search stage. This lends credence to the information-processing model, in which stages of processing are seen as producing successive transformations upon the information as it moves through them.

Note that Sternberg designed his experiment so that either result would have been informative. A good experimenter first asks: What are the possible outcomes of the experiment? What theories can be rejected or supported by the study? If the results do not distinguish between theories, they are not informative in the sense of reducing uncertainty about the psychological processes responsible for the results. The psychologist is primarily interested in what the experiment can indicate about psychological processing; behavior data are not sufficient in and of themselves. The experiments should be designed so that every possible outcome will be informative with respect to psychological functioning. Although Sternberg's modification of Donders' subtractive method avoids the difficulties of inserting or deleting a stage of processing, it can sometimes be used to estimate the duration of a mental process. Rather than manipulating whether or not a mental process occurs, it is possible to manipulate the number of times the process occurs. In the memory-search task, for example, the number of items in the memory set is varied.

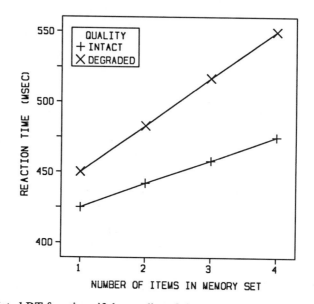

Figure 7. Predicted RT functions if the quality of the test stimulus offsets both the recognition stage and the memory search and comparison stage of processing in the search task.

If a serial memory search and comparison occurs, the number of times it occurs is a systematic function of the number of items in the memory set. Therefore, it is possible to estimate the time required for a single memory search and comparison. As an example, the slope of the linear function for "no" responses provides an estimate of this process for a serial search process. It should be noted that the additive-factor method will not always provide an estimate of the time for some mental processes. To achieve this goal, it is necessary to verify a particular model of the task and then to estimate the duration of a particular process in the model by manipulating the number of times it occurs.

Variations in Memory Search

Given recognition, memory search and comparison, and response-selection stages of processing in a memory-search task, the operations of the memory search and comparison stage should not change with relatively minor changes in the response-selection stage. Some experiments appear to have weakened this hope. Egeth, Marcus, and Bevan (1972) looked at the Sternberg memory-search task in a Donders type C task in which subjects responded only on "yes" trials. The memory set was either the digit 1 or the digits 1, 2, and 3. RTs were only 6 msec longer for the memory set of three digits than for the memory set of one digit. In the more typical B task requiring both "yes" and "no" responses, the RTs increased 70 msec with the memory set of three relative to the memory set of one item. This result indicates that the response-selection process is influencing the memory-search process. The C task requests only that the subject report presence of a letter, whereas the B task also requests a report for absence. Given this difference, changes in the memory-search process should not be unexpected.

Ogden and Allusi (1980) found that memory search and comparison and response selection were not independent in the Sternberg memory-search task. The linear increase in RT with increases in memory-set size was eliminated by asking subjects to verbally respond "yes" and "no" instead of the standard button-pushing task. In this case, the number of responses remains fixed but

---

Analysis of Variance

The analysis of variance is the best statistical tool to analyze experiments with two or more independent variables that are combined in a factorial fashion, as is required by the additive-factor method. The analysis essentially evaluates the treatment effect against the chance variability found in the experiment. Consider an experiment with two levels of an independent variable in which we test the subject three different times under each level so that we have three scores at each level. Assume that in two different experiments the scores are those given in the table below, where l_1 and l_2 are the two levels of the independent variable.

Experiment 1		Experiment 2	
l_1	l_2	l_1	l_2
80	100	73	87
60	90	70	87
70	80	67	93

In both experiments, the subject averaged 70 at l_1 and 90 at l_2. However, we have more confidence in the difference between l_1 and l_2 in the second experiment than in the first. In the first experiment, the difference (20) between l_1 and l_2 is not any larger than the difference between the three scores at the same level of l_1 or l_2. The differences between the scores at the same level of our independent variable must be attributed to chance variability since there is nothing the experimenter can point to as a causal factor. Since chance variability was so much larger in the first experiment than the second, we have more faith in the significance of the results in the second experiment than the first. However, statistical significance itself is not the major issue, and our analysis is focused on the psychological significance of a given result.

The analysis of variance provides the experimenter with an index of the size of the treatment effect measured against the chance variability in the experiment. In a two-factor design—an experiment with two independent variables—the analysis of variance provides this index for the effect of each of the independent variables and their interaction. The experimenter should design the experiment as carefully as possible to keep chance variability to a minimum. After the experiment, the statistical significance is computed using the analysis of variance. The task then is to evaluate the size of these effects and what these effects say about psychological processes and current models or theories of the processes. Our knowledge comes from evaluating the meaningfulness of the effects of independent variables rather than simply from their statistical significance.

---

the nature of the response is changed. Once again, a variable that should affect only one stage appears to influence some other stage of processing. On the other hand, several studies have failed to find any changes in memory search with changes in response requirements and others have found only quantitative rather than qualitative changes (Corballis, 1975; Kristofferson, 1975; Sternberg, 1975). Similar findings exist in visual search. Van der Heijden and La Heij (1982, 1983) explored the differences between Donders C task (go-no go) and Donders B task (yes-no and two alternative) in the visual-search paradigm. Although there were differences among the tasks, they were more accurately described as quantitative rather than qualitative.

These experiments reveal the inadequacy of the Donders subtractive method and the limitations in the Sternberg additive-factor method. It would be incorrect to assume that the difference in the type B and type C task is only due to the response-selection stage since the stage of memory search and comparison seems to change also. As noted by Külpe and many other critics around the turn of the century, the Donders subtractive method cannot be employed to study the operations of a single stage of processing. Changing the task can change the operations of that stage of processing. Therefore, changing the task from a type B to a type C task might change memory search. Within each of these tasks, however, the additive-factor method might still be valid. In fact, the additive-factor method was designed explicitly to overcome the limitations of the subtractive method. The additive-factor method acknowledged that one stage of processing might change with changes in the overall task of the subject. What has to be qualified is that the nature of the memory-search process in a type B task may not be found in a type C task. This result should not be too surprising or disheartening. A major question facing experimental psychology is the degree to which findings can be generalized beyond the specific experimental task. Exploring the difference between the type B and C tasks might not only reveal additional knowledge about these tasks but might provide insight as to the kinds of search processes found in more natural situations.

VISUAL SCANNING

About the time that Sternberg was doing his memory-search experiments, Neisser and his colleagues devised another paradigm that approached the study of memory search from a different direction (Neisser, 1963, 1964; Neisser, Novick, & Lazar, 1963). In Neisser's task, the subject was given a memory item, perhaps a letter of the alphabet, and told to find this item in a typed list of letters. Figure 8 provides a copy of sample lists from these experiments. The list contained a column of letters with usually four or six letters per row. Upon presentation of the list, the subject read (scanned) the list from the top and pushed a lever as soon as the memory letter was found. Reaction time was measured from the presentation of the list to the onset of the response.

```
ZBMX    JYRANF
YFJU    HGJDST
UXNT    LMHPBM
FBOS    YXQPYD
UWJE    RQLATE
TOBH    INTQDV
DJWR    BVPRKO
VFKE    KCVWDO
AXDC    EMQXCT
SFDP    XEKNWV
```

Figure 8. Sample lists for Neisser's scanning task.

Sternberg's additive-factor method allows us to determine the time for memory search by accounting for the times of other processes in the task. The slope of the function relating RT to the number of items in the memory set provides an index of memory search and comparison time. Neisser estimated search and comparison time in a similar fashion. However, in this case, the process is more accurately described as visual search and comparison since each new comparison requires visual identification of a test letter and memory comparison with a memory item. The independent variable in Neisser's task is the location of the memory letter in the test list. Reaction time should be a direct function of what row in the list contains the memory letter. Since the subjects begin scanning at the top of the list, we would expect RT to increase as the memory letter is placed lower down in the test list. Logically, each letter in the test list requires the same amount of processing until the subject finds the memory letter. For example, if the subject is looking for the letter K, we would expect that his search rate through the list would be constant. That is, the time to process the test letters should be independent of their serial position in the test list. Since the response-selection time should also be independent of where the subject finds the letter in the list, we would expect that RT should be a linear function of the serial position of the memory letter.

The results of Neisser's experiment, shown in Figure 9, support the logical analysis. Reaction time is well described by a linearly increasing function of position of the memory letter in the test list. The fact that the intercept of the function is close to zero shows that other processes such as response-execution time account for very little of the RT. The slope of the function provides an index of the time it takes the subject to recognize, to compare, and to select a response for each letter. That is to say, for the subject to perform the task correctly, he must process each test letter to the degree that he knows enough about whether it is or is not the memory letter and must select the appropriate response given this information. If it is not the memory letter, he goes on to the next letter; if it is, he pushes the lever. The estimate of search time is between six and seven letters per second, considering that each line had four letters. (The search time is also critically dependent on the similarity between the memory letter and test letters.)

Neisser's paradigm is very similar to the experimental task used by Sternberg. The memory item in Neisser's task is analogous to the memory set in Sternberg's task; Neisser's test list is analogous to Sternberg's test item. In Neisser's task, there is one memory item and many test items. In Sternberg's task, there can be more than one memory item, but there is just one test item. As you might expect, one task can be modified to be more directly comparable to the other. Neisser actually tested his subjects with more than one memory item, and multiple test items have been employed in the Sternberg task (Schneider & Shiffrin, 1977). Given Sternberg's results, we might expect subjects to perform Neisser's task by comparing each item on the presentation test list to the memory item in memory. Since they are instructed to start at the top of the list, they could proceed in serial order until a match is found. In Sternberg's task, the subject has several items in memory and one test item to be recognized and compared to the items in memory. In Neisser's task, the subject has one item in memory and up to 50 rows of letters to be compared to it. Reaction time in Neisser's task should vary, therefore, not as a function of the number of memory items, which is constant at one, but rather as a function of the position of the memory item in the list; that is to say, RT should vary as a function of the number of test items that must be searched before the subject reaches the one that corresponds to the item in memory. This function should be linear, as in Sternberg's task, i.e., each item to be searched should add a constant increment to the RT. In fact, Neisser's results confirm this prediction, indicating a linear increase in RT as the memory item is moved further and further down the list. Up to this point, Neisser's and Sternberg's experiments confirm each other nicely.

Having established the RT function in the case of one memory item, Neisser presented subjects with a larger number of memory items. For example, the subject would be given two letters, perhaps K and O, and told to respond as soon as he found either one in the list. We would expect, according to what both Sternberg and Neisser have shown so far about how subjects perform this sort of task, that each item in the list would be matched against one memory letter first, and then against the other, proceeding serially down the list, and generating a linear function that would have a steeper slope than the function with the same list and only one of the memory items. That is, twice as many comparisons will have to be made for the same number of test items, since now the subject has to check each test item against two memory items instead of just one.

This is not what Neisser found with practiced subjects. Although RT was a linear function of the position of the memory item in the test list, it did not vary at all as a function of the number of items in memory. An item that was one of ten memory items was found as quickly as the same item when it was the only one the subject was looking for. Subjects could search the test list for eight letters and two numbers as quickly as they could search for the letter K alone. This means that the rate of memory search and comparison was independent of the number of items in memory.

Neisser's results can be described by a slight variation on the content-addressable search algorithm discussed earlier. Subjects would ticket only the memory items in advance; negative items would remain unmarked. Therefore, each test item would take the search process to a specific location in memory corresponding to that test item. If it was ticketed, it would be a positive (memory) item, and the subject should push the lever. If it was unticketed, the subject could reliably conclude that it was a negative (nonmemory) item and proceed to the next test item. In this way, RT would not be dependent upon the number of items in memory. All that is required is a check of the status of each test item without referring to each of the memory items at all.

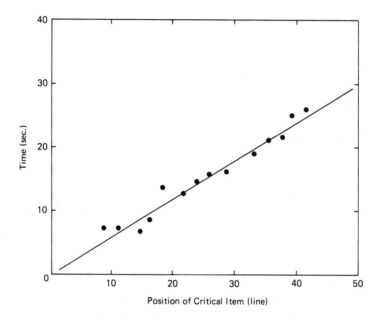

Figure 9. Reaction time as a function of the serial position of the memory item in the test list (after Neisser, 1967).

Neisser compared the performance of his subjects to that of employees in news-clipping services, who contract with clients to search the newspapers for any mention of clients' names. The people who perform this work learn to scan newspapers at astonishing rates. They report they do not need to read the material in the traditional sense. Somehow the clients' names just pop out at them. In the same way, Neisser's subjects reported that, after practice, the memory letters just leaped out at them from the list. According to our content-addressable search model, ticketing the items in the memory set has the phenomenological consequence of these items popping out, whereas unticketed items do not. With the content-addressable search, it was not necessary to compare each letter in the test list to the items in memory. Rather, the necessary information was present in the test item itself.

Differences between Sternberg and Neisser Tasks

The difference in the way the subjects performed these two tasks might reflect differences in the two experimental situations. Unlike Sternberg's subjects, Neisser's were practiced and highly motivated. They returned day after day and were able to decrease their overall RT remarkably. Moreover, the items which they had to keep in memory while searching the lists did not vary. A subject would be given ten memory letters; on one day he might look for five of these, and on another day he might look for all ten. Over time he learned the items quite thoroughly. Sternberg's subjects, on the other hand, came in once for a few hours. They had little practice with the search operation, and very little opportunity to rehearse the memory items. In addition, Sternberg emphasized perfect performance with his subjects, keeping the rate of errors down to about two or three percent. Neisser, on the contrary, allowed his subjects to make many errors, about 25 percent; the emphasis in his experiment was on speed of reaction.

Humans probably choose one of a number of search algorithms depending upon the conditions and requirements of the task at hand. If subjects are highly practiced with the memory set and errors are not critical, something analogous to a content-addressable search can be used. If accuracy is critical and the subjects are unpracticed, a serial search seems more appropriate. Kristofferson (1972a, b, c) and her colleagues (Kristofferson, Groen, & Kristofferson, 1973) systematically explored the effects of practice and error rates in both the Neisser and Sternberg search tasks and demonstrated that differences in practice and error rates are responsible for much of the difference originally found between the two tasks.

Specific Practice

An experiment performed by Graboi (1971) demonstrated the critical effect of specific practice on memory search. Graboi used Neisser's paradigm and English surnames as memory and test items. Subjects were given such names as Hicks, James, Blake, Klein, Allan, Brown, and Joyce to find in a list of similar names; the number of memory names could vary from one to seven.

Graboi first allowed his subjects to become very practiced with the same seven names. Each subject had seven items which he searched for in combinations from one to all seven in list after list, until he was highly practiced with these items. Measuring RT as a function of memory set size, Graboi found that there was some increase in time, but this increase was not a linear function. Subjects took longer to search with three memory items than with one, but beyond three items RT did not increase. Seven memory items took no longer than three; finding James in a list took no longer if the possible memory items were Hicks, James, Brown, Jones, Klein, Blake, and Joyce, than if they were Hicks, James, and Brown.

Subjects all reported that this was a skill they had learned. After so much practice, they felt they no longer gave the list the active attention they had at the beginning of the experiment; rather, they seemed to need only glance through the list, thinking of nothing in particular, to have the relevant names pop out at them.

Now Graboi gave subjects a new set of memory names and 15 minutes in which to study them. When the same subjects performed the same task with a different set of names, the RT was found to increase sharply with increases in the number of items in memory. Subjects who had had much practice in the task and who had learned to search for one set of items according to a content-addressable search, fell back on a serial search when presented with a new set of memory items. This study demonstrates that practice affects the type of search algorithm used.

Schneider and Shiffrin (1977) advanced our understanding of memory search by pinpointing an important variable influencing the type of search that is carried out. Using the standard Sternberg (1975) memory-search task, Schneider and Shiffrin (1977) asked subjects to indicate whether or not a test item is a member of a memory set of items. A test item identical to an item in the memory set is a target item and requires a positive response whereas a test item not in the memory set is a distractor and requires a negative response. The makeup and the number of items in the memory set were varied systematically. A critical variable for performance is whether the mapping between test items and responses is *consistent* or varied. With consistent mapping, the memory items are always chosen from the same superset ensemble of items, and these items are never presented as distractors. Table 1 illustrates a set of trials with consistent mapping. As can be seen in the table, the ensembles for the memory and distractor digits do not overlap. A digit tested as a positive item in one block of trials can never be tested as a negative item in another block of trials. In the varied mapping condition, the memory items are not constrained in this way. The same set of items are used for both the memory and distractor ensembles. Table 2 illustrates a set of trials with varied mapping. A memory digit in one block of trials can be a distractor in another block of trials.

Table 1. Illustration of consistent mapping. The target ensemble (1, 3, 5, 9) represents all the items (test digits) that can be used as positive items in the task. The distractor ensemble (2, 4, 6, 7, 8) represents all the items (test digits) that can be used as negative items in the task. The target set contains the positive items and the distractor set contains the negative items that can be used in a particular block of trials.

Block of 100 Trials	Target Set	Distractor Set
First	1 5 9	2 4 6 7 8
Second	3	2 4 6 7 8
Third	1 9	2 4 6 7 8

Table 2. Illustration of varied mapping. The target ensemble (1, 2, 3, 4, 5, 6, 7, 8, 9) represents all the items (test digits) that can be used as positive items in the task. The distractor ensemble (1, 2, 3, 4, 5, 6, 7, 8, 9) represents all the items (test digits) that can be used as negative items in the task. The target set contains the positive items and the distractor set contains the negative items that can be used in a particular block of trials.

Block of 100 Trials	Target Set	Distractor Set
First	1 5 9	2 3 4 6 7 8
Second	3	1 2 4 5 6 7 8 9
Third	1 9	2 3 4 5 6 7 8

The results showed that memory search is influenced by the consistency of the pairings between an item and a positive or negative response throughout the experiment. If the pairing's change randomly as they do in varied mapping, RTs increase with increases in memory-set size. If the memory-set items are never presented as nontargets as in consistent mapping, however, a relatively small number of trials (2100) is sufficient for the subjects to produce RTs independent of memory-set size.

An additional result reveals the importance of the history or the pairings between items and responses. Analogous to Graboi's manipulation, subjects, given practice with consistent mapping, were then asked to search for items that were previously nontargets in displays. These new target items were placed in a background of nontargets that functioned as targets during the previous practice during consistent mapping. Reversal of the target and nontarget sets after practice with consistent mapping produced a huge negative transfer. This task was found to be more difficult and time consuming than the original task without practice.

The memory-search experiments reveal several facts about human performance. First, the processing system is highly flexible. Memory search under one set of task conditions can change with changes in the task conditions. Thus, memory search can operate more efficiently with some response requirements than with others, as in the experiments discussed in *Variations in Memory Search*. Second, there is a strong trade-off between accuracy and RT, and it is only natural that a less accurate search will proceed more quickly and will be less influenced by the number of items in the memory set. Third, the history of the subject's training is critical to how the search is carried out. A consistent training with specific items mapped to specific responses will lead to a much more efficient search than will a varied mapping. This last observation reveals that the processing system can become highly efficient when there is a consistent mapping between some environmental event and some action. Thus, expert Ping-Pong players appear to place themselves to allow the same stroke to be made. Rather than attempting to learn a large number of strokes from different positions, they master just a few strokes from a small number of positions. One interpretation of this behavior is that the experts are placing themselves in positions in which they can execute consistent stimulus-response mappings.

ACCURACY AND RT METHODS COMPARED

Accuracy and RT are considered to be converging measures of human performance. We expect that a difficult task will take longer, and will also be less accurate if stimulus information or processing time is limited. Salthouse's (1981) study provided evidence for this hypothesis and for the information-processing stage model by comparing accuracy and RT paradigms. Visual information processing in a tachistoscopic task was contrasted with performance in a speed-accuracy RT task. The test stimuli were digits or symbols and the responses were key presses. In one experiment, for example, subjects responded with one key to the odd integers 1 to 9, and responded with another key to to the even digits 0 to 8. The stimulus duration was reduced to produce errors in the tachistoscopic task, but remained on until the subject responded in the speed-accuracy task. The effects in the two different tasks can be compared by measuring the improvement in accuracy with increases in time. The size of an effect in the two tasks was used to assess whether the influence of a particular independent variable was at an early stage or a late stage of information processing. As an example, manipulating the number of stimulus alternatives while holding the number of response alternatives constant produced a smaller effect in the tachistoscopic task than in the RT task. This result agrees with earlier research showing that perceptual processing is less influenced by number of alternatives than is response processing. Another reasonable finding was no effect of stimulus-response compatibility in the tachistoscopic task, but a large effect in the RT task.

Experimental Demonstration

We have stated that speed and accuracy are converging measures of human performance. That is, results found with one dependent measure should agree with those of the other. An experiment on shape perception provides a good example to illustrate the convergence of these two measures (Massaro, 1973). The experiment also allowed a test of the invariance hypothesis of shape perception (see Chapter 14). Following Donders, it was assumed that shape judgments involve a sequence of psychological processes (stages) between presentation of the stimulus and the observer's response. In fact, the Donders B type RT paradigm was used. There were two possible stimuli and two possible responses. On each trial, two test shapes were presented and subjects had to decide if they were the same or different in shape. The test figures were two-dimensional rectangular shapes cut out of plastic. The test figures had the same height but differed slightly in width. The observer was required to hit one button if the two figures had the same width and another button if they had different widths.

The independent variable was the orientation (rotation) of the figure in depth about the vertical axis. The dependent variables were the RT and the percentage of correct responses in the task. Three subjects were tested under speed instructions and three subjects were tested under accuracy instructions. As usual, the subjects given accuracy instructions were instructed to respond as rapidly as possible without making a large number of errors. These subjects were given feedback after each error trial. (As has been pointed out many times, these instructions cannot be followed exactly. If the subject is not making many errors, she is not responding quickly enough. These instructions are somewhat analogous to asking subjects to respond if a signal is present when they know there is a signal present on each trial.) The subjects given speed instructions were given feedback on their RTs. If any RT exceeded 1.3 sec, they were encouraged to respond more rapidly on succeeding trials.

Figure 10 shows a stage model of this task. The observer can be conceptualized as first determining the shape of each of the test figures in the perceptual-encoding stage. After perceiving the shape, some comparison must be made between the two test figures. The two figures will either be the same or will differ in shape. The observer then selects the response that agrees with the outcome of the comparison process. The simplest assumption is that each of these stages is independent and sequential as indicated in Figure 10. Each stage takes some finite time and gives information to the following stage. The time to complete a stage is independent of the time it takes to complete preceding or following stages.

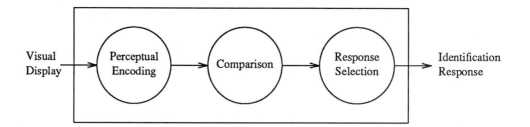

Figure 10. An information-processing model of the shape-judgment task.

Each trial was initiated by the opening of a rotating shutter that exposed the test figure. The subjects were sufficiently practiced in the task on the day before the actual experiment began. The subjects were then tested an hour a day for four successive days. Furthermore, all levels of the independent variables were presented randomly from trial to trial rather than between days or blocks of trials. The 14 possible combinations of 2 test figures x 7 rotation conditions were randomized within blocks of 14 trials. There were five blocks of trials per day, giving a total of 70 trials per day. The randomization of all events within a session is the best control for the effects of changes in motivation and strategies over the course of the experiment.

Before this experiment, it had already been demonstrated that increasing the rotation of the test figures would increase the difficulty of the task. Therefore, we would expect RT under accuracy instructions to increase with increases in angle of rotation. Similarly, accuracy under speed instructions should decrease with increases in angle of rotation. The top left panel of Figure 11 presents the mean RTs of the correct judgments for a subject given accuracy instructions as a function of angle of rotation of the two test figures. Increasing the angle of rotation increased RTs. The percentage errors are also shown in the bottom left panel of Figure 11. Although this subject was fairly successful in keeping her error rate to a minimum, there was some increase in error rate with increases in angle of rotation. This result is a common one in RT studies in which accuracy is stressed. Although the error rate is relatively low, there is usually a positive correlation between RT and percentage errors. What the correlation means here is that the RT function would have increased even more with increases in rotation if the subject had been successful in holding percentage errors constant at all levels of the independent variable.

The right panels of Figure 11 give the results for a subject tested under speed instructions. The bottom right panel shows that percentage errors increased with increases in angle of rotation. The top right panel of Figure 11 shows that RTs also increased somewhat with increases in angle of rotation, but not as much as for the subject tested under accuracy instructions. The results of the other subjects showed a similar pattern. To summarize, the outcome of the experiment is consistent with the idea that RT and accuracy are converging measures of performance. Both of these dependent measures have been central to the development of research and theory in experimental psychology.

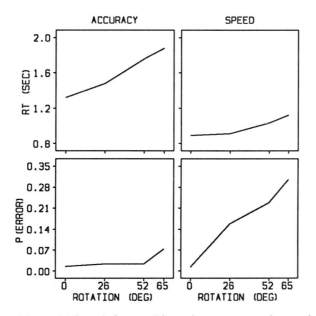

Figure 11. Mean RTs and P(error) for a subject given accuracy instructions (left panels) and for a subject given speed instructions (right panels) as a function of the angle of rotation of the two test figures.

Within-Subject Design

In the experiment just discussed, practiced subjects were tested under all experimental conditions repeatedly throughout the study. The first day was completely devoted to practice and the data disregarded. On the next four days the subjects received repeated presentations of all of the experimental conditions in a randomized fashion. This kind of experiment allows us to derive a function for each subject that relates RT or percentage errors to the levels of the independent variable. A between-group design in which different subjects are tested under different experimental conditions would be inefficient and inappropriate. The experiment can be considered a two-factor design with type of trial (same or different) and slant of figures as the two independent variables. To do a between-group design would require one group for each slant condition. The type of figure must be a within-subject variable so that subjects would have two responses available. Otherwise they could just hit the same button on each trial without looking at the figure.

In a between-group design, the experimenters would probably need at least five or ten subjects for each group to eliminate major differences due to different subjects in each group. However; they probably will never eliminate individual differences completely in this task. Subjects tested under just one experimental condition might employ different strategies than if they were tested under all conditions. Since subjects in the between-group design know the slant before the figure is presented, they might be able to short-circuit the normal shape perception process by simply operating on the size of the projected shape. Therefore, the between-group design does not control for differences in strategies under the different experimental conditions. This is the same reason that the experimental conditions are randomized from trial to trial in the within-subject experiment. If subjects knew which condition was to be presented, they might switch strategies. Randomizing the trials is the best insurance for the subject to operate within the same strategy under all experimental conditions. To assess any contribution of strategies, the experimenter could include another independent variable and vary systematically whether the orientation of the test figure is known before its presentation.

The subjects should be practiced on the task before the RTs are recorded, because other processes such as response selection and execution improve significantly and rapidly during the first 50 to 200 trials. Therefore, the average RT decreases markedly during this time. Since the early RTs are larger, they will contribute more to the overall average. Furthermore, early in the experiment, subjects usually make foolish mistakes, like hitting the wrong button even though they know the right answer. Early in the game they do not know what is involved and may feel threatened. The first series of trials is necessary to convince them that they can handle the task easily and to adopt a relatively constant level of motivation throughout the task.

Process Considerations

Although accuracy and RT provide converging measures of performance, they cannot be blindly interchanged for one another. The researcher must use an information-processing strategy in analyzing both dependent variables. In some cases, the two different variables will be tapping different processing stages and, therefore, the experimenter is faced with two different phenomena rather than converging measures of the same phenomenon. Converging measures are less likely to be observed when the accuracy and RT tasks change the stimulus conditions as well as the response instructions. Santee and Egeth (1982) give a nice example of how RT and accuracy do not measure the same aspects of performance, when stimulus conditions are varied between the two tasks.

The task they use is letter recognition of one of two alternative letters. Subjects were shown letters presented on opposite sides of a fixation point. Sometime after the onset of the test display, subjects were cued to report one of two letters. The independent variables were 1) the psychophysical similarity between the cued letter and the noncued letter and 2) whether the noncued letter was identical to the cued letter, was the alternative target letter, or was a nontarget letter. Short durations of the test letters were used to produce errors in the accuracy condition and we refer to this condition as a data-limited condition. A long display duration was used to produce essentially perfect performance in the RT condition, but subjects were instructed to respond as rapidly as possible without errors. We therefore call this condition a time-limited condition.

The processes involved are 1) lateral interference of similar letters on letter recognition and 2) response interference between target and noise items at response selection. Lateral interference occurred in the data-limited task and response interference in the time-limited task. If the noncued letter was identical to the cued letter, accuracy was lower than the case with different noncued letters in the data-limited task. In the time-limited task, RTs were longer when the noncued test letter was the alternative target. Thus, the results reveal lateral interference in the data-limited task and response interference in the time-limited task.

Although RT and accuracy do not provide converging measures of performance in the two tasks, the results can be explained within a model of information processing. Finding no effect of response interference in the data-limited task is reasonable. These subjects take their time in responding and simply optimize the accuracy of their choice. The stage of response selection should not be influenced by the similarity of the target and background items and neither accuracy nor RT (which Santee and Egeth do not report) should be influenced by the similarity manipulation in the data-limited task. In the time-limited task, subjects respond as quickly as possible without too many errors. Response interference is reasonable; presentation of the alternative target as the noncued test letter produces response interference analogously to the Stroop color-word task. In the Stroop task, printing a color word in the ink of another color disrupts a person's ability to name the color of the ink.

One might ask additionally, however, why one does not observe an effect of similarity of the two test letters on RT. That is, subjects should be somewhat slower when the noncued letter is identical to the cued letter relative to the case in which the two letters differ. To address the question, however, it is necessary to have a quantitative model of the contribution of lateral interference and response interference. It could be the case that the disadvantage of identical letters in perception is overcome by an advantage in response selection. For example, the identical background could have slowed down perceptual processing of the target item by 100 msec, but having the background identical to the target could have speeded up response selection by 300 msec. Supporting this interpretation, Shapiro and Krueger (1983) revealed significant but opposing effects of discriminability and bias due to the similarity of context letters to the test letter.

Given an information-processing description, the Santee and Egeth (1982) experiment does not challenge the common assumption that accuracy and RT are converging measures of human performance. Although it is easy to overlook the differences in the stimulus conditions in the accuracy and RT tasks, these differences could contribute to any differences that are observed. What the results make apparent is that data are meaningless without some kind of model analysis. One needs both information-processing models and fine-grained analyses of performance in the study of perception and action. A good theory will accommodate both accuracy and RT measures of performance.

SPEED-ACCURACY TRADE-OFF METHOD

The speed-accuracy trade-off method combines the logic of both accuracy and RT experiments, and offers a powerful method of study of human performance. This important new method involves the trade-off between speed and accuracy in an experimental task. Both the

Donders subtractive method and the Sternberg additive-factor method are based on relatively errorless performance by the subject. In addition, it is assumed that subjects in these tasks respond as quickly as possible without making errors. These requirements are seldom achieved exactly and probably only approximate what actually occurs in an experimental setting. Subjects are usually given the inconsistent instructions to "respond as rapidly as possible without making errors." If the subject does not make any errors, he or she is probably not responding fast enough.

To overcome these shortcomings, investigators have proposed speed-accuracy trade-off experiments. Although there are a number of variations of this basic approach, the critical feature is that both RTs and error rates are central to the data analysis and interpretation. In general, the procedure follows from the commonly held assumption that RTs and error rates are converging measures of performance. A more difficult task can be expected not only to take longer to perform but also to produce more errors. The assumption of speed-accuracy trade-offs is that the observer is also capable of trading accuracy for speed (or speed for accuracy) in most performance tasks.

Memory Search Revisited

In order to obtain a more detailed picture of the operations of the intervening processes between stimulus and response, it is necessary to generate speed-accuracy trade-off functions. The observer must perform the task at a number of speeds or RTs and, therefore, at a number of accuracy levels. An experiment by Reed (1976) illustrates one method of obtaining speed-accuracy trade-off functions in the standard Sternberg memory-search task. On each trial, the subject saw a list of items to be remembered. A two-second period followed the presentation of the memory set and preceded the presentation of the test item. The subject's task was to respond "yes" or "no" to whether the test item was one of the items in the memory set. Sometime after the onset of the test item, a response signal (a tone) was presented. Subjects were instructed to press the "yes" or "no" button "as fast as you can after hearing the tone signal." That is, subjects were expected to respond with the alternative they felt most likely to be correct at the time they heard the response signal, even if they were not completely sure of the correctness of their answer. The time between the presentation of the test item and the onset of the response signal serves as an additional independent variable in this task.

Reed used seven response-signal lags and manipulated this variable within subjects but between experimental sessions. Since three memory-set sizes were used, there were 21 unique experimental sessions consisting of the factorial arrangement of memory-set size and response-signal lag. It should also be possible to manipulate these variables within a given session. As an exercise, the student could devise counterbalancing and randomization schemes for both of these procedures.

In the standard RT task, RT is the primary dependent variable. In the standard accuracy task, accuracy is the primary dependent variable. In the speed-accuracy method, accuracy as a function of RT is the central dependent measure of interest. The RT is controlled by the response-signal lag. We would expect accuracy to increase with increases in the time between the test item and the response signal. Reed computed d' measures analogous to the d' measure of signal detection theory (see Chapter 12). As will be seen in that chapter, d' is a dependent measure that more directly reflects the amount of information that a subject has in a way that simple accuracy does not. Figure 12 shows that performance accuracy as measured by d' increased with increases in the lag of the response signal. The increase in accuracy with increases in time is best described by a negatively accelerating growth function. The absolute gain in accuracy with each additional increment in time becomes smaller and smaller as it approaches a ceiling. The ceiling is called an asymptote. Functions of this type are described by an asymptote which is the maximum level of performance and a rate of growth to the asymptote.

The question of interest is how memory-set size influences the function relating accuracy to RT. As can be seen in Figure 12, set size seems to influence both the asymptote and the rate of growth. The three functions level off at different d' values and the time at which this maximum is reached differs for the three functions. Smaller set sizes give larger asymptotes and faster rates of growth to the asymptote. This result replicates the results found in the standard RT task (see Figure 5) because increases in set size increases task difficulty in both tasks.

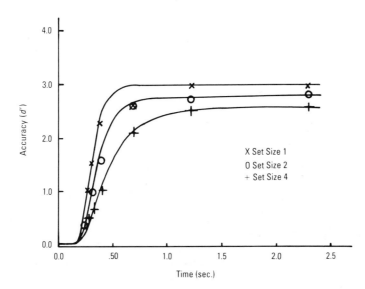

Figure 12. Group time-accuracy functions from each memory-set size and signal-lag condition of Reed (1976), along with curves generated from a negatively accelerating growth function.

Retrieval from Semantic Memory

Speed-accuracy trade-off functions also have been used to clarify the nature of retrieval from semantic memory. Given the superordinate category *bird*, people are faster deciding that *robin* is an instance of this category than an analogous decision for *chicken* (see Chapter 17.) Relative to *chicken*, robin is judged as a more typical instance of *bird* and is a more dominant associate to the category *bird*. The time course of retrieval of an instance and evaluation of the instance as a member of a category can be described by the same negatively accelerating growth function discussed in the previous section. In quantitative terms,

$$d' = \alpha(1 - e^{-\theta(t - \delta)})$$ (2)

where d' is the accuracy of retrieval after t sec, α is the asymptotic level of accuracy, θ is the rate of growth to the asymptote, and δ is the time intercept (or the time at which the function begins to grow above chance performance). In the equation, $(t - \delta)$ is defined as 0 when $t < 0$ and as $(t - \delta)$ when $t > \delta$.

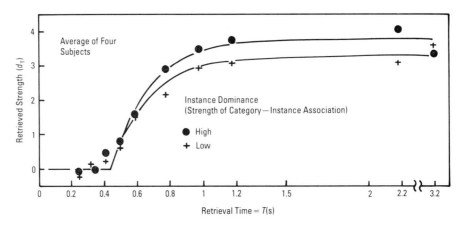

Figure 13. Speed-accuracy trade-off functions for category-example verification for high-versus low-dominance examples. Data are d' and t values for each lag averaged over four subjects. Lines are best-fitting exponentials with parameters derived from averaging the best-fitting values for each subject.

According to this equation describing the time course of retrieval, high-dominance associates may be retrieved at a faster rate θ than low-dominance associates or may have a larger asymptotic strength α relative to low-dominance items. The effects of dominance should be reflected in either different values of α or θ depending on whether the differences are due to rate of retrieval or asymptotic strength, respectively. In a typical experiment using the additive-factor method with high accuracy, RT is the primary dependent variable. Differences in RT cannot provide information about the degree to which the rate of retrieval or the asymptotic association strength is responsible. Either or both of these mechanisms may be responsible for the differences that are observed. To disambiguate these alternatives, Corbett and Wickelgren (1978) replicated a typical category-verification task using a speed-accuracy trade-off method. On each trial, the subject was given a superordinate category name followed two seconds later by a correct or incorrect example of that category. At some time after the onset of the example, a response-signal tone was presented. The subject was instructed to respond "yes" or "no" by pushing one of two keys approximately 1/5 second after the onset of the tone. Ten response-signal lags were used, and any of the ten lags could occur randomly on any trial within an experimental session. Of course, the test example and, therefore, its truth value were also selected randomly from trial to trial to keep the subject uncertain about the correct answer on any trial.

For the data analysis and evaluation of the two possible mechanisms given by Equation 2, it was necessary to derive d' values at each of the response-signal lags for each subject. Before doing so, it was important to verify that the subjects were able to follow instructions and respond within approximately 1/5 second of the response signal. If so, then it is reasonable to plot performance accuracy as a function of the total processing time measured from the onset of the test example and the onset of the response. The accuracy at each level of processing time was a d' measure, computed as in typical yes-no tasks (see Chapter 12). The probability of a "yes" response, given that the example was an instance of the category, is the hit rate, and the probability of a "yes" response, given that the example was not an instance of the category, is the false alarm rate. These d' values were computed for each subject at each level of processing time. In addition, separate d' values were computed for high-, medium-, and low-dominance examples of the category based on the Battig and Montague (1969) and Hunt and Hodge (1971) norms. In this case, only the hit rates can change with the test-example dominance, since examples that are not instances of the designated category cannot be defined with respect to dominance level.

Figure 13 gives the observed and predicted results for the high- and low-dominance examples. As expected, performance improved with increases with delay of the response-signal tone. The improvement is well-described by the function predicted by Equation 2. The results revealed that dominance differences were only reflected in α and not in θ, indicating that high- and low-dominance examples are retrieved and evaluated at the same rate, but that high-dominance items have a larger asymptotic association strength to their superordinate category. This interpretation clarifies the previous results of RTs differences when performance is at a very high accuracy. Given the differences in asymptotic association strength, subjects have to spend a longer time in memory retrieval and evaluation for low-dominance items to perform at the same accuracy as for high-dominance items. This result is consistent with the results of the series of experiments (discussed in Chapters 16 and 17) which show the important role or dominance (prototypicality) in categorization and memory.

10

Psychophysical Methods

Classical Psychophysics

Fechner's Psychophysical Methods
Method of Limits
Method of Adjustment
Method of Constant Stimuli
Choice of Stimulus Levels

Contemporary Psychophysical Methods
Staircase Method
Two-Alternative Forced Choice Task

The Threshold
Variability of the Threshold
Attitude of the Observer

Modifications to Keep the Observer Honest
Motivation of Observer

Normal Distributions and Ogive Curves
Subliminal Perception

*Psychophysics should be understood here as an exact
theory of the functionally dependent relations of body
and soul or more generally, of the material and the
mental, of the physical and the psychological worlds.*
Gustav T. Fechner (1860)

The methods developed by Donders and Sternberg have allowed us to partition the time between stimulus and response into a series of psychological processing stages. We now begin to study in more detail how these processes operate. The initial stage of processing is what we call detection and is very similar to the British empiricists' concept of sensation. The outcome of the detection process provides information about whether or not a stimulus, or stimulus property, occurred. Did you detect the monosodium glutamate (MSG) in the Chinese dinner? Did you hear the siren signaling? Did you see the smog in the foothills? All of these experiences depend upon the outcome of a detection process.

In addition to detecting the presence or absence of some environmental event, we are interested in the magnitude of this experience. Measuring the magnitude of sensation implies that we can discriminate one sensation from another. As we will see, discrimination has been one of the central methods used to determine the relationship between some stimulus variable and some experiential variable. Was there too much salt in the soup? How cold is the water? Is there enough light for comfortable reading? These questions concern the magnitude of sensation and its relation to some stimulus event. Traditionally, the study of the relationship between stimulus and sensation has been called psychophysics. The goal of this research has been to describe and understand the relationship between the physical stimulus signal and the psychological experience it creates.

Given the current advanced state of technology, the experimental psychologist is now able to control and measure the stimulus signal exactly. In contrast, the psychological sensation of the observer remains unobservable and the experimentalist must resort to asking the observer about her or his experience. From this answer, the experimenter must be able to derive a measure of the observer's sensation. The development of experimental and analytical techniques for deriving a measurement of sensation based on the response of the subject has gone hand in hand with theoretical advances, so that today the experimenter is able to measure the unobservable psychological experience of the observer.

CLASSICAL PSYCHOPHYSICS

In the mid-nineteenth century, Gustav T. Fechner, a physicist recovering from a nervous breakdown, took up the study of philosophy. At that time the fashion in metaphysics was materialism, but Fechner was not convinced by it. He rejected the notion that the mind was forever closed to the scientific explorations that had been developed for the study of the physical universe. On the contrary, to him it seemed certain that mind and matter were two aspects of one world. The mind was only a different sort of manifestation of the same universe (completely separated and different in kind, but in constant correspondence with the body). Thus, internal psychological experience should correspond directly to changes in the physical environment. These beliefs correspond to the epiphenomenalists' solution to the mind-body problem (see Chapter 1). It followed that internal experience could be studied through manipulation of the environment. Changes made in a stimulus under carefully controlled experimental conditions should be reflected directly in changes in sensation. Sensation, a mental event, could thus be an object for scientific study on the same level and under the same scientific constraints as physical phenomena.

Fechner's insight supposedly came in a flash before rising from bed on the morning of October 22, 1850 (Rosenzweig, 1987). Fechner inaugurated the study of psychophysics, the goal of which was to determine the laws of correspondence between the outer world and inner experience. For example, the sensory threshold seemed a clear case of the link between mental and physical phenomena. Since the time of the ancient Greeks it had been taken as self-evident that for each individual there is some value on a given stimulus dimension (sound intensity, for example) such that stimuli above this value produce a sensation, whereas stimuli below it do not. A sound that is one unit more intense than the individual's threshold is heard, and a sound that is one unit less intense goes unnoticed. No one had ever subjected the assumption of a sensory threshold to systematic experimental study; the threshold for sound intensity, or indeed for any other stimulus dimension, had never been determined for any individual. Yet here was a clear instance of the direct relationship between mental and physical events, one that could be observed and measured under controlled conditions.

Accordingly, Fechner set about studying individual threshold values. His first problem in this new science was to devise experimental methods for measuring the correspondence between the physical and mental worlds. The three experimental methods that he employed, (1) the method of limits, (2) the method of constant stimuli, and (3) the method of adjustment, were carefully described along with his results in the treatise *Elemente der Psychophysik*, published in 1860. These three methods continued to be used in all psychophysical research as recently as twenty-five or thirty years ago, when their inadequacies began to emerge and better methods were introduced. Indeed, Fechner's methods are still favored by some researchers and are assumed to be valid in some experimental and practical applications. These experimental methods will be discussed in some detail, showing in just what way they sometimes fail to provide the experimenter with a reliable measure of the observer's sensation. Following this discussion of classical psychophysics, a more recent and sophisticated method of psychophysical experiment will be presented. In the following two chapters, we shall discuss and evaluate alternative models of the psychological processes involved in the psychophysical task.

FECHNER'S PSYCHOPHYSICAL METHODS

To determine the threshold value along a given stimulus dimension, Fechner and his successors in classical psychophysics presented subjects with a stimulus and asked them to report whether or not they detected it. The independent variable in this simple experimental design is the intensity of the stimulus; the dependent variable is the subject's response. Fechner's three methods represent three different ways of presenting the stimuli and measuring the responses.

Method of Limits

In the method of limits, subjects are tested by presenting stimuli in an ascending or descending series of intensities. For example, an experimenter can choose a tone of a certain frequency and vary its intensity from trial to trial through a range that is both well above and well below what is known to be audible. On each trial, subjects are asked to say whether or not they heard the tone during a certain interval, and their answers are recorded. Somewhere on the continuum of intensities the subject's response should change. In an ascending series, the tone is presented at a weak enough intensity to assure that the subject will respond "no." Then, the tone is incremented by a small amount on each successive trial until the subject says "yes." In a descending series, the first tone is intense enough so that it is consistently detected and then made slightly less intense on each successive trial until the subject reports "no." Each series is always started at a different intensity so that the subject will not become accustomed to always changing his or her response at a given serial position in the series.

If the classical threshold model of sensation is correct, there will be a stimulus value along the continuum of values where the subject's response changes from "yes" to "no" or from "no" to "yes." This value should, therefore, correspond to the sensory threshold of the subject, the transition point between hearing nothing and hearing something. Fechner's original threshold model predicted that this value would be definite and unconditional.

Table 1 presents the results of a hypothetical experiment employing the method of limits to measure the detectability of a tone as a function of its intensity.

Table 1. Determination of the detectability of a tone as a function of its intensity by the method of limits.

Stimulus Intensity (arbitrary units)	Alternating Descending and Ascending Series									
5					Y					
4			Y		Y				Y	
3	Y		Y		Y		Y		Y	
2	Y		Y		Y		Y		N	
1	N		Y		N		Y			
0		Y	N				N	Y		
-1		N				Y		N		Y
-2		N		Y		N		N		N
-3		N		N		N		N		N
-4		N		N						N
-5		N								N
Threshold	1.5	-.5	.5	-2.5	1.5	-1.5	.5	-.5	2.5	-1.5

Threshold = average transition point

$$= \frac{1.5 - .5 + .5 - 2.5 + 1.5 - 1.5 + .5 - .5 + 2.5 - 1.5}{10}$$

$$= \frac{0}{10} = 0$$

The threshold intensity is taken as the halfway point between the two stimulus intensities at which the response changed from one category to the other. In the first descending series, the threshold intensity would be defined as 1.5 units.

As Fechner and all other experimenters using this method have found, no point exists in these data at which the response consistently changes from one category to the other. Instead, the transition point differs for the ascending and descending series and also varies from trial to trial within a particular type of series. Faced with this variance, Fechner and later experimenters have usually averaged the transition values and defined the threshold as the mean of all of the transition values. Clearly, these results indicate that the classical concept of a threshold will require modification.

Method of Adjustment

In the method of adjustment, the observer in the experiment controls the intensity of the stimulus. The task is to adjust the intensity of a stimulus until it becomes just perceptible. In the popular Békésy audiometer application of this method, the observer is required to maintain a tone of a given frequency at a barely detectable level. The observer sits listening to a tone whose intensity is slowly decreasing. The observer controls a button which increases the intensity of the tone when it is pressed. The task is to maintain the tone at a barely audible level. Thus, the subject presses the button as soon as the tone becomes inaudible and holds it down until it is audible again, at which point the button is released and the tone is allowed to decrease again. The subject is actually engaged in tracking a certain intensity, corresponding to the limits of his or her hearing. The experimenter can calculate the intensity that the subject attempts to maintain and thus arrive at an estimate of the subject's threshold for a tone of a given frequency. By testing the subject at a number of frequencies, it is possible to derive an audibility function relating the threshold intensity across the frequency range of hearing, as shown in Figure 1.

Method of Constant Stimuli

In the method of constant stimuli, the experimenter chooses a population of stimuli that differ in intensity around the limits of audibility. The subject is then given a series of trials in which the stimulus for each trial is chosen randomly from this set. (Although this stimulus set corresponds to the set of stimuli used in the method of limits, the constant stimuli method usually requires more trials than does the method of limits, since the experimenter can terminate the series after a response transition in the method of limits.) The experimenter records the responses to each stimulus and the dependent variable is the proportion of "yes" responses. As shown in Figure 2 the proportion of "yes" responses in a typical experiment rises continuously with increases in intensity. There is no precise threshold level; the subject is more and more likely to say "yes" as the intensity increases, but there is no clearly defined transition between "yes" and "no" responses.

Choice of Stimulus Levels

In these psychophysical methods, the experimenter must attend carefully to the levels of intensities of the independent variable. The series of intensities must be neither too close to one another nor too distant. Consider an experiment using the method of limits, for example. If the intensities of a series of seven stimuli are chosen so that they are very close to one another, no change will occur in the subject's response with changes in intensity. By contrast, if the intensities are chosen so that they are too distant, the change in the subject's response with a change in intensity will be too large and, therefore, will not be informative. In this case, the experimenter cannot interpolate—speculate on the responses for the intervening intensities—between the observed responses. For example, if a subject responds "yes" 5% of the time to one level of stimulus intensity and 90% of the time to the next level, the experimenter is not justified in interpolating between these values. Therefore, in this task, as in most psychological experiments, the experimenter must choose the levels of the independent variable cautiously.

Choosing the appropriate stimulus levels usually requires a series of miniature experiments. For example, in the method of constant stimuli, the experimenter might choose seven levels of intensity, the extremes of which are known to be well above and well below threshold. The

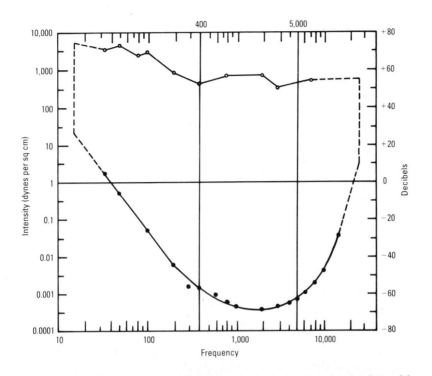

Figure 1. The range of hearing. The upper boundary shows the stimulus intensities which are high enough to produce sensations of pain or pressure in the ear region, a warning that the line of safe intensities is about reached. The lower curve shows the much smaller intensities which arouse a minimum sensation of tone at each frequency. The intensity scale at the left is in absolute units of pressure; that at the right is in relative units of energy, measured up and down from a central value. Data from 10 individuals of normal hearing (after Wegel, 1932; Wever, 1949).

experimenter presents these levels in random order and records the responses to each stimulus. The experimenter could easily find that the subject consistently responded "yes" to some of the stimulus levels and "no" to the other levels. Since the response of the subject changed in an all-or-none manner, does this result support Fechner's idea of a threshold? Not necessarily; the intensity levels may have been too far apart, with the result that some of the stimuli were too far above and too far below the limits of audibility. The experimenter should now choose seven new levels between the two levels at which the subject changed from "yes" to "no" responses in the first experiment. By repeating the experiment and continuing in this manner, the experimenter will eventually find the appropriate levels that allow a valid test of Fechner' all-or-none threshold concept. Before exploring studies of the threshold, we discuss some contemporary psychophysical methods.

CONTEMPORARY PSYCHOPHYSICAL METHODS

The central goal of psychophysical testing is usually to gain information about the psychometric function—that is, the function describing changes in the dependent variable as a function of the independent variable. For example, Fechner's psychophysical methods produce the probability of a detection response as a function of the intensity of the stimulus. One desirable

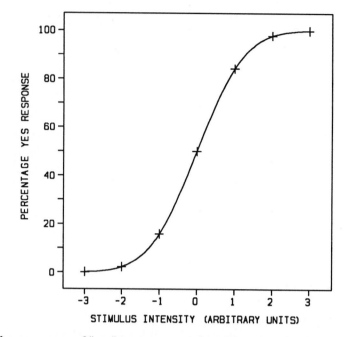

Figure 2. The percentage of "yes" responses as a function of the stimulus intensity of a tonal signal utilizing the method of constant stimuli procedure.

property of a dependent variable is sensitivity—a measure that changes with changes in the independent variable (Chapter 4). In Chapter 4, we noted that ceiling and floor effects are undesirable in psychological testing because they produce results in an uninformative range of performance. When subjects are at chance or at perfect performance, the independent variable can have no influence and its contribution is camouflaged. Evaluating Fechner's psychophysical procedures by this criterion, it is clear that many trials in a psychophysical task are uninformative. Eliminating these trials would enhance the efficiency of the task. Having an efficient task is particularly important in clinical settings in which tests must be performed very quickly.

Adaptive procedures have been developed to increase the efficiency of psychophysical testing (Cornsweet, 1962; Levitt, 1971; Taylor & Creelman, 1967; Watson & Pelli, 1983). The main feature of adaptive methods is that the test condition given on one trial is a function of the subject's performance on previous test trials. Fechner's original methods have a hint of adaptiveness, for example, the method of limits terminates an ascending series when the subject first says "yes, I detect it." Even the method of constant stimuli requires pilot testing to find the stimulus intensities that border on the subject's threshold.

Staircase Method

The most popular adaptive method is some variation on a staircase method. The staircase method is really a variation of the method of adjustment, except that the experimenter changes the intensity of the stimulus in the staircase method. Like the method of limits, the test begins with a stimulus well above threshold. The intensity is decreased on successive trials until the subject first fails to detect the stimulus. At this point, the intensity is increased on successive trials until the subject detects the stimulus. The direction is changed every time the subject's response changes.

After some testing, the intensities required for testing will stabilize within a relatively small range. Continued testing at this plateau for several trials will give a fairly good measure of the threshold. Figure 3 gives the results of a single subject tested with the staircase method.

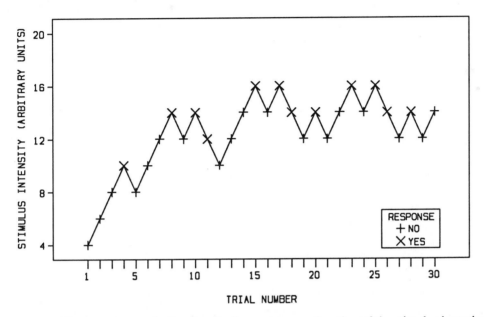

Figure 3. The occurrence of a "yes" or "no" response as a function of the stimulus intensity (in arbitrary units) of a tonal signal utilizing the staircase method.

It can be shown that the most efficient test stimulus is one that is at the subject's threshold (for example, the intensity that the subject detects 75% of the time). Of course, the experimenter does not know this intensity value, if she did, there would be no reason to do the experiment. However, the most probable value can be estimated using the Bayesian estimation procedure described in Chapter 16. The subject's performance on each successive trial gives additional information about the threshold value. With succeeding trials, the estimate becomes more and more reliable until it is clear that additional trials would provide no new information. The testing can then be terminated. This adaptive technique is simple, fast, and efficient and is easy to implement in a computer-controlled testing situation.

In addition to the subject's performance on previous trials, prior knowledge available to the experimenter can also be used (Pelli, 1987). The experimenter has information about previous findings on the the stimulus conditions of interest. The prior knowledge can be combined with the subject's performance to give a more efficient and reliable test than would be possible given just one of these sources of information.

Two-Alternative Forced Choice Task

Most of the limitations of Fechner's methods and the adaptive methods can be overcome by using a two-alternative forced choice task. The subject is given two observation intervals per trial, rather than just one. The signal is presented in only one of the intervals; the interval containing the signal on any trial is selected randomly. The two observation intervals can be marked by some cue, such as a light in an auditory detection task. A subject would see two successive lights separated by about a half a second. The task would be to report, on each trial, whether the auditory stimulus was in the first or in the second interval. In this task, subjects have to indicate one interval or the other; "I don't know" responses are not permitted.

Having two observation intervals guards against the systematic biases that might be present in single-interval tasks. We will see that subjects have biases that can influence the results. One subject might be reluctant to report that a signal was present. Another subject might be eager to report detection of the stimulus. These biases change the estimate of the threshold. Although there are modifications to keep the observer honest in psychophysical tasks, two intervals are considered to be safer. Even so, single-interval tasks are more efficient and, if carried out properly, are equally reliable.

THE THRESHOLD

Fechner had centered his study of the relationship between stimulus and sensation on the sensory-threshold concept. Below the threshold, changes in stimulation do not effect changes in sensation; sensation does not occur at all. That is, when the stimulus is at threshold, no sensation occurs. As stimulus intensity increases over this threshold value by the smallest amount, a noticeable sensation occurs. According to this model, data from an experiment in detection should correspond to the curve shown in Figure 4.

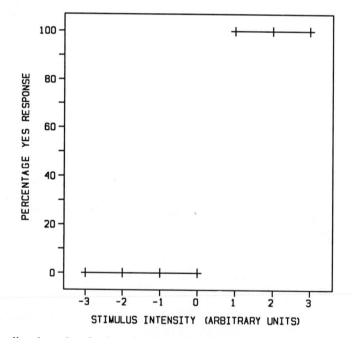

Figure 4. Predicted results of a detection experiment according to a simple threshold model.

As noted earlier, Fechner's actual results looked rather different from those predicted in Figure 4. The results presented in Table 1 and Figure 2 show that subjects are not completely consistent in the psychophysical task; they do not give the same response to the same stimulus trial after trial. However, the results in Figure 2 indicate that the observers have a higher probability of saying "yes" to the more intense than to the less intense stimuli. The graph of these data actually approximates an ogive curve (see box at end of chapter); the increase in the percentage of "yes" responses is less at the high and low values of sound pressure than in the middle.

If Fechner was disappointed to find that the sensation of an observer cannot be exactly predicted by knowledge of the intensity of the stimulus, the results he obtained were nevertheless reassuringly orderly and systematic. The probability that a stimulus exceeded threshold was directly related to the intensity of the stimulus. Thus, although his data did not support the assumption of his original model, that for each sensory system there is an absolute threshold of detection, the threshold could be applied if modified from an all-or-none to a probabilistic concept.

Variability of the Threshold

After looking at the results, Fechner defined the threshold as that point at which the observer detects the stimulus 50% of the time. This definition maintains the concept of a threshold but assumes that the threshold value varies from trial to trial. With this assumption, the results indicated that the threshold value varies in a very specific fashion. The function in Figure 2 shows that the variation is symmetrical; the momentary value of the threshold is just as likely to be above as below the defined 50% value. Figure 5 represents graphically the distribution of threshold values that will predict the results shown in Figure 2.

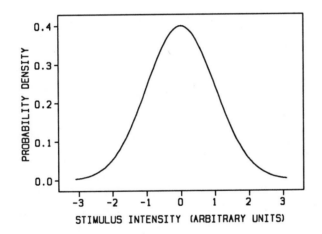

Figure 5. The probability distribution of momentary threshold values that will predict the results shown in Figure 2.

Noise in the sensory system might account for the variability in the threshold values that Fechner observed. Noise is a concept that will be used continuously throughout our psychological study. It is not unlikely that the momentary state of the sensory system would fluctuate rather than remain exactly constant. That is to say, although the subject is in a quiet room in the experiment, we can expect there to be a certain amount of background noise, for example, from the heating and ventilating system or the lights, and so on. This noise would most likely fluctuate according to a normal distribution. That there is internal noise in the sensory system is also likely. Our receptors are continuously firing at a low level even though no stimulus is present. The number of receptors firing could also vary randomly from moment to moment. Therefore, it seems probable that existing external and internal noise in the experimental situation will make itself visible in the results of the experimental situation. We shall see in Chapter 12 that the concept of noise is an important one in the most recent approach to the study of sensation and detection.

Although the threshold proved to be an elusive entity, it is still informative to determine those intensity values that are just noticeable or detectable. In actual practice, the experimenter defines the weakest stimulus that is detected 50% of the time. Some approximate values of the thresholds for the five senses are given in Table 2.

Table 2. Some approximate detection threshold values.

Sense Modality	Detection Threshold
Sight	A candle flame seen at 30 miles on a dark clear night (ca. 10 quanta).
Hearing	The tick of a watch under quiet conditions at twenty feet (ca. 0.0002 dynes/cm^2).
Taste	One teaspoon of sugar in 2 gallons of water
Smell	One drop of perfume diffused into the entire volume of a 3 room apartment
Touch	The wing of a bee falling on your cheek from a distance of 1 cm.

Normal Distributions and Ogive Curves

The normal distribution is a frequently encountered distribution in psychology and other scientific disciplines. If we set a radio dial between stations, we hear static, referred to as white noise. If we took isolated samples of this static, for example, recording 100 msec segments on a tape recorder, and measured the sound pressure level (SPL), we would find that the samples differed. A frequency distribution of the SPL for each sample could then be plotted. If we took a very large number of samples and converted our frequency histogram to a probability distribution, this distribution would approximate a normal curve. The curve would be symmetrical and would have the shape shown in Figure 5. If the probabilities of the normal curve from left to right were cummulated, we would produce the ogive curve shown in Figure 2.

Probability density, plotted on the y axis in Figure 5, can be thought of as analogous to relative frequency of occurrence. The probability density is an index of what proportion of the normal distribution is between two points on the abscissa. Consider the proportion of the distribution between 0 and 1 stimulus intensity. The probability density is equal to about .4 at 0 and about .24 at 1. The average density between 0 and 1 is about .34. (It is more than the arithmetic average since the curve is not linear between the points zero and one.) This means that there is about 34% of the distribution between these two points. In general, it is necessary to weight the difference between the probability density values by the distance covered along the abscissa. If the distance is .5, then the proportion of the distribution between the two points would be one half of the average probability density.

Attitude of the Observer

A far more serious problem posed for Fechner's model is the discovery that the probabilistic threshold could be affected by the attitude of the observer. An experimenter could raise or lower the threshold of the same observer by instructions, for example. If he or she instructed one group of observers that they were to respond positively only when they were absolutely certain that they had detected the tone, a much higher threshold would be obtained than that from a group not so instructed.

Smith and Wilson (1953) carried out an experimental demonstration of the influence of attitude on the measure of the threshold that is obtained. Three groups of subjects were given different instructions in a psychophysical task using the method of constant stimuli. One group was given an conservative attitude by instructing the subjects to report a stimulus only if they were absolutely certain that a stimulus was presented. Another group was instructed to report a stimulus if they had some inclination that a stimulus was presented. Another group was instructed to report a stimulus if they had even the slightest inclination that a stimulus was presented. Figure 6 gives the probability of report of the stimulus as a function of the stimulus intensity for the three different attitudes. Figure 6 shows that Smith and Wilson's (1953) subjects changed their detection responses in an orderly fashion as a function of instructions. Fewest detection responses were made with a conservative attitude and the number of responses increased systematically with a "liberalization" of attitude. Therefore, the threshold measure (the point at which the subject detects the stimulus 50% of the time) changed systematically with changes in attitude of the observer.

Although noise in the sensory system can account for the variability in the threshold that led to Fechner's probabilistic modification, nothing in Fechner's model can account for the effect of

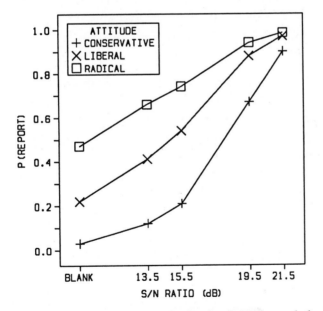

Figure 6. Percentage report as a function of stimulus intensity and the attitude of the observer. The bottom line corresponds to a conservative attitude, the middle line corresponds to a liberal attitude, and the top line corresponds to a radical (very liberal) attitude (results from Smith & Wilson, 1953).

attitude on the subject's response. According to this model, the threshold of detectability is wired into the sensory system. Whether or not a stimulus is detected can be determined only by the limits of that system and by variables that affect the sensory system. How could changes in attitude affect the measured sensitivity of the sensory system?

Because attitude can affect the observed threshold value, we face the problem that this measure can not be a valid index of the sensitivity of the sensory system. Logically, the sensory system probably does operate independently of the observer's attitudes and motivations. But the decision or response of the subject in a psychophysical task does not. What is needed is an index of the attitude of the observer so that the results can be corrected to account for this attitude. With this correction, the experimenter would have an independent measure of the sensitivity of the sensory system under study. The experimental methods that Fechner employed, however, can not provide such an index.

Consider, for instance, the fact that Fechner presented a stimulus on every trial. Some of his stimuli were assumed to be audible and some were not, but even on those trials in which no subject ever detected a stimulus, a stimulus was in fact presented. Very likely most subjects were aware of this or, if not, would sooner or later become aware of this circumstance as the experiment progressed. Perhaps they might realize that there was a higher probability that a stimulus was present than that it was not. Intuitively we would all expect a subtle change in the subject's response pattern given this knowledge. Even without reference to such an influence, however, there is the undeniable possibility that subjects could lie in this task. Knowing that a stimulus was always present, they could say that they detected it, on some trials, when in fact they had not. In fact, Smith and Wilson were able to estimate the attitude of their subjects and to adjust the results on this basis. The threshold values which resulted now supposedly represented measures of sensory performance uncontaminated by attitudes. We now turn to a formal method of accounting for the attitudes and motivations of subjects in psychophysical experiments.

MODIFICATIONS TO KEEP THE OBSERVER HONEST

A partial solution to the problem of the effect of attitude on the observer's performance, therefore, is to include no-signal trials in the experiment in which no stimulus is presented. The subject's task remains the same; he simply reports whether he detected a stimulus. If signal and no-signal trials are randomly presented, the subject has no cue to the presence or absence of the signal other than the sensitivity of his sensory system. A 2 x 2 confusion matrix, shown in Figure 7, is used to analyze performance in this task. The criterion of performance changes from "trials on which the stimulus is detected" in the classical methods to "trials on which a subject's response correctly reflects the real state of the world" in the new psychophysical method with no-signal trials.

There are, therefore, two kinds of correct trials: those in which a signal is present and the subject says "yes," called "hit trials," and those in which a signal is not present and the subject says "no," called "correct rejections." Incorrect trials are those in which a signal is present but the subject says "no"—equivalent to misses—and those in which no stimulus is present but the subject says "yes," called "false alarm trials." The experimenter tabulates the frequency of each of these four possibilities and computes the probability for each cell of the matrix. As the figure shows, only two of the probabilities are independent of each other: the two probabilities that come from different stimulus trials. The standard data analysis of this task employs the proportion of times the observer said "yes" given that a signal was present, $P(yes \mid signal)$, and the proportion of times the

Subliminal Perception

The concept of threshold can be traced back to the ancient Greeks and psychologists have traditionally called it *limen*, derived from the Greek work. Subliminal perception, then, translates as a perceptual experience that is below the threshold for the stimulus involved. To take an example from science fiction, Ballard's (1974) story, *The Subliminal Man*, depicts a society that is entirely dependent on a consumer economy, making it necessary to convince the public of the value of buying. To accomplish this, huge signs are placed along the expressways, displaying advertisements at durations too short to be seen, but somehow long enough to influence the commuter to BUY NOW. This concept of subliminal perception is critically dependent on the threshold concept that a barrier exists which must be exceeded before we become aware of the stimulus presented to the senses. Somehow, stimuli below this level have an effect, but we are unaware of the impact of the message.

One could, therefore, equate subliminal perception with perception without awareness. It cannot really be denied that we seem to continually process information without a conscious awareness. Walking with a friend while simultaneously carrying on an intellectual discussion requires the participants to avoid bumping into trees and walls, and tripping over curbs, holes, and other people. The participants have no trouble doing this although they may not be consciously aware of their decisions. Or to take another example, we continually learn about people through certain interactions without making conscious conclusions about the basis for our information. We find ourselves giving an opinion when, in fact, none had been developed consciously. These examples are meant to illuminate the difficulty of relating perceptual processing to conscious awareness. There are probably many states of awareness; hence, the dichotomous assumption necessary for the subliminal perception concept is not justified.

The concept of a threshold is itself the weakest link in the subliminal perception idea. In the chapters that follow we consider alternatives to Fechner's threshold concept. Chapter 12 presents evidence that persons have any one or more of a range of sensations to a given stimulus. The observer, therefore, always has some information about the stimulus situation, and there is no such thing as a stimulus going unnoticed because it is below threshold. Without a threshold barrier to overcome, subliminal perception is not a meaningful issue. Subliminal advertising need not worry us, either, although, as Freud pointed out, we must realize that some of our values and actions may be based on processing not immediately available to conscious introspection (see Chapter 2, Introspective Method).

observer said "yes" given that no signal was present, $P(yes \mid no\ signal)$. These are the two probabilities we will be concerned with; the results in the confusion matrix can be represented completely by these two alone, since each of the remaining two can be generated from these.

Consider an experimental situation in which the subject says "yes" on most trials, not because he actually hears the stimulus, but for other reasons; for example, he decides that the experimenter will present a stimulus on most trials. His hit rate, the probability that he says "yes" given a signal, will be very high. But so will his false alarm rate, the probability that he says "yes" given no signal. By contrast, if another subject actually heard the stimulus trials and responded "yes" to these trials and "no" to the blank trials, her hit rate would be high but her false alarm rate would be low. We can see that the correct measure of performance in this task must include some analysis of the relationship between these two probabilities. A high hit rate means one thing when the false alarm rate is low, and another when the false alarm rate is high.

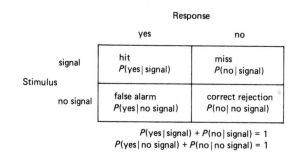

Figure 7. A 2 x 2 confusion matrix used to analyze performance in the yes-no signal detection task.

Motivation of Observer

Consider, for example, an experiment of 100 trials in which subjects are awarded five cents for every correct "yes" response and one cent for every correct "no" response. The signal is presented on one half the trials, and the subjects know this. If these subjects simply disregard the sensory information entirely and say "yes" on every trial, they will get every signal trial correct and receive $2.50. At the same time, every no-signal trial will be a false alarm, and they will not collect for any of these trials. The no-signal trials are worth only one cent, however; if they got all of them correct, they would receive only fifty cents. Obviously, it is better to bias one's response in this situation in favor of "yes," since a correct "yes" is worth more than a correct "no." Indeed, if the subjects attempt to respond simply on the basis of sensory information, then their unbiased performance must be 84% correct in order to earn slightly more than the amount they can earn by saying "yes" on every trial.

Since the experimenter controls the difficulty of the detection experiment, and since it is he or she who will have to pay, it seems the subject's wisest choice might very well be to say "yes" on every trial. The hit rate of a subject who so chooses—the probability of a "yes" response given the presence of a signal—will be 100%. Fechner would wish to conclude that the subject therefore detected the signal on every trial in which it was present. But we know that this is not the case because the false alarm rate is also 100%. Neither of these figures alone—the 100% hit rate nor the 100% false alarm rate—accurately reflects the sensitivity of the subject's sensory system.

Fechner, you will remember, experimented with inducing changes in the subjects' attitude by instructing them on how confident they should be before reporting that a signal was presented. In this way he could raise or lower the subject's probability of saying "yes" quite independently of the difficulty of the detection task. When a high confidence was required, the "probabilistic threshold"—the intensity at which the subject said "yes" half the time—was far greater than when he encouraged the subject to say "yes" with a low confidence. Clearly Fechner's subjects had some decision rule, held more or less consistently throughout the experiment, by which they selected their response given the sensation on a particular trial. In the earlier example, where hits were rewarded over correct "no" responses, the best rule might be to disregard the percept entirely or to respond "yes" to the smallest possible sensation. By changing the payoff, then, the experimenter could induce subjects to change their decision rule affecting the proportion of "yes" responses in a given experiment.

Fechner intended to study the relationship between the intensity of the stimulus and sensation, that is, how the subject's experience was dependent upon the stimulus environment. He assumed that the subject's response was a direct indication of the sensation, but by logical analysis we see that another stage of processing intervenes, the decision process. How an observer responds in a given psychophysical situation is influenced by factors other than the information in the sensation. An adequate method for the study of sensation or the detection process, therefore, requires that the operation of the decision system be understood so that we can account for its effect on the response. Some alternative solutions to the problem are presented in Chapters 11 and 12.

11

Sensory and Decision Processes

Stages between Stimulus and Response

Models of the Sensory System

High Threshold Theory
   Measure of Sensitivity
   ROC Curves
   Empirical Tests

General Two-State Threshold Theory
   Measure of Sensitivity
   ROC Curves
   Empirical Tests

   Probability and Combining Events
   Transition Matrices
   Classical Correction for Guessing
   Parameters

---

*A way is suggested to graft onto this sensory threshold
model a decision process which predicts in some detail
the biasing effects of information feedback, payoffs, and
presentation probabilities.*
R. Duncan Luce (1963)

The last chapter showed how our description of the observer's task in the psychophysical situation must include and account for two stages of information processing between stimulus and response. We must understand both the sensation stage and the decision stage before we can isolate the relationship between the stimulus and response. Fechner's original experiments do not allow for this possibility; his measure of sensitivity can be influenced by both the sensory system and the decision system. The results cannot discriminate between a change in the sensory system and a change in the decision system. We do not know whether a change in the measured threshold following some experimental manipulation is due to a change in the sensation or to a change in the decision rule.

STAGES BETWEEN STIMULUS AND RESPONSE

Figure 1 shows graphically the sequence of operations that is assumed to occur in the psychophysical task. Notice that contact with external events is limited for both stages. The sensory stage's input is the stimulus, which can be objectively observed and measured, but its output is an unobserved sensation, which can be represented by the value X. The value X is made available to the decision stage and is operated on before the subject tells the experimenter his answer. The output of the decision operation determines the response, but its input is the information value X given by the outcome of the sensory operation rather than by the stimulus itself.

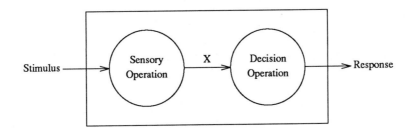

Figure 1. A flow diagram of the two operations that occur between stimulus and response in a detection task.

To understand the implications of this stage model, let us look more closely at the contribution of each stage to performance, and the variables by which each is affected. Each stage operates upon its input and transforms it. The stimulus information first enters the detection stage. This stage can be thought of as the operation of the sensory system. Its output is some value X that reflects two things: the properties (e.g., intensity) of the stimulus and the state (e.g., sensitivity) of the sensory system. This value X is the input to the decision or response-selection stage. This stage asks the question: Given X, which of the alternative responses is most appropriate? A decision is then made according to some decision rule and the response is then executed. The operation of transforming the stimulus into a sensory experience is performed at the sensory stage. For example, in auditory detection, the sensory system includes the hearing apparatus and other physiological structures that transform and carry the stimulus message. Therefore, the output of the sensory system—the sensation value—should be a direct function of the characteristics of the stimulus and the state of the sensory system.

By contrast, the operations of the decision stage are affected by variables that determine the appropriateness of a response, for example, knowledge of the experimental situation, payoffs, attitudes, and motivations. If we could measure the two processes independently, the outcome of each process should be affected only by the variables that influence that process alone. Accordingly, we expect the rule of the decision system to be independent of the intensity of the stimulus signal. Similarly, the sensitivity of the sensory system should be independent of the decision rule employed by the decision system.

In terms of our information-processing model, Fechner wanted to describe the relationship between the stimulus and the value X given by the sensory system. However, we cannot assume that we know this value merely by observing the response of the subject. The intervening decision stage may transform the information made available by the sensory stage in any number of ways. If we can determine the nature of the decision rule, however, we may be able to discount its effect and extrapolate the actual sensation or value X from the response information given by the observer.

MODELS OF THE SENSORY SYSTEM

Given this stage model of performance in the psychophysical task, we can formalize various models of the detection process. Any threshold model implies that the output X from the sensory system can take on only one of two possible values. If the stimulus intensity is greater than the sensory threshold, the sensory system outputs a sensation value s. If the stimulus intensity is below the threshold, the sensory system outputs the value n, since no sensation was experienced. In the all-or-none threshold model, a given stimulus intensity and the output of the sensory system are consistently related. If a stimulus intensity I is greater than the threshold T, the condition probability of s, given the stimulus, is one. This can be written $P(s \mid I > T) = 1$. Analogously, according to the all-or-none mode, $P(s \mid I \leq T) = 0$. That is, the probability of s, given a stimulus whose intensity is at or below threshold, is zero.

Fechner's original conception of psychophysics, then, was that the probability of a "yes" response, given a fixed stimulus, was either zero or one. But as we have seen, this expectation was not confirmed by the results. A stimulus near the "threshold" value will be reported as present on only some proportion of the trials. In order to save the concept of a threshold, it is necessary to propose a probabilistic threshold, which is assumed to be unstable. That is, the probability that a stimulus exceeds the threshold will not always be zero or one. It is assumed that, owing to noise in the sensory system, the threshold itself varies somewhat.

A given stimulus, then, due to noise in the sensory system may fall above threshold on one occasion, below it on another. Fechner's test tone, presented around the threshold value, will sometimes exceed the threshold and sometimes fall below it. The probability of the stimulus exceeding the threshold 80% of the time is .8. As the intensity of the stimulus increases, the probability of its being detected increases also. If we take two stimuli, S_1 and S_2, such that S_1 is more intense than S_2, we can ask: What is the probability that S_1 and S_2 give rise to s, a sensation output from the sensory system? This probability is no longer 1, but varies between 0 and 1. If the sensory system gives value s to S_1 eight out of every ten times it is presented, then the probability that S_1 gives rise to s is .8. We have said that S_2 is less intense than S_1; the probability that S_2 gives rise to s would therefore be less than .8.

The probabilistic concept is that the threshold varies from moment to moment, and that therefore a stimulus of given intensity will exceed it only with some probability. This viewpoint holds the promise of being consistent with Fechner's results; it explains the effect of noise in the system, and, as will be shown below, can be incorporated into a theory with a decision process. This high threshold theory can account for both probabilistic responses to a stimulus and changes in attitude on the part of the observer.

It is necessary to evaluate the high threshold theory and any alternatives in a signal detection task in which both signal and no-signal (noise) trials are presented. As noted previously, Fechner's classical methods cannot derive independent measures of the sensitivity of the sensory system and the decision rule of the decision system. In contrast, the signal detection task with noise trials allows the experimenter to derive indices of the two stages of processing that operate in the task. To do this she must first formalize the operations of these two stages of processing and, then, derive the indices of each process, based on this formal model. It is also necessary to provide evidence that the model adequately describes performance in the experimental task before the indices can be taken as valid measures of the two stages of information processing.

Probability and Combining Events

Probability theory provides a method of combining probabilistic events. The probability of two independent events occurring together is referred to as the conjunction ($\land$) of the events. The likelihood of both events occurring is simply the multiplication of the likelihoods of the independent events. If the likelihood of X is probability p and the likelihood of Y is q, then the likelihood of both events, $(l(X \land Y))$, is

$$l(X \land Y) = p \times q$$

The probability of either of two independent events occurring, is called disjunction ($\lor$). The likelihood of either event X or Y, $l(X \lor Y)$, is given by the addition of the independent events minus their conjunction

$$l(X \lor Y) = p + q - (p \times q)$$

HIGH THRESHOLD THEORY

In the high threshold theory, it is assumed that noise trials never exceed the threshold. Signal trials exceed the threshold with some probability (p), where $0 \leq p \leq 1$ and the value of p is directly related to the intensity of the signal. The decision system is assumed to operate according to the following algorithm: An observer will respond "yes" in the experimental situation with probability 1 when the stimulus exceeds the threshold and probability g when the stimulus does not exceed the threshold. As the observer is induced to say "yes" more often, he will increase the probability (g) of saying "yes" on those trials in which the threshold is not exceeded.

Assuming no-signal or noise (N) trials and signal-plus-noise (SN) trials, the two possible sensory states, s and n, correspond to whether the stimulus presented on that trial exceeded or did not exceed the threshold, respectively. Let p represent the probability that SN exceeds the threshold, that is, produces output s from the sensory system. Therefore, the probability that SN does not exceed the threshold, that is, produces output n from the sensory system, must be $1 - p$. Given that N cannot exceed the threshold, the probability that N produces output s is zero.

Therefore, N produces output n with probability 1. These assumptions of the high threshold theory can be formalized in a two-state transition matrix.

$$\textit{Sensory State}$$

$$\textit{Stimulus} \quad \begin{array}{c} \\ SN \\ N \end{array} \begin{array}{cc} s & n \\ \left[\begin{array}{cc} p & (1-p) \\ 0 & 1 \end{array}\right] \end{array}$$

The inputs in the transition matrix are the two stimulus events and the outputs are the two sensory states that can be produced by the sensory system. The entries in the transition matrix represent the probability of a particular sensory state given a particular stimulus trial. For example, the sensory state s will occur with probability p given stimulus SN. This matrix describes the relationship between the stimulus and the output of the sensory system, the first stage of the two-stage model shown in Figure 1. The experimenter does not have an observable measure of this output in the experimental task. The decision system intervenes between output of the sensory system and the observable response of the subject. Therefore, it is also necessary to describe the relationship between the output of the sensory system and the response of the subject. The high threshold theory assumes that the subject employs a specific decision rule that can be represented by a two-state transition matrix which describes the relationship between the output of the sensory system and the response of the subject.

$$\textit{Response}$$

$$\begin{array}{c} \textit{Sensory} \\ \textit{State} \end{array} \quad \begin{array}{c} s \\ n \end{array} \begin{array}{cc} yes & no \\ \left[\begin{array}{cc} 1 & 0 \\ g & (1-g) \end{array}\right] \end{array}$$

In this case, the transition matrix represents the relationship between the input to the decision system and its output. Since the input to the decision system is the output of the sensory system, the possible inputs are s and n. Given that the subject must make one of two responses on each trial, the outputs are limited to "yes" or "no." The entries in the transition matrix define the decision rule used by the decision system. In the high threshold theory, it is assumed that the observer always says "yes," given that the stimulus exceeded the threshold, producing sensory state s. Accordingly, the transition probability from s to "yes" is 1. The probability that the observer responds "yes" on trials in which the threshold was not exceeded is dependent on the motivations and attitudes of the observer and his or her knowledge of the likelihood of a signal trial. Therefore, the transition probability from n to "yes" is represented by the value g, which can take on values between 0 and 1.

Measure of Sensitivity

Given this model of the sensory and decision systems, how does the experimenter account for the contribution of the decision system and derive a true measure of the sensitivity of the observer in the experimental task? The measure of sensitivity, according to the high threshold theory, is the parameter p, the proportion of times the stimulus exceeded the threshold. The parameter p represents a true measure of sensitivity since it indexes exactly the relationship between the stimulus and the output of the sensory system. According to this two-stage theory, the operation of the sensory system is not influenced by the decision system. Therefore, the value p is uncontaminated by changes in the response bias of the subject; that is, p remains constant with changes in g. The value p can, therefore, be used as a dependent variable that describes the sensitivity of the sensory system, assuming this formal probabilistic threshold theory. Keep in

Transition Matrices

Transition matrices are used in this section because they are convenient forms for presenting theories with two or more intervening stages between stimulus and response. Each matrix represents one stage and has an input and an output. The entries in the matrices represent the probability of the output given (conditional upon) the input. Consider the two matrices:

$$A = input \begin{array}{c} \\ a \\ b \end{array} \overset{\overset{\textit{Output}}{c \quad d}}{\begin{bmatrix} p & (1-p) \\ q & (1-q) \end{bmatrix}} \qquad B = input \begin{array}{c} \\ c \\ d \end{array} \overset{\overset{\textit{Output}}{e \quad f}}{\begin{bmatrix} g & (1-g) \\ h & (1-h) \end{bmatrix}}$$

The matrix A has as input the events a and b and as output the events c and d. The entries represent the probabilities of the output given the input. Since there are only two possible outputs, the entries across the rows must add to 1.

If we were interested in the relationship between the inputs a and b and the outputs e and f, we would want to know the probability of output e given input a and so on. This relationship could also be represented in a 2 x 2 transition matrix with inputs a and b and outputs e and f. The entries in the matrix would be determined by multiplying matrices A and B.

$$AB = \begin{array}{c} \\ a \\ b \end{array} \overset{c \quad d}{\begin{bmatrix} p & (1-p) \\ q & (1-q) \end{bmatrix}} \times \begin{array}{c} \\ c \\ d \end{array} \overset{e \quad f}{\begin{bmatrix} g & (1-g) \\ h & (1-h) \end{bmatrix}}$$

$$= \begin{array}{c} \\ a \\ b \end{array} \overset{e \qquad\qquad\qquad f}{\begin{bmatrix} pg + (1-p)h & p(1-g) + (1-p)(1-h) \\ qg + (1-q)h & q(1-g) + (1-q)(1-h) \end{bmatrix}}$$

Put into words, event e can occur, given the event a, in two different ways: first, if event a produces event c and c produces event e —this occurs with probability pg; second, if event a gives rise to event d and d gives rise to event e —this occurs with probability $(1-p)h$. Therefore, event e can occur given event a with probability $pg +(1-p)h$, and so on for the other entries.

mind, however, that the high threshold theory must be shown to accurately describe performance on this task before this dependent variable can be used.

The high threshold theory can be tested against the empirical data in our psychophysical task. A series of trials is presented, randomly choosing between signal (SN) and no-signal or noise (N) trials. The observer might be tested for a series of 600 trials. The experimenter records the trial type and the response in a 2 x 2 confusion matrix (see Figure 7 in Chapter 10). Performance can be completely described in this task by the two independent probabilities: $P(yes \mid SN)$, the probability that the subject says "yes" given that SN is presented; and $P(yes \mid N)$, the probability that the subject says "yes" given that N is presented. These are our observed hit and false alarm probabilities, respectively.

The predicted values of these two probabilities can be derived from the assumptions of the high threshold theory. According to this theory, a hit—saying "yes" on an SN trial—can occur in one of two independent ways. First, if the signal exceeds the threshold and the subject says "yes"; second, if the signal does not exceed the threshold but the subject says "yes," anyway. This verbal description can be presented in terms of probabilities. The probability that the subject says "yes" on a signal trial is equal to the probability that the signal exceeds threshold and the subject said "yes," plus the probability that the signal did not exceed threshold but the subject said "yes," anyway. Stated mathematically:

$$P(yes \mid SN) = P(s \mid SN)P(yes \mid s) + P(n \mid SN)P(yes \mid n). \tag{1}$$

Substituting the entries of the transition matrices for the respective probabilities, we get

$$P(yes \mid SN) = p\,1 + (1-p)g. \tag{1a}$$

Analogously, we see that

$$P(yes \mid N) = P(s \mid N)P(yes \mid s) + P(n \mid N)P(yes \mid n) \tag{2}$$

$$P(yes \mid N) = 0 \times 1 + 1 \times g = g. \tag{2a}$$

These equations predict the hit and false alarm probabilities in terms of the high threshold theory. Given these equations, it is now possible to determine p, the measure of sensitivity according to high threshold theory. Since $P(yes \mid N) = g$, we can substitute value $P(yes \mid N)$ in place of g in Equation 1a, which gives

$$P(yes \mid SN) = p + [1-p]P(yes \mid N). \tag{3}$$

Multiplying and rearranging terms gives

$$P(yes \mid SN) = p + P(yes \mid N) - p[P(yes \mid N)] \tag{3a}$$

$$P(yes \mid SN) = P(yes \mid N) + p[1 - P(yes \mid N)] \tag{3b}$$

It follows that the value p is given by

$$p = \frac{P(yes \mid SN) - P(yes \mid N)}{1 - P(yes \mid N)} \tag{4}$$

Accordingly, given the hit and the false alarm probabilities, it is possible to derive a measure (p) of the magnitude of the sensation of the observer that is uncontaminated by the operation of the decision system. Before we can employ the measure p as an index of the sensitivity of the sensory system, however, it is necessary to demonstrate that the high threshold theory accurately describes our two stages of processing in the psychophysical task. A critical test of the theory is to hold the signal characteristics constant and to vary the decision bias of the observer. In this case, the experimenter performs a number of small experiments that differ only with respect to the instructions given the subject. In one case, the subject is instructed to be relatively certain that a signal was presented before he says "yes"; in another, he is told to say "yes" if he has the slightest indication that a signal was presented. These instructions, according to high threshold theory, are assumed to influence the value of g, the decision bias of the subject.

ROC Curves

It is possible to represent graphically the results from this hypothetical set of experiments in which the sensitivity of the observer remains constant and the decision rule changes. This representation, called a receiver operating characteristic (ROC) curve, plots the hit rate, $P(yes \mid SN)$, on the ordinate (y axis) as a function of the false alarm rate, $P(yes \mid N)$, on the abscissa (x axis). The ROC curve plots performance at one stimulus level but across a range of decision biases of the subject. According to the high threshold theory, an unbiased observer would

Classical Correction for Guessing

The mathematical formulation of high threshold theory given by Equation 4 is analogous to the classical correction for chance guessing, so often employed in psychological testing. The assumption here is that the observer either knows the answer or guesses randomly from the possible set of response alternatives. The chance factor is taken as $\frac{1}{n}$ where n is the number of possible response alternatives. Therefore, the classical correction for chance guessing is given by the equation

$$p = \frac{P(c) - 1/n}{1 - 1/n} \tag{5}$$

where p is the true proportion correct and $P(c)$ is the observed proportion correct in the experimental task. Equation 5 is identical in form to Equation 4; $P(c)$ is substituted for $P(yes \mid SN)$ and $\frac{1}{n}$ is substituted for $P(yes \mid N)$. We shall see throughout this volume that the assumption of all-or-none knowledge underlying the correction is seldom true. In many situations, people have partial but not complete information about some event such as Lincoln's birthday.

respond "yes" given SN trials with probability p and would never respond "yes" on N trials. Therefore, his performance would be represented by the point $(0, p)$. Hence, the ROC curve must intersect the ordinate at the value p when the abscissa is equal to zero. Now, as the observer becomes biased to respond "yes," both $P(yes \mid SN)$ and $P(yes \mid N)$ will increase accordingly. Equation 6, describing the relationship between $P(yes \mid SN)$ and $P(yes \mid N)$, is in the form of a linear equation: $y = a + bx$.

$$P(yes \mid SN) = p + (1 - p)P(yes \mid N) \tag{6}$$

Equation 6 shows that $P(yes \mid SN)$ is a linear function of $P(yes \mid N)$. Therefore, the ROC curve will be described by a straight line beginning from the point $(0, p)$. The most biased observer will be one that sets the value $g = 1$. In this case, $P(yes \mid N) = 1$ by Equation 2a and $P(yes \mid SN) = 1$ by Equation 6. It follows that the straight line must go through the upper right-hand corner of the ROC curve intersection at the point $(1,1)$. This analysis indicates a critical test of the high threshold theory: an ROC curve drawn through the results of the experiment manipulating the observer's decision rule should be a straight-line function similar to the one shown in Figure 2. In Figure 2, the intersection point on the ordinate would be our estimate of the value p, our index of sensitivity.

Empirical Tests

The prediction of the high threshold theory, that the ROC curve should resemble a straight line, fails empirical tests. Consider an early experiment performed by Smith and Wilson (1953). Using a method of constant stimuli with some blank trials, listeners were presented with auditory signals of various intensities. The signal to noise (S/N) ratio indexes the intensity of the signal in dB. The listeners were also tested with three types of instructions aimed at influencing their attitude and, therefore, their response biases. Subjects were asked to be very conservative, relatively neutral, and very liberal in their tendencies to report that a signal was present. Figure 6 in Chapter 10 gives the results of this experiment. It is possible to plot subsets of the results in terms of ROC curves. A given ROC curve would include the points for blank trials and a given S/N ratio for each of the three instruction conditions.

Figure 3 plots three ROC curves based on the results of Smith and Wilson (1953). Three ROC curves are plotted corresponding to S/N ratios of 13.5, 15.5, and 19.3 dB. The three points for each curve correspond to the three respective instruction conditions. From left to right, the

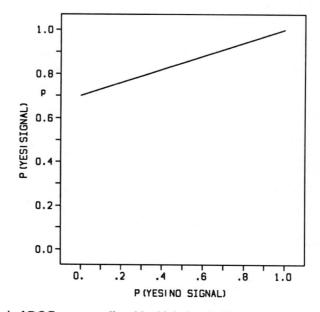

Figure 2. A typical ROC curve predicted by high threshold theory.

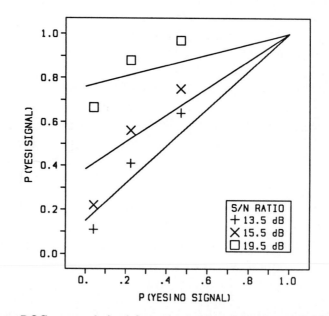

Figure 3. Three ROC curves derived from the results of Smith and Wilson (1953). The three points for each of the three S/N ratios represent from left to right the conservative, neutral, and liberal instructions.

points correspond to conservative, neutral, and liberal instructions, respectively. As can be seen in the figure, the shape of the ROC curves does not conform to the straight-line prediction of high threshold theory. The theory predicts that the points should fall on a straight line drawn through some point on the y axis and the upper right-hand corner intersection, the point (1,1). Figure 3 makes it obvious that the points do not fall close enough to the best fitting straight line. The average positive deviation between the predictions given by the best fitting straight line and the observed points is about 10%. The size of this deviation is considered to be much too large to be due to random variability. In addition, the differences between the predictions of high threshold theory and the observations are systematic. The theory underpredicts the hit rate at low false alarm rates and overpredicts the hit rate at high false alarm rates. The proper conclusion is that points cannot be described by a straight line.

The predictions of high threshold theory do not hold up to experimental test. Rather than dispensing with the concept of a threshold, however, some theorists have removed certain constraints in the high threshold theory. This allows the theory to be more flexible in its predictions even though a threshold is assumed. The first constraint that is removed is the high threshold theory assumption that noise trials cannot exceed the threshold. The alternative possibility we shall consider is that if there is a threshold, a substantial proportion of noise trials also exceeds the threshold. This possibility could result from noise in either the experimental situation or the sensory system. A second constraint of high threshold theory is eliminated by permitting the decision system to respond "no" when a stimulus exceeds threshold. We can formalize a general two-state threshold theory. This theory might provide a description of psychophysical experiments and deserves consideration.

GENERAL TWO-STATE THRESHOLD THEORY

In this formal model of a probabilistic threshold theory (Luce, 1963) the sensory system produces one of two possible values on each trial. These alternative outputs are tied to two stimulus alternatives, but in a probabilistic manner. Let N represent trials on which no signal or noise alone is present; SN represents signal-plus-noise trials. We refer to trials with a signal as signal-plus-noise, since the same noise present on no-signal trials should also be present on signal trials. Let s and n represent the sensory-system outputs, with s standing for the sensation produced when the threshold has been exceeded, and n for the sensation produced when it has not. Let p equal the probability that SN exceeds the threshold and produces output s; let q represent the probability that N exceeds the threshold and produces output s. These assumptions can be represented by the following two-state transition matrix:

$$\textit{Sensory State}$$

$$\textit{Stimulus} \quad \begin{array}{c} \\ SN \\ N \end{array} \begin{array}{cc} s & n \\ \left[\begin{array}{cc} p & (1-p) \\ q & (1-q) \end{array} \right] \end{array}$$

The input to the decision process is the output of the sensory system—the sensation s (stimulus exceeds threshold) or n (no signal is detected). The decision process is controlled by a decision rule. The operation of the decision rule is affected by the subject's knowledge of the likelihood of a signal (SN) trial, the reward contingencies in the experimental situation, and the attitudes and motivation of the observer. The output of the decision process prescribes the observable response of the subject in the experimental situation. The following transition matrix represents these assumptions:

$$\textit{Response}$$

$$\begin{array}{c} \textit{Sensory} \\ \textit{State} \end{array} \quad \begin{array}{c} s \\ n \end{array} \begin{array}{cc} \textit{yes} & \textit{no} \\ \left[\begin{array}{cc} f & (1-f) \\ g & (1-g) \end{array} \right] \end{array}$$

The value f represents the probability that subject responds "yes" given sensory input s; the probability that he responds "no" given sensory input s is thus $1 - f$. Similarly, g represents the probability of a "yes" response given sensory input n, and the probability of the "no" response given this input is $1 - g$. These probabilities, f and g, are determined by the class of variables mentioned above—those that influence the decision bias of the subject. For example, if observers won a nickel every time they correctly identified a signal present and lost 3 cents every time they missed a signal, they should be more likely to indicate "signal" on both SN and N trials. Or, if told that 9 out of 10 trials would be signal trials, observers should say "yes" most of the time, independent of which sensory state was elicited, if they want to maximize the number of correct answers. In this example, simply responding "yes" all the time would allow an observer to be 90% correct.

It should be noted that the high threshold theory merely represents a special case of the general two-state threshold theory. If g is made equal to zero and f is set equal to 1, the general two-state theory reduces to the high threshold theory. We can see that the general two-state theory *is* more general and, therefore, should be able to provide a better description of the results than does the high threshold theory. However, two additional parameters, g and f, must be estimated by the experimenter from the results. As we shall see, this limits the practical or heuristic value of the general two-state theory, since its estimates of sensitivity and decision bias cannot be derived from one set of hit and false alarm probabilities.

Thus, performance is determined by two processes, the sensory system and the decision system. The probability of a particular response, given a particular stimulus, cannot be calculated from either transition matrix alone. The first matrix gives the probability of each sensory state given the stimulus; the second gives the probability of each response given those sensory states. To find our two predicted response probabilities in the experiment—the hit rate (probability of "yes," given signal-plus-noise) and the false alarm rate (probability of "yes," given noise alone)—we must multiply these two matrices.

The predicted hit rate can be obtained as follows: The hit rate refers to the probability of a "yes" response conditional on an SN trial. An SN trial can give rise to one of two sensory states. Therefore, the probability of the "yes" response given stimulus SN is the sum of two probabilities: (1) the probability that stimulus SN elicited sensory state s and the subject said "yes," and (2) the probability that stimulus SN elicited state n and the subject said "yes." Hence the equation for the hit rate is:

$$P(yes \mid SN) = P(s \mid SN)P(yes \mid s) + P(n \mid SN)P(yes \mid n). \tag{7}$$

Substituting our parameter values for these probabilities, this equation can be expressed as:

$$P(yes \mid SN) = pf + (1 + p)g. \tag{7a}$$

The equation for the false alarm rate can be derived in the same manner, giving:

$$P(yes \mid N) = P(s \mid N)P(yes \mid s) + P(n \mid N)P(yes \mid n), \tag{8}$$

which we simplify as

$$P(yes \mid N) = qf + (1 - q)g. \tag{8a}$$

Measure of Sensitivity

In the general two-state threshold model, performance in a psychophysical task can be described by the values of the parameter estimates, since these determine our observed response probabilities. The probability p represents the probability that a signal trial exceeds the threshold. It is influenced, therefore, by variables affecting whether or not a stimulus exceeds threshold—

namely, the energy of the signal and the state of the sensory system. The probability of q is likewise dependent upon the properties of sensory variables—the background noise on no-signal trials, for example. The probabilities f and g, on the other hand, represent the probabilities of a particular response decision, given one or the other sensory state. These probabilities are affected by variables influencing the subject's decision rule. We expect f and g to increase as the observer becomes more biased toward the "yes" response. If we assume that the observer modifies this bias to optimize the decision making, then some simplifying constraints can be applied to the values f and g. With a bias toward correctly identifying SN trials, it would be optimal to give this response every time the sensory output is s, and to deviate from it only on occasions when the sensory output is n. The parameter f in that case is equal to 1. The value g, which is the probability of "yes" given n, would lie between zero and 1, and would increase with increases in the bias toward "yes." Likewise, with a bias toward "no" or correctly identifying no-signal (noise) trials, the value g is optimally set at zero and f lies between zero and 1.

An observer with no bias toward either response is assumed to map the output of the sensory system directly into a response. With this decision rule, a given sensory state would determine a given response with probability 1. Since in this case $f = 1$ and $g = 0$, Equations 7 and 8 give

$$P(yes \mid SN) = p, \text{ and } P(yes \mid N) = q. \tag{9}$$

These two probabilities, equal to p and q, respectively, represent performance of an unbiased observer in the signal detection task. According to the general two-state model, the index of performance of the sensory system is described by the values of p and q. Analogously, the values of f and g describe the decision rule of the subject in the experimental task.

ROC Curves

By varying the decision bias of the observer while holding sensory variables constant, we can also generate a hypothetical ROC curve that is predicted by the general two-state threshold theory. As mentioned above, the point (q, p) will represent performance of an unbiased observer in the psychophysical task. If the observer was biased to respond "no," the parameter g would be zero and f would vary from zero to 1. When both g and f are zero, $P(yes \mid SN)$ and $P(yes \mid N)$ are also zero, as can be seen in Equations 7a and 8a. It can also be shown that increases in f produce increases in $P(yes \mid SN)$ that are linearly related to $P(yes \mid SN)$, so that a straight line between the points—(0,0) and (q, p)—is obtained. Analogously, when f is equal to 1 and g increases from zero to 1, $P(yes \mid SN)$ increases linearly with increases in $P(yes \mid N)$ from the point (q, p) to the point (1,1). Figure 4 presents an ROC curve generated by the general two-state threshold model.

According to the general two-state theory, it is necessary to estimate four parameter values p, q, f, and g to predict the observed values of $P(yes \mid SN)$ and $P(yes \mid N)$. But it is not possible to derive a single set of these parameter values from a simple experiment with only these two observed response probabilities. That is to say, there is a whole family of values for each of the parameters that will predict the results accurately. Having only one point on the ROC curve does not uniquely determine the placement of the two lines predicted by the general two-state theory. At least two points are needed on the ROC curve to uniquely determine the placement of the two lines. (Two points are sufficient since the two lines must intersect at the points 0,0 and 1,1, respectively.) Any experiment, therefore, that is based on the model of the general two-state threshold theory must include measures of performance along at least two points on the potential ROC curve.

Empirical Tests

The results used to test high-threshold theory can also be used to test general two-state threshold theory. Smith and Wilson's (1953) results shown in Figure 3 were *not* well-described by high threshold theory. The hit rate associated with false alarm rates was overestimated by high

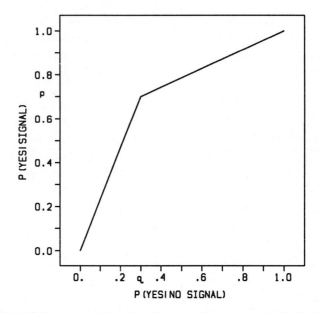

Figure 4. Typical ROC curve predicted by the general two-state threshold theory.

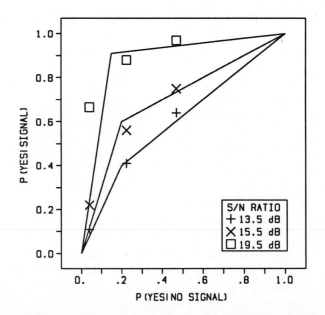

Figure 5. Three ROC curves derived from the results of Smith and Wilson (1953). The three points for each of the three S/N ratios represent from left to right the conservative, neutral, and liberal instructions. The lines give the predictions of the general two-state threshold theory.

threshold theory, and the hit rate associated with high false alarms was underestimated (see Figure 3). Although general two-state threshold theory should do somewhat better simply because it has the advantage of fitting an ROC curve with two connecting straight lines rather than just one, the

---

Parameters

Although the concept of a parameter is not easily articulated, an example of its use usually provides a sufficient explanation. Every quantitative description of some state of affairs has a set of parameters. As an example, Fechner's (1860) psychophysical law was formulated and expressed as

$$S = K \, log_{10} I$$

where S measures the magnitude of the sensation, I the intensity of the stimulus, and K is a constant of proportionality. In this model, K and I serve as parameters. The stimulus intensity I is directly measurable in that Fechner specified exactly how it should be measured. The value of K, on the other hand, can not be directly measured and, therefore, is a free parameter. In other words, Fechner's law can not predict the magnitude of sensation given the stimulus intensity until some K value is assumed. In testing the law, the obvious question is what K value should be assumed. The answer is the K value that optimizes the predictions of the law. Any other value would produce an unfair test of the law since it would always be possible to find a K value that would violate the predicted relationship. More specifically, we want to find the K value that minimizes the differences between the observed and predicted values. For Fechner's law a simple mathematical solution is possible; for more complicated models, iterative computer routines (e.g., Chandler, 1969) are available.

The predictive power of a model is determined by evaluating how much can be predicted relative to how much has to be assumed. To return to Fechner's law, it can not be disproven if it is tested at only one stimulus intensity. Regardless of the sensation S, some value of K exists to predict it exactly. This would not be the case with two or more levels of stimulus intensity. To the extent that a single free parameter K can predict the sensation at a large number of stimulus intensities, we gain confidence in the model. If Fechner's law holds for three or four intensity levels, we are somewhat impressed; if it holds across the complete range of perceptible intensities, we are very impressed. The student should be warned that there is no convenient measure of how well a model describes some set of outcomes relative to the number of free parameters needed to predict those outcomes. Usually, we are satisfied when one model does significantly better than other contenders, even though it has the same number or fewer free parameters.

---

question is whether it does significantly better. Figure 5 plots the predictions of the general two-state threshold theory for Smith and Wilson's (1953) results. General two-state theory improves on the description given by high-threshold theory by providing a somewhat better description of the relationship between the hit and false alarm rates. High threshold theory can be rejected in favor of general two-state threshold theory. Our evaluation of the general two-state threshold theory will be deferred until another conception of the signal-detection problem is presented in the next chapter.

The goal of this chapter has been to account for two stages of processing in a psychophysical task. A theory of psychological performance must describe the operations of each stage, and the experiment must be designed in a way that will allow a measure of performance for each of the processing stages. Although we are currently concerned with psychophysical problems, the approach should be taken as prototypical for all psychological problems. Every experiment in all areas of psychology requires a task with a number of processing stages, and each of these stages must be accounted for before the experimenter learns something about the exact process of interest. For example, learning tasks also require decision operations which must be understood and incorporated into the theoretical and empirical study of learning phenomena. Hence, our interest in the development of theory and experiment in psychophysics is not only for the purpose of studying psychophysical phenomena but also has the aim of establishing methods for making transparent all operations of the human mind.

12

Theory of Signal Detectability

Multistate Theory

Sensory System
Decision System

Dice Game Analogy

Value of Signal
A Priori Probability of Signal
ROC Curve
Measure of Sensitivity
Normal Distribution and z Scores
Measure of Decision Bias
Perceptual Bias versus Response Bias

Analysis of Signal Detection Experiment

Experimental Method
Data Analysis

Multistate versus Two-State Theory

Psychometric Functions
Confidence Ratings
A Priori Probability and Payoffs
Other Evidence

Likelihood Ratio
"Percent Correct" Invalid Index

---

*The methods that permit separating the criterion and
sensitivity measures, and a psychophysical theory that
incorporates the results obtained with these methods,
stem directly from the modern approach taken by
engineers to the general problem of signal detection.*
John A. Swets (1961)

There are only two possible states of the world in the psychophysical task: *SN* (signal present) and *N* (no signal). Accordingly, it is only natural to assume that there are only two possible outputs of the sensory system: *s* (sensation) and *n* (no sensation). That is, the signal either exceeds or does not exceed a threshold. However, according to a multistate theory—the theory of signal detectability (Peterson, Birdsall, & Fox, 1954)—many sensory states are possible.

MULTISTATE THEORY

The central assumption of multistate theory is that no threshold or barrier exists that must be overcome for a sensation. Rather, there is always some background noise in the sensory system, which always produces some positive sensation. The amount of noise fluctuates from moment to moment. Even though there are only two types of trials, many possible outputs of the sensory system can occur. The subject actually knows a different amount on each trial, a difference that can extend over a wide range. For a given stimulus event, the sensory system can output any of a number of sensation values corresponding to the magnitude of the sensation.

Sensory System

The transition matrix corresponding to the sensory system of multistate theory consists of two stimulus states and m sensory states:

$$
\begin{array}{c}
\textit{Sensory State} \\
\textit{Stimulus} \quad
\begin{array}{cc}
 & \begin{array}{cccccc} s_1 & s_2 & s_3 & \cdots & s_i & \cdots & s_m \end{array} \\
\begin{array}{c} SN \\ N \end{array} &
\left[\begin{array}{ccccccc}
p_1 & p_2 & p_3 & \cdots & p_i & \cdots & p_m \\
q_1 & q_2 & q_3 & \cdots & q_i & \cdots & q_m
\end{array} \right]
\end{array}
\end{array}
$$

$$\sum_{i=1}^{m} p_i = 1 \ , \qquad \sum_{i=1}^{m} q_i = 1$$

As can be seen in the transition matrix, a single (*SN*) gives rise to sensory state s_i with probability p_i and a no-signal (*N*) trial gives rise to this state with probability q_i. It is assumed that the sensory states are ordered in magnitude along some dimension, for example, the magnitude of sensation. In this case, the magnitude of sensation given by sensory state s_i is less than that given by sensory state s_{i+1} ($s_i < s_{i+1}$).

If s_1 is the smallest magnitude for a sensory state, then we would expect q_1 to be larger than p_1. In other words, it should be more likely for a no-signal trial to elicit sensory state s_1 than for a signal trial to do so. In contrast, if sensory state s_m is the largest magnitude of sensation, we would expect that $p_m > q_m$. Somewhere along the continuum of sensory states, then, the relative values of

p_i and q_i reverse. Furthermore, we might expect that the differences between p_i and q_i are smaller in the middle range of values of s_i than at the somewhat more extreme values.

Decision System

According to multistate theory the decision system is faced with any of a whole range of sensation values given by the sensory system. The task facing the decision system in the multistate theory might be expected to be more complex than its task in the threshold models. In a two-alternative task, however, the decision system can divide the range of sensory output into two classes: those that are smaller than some sensation value s_i and those that are larger than this sensation value. In multistate theory, these two sets of values are treated differently by the decision system. It is assumed that the decision system responds "no" for sensation values that are below the cutoff sensation value and "yes" for sensation values that are equal to or larger than this cutoff value.

In the formal model, it is assumed that the decision system chooses a cutoff or criterion value C such that if the sensory value s_i from the sensory system is equal to or exceeds this value, a "yes" response is executed; otherwise, the observer says "no." This decision rule can be represented by the following transition matrix:

$$\begin{array}{cc} & \textit{Response} \\ & \begin{array}{cc} \textit{yes} & \textit{no} \end{array} \\ \begin{array}{l} \textit{Sensory} \quad s_i \geq C \\ \textit{State} \quad\;\; s_i < C \end{array} & \begin{bmatrix} 1 & 0 \\ 0 & 1 \end{bmatrix} \end{array}$$

As can be seen in the transition matrix representing the decision system, the decision rule is assumed to be deterministic rather than probabilistic. Given a similar value from the sensory system, the response is determined with probability 1. This decision rule contrasts with the probabilistic decision rule of the general two-state threshold model.

DICE GAME ANALOGY

The exact predictions of multistate theory are not easily derived from the transition matrices of the sensory and decision systems because of the large number of sensory states. The theory, however, can actually be simulated (modeled), using a dice game analogy. For this analogy we imagine an experimenter with three dice, including one stimulus die. The stimulus die is imprinted on three of its sides with the value 3, and on the remaining three sides with the value 0. The other two dice in the game are normal dice with the values 1 through 6 on their six respective sides. The experimenter rolls the three dice and announces the sum of the values on their faces. A subject must decide, on the basis of the total value, whether the value showing on the stimulus die was a 3 or a 0.

The dice in this game are analogous to a trial in a signal detection experiment; the total dice value presented to the subject by the experimenter represents the sensation—the information from the sensory system. The subject in the dice game performs the task of the decision system, judging whether the stimulus die is 3 or 0 on the basis of the total value. Multistate theory assumes that the output of the sensory system is analogous to the total number of points obtained from the three dice. The decision system, given only the combined total, must say "yes" or "no" whether the stimulus die is showing a 3 (signal) or a 0 (no-signal), respectively. In this case we have a range of possible combined totals from 2 (0 + 1 + 1) to 15 (3 + 6 + 6). Given the total value of 2, the decision system can say "no" with absolute confidence. Similarly, it can say "yes" to the value of 15 with 100% accuracy. In fact, the combined values up to 4 could not occur if the signal die is 3;

and the combined values of 13 and over could not occur if the special die is 0. So up to 4, and over 13, the decision system can be 100% correct. For all values in between, the decision system cannot be absolutely certain of its decision.

This particular dice game can be analyzed in terms of a transition matrix of the sensory process. Since the dice totals are in the range of 2 to 15, and these correspond to the possible number of sensory states, we have 14 possible sensory states. Of course, there are only two possible stimulus trials, signal (3) or no signal (0). Therefore, the sensory process can be represented by the following transition matrix.

$$\begin{array}{c} \textit{Sensory State} \\ \begin{array}{cccccccccccccc} 2 & 3 & 4 & 5 & 6 & 7 & 8 & 9 & 10 & 11 & 12 & 13 & 14 & 15 \end{array} \\ \textit{Stimulus} \begin{array}{c} 3 \\ 0 \end{array} \left[\begin{array}{cccccccccccccc} 0 & 0 & 0 & 1 & 2 & 3 & 4 & 5 & 6 & 5 & 4 & 3 & 2 & 1 \\ 1 & 2 & 3 & 4 & 5 & 6 & 5 & 4 & 3 & 2 & 1 & 0 & 0 & 0 \end{array} \right] \end{array}$$

Each entry in the matrix is divided by 36.

For example, if the stimulus die is showing a 3, the probability that the sensory system will output a total value of 10 points is 6/36. In this case, $p_{10} = 6/36 = 1/6 = .17$.

The expected distribution of totals given that the stimulus die contains a 0 or a 3 are shown in Figure 1. The total number of points represents the output of the sensory system, the values given to the decision system. The subject in our dice game arrives at a decision choosing some criterion

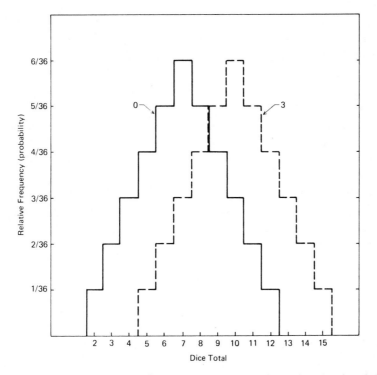

Figure 1. The expected distribution of totals as a function of whether the signal die showed 3 or 0.

value C, such that if the total is equal to or exceeds that value, she says "yes"; otherwise she says "no." As in the two-state models of detection, two processes in the multistate model contribute independently to the final result. The output of the sensory system is affected by the nature of the stimulus and the state of the sensory system. The decision rule is affected by the subject's knowledge of the probability of a signal trial, the payoffs in the experimental situation, and the attitude of the observer.

Value of Signal

In the dice game model of multistate theory, the nature of the stimulus can be changed by changing the stimulus die from 3 to 6. Again, the decision maker is told only the combined value showing on all three dice, and his task is to say "yes" or "no," given this combined value, whether the number showing on the die is 6 or 0. Changing the signal level from 3 to 6 changed the possible outputs of the sensory system, as represented by the total number of points showing on the three dice. The decision maker in this case can be certain that 6 is not present given 2, 3, 4, 5, 6, and 7, and that it is present given 13 through 18. The number of trials on which she can be absolutely certain has increased significantly and her performance should be correspondingly better.

The following transition matrix of the sensory system presents the relationship between the two stimulus trials and the sensory state outputted by the sensory system.

$$\text{Sensory State}$$

		2	3	4	5	6	7	8	9	10	11	12	13	14	15	16	17	18
Stimulus	6	0	0	0	0	0	0	1	2	3	4	5	6	5	4	3	2	1
	0	1	2	3	4	5	6	5	4	3	2	1	0	0	0	0	0	0

Each entry in the matrix is divided by 36.

Figure 2 presents the two distributions of total values from the sensory system. It should be noted that the distance between the two distributions corresponding to the 6 and 0 on the signal die is twice the distance between the 3 and 0 distributions shown in Figure 1. The absolute values on the stimulus die—the stimulus variables in the experimental situation—determine the values that the sensory system transmits to the decision system; the stimulus die values do not influence the operations of the decision system since the same decision rule or algorithm can be maintained.

It should be noted that the decision system must have the information about the range of values transmitted by the sensory system in order to apply its decision rule reliably. If the subjects did not know the range of values from SN and N trials, they would not know where to set the criterion and could not respond appropriately. In our dice game, the subjects are told the range of values in advance, so that they have the necessary information. In a real signal detection experiment, the subjects practice the task before the experiment so that they can learn the range of sensation values in the experiment. After each trial, feedback must be given about which stimulus event was presented, allowing the subject to learn the range of sensation values resulting from SN and N trials.

A Priori Probability of Signal

Other variables in the task affect the operations of the decision system. To illustrate, take up our dice game again with a 3 representing signal trials and a 0 representing no-signal trails. However, instead of a 3 appearing on three of the six sides, it now appears on five. This manipulation of the a priori probability changes the prior likelihood of a signal trial from 50% to $5/6 = 83\%$, but does not change the possible total values presented to the decision system. The a

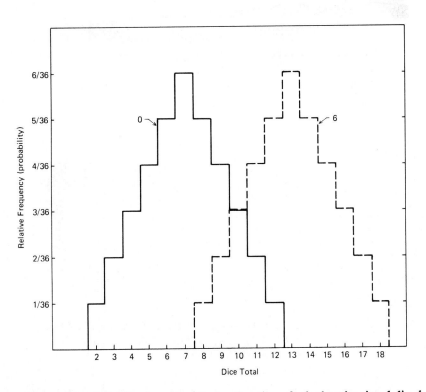

Figure 2. The expected distribution of totals as a function of whether the signal die showed 6 or 0.

priori probability refers to the likelihood that the stimulus die will contain a 3 before the dice total is known. On a given roll of the dice, the sensory system possesses no more or no less knowledge about the stimulus than it did when the 3 occurred on only three sides. The values transmitted by the sensory system, or the range of totals given by the three dice, does not change with changes in the a priori probability. All that has changed is the likelihood or the probability that any of the ambiguous values given by the sensory system represents the presence of a 3 on the stimulus die. This difference in a priori probability should accordingly change the rule of the decision system. The decision system should be biased to say "yes, a 3 was presented," much more often than in the previous example where 0 and 3 trials were equally likely.

To determine the relative frequency of possible totals with an a priori probability of a signal trial (3) being 5/6, we can simply weight the frequencies given when the a priori probability was 1/2. For each of the possible totals from the two normal dice, a signal (3) will be added to this total on 5/6ths of the trials, and no signal (0) will be added to the total on 1/6th of the trials. For example, given the total value 5 from the three dice, the relative frequency of a signal (3) will be five times the relative frequency of no signal. With equally likely signal and no-signal trials, the total 5 arises from 3 one out of five times, and from 0 four out of five times. If the a priori probability is 5/6ths, the total 5 will result from a signal trial five times as often relative to a no-signal trial. Therefore, multiplying the relative frequencies 1 and 4 for the total 5 by 5 and 1, respectively, gives the relative frequencies of 5 and 4 when the a priori probability is 5/6. The following transition matrix of the sensory system presents the relationship between the two stimulus trials and the sensory state.

Likelihood Ratio

In the mathematical formulation of the theory of signal detectability, the decision rule of the subject is assumed to be analogous to one in statistical decision theory. It is assumed that the decision system assigns conditional probabilities to the output of the sensory system. The decision system computes the conditional probability that the output s_i from the sensory system arose from an SN trial $P(s_i \mid SN)$, and the probability that it arose from an N trial $P(s_i \mid N)$. The likelihood ratio L is a ratio of these two probabilities:

$$L = \frac{P(s_i \mid SN)}{P(s_i \mid N)}$$

The decision system has a criterion value, so that if the likelihood ratio exceeds this value it responds "yes"; otherwise it responds "no." The unbiased observer would have a criterion value set at 1, the point at which it is equally likely that s_i came from an SN or an N trial.

The likelihood ratio can also be defined to take into account the a priori probability of an SN trial. In this case, the conditional probabilities are weighted by the a priori likelihood of that kind of trial. In this case,

$$L = \frac{P(s_i \mid SN)P(SN)}{P(s_i \mid N)P(N)}$$

This equation shows that L becomes large to the extent that $P(SN)$ is greater than $P(N)$. For a fixed criterion, more observations of L will exceed the criterion to the extent that $P(SN)$ is greater than $P(N)$. Accordingly, the probability of a "yes" response will increase when SN trials become more frequent. Observers are not completely optimal decision makers, however, since they usually respond "yes" much less frequently than they should when the likelihood of an SN trial is large. This result is consistent with people's failure to give sufficient weight to a priori knowledge in decision making, while giving too much emphasis to immediate or direct observations (see Chapter 15).

Sensory State

		2	3	4	5	6	7	8	9	10	11	12	13	14	15
Stimulus	3	0	0	0	5	10	15	20	25	30	25	20	15	10	1
	0	1	2	3	4	5	6	5	4	3	2	1	0	0	0

The entries in the first and second rows are divided by 180 and 36, respectively.

The transition matrix is identical to the matrix generated when the a priori probability of a 3 is 3/6. The number and the values of the sensory states are the same and the transition probabilities are identical in the two cases. Therefore, changes in the a priori probability would not change the expected distribution of totals shown in Figure 1. The sensory system only makes contact with the stimulus event on a trial. Therefore, manipulations in the a priori probability cannot affect the operations and hence the outputs of the sensory system. Accordingly, our measure of the sensitivity of the sensory system should not change with changes in a priori probability. Since the transition matrix for the sensory system does not change with changes in a priori probability, neither does the distribution of sensory states as plotted in Figure 1. Changes in a priori probability do not affect the relative frequency of occurrence of each total given the value 3 showing on the signal die; although it increases the number of signal (3) trials relative to no-signal (0) trials in the experiment, it does not affect the relative frequency of occurrence of each total given the value showing on the stimulus die. Therefore, a change in a priori probability does not affect the shape of the distributions or the distance between the means of the two distributions. This manipulation contrasts with the manipulation of signal intensity (6 or 3) which directly affects the distance between the two means of the distributions.

'Percent Correct' Invalid Index

Our measure of the sensitivity of the sensory system should not change with changes in a priori probability, nor with the placement of the criterion, since these changes do not affect the operations of the sensory system. We can see that the percentage of correct responses in the task cannot be used as a measure of the sensitivity of the sensory system. Assume that an observer knows that the a priori probability of a 3 is 3/6 in one case and 5/6 in another. If she simply responded on the basis of this information, she could achieve a performance of only 50% correct in the former case but could maintain a performance of 83% correct in the latter. She would simply respond "yes" on every trial regardless of the total value. Then if "percent correct" were used as a measure of the sensory system, we would conclude that the system was more sensitive with increases in a priori probability—an incorrect conclusion since the actual operations of the sensory system did not change.

Note that to use an optimal decision rule, the decision system must have access to the a priori probabilities in the experimental situation. The experimenter might either tell the observer the a priori probabilities or give the observer feedback from trial to trial so that he could discover this fact for himself. As noted, the decision rule can also be affected by the payoff in the situation. If the observer is rewarded for saying "yes" correctly by a greater increment than he is punished for saying "yes" incorrectly, it will pay off for him to say "yes" more often even when the probability is relatively low that "yes" is the correct response.

ROC Curve

According to multistate theory, the a priori probability of a signal trial (3) affects the decision system's choice of a criterion value. We can actually determine the receiver-operating characteristic predicted by multistate theory with changes in the criterion value. Figure 3 presents the $P(yes \mid 0)$ and $P(yes \mid 3)$ at each possible criterion value on the dice game task when the signal die contains a 3 for the signal trial and a 0 for a no-signal or blank trial. If the observer responds "no" all the time, $P(yes \mid 3) = 0$ and $P(yes \mid 0) = 0$. As the observer becomes more willing to respond "3", the $P(yes \mid 3)$ increases but so does $P(yes \mid 0)$ as demonstrated in Figure 3.

Measure of Sensitivity

Now it is necessary to provide a measure of the sensitivity of the sensory system that is invariant with changes in the criterion value. This measure is given by the distance between the means of the two distributions. How can this distance be calculated in a signal detection task? In this task, we are given the results represented by a confusion matrix. From our hit and false alarm probabilities, we can determine the criterion value of the subject with respect to the means of each of the two distributions and, therefore, compute the distance between the means of the distribution. Assume that in our experiment an observer responded $P(yes \mid signal) = .9$ and $P(yes \mid no\ signal) = .2$. The distribution for the signal trial, therefore, would be drawn so that 90% of it lies to the right of the criterion value. Similarly, the distribution for the no-signal trial would be drawn so that 20% of it lies to the right of the criterion value.

Normal Distribution and z Scores

Since the experimenter does not know the number or values of the sensory states in an actual experiment, multistate theory assumes that the sensory states are distributed normally in a bell-

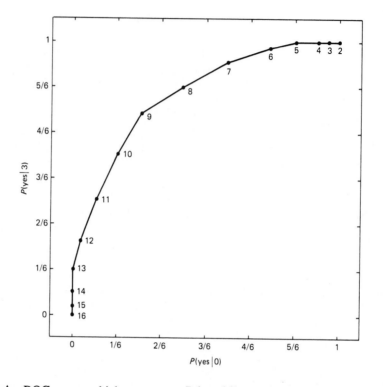

Figure 3. An ROC curve which represents $P\,(yes\,|\,3)$ and $P\,(yes\,|\,0)$ for each possible criterion value in the dice game task. The subject responds "yes"—a 3 was presented—if the total is larger than or equal to the criterion value. Otherwise, he responds "no."

shaped curve with variance equal to 1. This distribution is called the normal distribution and is shown in Figure 4. The normal distribution is similar to the distributions generated by the dice game but is drawn as a smooth curve since it can take on all positive and negative values, not just the integer values given by the dice game. The normal curve has a strict relationship between the area represented under the curve and the distance along the horizontal axis. Since the curve is symmetrical, 50% of the area lies to the right of the mean. The distance from the mean is given by z scores. Since we know the shape and the variance of the curve, we can compute a z score for each percentage of the area to the right or the left of the mean. Similarly, we can derive the percentage of the area between a point along the horizontal axis and the mean. Table 1 gives the distance between the mean and the criterion as a function of the percentage of the distribution between these points.

Accordingly, representing the distributions of sensory states by normal curves, we can compute the distance between the means of the two distributions. We use this distance called d prime and written as d', as an index of performance of the sensory system, since it remains fixed with changes in the criterion value. To the extent that the two distributions of sensory states differ from each other, d' will be large. To the extent that the two distributions are similar, d' will be small. In our hypothetical experiment we said that $P\,(yes\,|\,signal) = .9$ and $P\,(yes\,|\,no\ signal) = .2$. The hit rate of .9 means that the criterion was set so that 90% of the distribution of signal trials was to the right of the criterion (see Figure 5).

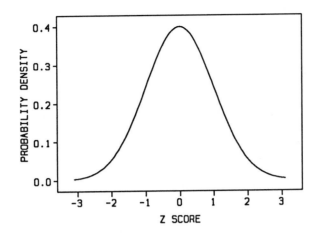

Figure 4. The normal distribution with a mean of 0 and a variance of 1.

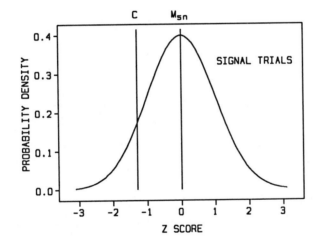

Figure 5. A graphic representation of the distribution for signal trials with the criterion C drawn so that 90% of the distribution is to the right of the criterion.

Figure 6 is a graphic representation of the normal curve of the no-signal distribution, with 20% of the curve to the right of the criterion C. The relationship between the two curves is given in Figure 7. Accordingly, the distance between the means is given by the sum of the absolute distance of A and B. To determine the distance B between the criterion point and the mean of the signal distribution, we want the value of the z score of a point that lies 90% to the left of the distribution or 40% to the left of the mean of the distribution, since the curve is symmetrical around the mean. Table 1 shows that the z score which represents this distance along the abscissa is -1.282. (The value is minus since the criterion lies to the left of the mean.) Analogously, to find the distance A of the same criterion point from the mean of the no-signal distribution, we want the distance between the mean of this distribution and a point that lies 30% to the right of the mean. This distance as shown in Table 1 corresponds to a z score of .842. Given that the criterion lies between the means of the two distributions, the distance between the means of the two distributions is given by the sum of the positive values of A and B. Therefore, the distance d' is given by the

Table 1. The z score distance and the ordinate values corresponding to the percentage of the distribution between the mean and the criterion value C. (If the criterion lies to the left of the mean, the z scores are negative.)

Percentage	Ordinate	z score	Percentage	Ordinate	z score
0	.399	.000	26	.311	.707
1	.399	.025	27	.304	.739
2	.398	.050	28	.296	.772
3	.398	.075	29	.288	.806
4	.397	.100	30	.280	.842
5	.396	.125	31	.271	.878
6	.394	.150	32	.262	.915
7	.393	.176	33	.253	.954
8	.391	.202	34	.243	.995
9	.389	.223	35	.233	1.037
10	.386	.253	36	.223	1.080
11	.384	.280	37	.212	1.126
12	.381	.306	38	.200	1.175
13	.378	.332	39	.188	1.226
14	.374	.358	40	.178	1.282
15	.370	.385	41	.163	1.340
16	.368	.403	42	.149	1.405
17	.362	.440	43	.134	1.476
18	.358	.468	44	.111	1.555
19	.353	.496	45	.103	1.645
20	.348	.524	46	.086	1.751
21	.342	.553	47	.068	1.882
22	.336	.584	48	.048	2.054
23	.331	.610	49	.027	2.327
24	.324	.643	49.5	.014	2.575
25	.318	.675	49.9	.003	3.085

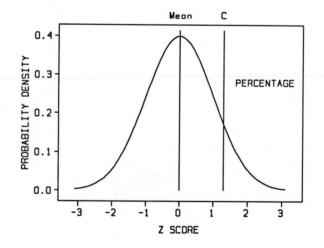

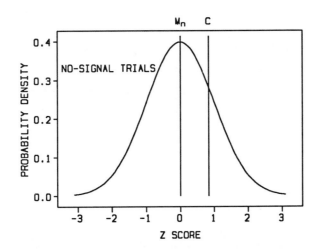

Figure 6. A graphic representation of the distribution for no-signal trials with the criterion C drawn so that 20% of the distribution is to the right of the criterion.

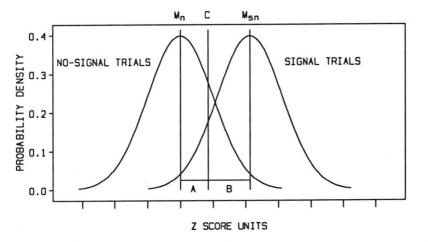

Figure 7. A graphic representation of the juxtaposition of the distributions in Figures 5 and 6.

sum of 1.282 and .842, which is 2.124. Our measure of performance in this hypothetical experiment (2.124) provides an index of the sensitivity of the sensory system that is uncontaminated by the exact placement of the criterion value. Given a fixed distance between the means, the calculation of this distance using z scores obtains the same distance value regardless of the placement of the criterion.

Measure of Decision Bias

The distance between the means provides a measure of sensitivity of the sensory system. Sometimes it is also informative to have a measure of the bias in the decision system. The most straightforward measure of this bias is simply the overall or marginal probability of a "yes" response. This probability lies between 0 and 1 and reflects the willingness of the observer to say "yes." To calculate the marginal probability of a "yes" response, we take the average of the conditional probabilities of a "yes" response given signal and no-signal trials, weighted by the probability of occurrence of the signal and no-signal trials.

$$P(yes)=P(SN)P(yes \mid SN)=P(N)P(yes \mid N) \tag{1}$$

This measure of $P(yes)$, then, indexes the willingness of the observer to say "yes," independent of sensitivity of the sensory system.

In our example illustrated in Figures 4 through 7, the probability of a signal trial is assumed to be .5. The hit and false alarm rates were .9 and .2, respectively. In this case, the decision bias would be equal to

$$P(yes) = .5 \times .9 + .5 \times .2 = .45 + .10 = .55$$

which indicates that the observer was biased to say "yes". A value of .5 for $P(yes)$ would index an observer that is unbiased, and values greater than or less than .5 would index the degree of bias of an observer.

Another measure of decision bias is to give the criterion value used by the subject. To compute the value, it is necessary to introduce a measure of the height of the criterion with respect to the signal and no-signal distributions. The height is measured by the probability density given for the y ordinate, as shown in Table 1. The criterion value is expressed in terms of beta (β), defined as

$$\beta = \frac{y(SN)}{Y(N)}$$

which is the probability density value of the criterion given for the signal distribution divided by the probability density value of the no-signal distribution. Returning to our example in Figure 7 with hit and false alarm rates of .9 and .2, $y(SN)$ is equal to .178 and $y(N)$ is equal to .280. Therefore:

$$\beta = \frac{.178}{.280} = .636$$

A β value of .5 indicates that the observer is biased to say "yes". A β of 1 represents an unbiased observer, and a bias to say no is given by a β value greater than one. The degree of bias is indexed by the degree to which β is larger or smaller than 1.

Perceptual Bias versus Response Bias

Although the distinction between sensitivity and bias is an important one, it is also necessary to distinguish between two types of bias. We have treated bias as a decision bias that must be controlled in psychophysical experiments. However, decision biases are important components of psychological judgment (see Chapter 18) and play an important role in research and theory. In addition, psychologists have recently acknowledged that a bias effect in a perception experiment is *not* artifactual or uninteresting. In fact, a bias effect can be as perceptual as a sensitivity effect. The privileged status of d' relative to β in psychophysical tasks is a historical accident. Communication engineers were interested in the transmission of information and not in perceptual experience. Thus, psychophysicists asked how well subjects could discriminate an auditory signal from noise without regard for what their experience might be. There are few acknowledgments of perceptual experience in the signal detection literature. As an exception, Tanner and Swets (1954) described the phenomenal impressions of their observers in a visual detection task. Increasing the a priori probability of a signal trial increased both the hit rate and the false alarm rate. The observers, in fact, reported that their responses were based on phenomenal seeing (and not a conscious guessing strategy). Given the limitations in introspective reports, however, the result cannot be taken as strong evidence for perceptual bias as opposed to just a post-perceptual decision bias.

Perhaps because of the difficulty of distinguishing between the two types of bias, signal detection theory blurs decision bias and perceptual bias. A particular judgment might be made more frequently because of a decision bias. If I am rewarded for saying signal given a signal and not taxed for saying signal given noise, I will say signal more often independently of my actual percept. However, it is logically possible that rewards or some other variable might actually increase the likelihood of a signal percept on both signal and noise trials. If I respond in concordance with my percept, I will say signal more often on both signal and noise trials. This perceptual effect will also be reflected in bias and not in sensitivity.

If a signal detection analysis is performed on an optical illusion, such as the Müller-Lyer figure (p. 278), the illusion would be primarily reflected in bias and not sensitivity. That is, we would see the Müller-Lyer figure with outgoing wings as longer than a control figure but our ability to discriminate line length would remain relatively intact. We should be able to discriminate two different line lengths from each other just as well in an illusory context as in a control condition. Perception would be illusory because we would see both lines as longer in the illusory context, but no loss of sensitivity would be present. Our discrimination of the two line lengths would not be compromised because we would still respond differentially to the two stimuli. Although signal detection theory distinguishes between sensitivity and bias, it cannot distinguish between the two types of bias. Luckily, there are empirical and theoretical techniques to address which type of bias is present (Cornine & Clifton, 1987; Ratcliff, McKoon, & Verwoerd, 1988), but an analysis of them is outside the scope of this chapter.

ANALYSIS OF SIGNAL DETECTION EXPERIMENT

The multistate theory provides a method of data analysis in order to provide a measure of the sensitivity of the sensory system that is independent of changes in the decision system. This method of analysis allows the experimenter to compare sensitivity values between experimental conditions even though the variables affecting the decision rule differ in the different situations. This method achieves Fechner's original goal: to relate the sensation of the observer to the stimulus situation although the response of the subject does not appear to be directly related to the stimulus situation.

Let us go over the basic design of the signal detection experiment in detail. First, an observation period is defined for the observer. For example, in an auditory detection task we can define the observation interval by turning on a light; during the light presentation the subject attends and then reports to the experimenter whether a stimulus tone was or was not presented. To preserve the subject's honesty, we present the tone on a random 50% of the trials.

Experimental Method

This experimental method and data analysis can be used in any two-stimulus-two-choice experimental task. For example, instead of the auditory alternatives of tone and no-tone, the subject could be asked to distinguish between two visual alternatives, the letters D and O presented briefly in a tachistoscope. On each trial, one of these two letters is chosen randomly and presented; the subject's task is to report which was presented. Here, instead of the magnitude of the sensation, the sensory system has a measure of the amount of O-ness and D-ness that was present on a given trial. We can think of the information available to the sensory system as falling on a single D-O dimension. A large amount of O-ness implies a small amount of D-ness and indicates that an O was more likely presented. Similarly, a large amount of D-ness implies a small amount of O-ness and indicates that a D was more likely presented. Given the complementary relationship between O-ness and D-ness, it is sufficient for us to specify the information available to the sensory system in terms of O-ness. Therefore, the amount of O-ness produced by either letter must fluctuate from trial to trial and, on occasion, the letter D will actually produce more O-ness than will the letter O on another occasion. Thus, just as in the dice game analogy, the two stimulus states of signal-plus-noise and noise alone could result in a range of possible combined total values, in this experiment the two stimulus alternatives of O and D can result in a number of different values of O-ness.

We think of O-ness, then, as a continuum on which the letter O will, on the average, produce more O-ness than the letter D. If we assume that the noise effect is randomly distributed in a bell-shaped curve, then the amount of O-ness perceived by the subject varies from trial to trial. Drawing the distribution of O-ness perceived by the subject for O trials and for D trials, Figure 8 shows that the two curves can

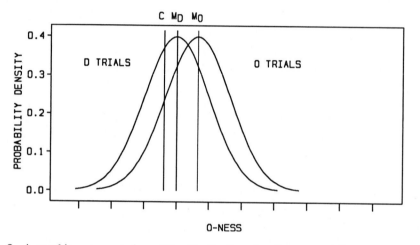

Figure 8. A graphic representation of the distributions for O-ness and D-ness.

overlap. This overlap represents the range of uncertainty in the information passed on to the decision system by the sensory system. Within this range the observer cannot be 100% correct but must establish a decision rule, or criterion, that translates "maybe" into "yes" or "no" with an optimal degree of accuracy. It is assumed that the observer establishes some criterion along the O-ness scale. Whenever the output of the sensory system exceeds this criterion value, the observer says O; otherwise he says D.

Data Analysis

After running repeated series of random trials, the experimenter sets up a confusion matrix with two stimuli and two responses. The stimulus can be O or D, and the observer can say O or D. The two independent probabilities are the probability that the observer said O, given that the stimulus presented was O (the hit rate), and the probability that he said O, given that the stimulus presented was D (the false alarm rate). We can count up these two outcomes over the course of the experiment and compute their probabilities. To compute $P(O|O)$, we first count up all the

Response

$$\begin{array}{cc} & \begin{array}{cc} O & D \end{array} \\ \textit{Stimulus} \begin{array}{c} O \\ D \end{array} & \left[\begin{array}{cc} F_1 & F_3 \\ F_2 & F_4 \end{array} \right] \end{array}$$

trials in which an O was presented (i.e., the sum of F_1 and F_2). Then the proportion of trials that the subject said O, given O, is the number of these trials (F_1) divided by F_1 plus F_2. Similarly, the proportion of D responses to the D stimulus is equal to F_4 divided by F_3 plus F_4. Our second independent probability of interest, $P(O|D)$, is equal to F_3 divided by F_3 plus F_4, or 1 minus $P(D|D)$.

If in a particular experiment the observer responded "O" 85% of the time when presented with an O, the probability of O given O is .85. If he responded "D" 35% of the time when presented with a D, the probability of D given D is .35 and the probability of saying "O" given D is .65. These independent response probabilities allow us to draw in the distributions for O and D on the O-ness axis (see Figure 8). The line drawn perpendicular to the axis represents the criterion (C). The criterion is the point along the O-ness continuum where the subject ceased to respond "D" and began to respond "O". Therefore, the normal distribution for the stimulus alternative D would be drawn so that 35% of it lies to the left of this line, representing the .35 probability of D given D. The distribution of O-ness for the stimulus letter O is drawn so that 85% of it lies to the right of the criterion line, representing the probability of responding with O given O.

Our goal is to find some sensitivity parameter for a dependent variable that is changed by variables affecting the sensory process, but is not changed by variables affecting the decision process. These conditions are fulfilled by employing the distance between the means of the two distributions. This distance is measured using the z scores of the normal distribution as shown in Figure 4. Imagine a subject in the same experiment who for some reason is especially partial to responding "O". The criterion will move to the left so that more of the O and D distributions will lie on the right of the line. That is, both the hit rate and the false alarm rate will increase. The distributions of O-ness on D trials and of O-ness on O trials will remain at the same distance from each other. The sensory system of this subject is able to discriminate O from D as well as she could with a different criterion, and the difference between the means of the two distributions expresses only this ability to discriminate.

On the other hand, imagine a different subject whose results show the same hit rate but a higher false alarm rate. The distribution of O-ness and O trials will be the same with respect to the criterion value; but a larger proportion of the distribution of O-ness on D trials must now lie to the right of the criterion, and the two distributions will therefore be closer together. This subject is less able to discriminate between the two letters than our first subject. If a third subject's false alarm rate is lower than that of the first subject, the D distribution is farther to the left of the criterion, and therefore the distance between the two means is greater. This subject is better able to discriminate the two letters than either of the other two subjects.

The distance between the two means therefore provides us with an index of the sensitivity of the subject; it takes into account both the hit rate and the false alarm rate and is completely independent of the decision rule the subject may use. This distance is called d' and can be computed by the following equation:

$$d' = z[P(yes|N)] - z[P(yes|SN)] \tag{2}$$

where $z[P(yes|N)]$ is the z score for the false alarm rate, $P(yes|N)$, and $z[P(yes|SN)]$ is the z score for the hit rate, $P(yes|SN)$.

In this equation, the sensitivity measure d' is obtained by subtracting the z score transformation of the hit rate from the z score transformation of the false alarm rate. In our sample experiment of discriminating D and O, the hit rate $P(O|O)$ was .85 and the false alarm rate $P(O|D)$ was .65. The 85% hit rate means that the criterion value was set so that there was 35% of the area of the O distribution between its mean and the criterion. Since the criterion is to the left of the mean, we take the negative z score for 35% in Table 1 (-1.037). The 65% false alarm rate places the criterion value to the left of the mean of the D distribution, with 15% of the distribution between its mean and the criterion value, giving a z score of -.385. Substituting these values in

Equation 2 gives

$$d' = -.385 - (-1.037) = .652$$

for the d' value in our sample experiment.

MULTISTATE VERSUS TWO-STATE THEORY

Multistate theory and two-state threshold theory differ significantly in their descriptions of performance in the psychophysical task. The major difference concerns the assumption of a threshold. Two-state threshold theory assumes that the signal on a given trial either does or does not exceed the threshold. Accordingly, the output of the sensory system can take on only one of two values. In contrast, multistate theory disposes of the concept of a threshold and assumes that the output of the sensory system can take on a whole range of values even though there are only two trial types. How do we decide between these two theories?

Psychometric Functions

As discussed in Chapter 10, the method of constant stimuli can be used to study the detection of a stimulus presented at intensities slightly below and above the threshold value. The method permits the investigator to determine the percentage of "yes" responses as a function of the stimulus intensity; this function is called the psychometric function. According to high threshold (two-state) theory, the threshold value should remain relatively constant with changes in the attitudes and motivations of the observer in the task. To test this prediction, Swets, Tanner, and Birdsall (1961) generated psychometric functions with five levels of signal intensity. One of the five levels was zero intensity, making it identical to a catch trial. In addition, the authors tested the subjects in separate sessions with different payoff matrices and a priori probabilities. According to high threshold theory, the threshold value, and therefore the probability of a true detection, should not change with changes in these variables. Since payoffs and the likelihood of a signal can only change the decision system, correcting for guessing should lead to equivalent results in the various conditions.

According to high threshold theory (see Chapter 10), the probability of a true detection, p, measures the proportion of times a particular stimulus exceeds the threshold. Since the probability of a "yes" response includes both true detection and guesses, it is necessary to correct for guessing. The "correction for guessing" was derived in Chapter 10 and is given by

$$p = \frac{P(Yes \mid SN) - P(Yes \mid N)}{1 - P(Yes \mid N)} \tag{3}$$

where p represents the probability of a true detection; $P(Yes \mid SN)$ is the probability of saying "yes" to a particular signal intensity, and $P(Yes \mid N)$ is the probability of saying "yes" to the zero-intensity stimulus. If high threshold theory is correct, the p value derived for a given signal intensity should remain invariant with changes in payoffs and a priori probabilities.

Figure 9 shows the psychometric functions for three different conditions in the Swets et al. study. As can be seen in the figure, the overall likelihood of a "yes" response changed systematically with changes in the a priori probabilities and payoffs. According to high threshold theory, the curves should be superimposed on one another if they are corrected for guessing. The correction for guessing is given by Equation 3, using the false alarm rate (the probability of a "yes" response given the zero intensity) for $P(Yes \mid N)$ in the correction. Figure 10 shows that correcting for guessing does not superimpose the curves and, thus, does not lead to equivalent estimates of p for each stimulus intensity. These results are strong evidence against the high threshold theory.

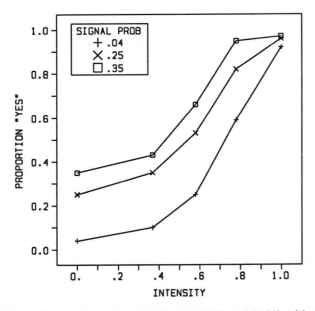

Figure 9. The relationship between the stimulus threshold and $P_N(A)$ with the proportion of positive responses to four positive values of signal intensity, $P_{SN}(A)$, and to the blank or zero-intensity presentation, $P_N(A)$, at three values of $P_N(A)$ (results from Swets, Tanner, & Birdsall, 1961).

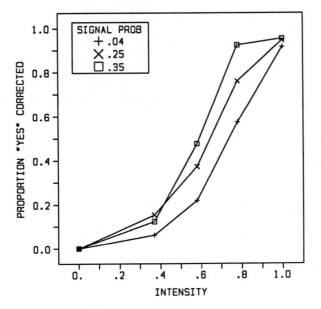

Figure 10. The relationship between the stimulus threshold and $P_N(A)$ with the three curves in Figure 9 corrected for chance success (results from Swets, Tanner, & Birdsall, 1961).

Confidence Ratings

The second source of evidence supportive of multistate theory comes from the phenomenological experience of observers in the signal detection task. They report that they seem to have more information on some trials than on others. If they were gambling, they would be willing to bet more on the correctness of some answers than others. To test this experimentally, studies have been done in which subjects have been provided with the means to record their degree of confidence about their response to each trial. These experiments follow from the fact that if observers have more information on some trials than on others, they should be able to estimate the degree of information reliably.

In the signal detection experiments, subjects are asked to rate their confidence in each "yes" or "no" judgment on a scale, for example, from 1 to 5. Thus one response "yes" might be accompanied by the rating 5, meaning the subject is very sure that a signal is out there; the same response on another trial might be rated 3 by the subject, and on a third trial rated 1, meaning that he is very uncertain, perhaps just guessing. His confidence could then be compared to his actual performance. The experimenter can look up the trials for each rating and compute the probability that the response was correct. According to multistate theory, if the subject says he is positive that a stimulus signal is out there, his response should almost always be correct. If he says he is not very certain, a correct response should be less likely. Overall, a positive correlation between confidence and accuracy is predicted because it is assumed that the sensory system has information about the magnitude of sensation. Actual confidence ratings done during experiments have yielded results that support the multistate model (Green & Swets, 1966; Swets, 1961). Threshold theory, on the other hand, cannot easily predict this result since the theory was not developed to predict confidence judgments. In its present formulation there is no immediate mechanism available to incorporate the results. In this regard, then, multistate theory is preferred since it is relevant to a larger class of psychophysical experiments and results.

A Priori Probability and Payoffs

Another way to distinguish between the two theories is to compare their quantitative predictions of performance in a signal detection task as a function of changes in the a priori probability of a signal trial, or of changes in the monetary payoffs in the experimental situation. As seen in the last chapter, the general two-state threshold theory predicts an ROC curve with two straight-line segments. In contrast, the multistate theory predicts a curvilinear ROC curve similar to that generated by the dice game presented in Figure 3. The results of experiments in audition, vision, and taste are consistent with the predictions of multistate theory (Linker, Moore, & Galanter, 1964; Swets, 1961; Swets, Tanner, & Birdsall, 1961).

Other Evidence

A straightforward test between multistate and two-state theories is an experiment in which the observer is asked to attend to four observation intervals on each trial. The signal is randomly presented in one of the four intervals on each trial. Two-state theory says that each interval either will or will not exceed the threshold. In contrast, multistate theory predicts that the observer will have a measure of the likelihood that the signal was presented in each of the intervals. The two-state sensory system can only categorize each interval in terms of a "yes" or "no," whereas in the multistate sensory system each interval's sensation state can take on many values. If we ask the observers to rank the four observation intervals in terms of the likelihood that the signal occurred in each of the intervals, we can ask what happens when the observation interval that contains the signal is *not* ranked first. Two-state theory would claim that the signal was not detected and, therefore, the signal interval should be ranked second, third, or fourth with equal probability. Multistate theory, on the other hand, would predict that the signal interval should be ranked second more often than third or fourth. The actual results agree with the predictions of multistate theory (Swets, Tanner, & Birdsall, 1961).

An observation by Nachmias and Steinman (1963) provides further evidence against the general two-state threshold model. They found that the estimate of q—the probability that the threshold was exceeded on noise trials—was not independent of the strength of the stimulus on signal trials. The estimated value of q decreased with increases in the intensity of the stimulus on signal trials. There is no way that two-state theory can handle this result since it assumes a fixed threshold; hence the probability that noise trials exceed the threshold must remain independent of the intensity of the signal on stimulus trials. In contrast, this result can be predicted by the multistate theory. If the subject establishes her criterion at the intersection of the signal and no-signal distributions, increasing the intensity of the signal will pull the distributions apart, increasing the hit rate and decreasing the false alarm rate simultaneously. (This result is exactly analogous to our previous description of the dice game in which the value of the signal was changed from 3 to 6.)

A final reason why most investigators have accepted the multistate theory over the two-state threshold theory is a practical or heuristic one. The two-state theory does not allow the investigator to derive an index of the operation of the sensory system from just one set of hit and false alarm probabilities, whereas the multistate theory does. Therefore, if experimenters want to use the two-state model they must simultaneously vary the a priori probability or the payoffs in the task to generate an ROC curve. Then they must fit the curve and estimate the values p and q in the task. This analysis increases the complexity of the experiment because usually the experimenter is interested in signal detection performance as a function of some other independent variable. Accordingly, using the two-state theory increases the number of subject hours by a factor of 3 or 4 over using the multistate model. Finally, the index d' describes sensory performance with only one value, whereas the two-state theory needs two values, p and q, to describe performance. Accordingly, the two-state theory only leaves us with something very similar to hit and false alarm probabilities, still making it necessary to analyze the relationship between the values p and q. We know performance is better to the extent that p is larger than q, or that the hit rate is larger than the false alarm rate. The theory of signal detectability allows us to reduce these independent observations into one value that represents a direct index of performance. Given the relative simplicity of multistate theory and the supporting evidence, it is now generally accepted by most investigators of sensory processes.

In summary, we have seen how the multistate theory can be used to derive an index of sensory performance that is unaffected by biases in the decision system. The decision system plays a role in all experiments, whether sensory, perceptual, mnemonic, or whatever. In each case, the experimenter wants an index of performance that is free from any decision bias. The multistate model allows this by using the d' index to describe what a sensory, perceptual, or mnemonic system knows under a given set of experimental conditions. In this case, the experimenter can observe directly the effects of the independent variable on the psychological process of interest. The advantages of the multistate theory are apparent in the analysis of experiments and the development of theory in current experimental psychology.

13

Scaling Psychological Processes

Scales
  Nominal Scale
  Ordinal Scale
  Interval Scale
  Ratio Scale

Classical Psychophysical Scaling
  Psychophysical Method
  Perceptual Magnitude and Discriminability
  Weber's Law
  Sound Discrimination

Sensation Magnitude
  Fechner's Model
  Magnitude Estimation
  Stevens' Power Model
  Questioning Assumptions

Functional Measurement
  Illusory Weight Judgments
  Experimental Test

Multidimensional Scaling
  Dissimilarity Ratings of Animals
  Animal Space

Logarithms
Dynes and Decibels
Stars and Category Judgments

Functional measurement thus leads to increased emphasis on
judgmental processes, decreased emphasis on scaling per se.
Norman H. Anderson (1970)

One of the most distinguishing attributes of people is our consistent evaluation of the world around us. We assess our looks, happiness, friends, food, work, and play. We believe that we can discriminate the differences between various wines and even assign numbers indicating the degree of difference. We consult ratings of restaurants, movies, and presidential candidates. In much of this chapter, we will be concerned with scaling our sensations to physical stimuli whose properties can be quantitatively measured. Therefore, we will ask how our sensation magnitude varies as a function of intensity of the stimulus. In other cases the scaling problem is not so straightforward. We might want to scale aesthetic judgments of works of art. In this case, there is no obvious external referent such as stimulus intensity as in the case of measuring sensation magnitude. In both situations, however, we aim to quantify some aspect of our psychological experience.

SCALES

Psychologists, as well as other scientists, find it useful to distinguish among four kinds of scales or types of measurement. As in our discussion of successive approximations to the experimental method, these four scales can be ordered with respect to desirable qualities. In addition, distinguishing among scale types illuminates many of the important features of scaling in psychological study.

Nominal Scale

A nominal scale does not measure; it only classifies. Objects with one attribute are given one name, those with another attribute are given another name. With a nominal scale, objects with a given property are treated identically. We cannot distinguish among the objects within a given category nor can we order the various categories in any systematic way. A person's friends can be considered to be a nominal scale. Each friend has a unique name but the name implies nothing whatsoever about the relationships among the friends. We could change or interchange the names of the friends and yet their relationships would not change.

Ordinal Scale

As might be predicted from its name, the ordinal scale carries information about order along a given dimension. However, it does not imply anything about the relative distances between adjacent members on this dimension. To return to the class of friends, one example of an ordinal scale would be to rank a number of friends on how assertive they are. This ranking would answer any question about who is more or less assertive relative to someone else, but it would not provide information about how much more assertive one person is than another. Accordingly, we can make greater than or less than statements about the ranked members, but we cannot provide information about degree. The amount of assertiveness between adjacent members on the ordinal scale is not specified.

Interval Scale

The interval scale improves on the ordinal scale by specifying the interval between objects. Rather than ranking our friends on assertiveness we might rate their assertiveness on a scale from 1 to 7. A rating of 1 would correspond to "very little," and a rating of 7 to "very much." The rater would be told that the rating should be an interval one; the distance between 1 and 2 should be equivalent to the distance between 6 and 7 in terms of amount of assertiveness. If the rater can follow these instructions, we have an interval scale of assertiveness. Therefore, we can make statements about the amount of assertiveness difference between two friends.

The interval scale lacks an origin, however. We do not know how much assertiveness the rating of 1 is above or below zero assertiveness. Without a zero point, we cannot make statements about assertiveness ratios between friends. If Mary is rated 2, John 4, and Sally 6, we can say that the difference between Mary and John is the same as the difference between John and Sally. We cannot say that John is twice as assertive as Mary or that Sally is three times as assertive as Mary.

It should be noted that the assumption of an interval scale cannot be easily tested. Although a rater may be told to use an interval scale, he or she may not be able to do so. Luckily, there are good techniques for testing the assumption of an interval scale, as for example, in the context of information integration and functional measurement (Anderson, 1974, 1981, 1982).

Ratio Scale

The ratio scale has a true zero point. Assume that one of our rater's friends is a robot who is programmed to have zero assertiveness. Our rater could be told this fact and could use this information in her ratings. In this case, the rater should be able to scale her friends on a ratio scale. If Mary is 2 units more assertive than the robot and John is 2 units more assertive than Mary, we are justified in saying that John is twice as assertive as Mary.

CLASSICAL PSYCHOPHYSICAL SCALING

In the early nineteenth century, physiologists began to study sensation in the experimental laboratory. Ernst H. Weber did a series of studies evaluating our discriminative ability to sense one stimulus as different from another. This ability was indexed by the concept of a just noticeable difference. How much did one stimulus have to be changed to become just-noticeably different from another? For example, by how little can two lines be made to differ and yet still be seen as different? On first blush, we might expect some straightforward answer such as one centimeter (cm) or even one millimeter (mm). Weber's significant finding was that the just noticeable difference was dependent on the overall length of the lines being discriminated. Observers are much more sensitive to small changes in short lines than in long lines. Weber found that people could notice about a 2% difference when the lines were presented simultaneously and about a 5% difference when the lines were presented successively (Geldard, 1953).

Psychophysical Method

It is not obvious which method Weber used to study just noticeable differences, but after Fechner's time the typical method was the method of constant stimuli. Comparative judgments for determining just noticeable differences require two stimuli, one called the standard and one the comparison. The standard is held fixed and the comparison is varied across a range of intensities bracketing those of the standard. The observer is given the standard and a given comparison stimulus and is asked to indicate which appears more intense. As an example, a standard tone of a given frequency is followed by a comparison tone of the same frequency and the subject reports whether the second tone was louder or softer than the first. As in absolute judgment, a large number of trials is given on each of the comparison stimuli.

In analyzing the results, the probability of a "louder" response, $P(louder)$, is the dependent measure. The observed percentage of "louder" responses is the best estimate of $P(louder)$. Since the observer is required to respond either "louder" or "softer", the probability of a "softer" response is just one minus the probability of a "louder" one. For a graphical representation, $P(louder)$ is plotted on the vertical axis as a function of the intensity difference between the comparison and standard plotted on the horizontal axis. As can be seen in some hypothetical results in Figure 1, $P(louder)$ increases systematically with increases in the differences in intensity between the comparison and standard. Two measures of performance are usually computed from these data. The point of subjective equality (p.s.e.) is taken as the intensity difference at the point of 50% louder judgments. Note that the p.s.e. may not be equal to the point at which the standard and comparison are equal in intensity. Psychophysicists do not have an accepted ready explanation of situations in which the p.s.e. differs from objective reality and it may be worthwhile for you to consider some of the reasons why this result might be observed.

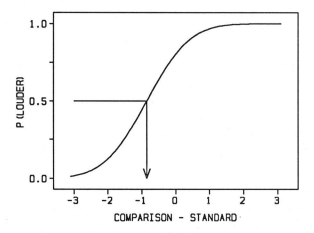

Figure 1. The proportion of louder judgments, $P(louder)$, as a function of the intensity difference between the comparison and standard. The point of subjective equality (p.s.e.) is the intensity difference at the point of 50% louder judgments.

The second measure of performance is the just noticeable difference (j.n.d.). Intuitively, we want that intensity difference that the subject notices reliably about half the time. By notices reliably, we mean the ability of the subject to systematically report the direction of the intensity difference. A value of 50% would be a completely unsystematic report whereas values of 0% or 100% are completely systematic. Half way between a systematic and unsystematic report is, therefore, either 25% or 75%. Following this logic, investigators have taken this to mean the 25% and 75% values of $P(louder)$. To compute the just noticeable difference, we take the absolute difference in intensity between the stimulus values for the 25% and 75% judgment points and divide this absolute difference by 2. Figure 2 illustrates computation of the just noticeable difference using this method. The measure is a reasonable one and it gives the intensity difference that the subject reliably discriminates about half the time.

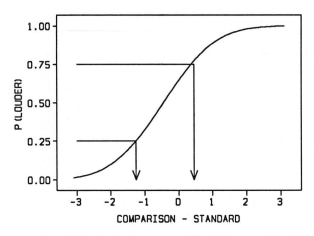

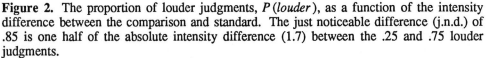

Figure 2. The proportion of louder judgments, *P* (*louder*), as a function of the intensity difference between the comparison and standard. The just noticeable difference (j.n.d.) of .85 is one half of the absolute intensity difference (1.7) between the .25 and .75 louder judgments.

Logarithms

Consider the case in which each of the successive levels of an independent variable is 10 times the value of the preceding level. If the first level was 1 unit, the following six levels would be 10, 100, 1000, 10,000, 100,000, and 1,000,000 units, respectively. Rather than dealing with these large numbers, they are more easily expressed as logarithms to the base 10. The seven levels (X) of our independent variable are easily expressed in terms of 10 raised to the appropriate power Y.

$$X = 10^Y$$

The seven levels would be 10^0, 10^1, 10^2, 10^3, 10^4, 10^5, 10^6, respectively. The logarithms of our values X are the respective powers Y of the value 10. In this way we define Y as the logarithm of X to the base 10 as

$$Y = \log_{10}X.$$

Then the logarithm Y of X to the base 10 is the power to which we must raise 10 to get X. In other areas of psychological study, it is useful to use logarithms to other bases besides 10. The same general principles hold, so that Y is the logarithm of X to the base b.

$$Y = \log_b X.$$

As in the measurement of absolute thresholds, there is also a criterion or decision problem with traditional psychophysical methods in the measurement of just noticeable differences. The motives of the subject are unknown and these may bias the results in various ways. Subjects may be relatively unmotivated and perform haphazardly in the task. In one string of trials, subjects may be biased to say "louder"; in another string of trials, the bias might change to the "softer" response. This kind of strategy would make the results more random and would give the impression of a relatively indiscriminate loudness sense. It has been shown that payoffs for correct responses in the task can double the sensitivity of the observer in the task. By rewarding subjects for correct louder and softer judgments, the just noticeable difference can be decreased by about one half. In addition any systematic bias in the p.s.e. is usually attenuated with correct feedback and payoffs in the experimental task. It should be noted that the payoffs need not always be monetary; in some cases subjects will show similar improvements by being informed on each trial with respect to the correctness of their response.

Perceptual Magnitude and Discriminability

Psychophysical measurement has consistently relied on two aspects of perceptual behavior: magnitude and discriminability. Consider an experiment that varies several cues to depth (Chapter 14). Increasing the number of cues specifying some distance between the objects might not only increase the perceived depth, but might also enhance the discriminability of the judgment. The average perceived depth would be a measure of perceptual magnitude. Discriminability would be indexed by several factors. Better discriminability by an observer would be reflected in lower variability in his or her judgments, more confidence in them, and less processing time to make them. For example, motion might also be expected to enhance the resolution of the displays (i.e., increase the discriminability in perception) in addition to changing the perceived depth. The p.s.e. gives a measure of perceptual magnitude and the j.n.d. gives a measure discriminability.

Weber's Law

Even more encouraging to the development of an exact science of sensation, Weber observed an elegant relationship between the just noticeable difference of a stimulus and its absolute magnitude. This relationship has come to be known as Weber's law and is expressed both verbally and quantitatively. Verbally, the law is that an increment in intensity of a stimulus becomes just noticeable when it is made a fixed percentage more intense than the original stimulus. That is, the just noticeable difference is a constant when measured relative to the absolute intensity of the stimuli. In mathematical terms, this form of Weber's law can be expressed as

$$\frac{dI}{I} = K \tag{1}$$

where dI is the just noticeable intensity change in a stimulus of original intensity I, and K is a constant value for a given intensity continuum. Thus, if K were equal to .05 for loudness sensation, the intensity of a sound must be increased or decreased by 5% (.05 = 5%) to be noticed. This relationship captures the fact that a weaker stimulus requires a smaller absolute stimulus change in order to be noticed. An observer notices a smaller absolute change in a weak than in a strong stimulus.

Consider the implications of Weber's law for the discrimination of line length. If a person could just notice a 5 mm increase in a line 10 mm long, the value of K computed from Equation 1 would be equal to

$$\frac{5}{10} = .5 \tag{2}$$

If Weber's law holds, then that person should be able to notice a 50% (.5 = 50%) increase in lines of any length. In this case, a line of 100 mm would have to be increased by 50 mm in order for a difference to be noticed. Figure 3 gives the just noticeable differences for lines of 0 to 150 mm in length. Equation 1 can be rewritten as

$$dI = KI \tag{3}$$

which is a linear function of the form $y = ax$. As can be seen in Figure 3, the just noticeable

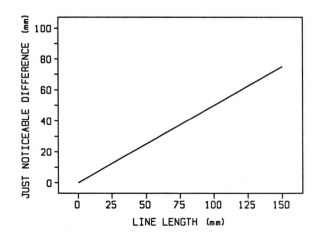

Figure 3. The just noticeable difference of line length as a function of length of the line.

difference predicted by Weber's law follows a linear equation. The slope of the function as measured by the amount of change in Y (the vertical distance) divided by the amount of change in X (the horizontal distance) gives Weber's constant K. There is a 5 mm change in y with each 10 mm change in X, producing the Weber constant of .5.

Sound Discrimination

Subjects can notice about a 1 or 2 dB difference for sounds across the range of normal speaking intensity. A constant dB change is in agreement with Weber's law because dB is already a log scale. Therefore, an absolute difference on this scale reflects a fixed proportional difference on a linear scale. However, contrary to Weber's law, a slightly larger dB change is needed for very soft sounds and for relatively high and relatively low frequencies. This result reflects the well-known observation that Weber's law tends to break down at the extremes of the stimulus continuum.

SENSATION MAGNITUDE

Weber's law describes our discrimination ability, but it does not describe the magnitude of our sensation. That is, we not only discriminate a louder sound from a softer sound, the magnitude of the sensation is greater for the louder sound. A model must describe the relationship between the stimulus intensity and sensation magnitude in an analogous manner to Weber's law describing the relationship between the stimulus intensity and discrimination ability. In addition to Fechner's seminal work in developing psychophysical methods (see Chapter 10), he formalized a specific model of the psychophysical relationship between stimulus intensity and sensation magnitude.

Fechner's Model

In addition to the concept of a threshold, Fechner had a specific idea of the relationship between the intensity of stimulation and the magnitude of sensation. Fechner believed that a simple relationship held between the intensity of a stimulus and the magnitude of a sensation. He was aware of Weber's experiments which showed that the just noticeable difference is not an absolute change but a relative one. Fechner accepted as true Weber's law which implies that the

---

Dynes and Decibels

A dyne is a measure of force or pressure, and dynes/cm^2 measures the amount of pressure per square centimeter. One dyne of force applied to a mass of 1 gram for 1 sec will move it a velocity of 1 cm per sec.

Since dynes/cm^2 is an unwieldy unit of measurement, researchers and practitioners have transformed the sound pressure from dynes/cm^2 to decibels. A decibel is a unit that describes the sound pressure of a sound wave relative to some other sound pressure value. The decibel, therefore, refers to a sound pressure ratio and is equal to 20 times the logarithm to the base 10 of that ratio. Accordingly, 100 times the sound pressure is equivalent to 40 dB since 20 times $\log_{10} 100$ equals 40. A doubling of sound pressure gives an increase of 6 dB since 20 times $\log_{10} 2=6$. The reference sound pressure level is usually taken to be .0002 dynes/cm^2, since this value approximates the limits of audibility.

The value .0002 dynes/cm^2 is equal to the atmospheric sound pressure of a 1000 Hz tone that is barely detectable. Sixty dB with a reference source pressure of .0002 dynes/cm^2 would be equal to 1000 times .0002 dynes/cm^2, or .2 dynes/cm^2, which is roughly equivalent to conversational speech at a distance of 3 ft.

---

intensity change necessary for a just noticeable difference is a constant proportion of the absolute intensity level. Fechner went significantly beyond Weber's law in assuming that the just noticeable difference could be treated as a unit of sensation. Measurement was the keystone of science; measurement of sensation required a measuring unit (a metric) and the best candidate was Weber's just noticeable difference. Fechner's critical assumption was that all just noticeable differences were subjectively equal. For the physical scale of length, the inch between 1 and 2 is equal to the inch between 20 and 21 and the same was assumed for sensation differences. The sensation magnitude corresponding to the just noticeable difference at a stimulus intensity of 10 should be equal to the sensation magnitude corresponding to the just noticeable difference at an intensity of 100.

By extending Weber's law in this way and by including the concept of a threshold, Fechner derived the following equation relating stimulus and sensation

$$S = K \log_{10} I \tag{4}$$

where S measures the magnitude of the sensation, I is equal to the intensity of the stimulus, and K is a constant of proportionality.

The value of K determines how quickly sensation grows with increases in $\log_{10} I$. Larger values of K would correspond to smaller just noticeable differences which would be analogous to smaller values of Weber's constant. The smaller the just noticeable difference, the smaller the value of Weber's constant, and, therefore, the more quickly sensation should increase with increases in $\log_{10} I$.

It might be worthwhile to demonstrate how Fechner's model is applied. Assume that K is equal to 1.5 and that I is 10 units.

$$S = 1.5 \times \log_{10} 10$$

$$S = 1.5 \times 1$$

$$S = 1.5$$

In this case, a stimulus of 10 units gives a sensation value of 1.5 units (the logarithm of 10 is 1). If we increase the stimulus to 100 units, we double the sensation value.

$$S = 1.5 \times \log_{10} 100$$

$$S = 1.5 \times 2$$

$$S = 3$$

Another increase by a factor of 10 does *not* double the sensation value, since

$$S = 1.5 \times \log_{10} 1000$$

$$S = 1.5 \times 3$$

$$S = 4.5$$

These cases illustrate the basic idea of Fechner's model. Equal proportional changes in the magnitude of a stimulus produce equal absolute changes in the magnitude of the sensation. In our example, increasing the intensity of the stimulus 10 times adds 1.5 units to the sensation value.

In Equation 4, the stimulus intensity, I, is measured with the threshold value (I_t) as the unit of measurement. Recall Fechner's critical assumption of a threshold, that stimulus intensity at or below which no sensation occurs. To incorporate this assumption into his model, the intensity of the stimulus is measured with the threshold intensity as the unit of measurement. Using the threshold as the unit of measurement allows the prediction of no sensation when the stimulus intensity is at or below the threshold. Otherwise, any intensity, no matter how weak, would always produce some sensation. Accordingly, the value I substituted in Equation 4 is a ratio of the absolute intensity of the stimulus to the threshold value. For example, if the threshold of sound intensity for a subject corresponds to a sound pressure of .0002 dynes/cm^2, each value of I is obtained by dividing the sound pressure value of the stimulus by .0002 dynes/cm^2. Therefore, when the stimulus presented is at threshold value:

$$S = K \log \frac{.0002 \text{ dynes /cm}^2}{.0002 \text{ dynes /cm}^2} \tag{5}$$

$$= K \log 1 = K \times 0 = 0$$

Equation 5 predicts no sensation when the stimulus is at the threshold value. Therefore, Fechner developed a scale with a zero point in addition to the assumption that S could specify the precise intervals between various sensations. This means that Fechner's scale was assumed to be a ratio scale; statements about both intervals and ratios should be meaningful. One sensation could be said to be 10 units larger than another and also to be twice the value of a third.

To give an example of Fechner's model, consider the results in Figure 3, in which Weber's constant is .5. The magnitude of a stimulus that is just noticeably different from a reference stimulus must be 1.5 times the absolute intensity of the reference stimulus. If we assume that the threshold value is 20 units, then we can plot the sensation value in terms of the number of just noticeable differences. Figure 4 shows that the sensation value grows more and more slowly as the stimulus magnitude gets larger. We saw that Fechner's model predicts a linear function between sensation and the logarithm of stimulus magnitude. Table 1 gives the log values and Figure 5 gives the graphical plot. The function in Figure 5 illustrates Fechner's model: sensation is proportional to the logarithm of the magnitude of the stimulus. Fechner's model predicts a linear function when the sensation value is plotted on a linear scale and the stimulus magnitude is plotted logarithmically, as seen in Figure 5.

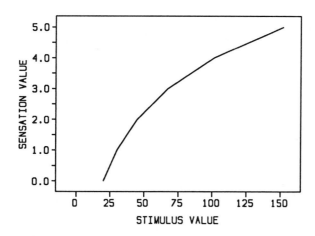

Figure 4. The sensation value, measured in terms of the number of just noticeable differences, as a function of the stimulus value according to Fechner's model. The threshold I_t is assumed to be 20 and $K = 5.68$.

Table 1. Predictions of perceived stimulus magnitude according to Fechner's model, $S = K \log(\frac{I}{I_t})$. The threshold value I_t is assumed to be 20 and $K = 5.68$.

Stimulus Value (I)	Log Stimulus Value (log $[I/I_t]$)	Sensation Value
20.000	.00	0.0
30.000	.18	1.0
45.000	.35	2.0
67.500	.53	3.0
101.250	.71	4.0
151.875	.88	5.0

for example, $S = 5.68 \log(\frac{30}{20}) = 5.68 \log 1.5 = 5.68 \times .18 = 1.0$

Fechner's psychophysical methods did not allow the experimenter to measure sensation directly. Rather, the sensation had to be inferred from the measurement of the threshold and the just noticeable difference. Consider Weber's experiment on the just noticeable difference of lines of various lengths. Figure 3 presents some hypothetical results following Weber's law; the just noticeable difference is 50% of the length of the line. Fechner assumed that the just noticeable differences could be added to describe the sensation to a given stimulus dimension. Therefore, these results can be replotted in terms of Fechner's model which assumes that sensation grows with the logarithm of line length.

$$S = K \log_{10} I \tag{6}$$

Looking at Figures 4 and 5, and assuming that the stimulus dimension is line length, then a line length of 101 mm looks significantly longer than twice as long as the 45 mm line. Accordingly, Fechner's scaling based on the summation of just noticeable differences did not agree with our everyday experience and people were quick to propose alternative solutions.

Fechner's model that summates just noticeable differences to give the magnitude of sensation was not easily put to experimental test. The methods of sensation measurement were indirect;

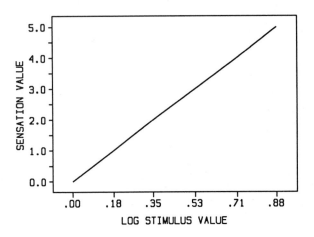

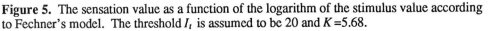

Figure 5. The sensation value as a function of the logarithm of the stimulus value according to Fechner's model. The threshold I_t is assumed to be 20 and $K = 5.68$.

Stars and Category Judgments

Fechner's Equation 4 captures an important relationship between light intensity and the magnitude of visual sensation. Equation 4 specifies a logarithmic relationship between the magnitude of the sensation and the intensity of the stimulus. This means that it takes a much larger increase in the intensity of a bright light than of a dim light to give the same increase in the magnitude of the sensation. The subjective classification of the brightness of the stars by the ancient astronomer, Hipparchus, illustrates this fact. Wishing to describe the brightness of stars, Hipparchus placed the stars in six or seven categories based on their apparent brightness. The first category contained the stars that were barely visible and each succeeding category contained stars that were perceived to be one order of magnitude brighter than the stars in the previous category. When precise measurement became possible, it was found that the physical intensity of the stars in each category was about 2 1/2 times more intense than the intensity of the stars in the preceding category. If the physical intensity of the stars in the first category is arbitrarily defined as 1 unit, then the stars in the second category would be 2 1/2 units of intensity. The physical intensity of the stars in the third category would be 2 1/2 x 2 1/2 or 6 1/4 units and so on. This means that, as described by Equation 1, equal increments in sensation required equal ratios between the stimulus intensities.

Hipparchus may have been the first person to implement the category scaling method which became very popular at the end of the nineteenth century. The observer is to judge the relative magnitudes of a series of stimuli. Judgments are made in terms of a set of categories, for example, the first seven integers. The task is to distribute the stimuli across the seven categories from weakest to strongest in sensation magnitude. The important and most difficult part of the task is to keep sensation differences between adjacent categories as subjectively equal. The sensation difference between stimuli in categories two and three must be the same as the sensation difference between stimuli in categories six and seven. The subject is tested with each stimulus a number of times and the average of the category values that were assigned to a given stimulus is taken as the sensation value.

---

subjects were asked to detect the presence of a stimulus or to report the just noticeable difference between two stimuli. There were no proven methods for measuring sensation directly. What was needed was another method of deriving a scale of sensation and to see if this scale agreed with

Fechner's log scale. These direct scaling methods were devised and Fechner's theory could be put to experimental test. The two most popular methods have been category scaling and magnitude estimation.

Magnitude Estimation

The best known and most easily used method is called magnitude estimation. Consider an experiment carried out by Stevens and Marks (1971). How the warmth sensation varies as a function of thermal stimulation was the psychophysical question. Figure 6 illustrates the experimental situation. A projector lamp was used to radiate the forehead. An aperture and a shutter were used to control the area and duration of the stimulation. In order to derive a meaningful scale of the warmth sensation, it was necessary to test the subject with a large number of intensities across a large range of intensities. By testing pilot subjects, the experimenters were able to determine the proper number and spacing of the stimuli necessary to cover the psychological range of the warmth sensation. The experimenters chose 60 stimuli and tested every subject once on every stimulus on each of two days. The instructions to the subjects were as follows.

> I am going to present a number of heat stimuli to your forehead. Your task is to judge how warm each stimulus feels to you by assigning numbers to stand for the degree of apparent warmth. To the first stimulus, assign whatever number seems to you most appropriate to represent the degree of warmth. Then, for succeeding stimuli, assign other numbers in proportion to warmth. If one stimulus seems three times as warm as another, assign a number three times as great; if it feels one fifth as warm, assign a number one fifth as great. Any type of number—whole number, decimal, or fraction—may be used (after Marks, 1976).

This experiment is typical of most studies using the magnitude estimation procedure. In some experiments, subjects are given a standard stimulus and told to assign it some numerical value such as 100. All other stimuli are assigned numbers with respect to this standard. In addition, the standard can be presented on every trial preceding the test stimulus or made available whenever the subject requests it. Given the tedious nature of judging warmth in this task, it was not feasible to use a standard stimulus since it might prolong the experiment beyond what would be considered reasonable by the subject. Figure 7 presents some of the results of this experiment. The results are plotted on a linear-linear, a linear-log, and a log-log scale.

As can be seen in Figure 7, Fechner's model is not correct for warmth, nor is it correct for a variety of other sensations. The results plotted on a linear-log scale do not follow a linear function. Interestingly, the results on a log-log plot do seem to be linear. Fechner assumed that equal differences in just noticeable differences give rise to equal sensation differences. That is, the sensation difference between 20 and 25 j.n.d. is the same as the difference between 60 and 65 just noticeable differences. This assumption does not predict the relationship between sensation and intensity as measured by the method of magnitude estimation.

Stevens' Power Model

The most influential alternative to date was proposed by S. S. Stevens in 1960, one hundred years after Fechner published his *Elements of Psychophysics*. The title of the article by Stevens was "To Honor Fechner and to Repeal His Law." Actually, Stevens was objecting to Fechner's indirect methods of measuring sensation and he proposed some direct methods that had been in practice for some time. In terms of the psychophysical law, a slightly different assumption was

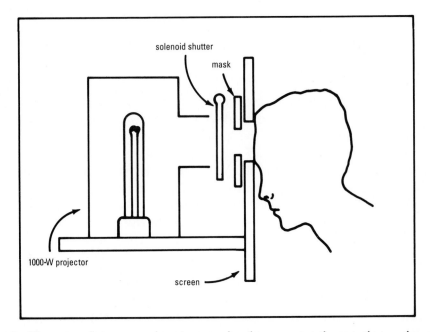

Figure 6. The setup for an experiment measuring how a warmth sensation varies as a function of the thermal stimulation applied to the forehead. Level of intensity is controlled by adjusting the voltage to the 1000-W lamp, and the areal extent of stimulation is controlled by varying the size of the aperture in the mask (after Marks, 1976).

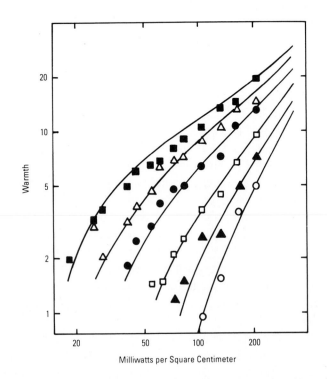

Figure 7. Magnitude estimation of warmth as a function of the radiant intensity (milliwatts per square centimeter) applied to the forehead. The different curves correspond to different areal extents of the stimulation (after Marks, 1976).

made by Stevens and represents his well known power law. The assumption is that equal ratios of just noticeable differences give rise to equal sensation ratios. Therefore, the ratio of 25 to 20 is 5 to 4, and an equivalent ratio would be 60 to 48 just noticeable differences. Accordingly, the sensation magnitude between 20 and 25 is equivalent to that between 48 and 60. The power function says that the sensation S is equal to a constant times K the stimulus intensity I raised to some power n.

$$S = KI^n \tag{7}$$

Power functions plotted on a log-log scale are linear. Taking logarithms of both sides of Equation 7 gives

$$\log S = \log K + n \log I \tag{8}$$

which is a linear equation of the form

$$y = a + bx \tag{9}$$

The intercept is K and n is the slope of the linear function plotted on a log-log scale. Figure 8 illustrates that the power function seems to be a good representation of the magnitude estimation of a variety of stimulus dimensions (Stevens, 1961). The slopes of the linear functions are informative. Our magnitude of length follows fairly closely the actual length, as we might expect. Our estimation of brightness, however, grows much more slowly with increases in the intensity of light. This should not be surprising if you have noticed that a 100-watt bulb does not appear twice as bright as a 50-watt bulb. Finally, our reaction to electric shock is extremely sensitive to increases in intensity, as we would hope.

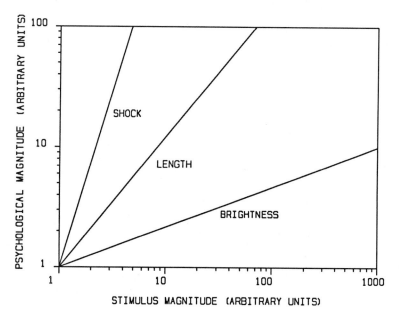

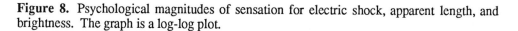

Figure 8. Psychological magnitudes of sensation for electric shock, apparent length, and brightness. The graph is a log-log plot.

Questioning Assumptions

The implicit assumption in the method of magnitude estimation is that subjects are capable of generating an interval scale of sensation values. In this method, for example, a stimulus assigned the value 200 is supposed to be perceived as 100 units more intense than a stimulus assigned the value 100. Similarly, this 100 units of sensation difference is assumed to be the same as the 100 units of sensation difference separating the sensations 400 and 500 assigned to two other stimuli. Although numbers may have interval scale properties mathematically, they may not have these properties psychologically. Subjects may be biased in their use of the number scale and these biases could distort the results in a magnitude estimation experiment. Accordingly, the investigator must validate the interval properties of the scale that is used to represent sensation values.

Much to the credit of researchers utilizing the method of magnitude estimation, the procedure has been evaluated in situations without the use of numbers. The experiments involve the use of cross-modality matching. Subjects are asked to adjust the intensity of a stimulus in one modality so that its sensation is equal to the sensation given by the test stimulus of another modality. For example, the intensity of a tone is adjusted so that its sensed loudness is equal to the sensed brightness of a test light. These experiments also support the idea of a power law relationship between stimulus and sensation.

FUNCTIONAL MEASUREMENT

The procedures of functional measurement developed by Norman H. Anderson (1974, 1981, 1982) allow a direct evaluation of the properties of the scale used by subjects in their sensation judgments. Anderson proposes a good method to measure simultaneously the nature of the judgmental process and the scale that is used. By complicating the experiment, the investigator is able to test hypotheses concerning the judgmental process that is used. If the results are consistent with a particular judgmental process, they also provide support for the use of an interval scale in the task. The critical procedural innovation is the use of factorial designs in which two or more independent variables are manipulated independently. Figure 9 gives a graphical representation of a factorial design in which the row variable, weight of one object, is crossed with the column variable, the weight of a second object. The task of the subject is to estimate the combined weight of the two objects when they are lifted one immediately after the other.

It seems reasonable to expect that the subject will estimate the weight of both objects by adding the estimated weights of the two objects. To express the process algebraically, denote the stimulus object corresponding to the row variable as A_i; the stimulus object in the column variable will be denoted by B_j. The subject is tested with each pair of objects corresponding to each cell in the design. Each cell in the design is designated by the quantity (A_i, B_j). The subjects estimation of combined weight is denoted by R_{ij}. The subject's estimated weight will seldom correspond to the actual weight and the additive process describes the operation on the subjective weight values. To distinguish these from the actual stimulus weights, they are denoted with lowercase letters. Also, because of possible inaccuracies in the use of the external response scale, the actual estimated weight, r_{ij} may differ from the external response, R_{ij}.

The idea of adding the two weights to obtain the estimated weight can be expressed as

$$r_{ij} = a_i + b_j \tag{10}$$

This psychological process can be expressed in a simple stage model. The sensory stage transforms A_i and B_j into the weight experiences a_i and b_j. At the integration stage, these values are recalled and then added together to obtain an interval judgment of estimated weight, r_{ij}. This decision is

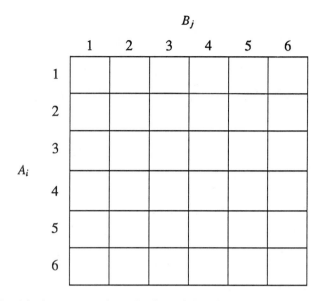

Figure 9. Graphical representation of a factorial design of two independent variables with six levels of each variable.

then mapped into an observable response by the response selection and execution process. All of these processes are unobservable; we know only the actual weights of the two objects and the actual response of the subject. The functional measurement approach allows the possibility of discovering both the psychophysical relationship mapping object weight into weight sensation and the rule used by the subject to combine the two sensed weights.

The use of functional measurement is analogous to the use of the Sternberg additive-factor method. Factorial designs are used in both situations. In addition, the results are informative with respect to more than one issue simultaneously. In the additive-factor method, additive effects of two independent variables are consistent with 1) the idea of successive stages of processing, and 2) the idea that the independent variables had their effects on different stages of processing. In functional measurement, additive effects support the idea that 1) an additive rule was used to add the two perceived weights, and 2) the subject used an interval scale in responding.

Analogous to the additive-factor method, the critical result in functional measurement is whether the response curves are parallel in a two-dimensional plot of the two factors. If the curves are parallel, the mean estimates of the row objects will be on an interval scale. Similarly, the means of the responses to the column objects will be an interval scale of the subject's sensations of object weight. This interpretation of parallel curves can be justified since both an interval scale and the additive combination rule must be used in order to obtain parallel curves. Additive results would not occur if only one of these conditions held. That is, an interval scale with a nonadditive combination rule would produce nonparallel curves as would an additive combination rule with a scale that did not have the interval property. There is a very remote possibility that additive results might be obtained if both conditions did not hold since the distortion in the interval scale might just cancel the nonadditivity of the combination rule. However, we would not expect this unlucky canceling to occur in repeated experimental tests using different conditions and different subjects. Therefore, parallel curves for each of a group of subjects provide strong support for the additive combination rule and the use of an interval scale. Figure 10 presents some hypothetical results, assuming the use of both an additive combination rule and the use of an interval scale. These

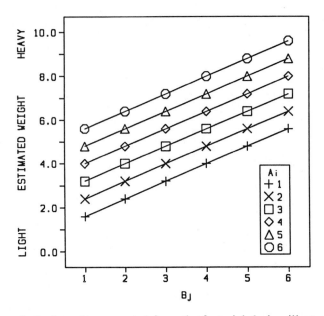

Figure 10. Hypothetical results generated from the factorial design illustrated in Figure 9, assuming an additive combination rule and use of an interval response scale.

results allow the experimenter to compute the psychophysical function relating real weight to estimated weight. A psychophysical function can also be derived from the results in Figure 10. These results could then be used to evaluate various psychophysical models. The advantage is that the investigator can be much more confident that sensation was, in fact, measured on an interval scale.

Illusory Weight Judgments

The use of functional measurement will be described in the context of the size-weight illusion (Anderson, 1970). The size of an object can influence its perceived weight, making the judgment of weight illusory. A pound of feathers is subjectively lighter than a pound of lead. We expect objects to weigh more as they increase in size and this expectation influences their perceived weight. If we have high expectations about an event, we are more likely to be disappointed than if our expectations are minimal. This is a contrast effect. Anderson formulated a model of this contrast effect to allow an experimental test. Two values contribute to the perceived weight of an object: a heaviness value (h) directly related to the actual weight and independent of size and a heaviness value (h^*) which is a perceived weight dependent upon perceived size. The actual perceived or judged weight (J) is then a weighted average of these two values, giving the equation

$$J = w_1 h + w_2 h^* \qquad (11)$$

where w_1 and w_2 are the weights given the two heaviness values, respectively. (Unfortunately, we must refer to two kinds of weights: the actual weights of the blocks and the weights given the heaviness values in the model.) A contrast effect is operative in the size-weight illusion; to the extent h^* is large, J must be small. This means that w_2 must be negative, in which case larger values of h^* would lead to smaller values of J.

$$J = w_1 h - w_2 h^* \tag{12}$$

If it is also assumed that the subject averages the h and h^*, the weights w_1 and w_2 must sum to unity, producing the equation

$$J = (1+w)h - wh^* \tag{13}$$

which is mathematically equivalent to

$$J = h + w(h-h^*) \tag{14}$$

Equation 14 shows that the predicted judgment is dependent on two factors: the actual perceived weight h, independent of size, and the difference between h and the size-based expectancy h^*. To the extent that h^* is larger than h, a contrast illusion is operative. The size of the illusion is also dependent on w, the weight attached to the expectation. If w were zero, no illusion would be operative, since the judgment would be completely determined by h.

Experimental Test

Anderson's (1970) experimental procedure shows how factorial designs can be used to provide a quantitative test of mathematical formulations of specific theories. Subjects were required to judge the heaviness of blocks. The two independent variables in the experiment were the weight and size of the blocks. Three different weights and five different sizes were chosen, giving 15 blocks in all. Subjects lifted each block and estimated its weight by marking a slash on a horizontal line from left (lightest) to right (heaviest). Two end anchors, one much lighter and one much heavier than the test blocks, were first presented for lifting and the subjects were told to respond near the left and right ends, respectively, for these stimuli. The perceived weights of the test blocks, therefore, would lie between these two values. The subjects judged each of the objects presented in randomized trials. The mean ratings of the blocks in terms of the distance from the left of the line to the slash are presented in Figure 11. The results show that the size of the block had a significant contrast effect on its perceived weight. A block of a given weight was perceived as heavier when it was smaller in size. The second significant effect is that the actual weight of the block influenced its perceived weight.

How does the preceding mathematical formulation relate to the results of the present experiment? Equation 13 states that the judged weight is a weighted composite of two factors. To know the predicted value of J for any experimental condition, it is necessary to have values of the parameters w, h, and h^*. With only one experimental condition these values cannot be determined, since many different values of the three parameters values could be combined to give J the value that was observed. Therefore, the experiment must be designed so that unique values for the parameters w, h, and h^* can be estimated, and it can be determined whether a set of parameter values exists to provide a good description of the observed results.

In his factorial design Anderson employed three levels of actual weight. Since it is assumed that the actual weight will affect h, we must have a different value for h at each of the three levels of weight. Second, it is assumed that the size of the block affects h^* and we must estimate five different h^* values for the five unique block sizes. Finally, we must estimate a value of w which is assumed to remain constant under all experimental conditions. The value of w could be affected by the instructions or attitude of the observer, but it should not be affected by the different experimental conditions, since the subject's attitude should not change as a function of different sizes S or weights W of the blocks. Table 2 presents the equations for the 15 conditions in Anderson's experiment.

Now we must find values for h_1, h_2, h_3, h^*_1, h^*_2, h^*_3, h^*_4, h^*_5, and w that give the closest correspondence between our observed values of J and the predicted values given by these equations. This can be done by utilizing a high-speed digital computer that performs a search for the best values. The program is given a range of values for each parameter and tries out different values in the range in order to give the closest correspondence between the observed and predicted scores. One index of correspondence is the average squared difference between the predicted and observed values. When the parameter values are found that best describe the observed data, some index of how well the predicted results match the observed can be computed. For example, the experimenter can determine the average percentage deviation between predicted and observed results.

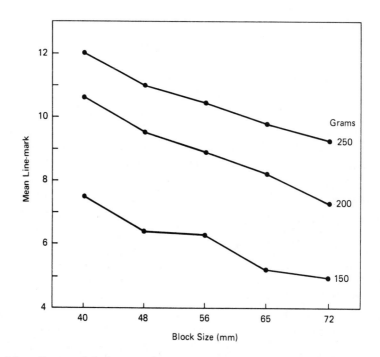

Figure 11. Mean line-mark judgments for the three values of block weight (in grams) as a function of block size.

In Anderson's experiment, 9 parameters must be estimated from the data in order to predict 15 data points. It is possible, therefore, to disprove the theory. More specifically, the equations in Table 2 show that the effects of block weight and block size should be additive. That is to say, the judgment is an additive combination of a heaviness value based on h and one based on h^*. Accordingly, if we plot the judged weight as a function of actual weight and block size, the theory predicts a series of parallel curves. Hence, it is possible to test the theory by observing whether there is a significant interaction between the independent variables of actual weight and block size. We saw in Figure 11 that the observed curves are parallel, supporting this quantitative formulation of the size-weight illusion.

Table 2. Predicted judgments (J) for each factorial combination of five sizes (S) and three weights (W) used in the Anderson (1970) study.

Size	Weight	Prediction
S_1	W_1	$J = (1+w)h_1 - wh_1{}^*$
S_1	W_2	$J = (1+w)h_2 - wh_1{}^*$
S_1	W_3	$J = (1+w)h_3 - wh_1{}^*$
S_2	W_1	$J = (1+w)h_1 - wh_2{}^*$
S_2	W_2	$J = (1+w)h_2 - wh_2{}^*$
S_2	W_3	$J = (1+w)h_3 - wh_2{}^*$
S_3	W_1	$J = (1+w)h_1 - wh_3{}^*$
S_3	W_2	$J = (1+w)h_2 - wh_3{}^*$
S_3	W_3	$J = (1+w)h_3 - wh_3{}^*$
S_4	W_1	$J = (1+w)h_1 - wh_4{}^*$
S_4	W_2	$J = (1+w)h_2 - wh_4{}^*$
S_4	W_3	$J = (1+w)h_3 - wh_4{}^*$
S_5	W_1	$J = (1+w)h_1 - wh_5{}^*$
S_5	W_2	$J = (1+w)h_2 - wh_5{}^*$
S_5	W_3	$J = (1+w)h_3 - wh_5{}^*$

MULTIDIMENSIONAL SCALING

Psychophysical scaling is aimed at establishing relationships between objective and subjective dimensions. The dimensions do not have to be limited to physical properties of stimuli such as intensity, but can refer to semantic properties such as the meaning of words. There is a mathematical procedure called multidimensional scaling (MDS) that seeks to describe the relationship among a set of stimuli such as words. Multidimensional scaling, or MDS, is a promising method for imposing some order on otherwise apparently complex results. To take an example from Kruskal and Wish (1978), suppose you have a map of the United States. It is possible to determine the relative distances between all pairs of cities represented on the map. One could construct a table listing the distance between each pair of cities. For example, the distance between Albuquerque and Denver is 9.6 cm on my map. The distance between Denver and Salt Lake is 10.2 cm and the distance between Albuquerque and Salt Lake is 13.6 cm. From this table, the relative distance between cities could be determined. Note that, without a scale, we do not know the actual distance. Our measures give us only relative distances. Thus, for example, we know that the distance between Albuquerque and Salt Lake is about 42% greater than the distance between Albuquerque and Denver.

Given a table of distances between cities, it is a much more difficult problem to construct a map showing the relative locations of the cities. For just the three cities in our example, making a map would be relatively easy. A triangle could be constructed out of the three distances. With a larger number of cities, the task gets much more complicated. With just 10 cities, there are 45 distances between all possible pairs. In general, the number of distances is equal to number of cities (n) taken two at a time $\{n!/\{(n-2)!2!\}$, where $n!$ is n factorial). MDS is a procedure for solving a problem of this type. In addition, it can be performed on any measure of distance or proximity—even psychological measures having considerable variability. The solutions given by MDS are not limited to two-dimensional ones. Ideally, the procedure finds the optimal number of dimensions to describe the relative proximities among the objects of interest. The stimuli are placed in the Euclidian space so that the distance between two stimuli in the space represents a measure of the similarity of the stimuli.

One important assumption of MDS is that the proximities are symmetrical. This is a reasonable assumption in many cases. The distance from Denver to Salt Lake is the same as the distance from Salt Lake to Denver. There are clear violations of this assumption in other domains. The perceived similarity of Cuba to the Soviet Union is much greater than the perceived similarity of the Soviet Union to Cuba (Tversky, 1977).

MDS only requires some measure of the proximities among the objects of interest. These proximities can be determined from standard psychophysical tasks, such as similarity ratings or confusion matrices. The analysis gives a geometric configuration of the objects, similar to the layout of cities on a map. There are also methods for determining the number of dimensions required for a reasonable description of the objects. In general, increasing the number of dimensions will give a better description because of an increase in the number of free parameters (see Chapter 10, Parameters). Thus, it is important to require as few dimensions as necessary. The underlying structure of the objects is best revealed when there are relatively few dimensions.

Finally, it should be noted that this MDS solution to a single set of distances gives only the relative proximities in the dimensional space. The location of the axes in the solution are not meaningful. The experimenter must rotate the axes to make sense of the results. For example, a two-dimensional solution to the problem of 10 cities is given in Figure 12. It is only our knowledge of geographic north-south and east-west directions and our knowledge of the absolute location of one of the cities that allows us to rotate the axes and to express the cities in a geographic space shown in Figure 12.

Dissimilarity Ratings of Animals

Henley (1969) used the MDS technique to study the structure of long-term memory. She was interested in the relationship between animal names. A dog has certain properties or features that distinguish it from a horse and so on. Henley asked, what dimensions are important in the meaning of animal names? For example, how does a mouse differ from an elephant? Most people would agree that size is the most distinguishing factor between these two animals. In contrast, a deer and a gorilla seem to be about the same size, but differ in ferocity. To get subjects to compare animals in this way, Henley asked them to rate the amount of dissimilarity between two animals on a scale from 0 (no difference) to 10. She used 30 animals and presented subjects with all possible pairs one pair at a time.

The dependent measure in this experiment is a matrix of dissimilarity ratings. The dissimilarity of each animal to every other animal would be represented by a number between 0 and 10. The investigator faced with a dissimilarity rating for all possible pairs of 30 animals is unable to determine how many dimensions were important in the subject's ratings. As we have seen, multidimensional scaling can be used to represent the animals in an n-dimensional Euclidean space so that the distance between two animals would be directly related to the rated amount of dissimilarity. In addition, the analysis provides the representation with the smallest number of dimensions possible. In our earlier example, we said that subjects might judge the dissimilarity of the animals on the basis of only size and ferocity. In this case, the multidimensional scaling routine

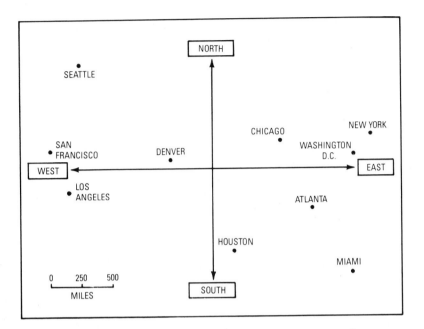

Figure 12. Spatial relationship among cities given by MDS of the distances among the cities (rotated axes).

would indicate that the animals can best be represented in a two-dimensional space. The multidimensional routine does not label the dimensions but simply places animals in the space. The experimenter must use some ingenuity in finding dimensional names or concepts that describe the placement of the animals. The experimenter would be justified in labeling the two dimensions *size* and *ferocity* if the animals were arranged from small to large and gentle to fierce, respectively, on the two dimensions. The relationship between the animals could then be seen directly on a simple two-dimensional plot. Animals judged to be very dissimilar would be very distant spatially, whereas animals judged to be similar would be represented very close together.

Animal Space

Henley found that three dimensions were necessary to describe the dissimilarity ratings of the animals. Three dimensions or attributes seemed to be important to the subjects in rating dissimilarity. Figure 13 plots the spatial relationship between her selected set of animals in a way that best describes the dissimilarity ratings. The three dimensions seem to correspond to the attributes of size, ferocity, and humanness, although it may not be possible to describe each dimension in terms of a single word. The dimensions may be more complex and difficult to specify exactly. This spatial structure was also found when other methods, such as a method of association, were used. In this case subjects were required to respond with the animal word that came to mind upon presentation of a test word. The test words were the 30 animal names. In this instance, animals were considered to be similar to the extent that they were given as responses to each other. The multidimensional scaling routine revealed the same structure for these responses as for the dissimilarity ratings. Henley's results reveal that it is reasonable to represent the conceptual codes of animals in a multidimensional space with roughly three dimensions.

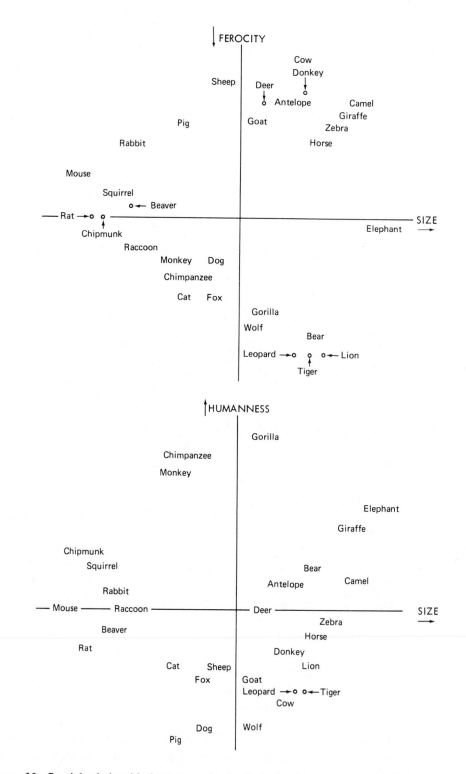

Figure 13. Spatial relationship between animals along the dimensions that best describe the dissimilarity ratings (after Henley, 1969).

PART THREE

Perception and
Cognition

14

Visual Perception

Light

The Eye

Eye Movements
  Nystagmus
  Saccades
  Accommodation
  Vergence

Perception and Knowledge

Cues to Depth
  Size in Picture Plane
  Height in Picture Plane
  Lighting and Shadow
  Interposition
  Linear Perspective
  Surface Texture
  Simplicity of Figure
  Motion Parallax
  Binocular Disparity
  Panum's Area
  Vergence
  Ambiguity and Integrating Cues

Size Constancy
  Inductive Inference
  Invariance Hypothesis

Shape Constancy
  Invariance Hypothesis
  Perceptual Processing Time

Optical Illusions
  Illusory Contours
  Reversibility
  Impossible Scenarios
  Knowledge and Perception
  The Moon Illusion
  Constancy Scaling
  Geometrical Illusions Revisted
  Total Impression Theory

How Well Do We See?
Hermann von Helmholtz

---

*So, Socrates, you have made a discovery—that false
judgment resides, not in our perceptions among
themselves, nor yet in our thoughts, but in the fitting
together of perception and thought.*
Plato's Theaetetus

The perception of the visual world appears to be direct and straightforward. We easily recognize objects of different sizes, shapes, and colors at varying distances and orientations in the real world. The act of visual perception is so familiar that, upon introduction to the topic, many students do not see the necessity of psychological investigation. Our phenomenological experience might easily lead to the position that we see the world in a certain way because that's the way the world is. This position is sometimes referred to as naive realism. Perception, therefore, simply involves walking up to an object and resonating to the information that is contained within it.

Nevertheless, eye contact with the visual world is not sufficient to see it in an orderly, organized, and predictable way. Gregory (1966, 1987) reports the experiences of a man who, blind from the age of ten months, had his sight restored at the age of fifty-two. (The corneas of his eyes were opaque and this deficit was corrected with cornea transplants.) After the surgery, he could recognize only those objects that he had previously learned by touch. For example, he had been taught to read uppercase letters by touch at school. With restored sight, he could recognize uppercase letters but not lowercase. When he was shown a simple lathe, he could not recognize it or see it clearly although he knew what a lathe was and how it functioned. When he was allowed to touch it, he closed his eyes and ran his hands over the parts of the lathe. Afterwards, when he stood back and observed it, he said, "Now that I've felt it I can see it." Apparently this man had learned a set of operations which allowed him to see the world by touch but not by sight. But after learning about the shape and function of a particular object by touch, he could use this information to see the object as it should have been seen. Without knowing what to look for, or how to look for it, the object could not be perceived. This example, given its complexity, is meant only to show that visual perception is a complicated and time consuming process that deserves careful psychological study. We begin our discussion of the interaction of the stimulus world and the perceiver with light and the eye.

LIGHT

Light is radiant energy which makes up only a minute part of the electromagnetic spectrum. Along this spectrum energy is described by its wavelength and its intensity. The visible part of the spectrum contains wavelengths longer than X-rays and ultraviolet waves and shorter than radio waves and infrared waves.

Within the visible portion of the electromagnetic spectrum, the intensity of light is primarily responsible for its perceived brightness. The wavelength mainly determines which hue, usually called color by the layman, is perceived. White light is a combination of all visible wavelengths. When it enters a prism, it slows down and is bent, since the medium of the prism is denser than air. The amount of bending differs for the different wavelengths making up the white light, producing a rainbow on the other side of the prism. White light leaves a prism as different hues, ranging from violet, blue, green, yellow, orange, to red. The wavelengths of these hues range between 400 and 700 nanometers (nm). [One nm is equal to one billionth of a meter.]

A description of the electromagnetic spectrum in terms of waves does not describe or explain all of its known properties. Accordingly, physical scientists find it useful to describe light in terms of a quantum theory. This theory assumes that radiant energy is emitted in discrete units, one at a time, not in a continuous train of waves. Each unit or particle of energy is called a quantum. Although the quantum theory solves many of the physicists' problems, they still find it necessary to treat light as a wave phenomenon in some situations. Both theories are also utilized by psychologists studying light detection, as we observed in the discussion of the minimum light needed for seeing (Chapter 3, Seeing Light under Optimal Conditions).

THE EYE

The appropriate stimulus for seeing is light entering the eye. Figure 1 illustrates that when light enters the eye, it first passes through the cornea, the protective window of the eye. The curvature of the cornea and the shape of the lens focus the light entering the eye so that a reasonably accurate inverted picture of the visual field is formed on the retina, the back of the eye. Before light reaches the retina, however, it has to pass through the nerve fibers connected to the light receptors, since the nerve fibers lie directly in the path of the incoming light. The retina contains the rods and cones, the light-sensitive receptors. The cones are packed at the center of the eye, called the fovea, whereas the rods are more prevalent in the periphery. The rods and cones transform the light into nerve impulses as a result of their photochemical reaction to the light. These impulses are passed on to the brain via the optic nerve fibers.

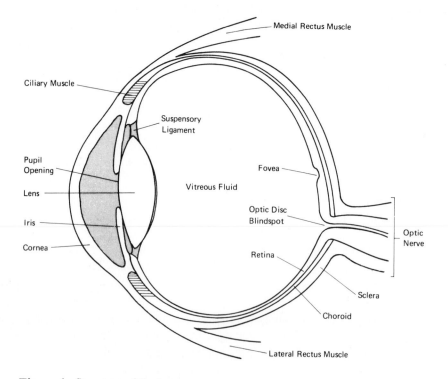

Figure 1. Structure of the human eye.

EYE MOVEMENTS

An important feature of seeing is that the eyes are not static, but move in a variety of ways. Eye movements play an important role in our visual experience. Experimenters must be careful to account for these eye movements in their experiments. We distinguish four classes of eye movements, each of which has unique characteristics and different consequences for our visual experience.

Nystagmus

The eye has a fine high-frequency tremor or nystagmus. This movement is an involuntary rapid oscillation of the eyeballs of between 30 and 100 cycles per sec of arc. Accordingly, the retinal image of a scene is continually jerking (moving) slightly on the retina, even though one usually sees a stable world.

Nystagmus appears to have no important function in visual processing. It is best thought of as meaningless background noise in the visual system. In no way does nystagmus help one to encode information, nor does it add to the information in the visual stimulus. The assertion of some investigators that these small, high-frequency oscillations allow the light pattern to hit more receptors and, therefore, improve the figure-ground contrast is unfounded. When an image is stabilized on the retina, so that nystagmus is eliminated, visual acuity is just as sharp as with normal nystagmus movements (Keesey, 1960).

Saccades

A second kind of eye movement, called saccades, are much larger movements than high-frequency nystagmus and do not occur more frequently than 4 or 5 times per sec. Viewing a painting, for example, the eyes jerk across the painting and the viewer obtains a succession of discrete looks during the fixation time between eye movements. The saccadic eye movement is programmed by the viewer before it is initiated. Once it begins, the direction and distance of the movement cannot be modified. The movement is called ballistic and is very rapid, covering about 360 degrees per sec for large eye movements.

Again, in normal perception, we are not usually aware of this very fast eye movement. Perception is suppressed during the saccadic eye movement, and the views from successive fixations are integrated into a continuous picture. Since saccadic eye movements are extremely fast, the image of the visual scene moves rapidly across the retina. We do not notice this for at least two reasons. One is that the stimulation from any point on the visual scene occurs only on a given point on the retina for a brief period of time so that the intensity of the stimulation is very low. The second reason is that very little time elapses to process the stimulation once initiated, since it is replaced immediately by another part of the visual scene.

Saccadic eye movements are critical for visual perception. It is important to refresh our view of the world every 1/4 sec or so; otherwise, it might disappear entirely. This is demonstrated in the painting *Minimum* by Alexander Liberman (Figure 2). Fixating on a point in the center of the painting will cause the thin circle to blend with the background and disappear. The small saccadic movements when we try to hold our fixation steady do not change the visual scene significantly, indicating that simple scenes can be made to disappear with steady fixation. This demonstration shows that nystagmus movements, which cannot be controlled voluntarily, are not sufficient to maintain the appearance of the scene, again demonstrating their lack of function.

Figure 2. *Minimum* by Alexander Liberman.
1949. Enamel on composition board, 48 x 48". Collection, The Museum of Modern Art. Gift of Samuel I. Newhouse Foundation, Inc.

Accommodation

Accommodation is not a movement of the eye itself, but involves adjustment of the crystalline lens of the eye (Figure 3). The curvature of the lens is changed to bring an image into sharp focus (analogous to the focusing of a camera). When an observer is viewing a near object, the curvature of the lens is increased to increase its refractive power. When the object is farther from the viewer, the lens curvature of the lens is decreased to decrease its refractive power.

Figure 3, *Cinematic Painting* by Wolfgang Ludwig, is appropriately titled; no matter how much we try to stabilize the scene, the centers of the two patterns do not remain stable. Has the artist, therefore, succeeded in devising a scene that takes advantage of the eye's movement? Normally, the visual scene has a more defined figure-ground relationship, and small eye movements go unnoticed. In the painting, however, the lines become very fine towards the middle of the patterns so that acuity breaks down. The thin portion of the line becomes fuzzier at the center and the viewer tends to see a gray patch that vibrates.

One test of the eye movement explanation of visual effects in Figure 3 is to produce in a dark-adapted subject an afterimage of the painting, by illuminating it with a very short and bright light. The electronic flash used in photography is excellent, since it presents the light in less than 1 msec. In this case, eye movements cannot change the position of the image on the retina as they do

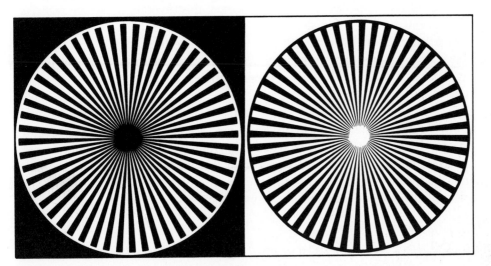

Figure 3. *Cinematic Painting* by Wolfgang Ludwig.
1964. Oil on composition board, 24¼ x 48¼. Collection of the artist.

in normal viewing. If a positive afterimage is obtained, the viewer can observe whether she experiences any movement within the patterns. If she does not, this provides good evidence that eye movements are, at least, partially responsible for the effects observed in Ludwig's disturbing painting. Some corroboration for this comes from Evans and Marsden (1966), who showed that movement in patterns similar to Ludwig's painting disappeared when viewed as positive afterimages.

Another possible cause of the movement in Ludwig's painting could be fluctuations in the accommodation of the lens of the eye. In order to bring a retinal image into sharp focus, the curvature of the lens must be changed, that is, it must accommodate. When the object is brought closer to the viewer, the lens must accommodate at a larger curvature in order to focus the image properly on the retina. The method of stabilizing the retinal image by a bright flash producing an afterimage would not only eliminate nystagmus and saccadic eye movements, but would also eliminate movements of the retinal image due to fluctuations in accommodation. Therefore, any or all of these movements could be responsible.

Another method of stabilizing the image on the retina projects the image on a contact lens. The contact lens moves with movements of the eye so that the image on the retina does not change its position with eye movements. Although this method eliminates changes in the retinal position due to eye movements, it does not eliminate changes in the image produced by changes in accommodation. Therefore, using this stabilization method when observing the painting could isolate the critical variable. If nystagmus or saccadic eye movements were responsible, no movement should be visible. MacKay's (1957) observations implicate accommodation as the responsible mechanism, since he observed movement of similar figures using the contact lens stabilization technique.

Millodot's (1968) observation also tends to support the accommodation hypothesis. His experiment was based on the observation that the momentary fluctuations in accommodation were smaller when objects were viewed at greater distances. Accordingly, the perceived movements should be larger when the figure is viewed at a shorter than a longer distance if accommodation is responsible for the effect. His observations supported this hypothesis when subjects viewed concentric circles drawn within one another. Furthermore, one of his subjects who had no accommodation in one eye, only saw the illusion with the other eye. These observations point to accommodation changes rather than nystagmus eye movements as responsible for the movement seen in Ludwig's painting and in Millodot's concentric circles.

Vergence

The two eyes are normally rotated to fixate on a given point in space. Vergence eye movements change the point of fixation in space. Convergence of the eyes involves rotating the eyes inward to fixate on a near object. Divergence of the optical axes increases the depth of the point of fixation in space. Vergence eye movements are about ten or twenty times slower than saccades and occur independently of saccadic eye movements.

PERCEPTION AND KNOWLEDGE

Visual perception involves the interaction of two sources of information available to the perceiver. The first is the visual stimulus available to the visual sensory system and the second is the knowledge of the perceiver. An example of how the visual information available to the observer and his knowledge interact in perception is illustrated by a passage taken from Defoe's *Robinson Crusoe*.

> When, one morning the day broke, and all unexpectedly before their eyes a ship stood, what it was was evident at a glance to Crusoe. But how was it with Friday? As younger and uncivilized, his eyes were presumably better than those of his master. That is, Friday saw the ship really the best of the two; and yet he could hardly be said to see it at all.

What Crusoe possessed that Friday did not was knowledge of how to operate on the visual information transduced by the eye in order to recognize a ship on the horizon. Without these operations, the visual input was not sufficient for perception of a ship.

Recall that Gregory's patient could not see the shape of an object accurately if he first did not learn about it by touching it. Similarly Crusoe's man Friday was not able to discern a ship on the horizon, being young and inexperienced on the seas. These observations agree with the statement of William James, who said we can perceive only what we have preperceived. Gregory's patient was able to build up a memory representation of the object by touching it, which later facilitated his visual perception of it. Crusoe's experience allowed him to spot the ship with very little visual information. Our knowledge continually facilitates perception by allowing us to build a figure-ground relationship with the processing of a minimal amount of visual information.

To perceive a figure-ground relationship it is necessary to have information in memory to help identify what is seen. The left panel of Figure 4 shows a lithograph by Roy Lichtenstein. By viewing the work from a distance, the dots can be mixed in the way intended by pointillist painters, such as Seurat. But Lichtenstein's print is ambiguous and usually is not perceived at first glance. Even its title, *Cathedral #3*, does not help most observers. The most help comes from viewing Claude Monet's *Rouen Cathedral* (right panel of Figure 4), which Lichtenstein used as a model for his lithograph. With an idea or conception of what we should see, we have no problem seeing the intended figure-ground relationship.

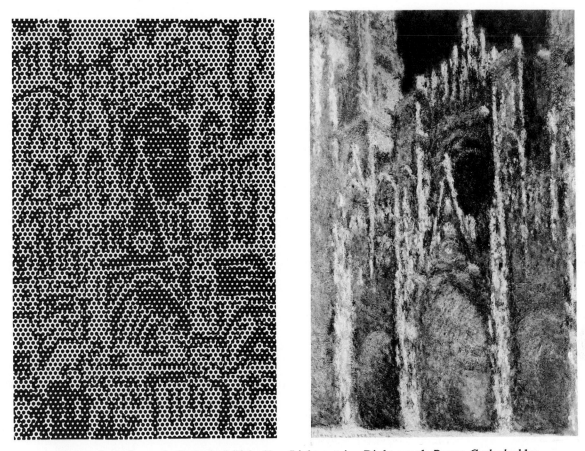

Figure 4. Left panel: *Cathedral #3* by Roy Lichtenstein. Right panel: *Rouen Cathedral* by Claude Monet.

(Left) Gemini G. E. L., Los Angeles, California, 1988.   (Right) Art Resource, New York.

As noted earlier, in visual perception both the visual stimulus and the knowledge of the observer are essential ingredients. One problem that has intrigued philosophers and psychologists for centuries is how to see a three-dimensional world given only a two-dimensional visual image. This problem is easily resolved if we recognize the contribution of what the observer knows. Gregory's patient, we noted, could not perceive the visual input accurately in three dimensions. Here we discuss how the knowledge of the observer takes advantage of visual features, or cues in the visual scene, to perceive a three-dimensional world.

CUES TO DEPTH

There are many cues that aid us in perceiving a three-dimensional world. Some cues are referred to as two dimensional because they are not dependent on actual depth relationships. Some cues are called monocular because they do not have to be viewed binocularly. The role of of a given cue could be localized in abstract art, if the artist makes only that one cue available. Its perceptual consequences can thus be viewed directly.

How Well Do We See?

As in Star Wars, suppose you entered light space and landed in a completely novel universe. The beings there just happen to be Homo sapiens and could communicate in earthly tongues, such as the king's english. The central concern of these beings is to understand what it is like living on Earth. To begin, they ask about our physical, botanical, and biological environs. How accurate would you be in your descriptions? For example, how would you describe butterflies, grasshoppers, and mosquitos? Or, more relevant to this world, a midwesterner goes to the Southwest, meets a native, and has to explain the differences in geographical and botanical milieu. How well would you succeed at this? Some measure of success might reveal how well you see beyond simply avoiding bumping into objects and falling down steps.

Size in Picture Plane

The first perspective cue we consider is size. Relative size is a cue that can be used for determining relative depth. Discs perceived in Figure 5 seem to be at different distances from the viewer. The larger discs appear closer; the small ones appear far away. This painting has no other cue to depth but size, indicating that relative size is a powerful depth cue. Usually, larger things appear nearer than smaller things. This phenomenon can also be observed in the moon illusion. The moon at the horizon looks both large and close, whereas the moon at the zenith appears small and far away.

Height in Picture Plane

Height in the picture plane tends to covary with distance from the viewer. Objects on the terrain will be higher in the picture plane to the extent they are farther away. Perhaps the filled discs at the top of Figure 5 appear larger to you than those at the bottom of the figure. Artists employed this cue to convey depth long before many of the other cues were discovered.

Lighting and Shadow

The change in lighting and detail of objects is a cue to their depth. The appearance of an object is fuzzier and less detailed with increasing distance from the viewer. We have no problem perceiving a weeping willow in the pastel by Wayne Thiebaud (Figure 6). The differential lighting and the shadow convey a message of figure, ground, and depth. Of course, contemporary artists were not the first to use shadow as a perspective cue. In fact, lighting and shadow were used as cues to depth long before linear perspective cues. Thiebaud, however, by eliminating other depth cues in this work, demonstrates that the nature of the lighting is a sufficient cue for depth.

Interposition

Figure 7, *Black Cross, New Mexico* by Georgia O'Keeffe, demonstrates the role of interposition in perceiving depth. One cue to depth in the real world is that an object appearing in front of, or interposed, between you and another object is perceived as nearer. It is very easy to perceive the black cross and the mountains extending in depth, because the cross is interposed in front of the mountains and each mountain covers another mountain behind it.

Linear Perspective

Linear perspective is a very important cue to depth. Two converging lines are usually perceived as extending in depth if they are assumed to be parallel in the actual three-dimensional scene. Victor Vasarely uses perspective very nicely in the painting shown in Figure 8, which gives

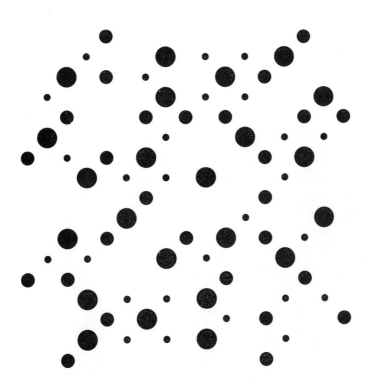

Figure 5. *White Discs I* by Brigit Riley.
1964. Private collection, Mrs. Robert B. Mayer.

a receding hallway effect. Because it is usually assumed that hallways do not change their shape, the converging lines, conveyed by the rectangles become smaller, allow the viewer to look down the hallway receding into the distance. In this painting, it is difficult to compete against the linear perspective cues by trying to see the narrow part of the hallway as actually closer.

Surface Texture

Another cue for depth is surface texture. If the texture of an object remains constant, then as it recedes into the distance the gradient of the texture appears smaller. In *Equivocation* by Benjamin Cunningham (Figure 9), the relative sizes of the squares give a cue to their distance, since it is usually assumed that the texture of the object is made of constant size squares. The object must be receding in depth if the squares become smaller. The change in the projected size of the squares is called a texture gradient. Texture gradients provide information about relative depth and simultaneously give a cue to the slant of the surface. Cunningham's work shows that texture gradients can convey not only relative depth but the actual shape of the surface seen in depth. Texture allows Cunningham to display a fascinating three-dimensional scene in only two dimensions. Rosinski and Levine (1976) demonstrated that texture gradients were functional in the perception of the slant of surfaces.

Figure 6. *Weeping Willow* by Wayne Thiebaud.
Allan Stone Gallery, New York.

Simplicity of Figure

In *Betelgeuse I* by Victor Vasarely (Figure 10) the depth we see is dependent on the figure we see. We tend to perceive as figure the simplest possible object in the real three-dimensional world. In other words, it is easiest to see those objects that are familiar or simple—circles, squares, rectangles, and so on.

The simple or good figure—such as the circle—is most easily seen, and the perceived depth is made congruent with this perception. An ellipse is more likely to be seen as a circle rotated in depth. By contrast, circles are seen as flat, in a plane parallel to the viewer's forehead. Figure 10 shows that different depth relationships can be seen in the same two-dimensional representation, depending upon the simplicity of the possible figures in the three-dimensional world.

Motion Parallax

Moving around objects in space provides information about their depth. How does motion parallax work? Assume that you are fixated at an object in space, as illustrated in Figure 11. You move from right to left and remain fixated on the object. Objects closer to you than the fixation object will appear to move in the opposite direction of your movement with respect to the fixation

Figure 7. *Black Cross, New Mexico* by Georgia O'Keeffe.
1929. Oil on canvas, 99 x 77.2 cm. The Art Institute Purchase Fund, 1943.95. © 1988 The Art Institute of Chicago. All Rights Reserved.

object. Objects farther from you than the fixation object will appear to move in the same direction as your movement with respect to the fixation object. Also, the speed of movement depends on the relative proximity between you and the fixation object. The greater the distance, the greater the speed. Motion parallax can also be thought of as a modulator or magnifier of other cues to depth. Perspective and texture cues create an optical change during motion that is sometimes referred to as motion perspective.

Binocular Disparity

Two eyes present us with two views of the visual world. These two views can serve as a cue to depth. When the eyes are looking at a point in infinity, the line of sight of the right eye is parallel to the line of sight of the left eye. In this case, the same image falls on each retina and stimulates corresponding retinal points. Corresponding retinal points are linked by the fibers of the optic tract to a common locus in the visual projection area of the cortex. For example, when one observes the sky at night and fixates on a star, the images of all the stars would fall on corresponding retinal points. But when one fixates on an object closer in space like the page of a book, only some of the objects in space will produce images that fall on corresponding retinal

Figure 8. *Vonal-KSZ* by Victor Vasarely.
1968. 78¾ x 78¾. Réunion des Musées, Paris.

points. The loci of all points in space which stimulate corresponding retinal points is defined as the horopter. When the eyes are fixated on a point in space, the horopter approximates a circle passing through the points of fixation and the center of curvatures of the two eyeballs (shown in Figure 12). The perception of the points in space is critically dependent on their distance from the horopter. Points on or near the horopter are seen most clearly; points farther from the horopter appear blurred and sometimes double images can be seen. Figure 13 depicts Peter Paul Rubens' view of an early study of the horopter.

To demonstrate the horopter, put a coin in each hand, and hold out both hands side by side. Maintain your fixation on one coin while moving the other slowly closer or farther away. Do not change your fixation—concentrating on the writing of the coin may help. You should notice blurring of the moving coin as it is moved off the horopter of the coin that is fixated. The binocular

Figure 9. *Equivocation* by Benjamin Cunningham.
1964. Synthetic polymer paint on composition board, 26 x 26". Collection, The Museum of Modern Art, New York. Larry Alrich Foundation Fund.

disparity created by objects placed off the horopter provides information about their relative locations in depth.

Panum's Area

The recognition process can only read out or resolve the figure-ground relationship of the points in space that are sufficiently close to the horopter. Exactly how close was first determined by Panum, and this area is called Panum's area. Panum's area includes the nearest and farthest points that can be seen clearly without blurring. Panum defined this area in terms of the angle of vergence—the angle given by the intersection of the two lines of sight as shown in Figure 14. To determine Panum's area at a given fixation, we subtract the angle of vergence given by the farthest points that can be seen clearly from the angle of vergence given by the nearest points. Panum defined this area to be about 6 to 10 min of visual angle.

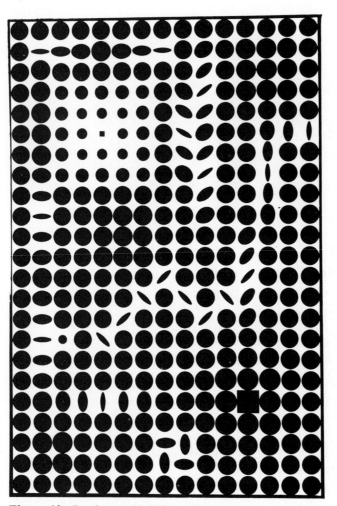

Figure 10. *Betelgeuse I* by Victor Vasarely.
1957. 195 x 130 cm. Réunion des Musées, Paris.

Vergence

Information about the vergence posture can serve as a cue to the depth of the fixated object. Descartes explained this possibility using the analogy of a blind person holding two sticks, one in each hand (Owens, 1987). The sticks are placed to intersect at the location of the object being fixated. Knowing the distance between the hands and the angle of rotation of the two sticks, the distance to the object can be computed. The angle of vergence of the eyes can also provide depth information. If the observer is fixated on an object, then that object is farther away to the extent that the angle of vergence is small. Obviously, the visual system does not know the angle of vergence directly, but it does receive feedback from the eye muscles signaling how much the eyes are rotated inward.

To experience the effects of the vergence cue to depth, find the typical chain-linked fence or some other similarly textured surface. Now converge the eyes to fixate a point in space in front of

Figure 11. Motion parallax. When a person moves, objects at varying distances from the observer will appear to move in different directions and at different speeds.

the fence. Although your view might be blurred at first, the pattern should pop out and appear closer to you. More importantly, the pattern now appears much smaller than it did previously. The decrease in apparent size of the pattern is consistent with the size-distance invariance hypothesis (p. 274), in which the perceived size of an object decreases with decreases in perceived distance. The decrease in apparent size when the pattern appears close shows that vergence functions as a cue to perceived distance. Similar to vergence, accommodation (variations in the curvature of the lens) can also contribute to perceived distance.

Ambiguity and Integrating Cues

You might not have been totally convinced by the preceding demonstrations of cues to depth. With good reason. Each cue to depth is somewhat ambiguous, in that it does not guarantee a particular depth. An object that is higher in the picture plane is not necessarily farther away. My video display terminal is higher in the picture plane than a painting on the wall behind it, and yet I still see the video display as closer. Other cues apparently override this height cue, so that my perception is fairly veridical.

The best way to think about these cues is *ceteris paribus*—all other things equal. Height is a cue (clue) to depth because, on the average, objects higher in the picture plane will be farther away. Information is not packaged in guarantees. As in our discussion of information theory (Chapter 1), the cues can be said to reduce uncertainty because they eliminate alternatives. Consider the example of guessing the outcome of a sequence of coin tosses. No question is sufficient for determining the answer. All of the questions together, however, give the answer. An analogous

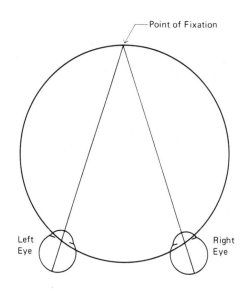

Figure 12. The horopter approximates a circle passing through the point of fixation and the centers of curvature of the two eyes.

Figure 13. Rubens' drawing of the original horopter apparatus of Franciscus Aguilonius (1613). As can be seen in the drawing, the student assistants were extremely enthusiastic and took an active interest in their mentor's work.

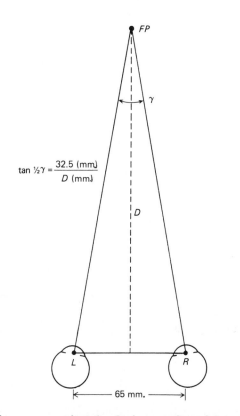

Figure 14. The angle of vergence γ given by the intersection of the two lines of sight at the fixation point *FP*. The eyes *L* and *R* are assumed to be 65 mm apart.

situation exists with respect to cues to depth (or influences on performance in other domains). No depth cue is sufficient, but the combination of all cues presents an unambiguous situation. Realist paintings are usually unambiguous, for example, because the painter usually exploits many depth cues to convey the scene.

Our impressive resolution of the visual world might be a consequence of having multiple sources of information about it. The prototypical experiment in visual perception has been to eliminate or to hold constant all potential cues but one, vary the cue of interest, and to observe its behavioral consequences. The single-factor design is weak in information value, however, because it cannot measure the relative salience of the cues nor address the processing of multiple cues. Given that all cues but one are neutralized, the single-factor design might not give a valid estimate of the contribution of the cue being manipulated. Following the logic developed in this text, cues to depth are best studied in factorial designs in which several cues are varied independently of one another.

Bruno and Cutting (1988) varied four cues to perceived depth in a factorial design, and used some of the techniques of functional measurement and multidimensional scaling (see Chapter 13). The four sources of monocular information were size in the picture plane, height in the picture plane, interposition, and motion parallax. Among other things, these sources of information or cues specify the (exocentric) distance between two objects. Subjects judged the distance between two test objects. Bruno and Cutting's (1988) experimental analysis of exocentric distance is a step forward because it improves on the classic single-factor design. The results of the judgments indicated that each of the four sources of information influenced the judgments; no single source of information dominated the others. Although beyond the scope of this discussion, the results also illuminated how depth cues are processed and combined. This experimental approach offers a promising attack on a old problem in visual perception.

SIZE CONSTANCY

Cues to depth allow us to impose a meaningful and veridical interpretation of our visual world. Consider the problem of the perceived size of objects. If we ask observers to judge the size of a series of objects at varying distances, the observers might respond, "In order to accurately judge the size of planes we first have to know how far away they are?" Such an observation expresses the fact that, in order to judge size accurately, distance must be taken into account. Holway and Boring's (1941) experiment was designed to show that accurate perception of distance is necessary for accurate perception of size.

The subject in the experiment sat at the intersection of two long hallways connecting at a right angle. A disk of light that was adjustable in size, called the variable disk, was placed in one hallway 10 feet away from the observer. In the other hallway, a standard disk was placed from 10 to 120 feet from the observer. The size of the standard disk was increased with increasing distance so that it always subtended a visual angle of 1 degree. That is, the standard disk was inches and 10 feet and its size had to be doubled with every doubling of distance. The subject's task was to adjust the size of the variable disk of light so that the two disks appeared to be the same size. The independent variable was the distance of the standard disk from the observer and the dependent variable was his or her setting of the variable disk.

There are two orderly ways the subject can operate in this task. The subject can adjust the variable disk so that its real size is the same as the standard disk or so that the variable disk subtends the same visual angle as that subtended by the standard disk. When the standard and variable disks are the same distance from the observer, both strategies will give the same response. The responses of the two strategies diverge as the distance of the standard disk is increased. Figure 15 shows the predicted adjustments of the variable disk using these strategies as a function of the distance of the standard disk. We call the strategy of matching the true size of the standard disk *size constancy* and the strategy of matching the retinal size *retinal size match*. If the subject shows size constancy, the apparent size of the standard disk follows its true size, whereas a retinal size match follows its retinal projection.

When Holway and Boring did this experiment under conditions of normal binocular (1) or monocular (2) viewing, the subject's adjustments of the variable disk matched the actual size of the standard disk. In Condition (3) however, when the subject had to view the standard disk monocularly through an artificial pupil—a small hole that eliminated some depth cues, such as the sides of the hallways—the judgments fell somewhere between the two strategies. When additional depth cues were eliminated by removing reflections in the hallway (4), the judgments were almost equivalent to the retinal size match. These results reveal that the apparent size of an object is critically dependent upon its perceived distance. If distance cues are available, subjects tend to perceive size veridically; when these cues are eliminated, performance deteriorates and tends towards a retinal size match.

Holway and Boring's experiment demonstrates that we are capable of perceiving the true size of an object at different distances. Their experiment was somewhat unnatural in the sense that the size of the standard was changed at different distances in order to maintain a fixed visual angle of 1

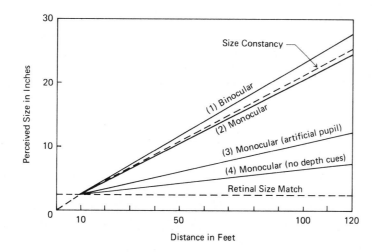

Figure 15. The perception of size as a function of the distance of the object from the observer. The different conditions are described in the text (after Holway & Boring, 1941).

degree. Holway and Boring had to increase the size of the standard by a factor of 2 for every doubling of distance. The experimenters could have carried out their study in another manner by having subjects judge the same objects at different distances. They would have found that the same object can be perceived as the same size at different distances, which changes the retinal size significantly. Both results show that some process operates to incorporate distance information in the perception of size.

Inductive Inference

How can we account for veridical perception despite the changes in retinal information? Helmholtz, in the middle of the nineteenth century, proposed a solution which is still influential in much of today's research and theory in visual perception. Helmholtz first made a distinction between sense impressions and perceptual judgments. This distinction made by Helmholtz corresponds to the distinction made earlier by Reid between sensation and perception. Sensation was the raw impression made by an object, whereas perceptual judgments involved a further step in which the sense impressions were supplied with meaning. Helmholtz's significant contribution was the process he proposed for going from sensation to perception. He stated that our perceptions were determined by inductive inference—an unconscious mental process in which we derive inferences from our sense impressions. Inductive inference in perception was assumed to be analogous to the process of inference in more abstract mental functioning, such as inferences that can be made from a set of assumptions using laws of logic.

In making a distinction between sensations and perceptual judgments based on inductive inference, Helmholtz may have implied that there were two successive stages involved in the perceptual process. Helmholtz (1867) said, "We shall succeed much better in forming a correct notion of what we see if we have no opposing sensations to overcome, than if a correct judgment must be formed in spite of them." In our interpretation of Helmholtz, then, the first stage would involve the operations necessary for the sensations to become apparent. The second stage would involve the formation of a perceptual judgment based on inductive inference. In the formulation, the process of inductive inference must occur after the process of sensation, since inference operates on the output of the sensation stage. This model is illustrated in Figure 16.

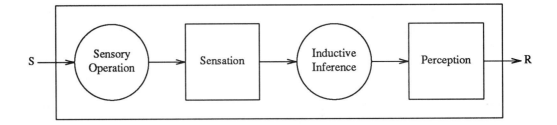

Figure 16. Stage model representing Helmholtz's two-stage theory of perception. The operations of the first stage produce a sensation that becomes available to the second stage, the operation of inductive inference. The outcome of inductive inference is the conscious perception that can be reported by the observer.

Hermann von Helmholtz

A German physicist and physiologist, Helmholtz, lived from 1821 to 1894. In addition to many outstanding contributions to mathematical and experimental physics, this scientist wrote seminal treatises in vision and audition. These volumes are surprisingly current today, more than 100 years after their original publication (Hurvich & Jameson, 1979). The ophthalmoscope used by your eye physician has not changed much since Helmholtz's invention of it. It is interesting that Helmholtz, a highly knowledgeable physicist and physiologist, gave equal if not greater importance to psychological processing. Sensations could be interpreted in various ways depending on the situational context and previous experience of the observer. As an example, Helmholtz attributed the processes involved in size and shape constancy to internal psychological events rather than to peripheral visual processing. Helmholtz's highly influential idea of unconscious inductive inference is still advocated by many today (Gregory, 1986; Rock, 1983; 1985).

Invariance Hypothesis

A more specific application of Helmholtz's theory of inductive inference is the invariance hypothesis (Beck & Gibson, 1955; Hochberg, 1971; Koffka, 1935). The invariance hypothesis is a descriptive process that accounts for veridical perception, the fact that the perceived object usually corresponds to the real object even though the retinal input changes with changes in the object's distance and orientation. The invariance hypothesis of object perception uses laws of projective geometry to describe the stimulus circumstances that can provide veridical perception of an object.

The invariance hypothesis of size perception provides the object's true size by incorporating retinal (projected) image size and distance in an algorithm taken from the laws of projective geometry. In this case, size perception also follows a two-stage process similar to the process of inductive inference (see Figure 17). Distance cues and the projected image of the object enter the sensory system, are processed there, and transformed into actual value of distance and retinal image size. These values are then inserted in an equation called an invariance algorithm, which computes the size of the object. The invariance algorithm says that for a fixed retinal image, the perceived size of an object is directly proportional to its perceived distance D. Expressing the invariance hypothesis mathematically gives the equation

$$S = K \times D \qquad (1)$$

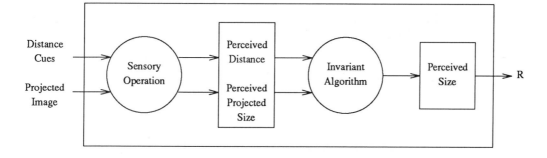

Figure 17. A two-stage process representing the invariance hypothesis of size perception.

where K is the constant of proportionality. For example, if K is .1, then the perceived size S is always one tenth of perceived distance (for a fixed projected size). This equation accurately predicts the results of the Holway and Boring experiment under the different conditions of viewing. When distance cues are available so that distance should be perceived veridically, the observers' judgments should be on the straight line generated by Equation 1. As cues to distance are removed, the sensory system cannot resolve a value for the distance D. In this case, the true size cannot be computed and the observers simply match the retinal images of the two disks.

SHAPE CONSTANCY

Analogous to perceived size, perceived shape usually corresponds to objective shape, even though the retinal input changes with changes in spatial orientation of the object. Consider the retinal projections of a coffee cup as the cup is rotated in depth. When the viewer is looking directly inside the cup, so that the plane formed by the rim of the cup is parallel to the viewer's forehead, the projected image of the rim of the cup is a circle and, of course, a circle is seen. However, as the cup is rotated into an upright position, the projected image of the rim of the cup becomes elliptical until only a line is projected when the plane of the rim of the cup is perpendicular to the observer's forehead.

The most striking observation is that the rim of the cup continues to appear circular as the cup is rotated despite the projective transformations of the retinal image. We might assume that the observer has independent access to the object's real shape and that this accounts both for constancy and veridicality. For example, with a coffee cup, context cues such as the handle and other identifiable characteristics indicate that the object is a coffee cup. With these cues, the observer could infer directly that the rim of the cup is circular. In this case, the projected image transformations could be ignored and a circular rim perceived because this perception agrees with what is known about coffee cups. However, the appeal to nonvisual knowledge cannot account completely for shape constancy and veridicality since redundant cues are not in fact necessary for the perception of true shape. If, instead of the rim of a cup, a plain circular ring is viewed under different rotations, shape constancy and veridicality will still be found.

Without additional context cues, the spatial orientation of an object must be incorporated in the perception of shape. Analogous to size perception, we would expect that elimination of orientation cues would interfere with true shape perception and the observation would tend towards a retinal image match. In fact, a number of studies of shape perception have shown that shape constancy breaks down when cues to orientation are reduced or eliminated entirely (Epstein & Park, 1963; Winnick & Rosen, 1966). This analysis indicates that, analogous to the judgment of size, one cannot tell the true shape of an object without accounting for its spatial orientation.

Invariance Hypothesis

The invariance hypothesis of shape perception provides the object's true shape by incorporating retinal image shape and spatial orientation (slant) in an algorithm based on the laws of projective geometry. This hypothesis can also be interpreted as a two-stage process, illustrated in Figure 18. Depth cues of the object and its projected retinal image provide the sensory operation with information on slant and projected shape, respectively. The sensory system processes these two inputs and gives values of perceived slant and projected shape. These values are then inserted into the invariance algorithm, which then gives a unique value of perceived shape. Mathematically, for a fixed projected image, perceived shape S is some function of perceived orientation O.

$$S = F(O)$$ (2)

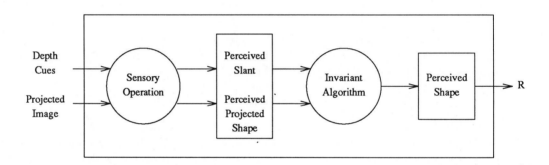

Figure 18. A two-stage process representing the invariance hypothesis of shape perception.

The invariance algorithm resembles Helmholtz's process of inductive inference, since its operation occurs after the process of sensation and operates on the values given by that stage. The invariance hypothesis of shape perception can account for veridical perception of shape. The model illustrated in Figure 18 and expressed in Equation 2 shows that perceived shape is uniquely determined by projective shape and apparent slant (Koffka, 1935; Beck & Gibson, 1955). The projected shape is available in the retinal image and apparent slant is determined by depth cues. Support for the invariance algorithm has been found in two paradigms. First, investigators have shown a direct functional relationship between perceived shape and apparent slant as predicted by Equation 2. Second, as noted earlier, shape constancy breaks down when cues to orientation are removed (Epstein, 1973; Epstein & Park, 1963; Winnick & Rosen, 1966).

Perceptual Processing Time

The classical formulation of inductive inference and the invariance hypothesis viewed perception as a relationship rather than a process which occurs over time. Our stage-model approach enables us to clarify the early theories more explicitly and to subject them to new experimental tests. One important variable in the information-processing model, but not central to the invariance hypothesis is the role of time for perceptual processing. If observers lack depth information, they tend to see the frontoparallel projection (retinal image match in the Holway & Boring, 1941, study). We might expect that processing time would also be important for seeing objects in depth. In an early study, Leibowitz and Bourne (1956) varied the exposure duration of a circle rotated in depth. When a circle rotated at 30° from the frontoparallel was presented for 100 msec, subjects saw the figure as an ellipse corresponding to the projection of the circle. Although Leibowitz and Bourne (1956) did not ask for slant judgments, Epstein, Hatfield, and Muise (1977) asked for slant as well as shape judgments in a similar task. As will be discussed in Chapter 15, exposure duration cannot be taken as a direct index of processing time and, therefore, the authors manipulated the stimulus onset asynchrony (SOA) in a backward masking task. Without a masking stimulus, a short exposure of around 80 msec was sufficient for good shape constancy. Observers saw a circle rotated in depth rather than an ellipse in the frontoparallel plane. Following the test presentation with a masking stimulus, however, reduced shape constancy considerably even when the mask was delayed by 50 msec. Even more to the point was the observation that the mask also led subjects to underestimate the orientation of the stimulus figure. The perception of shape was reasonably well predicted from the perception of slant of the figures.

Epstein et al. (1977) proposed that the time available for processing was the critical variable in their task. Given that subjects made reasonably good projective shape matches, this means that the mask did not disrupt the processing of contour information. It is probably the case that the simple contour information had been processed by the time of the onset of the mask. The disruptive effect of the mask derived from its interference with processing the orientation of the test figure. Insufficient processing time led to perception of a relatively flat or two-dimensional view and, therefore, subjects tended to match perceived shape of the test figure with its projective shape. In further experiments, Epstein and Hatfield (1978a, 1978b) replicated these results and also provided evidence for dichoptic masking (presenting the test stimulus to one eye and the masking stimulus to the other eye). These results show that, in addition to stimulus information or cues to depth, processing time is also necessary to achieve a three-dimensional view of the visual world.

OPTICAL ILLUSIONS

Usually, the many features of the scene are sufficient for the phenomenological experience of size, shape, and so on. In addition, in normal perception the visual features are interpreted correctly and experience is veridical; that is to say, it accurately represents the scene as it is. Sometimes, however, the visual features give misleading information so that phenomenological experience does not accord with the way things are. In this case, we say we have experienced an optical illusion.

Optical illusions are not only fun but important in the study of perception. Understanding the mechanisms or processes that underlie illusory perception should give some insights into such basic perceptual processes as form and space perception. For example, how is it that three-dimensional shapes in space can be seen when only a two-dimensional representation is given? The most popular illusions are geometric such as the Müller-Lyer, Ponzo, and Poggendorf figures shown in Figure 19. However, new illusions continue to be discovered and the impossible figures are gaining in popularity. The left object in Figure 20, known as a "blivet," appeared on the cover of the March, 1965, issue of *Mad Magazine*. The cover showed Alfred E. Neuman, with two extra eyes, trying to balance a blivet on his index finger. The *National Lampoon* also did a take-off on apparent illusions that were not actually illusory. For example, although the blivet shown on the right in Figure 20 is not impossible, it could easily seem so, since it is so difficult to resolve in just one or two glances.

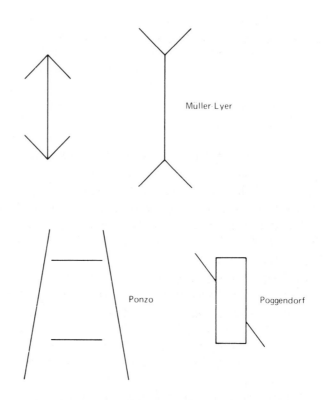

Figure 19. Popular illusions. In the Müller-Lyer illusion, the central axis is perceived as longer with the wings directed outward than inward. In the Ponzo illusion, a horizontal line is perceived as longer when it is farther along the converging railroad tracks. In the Poggendorf illusion, two segments of a continuous line do not appear to intersect.

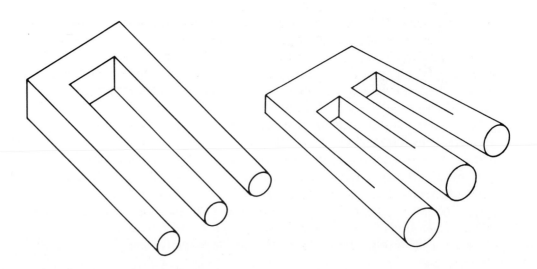

Figure 20. The blivet on the left could not exist in a three-dimensional world. The illusory blivet on the right could exist in a three-dimensional world.

Illusory Contours

The visual system does not always need complete information to form a figure-ground relationship. Figure 21 (*Capella II* by Vasarely) shows how very easy it is to see shapes as complete even though they are not. The borders of the squares and circles are not continuous even though we see them that way. We can fill in the missing parts to form a figure-ground relationship that is meaningful. Vasarely demonstrates this perceptual process in a very simple situation; we might expect from this demonstration that the process also plays a role in seeing the three-dimensional world.

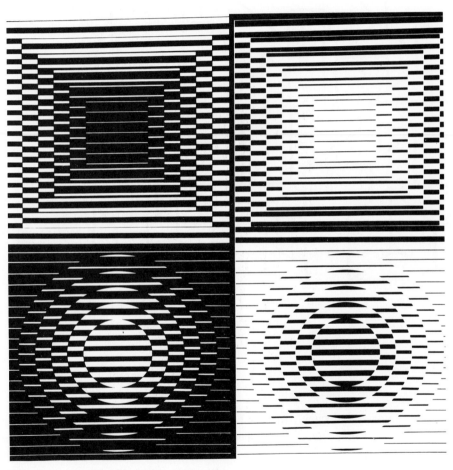

Figure 21. *Capella II* by Victor Vasarely.
1967. 130 x 195 cm. Réunion des Musées, Paris.

Reversibility

In Figure 22 (Al Held's *Blk/Wt #16*) we see that a given two-dimensional display can be interpreted in different ways. The boxes do not remain fixed; the top of one box may become the bottom of another, and so forth. Looking at a particular box, if an intersection of two sides appears nearer to you, try to reverse it so that it now appears farther away. In other words, instead of looking at the outside corner of a box, look at the intersection as the inside corner of a room.

Held's painting shows that, given a fixed two-dimensional scene, we can interpret it in a variety of ways. Our perceptions, then, are not always determined by the visual information present in the scene. In a number of situations, we perceive what we expect, desire, or try to see.

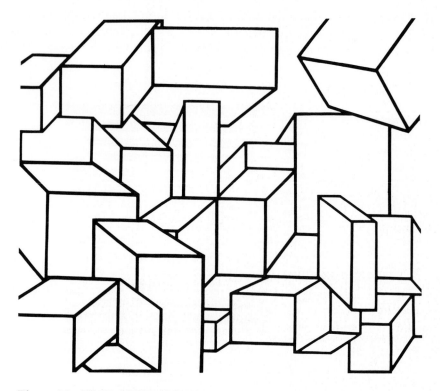

Figure 22. *Blk/Wt #16* by Al Held.
1968. Everson Museum of Art, Syracuse, New York.

Impossible Scenarios

Two-dimensional perspective cues can also be used to create impossible three-dimensional scenes. Figure 23, *Satire on False Perspective*, an engraving by William Hogarth (1754) presents an impossible town scenario. Although the depth relationships in any small portion of the engraving are reasonable, combining the various scenes boggles the mind. Artists usually incorporate two-dimensional depth cues to convey realistic three-dimensional scenes. In this engraving, Hogarth has done the opposite; he has used the depth cues to make the scene impossible.

Illusions are not restricted to perceptions of two-dimensional scenes but can also be found in three-dimensional representations. Furniture designers and architects often distort their creations from their geometrical or pure forms to take into account certain perceptual distortions. For example, the arm of a chair usually looks most pleasing when it appears parallel to the floor. In some chair designs, the front of the arm is made higher than the back in order to counterbalance the sloping seat and back of the chair.

The artist employs a number of visual devices in his painting to represent a three-dimensional scene in two dimensions. Perception of depth relationships in painting can be considered illusory since they do not actually exist in the real world. The term illusory, however, is usually given to perception that does not agree with another measure of the visual scene. For example, Figure 24 is

Figure 23. *Satire on False Perspective* by William Hogarth.

a photograph of the Palazzo Spada restoration by the well-known Renaissance architect Borromini. The photograph indicates that a viewer standing at one end of the palazzo sees a long colonnade, beyond which is a large open space with a life-size statue at the far end. However, in actual fact, Borromini had only a limited area and expanded the available space by magnifying the perspective features. Rather than erecting all the columns the same size as we would expect, he made them shorter, thinner, and closer together as they were placed farther from the observer. Moreover, the statue at the far end of the palazzo is not life size, but was reduced by about one half. Hence, the colonnade is perceived as much longer than it is, making the statue seem much farther away than it actually is. Figure 25 is a photograph of the same scene with a person in it. Here we see that something is wrong. It can be said, therefore, that Borromini achieved an illusory situation, since our perception of it conflicts with its actual physical representation.

Figure 24. Palazzo Spada colonnade and statue.

Knowledge and Perception

Illusions continue to persist even though we know what we are seeing is illusory. Figure 26 gives an example of a man holding an umbrella over himself and a woman (Kanizsa, 1969). The shaft of the umbrella appears to be extended through the woman's hair even though we know this cannot be the case. Here we have a stimulus property of the display playing a larger role in what is seen than knowledge of the observer. The umbrella shaft and the hair are the same color and the viewer must fill in the outlines of the object that is in front of the other object. Apparently, it is easier to fill in the outlines of the shaft in front of her hair. In the first case, only a very small area has to be filled in, whereas completing the outlines of the shaft requires filling in a very large area.

Figure 25. Same scene as Figure 24 with a person alongside the statue.

Figure 27 presents another impossible scene of this type. These examples stand in marked contrast to those in the last chapter in which knowledge critically influenced what was perceived. The stimulus properties in Figures 26 and 27 determine what is seen and our knowledge is unable to influence this impossible interpretation. Both the stimulus characteristics and the knowledge of the observer are important contributions to our experience of the visual world.

The Moon Illusion

On evenings when the sky is clear and the moon makes an appearance, one might say, "Look at that huge moon." This observer probably would be looking towards the horizon; the key word here is "huge." If the moon is overhead at the zenith, one might say, "The moon is out," or "full,"

Figure 26. Our knowledge of the way things should appear is not foolproof (after Kanizsa, 1969).

or "lovely," but the adjective would probably not be in terms of size because the perceived size of the moon at the zenith is not impressive and appears significantly smaller than the horizontal moon. The moon illusion has been represented in a number of paintings; apparently the artists were unaware of their illusion.

For example, Van Gogh's *The Sower*, a scene showing a farmer sowing his fields near a tree, has an enormous moon at the horizon. Comparing the painting to a hypothetical photograph of the scene, it can be shown that in relation to other details of the painting, Van Gogh made the moon ten times larger than it should have been. The perception of a larger horizontal than zenithal moon is illusory, since the moon reflects the same size image at the horizon and zenith. One way to see this is to photograph the moon in different celestial positions. Cameras are not sensitive to the moon illusion and record the same size image at the horizon as at the zenith. However, the photographer must be sure to measure the size of the images physically since some people report a moon illusion even in photographs.

Constancy Scaling

The moon illusion has been known and discussed at least since the time of the astronomer Ptolemy in the second century (Ross & Ross, 1976). Roger Bacon in the thirteenth century proposed that the apparent distance of the moon is responsible for its perceived size. The horizontal moon viewed across a terrain appears farther away than the zenithal moon, which is viewed through empty space. This explanation rests on the perceptual phenomenon of size constancy which illustrates that an object retains a relatively constant apparent size at different distances from the observer. As one moves towards an object, the size of the retinal image increases so that if the distance is halved, the retinal image doubles in size. Psychologists have,

Figure 27. What properties of the visual scene are responsible for its impossible interpretation (after Kanizsa, 1969)?

therefore, proposed a psychological mechanism which operates to evaluate the size of the retinal image of an object with respect to the perceived distance of the object. This mechanism is referred to as constancy scaling since it scales the size of the image based on perceived distance.

How does constancy scaling account for the moon illusion? If the view of the moon gives more depth cues at the horizon than overhead, it should appear larger at the horizon. The moon gives the same retinal image at both locations; constancy scaling must expand the image of the horizontal moon more than the zenithal moon since the horizontal moon appears farther away due to the depth cues. In this view, the moon illusion simply reflects a valuable perceptual process, constancy scaling, which is led astray when faced with the moon.

To overcome the experimental difficulties in studying the real moon, Rock and Kaufman (1962) developed an apparatus in which artificial moons could be seen against the sky. Observers could then be asked to compare directly a moon seen at the zenith with a moon seen at the horizon. The subjects observed a standard size moon in one sky position and determined when another variable comparison moon in another position was equal to it in size. The method of limits was used to change the size of the variable moon. The dependent variable was the actual size of the zenithal moon divided by the actual size of the horizontal moon when the two moons were perceived to be equal.

Rock and Kaufman found that the two moons were seen as equal in size when the zenithal moon was about 1½ times larger than the horizontal moon. Furthermore, they found no significant effect of eye elevation using their experimental setup. They also showed that the view of the terrain was a necessary condition for the moon illusion. If the view of the terrain was eliminated by requiring the subject to view the moon through a small aperture in a large piece of cardboard, the moon illusion was eliminated. In this case, the horizontal moon was perceived as the same size as the zenithal moon. Rock and Kaufman believed that they had established unambiguous support for the idea that the moon appears farther away at the horizon than at the zenith and that the constancy scaling mechanism operates to enlarge the retinal image of the horizontal moon relative to the zenithal moon. However, Rock and Kaufman did not provide any direct evidence that the moon at the horizon is actually seen as farther away than the moon at the zenith. To support the theory directly, we must show that the moon or other objects are seen as being farther away at the horizon than at the zenith.

However, one also hears how near the moon appears at the horizon: "It looks as if it's just behind that building." Boring (1943) and his colleagues at Harvard University tested our phenomenological experience by asking people to judge the relative distances of the horizontal and zenithal moon. The observers tended to see the zenithal moon as farther away than the horizontal moon. This result led Boring to reject the constancy-scaling explanation of the moon illusion. Earlier we said that the moon at the horizon also impresses us because of how near it appears. How can the moon appear near, when, at the same time, depth cues such as the terrain provide distance cues for constancy scaling? Rock and Kaufman (1962) handle this paradox by claiming that the subject may not be consciously aware of the registered distance used by the constancy scaling mechanism. Therefore, when asked to evaluate the distance of the moon, a person does not report the registered distance used for constancy scaling but rather bases this judgment on the conscious perceived size of the moon. The evidence for this assumption is that subjects presented with two moons, one much larger than the other, always report the smaller moon as farther away, regardless of its location in the sky. This is analogous to our observation of the size of the discs shown in Figure 5. For Rock and Kaufman, this shows that the larger moon will be seen as nearer, without reference to other factors that produce differences in perceived distance. The constancy scaling explanation of the moon illusion attained credence in the scientific community and also has been proposed for a number of other illusions.

Geometrical Illusions Revisited

The size constancy explanation known as perspective theory has been applied to the standard geometrical illusions by R. L. Gregory (1963, 1966, 1968). Perspective theory considers the geometric illusion figures to be similar to two-dimensional projections of three-dimensional figures. These projections, like three-dimensional scenes, contain perspective cues for depth and are best illustrated by the Ponzo, or railroad track, illusion (see Figure 19). The lines, as they approach one another, give cues for increasing depth as in three dimensions. The depth cues are assumed to trigger constancy scaling, which in this case is operating inappropriately because the actual scene is two dimensional. However, as in three dimensions, constancy scaling will operate to increase the apparent size of parts that appear distant and to decrease the apparent size of parts that appear near. The figure itself need not be perceived as having depth because constancy scaling could be triggered by the perspective features directly.

Although some geometrical illusions contain perspective cues that could give the observer depth information about parts of the figure, not all illusions contain perspective features. This is best illustrated by the dumbbell variant of the Müller-Lyer. The illusion is easily demonstrated with three coins or discs. Place the three coins in a row and have the observer slide the middle coin down until the distance AB seems equal to the distance CD, as in Figure 28. This illusion demonstrates that perspective theory cannot account for all geometrical illusions, because some illusions do not contain perspective cues. However, it is still necessary to test the perspective theory to account for other two-dimensional illusions. The standard Müller-Lyer figure is a good place to start because the processes operating with this illusion might also be operating in the dumbbell illusion.

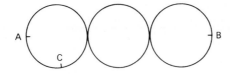

Figure 28. The dumbbell illusion is demonstrated by placing three coins in row and requiring the subject to slide the middle coin down until the distance AB is equal to the distance CD. Although the distances appear to be about equal, AB is 20% longer than CD.

Perspective theory assumes that Müller-Lyer figures are similar to projections of typical three-dimensional objects. For example, Figure 29A—with the wings directed outward—is similar to a projection of the corner of a room, where the central axis corresponds to the corner and the outside wings correspond to the intersections of the walls with the ceiling and with the floor. Due to the effect of the wings as perspective cues, the central axis is judged as if it were farther away than the wings. According to the theory, constancy scaling operates, and increases the apparent length of the central axis. Figure 29B—with the wings directed inward—has the perspective cues of a projection of an outside corner of a building. The central axis is thus judged as if it were closer than the wings and, therefore, appears smaller due to constancy scaling. Gregory (1968) presents evidence which he interprets as directly supportive of the perspective theory explanation of the Müller-Lyer illusion. He asked observers to make depth judgments of Müller-Lyer figures illuminated without a visible background so that they appeared suspended in space. To eliminate binocular cues to depth, the figures were viewed with one eye. Subjects judged the distance of the central axis of figures with ingoing and outgoing wings. The results, as predicted by perspective theory, showed that the axis with ingoing wings was judged as nearer than the axis with outgoing wings. However, although these results are in agreement with perspective theory, they cannot be taken as evidence that the perceived depth of the central axis influenced its perceived length. Gregory's observation is a correlational one so that no conclusion about causation can be reached (see Chapter 3, Correlational Relationship).

The perspective theory account of the Müller-Lyer illusion has been put to a number of experimental tests. Waite and Massaro (1970) observed that perspective theory makes an interesting prediction about the size of the central axis of the Müller-Lyer figures. Since the figure with outward-directed wings contains perspective features that make the central axis appear more

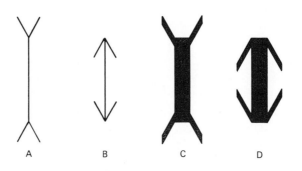

Figure 29. The standard Müller-Lyer figures and the same figures with an enlarged width of the central axis.

distant, constancy scaling should affect both the apparent length and the apparent width similarly. That is, if constancy scaling is responsible for the illusion, then both the apparent length and the apparent width of the central axis should be increased.

However, observing the standard Müller-Lyer figure, there are no noticeable differences in the apparent widths of the central axes. These lines are relatively fine and any change—a 20 percent increase or decrease in the apparent width, for instance—would not be noticed. One way of overcoming this difficulty is to increase the width of the central axis. Any distortion of the width should now be discernible. If we assume that a change in the width does not make a significant change in the perspective cues—the wings and their directions—available in the Müller-Lyer figures, constancy scaling should also operate in the modified figures. According to perspective theory, both the length and the width of the central axis should change with changes in the directions of the wings. Waite and Massaro, therefore, required length and width judgments of modified Müller-Lyer figures, two of which are shown in Figures 29C and 29D.

In the Waite and Massaro (1970) study, a number of modified figures with inward and outward wings were used. Four different sizes of the central axis were used so that subjects would not learn that all the figures had the same size central axis and respond accordingly. Figures were projected one at a time onto a screen and the subjects were told to judge the apparent length and width of the central axis of each figure. The response sheet contained a horizontal and vertical line which met at a point near the upper left corner of the sheet. The subject made his judgment by making a mark on each line to indicate the length and width of the central axis. Each subject judged each of the figures a number of times in randomized blocks of trials.

The results agreed exactly with what one observes phenomenologically in Figures 29C and 29D. The distortion of the width of the central axis is in the opposite direction of its length. That is, the figure with outward-directed wings appears longer than the figure with inward-directed wings, as is predicted by perspective theory. However, the apparent width of the figure with outward-directed wings is slightly smaller than the apparent width of the figure with inward-directed wings. The fact that there was a significant distortion of the length of the central axis of the figures as a function of the direction of the wings supports the assumption that the modification of the figures did not significantly change the visual features of the Müller-Lyer figures. That is to say, since the illusion of the length of the central axis is the same in the modified figures as in the normal figures, the same mechanism is probably responsible. The Waite and Massaro (1970) study, then, appears to provide a critical rejection of perspective theory; the explanation of the Müller-Lyer illusion must be found elsewhere.

Total Impression Theory

Restle (1970) has utilized the general total impression theory to provide an explanation of the moon illusion. Restle assumes that the size of an object is always judged relative to other extents in the visual field. This assumption is similar to the contrast mechanism used to explain the size-weight illusion (see Chapter 13, Illusory Weight Judgments). According to Restle's application of the relative size hypothesis to the perception of the moon, the significant context effect is the empty space between the moon and the horizon. The moon appears small at the zenith because it is surrounded by large empty space, whereas the moon near the horizon appears large due to the small space between the moon and the terrain. Restle (1970) was able to predict many of Rock and Kaufman's results quantitatively with his mathematical formulation of this assumption.

We have discussed two widely different theories for visual illusions. Constancy scaling is appealing because it attempts to relate mechanisms found in normal visual perception to illusory perception. In contrast, the total impression theory has not been utilized much in the study of normal perception, and it is unlikely to be accepted by the scientific community until it has been made relevant to much more of normal visual functioning. In the future, we can expect that innovative research and theory in the study of visual illusions will go hand in hand with the study of normal perception. We might predict, also, that neither constancy scaling nor total impression theory will be the final answer since research, like perception, requires a constant revision and reconstruction of our hypotheses about the nature of reality.

15

Testing Theories of Attention

Broadbent Model

    Short-Term Store
    Limited Capacity Processor

Split-Span Experiments

    Gray and Wedderburn Study
    Questioning Assumptions

Shadowing

    Information Coming Through
      Unattended Channel
    Unconfounding Recognition
      and Memory
    Attending to the Unattended
      Channel

Deutsch/Norman Model

Location of Selective Filter

    Testing the Broadbent and
      Deutsch/Norman Models

Treisman Model

    Attenuation
    Two Levels of Selection

Neisser Model

Kahneman Model

Norman/Bobrow Model

    Multiple Resource Pools

Attention and Processing Stages

    Detection and Recognition
      Processes
    Precueing Detection and
      Recognition
    Feature and Conjunction Search

_____

    Attending Infants

_____

A shift of the selective process from one class of
events to another takes a time which is not negligible
compared with the minimal time spent on any one class.
Donald E. Broadbent (1958)

The attitude of the experimental psychologist to attention provides an index of his or her theoretical biases. The introspectionists considered attention a focal point for psychological study and studied such phenomena as sensory clearness and prior entry as a function of attention. That is, do we see something more clearly or sooner when we are attending than when we are not attending? William James, for example, observed how the surgeon sees the blood flow from the arm of a patient whom he is bleeding before he observes the knife pierce the skin. James, more than anyone, made attention an engaging and respectable area of psychological inquiry.

The Gestalt psychologists had no need for attention, since they believed that the properties of the stimulus array were sufficient to predict the perceptual response to it. Strict behaviorists dismissed the concept of attention as something unobservable and therefore not worthy of experimental study. As pointed out by Lovie (1983), however, empirical work on attention continued at a substantial pace during the behaviorist era in America. However, attention was not a central issue in the description of stimulus-response relationships in the Gestalt and behaviorist schools of psychology. So, in 1958, when attention was receiving little attention from American psychologists, a book written by a British psychologist, Donald Broadbent, provided a renaissance for employing the concept of attention to describe how humans perceive and remember inputs from the senses.

BROADBENT MODEL

Broadbent's model, illustrated in Figure 1, focused on the flow of information between stimulus and response. Information enters this system through the senses and passes into a short-term store, a temporary buffer or storage structure whose purpose is to hold information until it can be processed further. This buffer, in effect, extends the duration of a stimulus; for example, the light from a camera flash maintains its effects beyond the time the light stimulus actually exists. Some structure of this sort is responsible for the fact that a lighted cigarette or a finger moved rapidly back and forth is perceived as being in several places at once.

Broadbent assumed that stimuli could be partitioned into separate classes or channels of events as, for example, auditory and visual stimuli. Auditory stimuli coming from the left or the right could also be considered as different channels. As can be seen in Figure 1, Broadbent further assumed that the passage of information through the short-term store preserved these channels of information. A filter could then operate by selecting information on the basis of these separate channels or classes of information. All of the outputs from the buffer must pass through the selective filter device before reaching the limited capacity channel. The limited capacity processor is the workhorse of the system and operates on or processes the information made available by the selective filter. The limited capacity processor can be thought of as an analog of a computer's central processor. It also corresponds to James' span of consciousness—what is experienced as happening now. This process operates on the information in the short-term store and transforms it into more abstract or meaningful information. The processing of the limited capacity channel was

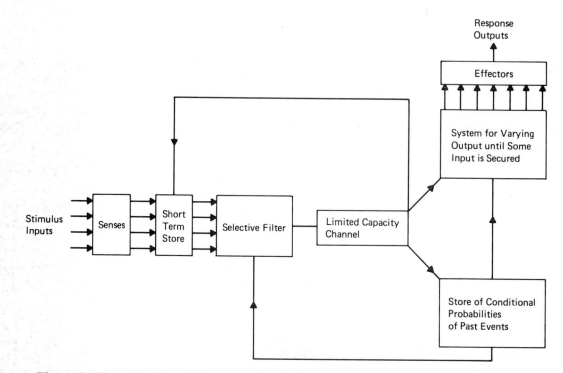

Figure 1. Flow of information between stimulus and response as illustrated by Broadbent (1958).

equated with the process of attention; that is, to the extent a channel of information is being processed here, it is being attended to.

Short-Term Store

According to Broadbent, the processing that occurs up to the filter can take place simultaneously or in parallel across the different channels of information. In contrast, the processing of the limited capacity channel must operate serially across the different stimulus channels. That is to say, the processing by the senses into short-term store occurs simultaneously across the different stimulus channels, whereas the limited capacity processor can only operate on one channel at a time. The short-term store can hold the information from both auditory and visual inputs, or from two different speakers at a cocktail party; in short, from all the sensory stimuli that may surround one at a given time. This implies that the system is not limited in the amount of information that can be processed by the senses and stored in short-term store. The transformation and storage of the sound pressure vibrations of a symphony occur in the same way whether or not one is attending to the music. It is the limited capacity channel that is limited in the amount of information it can process. A filter between it and the buffer allows it to attend to only one source of information at a time. Thus, for example, at a cocktail party, the buffer may be storing the stimulus characteristics of two conversations, but the listener can pay attention to only one of them. Only one can pass through the filter to the limited capacity channel, where it can be recognized, possibly rehearsed, and then perhaps transferred to the motor effectors, where an appropriate response can be initiated.

Broadbent assumed that information could last in the buffer on the order of seconds without being processed by the limited capacity channel, after which it would decay. Thus, the very fact that the limited capacity channel is processing one channel of information tends to ensure that the information from other channels will be lost. However, the central processor could switch attention and resolve the last couple of seconds of information on the unattended channel.

The filter has flexibility; obviously we can switch our attention from one stimulus source to another. The features that identify a channel of information also define channels of information in short-term store. The representation of these features in short-term store can be used by the central processor in switching attention. Broadbent proposed that the physical features of the stimuli are the critical features defining a channel of information. Thus, the filter will be open to a certain spatial location in the environment, filtering out all other locations. It can also select a particular voice out of several, and the task of selecting will be easier if the selected voice is female and the other male. It can pass speech and filter out a pure tone that accompanies it; or it may pass the tone over the speech. In all cases, it has some physical feature to guide the central processor.

Limited Capacity Processor

Broadbent's processing system is limited at the stage of the limited capacity channel. The filter protects the processing at this stage by allowing it to concentrate its limited capacity on one channel. The buffer is utilized to hold information from other channels, so that when the serial processor is done attending to one channel, it can return to process another. Attending to one thing does not necessarily mean, therefore, as James said, that everything else is lost. If the processor can get back to the buffer soon enough, before the second channel decays, it can process it. Thus, the buffer provides some flexibility to the system; it allows it, in a sense, to deal with two simultaneous stimuli if the first can be processed before the second has decayed from the buffer. However, Broadbent further assumed that switching of attention between channels takes some substantial amount of time. In this case, processing information from two channels would always take longer and would be less efficient than processing the same information from one channel.

SPLIT-SPAN EXPERIMENTS

Broadbent's theory was based on a series of experiments, now known as the split-span experiments. The studies took advantage of the ability to distinguish easily the location of an auditory stimulus presented over a headphone on the left ear from another stimulus presented over a headphone on the right. Sound presented to the left ear is localized to the left whereas the same sound to the right ear is localized to the right. Different sounds presented to the two ears is referred to as a dichotic presentation. The two ears can, therefore, function as two different channels of information in Broadbent's model. (This is not true of the eyes since, if both eyes are open, we cannot discriminate which eye is being stimulated.)

Broadbent (1954) presented auditory messages over the headphones, feeding a different message into each ear. In one ear he would present three digits, say 7, 4, and 3. Simultaneously, he presented three other digits in the other ear, say 8, 2, and 6. The rate of presentation to a given ear was two digits per second, so that the total presentation time was 1½ seconds. The task of the subject was to listen to each list and then to write down as much of it as could be remembered. Given this task, the subject could recall the digits in one of two different ways. First, he could recall the digits by ear of presentation; all three items presented to one ear, then the other three presented to the other ear. In our example, a correct response would be the serial recall 7, 4, 3, 8, 2, 6. Second, subjects could recall the items according to their chronological order of presentation.

The digits had arrived in pairs, one at each ear simultaneously, and the subject would record the digits within each pair in either order. But both digits of a pair would be reported before moving on to the next pair; thus, 7, 8, 4, 2, 3, 6 would be a correct recall by temporal order.

It was well known that subjects could serially recall a list of six digits, presented at a rate of two per second with a total presentation time of 3 seconds, with about 95% accuracy. The subjects could correctly recall 19 out of 20 lists. Broadbent's (1954) modification of this paradigm, by splitting the source of the digits, lowered performance significantly. Faced with digits arriving simultaneously at the two ears, subjects recalled all of the digits in a list correctly only 65% of the time. Most importantly for Broadbent's model, correct recall of the list almost always involved recalling all of the digits presented on one ear before recalling any of the digits on the other ear. In another condition of Broadbent's (1954) experiment, subjects were required to recall the items by order of presentation—the first item in each ear followed by the second item in each ear, followed by the third. These subjects were able to correctly recall the entire list only 20% of the time. These results together indicate that people prefer to recall simultaneous lists of words according to their ear of presentation. The subject will report words presented to one ear before those presented to the other. In addition, people are better at this kind of recall than at recall based on the temporal order of presentation.

Broadbent interpreted the difference between the two kinds of recall as reflecting the necessity of switching attention more frequently in the second recall condition than in the first. In the first condition, the subject would monitor one location and then identify the items as they were presented. After identifying these three items, attention can be switched to the information from the second ear before it decays from the buffer or short-term store. The total time between the end of the list and its complete identification includes the time required to switch attention from the first to the second ear and the time required to recognize the digits presented to that ear. Given that the items in short-term store could decay, this could reduce performance from that obtained when the list was presented over one source.

When the subject is required to report the items by their temporal order, however, the subject has to switch attention at least three times. He could attend to one ear and recognize the first digit, then switch to the second ear to process the first digit on that channel. Next, the limited capacity processor could recognize the second digit on the second ear without switching, but would have to switch once again to read out the second digit of the first ear. The processor could remain on the first ear for the last digit and then switch to the second ear for the final digit. In all, the limited capacity processor would have to switch its attention three times in this condition. When recall is by ear of presentation, on the other hand, the limited capacity processor has to switch its attention only once. This would increase the time required for identification of the items and would lower the chances of reaching the end of the list before the information in the short-term buffer faded away.

Broadbent's (1954) results are consistent with his limited capacity filter model of selective attention. As noted in our discussion of verification and falsification in scientific inquiry (Chapter 5), the split-span experiments can not verify the theory; they simply fail to falsify it. Other researchers might be expected to be particularly eager to falsify the model.

Gray and Wedderburn Study

Among the first to respond to Broadbent's publication of his model were two Oxford undergraduates, Gray and Wedderburn (1960). They took issue with the assumption of Broadbent that the two ears must function as channels that require switching time between them. It might be easier, they reasoned, to process information alternately across the ears if it was advantageous to do so. To bias the task in this direction, the experimenters made the lists more meaningful when they alternated across the ears than when they did not. They modified the split-span experiment by choosing the six stimulus items from two semantic categories: for example, three digits and three words. Each successive pair contained one word and one digit and the words and digits were alternated across ears. The words also had certain sequential constraints; for instance, one of their three-word sequences was dear, aunt, Jane, earning their experiment the name of *The Dear Aunt Jane Task*. In all other respects, they replicated Broadbent's experiment; the items were presented in pairs, one in each ear, at a rate of two pairs per second. Subjects would hear "3, aunt, 8" in the right ear and "dear, 2, Jane" in the left ear. Their task was to recall all six items in any manner they wished. Gray and Wedderburn found that subjects were just as likely to recall the items correctly when they reported the items by alternating between the ears as when they reported the items by spatial location.

Gray and Wedderburn's results contradicted the most straightforward form of Broadbent's model. Their results demonstrated that the ears do not always function as different channels of information. Recall that Broadbent argued that channels of information are defined with respect to physical stimulus characteristics. The channels exist in the short-term store before the information is processed by the limited capacity processor. Since it is the central processor that is responsible for deriving meaning from the stimulus, meaning should not influence the switching time in the split-span studies. The semantic variables of superordinate category and sequential constraints between words should not have influenced the results if Broadbent's original formulation was correct.

Needless to say, Broadbent's model requires modification and a good scientist will patch up the model as necessary to make it conform to the reality of experimental results. Broadbent admitted that perhaps the concept of channels was too narrowly defined in the original model. Broadbent may have begun with the strictly empirical notion that most of the meaningful order in our experience is out there in the stimulus. However, it appeared that a semantic category could influence performance in the same way as physical channels. Broadbent and Gregory (1964) argued that selection of a class of an item must also take switching time. Therefore, switching between items on the same ear because of category class eliminated the advantage of recall by physical location in the split-span task with letters and digits. This means that recall by physical location should be disrupted when the items alternate between categories on a given ear. Consistent with this interpretation, subjects recalled the entire list correctly about 20% of the time under both recall conditions, which is much lower than the 65% correct recall by physical location in Broadbent's original (1954) study.

Questioning Assumptions

Let us analyze the split-span task in terms of a general information-processing model. We assume that recognition and memory are vital information-processing stages in the task. Each item must be recognized, that is, identified, and stored in memory from which it must be retrieved at the time of response. Performance in this task is, therefore, dependent upon both of these processing stages. Experimenters do not have a direct measure of performance at either of these stages; they only have some overall measure of performance. Unless investigators can account for each stage of processing in the task, they cannot state with certainty the implications of the results.

The critical independent variable in the split-span experiments has been the order in which the subject is required to report the items. Broadbent assumed that this manipulation should affect only the recognition stage while not directly influencing the memory stage. In this assumption, Broadbent probably was influenced to a greater extent by his model than his intuition or his phenomenological experience in the task. Consider the split-span task from a generally naive point of view. Subjects are presented with six digits, three to each ear, within 1½ sec. They are required to report the digits back in one of two ways: temporal order or ear of arrival. The performance differences may not reflect differences in recognition but rather differences in memory and retrieval. One question Broadbent did not ask was: How long does it take to perceive a digit? He assumed instead that the time could extend well beyond the presentation time; in fact, over 1½ sec after a digit had been presented. Recall that subjects who reported by ear of arrival were assumed to recognize all of the digits in one ear before switching to the other.

As an alternative explanation, it could have been the case that all of the digits were recognized as they were presented in both recall conditions. The differences in performance reflected differences not in recognition, but in memory. Subjects in the split-span tasks must not only recognize and remember the names of the items but also their ear of arrival or temporal order, depending upon the recall condition. This interpretation of the split-span task locates performance differences at the memory stage, which makes the experiments irrelevant to Broadbent's model. We might argue that subjects would find it easier to remember the ear of arrival of the digits than their temporal order. Each digit must be stored in memory with some information relevant to recall. In the recall by temporal order condition, subjects must remember whether each digit came first, second, or third. In recall by ear of arrival, they only have to remember if each digit came from the left or right ear. Since alternative interpretations are possible, the manipulation of order or report in the split-span experiments does not speak to Broadbent's model or any other model of the recognition process.

SHADOWING

At about the same time of Broadbent's research, an experimental task known as shadowing, was devised by Cherry (1953). This task appeared to offer a flexible and reliable approach to the study of attention. Subjects were presented with a continuous auditory message, usually at a fairly rapid rate such as 150 words per minute. Their task was to repeat back every word of the message verbatim. This was found to be least difficult when the message was simple English prose that contained all the semantic and syntactic constraints of the language. Subjects in this case, instead of repeating each word as it came in, seemed to shadow by phrases, repeating two or three words at a time, so that a lag appeared between the message and the subject's response. When the words of the message were in random and unconstrained order, the shadowing task became much more difficult and subjects in this case repeated the message word by word, rather than phrase by phrase. In a sense they could not predict what was coming next and operated on each word separately. The central assumption underlying the shadowing task is that the difficulty of the act of shadowing absorbed the subject's attention.

Information Coming Through Unattended Channel

The immediate problem that interested Cherry and others using his paradigm was the nature of information from an unattended channel that can get through to consciousness when subjects are devoting their attention elsewhere. Like Broadbent, Cherry used the two ears as separate channels and presented a different message to each ear through headphones. The subject shadowed one of the messages while the experimenter introduced various changes in the message on the unattended channel. After a brief period of shadowing the experimenter would break in and ask the subject if he had recognized anything peculiar on the unattended channel.

Cherry (1953) and Cherry and Taylor (1954) found that subjects noticed a change in voices on the unattended channel, especially changes in the sex of the speaker. They noticed a nonverbal event—for instance, a tone. More significant, however, was what they failed to notice. They missed changes in the nature of the material on the unshadowed ear; the investigators could switch the message from a passage in a science fiction novel to poetry, then to a physics text. They could reverse the speech for a while. They could even change the language on the message from English to French and back again without the subjects being able to report the change. These results were seen to support Broadbent's theory; they indicated that subjects, when attending to one channel, notice only gross changes in the physical characteristics of input on another channel. They notice a change from a male to a female speaker, and from speech to pure tones. But they miss changes that would require some perception of the meaning of the stimulus. The initial results of these rather informal experiments tended to locate the filter after the gross physical characteristics of the stimulus were detected, and before recognition of it.

Like Broadbent's split-span task, however, the shadowing task confounded the memory and recognition stages, as was pointed out by Norman (1969). He argued that, after all, subjects were required to remember what had occurred on the unshadowed message some unspecified time after it was completed. Moray (1959) previously had found that subjects could not remember English words that were repeated 35 times on the unshadowed channel. Norman (1969) pointed out that subjects in this experiment continued to shadow for roughly 30 seconds after the last test word was presented in the list. Rather than concluding from Moray's results that the words were not recognized on the unattended ear, one could argue that the words were perceived accurately but were forgotten by the time of the test.

In fact, there were some observations indicating that meaning did get through on the unshadowed channel, especially when very little memory was required. Some of Moray's (1959) subjects did remember hearing their names on the unattended channel, which we might expect to be easier to remember than random lists of words. In another study, Treisman (1960) showed that a meaningful series of words, when split between the two ears, could induce the subject to shadow the meaningful sequence rather than the sequence of words presented on the attended ear. Some subjects did not even notice that they had switched ears to follow the meaningful message.

Unconfounding Recognition and Memory

Given the confounding of recognition and memory stages in the earlier shadowing experiments such as Moray's, an experiment was designed by Norman (1969) that would allow him to evaluate the recognition and memory stages separately. Practiced subjects shadowed a continuous sequence of monosyllabic words spoken in a female voice at a rate of 2 per second. In the memory conditions, a test list of six two-digit numbers was presented in a male voice on the unshadowed channel at a rate of 1 per second. The test list was followed by a tone either immediately or after a 20-second delay. A probe number followed the tone and subjects indicated whether this number had appeared in the preceding list. On two thirds of the trials, the probe number was equal to one of the numbers on the preceding list; on the other one third it was not. This paradigm allows the investigator to distinguish between recognition and memory stages as discussed in Chapter 17. Using d' as a measure of memory performance, we can determine the memory for each item in the six-item list. The results in Figure 2 show a significant amount of memory for the last couple of items in the list if the subjects are tested immediately. This means that these items must have been recognized. However, if the probe test is delayed through 20 seconds of shadowing, no memory remains for any of the items. Clearly, delaying the test of memory is an invalid measure of whether the items on the unattended channel were recognized. To provide a true index of recognition the investigator must account for the forgetting that takes place between presentation and test.

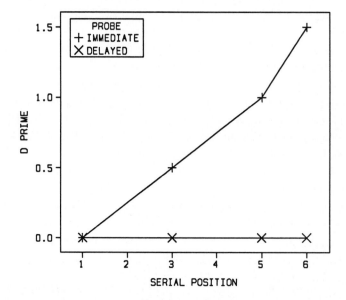

Figure 2. Memory performance an indexed by d' values as a function of serial position when the probe item is presented immediately or after a delay of 20 seconds of shadowing (taken from Norman, 1969).

Attending to the Unattended Channel

Norman's result indicates that subjects are able to recognize the meaning of words on the unshadowed channel. An impressive demonstration that messages presented to the unshadowed ear are processed for meaning was carried out by MacKay (1973a). Subjects shadowed sentences containing ambiguous or polysemous words (words with multiple meanings). A word was presented to the unshadowed ear simultaneously with the presentation of the ambiguous word on the shadowed ear. For example, subjects might shadow the sentence, "The man approached the *bank*." Simultaneously with the presentation of *bank*, either *money* or *river* would be presented to the unshadowed ear. When subjects were asked later to select a sentence that was a paraphrase of the shadowed sentence, they were more likely to choose a sentence that was a paraphrase of the meaning given by the word on the unshadowed channel. Both the Norman (1969) and MacKay (1973a) studies demonstrate that subjects can recognize the meaning of words on the unshadowed ear, although we cannot be certain that they do so without the help of attention. Norman monitored the shadowing performance of his subjects carefully and did not report an increase in shadowing errors when the memory list was being presented. Even so there is simply no evidence that shadowing the message on one ear prevents attending to parts of the message on the unattended ear. Similarly, we cannot conclude that MacKay's subjects recognized the word on the unshadowed ear without some switch of attention. Switching attention was possible and is not inconsistent with the additional finding that subjects did not remember the words on the unshadowed ear. Subjects will forget words whether or not they are attended to.

In most experiments, shadowing is easy and performance is extremely good, so that brief switches of attention will not necessarily lead to an increase in shadowing errors. One solution would be to make shadowing difficult with a substantial error rate; switching of attention should then be reflected in an increase in shadowing errors. Until such an experiment is carried out, no firm conclusions can be reached. The shadowing experiments, therefore, indicate that meaning can get through on the unshadowed channel, but we cannot say this occurred without attention.

DEUTSCH/NORMAN MODEL

Broadbent's model of information processing generated a good deal of research, leading to refinement of the model and more research. Here we have an example of how the insights of a scientific investigator can influence the course of experimental research and theory. Although we criticized the basic experimental approach, it can be readily modified to disentangle the stages of information processing in the task and, more importantly, to determine which stages are influenced by attention. Experimentation and theory go hand in hand in scientific research. Broadbent's theory followed from the split-span studies and generated further research in this area. Rather than working within Broadbent's general theoretical formulation, other investigators developed contrasting theories. Broadbent (1958) proposed that the attention of a limited capacity processor was necessary for recognition, whereas some research appeared to show that recognition could occur without complete attention. These results spurred others to devise a model that could account for recognition without attention.

Deutsch and Deutsch (1963) proposed that *all* information is recognized before it receives the attention of the limited capacity processor. Figure 3 presents a formal model of the Deutsch and Deutsch assumption as elaborated by Norman (1968). In this model, recognition does not require the processing of a limited capacity processor. Rather, the meaning of all inputs can be derived simultaneously or in parallel. It is only then that the processing system becomes limited in capacity and the selective attention operation becomes necessary. Instead of using a physical channel as a basis for selection, however, the pertinence of the information is analyzed. The recognized items that have the highest level of relevance or pertinence are selected for further processing. It is only at this stage that information processing becomes limited in capacity. The criterion for selection is pertinence, some ongoing aim of the processing system that enables it to select or reject information according to relevance.

The central assumption of the Deutsch/Norman theory is that all items are recognized, even those presented to the unshadowed ear in a shadowing experiment. This means that the subject should know the words being presented on the unshadowed ear. If he is asked immediately, he should be able to repeat the word just spoken on that channel. But because he has been instructed to shadow the other message, which absorbs his attention, he cannot process the unattended message any further than recognition. The latter gets into short-term memory only for a brief period and is forgotten very quickly. These implications were supported by Norman's (1969) observations that subjects could remember the last couple of words on the unattended ear only if they were tested immediately, not after a short period of shadowing.

LOCATION OF SELECTIVE FILTER

The critical difference between this theory and Broadbent's is the location of the selective-attention mechanism. In Broadbent's model, all information available to the senses gets into the sensory buffer and remains there for two seconds or so. The limitation of the system is imposed between the sensory store and the recognition stage. Recognition is thus strictly limited by the selective filter since it needs the active attention of the limited capacity processor. In the

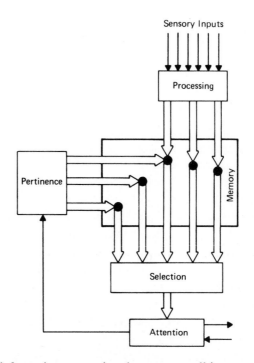

Figure 3. A model of information processing that assumes all inputs are recognized before selection occurs. All sensory inputs receive perceptual processing and are recognized; that is, they excite their representations (indicated by solid circles) in memory. Other factors influence which stored representations have high pertinence. The recognized items selected for attentive processing are those having the greatest pertinence to the task at hand (after Norman, 1968).

Deutsch/Norman model, on the other hand, information entering sensory store makes contact with meaning in long-term memory without the attention of a limited capacity processor; all information available to the senses is thus identified and made meaningful before attention operates. Recognition does not require central processing capacity in this model, but remembering and/or responding to the information does require it. We are able to respond best when responding to only one channel of information, for example, a sentence; with more than one channel, performance deteriorates. In the Deutsch/Norman model, we can recognize all the stimuli entering the sensory store at the same time.

Figure 4 locates the filters of the two models in terms of our general information-processing model. Broadbent's theory says that the recognition process requires the attention of a central processor which is limited in capacity. Therefore, we cannot recognize two items as well as one. In contrast, the Deutsch/Norman theory says that only the rehearsal and response-selection processes require the attention of a central processor which is limited in capacity; the process of recognition occurs without allocation of processing capacity. We, therefore, can recognize two items as well as one but can only rehearse and respond to a limited number.

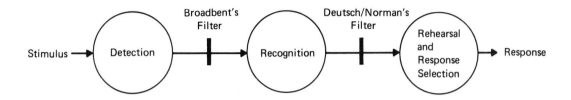

Figure 4. The location of the filters of Broadbent and Deutsch/Norman models in terms of our general information-processing model.

Testing the Broadbent and Deutsch/Norman Models

Treisman and Geffen (1967) designed a test between the two models. Are all incoming words recognized whether or not they are attended. Subjects shadowed a message in one ear while simultaneously another message occurred in the opposite ear. Besides repeating back one of the messages, they performed a second task at the same time. Subjects tapped whenever they heard one of a set of target words in the message. The target words could occur in either message, shadowed or unshadowed, and a tapping response was required in either case. The subjects thus had two tasks, to shadow the designated message and to respond to targets occurring in either message.

The target words were of two kinds: specific words or categories. In one condition, the subjects simply were told to tap to a specific word, such as "green." In others they were told to respond to a class of words, such as any color or any part of the face. On any shadowing trial there was only one target, or one class of targets.

Treisman and Geffen reasoned that, in Broadbent's model, recognition requires attention; therefore we can lock in the subject's attention by requiring him to shadow the message arriving at one ear, and he should not be able to notice target words or classes presented to the opposite, unattended ear. On the other hand, targets presented in the attended message should be easily recognized; they should get through the filter and should not require any additional processing to that necessary for the shadowing task itself. Broadbent's model predicts, therefore, that performance of the tapping response should be poor for targets on the unshadowed channel and very good for targets in the shadowed message.

In the Deutsch/Norman model, there is no filter at the recognition level; recognition does not require attention, and therefore the words will be recognized as easily in the unshadowed as in the shadowed ear. On the other hand, it does take processing capacity to respond in this model, and in this case all the processing capacity might be used in the task of shadowing. Very little, if any, might be available for the tapping response for either ear. In this case, performance of the second task should be poor for both the shadowed and the unshadowed messages. A second possibility is that recognition of a target word would have high pertinence, which would be sufficient for the observer to switch his attention and tap to the target word in both channels. In this case, the tapping response obtains higher pertinence than shadowing, and tapping performance would be good at the expense of accurate shadowing. However, regardless of the pertinence of tapping, there is no apparent reason that tapping performance should differ in the attended and unattended ears since targets are recognized equally well in both ears.

The actual results of the Treisman and Geffen experiment fit the predictions of the Broadbent model. Subjects were able to respond to 87% of the target words in the shadowed message, but to only 8% of the targets in the unshadowed message. This was strong evidence for Broadbent and against Deutsch/Norman. Moreover, on most of the instances that went to make up the correct responses for the unshadowed message, performance of the shadowing task was disrupted; subjects made an error in the shadowing response, delayed it, said the wrong word, or skipped a portion of it entirely. This disruption seemed to indicate that when subjects did recognize and respond to targets on the unattended channel, the processing capacity available to the shadowed channel was reduced. In contrast, tapping to targets on the attended channel did not disrupt shadowing of that channel. Thus, it might be argued that the subjects had to switch attention in order to recognize the few targets that they did recognize on the unshadowed channel. Since subjects knew that targets would occur on the unshadowed channel, it seems reasonable that every now and then they would switch attention, checking for targets on that unattended channel.

Creators of theories do not give them up easily. Deutsch and Deutsch (1967) promptly responded that Treisman and Geffen's experiment was poorly designed. They had neglected the critical factor of pertinence in the Deutsch theory. The judgment of whether or not to respond to recognized information is influenced by anything that contributes to the subject's sense of what is relevant. By instructing subjects to shadow words in the message to one ear, Treisman and Geffen had emphasized the importance of words coming to that ear. These words would be considered more relevant, in a general way, throughout the task. The data of this experiment were thus attributed to a tendency, induced by the experiment itself, to inhibit responses to words on the unattended channel, and not to a failure to recognize them. But why should subjects inhibit a simple tapping response to words recognized on the unattended channel when they could easily manage this response along with the shadowing response when the stimuli came in on the same channel?

Deutsch and Deutsch argued that it was the shadowing instructions that gave different pertinence values to targets on the different ears. A test of this criticism of the Treisman and Geffen study might be made by eliminating the shadowing instructions, thus having subjects attend to one message without repeating it. This would equal the pertinence of attended and unattended targets. If we could assume that their attention was indeed locked in on the designated message, even though they were not required to respond to it in a way that ensured this, then, according to Broadbent, performance of the tapping response ought to be the same as when the shadowing response is required. On the other hand, if we could assume that the instructions to tap to the targets on both channels equated their pertinence, Deutsch and Deutsch would predict that subjects would respond to all targets in both the attended and the unattended messages. Moray and O'Brien (1967) actually carried out this experiment. They had subjects attend to (but not shadow) a random list of letters in one ear while simultaneously another list of letters was presented in the other. They were instructed to push a button to digits that could occur in either channel. In Moray and O'Brien's study, more digits were recognized in the attended than in the unattended ear, even though no shadowing was required, thus continuing to support Broadbent.

If Treisman and Geffen's interpretation of the results is correct, supporting Broadbent's theory, then one would expect that nonverbal targets of distinctly different physical characteristics would produce a different effect. This experiment was done by Lawson (1966); the design was the same as Treisman and Geffen's except that, instead of target words, subjects were told to tap to clicks or brief tones embedded in both the shadowed and unshadowed messages. The task was identical to Treisman and Geffen's in all other respects. Nonverbal targets should be noticed, according to Broadbent, as they can be easily distinguished from the other verbal items in the messages without the attention of the limited capacity channel. They should not, however, according to Deutsch and Deutsch, be treated differently than verbal targets because Treisman and

Geffen's earlier results were presumably due to differences in pertinence, which would be the same in this study. Lawson's results revealed that subjects were able to respond to the nonverbal items independently of the channel in which they were presented, adding weight to the Broadbent theory. It is difficult to see how the Deutsch/Norman theory can provide a consistent account of both the Treisman and Geffen results, on the one hand, and Moray's and Lawson's results, on the other.

TREISMAN MODEL

In spite of this additional evidence in its support, the Broadbent theory could still not account for the fact that some meaning does get through on unattended channels. It is evident that both theories interpret attention, or the limitation of the system, too narrowly. Treisman, whose experiments have been important in demonstrating the problem of both theories, has argued for a third one that incorporates elements of both (Treisman, 1960, 1964). Her alternative, in a sense, allows information to be selected at both the physical and meaningful levels, but there are important differences in the way she sees the operation of the selection process.

Attenuation

The primary difference in Treisman's model is that the filter is not all-or-none, as in the Broadbent and Deutsch/Norman models. A certain probability always exists that some information on the unattended channel can get through. Treisman used the word attenuation to describe the filter's operation on the unattended channels; information on these channels is attenuated, rather than filtered out. The word was an unfortunate choice, as it is usually understood to mean something done to the information content. It suggests that information is reduced by the filter; that a tone, for instance, is made less intense. Treisman was now open to the criticism that once a channel had been attenuated, a portion of its message could not get through in its original intact state, as it evidently could in shadowing and other experiments.

What Treisman might have actually meant, however, was not that the filter reduced the amount of information available in the unattended channel but, rather, that it did not allow that information to be completely analyzed (however, see Solso, 1988). A particular signal can have a number of features: if it occurs on the attended channel, most of them will be analyzed; if it occurs on the unattended channel, only a portion of them will be processed. Only a few features, however, are presumably necessary to identify highly meaningful or overlearned material, and therefore such material occurring on the unattended channel can be expected to be recognized. That is, a subject attending to one channel might be actually processing about 10% of the information coming in on the other channel. This might be enough to allow her to identify her own name, or a word that is highly predictable from preceding context, but it is usually insufficient for recognition of any of the other words in the unattended message. A better concept for this than attenuation would be that of a probabilistic filter. The advantages of the concept of a probabilistic filter are analogous to those of a probabilistic threshold, as discussed in Chapter 10. There is a much higher probability of words in the shadowed message being recognized than words in the unshadowed message, since a larger portion of the attended message is processed for recognition.

Two Levels of Selection

The second point about Treisman's model is that selective attention can operate on two levels. Selection can take place along certain channels of information, as in Broadbent's original model. The filter is guided by distinctive physical characteristics; for example, the filter can select a particular voice out of several. Broadbent (1970, 1971) calls this stimulus set—subjects are set to receive stimuli from a certain stimulus channel. Selective attention also can operate at the level of meaning, in which case subjects must recognize the stimulus before they select or reject it. For example, if subjects were instructed to remember only the animal names in a list of words, they would have to recognize each word before they could decide whether they should study it further. Broadbent calls this response set. In this case, the subject is set to respond to stimuli that have a certain meaning. These two levels of selection correspond directly to Broadbent's and Deutsch/Norman's levels of selective attention. In Broadbent's (1971) most recent statement, Treisman's modification is accepted completely.

Thus, attention in Treisman's model is hierarchical. A stimulus can be first analyzed with respect to its gross physical features; if it occurs on a selected channel, a stimulus will have a higher probability of being recognized than if it occurs on an unselected channel. That is, if it occurs on a selected channel, a higher proportion of its features will pass through the filter than if it is on an unselected channel. The determining factor for the filter at this level is stimulus quality represented by physical location, voice characteristics, or any other gross stimulus characteristic. Information that is rejected at this level will not be perceived. Information that passes through the first level of the filter is recognized but may still be rejected after its relevance is determined, as in the Deutsch/Norman model. Information that is rejected at this second level will not be rehearsed and remembered, nor acted upon.

NEISSER MODEL

Neisser (1967, 1976) offers an alternative explanation of the act of attention. Neisser sees most behavior as the result of two successive stages of processing. The first stage is preattentive, in which certain global aspects of the stimulus input can be determined. For example, an object may be isolated from its background, that is to say, detected without being recognized. To determine the exact shape of the object, however, the second stage of processing is required. Neisser calls this process analysis-by-synthesis and holds that this constructive process is what we normally refer to as the mechanism of attention itself.

Neisser assumes that the analysis-by-synthesis process can be completely focused on one channel regardless of the events occurring on the other channel. This assumption does not hold in certain situations, however. Consider an experiment carried out by Treisman (1964) in which the subject was required to shadow a message presented to the right ear. Treisman tested the subject at two interference conditions by presenting two additional messages that could be ignored. In the first, these two interfering messages were presented to two separate channels: to the left ear and to the middle of the head (by presenting this message to both ears simultaneously). In the second condition, both interfering messages were presented to the same channel together. The results showed that shadowing performance was much poorer when the interfering messages were presented to separate channels than when they occurred on the same channel. Processing on the unattended channels was found to require processing capacity (attention), so that two separate inputs would produce more interference than one. Neisser's model cannot handle this result since the analysis-by-synthesis process is assumed to operate only on the attended channel. Whatever analysis occurred on the unattended channels should have resulted from the preattentive process. In Treisman's experiment, it seems evident that some additional processing capacity was required to reject two irrelevant locations instead of just one. By equating attention with the single processing stage of analysis-by-synthesis, Neisser's model does not provide a process to deal with attentional effects at other stages of information processing.

Neisser rejects limited capacity because people can develop incredible skills that should not be possible if we are limited in capacity. I watched a juggler in the Moscow Circus keep six soccer balls airborne—does he have more capacity than me? Without a doubt, we increase our apparent capacity with practice, and psychologists have turned their attention to this phenomenon (see Chapter 18). Advocates of limited capacity aren't persuaded by these results because they know that the system has to break down as more and more is demanded from it (Broadbent, 1982). Skilled basketball players believe that they can dribble without attention; yet performance of a second task is interfered with by dribbling. After considering two limited-capacity theories that are the antithesis of Neisser's view, we will review recent critiques of the concept of limited capacity.

KAHNEMAN MODEL

An effort theory of attention was developed by Kahneman (1973). This theory is similar to previous theories with respect to the notion of limited capacity. Effort is the process of determining how much capacity is available and is involved in the allocation of the capacity. According to Kahneman, the capacity available is not fixed but can be influenced by such variables as task difficulty. We have all experienced an increased effort when competing against a particularly challenging opponent. If experimenters design their experiments to be interesting and challenging in similar ways, the results might provide new insights into attentive mechanisms.

Kahneman (1975) presents some experiments as support for his effort theory of attention. Simultaneous lists of words were presented to the two ears, and subjects were given a memory test after the lists were presented. Subjects did not recognize items from the unattended ear in the subsequent memory test, but we cannot conclude that these items were not identified at presentation. They may have been and simply forgotten at a very fast rate because of a lack of rehearsal. The heavy involvement of rehearsal and memory in these experiments precludes any unambiguous interpretation with respect to attentional effects at particular stages of processing. This problem was analyzed in more detail in the discussion of Norman's (1969) important study.

NORMAN/BOBROW MODEL

Following the lead of Kahneman (1973), Norman and Bobrow (1975) offered a new means of looking at attentional phenomena. The central feature of their theory is the distinction between data-limited and resource-limited processes. In the performance of a complex task, behavior might be expected to be related to the amount of resources (such as effort) devoted to the task. Performance would improve up to some point with increases in the allocated resources. In some tasks, however, applying more resources does not improve performance; these tasks are called data limited. Some tasks might become data limited very quickly with increases in resource allocation. Other tasks might be resource limited across a wide range of resource allocation.

Norman and Bobrow (1975) offer this view as an alternative to the stage theories, which address what stages of processing are influenced by attention. Consider the experiments carried out by Treisman and Geffen (1967) and Lawson (1966) discussed previously. Recall that subjects shadowing words in one ear in the Treisman and Geffen (1967) study had difficulty recognizing target words presented simultaneously to the other ear. In contrast, Lawson's (1966) subjects were able to detect target tones presented in the unshadowed ear under similar conditions. Rather than interpreting the results in terms of the detection of the physical characteristics of the nonverbal target tones in the Lawson study as opposed to the necessity of word recognition in the Treisman and Geffen study, Norman and Bobrow assume that the tone detection process becomes data limited much sooner than the word recognition process.

Attending Infants

Ingenious methods have been devised to study psychological processes of infants. Consider the problem of selective attention in which observers are asked to selectively process one of two events. How can infants be instructed appropriately and how is performance evaluated? Neisser and Becklen (1975) studied selective looking by superimposing two natural events (such as the three-man ball game and the handclapping sequence shown in Figure 5). The observer's task is to follow one of the episodes and to press a key to indicate each occurrence of a critical event such as a ball throw. Adults can perform this task easily whereas they find it difficult to follow both events simultaneously.

Bahrick, Walker, and Neisser (1981) devised solutions to two obstacles in the study of selective looking in infants. First, how do we know what the infants are attending to when presented with superimposed episodes. Second, how can we evaluate what the infants learned about the episode that was selectively processed. Spelke (1979) had already shown that infants shown two films side by side will tend to look at the film corresponding to the soundtrack that is played. In this case, eye movements reveal where the infants are looking. As Spelke observed, infants perceive a correspondence between the visual and auditory dimensions of the film and look at the film that is appropriate to the sound track being heard. Accordingly, infants could be instructed to follow one of two superimposed episodes by playing the appropriate sound track. With respect to what the infants saw during selective looking, the authors capitalized on the common observation that infants get bored. Infants who have looked at a single sound film will tend to look at a new silent film when the old film is shown along with it also in silent form. Accordingly, the authors could present two superimposed films and then the two films side by side. Eye movements would then reveal which film was more novel to the infant.

Four-month-old infants were tested in the experiment. Two films were shown superimposed on the same screen along with the soundtrack of one of the films. In the following test period, the films were shown silently side by side and infants choose to look at the previously shown silent film. The result shows that the infants learned more about the film with the corresponding sound track when two films are superimposed. This result shows that infants can selectively follow one of the two superimposed visual episodes. Walker et al. conclude that this is a characteristic of perception and that it is innate rather than learned. The authors also conclude that selective attention is not a separate process or ability but is best revealed by understanding the perceptual and memory processes.

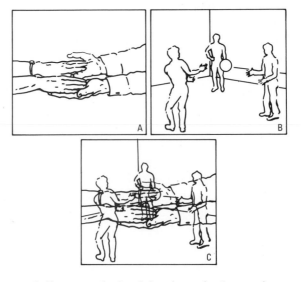

Figure 5. A three-man ball game and a handclapping episode superimposed on one another.

Although Norman and Bobrow (1975) offer a framework for the discussion of attention, their view appears to be untestable in its present form. It seems that any result can be explained by simply assuming different performance-resource functions. In addition, the authors allow for differential allocation of resources to various tasks by subjects. A high-priority task will be allocated more resources and, therefore, will tend to be data limited relative to a low-priority task. Since the experimenter can never be sure of how much resources have been allocated to a particular task, many results might be possible. Accordingly, no experimental result can be taken as negative evidence. Norman (1976) appears to accept the idea of a limited capacity at both early and late stages. In effect, Norman and Bobrow (1975), like Broadbent (1971), accept Treisman's modification of Broadbent's theory, while offering a new language for discussing attention effects. In terms of scientific endeavor, however, their view discourages tests of alternative hypotheses of attentional effects in human information processing. Until the Norman and Bobrow (1975) view can be formalized into explicit testable hypotheses, its usefulness as a theory of attention is limited.

Multiple Resource Pools

In several theoretical developments, limited capacity has been reformulized in terms of resources (Navon & Gopher, 1979; Wickens, 1980). Information processing is assumed to be limited by the total resources that can be allocated to performance. However, rather than a single resource, the theories assume multiple resources. In this framework, there would be separate resource pools for auditory processing and visual processing, for example. One limitation with this approach is that a theory with multiple resources might not be testable. Navon (1984) has even suggested that multiple resources might turn out to be excess theoretical baggage, analogous to a soup stone in the culinary arts. According to a Russian folktale, a soup stone makes a delicious soup, all you have to do is add boiling water, vegetables, meat, and spices.

One empirical test of multiple resources appears to have been successful. Given the assumption of multiple resource pools (Navon & Gopher, 1979; Wickens, Sandry, & Vidulich, 1983), performance should be improved to the extent multiple sources of information can be presented to different systems utilizing different resource pools. Thus, presenting one message visually and one auditorily should lead to better performance than presenting the two messages in a single modality. However, resource theory is not easily applied because it does not specify how people evaluate and integrate multiple sources of information. Thus, resource theory cannot predict that making a sequence of auditory tones more distinctive in pitch and spatial location disrupts tapping performance Klapp, Hill, Tyler, Martin, Jagacinski, and Jones (1985). On the other hand, tapping to a sequence of tones requires some integration of the tones into a single stream. Separating the tones by pitch and spatial location can disrupt this integration process. This example illustrates the value of analyzing performance in terms of the psychological processes involved in pattern recognition and action, and not simply in terms of the resources available for processing. We will find that addressing the issue of evaluating and integrating multiple sources of information will clarify the processes involved in recognition and categorization (Chapter 16), memory (Chapter 17), judgment (Chapter 18), and understanding spoken and written language (Chapters 19 and 20).

ATTENTION AND PROCESSING STAGES

Theory and research go hand in hand in psychological inquiry. We have presented and evaluated six models of attention, each of which attempts to account for the selective nature of information processing. In Broadbent's original model, attention is controlled by a filter that regulates the amount of information flowing past one point in the information-processing chain. At any point in time it permits only one channel of information to pass through to the processes that come after it; the system is always devoting 100% of its processing capacity to the selected channel and none to those that are rejected. In the Deutsch/Norman model, all inputs are recognized completely, and selection takes place afterwards. Treisman combined these two levels of selection into one model and argued that information could be partially filtered (attenuated) at two levels of information processing. Neisser's model equates attention with the constructive process of analysis-by-synthesis. Kahneman (1973) utilizes the concept of effort to explain performance in simultaneous tasks. Norman and Bobrow (1975) use task difficulty and the concept of resources as explanatory constructs.

There is little real dispute that the human information-processing system is limited in its capacity. Given this fact, the task then, with respect to attention, is to first clarify the stages necessary to the processing of information between stimulus and response. Then we can ask which stages of information processing have a limited capacity and, within each stage, which experimental and stimulus variables affect the processing capacity requirements of that stage. We can follow up by asking at each stage whether or not the system is limited at this point, whether it can perform this particular operation on more than one item at a time without loss of efficiency in the processing of any of them. If we have properly defined and distinguished each stage, it should be possible to devise experiments that test for the limitation at each stage, while controlling for the processing contributions of other stages.

Within this framework, the intervening processing between stimulus and response is made up of a series of processes, or stages, wherein the information undergoes ever more complicated analyses. Each stage receives its information from the last, acts upon it independently of the others, and sends it on to the next in a transformed state. Thus, information in this system is thought of as undergoing a series of transformations that, in a sense, ultimately transform the stimulus input into a response.

Following Broadbent's model, the system is provided with a number of channels along which information can enter. The process of monitoring these channels is detection. Detection, the simplest of the stages we shall consider, asks merely whether something is out there or not. Its analysis consists of determining whether or not a change has taken place in the steady-state level of a given channel. When a state of noise background changes to a state of signal plus noise, and the system registers that change, the system is said to have detected it. Specific memory for a stimulus need not be involved at all in this process, which merely looks for any change in the environment. Thus, we can detect a stimulus that is too faint to be recognized completely. We have often heard or seen something without determining what it was.

Detection and Recognition Processes

Attention must be articulated with a specific information-processing model of performance. Taking this tack, we must define the important stages of processing before we ask questions about attention. Throughout the history of psychology, as mentioned several times in this book, it has been valuable to distinguish between detection and recognition. This distinction is necessary to understand performance in several situations.

Consider an experiment involving an observation interval on each trial (Bland & Perrott, 1978). The experiment involved two tasks. In the detection task, a 10-msec pure tone was presented on half of the trials, and nothing was presented on the other half. The subjects indicated whether or not a test tone had been presented. The observation interval was always followed by a 150-msec masking tone after a variable silent interval. In the recognition task, a test tone was presented on every trial. The test tone was equally likely to be high in pitch or low in pitch. The subject's task was to identify the tone as high or low in pitch. As in the detection task, the test tone was followed by a masking tone after a variable silent interval. Given two alternatives on both tasks, accuracy of performance can vary between 50% and 100%. As can be seen in Figure 6, detection and recognition follow two different time courses. Detection performance reaches asymptote (the highest level of performance) at around 50 msec, whereas recognition does not reach this level until 310 msec of silence between the test and target tones. The experiment demonstrates the important difference between detection and recognition processes (consistent with the seminal results of Donders discussed in Chapter 7). This difference sets the stage for questions of limited capacity and selective attention at each of these two processing stages. Two questions can be asked about the process of selective attention at the level of detection. First, is there a limited amount of processing capacity available for detection that can be allocated to a particular stimulus channel? For example, can we detect a visual and auditory stimulus simultaneously as well as either stimulus alone? Second, can the processing interfere with the detection process? For example, do we detect signals as well when we are also rehearsing a set of numbers for later recall? In an analogous way, these same two questions can be asked about the recognition process. The answers to these questions will determine to what extent attention operates at each of these stages of information processing.

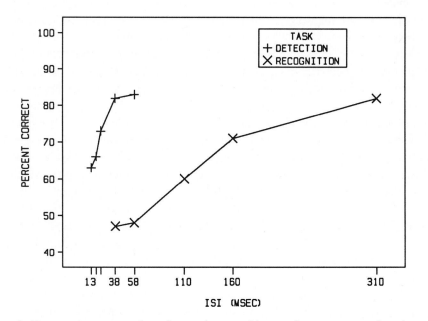

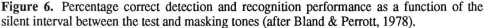

Figure 6. Percentage correct detection and recognition performance as a function of the silent interval between the test and masking tones (after Bland & Perrott, 1978).

Precueing Detection and Recognition

There is a long history of research on how prior information can influence the perception of an event. Most recently, Posner (1980) and others have used a precueing paradigm to study how attention influences the processing of visual displays. In one task, an observer is cued that a target light will more likely occur to the left or right of fixation. The reaction time (RT) to respond to the target is shorter when the target occurs in the predictable relative to the unpredictable location. This result can be analyzed within the framework of signal detectability discussed in Chapter 12. The RT advantage for the predictable location could be a sensitivity effect or a criterion effect. The precue might actually enhance sensitivity to the target. On the other hand, the RT advantage might reflect the use of a more liberal criterion for initiating a response to a target in a predictable relative to an unpredictable position (Duncan, 1981; Sperling, 1984). An information-processing analysis dictates a test between these two alternatives. As an example, these two alternatives might be tested using the logic of the additive-factor method (Chapter 8).

Feature and Conjunction Search

Memory and visual search tasks (Chapter 9) have been used to study attention (Schneider & Shiffrin, 1977; Treisman & Gelade, 1980). The search task has been used to study differences in the detection of a single property of an item versus the recognition of an item having two or more properties. Treisman and Gelade (1980, Experiment 1) asked subjects to perform a feature search and a conjunction search. In feature search, subjects had to find a blue letter or the letter S. In conjunction search, subjects had to find a green T. In both conditions, the negative items or distractors were green X or brown T. The logic underlying the two types of search is as follows. A single feature of an item is sufficient for a positive response in the feature search. That is, if the subject detects any blue letter or any letter S, then a positive response can be made. On the other hand, the presence of two features in the same letter is necessary for a positive response in conjunction search.

The number of items in the display is the independent variable of interest. If there is something inherently difficult about putting together two features of a single letter, then conjunction search should be more difficult than feature search. Increasing the number of items in the display should be much more detrimental to conjunction search than to feature search. Figure 7 gives the results of a feature search and a conjunction search task. As can be seen in the figure, there are large differences in the two types of search. For positive trials, the time for feature search remains fairly independent of the number of items in the display whereas the time for conjunction search grows linearly with the number of items in the display. For negative trials, RTs increase for both feature and conjunction search, but at a much larger rate for conjunction search than for feature search.

Given these results and several others (Treisman, 1986), Treisman has proposed that conjunction search requires selective attention whereas feature search does not. Attention can only be directed serially to a single item (or a group of items) at a time. Thus, conjunction search grows linearly with the number of items in the display. Feature search can be carried out in parallel, and thus remains independent of display size. Attention is not necessary for the detection of a single feature but is necessary for the integration of several features. Attention, therefore, apparently operates differently in the detection of a single feature and in the recognition of an item having two features. In terms of our information-processing stage model, attention operates at recognition, but not at detection.

Attention remains one of the biggest challenges to experimental psychologists. Perhaps we will know that we have made real progress in psychological inquiry when we improve on James'

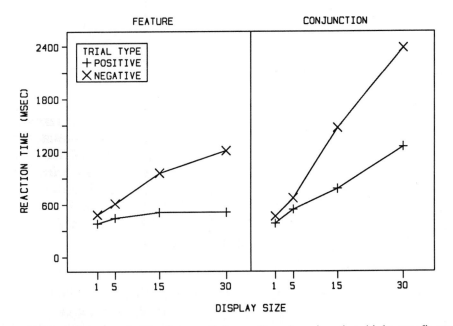

Figure 7. Reaction time in the feature (left panel) and conjunction (right panel) search tasks, as a function of display size for positive and negative test trials (from Treisman & Gelade, 1980).

description of the phenomenon. James also said that everyone knows what attention is; however, one hundred years of research reveals that everyone knows except those who want to know. We will find that we have been more successful in delineating the operations of specific psychological processes than in pinning down the concept of attention. We begin in the next chapter with the processes involved in recognition and categorization.

16

Recognition and Categorization

Recognition and Perception

Pattern Recognition
> Template Matching
> Feature Analysis

Concepts and Categorization

Classical Theory

Tests of Classical View
> Typicality Ratings
> Instance Generation
> Sentence Verification
> Priming
> Feature Generation
> Processing Well-Defined Concepts

Probabilistic Theory

Exemplar Theory

Summary Descriptions versus
> Exemplars

The Fuzzy View
> Evaluation
> Integration
> Decision
> Prototypical Task
> Fuzzy Logical Model of
>> Perception (FLMP)
> Connectionist Model of
>> Perception (CMP)
> Cups and Bowls
> Cups and Bowls in Factorial
>> Combination

Development of Categorization
> Fine-Grained Analyses

Category Knowledge
Fuzzy Logic

---

*A stone is shape, color, weight, and kind of substance
in complicated relation. When such descriptive ultimates
are general properties which can vary continuously or
discretely, when they are, in short, parameters, they may,
if one chooses, be called attributes of the object described.*
E. G. Boring (1942)

Oliver Sacks (1987) describes a distinguished music singer and teacher, who sometimes found himself unable to recognize the simplest and most familiar patterns. Here was a man of cultivation, imagination, and charm, who had no noticeable deficit. However, having decided to leave, he looked around for his hat, reached out and took hold of his wife's head, and tried to lift it off, to put it on. Mistaking his wife for a hat was pathetic enough to inspire Sack's to entitle his engaging anthology of clinical neurology dysfunctions, *The Man Who Mistook His Wife for a Hat and Other Clinical Tales.* What critical ingredient could this poor gentleman have lost from the recipe of categorizing and imposing order on the blooming, buzzing confusion around us? This chapter cannot answer this question, but it should help inform us about the various knowledge structures and psychological processes involved in perceiving, recognizing, and categorizing the world around us.

What does recognition and categorization accomplish? First, it reduces the complexity of an ever changing environment. As said so eloquently by the Greek philosopher, Heraclites, no one sets foot in the same river twice. Although the river changes constantly, much about it does not change. Thus, it is not inappropriate to treat it equivalently at different times. Categorization, in this case, allows different instances to be treated identically. Second, categorization entails identification and pigeonholes an event. Although each of us speaks the same word differently, the listener can interpret the different patterns as having the same meaning (see Chapter 19). Third, categorization facilitates learning by allowing us to transfer our experience from previous encounters with that category. Expert physicists classify problems in physics in terms of higher-order categories that are oblivious to novices. Novices see problems as similar if they have similar surface features, such as problems involving blocks on an inclined plane versus problems involving rotation of objects. Experts, on the other hand, see problems as similar if they involve similar theoretical concepts, such as the conservation of energy or Newton's second law. Fourth, categorization specifies an action that might not otherwise be carried out. Categorizing the intention of a large dog chasing you while cycling determines whether or not some defensive action is necessary. Finally, categorization allows us to order and relate classes of events. Number categories enable us to order and relate a dozen to a baker's dozen irrespective of whether the objects involved are cookies or doughnuts.

RECOGNITION AND PERCEPTION

Our perception corresponds to our phenomenal impression of some event whereas our recognition of the event refers to some categorization of the event. Rock, Shallo, and Schwartz (1978) carried out a series of experiments to evaluate the role of recognition in determining the perception of depth in pictures. Consider the two drawings in Figure 1. The drawing on the left includes a texture gradient of the waves since they decrease in size with increases in distance.

Category Knowledge

One of the most apparent properties of perception, memory, and thinking is the formation and use of categories of information. We ask a friend to have a chair, not to sit on a particular reinforced cushion supported by four legs. Children tend to think in terms of categories before they differentiate between members of a category. A delightful observation that I encountered was on an outing with a park naturalist. Upon hearing what was obviously a bird song to all of us, the naturalist asked, "Listen, can anyone identify that?" A young child said very quickly, "It's a bird." Although category information can make processing more efficient, it can also be less exact. It is important to determine whether the animal in the distance is the vicious dog that tried to bite you the last time you rode your bike down this street. Psychologists have used a variety of information-processing tasks to assess the nature of our category knowledge and how it is used in psychological processing.

The child's interpretation of the naturalist's question also reveals that there is a preferred level of categorization. Rosch (1978) has referred to this level as the *basic* level. Birds is a basic category, whereas finches would be considered a subordinate category and reptiles a superordinate category. Thinking and communication achieves the most with the least effort, when it occurs at the basic level. As observed by Rosch, satire and snobbery is communicated when there is an overabundance of category usage at the subordinate level. Consider the following passage

And so, after putting away my 10-year-old Royal 470 manual and lining up my Monggol Number 3 pencils on my Goldsmith Brothers Formica imitation-wood desk, I slide into my squirrel-skin L. L. Bean slippers and shuffle off to the kitchen. There Holding Decades in my trembling right hand, I drop it *plunk* into my new Sears 20-gallon, celadon-green Permanex trash can.

Relative size is also present: the nearer ships are larger than those farther away. Although slightly more difficult to see in these reproductions, interposition and shadow are also present in the drawing on the left. All of these pictorial cues to depth have been eliminated in the drawing on the right and yet our phenomenal experience of this drawing is similar. Both drawings give a relatively good impression of an ocean scene receding away from the viewer. If depth cues are necessary for perceiving depth in pictures, then we should perceive less depth in the right panel than in the left. If recognizing the photograph as an ocean scene is responsible for perceived depth, then there should be no difference in the perceived depth in the two drawings. These hypotheses were tested by the authors.

In order to measure the perception of depth in these pictures, Rock et al. (1978) utilized the well-known relationship between perceived depth and perceived size. If two identical objects are presented at an equal distance from an observer, the one seen as farther away will also be seen as larger. The pictures had white squares in their upper and lower portions and observers were asked to compare the apparent size of the upper square with that of the lower square (see Figure 1). The method of limits was used to measure the apparent size of the squares. The top slide was the standard and the bottom was the comparison. The slides were arranged in a carousel projector in order of size of the comparison square. The observer advanced the slides to the one that gave equal apparent sizes of the two squares.

The authors claim to demonstrate that cues to depth are not necessary for pictorial depth perception. If depth cues are necessary for perceived depth, we should expect very different results for the two drawings. A significant size illusion should occur only in the drawing with depth cues. Subjects should see the top square as larger than the bottom square in this drawing but not in the drawing without depth cues. But as you might predict from your own perception of these drawings, an identical illusion was found in both drawings. The size illusion was about 13% in both

Figure 1. The drawing on the left has several cues to depth present. The drawing on the right does not have these cues to depth.

drawings, the top square was seen as about 13% larger than the bottom square regardless of the presence or absence of depth cues.

The authors go on to argue that recognition of a scene is a critical stage in perceiving depth in pictures. To provide evidence for this argument, observers were shown photographs of natural scenes and made size judgments of superimposed squares as in the first experiment. The important result was that a size illusion only occurred for observers that recognized the scene correctly. When it was not recognized, no illusion occurred. For example, to see the top square as larger than the bottom in a photograph of a landscape, it was necessary to see the scene as a landscape. Therefore, correct recognition is a necessary condition for the perception of depth and, therefore, the appropriate illusion of size.

There are several limitations with the conclusions reached by Rock et al. (1978). In contrast to the authors' assumption, the drawing on the right of Figure 1 is not without depth cues. Height in the picture plane is a powerful cue to depth, and this cue is present in both drawings. In addition, the conclusion that recognition is necessary for the perception of depth cannot be completely true because we have observed in Chapter 14 that subjects are influenced by depth cues in displays that are not recognized as a particular scene. My feeling is that the percept and recognition emerge in parallel rather than successively.

PATTERN RECOGNITION

We use several terms to describe roughly the same phenomenon. Recognition means cognizing something we cognized previously. Identification means mapping a unique stimulus into a unique response. Categorization means mapping several noticeably different stimuli into the same unique response. For example, a child recognizes a dog she has seen before, identifies it as Fido, and categorizes it as a dog. Recognition, identification, and categorization appear to be central to perceptual and cognitive functioning. We consider these three acts to entail the same fundamental processes. All of these can be characterized as choice or pattern recognition situations in which the subject, given a stimulus, chooses one of a set of alternative responses (Bush, Galanter, & Luce, 1963). Pattern recognition has been found to be fundamental in such different domains as playing chess, examining X-rays, and reading text (Chase & Simon, 1973; Lesgold, 1984a, 1984b).

It is important to consider the extent that the processing of a pattern depends on the empirical domain involved. Does the recognition of a chessboard configuration involve the same processes as recognition of the spoken syllable /ba/. We take the view that pattern recognition involves similar operations regardless of the specific nature of the patterns. The developmental progression of the processes involved in pattern recognition is also addressed. Piagetian theory (1970) would lead to the expectation of a qualitative change in pattern recognition across different stages of development. Another influencial developmental theory is that young children perceive, recognize, and categorize events and objects in terms of undifferentiated wholes. It is only with development that the parts and dimensions of objects are noticed. Finally, it is necessary to evaluate the methodological and theoretical frameworks for studying pattern classification behavior. We begin with two general schemes for pattern recognition, called template matching and feature analysis, respectively.

Template Matching

Template matching is a form of holistic recognition in which the units of analysis are equivalent to the patterns to be recognized. A child's toy robot that recognizes a few voice commands is programmed to recognize by template matching. The toy, that sells for about 50 dollars, has a learning mode and a performance mode. In the learning mode, specific voice commands are linked with specific behaviors. The behaviors are moving forward or backing up, turning left or right, stopping, greeting, and lifting up or down. The commands can be words or short phrases, such as *move forward*, *back up*, *turn right*, *left turn*, *stop*, *hello*, *lift it up*, and *put them down*. Notice that I chose the commands to be very different from one another; distinctive alternatives make the task easier than similar alternatives.

The robot stores a template of each of the commands in terms of the waveshape of the speech pattern (see Chapter 19 for a discussion of sound). Each template is hooked up with the appropriate behavior pattern specified by the teacher. Having learned the eight commands, the robot can be placed in its performance mode. The speaker utters one of the commands, and the robot performs one of the actions. It accomplishes this feat by matching each of the templates in memory with the waveform of the new command. It behaves in accordance with the template that gives the best match with the command.

The recognition of printed letters by template matching is easier to visualize than is speech recognition. The template for a letter would be superimposed over the test letter and all the deviations would be measured. The template that gives the smallest deviations would be the winner. Speech recognition by the robot works in the same manner.

There are several limitations in recognizing patterns by template matching. All of these come about because the template matching routine is blind to the unique properties or features of most patterns. For most patterns, some features are critical for recognition and some are irrelevant. Template matching has no method to ignore or adjust for the irrelevant features of the pattern and utilize the critical features. The toy robot does not know that we speak at different rates, with different voices, and with different dialects. All of these differences will contribute to a mismatch between the specific templates stored in memory and new commands. As long as the matching routine operates on a holistic comparison, it cannot compensate for the irrelevant variation that is found in most patterns. Hence optimal performance by the robot occurs when the commands are given by the original teacher speaking at the same rate.

A related limitation in template matching is that it fails to take into account the nature of the fit between the template and the test pattern. Consider a case in which there is only partial information about the test pattern. A third of the letters H and N can be eliminated by either removing the middle line or by making the letters out of dots. However, we cannot recognize the letters in the first case, but we can in the second. We know enough to dismiss missing information (or noisy information) when it is uncorrelated with the pattern, but not when the nature of the pattern is changed. Simple template matching routines have no algorithm to make decisions about the nature of the variation that is observed.

Finally, template matching becomes unwieldy when the number of patterns to be discriminated is large. The toy robot does an acceptable job with eight patterns, but would have difficulty with a few hundred. A child, on the other hand, understands (but does not necessarily obey) an unlimited number of commands. The chess masters (discussed in Chapter 18) recognize thousands of board positions. Given these limitations, psychologists have turned to feature analysis for a more realistic description of pattern recognition in humans.

Feature Analysis

Before beginning our discussion, it is important to acknowledge that feature analysis is not a panacea for the difficulties faced by template matching. Feature analysis does not take the patterns themselves as the smallest unit of analysis as is the case in template matching. Each pattern is represented in memory in terms of several component parts. Thus, the command *go forward* might be described in terms of the words that make it up, or the syllables, or some other set of components. Recognition would now involve matching these component parts or features to the test pattern. Feature matching is not a panacea because matching of the features reduces to matching a set of mini-templates. Feature analysis might be just as susceptible to error as is template matching.

It is informative to describe three historical influences on the acceptance and development of feature analysis. These influences come from linguistics, neurophysiology, and artificial intelligence.

Four decades ago, linguists depended heavily on the concept of a *phoneme*. The phoneme was considered as the minimal speech segment that could change the meaning of a word. For example, the word *bet* has three phonemes /b/, /ɛ/, and /t/. To confirm this, we change the /t/ to /d/ and get *bed*, the /ɛ/ to /æ/ to get *bat*, and the /b/ to /m/ to get *met*. All languages of the world can be described by about 50 or 60 phonemes. The phoneme was conceptualized as a fairly holistic unit until linguists of the Prague school came up with the concept of distinctive features (Fromkin & Rodman, 1988). Now all of the phonemes could be described in terms of a set of about a dozen distinctive features. Each phoneme was described in terms of the presence or absence of each of these features. These features are discussed in greater detail in Chapter 19. For our purposes, the distinctive feature analysis offered an alternative to template matching. Speech recognition could be carried out, not by template matching of phonemes, but by feature analysis of the distinctive features making up the phonemes.

The second influence is found in the seminal and well-known work of Hubel and Wiesel, which led to the Nobel Prize. The receptors in the eye transduce the electromagnetic energy in the light into neural responses that are passed up the visual pathways to the cells in the visual cortex. The neural responses are brief electrical discharges that can be recorded by an electrode connected to an electronic amplifier. The output of these cells can be both seen and heard. Recording from the visual cortex of a cat, Hubel and Wiesel (1962) found single cells with amazing properties.

Anesthesized cats viewed various visual displays while electrical recordings were made from single cells. The researchers found that single cells were selectively sensitive to different aspects of the visual input. One set of cells became known as *simple* cells; these cells were essentially edge detectors. The critical property of the stimulus to elicit a response is a border between light and dark. Other simple cells were line detectors or slit detectors, both of which can be considered modifications of edge detectors. They gave a burst of electrical pulses when an edge was presented to a specific location on the retina. These cells were orientation-specific in that the border that produced a response had to have a specific orientation. A simple cell monitors a fairly precise location on the retina in terms of responding to the stimulus. The *receptive field*, defined as the sensitive area, is small for simple cells.

Another set of cells, called *complex* cells, were more selective in their response. They would respond only to lines of particular width and orientation; complex cells might be considered to be monitoring fairly abstract properties of the stimulus. In addition, many of these cells preferred some movement of the line, and the line moving in a given direction. Their receptive fields were significantly larger than those of simple cells. Finally, *hypercomplex* cells were even more discriminating in that the lines also had to be a given length. The receptive field of these cells were very large. Here before our eyes, or at least the cat's, was a physical instantiation of feature analysis. The feature analysis also appeared to be hierarchical—simple cells would talk to complex cells, which would talk to hypercomplex cells, and so on, eventually leading to a cell that would recognize your grandmother.

The influence from artificial intelligence is found in Oliver Selfridge's (1959) engaging pandemonium model. Without linguistics or neurophysiology to guide him, Selfridge settled on an older and more venerable tradition—the behavioral influence of demons. In Selfridge's model, the demons have their influence by shouting causing much pandemonium in pattern recognition. For recognizing letters of the alphabet, Selfridge utilized four types of demons arranged in hierarchical order. An image demon would transduce the stimulus and send it on to the feature demons. The feature demons correspond to mini-templates that are looking for themselves in the pattern. Each demon shouts in direct proportion to a match. Letter demons, corresponding to each letter of the alphabet, listen to the feature demons. These letter demons know what features make them up, and also shout to the extent their appropriate feature demons are shouting. The buck stops at the decision demon. This egotistical entity monitors the shouting of the letter demons, and decides in favor of the loudest shouting demon.

The three influences from linguistics, neurophysiology, and artificial intelligence encouraged psychologists to develop feature models of pattern recognition and categorization. Several characteristics (or features) of the psychological models exemplify this influence. First, a description of a pattern is in terms of component parts, as opposed to a holistic template. Although we experience an object as an integral whole, it is reasonable to describe the properties of size, shape, color, and texture independently of each other. Second, these parts or features take on different values for different patterns—the features differentiate the patterns from one another. Thus, some apples differ only in color whereas some trees differ in size, shape, and color, and so on. Third, the features are arranged hierarchically, with the smallest features grouped into a somewhat larger feature, the somewhat larger feature grouped into an even larger feature, and so on. The shape of a table is made up of component shapes and these component shapes are made up of component lines and angles (Biederman, 1987). In this scheme, a pattern in one domain is simply a feature in another; for example, a phoneme made of distinctive features is a feature for distinguishing word patterns. We now proceed to an analysis of theories of the representation of concepts and how instances are categorized as members of a conceptual class.

CONCEPTS AND CATEGORIZATION

Concept is defined as an abstract idea derived from specific instances. Accordingly, then, my concept of square is an abstraction from my experience with specific squares. Categorization of a new object as a square must involve evaluating the object against my abstract idea of squares and other relevant ideas—and finding that square gives the best match to the object. A psychological theory must address the mental structure of concepts and the psychological processes involved in categorization. We consider four classes of theories: classical, probabilistic, exemplar, and fuzzy. These theories differ with respect to several important assumptions about the representation and processing of categories, as illustrated in the binary oppositions illustrated in Figure 2.

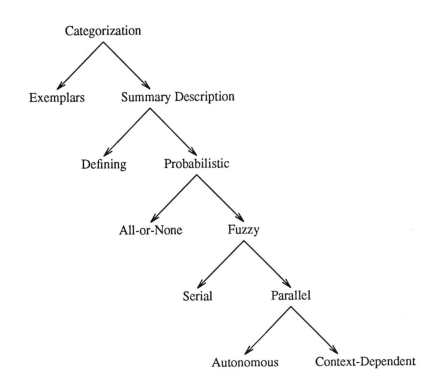

Figure 2. Tree of wisdom illustrating binary oppositions central to the differences among theories of concepts and categorization.

The first issue involves how concepts are represented psychologically. Theories can be partitioned into two classes. Most theories assume that each category is represented by some sort of summary description. Contrasting theories at this level are those that assume that a category is represented by the exemplars that make it up. Within the class of summary descriptions, an issue is whether there exists a set of defining properties or features for category membership. Defining properties would be necessary and sufficient for membership. Another issue concerns the features themselves: Is a feature either present or absent, or is it present to some degree? Analogous to memory search (Chapter 9), we can ask whether concepts and features are processed serially or in parallel. And finally, it is of interest to determine whether categorization proceeds autonomously, or whether it is context-dependent. We will allude to these questions in our presentation and evaluation of theories of concepts and categorization.

CLASSICAL THEORY

According to the classical view, every concept is defined by a set of necessary and sufficient features for category membership. Aristotle championed the classical view in his belief that each concept could be defined by essential features. The mental representation of a concept is a summary description of those characteristics that are defining for category membership. Defining characteristics are necessary and sufficient characteristics. A square, according to the classical view, would have four defining characteristics. It would be a closed figure with four sides that are equal in length, and the four sides would intersect to give equal angles. Any geometric figure with these characteristics would be categorized as square. Any geometric figure with at least one of these characteristics missing would be categorized as not a square.

TESTS OF CLASSICAL VIEW

The classical view of concepts and categorization appears to describe our processing of an object, such as a square. Most psychologists throughout the first half of this century accepted this classical view of concepts and categorization. For example, the seminal experiments carried out by Bruner, Goodnow, and Austin (1956) used geometric objects for test figures, and correct categorization of the objects required a set of defining features. In the 1960s, however, Eleanor Rosch (1975, 1975b; Rosch & Mervis, 1975) initiated a series of experiments that have revolutionized psychologists' thinking about concepts and categorization. Her experiments represented a converging series of tasks that were remarkably revealing about the nature of concepts and categorization. We will consider five different tasks that have been used to address this question.

Typicality Ratings

Consider the category, fruit. Rate on a scale from 1 to 9 how good an example an apple is of the category, fruit. A rating of 1 indicates that it is a very good example of the category, whereas a rating of 9 indicates that it is a very poor example of the category. A rating of 5 indicates that it is an average example of the category, and so on for the other ratings. How good an example of the category, fruit, is an apricot? How good of an example of the category, fruit, is a tomato? How good an example is an avocado?

As you may have guessed from this exercise, not all instances are equally good members of a category (Rosch, 1975a, 1975b). Some fruits appear to be better exemplars of the category than others. There is even very good intersubject agreement on the relative goodness of category membership. This result threatens the classical view of concepts. If concepts are defined by necessary and sufficient characteristics, then one instance of the category should be as good as another. There is no mechanism within the classical view to describe how the instances of a category could differ in terms of their relative goodness of category membership.

Instance Generation

Subjects have been asked to list all of the instances of a category that they can think of (Battig & Montague, 1969). Subjects recall some instances much more often than they recall other instances. For example, apple would be listed as a fruit more often than avocado. In addition, for those subjects that generated both apple and avocado, it would usually be the case that apple would be listed earlier in the list than avocado. Thus, instance generation reveals very much the story revealed by typicality ratings. Not all instances appear to be equally good members of a category.

Sentence Verification

Respond "True" or "False" as quickly as possible to the following statements:

"A dog is an animal."
"A lizard is an animal."
"A trout is a fish."
"A whale is a fish."
"A chair is a fish."

The reaction times (RTs) of the true and false responses to these statements differ greatly, depending on the nature of the statement. As will be discussed in Chapter 17, the RTs appear to be a function of the goodness-of-match of the instance to the category. Like the typicality-ratings and the instance-generation experiments, the sentence-verification task reveals that not all instances of a category are equal. It takes longer to verify that a nut is a fruit than an apple is a fruit.

Priming

In a priming task, a subject is given a priming stimulus followed by a test stimulus. The question of interest is, "To what extent does the priming stimulus influence the processing of the test stimulus?" Consider a naming task in which the subject is required to simply name a word when it is presented in a tachistoscope (Massaro, Jones, Lipscomb, & Scholz, 1978). The word is presented upside down to make the recognition process more difficult. The priming stimulus is a category name, such as fruit, furniture, bird, tool, and so on. The test words are instances of these categories. The dependent measure is the reaction time recorded from the onset of the test word. Two classes of test words are chosen. For the class, "Good Exemplars," the test items were given very high ratings in the typicality task. That is, subjects indicated that these items were good examples of the category in question. The "Poor Exemplars" were rated as bad members of the category. Examples of the good and poor exemplars are given in Table 1.

Table 1. Examples of the categories and good and poor exemplars of the categories used in the Massaro et al. (1978) task.

Category	Good Exemplars	Poor Exemplars
Furniture	Chair Sofa Table	Rug Stove Counter
Fruit	Orange Apple Banana	Prunes Date Avocado
Birds	Robin Sparrow Bluejay	Owl Buzzard Flamingo

Previous research has established that a priming stimulus can facilitate naming of a test word (Becker & Killion, 1977; Meyer, Schvaneveldt, & Ruddy, 1975; Sanford, Garrod, & Boyle, 1977). The present question is the extent to which the priming stimulus facilitates processing of the rotated test stimulus, as a function of exemplar goodness. The test items are either good or poor exemplars, and half of the trials in the task are primed and half are unprimed. As can be seen in Figure 3, the priming stimulus facilitates the naming of the rotated test word. Thus, subjects are able to utilize this additional source of information to speed up their naming of the test word. We might expect that priming should be more effective to the extent the category concept and the exemplar share semantic features. It follows that priming should facilitate naming of the good exemplars more than naming of the poor exemplars. Figure 3 shows that the prime facilitated the processing of good exemplars more than it facilitated the processing of poor exemplars. Thus, we have evidence that the mental relation between a category concept and its exemplars is not equal across the class of exemplars. There appears to be a closer relation between the category concept and good exemplars of the category than between the category concept and poor exemplars in the category.

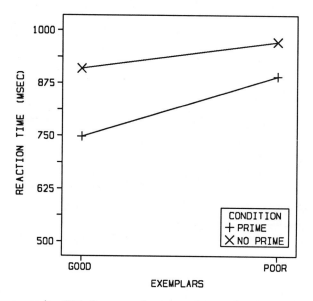

Figure 3. Average naming RTs for rotated test words as a funciton of exemplar goodness and whether or not a priming stimulus was presented (after Massaro et al., 1978).

Feature Generation

In another experimental attack on the nature of representation of concepts, subjects are asked to list features of a concept. Thus, for example, subjects might be given the concept, furniture, and be asked to list as many features as possible (Hampton, 1979; Rosch & Mervis, 1975). The results of this type of experiment indicate that subjects list many non-necessary features of the concept. For example, subjects might list the fact that furniture is found in a house, or in a living room, or is made of wood. Although the characteristics of being found in a house and perhaps being made of wood are typical of many instances of furniture, they are not necessary and sufficient features of the concept, furniture.

Processing Well-Defined Concepts

An impressive variety of tasks indicate that the classical view of concepts and categorization appears to be wrong in the domain of everyday concepts, such as fruit and furniture. The judgments of these natural concepts produce graded responses representing the degree to which instances represent the concepts. Armstrong, Gleitman, and Gleitman (1983) challenge the interpretation of these results, however. If this interpretation is correct, Armstrong et al. propose that categories that are well-defined should not produce graded responses because graded responses have been interpreted to mean that the concepts being judged are not well defined. A strong prediction, they reason, is that well-defined concepts, with necessary and sufficient descriptions, should not yield graded responses in terms of the degree to which an instance of the concept represents the category.

Armstrong et al. (1983) chose well-defined categories such as odd number, geometric figure, and female. An odd number seems to have a clear definition, namely an integer not divisible by two without a remainder. Analogously, geometric figure and female seem to be well-defined. What may come as a surprise to some of the readers is that instances of these categories were not rated as equally good members or exemplars of the category. Subjects rated 7 as a more typical odd number than 731. Analogously, a square is viewed as a much more prototypical geometrical figure than is a trapezoid or an ellipse. And finally, a policewoman is seen as less typical of the category female than is a mother.

Armstrong et al. (1983) conclude that the graded results with natural concepts cannot be taken as evidence against the classical view of concepts because the same results are found with well-defined concepts. However, I do not see any qualitative difference between the concepts odd number or female and those of bird or furniture. Consider the concept female, employed by the authors because they believe that this concept is well-defined. This interpretation contrasts sharply with our impression of the concept. No one would argue with the idea that some people are more representative of the category female than are others. The value of a continuous measure of androgeny, which can be measured both psychologically and physiologically, provides support for the idea of the gradedness of the property female. By these criteria, it is a mistake to consider female as a well-defined concept that should not give graded responses in terms of judgments of category membership. Thus, the classical view of concepts appears to be wrong for both natural and well-defined concepts and it is necessary to consider alternative theories of concepts and categorization.

PROBABILISTIC THEORY

The concept, square, is easy to think about and to describe. What about the concept of game, however? The well-known philosopher, Ludwig Wittgenstein (1953), used this example to argue that the classical view of concepts is inadequate. Wittgenstein (1953) proposed that our concepts are not neatly organized as implied by classical theory. It is informative to read some of his famous discussion of the meaning of game.

> Consider for example the proceedings that we call "games." I mean board-games, card-games, ball-games, Olympic games, and so on. What is common to them all?—Don't say: "There must be something common, or they would not be called games'"—but LOOK AND SEE whether there is anything common to all. And the result of this examination is: we see a complicated network of similarities overlapping and criss-crossing: sometimes overall similarities, sometimes similarities of detail. I can think of no better expression to characterize these similarities than "family resemblances"...

It is difficult to come up with a list of necessary and sufficient features or characteristics for defining some event as a game. For example, one might say a game involves competition. We can think of some games, such as crossword puzzles, that do not appear to involve competition. Of course, we can also stretch the notion of competition, because it is a concept that cannot be defined with respect to necessary and sufficient characteristics. Here we seem to have reached Gödel's strange loop (Hofstadter, 1979). We want to talk about concepts, but we have to use concepts to talk about them.

The probabilistic view of concepts builds on Wittgenstein's observations but attempts to make them more formal. According to the probabilistic view, no characteristic is necessary or sufficient for a given concept. However, an instance is a member of a category to the extent that it has characteristics in common with a description of the category. Thus, a category will be characterized by a whole host of characteristics. An object will be considered an exemplar of the category if it shares a criterial number of features characterizing the category. At face value, the probabilistic view appears to be consistent with the results of the experiments that we have discussed. We will return to an evaluation of the probabilistic view after the other two views of categorization have been discussed.

EXEMPLAR THEORY

The exemplar view rejects the psychological reality of the definition of concept. The exemplar view rejects the idea that a summary description characterizes a concept. According to the exemplar view, a concept is nothing more than the instances of the concept that a person has experienced (Brooks, 1978; Medin & Schaffer, 1978). Consider the concept, suicidal patient, from the perspective of a clinician. No single summary description can encompass all suicidal patients. Patients may be suicidal because they are despondent over some event, such as the loss of a loved one. They may be terminally ill. They may be individuals who consistently place themselves in life-threatening situations, and so on. A clinician on the lookout for a suicidal patient would not be helped by trying to utilize a summary description that captures the commonalities among all possible suicidal tendencies. On the other hand, the clinician might use the exemplars that she and her colleagues have observed to be suicidal. Faced with a new patient, the clinician, then, would look for the similarity between this patient and some other patient who was suicidal. To the extent that the current patient is highly similar to a previous suicidal patient, the clinician has good evidence that this patient may be suicidal. The exemplar view captures anecdotes about the behavior of clinicians. Medical doctors, for example, appear to be very good at spotting a rare illness, given some symptoms, when they have had specific experience with those symptoms in the past.

SUMMARY DESCRIPTIONS VERSUS EXEMPLARS

Is a test instance evaluated against summary descriptions of previous instances or direct representations of previous instances (exemplars)? For some domains, like everyday objects, the high frequency of occurrence of the instances would seem to make an exemplar-based representation unmanageable. Homa, Sterling, and Trepel (1981) propose that it is only in the initial learning of a concept that the representation might be limited to exemplars. Continued learning would lead to a summary-based representation.

A summary description cannot represent all categories. As noted by Fried and Holyoak (1984), the category of things stored in my attic is not easy to represent by a summary description (if the goal is to distinguish this category from others, such as things stored in my basement). In this case, a list of each item seems necessary. A summary description might not be represented, if it is not useful, as when the category's instances are highly unrelated. Subjects might also fail to generate summary descriptions even if reasonable descriptions are possible. This might occur when there are only a few instances per category or when the instance learning is stressed and the category structure is disguised.

In typical learning situations, however, summary descriptions play an important role in learning, memory, and categorization. Consider an experiment carried out by Clapper and Bower (1988). Subjects learn about stars. First, they learn about red, green, and blue stars that have unique properties. Red stars might have two properties and blue stars might have four other properites. Subjects then learn about specific stars; for example, Altair has five properties. A specific star had two types of properties: common and distinctive. Common features are those that belong to a superordinate color category. Distinctive features are those that are unique to a specific star. Four of the five properties of Altair are common because they belong to blue stars. The fifth property would be a distinctive feature unique to the star Altair. Categorization of these specific stars revealed that subjects did indeed exploit knowledge about the superordinate color categories of stars.

Subjects saw word pairs consisting of a specific star and a property. They responded as quickly as possible whether the star had that property. The time it takes to verify true statements of this form depends on the number of facts known about a particular object. This result is similar in form to other results involving memory search (Chapter 9) and sentence verification (Chapter 17). It has been called a fan effect because the increase in RT with increases in the number of associated facts with an object supposedly results from the increase in the number of facts emanating from the representation of the concept in a semantic network in memory.

The fan effect was used to measure the influence of common and distinctive features on RT. The question of interest is whether knowing the the color categories of stars will reduce the fan effect. In fact, RT to verify a star-property pair increased with the number of distinctive properties associated with that pair, but remained independent of the number of common properties. Subjects benefit from knowing that Altair is a blue star with an additional property. They do not remember Altair directly in terms of its five properties, as would be expected from an exemplar theory. If they did, RT should have also increased with the number of common features. In summary, both summary-based and exemplar-based processes appear to be involved in recognition and categorization (Busemeyer, Dewey, & Medin, 1984; Elio & Anderson, 1981; Estes, 1986; Hintzman & Ludlam, 1980). For example, Fried and Holyoak (1984) present evidence that subjects can learn not only the ideal values of a category but also the distribution of exemplars of that category.

THE FUZZY VIEW

Based on the empirical and theoretical developments in categorization research, it is possible to develop a framework for a general theory of concepts and categorization. The framework articulates the stages of processing in pattern recognition and categorization in the spirit of the information-processing approach. The framework also builds on certain "facts" of memory, learning, and decision making that will be discussed in the following two chapters.

The theoretical framework takes a stand on the binary alternatives listed in Figure 2. The representation of a concept is in terms of a summary description of probabilistic characteristics. However, the summary description can be embellished to allow information about exemplars to be represented. Given some object or event, a person has continuous (fuzzy) rather than just all-or-none information about the degree to which each characteristic is represented in the object. The category alternatives and the characteristics of the categories are evaluated in parallel, rather than serial order. Finally, the categorization of an instance is not autonomous; the categorization is sensitive to context. Having degrees of tallness, for example, it is possible to categorize the same person as tall in one cohort group and as short in another.

According to the theoretical framework, well-learned patterns are recognized in accordance with a general algorithm, regardless of the modality or particular nature of the patterns. Categorization is described by three stages of processing: feature evaluation, feature integration, and decision, as illustrated in Figure 4. In the first stage of processing, properties of the object are evaluated with respect to the relevant categories. The second stage involves combining or integrating these properties in order to determine the overall goodness-of-match of all of the properties with the summary description of each category. The third stage involves making some identification decision based on the relative goodness-of-match of the information with the relevant summary descriptions of the categories. We now consider the three operations of evaluation, integration, and decision in more detail.

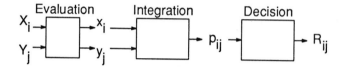

Figure 4. Schematic representation of the three operations involved in categorization.

Evaluation

The fuzzy view has the stipulation that the characteristics of a category cannot be considered to be all-or-none (present or absent). Like the multistate view of psychophysics (Chapter 12), the fuzzy view rejects the threshold concept that people are limited to just two levels of information about some property of the physical world. Consider the characteristic of baldness. We might think that a person could be classified as either bald or not bald. However, there are many degrees of baldness. This situation is most convincingly demonstrated by considering a senator who had very few hairs. (This senator should not be confused with a Wisconsin senator who gave golden fleece awards to qualified scientists engaged in important research projects.) Most people would classify him as being bald. The senator then had a hair transplant operation and, over time, he grew more and more hair. At this point in time, the senator has a lot of hair. The question is whether there was a point in time in which the senator went from being completely bald to being not bald. Everyone would agree that adding a single hair would not make a bald person not bald. With successive addition of single hairs, though, eventually the person would become not bald.

There is no catastrophic change from being bald to not bald, but rather baldness is a continuous characteristic that changes as a function of the number of hairs. Someone with many hairs can be considered not bald. Someone with few hairs can be considered bald. However, there is an ambiguous region in between in which there is a degree of baldness rather than all-or-none baldness. Figure 5 illustrates the truthfulness of baldness as a function of the number of hairs. Thus, the fuzzy theory considers that each characteristic can be considered to be represented to some degree in a certain instance. Thus, categorization of the instance as a member of a category is much more complex than in the case in which it was sufficient to determine whether the characteristic was simply present or absent. What is needed is a process by which this continuous degree of presence can be evaluated and integrated with other characteristics also represented in continuous form to determine whether or not an instance fits a particular category.

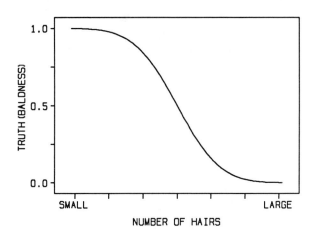

Figure 5. The truthfulness of a person being bald as a function of the number of hairs on his head.

Fuzzy Logic

In fuzzy logic, propositions are neither entirely true nor entirely false but rather can be represented by continuous truth values. For example, we might say that a team is having a relatively good season or that a meal is somewhat spicy. Ordinary logic would require that the team be performing well or not and that the meal is either spicy or it isn't. The theory of fuzzy logic (Zadeh, 1965; Goguen, 1969), on the other hand, allows us to represent the continuous nature of things. In fuzzy logic, we can construct a membership function: for example, short(x) that is true to the extent that item x is a member of the set short. It should be noted that fuzzy truth is different from probability. If we say that a whale is a fish to degree .2, that does not mean that there is a .2 probability that a particular whale is a fish. Rather, it is true that the whale is a fish to degree .2. Furthermore, when we say a whale is a fish to degree .2, we are not necessarily any less confident of this proposition than we are of the proposition that a robin is a bird to degree .99.

Integration

Having established that categorizers have continuous information about some property, it is necessary to account for how multiple properties are combined or integrated. The most venerable method for combining multiple sources of information is given by a theorem attributed to Reverend Thomas Bayes. The theorem is cast in terms of the probability of a given hypothesis being true given some evidence. For our purposes, the evidence would correspond to information that the perceiver has about some object and the hypothesis would correspond some some category. A simplified version of Bayes theorem states that

$$P(H_1|E) = \frac{P(E|H_1)}{\sum_i P(E|H_i)} \tag{1}$$

where $P(H_i|E)$ is the probability that some hypothesis H_i is true given that some evidence E is observed and $P(E|H_i)$ is the probability of the evidence E, given the hypothesis H_i is true.

The likelihood of hypothesis H_1 given some evidence E is equal to the likelihood of the evidence given the hypothesis divided by the sum of analogous likelihoods for all possible hypotheses. There are multiple sources of evidence relevant to a hypothesis in the same manner that there are multiple features relevant to categorization. Bayes theorem specifies how different sources of evidence are combined. Given two independent pieces of evidence E_1 and E_2 and equal a priori probabilities, the probability of a hypothesis H_1 is equal to

$$P(H_1|E_1 \text{ and } E_2) = \frac{P(E_1 \text{ and } E_2|H_1)}{\sum_i P(E_1 \text{ and } E_2|H_i)}$$ (2)

$$= \frac{P(E_1|H_1) \times P(E_2|H_1)}{\sum_i P(E_1|H_i) \times P(E_2|H_i)}$$

As a model of integration, Equation 2 is based on several assumptions. First, the a priori probabilities of all relevant response alternatives are equal. Second, it is assumed that the sources of evidence are evaluated independently of one another. That is, the evidence made available by a given source of information does not change with changes in the other sources of information. Given these assumptions, the equation with two sources of evidence follows from probability theory in which the probability of the joint occurrence of two independent events is the multiplicative combination of the probabilities of the separate events. The probability of two heads in two tosses of a coin is the multiplicative combination of the probability of a head on each toss.

Following Bayes theorem, we have specified how different sources of information are integrated and combined in categorization. Another important contribution, however, is the relative frequencies of the occurrences of the different categories (Estes, 1986). Categorization is dependent on the a priori frequency of occurrence of the categories, as is readily apparent in the strong effect of base rates or a prior probability in signal detection tasks (Chapter 12). Bayes theorem also specifies how the prior probability of occurrence is integrated with the other information. Incorporating a priori probability of occurrence into Equation 2 gives

$$= \frac{P(E_1|H_1) \times P(E_2|H_1) \times P(H_1)}{\sum_i P(E_1|H_i) \times P(E_2|H_i) \times P(H_i)}$$ (3)

where $P(H_i)$ is the a priori probability that hypothesis H_i is true. Equation 3 reveals that frequency of category occurrence is treated by the integration process as an additional (and independent) source of information. This information is integrated with other sources of information. Context can function similarly to a priori probability. Analogous to relative frequency, situational context can influence categorization. Within the context of Bayes theorem, context would also function as an additional (and independent) source of information. Support for this conceptualization can be observed in the role of context effects in perception and categorization. A sentence context constraining a word functions as an independent source of information for its recognition (see Chapters 19 and 20). Both relative frequency and context can be viewed as informative sources of information influencing perceptual categorization.

Decision

Equation 3 specifies the outcome of integration. The predicted response then depends on the operation of the decision process. We build on the foundation of the theory of signal detectability (developed in Chapter 12) to describe how the decision in a categorization situation occurs. The decision operation maintains a criterion value that is used to assess the outcome of the integration process. In a task with two alternatives, for example, the outcome is compared to the criterion. If the outcome exceeds the criterion, one of the alternatives is selected. Otherwise, the other alternative is selected.

If an exemplar is considered to be a member of a category only to some degree, then asking for a yes-no decision might be expected to produce inconsistent responses. McCloskey and Glucksberg (1978) asked college students to make membership decisions about exemplar-category pairs, such as apple-fruit. For items of intermediate typicality, a subject's decision varied over time. Thus, a student might say that a tomato was a fruit on one day and say it was not a month later. The variability in categorization decisions could result from either variability in evaluation and integration of the information or from the decision process. If the decision criterion fluctuates randomly from moment to moment (Carterette, Friedman, & Wyman, 1966), for example, then the same outcome of integration could lead to different categorizations.

Prototypical Task

Consider a typical categorization task manipulating two sources of information with a number of levels of each source of information. A factorial design is used to generate all stimuli representing all combinations of the two sources of information. Consider, for example, how a range of letters between G and Q can be created when the obliqueness of a line and the openness of the gap in the letter Q are varied across seven levels each (Figure 6). Seven levels of openness are created by removing 0, 2, 3, 4, 7, 9, and 10 points from the oval of the capital letter Q. Similarly, the obliqueness of the line varies between the horizontal and 10.8, 20.9, 28.9, 37.9, 50.7, 60.9 degrees of obliqueness measured from the horizontal. The resultant 49 test letters make up the factorial design. The test items are presented to subjects in randomized order and repeatedly for a series of test trials. Subjects are asked to categorize the test letters as G or Q.

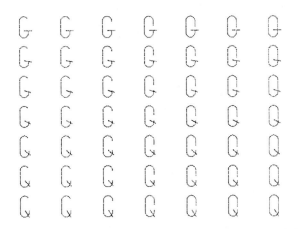

Figure 6. Forty-nine Q/G test letters created by varying the obliqueness of the straight line (row factor) and the openness of the gap in the oval (column factor).

Massaro and Hary (1986) actually carried out the prototypical task that we have described. Nine subjects saw each test letter (Figure 6) for 400 msec 12 times in random order. On each trial they labeled the test letter as a "Q" or a "G" and probability of a Q response for each test letter is the dependent variable. Given that the Q and G identifications sum to one, P(Q) for each test letter completely represents the identification judgments. Thus, we have 49 independent observations to describe the 49 test letters. The predictions of a model can be fit to the data of the individual subjects using the a parameter-estimation program, such as STEPIT (Chandler, 1969). A model is defined in STEPIT as prediction equations which contain a set of unknown parameters. STEPIT minimizes the deviations between the observed and predicted values of the models by iteratively adjusting the parameters of the equations. Root mean square deviation (RMSD) values index the overall goodness-of-fit of the model. This value is the square root of the sum of the squared deviations of the predicted and observed values. The smaller the RMSD value, the better the fit of the model.

Fuzzy Logical Model of Perception (FLMP)

There are several psychological models of categorization that incorporate the principles developed within the fuzzy view. One model is called a fuzzy logical model of perception (FLMP). Within this framework, well-learned patterns are recognized in accordance with a general algorithm, regardless of the modality or particular nature of the patterns (Massaro, 1987; Oden, 1981). The model consists of three operations, as illustrated in Figure 4: feature evaluation, feature integration, and decision. Continuously-valued features are evaluated, integrated, and matched against prototype descriptions in memory, and an identification decision is made on the basis of the relative goodness-of-match of the stimulus information with the relevant prototype descriptions.

Central to the FLMP are summary descriptions of the perceptual units (Oden & Massaro, 1978). These summary descriptions are called prototypes and they contain a conjunction of various properties called features. A prototype is a category and the features of the prototype correspond to the ideal values that an exemplar should have if it is a member of that category. The exact form of the representation of these properties is not known and may never be known. However, the memory representation must be compatible with the sensory representation resulting from the transduction of the input. Compatibility is necessary because the two representations must be related to one another. To recognize an object, the perceiver must be able to relate the information provided by the object itself to some memory of the object category.

Prototypes are generated for the task at hand. The sensory systems transduce the physical event and make available various sources of information called features. During the first operation in the model, the features are evaluated in terms of the prototypes in memory. For each feature and for each prototype, feature evaluation provides information about the degree to which the feature in the speech signal matches the corresponding feature value of the prototype.

Given the large variety of features, it is necessary to have a common metric representing the degree-of-match of each feature. Two features must share a common metric if they eventually are going to be related to one another. To serve this purpose, fuzzy truth values (Zadeh, 1965) are used because they provide a natural representation of the degree-of-match. Fuzzy truth values lie between zero and one, corresponding to a proposition being completely false and completely true. The value .5 corresponds to a completely ambiguous situation whereas .7 would be more true than false, and so on. Fuzzy truth values, therefore, not only can represent continuous rather than just categorical information, they also can represent different kinds of information. Another advantage of fuzzy truth values is that they couch information in mathematical terms (or at least in a quantitative form). This allows the natural development of a quantitative description of the phenomenon of interest.

Feature evaluation provides the degree to which each feature in the stimulus matches the corresponding feature in each prototype in memory. The goal, of course, is to determine the overall goodness-of-match of each prototype with the stimulus. All of the features are capable of contributing to this process and the second operation of the model is called feature integration. That is, the features (actually the degrees of matches) corresponding to each prototype are combined (or conjoined in logical terms). The outcome of feature integration consists of the degree to which each prototype matches the stimulus. In the model, all features contribute to the final value, but with the property that the least ambiguous features have the most impact on the outcome.

The third operation is decision. During this stage, the merit of each relevant prototype is evaluated relative to the sum of the merits of the other relevant prototypes. This relative goodness-of-match gives the proportion of times the stimulus is identified as an instance of the prototype. The relative goodness-of-match could also be determined from a rating judgment indicating the degree to which the stimulus matches the category. The decision operation is modeled after Luce's (1959, 1977) choice rule. In pandemonium-like terms (Selfridge, 1959), we might say that it is not how loud some demon is shouting but rather the relative loudness of that demon in the crowd of relevant demons. Two important predictions of the model are 1) two features can be more informative than just one and 2) one feature has a greater effect to the extent the other feature is ambiguous.

The three operations between presentation of a pattern and its categorization, as illustrated in Figure 4, can be formalized mathematically. Feature evaluation gives the degree to which a given dimension supports each test alternative. The physical input is transformed to a psychological value, and is represented in lowercase, e.g., X_i would be transformed to x_i, and analogously for dimension Y_j. Each dimension provides a feature value at feature evaluation. Feature integration consists of a multiplicative combination of feature values supporting a given alternative A_{ij}. If x_i and y_j are the values supporting alternative A_{ij}, then the total support p_{ij} for the alternative A_{ij} would be given by the product $x_i\, y_j$.

The third operation is decision, which gives the relative degree of support for each of the test alternatives. In this case, the probability of an A_{ij} response given $X_i\, Y_j$ is

$$P(A_{ij}\,|X_i Y_j) = \frac{x_i\, y_j}{\Sigma} \tag{4}$$

where Σ is equal to the sum of the merit of all relevant alternatives, derived in the same manner as illustrated for alternative A_{ij}.

Given a test letter, the feature evaluation stage determines the degree to which the Q and G alternatives are supported by the visual information. Using fuzzy truth values, a value between zero and one is assigned to the obliqueness and openness dimensions, indicating the degree to which these features support the Q and G alternatives.

The features values of openness and obliqueness are then integrated by the Q and G prototypes. The prototypes are defined by:

Q: Not (Open Oval) & Oblique Line
G: Open Oval & Horizontal Not (Oblique Line)

Given a prototype's *independent* specifications for the obliqueness and openness features, the value of one feature cannot change the value of the other feature at the prototype matching stage. Using the definition of fuzzy negation as 1 minus the feature value, we can represent the prototypes in terms of openness and obliqueness:

Q: (1 - Openness) & Obliqueness
G: Openness & (1 - Obliqueness)

The integration of the features defining each prototype can be represented by the product of the feature values (Massaro & Oden, 1980; Oden, 1979, 1984a; Oden & Massaro, 1978). In this case, the goodness of a Q or G alternative can be represented by:

$$G(Q) = (1 - t(Openness)) \times t(Obliqueness)$$
$$G(G) = t(Openness) \times (1-t(Obliqueness))$$

where G(•) represents the goodness-of-match of a test letter to the Q or G alternatives and t(•) is a function that determines the truth value of a particular feature: the degree to which a gap is open or a straight line is oblique.

If Q and G are the only valid response alternatives, the decision operation determines their relative merit leading to the prediction:

$$P(Q) = \frac{G(Q)}{G(Q)+G(G)} \tag{5}$$

where $P(Q)$ is the predicted probability of a Q response to a particular test letter shown in Figure 6.

Fourteen parameters are necessary to fit the FLMP to the 49 data points: seven parameters for each level of obliqueness and openness. The parameters represent the degree to which the obliqueness and openness features match the Q alternative. The predictions of the model are given in Figure 7. The predictions do very well in capturing the trends in the data. The RMSDs for the two subjects were .0312 and .0543, respectively, meaning that the predictions were within a few percent of the observations. More generally, the results reveal that letter recognition can be described in terms of the evaluation and integration of independent features with respect to prototypes in memory. The decision is based on the relative goodness-of-match of the featural information with the prototypes.

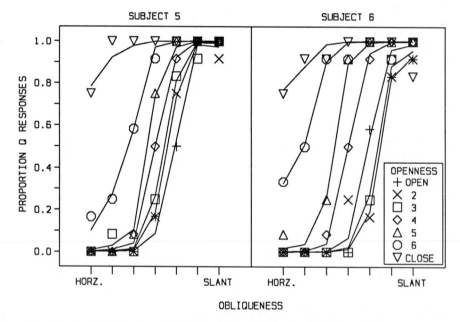

Figure 7. Observed (points) and FLMP predicted (lines) proportion of Q responses for 49 Q/G test letters created by varying the obliqueness of the straight line and the openness of the gap in the oval (results of two subjects from Massaro & Hary, 1986).

Both independent variables influenced the judgments in the expected manner. Decreasing the gap in the oval and making the straight line more oblique increased the likelihood of a Q response. In addition, there is an informative asymmetry in the openness of the gap. When the gap is fairly open, changing the straight line from horizontal to oblique changes the judgment from G to Q. When the gap is closed, however, the test letter is usually judged as Q, and the obliqueness has very little effect. Readers have difficulty accepting that a closed oval could be a part of G, regardless of how horizontal the straight line is.

Connectionist Model of Perception (CMP)

Recently, there has been a revived interest in constructing information-processing models out of neural-like units (Hinton & J. A. Anderson, 1981; Rumelhart & McClelland, 1986). The motivation is that these models offer better representations of what the brain is actually doing than more traditional stage models. Given how little is known about the neurophysiological level, however, the strongest test of either type of model will still be at the behavioral level. The information is assumed to exist in the form of activations and inhibitions of neural-like units. All knowledge in the system is contained in the connections among the units and the operations that map the input into the output. The units interact with one another via connections among the units. The connectivity is implemented by positive and negative weights among the units so that the activation of a given unit can activate or inhibit other units. Connectionist models are constructed and programmed by constructing units at different layers, such as an input and an output layer. This connectionist architecture has been used to model a broad variety of psychological phenomena (McClelland & Rumelhart, 1986).

Recognition and categorization are easily modeled within the framework of connectionist models of perception (CMP). The CMP is assumed to have an input layer and an output layer, with all input units connected to all output units. It is assumed that each level of each dimension is represented by a unique unit at the input layer. Each response alternative is represented by a unique unit at the output layer. In a *local* representation, there would be an unique input unit for a unique property of the stimulus. Similarly, there would be unique output units, representing the responses in the task.

The CMP is assumed to have an input layer and an output layer, with all input units connected to all output units. Each level of each source of information is represented by a unique unit at the input layer. Each response alternative is represented by a unique unit at the output layer. Figure 8 gives a schematic representation of two input units connected to two output units.

An input unit has zero input, unless its corresponding level of the stimulus dimension is presented. Presentation of an input unit's target stimulus gives an input of one. The activation of an output unit by an input unit is given by the multiplicative combination of the input activation and a weight w. With two active inputs X_i and Y_j, the activation entering output unit A is $x_i + y_j$, where $x_i = w_i X_i$ and $y_j = w_j Y_j$. The activation entering output unit B would be $-x_i + -y_j$, since $x_i = -w_i X_i$ and $y_j = -w_j Y_j$. The total activation leaving an output unit is given by the sum of the input activations, passed through a sigmoid squashing function

$$A_{ij} = \frac{1}{1 + e^{-[x_i + y_j]}}$$

$$B_{ij} = \frac{1}{1 + e^{[x_i + y_j]}}$$

A connectionist model does not specify completely the input-output relationship. The output activations have to be mapped into a response, and Luce's choice rule is usually assumed to describe this mapping (McClelland & Rumelhart, 1985). Taking this tack, the activation A_{ij}

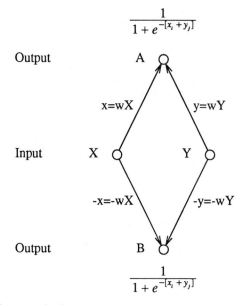

Figure 8. Illustration of connectionist model with two input units and two output units.

transformed into a response probability by Luce's choice rule gives

$$P(A \mid X_i \, Y_j) = \frac{\dfrac{1}{1 + e^{-[x_i + y_j]}}}{\Sigma} \tag{6}$$

where $\Sigma = \dfrac{1}{1 + e^{-[x_i + y_j]}} + \dfrac{1}{1 + e^{[x_i + y_j]}}$

The connectionist model can also be tested against the results in the same manner as the FLMP. A unique input unit is assumed for each level of the two independent variables, giving a total of 14 input units. Two output units are assumed to represent the response alternatives G and Q. All input units are connected to all output units, and the strength of the connections are specified by weights. It turns out that this specific CMP is mathematically equivalent to the FLMP formalized in the previous section. Thus, the FLMP predictions given in Figure 8 are also predictions of the CMP.

Cups and Bowls

Labov (1973) generated the set of containers shown in Figure 9. As can be seen in the figure, the containers resemble cups, glasses, and bowls to various degrees. Every container can be said to have some degree of cupness, and some containers have much more than others. Labov (1973) and Oden (1981) were concerned with devising a definition of cup that would distinguish a cup from other types of containers. They acknowledge that there is no set of necessary and sufficient features, but they are confident that some sort of summary description could be functional in the categorization of objects. One definition of cup is given by the logical proposition given in the following description,

cup   :   [(Dishware) & (Liquid Container) & (Not (Wide))
          & (Width = Depth) & (Has Handle)]

As can be seen in the definition, the features describing cup are reasonable and allow a cup to be distinguished from a bowl and a glass. Definitions of these latter two objects are given in the following two descriptions,

bowl : [(Dishware) & (Liquid Container) & (Wide)
            & (Not(Has Handle))]

glass : [(Dishware) & (Liquid Container) & (Not (Wide))
            & (Deep) & (Not(Has Handle))]

Figure 9. Labov's cups. Note that for Labov all cups have handles.

Cups and Bowls in Factorial Combination

Following the advances in experimental methodology developed earlier, an ideal method to study categorization is the use of factorial designs. Oden extended the universe of Labov's containers by varying properties in a factorial design. Four values of the width of the container were crossed with six values of the depth of the cup to give 24 unique objects, as illustrated in Figure 10. In addition each of these containers was drawn with and without handles. These 48 objects were presented to subjects in a categorization and a rating task. Subjects carried out both a categorization task and a rating task. In the categorization task, the subjects simply identified the object. In the rating task, subjects were instructed to rate the relative degree to which each object was a cup as opposed to a bowl. The term cup was used generically to include both drinking glasses and cups. The rating scale was a continuous line ranging from "definitely a cup" to "definitely a bowl." The rating was given a numeric value by transforming the distance of the judgment along the line into a number between 0 and 1.

Figure 11 presents the mean judged cupness as a function of the three variables in the experiment. As can be seen in the figure, all variables influenced the judgments. Not surprisingly, people judged a container more like a cup than a bowl if it had a handle. Taller containers were judged more like cups, as were narrow containers. Cups with handles were judged as better cups than cups without handles. There is also an interaction among the variables, indicating that the ideal size of cups differs for containers with and without handles. Without a handle, increasing the depth and height increases cupness. With a handle, increasing the depth decreases the cupness of narrow vessels and increases the cupness of wide vessels.

Figure 10. The 48 containers generated by the factorial combination of height, width, and handle (after Oden, 1981).

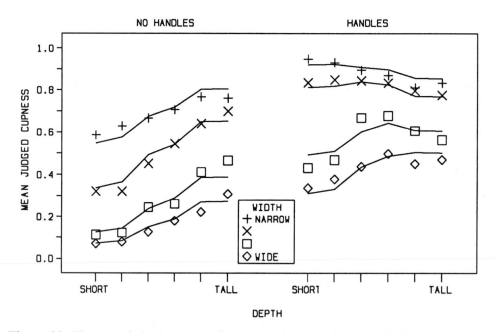

Figure 11. The mean judged cupness of each container as a function of height, width, and handle (after Oden, 1981).

The predictions of the FLMP are also given in Figure 11. To describe the judgments, it was assumed that a cup could be either a cup or a drinking glass (as given by the logical propositions for these objects),

generic cup   : [(Cup) or (Glass)]

The good description of the results by the model indicates that people are able to evaluate instances disjunctively. That is, a drinking vessel can be evaluated in terms of whether it is a good cup or a good drinking glass. If it matches either of these prototypes, then it is a good match to the generic concept cup.

DEVELOPMENT OF CATEGORIZATION

The processes involved in recognition and categorization might change across development. There is a long tradition in developmental theory centered around the idea that the child progresses from holistic to dimensional processing (James, 1890; Shepp, 1978; Smith & Kemler, 1978; Werner, 1957; Wilkening & Lange, 1987). This view claims that children have a natural tendency to perceive multidimensional stimuli as unstructured, integral wholes. Preschool children are claimed to process certain objects holistically whereas adults process the same objects analytically (Shepp, 1983; Smith & Kemler, 1977, 1978).

The evidence for holistic processing in children is based on a classification task of the following form. The child or adult subject is presented with three objects, such as the ones in Figure 12, and is asked "to put together the two objects that go together." The objects are constructed to vary on two dimensions, such as shape and color. Two of the three objects are identical on one of the dimensions, and are very different from one another on the other dimension. Two of the three objects are fairly similar to one another on both dimensions.

Consider the perceptual categorization of objects varying in size and brightness (Smith & Kemler, 1977). Older children and adults tend to group two objects together if they have the same size even if they differ greatly in brightness. Similarly, older children and adults tend to group two objects of the same brightness even if they differ greatly in size. These choices supposedly indicate that older children and adults perceive the separate dimensions of size and brightness. Younger children, on the other hand, tend not to group two objects that are equivalent on a given dimension. Instead, younger children tend to group two objects that differ by relatively small amounts on both dimensions. These results are usually interpreted as the younger child's failure to perceive the separate dimensions of size and brightness, implying holistic perception for young children.

However, ther is another interpretation of these findings. It is possible that the dimensions of size and brightness are evaluated independently by both young children and adults. The different results may simply reflect different strategies in the grouping task at the different developmental levels. Consistent with this interpretation, Kemler and Smith (1978) found that young children could treat size and brightness as independent dimensions to learn a higher-order conceptual rule. Moreover, contrary to what might be expected from holistic perception, Ward (1980) found that five-year olds had no difficulty making dimensional judgments given length and density.

Ward (1983) and his colleagues (Ward, Foley, & Cole, 1986) have offered an alternative to the developmental explanation. The central assumption is that the processing of the test stimulus makes available the overall similarity of the items at an earlier stage of processing than the information on specific levels of component dimensions. This interpretation can be formalized within the general framework of pattern recognition developed in this chapter. Early in feature

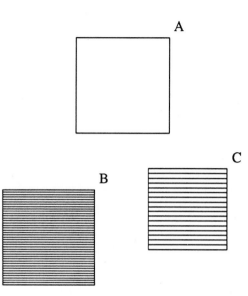

Figure 12. Illustration of a classification task in which the subject is asked to pick the two objects that go together. Picking A and B is called dimensional identity and picking B and C is called overall similarity. Choosing A and C has been called anomalous or haphazard; however, even this choice can reflect a systematic classification strategy. If the subject selectively attends to the brightness dimension, A and C would be picked if they are perceived as the pair of objects most similar in brightness.

evaluation, the perceiver would have some information about each feature (dimension) but the information would not be sufficient to inform the perceiver about the identity of two stimuli on a given dimension. Integration of the separate features (dimensions) occurs continuously as the featural information is being evaluated. Thus, integration could occur and a response could be initiated before the identity along one of the dimensions is noticed at the featural level. If the response is made at this point in processing, the observer would be more likely to group the two items with the largest overall similarity (objects B and C in Figure 12). Objects A and B would not be picked unless the subject took sufficient time to notice their identity in size *and* used this identity as a basis for the judgment. In this case, subjects would respond on the basis of this identity rather than on the overall similarity resulting from the integration of the different dimensions.

Notice that this explanation of the results does not assume holistic processing in one case and analytic processing in the other. The same processes occur in both cases: independent evaluation of features and integration of these features. A decision operation would be responsible for the different results that are observed. In the case of grouping by overall similarity, the decision is based on the integration of information along both dimensions. In the case of grouping by identity on a given dimension, the decision is based on the identity information made available at the level of feature analysis. No loaded terms such as holistic and analytic are necessary to describe the processing.

Fine-Grained Analyses

Wilkening and Lange (1987) overcame the shortcomings in previous research by carrying out a fine-grained analysis of the results of each of the children in the experiment. The test objects in one set of studies were pictures of dwarfs. The dwarfs varied in brightness and in the size of their belly. There were 3 different brightnesses and 4 different sizes, giving a total of 12 test objects. Before the experiment, a very small, dark dwarf and a very large, bright dwarf were shown to the children. The children were told that eating 20 magic candies transformed one of the dwarfs into the other. The children were shown a rating scale that consisted of a linear row of 20 candies. The original dwarf was shown at one end and the transformed dwarf at the other. For each test dwarf, the children were instructed to guess how many magic candies the dwarf might have consumed. In order not to bias the results, no mention was made of the dimensions size and brightness.

Each child judged each of the 12 test dwarfs several times, allowing single-subject analyses. The results showed that children did not judge the test dwarfs holistically, as predicted by the holistic hypothesis. A task requiring direct judgments of an object reveals that children can perceive objects in terms of their component parts. Asking subjects to group objects together can mislead the experimenter into believing that holistic perception occurred. Children might simply evaluate and integrate the dimensions differently from adults, when faced with the task of indicating which two objects go together.

In a second experiment, Wilkening and Lange replicated the traditional classification task with the dwarf objects. Replicating previous results using this paradigm, the children gave significantly more holistic responses than the adults. However, analyses of individual-subject data revealed that almost all subjects processed the stimuli dimensionally. The children tended to group together the two dwarfs that were the most similar on one of the two dimensions. About half of the children always based their judgments on size and about half based their judgments on brightness.

Children appear to be using only one dimension throughout the course of the classification task in which the child is asked to pick the two objects that go together. Consider the test display illustrated in Figure 12 and a child attending to the size dimension. Two of the three objects are identical in size, and she would group these two together. In this case, the experimenter would conclude that the child had made a dimensional response (i.e., behaved as an adult). Now consider a test display in which two objects are identical in intensity and all three objects differ in size. The same child would now group together the two objects that differed only slightly in size independently of their brightness. If these two objects are relatively similar in brightness, the judgment would be classified as a holistic response. If these two objects are relatively dissimilar in brightness, the judgment would be classified as a haphazard response. This example reveals the danger of interpreting judgments as dimensional, holistic, or haphazard in the classification task.

The rating judgment task used by Wilkening and Lange (1987) indicate that children perceive objects in terms of their parts. Different tasks will encourage differences in terms of how the information about the parts is used to make a judgment. At no time does the child appear to be confronted with an unanalyzable whole.

Memory

Decay Theory

Interference Theory

Tests between Theories
  Peterson and Peterson Task
  Broadbent and Gregory Study
  Conflicting Results and
    Distinguishing among Stages
  Probe Recall

Perceptual Processing Theory
  Experimental Test

Levels of Processing
  Processing for a Good Memory

Episodic versus Semantic Memory
  Direct versus Indirect Measures
  Dissociation Method
  Becoming Famous Overnight
  Episodic Priming of Identification

Long-Term Memory
  Forgetting
  Tip of the Tongue
  Blocking Lexical Access

Structure of Semantic Memory
  Network Representation
  Confounding of Co-occurrence
  Confounding of Similarity
  Confounding of Category Size
  Confounding of Familiarity
  Category Size Revisited
  Typicality Revisited

Evaluating Memory Processes
Picture Memory
Hermann Ebbinghaus
Structure and Process

Ghost: *Adieu, adieu! Hamlet, remember me.*
Hamlet: *Remember thee!*
          Ay, thou poor ghost, while memory holds a seat
          In this distracted globe. Remember thee!
          Yea, from the table of my memory
          I'll wipe away all trivial fond records
          All saws of books, all forms, all pressures past,
          That youth and observation copied there;
          And thy commandment all alone shall live
          Within the book and volume of my brain
          Unmix'd with baser matter: yes, by heaven!

In our model, synthesized visual and auditory memory can be transformed by the secondary recognition process into names held in generated abstract memory. This memory is called *abstract* because it is not modality-specific; it is called *generated* because the secondary recognition process involves an active generation of the synthesized information into abstract symbolic form. In this chapter, we attempt to analyze the way the forgetting of symbolic information happens in generated abstract memory. Analogous to other memories, there are two primary causal contenders: decay and interference. Decay theory was first presented systematically in Broadbent's (1958) model of information processing (see Chapter 15). Interference theory has its origin in the concept of association outlined by the British empiricists. Both of these theories will be presented, followed by experimental tests between the theories.

DECAY THEORY

In Broadbent's model, incoming stimuli are held in a preperceptual form along various channels. The recognition process reads out the information along one channel at a time, so that identification can take place. However, rather than passing on this transformed information to another storage structure, it is recirculated back through the original storage. This assumption eliminates the value of the information-processing approach. Information in preperceptual form certainly differs from the name information after recognition has taken place, and the storage characteristics and forgetting of both kinds of information should be both qualitatively and quantitatively different. Given this qualification, it is still possible to evaluate how forgetting of name information is assumed to occur in terms of Broadbent's model.

In Broadbent's formulation of decay theory, name information decays passively over time unless it is operated on; that is, unless it is rehearsed by the central processor. To cause forgetting, it is sufficient to distract the central processor away from this information so that its decay takes place. The activities of the central processor in the processing of new information do not in any way interfere with the previous information; the neglect of the old causes forgetting. No forgetting will occur if the central processor is allowed to devote attention to the relevant information during the forgetting interval. Because the central processor is limited in capacity, some forgetting usually occurs, as the processor is incapable of processing new information and maintaining its attention on the old.

INTERFERENCE THEORY

In contrast to decay theory, interference theory assumes that no forgetting will occur unless intervening activity has a direct effect on the information in memory. The interference theory of forgetting assumes that two events occurring together in time become associated or linked together. Memory in this context functions to maintain the association between the two events. Using a stimulus-response model, interference theorists interpreted the two events as consisting of a stimulus and a response. The subject learns to associate stimulus (S_1) with response (R_1), or certain features of the stimulus to the response. If the subject is required to learn to respond to a second stimulus, S_2, with the response R_2, it is probably safe to assume that the second stimulus has some features in common with the first. This similarity between the two stimuli means that there are features in one stimulus that are associated with the response of the other. S_2 is like S_1 in some respect, and when S_2 is presented, the features that it has in common with S_1 will evoke not only R_2, but also R_1. Thus, the similarity in the two stimuli produces competition between the two responses. In this way the learning of a new set of associations interferes with memory for an older set. This interference is called retroactive interference.

TESTS BETWEEN THEORIES

The critical difference between decay and interference theory, therefore, is in the way people forget. Decay theory says that one forgets when one is unable to rehearse, or chooses not to do so. The memory trace fades automatically over time unless it is renewed. Interference theory assumes that forgetting occurs when a stimulus-response association is weakened by the learning of another association. If no new material is learned, the subject would remember a given association permanently. This does not happen because we continuously learn new information that interferes with the old. Similarly, an old set of associations can retard the learning of a new set. This interference is called proactive interference.

Peterson and Peterson Task

If you are the typical age of an undergraduate and your parents took a psychology course a couple of decades ago, they might have participated in the following kind of experiment. They would be asked to remember three spoken letters on a given trial. This easy task was made difficult by requiring the subjects to count backward by threes, starting with a three-digit number that occurred immediately after presentation of the consonants to be remembered. On a given trial a subject might hear the letters *hjc* followed by the number 506. Counting backwards by threes the subject would then begin saying 503, 500, 479, and so on. Sometime later a light would go on and the subject would be asked to report the items that were originally presented. This experiment was invented by Lloyd and Margaret Peterson and carried out at Indiana University in the late 1950s, and called the Peterson and Peterson task.

The results of an experiment published by Peterson and Peterson (1959) are shown in Figure 1. As can be seen in the figure, subjects display a dramatic amount of forgetting over the retention interval when they are required to count backwards by threes. We have all experienced looking up a telephone number and being distracted and forgetting the number. Evidently, we must rehearse verbal information to keep it available in short-term memory or else devise a way of encoding it so that no rehearsal is necessary. The investigators interpreted the rapid rate of forgetting as being due to time without rehearsal.

The Peterson and Peterson task generated an immense amount of interest and much controversy. The controversy centered around whether forgetting was due to decay or interference. Peterson and Peterson argued that the results supported decay theory since it was difficult to see

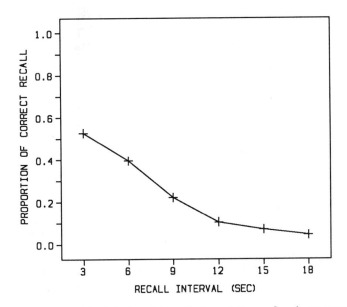

Figure 1. The proportion of trials in which all three letters of a three-consonant trigram were recalled correctly as a function of retention interval, when this interval was occupied by backward counting to prevent rehearsal (results from Peterson & Peterson, 1959).

how counting backwards could produce interference with letters in the memory. In their view the counting backwards task simply prevented the subject from rehearsal. Interference theorists, on the other hand, were quick to respond that interference was occurring in the Peterson and Peterson task.

Recall that interference theorists distinguish between retroactive and proactive interference. The natural interpretation of forgetting in the Peterson and Peterson task would be retroactive interference. That is, the counting on a given trial interferes with memory of the test letters. However, interference theorists claimed that proactive interference was also responsible for forgetting in the Peterson and Peterson task. In this case, proactive interference means the learning of test letters on early trials interferes with the learning and memory for items on the later trials.

Keppel and Underwood (1962) pointed out that Peterson and Peterson's subjects had two practice trials before the experiment proper. These two practice trials may have been sufficient to produce the proactive interference responsible for the forgetting in their task. Keppel and Underwood repeated the Peterson and Peterson task and looked at performance across the first three trials. They tested three groups of subjects and assigned them to different orderings of three retention intervals: 3, 9, and 18 sec. The results showed that there was essentially no forgetting on the first trial, whereas by the third trial there was a considerable amount of forgetting between 3 and 18 sec (see Figure 2). Decay theory has no explanation for the lack of forgetting on the first trial along with the significant forgetting on the third trial. If forgetting is due to time alone, then other contributions such as the number of previous trials should have no effect. On the other hand, interference theory has the mechanism of proactive interference. It is reasonable that the association learned on previous test trials would interfere with learning and memory of new test items. The evidence for proactive interference in the Peterson and Peterson task is detrimental to decay theory.

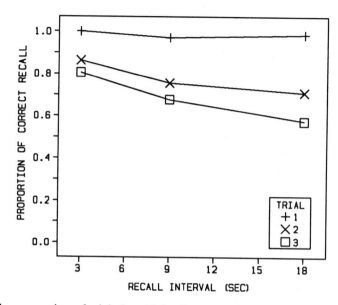

Figure 2. The proportion of trials in which all three letters of a three-consonant trigram were recalled correctly as a function of retention interval and the trial number (results from Keppel & Underwood, 1962).

Broadbent and Gregory Study

In 1965, Broadbent and Gregory showed how forgetting seemed to be more dependent on the attention of the central processor than on the learning of new associations. Subjects were given a dual task. On each trial, subjects listened to 10 letters presented at a rate of 1 letter every 5 sec. Within each set of 10 letters, 1 letter occurred twice, whereas none of the other letters were given more than once. At the end of the presentation, the subject reported which letter had occurred twice. This task required the subject to recognize and remember each letter and to determine if it was presented previously.

Simultaneously with this task, subjects were also required to perform a choice RT task. Subjects held the index finger of each hand on one of two buttons during the experiment. The buttons consisted of a ring, through the center of which a vibrating rod projected. The rod vibrated from time to time between the letter presentations. Under one condition, whenever one of the rods was felt to be vibrating, the subject was to press down on that same button. Under a second condition, when one rod vibrated, the subject was required to press the button under the finger of the opposite hand. Thus, under the compatible response condition, when the left button vibrated the subject pressed it with the finger of the left hand. Under the incompatible response condition, when the left button vibrated the subject pressed the right button.

According to Broadbent's decay theory, if the task of responding to the vibrating buttons reduces the processing capacity available for the letter memory task, then the second condition should reduce it more than the first. Subjects had longer RTs on the button-pushing task in the incompatible response condition, showing that this condition was indeed more difficult. Performance in the memory task should, therefore, be worse when the button-pushing task is being done under the incompatible response condition. This is in fact what Broadbent and Gregory found: memory performance was 85% and 59% correct under the compatible and incompatible response conditions, respectively. According to Broadbent's model, the subject had more time to perceive, rehearse, and update the letters in memory in the compatible response condition. This result makes more sense in terms of decay theory than in terms of interference theory. It is plausible that performance in the button-pushing task prevented rehearsal of the test items in the memory task. But it is very difficult to see how the vibration in the second task could have enough features in common with the letter stimuli to cause response competition and hence forgetting.

Conflicting Results and Distinguishing among Stages

The Peterson and Peterson task and the dual task of Broadbent and Gregory (1965) gave different answers to the question of decay or interference. It appears that neither theory in its simple form will be adequate. In addition, any theory of forgetting must be embedded in an information-processing model of the separate stages in the typical memory task. One popular test between these two theories was to vary the rate of presentation of a list of verbal items and to ask subjects to recall them immediately. Experimenters reasoned that faster rates should lead to less forgetting according to decay theory because there would be less time between presentation and test. However, early experimenters failed to realize that there were two important psychological processes in the task. The two processes are also referred to as storage and retention, respectively. The rate of presentation might affect both of these processes in different ways so that the results would not be informative with respect to the nature of the forgetting process.

A second problem with these studies is that subjects were permitted a free recall; hence their rehearsal and report strategies were not under experimental control. This paradigm does not allow one to describe the forgetting that occurs, since the actual forgetting interval and the interference activity varies, depending upon the strategy of the subject. It is necessary to devise an experimental paradigm that can measure storage and retention directly as a function of either time or the number of interfering items. One suitable paradigm is a probe recognition or recall task in which the subject's rehearsal is directed by the experimenter and he or she reports on only one item per trial.

Probe Recall

Waugh and Norman (1965) employed a probe recall study in which subjects were presented with a list of items followed by a test item and had to report the item that followed the test item in the preceding list. Waugh and Norman explicitly instructed their subjects to concentrate on the current item being presented and not to rehearse earlier items in the list. This instruction was given to eliminate differences in rehearsal for the different items as a function of serial position. Accordingly, any differences in memory performance as a function of serial position could be attributed to some other variable than amount of rehearsal. The experimenters could, therefore, determine whether time or number of items is a better predictor of changes in memory, thus providing a test between interference and decay theories.

Waugh and Norman's test of interference and decay theories was to vary the rate of presentation of the list and to compare the forgetting functions under two rates. The forgetting function was determined by systematically testing the subject for different items in the preceding list. A list of 15 digits was presented at a rate of 1 or 4 digits per sec. There were 1, 2, 3, 4, 5, 6, 8, 10, or 12 digits between the tested item and its presentation in the list. Figure 3 presents the percentage of correct recall as a function of the number of interpolated digits between a digit's original presentation and its test under two rates of presentation. The results show how quickly forgetting occurs at both rates of presentation. However, the two predicted curves describing the points illustrate a systematic difference between the forgetting functions under the two rates of presentation.

The predicted function describing forgetting at a rate of presentation of 4 items/sec starts out lower and ends up higher than the function describing forgetting when the items are presented at 1/sec. The intersection at the ordinate provides some measure of the original perception and storage

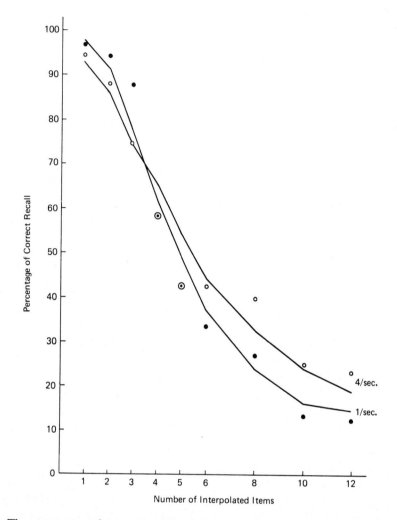

Figure 3. The percentage of correct recall as a function of the number of interpolated items between presentation of the digit and its test under two rates of presentation (after Waugh & Norman, 1965). The lines are predicted functions given by Massaro (1970).

of the digits, whereas the slope of the curves should provide an index of the retention or rate of forgetting. According to this analysis, the items presented at l/sec were better stored but forgotten faster than the items presented at 4/sec. Thus, the results illustrate the importance of our stage analysis of the memory task. Every memory task contains both storage and retention stages which must be isolated in both the experimental design and theoretical description. The Waugh and Norman task allows us to see the contributions of each of these stages independently, whereas the earlier free recall experiments did not. Accordingly, it is clear that the results must be described by a theory that can account for the differences in the original storage and the differences in forgetting rates under the two rates of presentation. A simple decay or interference theory based on only time or number of items will not suffice.

PERCEPTUAL PROCESSING THEORY

One theory that describes these results has been presented by the author (1970). The theory is similar to the analysis presented in the previous chapters on auditory and visual memory. In describing storage and forgetting in synthesized auditory and visual memory, the concept of familiarity is used. Here, we use a similar concept called memory strength as an index of how well the subject remembers what is required in the task. In Waugh and Norman's (1965) task, the subject was given a probe item and asked to give the item that followed it in the preceding list. We assume that the probe item is associated in different degrees to a number of different items in the preceding list, because of the contiguity between their presentations. Figure 4 illustrates some possible differences in association values to a probe item.

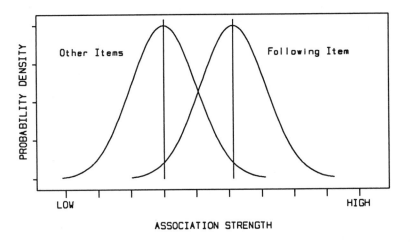

Figure 4. The distribution of association values to the probe item for the item that follows the probe and other items in the possible set of alternatives.

As can be seen in the figure, we expect the item following the probe item to have the highest association to the probe item. However, because of fluctuations in this value from trial to trial, the association is represented by a distribution of values rather than a fixed value. This procedure is exactly analogous to the concept of noise used in multistate theory (Chapter 12). Other items would, on the average, have smaller associations to the probe item. The subject's decision rule would be to respond with the item that has the highest association to the probe item. Most of the time, the item following has the highest association value and the subject will recall it correctly. However, as the association between the probe item and the following item is forgotten, all of the digits seem to be equally associated to the probe item. In effect, the distributions in Figure 4 are pushed closer together so that the subject becomes more likely to respond with a wrong item.

The two main assumptions of the above-mentioned theory describe changes in memory strength of an item as a function of perceptual processing. Perceptual processing simply refers to the analysis of information in a sensory input used to recognize and remember the stimulus. We have seen that recognition requires an analysis of the input held in storage so that a match can be found in long-term memory. After identification of the item, further perceptual processing is necessary to remember or store the item. For example, to perform correctly in the Waugh and Norman study, the subjects must remember the sequential order of the items so that they will be able to recall the item that followed the probe item in the preceding list. The first assumption of the theory is that memory for an item is directly related to the amount of perceptual processing of that item. Since an item is processed during its presentation, memory strength will increase with increases in the presentation time of the item. The second assumption is that memory for an item is inversely related to the amount of perceptual processing of other items. Accordingly, the amount of interference that a retroactive item produces will increase as the duration of the retroactive item increases.

Experimental Test

These two assumptions qualitatively predict Waugh and Norman's results. The first assumption predicts that the items presented at 1/sec will have more memory strength after their presentation than will items presented at 4/sec. The longer the presentation time of an item, the more time the subject rehearses it, providing a stronger memory trace at presentation. The second assumption predicts that the degree of interference with earlier items produced by a new item is directly related to the amount of processing the new item receives. Since items presented at 1/sec. receive more processing, they will interfere more with earlier items than items presented at 4/sec A quantitative formulation of the theory also gives a good quantitative description of the results (Massaro, 1970). Although the theory provides a good forgetting rule, much is still to be learned about the processes of storage and retention in short-term memory.

Evaluating Memory Processes

In our study of memory, we have relied on experimental procedures that control exactly the events between presentation of a memory item and its later test. There are critical design problems with other procedures, such as a free recall test in which the subject recalls all of the words in any order. Faced with the free recall protocol of a subject, the experimenter cannot isolate the psychological processes responsible for performance. Memory for an item is a joint function of perceptual, mnemonic, and decision processes and each of these must be evaluated exactly to make sense of the results.

As an example, consider the problem confronting the experimenter when the rate of presentation is varied in a free recall task. Subjects might be presented with a list of 24 words at a rate of 1 or 2 sec per item. We know that the additional study time should enhance the storage of each of the items in memory. This same additional time, however, will also produce additional interference with the retention of other items in the list. The helpless experimenter has no way of determining the contributions of each of these processes; hence, it is not possible to develop an understanding of how each of these processes operates.

LEVELS OF PROCESSING

We have seen how a stage model distinguishing between storage and retention clarifies the contributions to memory and forgetting. In 1972, Craik and Lockhart challenged the information-processing approach. Levels of processing was offered as an alternative to the standard information-processing stage model. A lot of people saw this view as an alternative to the stage model and pursued the study of memory in the levels-of-processing framework. The major assumption is that our persistence of memory is dependent upon the level (or depth) of processing imposed on the information. To the extent that you process information to a deep level, you should show good memory. To the extent that you have only processed it superficially, you should show relatively bad memory. Is this view a more promising way to explore how people function on a psychological level or is the stage model still useful in our quest for psychological understanding?

The following experiment was done in the levels-of-processing framework (Craik & Tulving, 1975). Subjects were presented words one at a time and they were asked questions about these words; the experimenters manipulated the kind of questions asked. If subjects answer questions about the meaning of a word, they should show better memory than if they are asked questions pertaining to the surface or superficial level. Given the word *apple*, for instance, the subject would be asked one of three questions:

1. Does it have capital letters?
2. Does it rhyme with ?
3. Does it fit in the sentence "The boy ate the green _____" ?

To answer the first question, only the letters of the word are relevant. The second question requires, at least, a speech level of analysis. Some spoken form of the word must be evaluated. The third question requires semantic processing in that we have to find the meaning of apple and evaluate whether or not it would fit in the sentence.

After the subjects went through a series of test words, they were given a surprise recognition memory test. They were given the test words along with new words and asked whether or not each of these words had occurred previously in the experiment. That is, a yes-no recognition memory test was used to evaluate memory. To the extent subjects can discriminate the old words from new words, they show good memory. Memory was a direct function of the depth to which the item was processed as determined by the question imposed by the experimenter. It is also important to show that it is the nature of the question that was asked and not necessarily the amount of time the subject spent with the word that is important. And, in fact, the experiments supported this supposition. The depth-of-processing idea seemed productive in that it led to a new kind of experiment that had not been previously done.

The levels-of-processing framework can be used to reinterpret traditional kinds of experiments. Consider the standard serial position curve in a free recall experiment. In terms of the levels-of-processing framework, we don't have to interpret these differences as a consequence of short-term and long-term memory. The items at the end of the list were simply processed to a relatively superficial level, whereas the items earlier in the list were processed to a deeper level. This makes some sense because the subject outputs these final items immediately in recall upon reading the list.

In another levels-of-processing experiment, the subjects were required to generate a verbal associate to each item as it was presented. Given the word *apple*, *tree* might be a response. If asked to recall the words but not the associates, recency is not observed in the experiment. This association task requires a more elaborate encoding for all items and the recent items are no longer favored in free recall. The levels-of-processing framework appeared to provide a very productive way to look at the world of memory research. Developmental differences in memory might also be explained by levels of processing. The improvement in memory with age may not be a structural difference but simply the kind of processing imposed on the material. As an example, young children do not necessarily employ optimal kinds of encoding. Their metacognition or awareness of how well their memory works is usually overly optimistic, they believe they will remember even if they do not encode the events to a deep level of meaning.

After a short honeymoon with this point of view, a number of researchers became very critical. The problem faced in evaluating this kind of theory is whether or not it is really testable. Sometimes the theory seems to be nothing more than a brief statement of what is observed. There is also the problem of measurement of the depth of processing. There is no independent assessment of depth of processing other than by memory performance (Baddeley, 1978). The only way you know how deep something is processed is how well it is remembered. That is, the notion of depth of processing is circular.

One distinction in the levels framework was whether an item was being rehearsed in maintenance form or elaborative form. The original argument was that maintenance rehearsal involving the simple repetition of items, without any kind of elaboration, would not improve memory. Elaborative rehearsal is usually more effective than maintenance rehearsal. However, people do show better retention if they spend more time doing maintenance rehearsal. For example, simply repeating to yourself a new acquaintance's name now and then after you meet will lead to much better retention of their name. We saw that rate of presentation affects memory storage in the probe recognition task. In contrast to the levels-of-processing prediction that nonelaborative rehearsal should not improve memory, there is a variety of evidence that it does (Baddeley, 1978; Nelson, 1977).

Processing for a Good Memory

Although the levels-of-processing approach is not a good alternative to a stage model, it did generate research that is informative with respect to what it takes to improve memory. Levels of processing addressed how information is placed in memory. With this focus, we will describe four properties of processing that lead to good memory. The first property is *spread of encoding*. To the extent that some new information is encoded in an elaborate way with respect to your knowledge base, there is a better chance of remembering it. When experimenters asked questions about items presented for memory, subjects show better memory for items given "yes" than "no" answers. If a subject is asked whether a word fits in a particular sentence, a negative answer can be based on a disagreement in syntactic or semantic structure. Little new knowledge is gained. On the other hand, a "yes" answer makes syntactic and semantic sense and some new knowledge is gained. That is, there is larger spread of encoding. If subjects are asked more complex sentences, they show even better memory.

The second dimension is what is called *encoding distinctiveness*. Subjects are asked either rhyming questions or semantic questions to each of a list of 24 words. For a first group of subjects, 20 of the words are given rhyming questions and 4 of the words are given semantic questions. For a second group, 4 of the words are given rhyming questions and 20 of the words are given semantic questions. According to the depth-of-processing notion, we should get better memory for words given semantic questions than words given rhyming questions. And, in fact, there was an overall advantage of words given semantic questions relative to words given rhyming questions. However, there was a nice interaction; words that were encoded in a more unique way in the experiment were better remembered. Subjects in the first group revealed better memory for the words given semantic questions. For the second group, the rhyming words, because there were only 4, turned out to show better memory than the 20 words, given the semantic question. If there is some event that you want to remember, encode it in some unique way relative to surrounding events.

The third property is *compatibility between learning and recall*. Consider the experimental demonstration of this property. Subjects are asked questions about rhymes or semantic questions. In the recognition memory test, subjects were asked to pick words that rhyme or were similar in meaning. The learning part of the task is similar to what we've been doing. A subject is given a test word "mate" and the question, "Does this word rhyme with 'wait'?" Or does this word fit in the sentence, "The _____ sailed off to sea last Monday." In the recognition test, there are two kinds of recognition tasks. In one case, a subject is given words like "sailor" and asked to come up with a word from the original test similar in meaning. For the second kind of test, a subject is given a word like "cake" and asked to think of a word that was on the original test that rhymes with it. Subjects must retrieve a word from a previous presentation via similar meaning or similar sound. The critical thing is whether the learning involves the same kind of encoding that was required in the test. When there is a match between the learning and the test, subjects do better than when there is a mismatch.

The fourth property that leads to good memory is the amount of *attentional resources* dedicated to the encoding of information. As your grandmother could tell you, if you pay more attention, you show better memory. Subjects performing encoding tasks are given a secondary task such as responding to a signal. Subjects are told to respond as quickly as possible when the signal is presented during the time of the encoding task. Responding to the signal is slower in the semantic task than in the rhyming task. If the reaction time is thought of as reflecting how much attention is given an encoding task, the semantic questions seem to be taking more attentional resources than the rhyming questions.

EPISODIC VERSUS SEMANTIC MEMORY

In a memory task, subjects usually report something about the previous presentation of an item or event. For example, a probe recall task asks subjects to report the item that followed a probe item in the learning session (see section on Probe Recall). A recognition task asks whether a given item was presented during the learning session. Identification, on the other hand, involves retrieving a word and its meaning regardless of when the word was previously experienced. The prototypical memory task, therefore, involves memory for a specific episode of experience whereas an identification task is not tied to any specific episode. Identification depends, supposedly, on only the perceiver's semantic knowledge. There seems to be sufficient plausibility to distinguish between semantic and episodic memory, and this distinction has driven much research in the last decade (Tulving, 1972, 1986).

Direct versus Indirect Measures

The differences between semantic and episodic memory have centered around studies using direct and indirect tests of memory. Subjects are given some episodic experience, called a target episode. Sometime later they are given a test. Experimental tests having instructions that make direct reference to the target episode are called direct tests. Those tests that do not make any reference to the target episode are called indirect tests (Johnson & Hasher, 1987; Richardson-Klavehn & Bjork, 1988). A schematic diagram of these two types of memory tests is given in Figure 5. The subject is given some target episode and some time later is given a memory test. The instructions in the memory either refer to or do not mention the target episode.

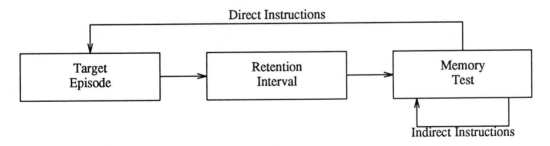

Figure 5. Schematic diagram of direct and indirect memory tests.

Table 1 gives a taxonomy of direct and indirect memory tests. Many of these tests should be familiar from the previous chapters. The studies on RTs, such as Sternberg's memory-search task, are direct tests of memory. The memory experiments discussed up to now have primarily been direct tests of memory, in which subjects are instructed to remember some episode and later tested for their memory of it. Free recall, cued recall, yes-no recognition, and forced choice recognition are direct tests of memory. We have also discussed a variety of indirect tests of memory. Indirect tests of memory include pattern recognition, categorization, perceptual identification, word fragment completion, problem solving tasks, and evaluative judgments.

Table 1. A taxonomy of direct and indirect memory tests.

Type	Tests	Examples
Direct	Recall	Cued Recall Free Recall
	Recognition	Yes-No Judgments Forced Choice Judgments
	Relearning	Repeated Study Sessions
Indirect	Priming	Perceptual Identification Word Fragment Completion
	Procedural Skills	Problem Solving
	Non-Verbal Changes	GSR (Galvanic Skin Response) Orienting Response
	Evaluative Responses	Liking Judgments Familiarity Judgments

Although the experimenter can manipulate instructions in this binary fashion, the actual memory test probably engages retrieval of the target episode to various degrees. As an example, consider a student taking the college entance examinations. The student studied specifically for these tests, and this study episode might be considered the target episode. However, performance on the examination can be influenced and should be influenced by other knowledge in memory— supposedly gained from other episodic experiences. In general, any memory test might be expected to be influenced to some degree by both the target episode and knowledge gained from nonspecific episodes.

There are not pure direct and indirect memory tests. Every test taps into specific episodic experiences and general knowledge to various degrees. Consider a creative variation on the Sternberg memory search task, which we have classified as a direct test. The digits chosen for the memory list are 1, 2, 3, and 4. In this case, RT is not significantly longer than it is for a memory list of just one digit. Rather than searching episodic memory, the subject can short circuit the process by asking whether the test digit is greater than four. In this case, the subject is using general knowledge to perform the task rather than attempting to retrieve a specific episode. In an analogous manner, one can see how an indirect memory test can be easily influenced by recent episodes. In problem solving, for example, the solution to a novel problem might follow directly from how a similar problem was previously solved.

Dissociation Method

Direct and indirect memory tasks have been used to study the differences between episodic and semantic memory. If these are two fundamentally distinct memories, then it should be possible to observe differences in terms of how the two memories work. At the heart of this research is the dissociation method. A dissociation is said to occur if an independent variable influences performance in one task, but not in another task, or if it influences performance in different directions in the two tasks. A double dissociation involves two opposing dissociations: two independent variables that have opposite effects across the two tasks. Table 2 illustrates the strongest possible double dissociation.

Table 2. Illustration of the strongest possible double dissociation. Two independent variables X and Y operate differently in two different tasks A and B.

Test	Independent Variable	Outcome
A (Recognition Memory)	X (Read)	Poor Performance
	Y (Generate)	Good Performance
B (Identification)	X (Read)	Good Performance
	Y (Generate)	Poor Performance

Jacoby (1983) was able to create a double dissociation. Subjects were given two types of learning episodes and two types of memory tests. Subjects studied consonant-word pairs, such as *xxx-COLD* in a learning condition, called the *Read* condition. In a second learning condition, called the *Generate* condition, the subjects generated associates to words, such as *HOT-???*. The memory test involved either recognition memory or perceptual identification. Figure 6 gives the results of a crossover interaction. Reading the words gave poorer performance than generating the words when memory was tested by a recognition memory test. The opposite occurred when the influence of the target episode was tested by perceptual identification: performance was best for the condition in which the test words were read rather than generated.

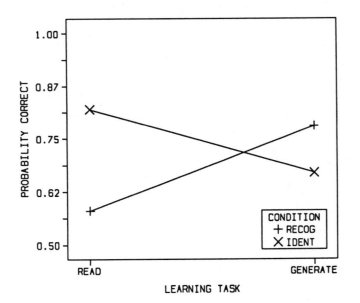

Figure 6. Accuracy in a recognition memory test and a perceptual identification test as a function of reading or generating the words during the learning task (results taken from Jacoby, 1983).

Tulving (1985) has taken dissociation results as support for two separate memory systems. Perceptual identification is based on semantic memory and recognition memory is based on episodic memory. There are, however, at least two alternative possibilities. Both alternatives assume that there is just a single memory underlying performance on both episodic and semantic memory tasks. The first alternative places the difference at retrieval; the second places the difference at decision. Different tests would only naturally present different retrieval cues that are differentially capable of accessing the appropriate memory. Differential access would lead to different memory performance. The second explanation assumes that retrieval is equivalent in the two tasks, but that the different decisions required by the two tasks are different functions of the memory that is retrieved.

Learning requires the processing of specific episodes in a manner that produces memories that, in some sense, summarize the episodes. Our semantic memory of beaches would be bogged down if every episodic detail were included. Rather, we generalize across episodes to achieve some reasonable summary description of beaches, not unlike the summary descriptions described in the categorization of objects and events (Chapter 16). If there are episodic and semantic memory systems, they must talk to one another constantly. A child learning arithmetic or reading spends hundreds of hours on specific tasks to acquire a general skill. Is this distinction sufficient to warrant a distinction between knowledge of these task experiences (episodic memory) and knowledge of the skill (semantic memory)? I think not. A more productive interpretation might be one in which there is a continuum between episodic memory and semantic memory. Any memory has shades of both episodes and generalizations. Within this framework, our memory performance is differentially dependent on specific memories and generalizations of these memories. Two memory systems are not required to implement this situation. The sources of information currently available and the quality of the memory will determine memory performance. Given specific episodic retrieval cues, our semantic memory will be highly episodic. Without good episodic information, memory for a specific episode might be greatly influenced by generalized semantic memory. We are not engaging different memory systems in the two situations, but simply exploiting whatever information is available.

Our analysis of pattern recognition and categorization in Chapter 16 was also consistent with the idea of a single memory system supporting both episodic and semantic memory. We call pattern recognition both recognition and identification. Put another way, no one has articulated how recognizing a semantic episode would differ from recognizing an episodic episode within the framework of a specific process model. That is, what specific operations would differ in the two situations. Analysis of the problem in this manner would probably convince the investigator that similar processes are engaged in episodic and semantic memory tasks, but that different sources of information might be used, retrieved, and acted on.

Two implications emerge from this task analysis. First, it is difficult to imagine how a given task can be said to measure *only* episodic or *only* semantic memory. Our memory simply cannot be partitioned up into these two types of discrete packages. Second, the work might be informed by developments in categorization research. Neither an exemplar-based or a summary-based representation appears to be sufficient for categorization. Both appear to be involved in the same manner that both episodic and general representations are involved in remembering.

Becoming Famous Overnight

The recent memory research using indirect measures of memory has broadened our understanding of several phenomena. One set of findings converges nicely with our criticisms of the introspective method (Chapter 2). The influences on our behavior are not always consciously available to us. Previous experiences influence later performance even though we are not aware of what experiences are having the influence. As described by Jacoby and Kelley (1987), we are awash in uncommon influences. We can become famous overnight. Jacoby and Woloshyn (1987) asked subjects to read a list of names of fictitious people. In one condition, subjects devoted their full attention to this task. In the divided-attention condition, subjects also performed another task simultaneously with the reading of the names. Sometime later, both groups of subjects were asked whether various people were famous. Included among the names of real people were names of fictitious people who were or were not on the original reading list.

Table 3 gives the results. Subjects were able to discriminate famous from nonfamous people to some extent in all conditions. However, their impression of the fame of fictitious people depends on whether the subjects have seen their names previously and the condition of processing the names. If full attention was devoted to the processing of the names, the subjects were better able to spot a fictitious name they had previously seen. Under full attention, the false alarm rate to nonfamous people was lower to old names than to new names. With divided attention during the processing of the names, however, subjects judge fictitious people whose names they had seen before as famous more often than new fictitious people. Under divided attention, the false alarm rate was higher to old names than to new names. Without being able to remember exactly the context in which you have experienced someone's name, familiarity with it is a good predictor of how famous we think that person is. The research supports the old adage, "I don't care what you say about me, but just spell my name correctly."

Table 3. The probability of judging a name as famous (adapted from Jacoby & Kelley, 1987).

	Type of Name		
	Famous	Nonfamous	
Study Condition	New	Old	New
Full Attention	.62	.19	.31
Divided Attention	.49	.27	.17

Episodic Priming of Identification

A perceptual identification task is used to investigate long-term priming effects. Subjects are presented with a list of words to be studied. Sometime later, they are presented with test words, each flashed briefly on a screen and masked. The task is to identify each word. Typical results show that the likelihood of correctly identifying the word is greater for words previously studied than for words not previously studied. Ratcliff, McKoon, and Verwoerd (1988) asked if this advantage would be located in sensitivity (d') or criterion (β) dependent measures of the theory of signal detectability (i.e., the multistate theory of Chapter 12).

A specific example might consist of a sentence that mentions the word *died*, which is then later presented as a test word. A positive priming result would consist of a greater likelihood of the subject identifying this word correctly relative to a new control word, such as the test word *lied*. In the forced choice task, the two alternatives *died* or *lied* are presented after the test and masking stimulus. Thus, there should be two types of test trials: signal trials will present *died*, catch trials will present *lied*. In both cases, subjects will choose from the response alternatives *died* and *lied*. According to the theory of signal detectability, the context sentence can have one or two types of effects. If the context sentence enhances the discrimination of the words within the sentence from other words, then subjects should be better able to discriminate *died* from *lied*. Enhanced discriminability would lead to an increase in d', which would be reflected in a higher hit rate with no increase in the false alarm rate. The context sentence might also increase the likelihood of the subject responding *died* on both signal and catch trials. Both of these results might also occur.

Ratcliff et al. (1988) replicated previous results, showing that the likelihood of correct identification was greater given priming of the test word by a context sentence. However, the forced choice task revealed that the effect was not on d', but on β. In one experiment, the hit rate was .89 given a word that had occurred in a priming sentence. The false alarm rate was .35. If the word had not occurred in the context sentence, the hit rate was .80 and the false alarm rate was .27. Thus, the overall likelihood of choosing *died* was $(.89 + .35)/2 = .620$ given its occurrence in a priming context sentence and $(.80 + .27)/2 = .535$ if it had not occurred earlier in a context sentence. There is a significantly greater likelihood of responding *died* given its occurrence in a prior context sentence for both of the test alternatives *died* and *lied*.

In contrast to the positive effect on β, prior occurrence in a sentence context did not influence d'. The results, therefore, show that a sentence context biases the perceptual system in the direction of seeing a particular test item that has been seen in the recent past; the sentence context does not enhance the ability of the perceptual system to discriminate that word from similar words. It would be amazing if it did. The perceptual bias is probably productive in the real world because there are many cases in which a word is repeated in text (or conversation), but it is unlikely that a similar word would be presented. Thus, a bias can increase the efficiency of processing, without a significant cost.

LONG-TERM MEMORY

Our study of the early stages of information processing is heavily dependent upon certain implicit assumptions about long-term memory. The psychological processing of a stimulus event is continually interpreted in terms of the knowledge the observer brings to the given task. For example, subjects utilize the spelling rules of English orthography to facilitate the perception of letter strings. Language users also utilize phonological, syntactic, and semantic rules in the processing of language. All of this information must be stored in long-term memory, making its capacity much larger than the other storage structures studied earlier.

Forgetting

How do we go about studying long-term memory? One method is to present subjects with material to be learned, and then wait a sufficiently long period of time before testing to ensure that whatever information is recalled is recalled from long-term memory. Analogous to our short-term memories, this approach should allow us to determine how forgetting occurs in long-term memory, the nature of memory-search strategies in long-term memory, and possibly the form of the structure of long-term memory. Wickelgren (1972) has measured the forgetting of long-term memories over a time span up to two years. His studies utilize the same methodological and procedural techniques that we analyzed in studies of short-term memory. The interested reader is referred to the original paper for the methodological details and results. We concentrate on experimental paradigms that have not yet been discussed for our studies of long-term memory.

Tip of the Tongue

One unique approach to the study of long-term memory is to ask subjects what they already know, rather than to have them learn something new. Brown and McNeill (1966) capitalized on a phenomenon that we all have experienced: a "tip of the tongue" (TOT) state. In this state, an individual is unable to remember a word that he is sure he knows. The experience that he knows this particular word is usually accurate, because he may eventually recall the word days later, be

Picture Memory

Potter and Levy (1969) studied recognition memory for color pictures of typical scenes of people, animals, food, and so on. Each subject viewed a sequence of 16 pictures at rates of presentation that varied from 8 pictures per sec to 1 picture every 2 sec. The subject was then given 32 pictures, 16 identical to those in the list and 16 new pictures. The task was to go through this group of pictures indicating whether or not each picture was in the preceding list. The results showed a very low false alarm rate (saying a picture was in the preceding list when it was not) at all presentation rates. In contrast, the hit rate improved substantially from 15% at 8 pictures per sec to 93% at 2 sec per picture. The first 333 msec of the picture appeared to be the most critical for retention; the hit rate was almost 60% at this rate of presentation. The last picture in the list was better recognized at all presentation rates, showing that the subjects were able to continue processing this item after the slide was turned off.

Potter and Levy's results show that subjects have a good memory for pictorial information even when this information is presented at relatively fast rates of presentation. With slower rates of about 5 sec per picture, Nickerson (1965) and Shepard (1967) showed extremely good recognition memory for lists of hundreds of pictures. In Nickerson's task, the hit rate was .87 and the false alarm rate was .02. Shepard showed increased sensitivity by using a two-alternative forced choice task. In this case, the subject was presented with an old and a new picture and was asked to indicate which one was in the preceding list. Subjects in this task were 97% correct. Haber (1970) carried Shepard's study to an extreme by asking his subjects to look at 2560 photographic slides over the course of several days. Haber's patient and courageous subjects averaged about 90% correct in a forced choice recognition task. These experiments demonstrate that visual memory for complex scenes is extremely good when we are tested with a recognition procedure. This visual memory also seems to improve memory performance substantially when subjects form images of words rather than trying to remember the words in purely linguistic form (Paivio, 1971).

Hermann Ebbinghaus

Ebbinghaus (1885) established the experimental study of verbal memory and learning at the turn of this century. He was totally committed to the experimental method as the appropriate framework for the study of mind. His major contribution involved applying the techniques of one area to another; in this case, Ebbinghaus extended the methods of psychophysical measurement to study learning and retention of verbal material. His theoretical approach was rooted in the tenets of British associationism in which frequency of experience of events played a central role (Postman, 1968).

The association to the name Ebbinghaus for most students is the nonsense syllable, which Ebbinghaus used in his experiments. He knew that ordinary words would already have a plethora of previous associations and these would contaminate their learning and retention. Since that time, we have seen that even nonsense syllables differ with respect to how much meaning they bring to the mind of the participant (Underwood & Schulz, 1960). And as Ebbinghaus would have predicted, the association value and meaningfulness of nonsense syllables are important determinants of how easily they are learned and remembered. Although today's research in verbal learning and memory has advanced considerably in method, theory, and application, the general framework owes its existence to Ebbinghaus and the solid foundation that he established.

able to recognize it correctly, or be able to give partial information about the word. Brown and McNeill successfully induced the TOT state in some subjects some of the time by presenting them with a definition of an uncommon English word and asking for the word. Subjects, given the definition of a word, sometimes entered the TOT state. In this state, subjects were in mild torment trying to recall the correct word. Brown and McNeill encouraged their subjects to give all of the words that came to mind; the subjects were also asked the first letter and the number of syllables of the word they were trying to remember.

Given the definition of *sextant,* "a navigational instrument used in measuring angular distance, especially the altitude of the sun, moon, and stars at sea," the TOT state was induced in 9 out of 56 subjects. Some of the words subjects gave were *astrolabe, compass, dividers, protractor, secant,* and *sexton.* The first four words are similar in meaning to the target word, whereas the last two are similar in sound and spelling. Some of the words similar in meaning could be traced directly to certain parts of the definition. For example, *protractor* is used in measuring angular distance but, of course, not the stars at sea. The semantic confusions show that words with similar meanings can be thought of as being stored and/or retrieved together or substituted for each other.

The similar sounding items show that the perceptual description of words must be stored along with their meaning. We can assume that some subjects were able to retrieve the correct concept given the meaning, but had only partial information about the perceptual properties of the word corresponding to that concept. Analyses of the physical similarity between the correct word and the words recalled that were similar in sound indicated that the number of syllables of the word, the primary stress of the word, and its first and possibly its last letter were the most prevalent features. This result shows that subjects can have partial information about the sound of a word corresponding to a concept, with certain attributes more prevalent than others. The final interesting result of the Brown and McNeill (1966) study is that subjects knew how much they knew. That is, subjects knew that similar sounding words were not correct but that they were, in fact, similar sounding.

Blocking Lexical Access

Woodworth (1938) collected naturally occurring TOT states and observed that people in TOT states often retrieved a word that was perceptually similar to the target word. This incorrect word seemed to block retrieval of the correct (target) word. Jones and Langford (1987) followed up on this observation and offer some evidence that the perceptual properties of words might have some priority over the conceptual properties during their retrieval. Subjects were placed in a "tip of the tongue" state and then given a potential blocking word. The potential blocking word was either unrelated, perceptually related, conceptually related, or both perceptually and conceptually related to the target word. Four definitions and examples of the four types of blockers are

(1) Something out of keeping with the times in which it exists. The word *anniversary* is both semantically related and perceptually related to the target word *anachronism.* (2) To steam food, particularly meat, slowly in a closed container. The word *bride* is only perceptually related to the target word *braise.* (3) Female spirit whose wail portends death. The word *ghost* is only semantically related to the target word *banshee.* (4) House of rest for travelers or for the terminally ill, often kept by a religious order. The word *equipment* is neither semantically related nor perceptually related to the target word *hospice.*

On each trial, subjects were given a definition followed immediately by one of the potential blocking words. The question of interest was to what extent properties of the blocking would influence the likelihood of entering a TOT state. Perceptually related blockers produced significantly more TOT states than perceptually unrelated blockers. However, the semantic relatedness of the blockers to the target word had no effect. It is also of interest that the word frequency of the blockers had no effect. The results offer some support for two successive stages in the retrieval of a word. The first stage would be the access to only partial information about the perceptual description of the word. This first stage would make available those features that are typically found in a TOT state, such as the first letter and the number of syllables in the word. Retrieving a word's complete identity requires the second stage. The second stage does not always successfully lead to retrieving a word's complete representation—a TOT state. The perceptually related blocker misleads the second stage by directing it to the wrong alternative. A semantically related blocker supposedly does not mislead the second stage because it activates the same pool of words activated by the definition of the target word.

An interesting extension of this study would be to present a blocking stimulus that is perceptually similar to the target word, but one that is a pseudoword. For example, *breem, boffill,* and *hargal* are pseudowords that are perceptually related to *braise, banshee,* and *hospice,* respectively. If the detrimental effect of a perceptually related blocking word results from misdirecting the lexical search to the wrong word, then perceptually related pseudowords should produce no interference. A pseudoword should be ineffective because it does not access any particular word in the subject's lexicon. On the other hand, if a pseudoword functions in the same manner as a real word, then the explanation would require modification. The interference of a perceptually related stimulus (whether a word or a pseudoword) might be due to interference in the production of the target word, rather than accessing the word in memory.

Structure and Process

When we do an experiment to illuminate the nature of long-term memory, there are a number of psychological processes entailed in that experimental situation. Depending on the assumptions about the processing that is going on, one might arrive at different conclusions about the actual structure. In other words, structure and process are tied up together and sometimes it is difficult to isolate these two components. If you assume a process of a particular nature, you'll reach one conclusion about the structure; if you assume the process is of a different nature, you will arrive at a different conclusion about the structure. In some cases, structure and process are confounded, and the ingenious experimenter has to pull these two apart.

STRUCTURE OF SEMANTIC MEMORY

Although there is no compelling reason to view semantic and episodic memory as different memory systems, the distinction is still helpful. Semantic memory refers to our knowledge independently of how that knowledge was acquired. For example, we know that there are seven days in a week, but we can't remember how we acquired this information. Episodic memory refers to memory of specific events such as who was at our last birthday party. The forgetting tasks discussed at the beginning of this chapter addressed the retention of episodic memory: subjects had to report what test items occurred on a particular trial. The indirect tests of memory that have been recently used, however, tap into knowledge that is not tied to a specific episode (although performance can be influenced by that episode).

The structure of semantic memory can be studied in terms of measuring the time it takes people to perform certain operations. From the times to perform these operations, psychologists have learned something about the representation of information in long-term memory. Ross Quillian developed a network model of semantic memory for the representation of knowledge (Quillian, 1968). Collins and Quillian (1969) carried out an experiment to evaluate whether people's representation was similar to the representation defined by Quillian's computer simulation. The two features of the model are, first, that knowledge is stored hierarchically, and second, that there is a cognitive economy in the storage of information. That is, knowledge is stored at different levels with connections between the levels and in a way that is nonredundant. If information about something is stored at one level, that knowledge is not replicated at another level. Information stored about the category bird is true of all birds. Given an instance of bird, like a canary, you would not replicate bird information with the storage of this specific instance.

Network Representation

Figure 7 illustrates three levels of representation: a subordinate level, canary; a basic level, bird; and a superordinate category, animal.

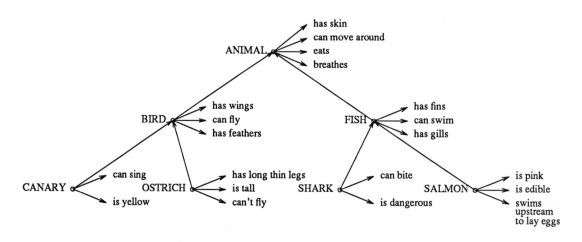

Figure 7. Hypothetical memory structure of a three-level hierarchy (adapted from Collins & Quillian, 1969).

Stored with animal are those things that distinguish animals from plants. Animals move around, eat, breathe, and so on. Birds can fly, have wings and feathers. Of course, canaries have many of the things that birds and animals have, but this information isn't stored at the canary level. It is stored only at the appropriate higher-level category. The unique information about canaries is that they can sing and that they are yellow.

In the Collins and Quillian experiment, subjects were given sentences of the form: "A canary is a bird," "A canary is an animal," "A canary is a canary," or "A canary is a furniture." Presented with a sentence, subjects would have to respond "true" or "false" as quickly as possible. The RT from the onset of the sentence to the onset of their decision was taken as a dependent measure. This time was used to illuminate the nature of the processing and the nature of the semantic representation of semantic knowledge. There were two kinds of sentences, category sentences like, "A canary is a bird," and property sentences like , "A canary can sing." The primary independent variable in the experiment was derived from Quillian's computer simulation model. This was the number of levels between the subject and the predicate in the test sentence. The sentence, "A canary can fly," cannot be answered in the same way as the sentence, "A canary can sing." The property to fly is stored with birds. To answer this question, the answer is not stored at the canary level, but at the bird level. We have to move from the canary node to the bird node before we can access the appropriate information. We might expect that it would take longer to evaluate the sentence, "A canary can fly," than, A canary can sing." In order to verify, "A canary can fly," it is necessary to move from the canary level to the bird level.

The results supported the network representation, illustrated in Figure 7. Figure 8 shows that it took longer for subjects to judge truthfulness of property sentences like, "A canary has skin," than a sentence, "A canary can fly." Similarly, for category sentences, "A canary is a bird," is slightly faster than, "A canary is an animal." These results were used to support the two critical assumptions of Quillian's network representation. First, a hierarchical representation describes semantic memory; we organize our knowledge in terms of categories and store the properties of items with their categories. Second, cognitive economy characterizes semantic memory. If we know all animals have skin, we do not replicate that knowledge at each instance of animal. We can derive this knowledge for bird from a bird being an animal and an animal having skin.

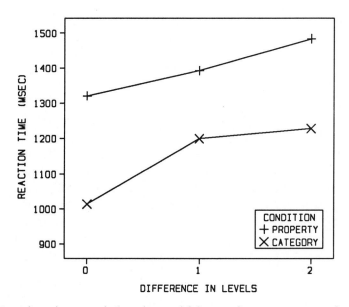

Figure 8. Reaction times to judge the truthfulness of sentences as a function of the difference in levels of the subject and predicate.

Confounding of Co-occurrence

One of the challenges of experimental research is the inevitable confounding of variables. When an experimenter manipulates one thing, such as hierarchical level in the Collins and Quillian (1969) experiment, something else is also varied. The first variable that was pointed out was frequency of co-occurrence of two concepts. The idea was that two concepts closer in hierarchical level in the Quillian model tended to occur more frequently together. As an example, canary and yellow co-occur more often than canary and animal.

Given the discovery of this confounding, the typical strategy is to perform an additional experiment to pull apart these variables. One such experiment was carried out by Conrad (1972). First, the author had to assess how often people will experience these things occurring together. Two hundred college sophomores were asked to describe categories such as birds, furniture, and so on. The number of subjects who used a given property describing a category was taken as an index of frequency of co-occurrence of that property with the category. If many subjects describe an animal having skin, there would be a high frequency of co-occurrence between animal and skin. If very few people say a bird has skin, there would be a low frequency of co-occurrence between bird and skin. One experiment consisted of sentences that were either low or high in frequency of co-occurrence and differed by 0, 1, or 2 hierarchical levels. Table 4 gives examples of the true sentences used in the experiment.

Table 4. Examples of the true sentences used in Conrad's (1972) experiment, as a function of the difference in levels between the category and the property and high or low frequency of co-occurrence between the category and the property.

Difference in Levels	High Frequency	Low Frequency
2	A shark can move.	A salmon has a mouth.
1	A bird can move.	A fish has eyes.
0	An animal can move.	An animal has ears.

Figure 9 presents the mean RT as a function of both frequency of co-occurrence and the number of levels separating the subject and predicate. In terms of RT to say "true" to these sentences, the major differences are due to frequency. People are slowed down if they don't think of a property as being associated with a given category. The number of levels separating the property and category is not important. Subjects are faster at verifying that, "A shark can move," than, "An animal has ears." According to the network organization, however, the property "can move" is stored two levels away from shark and is stored at the same level as animal. The observed RT is opposite that predicted by the network model. The reason is that "can move" co-occurs more frequently with shark than the property "has ears" co-occurs with animal. Conrad's results, therefore, provide strong evidence against a hierarchical organization of semantic memory.

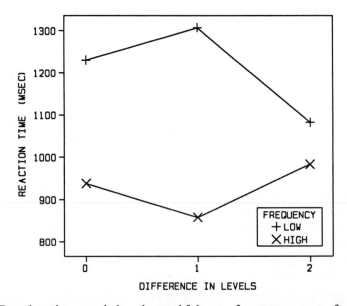

Figure 9. Reaction times to judge the truthfulness of sentences as a function of the difference in levels of the subject and predicate. The two curves give the results for low and high frequency of co-occurrence.

Confounding of Similarity

Schaeffer and Wallace (1970) and Glass and Holyoak (1975) also presented some problematical results. They found that false decisions gave just about the opposite kind of result as true decisions. People are much faster in responding "false" to, "A canary is a furniture," than to, "A canary is a mammal" (see Figure 10). According to the strict hierarchical model and cognitive economy, we would expect just the opposite result. It should take subjects a longer time to get to furniture traveling from canary through this hierarchy than it does to get to mammal. Semantic similarity seems to play a role. That is, subjects are able to see immediately that canary and furniture are very dissimilar. These two concepts could not be related in any kind of category relationship. On the other hand, canary and mammal are more similar and, therefore, subjects need more processing to reject this as a false sentence.

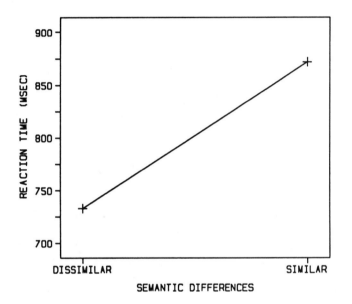

Figure 10. Reaction times to judge whether two words are members of the same category as a function of the semantic difference between the two words (adapted from Schaeffer & Wallace, 1970).

These data seem to indicate that the network model structured by cognitive economy is not a good one to represent semantic information. An alternative proposed by Smith and his co-workers in 1974 is a semantic features model. According to the semantic features model, a category is not stored with properties in memory, but rather each concept has features that describe that concept. These features range from defining features to characteristic features. Defining characteristics might be considered to be essential to the category. Characteristic features might be considered to be accidental. For example, robins have defining characteristics of bipeds, wings, and a particular color. A characteristic feature might be that they perch in trees or that they are not domesticated.

All members of a given category are not equally good members of that category. In speech perception, not all /ba/s are equally good /ba/s. Some are better than others. Robin is a prototypical bird, whereas an ostrich may not be very prototypical. Subjects given the sentence, "A robin is a bird," evaluate the features associated with robins and the features associated with birds. To the extent that there is a good match between the features of these two concepts, a "true" response is made. To the extent that there is a mismatch, you would expect subjects to respond "false". This comparison is analogous to how subjects evaluate features in a speech sound and compare the match of these features to prototypes in memory (see Chapter 16).

How do we determine the semantic features for a given concept? One method is to ask people to tell you how related they feel one concept is to another concept. For example, people can be asked to indicate, on a scale of 1 to 7, how related are birds and robins? All possible pairs of the concepts would be presented, and a multidimensional analysis can be carried out on the rating responses. From the multidimensional analysis, the relationship between the concepts and the features that are responsible for these relationships can be revealed.

Smith, Shoben, and Rips (1974) explicated a specific process model that operates on semantic features. This model is illustrated in Figure 11.

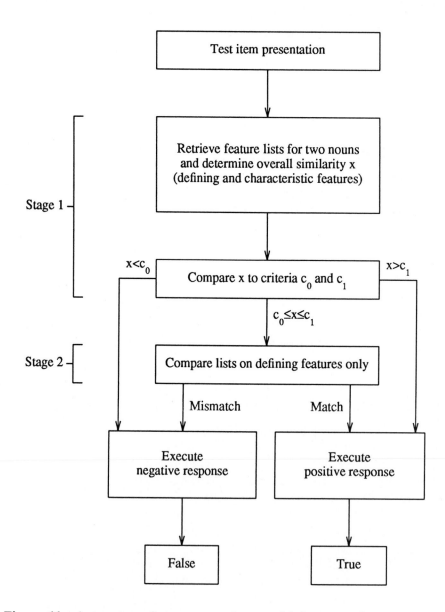

Figure 11. A two-stage feature comparison model for semantic categorization tasks (adapted from Smith, Shoben, & Rips, 1974).

Consider the test item presentation, "A canary is a bird." At Stage 1 the features for these two concepts, canary and bird, are retrieved. At Stage 1, the overall similarity between their features is determined. If the features are highly similar to one another, then you are probably pretty safe in executing a true judgment. If the features are highly dissimilar from one another, you are probably fairly safe in executing a false judgment. If the features are somewhere in between in terms of their similarity to one another, then you probably have to do something else to make a true or false judgment. The observer has two criterion values, C_1 and C_0. The comparison produces some degree of match. If the degree of match is very extreme, then that would be to the right of C_1. A "true" response could be executed right away. On the other hand, if there is a gross mismatch, that would be to the left of C_0. A false judgment would be appropriate. For many comparisons, however, the matching value will be between C_0 and C_1. In order to make a decision, the subject must go on to Stage 2. At Stage 2, concepts are compared on essential or defining characteristics. Adding Stage 2 increases the RT.

To compare their model to the network model, Smith et al. (1974) first had to find a measure of relatedness between concepts. That is, how typical are instances with respect to their superordinate categories? Subjects were given instances and asked to generate their superordinate categories. As you might expect, the category insect was generated more frequently than the category animal, given the instance butterfly. These productions were used as an index of semantic relatedness between an instance and a superordinance category. Smith et al. proposed that semantic relatedness was responsible for the fact that people can respond faster to some sentences than others. People are faster at saying that a sparrow is a bird than at saying that a sparrow is an animal. The reason is that sparrows and birds are more semantically related than sparrows and animals. The reason is not because birds are only one level up from sparrows and animals are two levels up from sparrows in a hierarchical representation.

Confounding of Category Size

It should be noted that a heirarchical representation is necessarily confounded with differences in category size (Landauer & Freedman, 1968; Landauer & Meyer, 1972). As differences in the number of levels separating two concepts change, so do differences in category size. Subjects might take longer to verify that, "A sparrow is an animal," than to verify that, "A sparrow is a bird," because birds make up a smaller category than do animals.

Smith et al. (1974) were able to pull apart category size from semantic relatedness with test sentences that consisted of an independent variation of category size and semantic relatedness. For the Set 1 items in the left-hand column of Table 5, the smaller category is more similar to the instance than is the larger category. For butterfly, insect is a smaller category than animal. In addition, insect is more similar to butterfly than to animal. There are two reasons why subjects should respond faster to the sentence, "A butterfly is an insect," than to the sentence, "A butterfly is an animal." The first reason is that insect is a smaller category. The second reason is that butterfly is more semantically related to insect than it is to animal. For the Set 2 items in the right-hand column of the table, the larger category is more similar to the instance than is the smaller category. Aluminum is more semantically related to metal than it is to alloy. Analogously, cantaloupe is more related to fruit than it is to melon.

According to Smith et al., similarity should play a bigger role in the judgment than category size. As you can see from the RTs in Table 5 and Figure 12, this is exactly what is found. When the instance is more similar to the smaller than the larger category, the smaller category is responded to 147 msec faster than is the larger category. From these results, you might conclude

Table 5. Mean correct RT (in msec) as a function of category size, separately for triples in which the smaller category was more similar to the test instance (Set 1), and for triples in which the larger category was more similar to the test instance (Set 2).

Smaller category more similar - Set 1			Larger category more similar - Set 2		
Instance	Smaller category / Larger category	Reaction time	Instance	Smaller category / Larger category	Reaction time
butterfly	insect	1077	aluminum	alloy	1267
	animal	1325		metal	1144
collie	dog	969	cantaloupe	melon	1174
	animal	1117		fruit	974
copper	metal	977	cathedral	church	1027
	mineral	1253		building	1167
copperhead	snake	1083	chimpanzee	primate	1298
	reptile	1398		animal	1017
daisy	flower	1036	Coca-Cola	pop	1009
	plant	996		drink	897
door	entrance	1103	diamond	jewel	1135
	opening	1081		stone	1101
lemonade	drink	1022	drum	percussion instrument	1292
	liquid	1041		musical instrument	1042
minute	unit of time	1277	fork	silverware	1122
	unit of measurement	1546		utensil	1023
pear	fruit	889	guitar	stringed instrument	1089
	food	1164		musical instrument	1095
potato	vegetable	1058	harvard	university	978
	food	983		school	1000
sparrow	bird	975	scotch	liquor	1043
	animal	1312		drink	988
toe	part of foot	1235	topaz	gem	1143
	part of body	1172		stone	1130
willow	tree	1065	wool	cloth	921
	plant	1290		material	1170
Mean	Smaller category	1059	Mean	Smaller category	1115
	Larger category	1206		Larger category	1058

that the reason is category size. However, the larger category is responded to 57 msec faster than the smaller category when the larger category is semantically more similar to the instance than is the smaller category. What appears to be important in this experiment is semantic similarity. The larger effect of semantic similarity with Set 1 than Set 2 items could be due to differences in semantic similrity and/or category size. Semantic similarity corresponds to the perceived

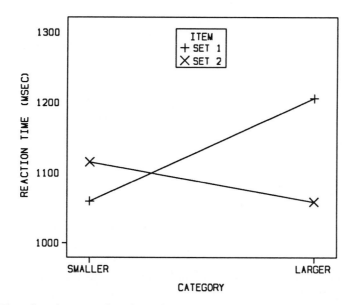

Figure 12. Reaction time as a function of relative category size and relative similarity. In Set 1 items, the instance is more similar to the smaller than the larger category. In Set 2 items, the instance is more similar to the larger than the smaller category.

relatedness or similarity between an instance and a category. It is not familiarity. You may be highly familiar with birds, but that is independent of how similar you think a canary is to a bird and how similar you think an ostrich is to a bird. Familiarity is a property of a word or concept independently of its relationship to other words or concepts.

Confounding of Familiarity

At an intuitive level, we might expect familiarity to be an important variable in our processing of linguistic and conceptual information. I feel more familiar with the category metal than with the category alloy. This difference in familiarity might be expected to contribute to performance in the sentence verification task. McCloskey (1980) alerted the scientific community about the role of familiarity in previous studies of semantic memory. His argument was that the effect of semantic relatedness in the Smith et al. (1974) studies was really a result of familiarity. When familiarity is properly controlled, semantic relatedness has no effect and category size once again reveals itself as an important variable in the sentence verification task.

The importance of McCloskey's research is that it makes apparent the stages of processing in the verification task. Previous work did not utilize the important framework offered by Sternberg's additive-factor method. Consider the subject faced with a sentence such as, "A canary is a bird." Three important processes are involved in the verification of this sentence. The subject must recognize the subject, recognize the predicate, and evaluate the relationship between subject and predicate. Previous studies have made the implicit assumption that any differences in RT are entirely due to the third process of evaluation. However, we can see easily that familiarity might be an important variable influencing the process of recognizing the subject and predicate terms in the sentence.

McCloskey argued that the semantic relatedness ratings of Smith et al. were not valid measures of the semantic relatedness of the subject and predicate terms. Contrary to the ratings observed by Smith et al. (1974), true semantic relatedness was higher for instance-small than for instance-large category pairs for both Set 1 and Set 2 items. Recall that the subjects were faster for small than for large categories for the Set 1 items, whereas the reverse was true for the Set 2 items (see Table 5). Therefore, the Set 1 results were consistent with both semantic relatedness and category size explanations of verification time, whereas the Set 2 results are *inconsistent* with both explanations. Something must be amiss, and McCloskey proposed the hypothesis that familiarity is critical for the recognition of the category concepts.

Subjects rated the familiarity of the categories used in the Smith et al. (1974) study. Subjects made rating judgments on a 7 point scale on which 1 is completely unfamiliar and 7 is completely familiar. Sure enough, the small categories in the Set 2 items were less familiar than the other 3 groups of items. Table 6 shows that the Set 2 items are rated as less familiar than the other 3 types of items. Thus, it is possible that the slow RTs to these items were due to their unfamiliarity rather than to semantic relatedness.

To test this hypothesis, McCloskey made a slight modification in the presentation of test sentences in the verification task. Sometimes small variations in the experimental task can be highly illuminating. McCloskey's task is illustrated in Figure 13. Subjects were first presented with a category and told to push a button when they comprehended it. The RT in this task is called the comprehension time. The test instance was presented 500 msec after the subject hit the button. The subject's task was then to hit a yes or no button signifying whether or not the test instance was a member of the category. The RT in this task is called the verification time. McCloskey used the items of Smith et al. presented in Table 5.

Table 6. Comprehension times, verification times, and familiarity ratings in the McCloskey (1980) study as a function of category size, separately for Set 1 items (triples in which the smaller category was more similar to the test instance), and for Set 2 items (triples in which the larger category was more similar to the test instance).

Set	Category Size	Comprehension Time	Verification Time	Familiarity Ratings
1	small	1073	688	5.56
	large	1072	793	5.33
2	small	1222	664	4.60
	large	1088	725	5.22

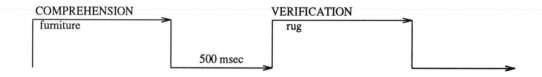

Figure 13. Illustration of the comprehension and verification tasks in the McCloskey (1980) study. Comprehension RT is the time between presentation of the category and its comprehension (as indicated by a button push). Verification RT is the time between presentation of the instance and its verification of membership in the category.

Table 6 gives the comprehension times and the verification times for Set 1 and Set 2 items. The comprehension times were longer for the small than for the large category for the Set 2 items, whereas there were no differences due to category size for the Set 1 items.

For verification times, subjects were faster for the smaller categories for both Sets 1 and 2. By removing the contribution of comprehension time, McCloskey demonstrated that semantic relatedness is not responsible for the RT differences observed by Smith et al.

Category Size Revisited

What about category size? McCloskey evaluated whether familiarity might be responsible for the category size differences. Subjects were asked to rate the familiarity of the category terms used in these experiments. What McCloskey found was that the ratings exhibited a pattern very similar to the comprehension RTs shown in Table 6. The small category in Set 2 is the least familiar and also shows the largest comprehension times. On the other hand, the familiarity ratings do not seem to account for the true verification times. The large categories give longer verification times for both Set 1 and Set 2 items. Given that familiarity cannot account for these differences, category size may be the effective variable. Thus, verifying that an instance is a member of a category appears to be a positive function of the size of the category. This conclusion should not be surprising given the powerful effect of category size in memory search (see Chapter 9).

Typicality Revisited

What about typicality? In Chapter 16, we saw that typicality is an important influence on how easily and quickly subjects classify an object as an instance of a category. Category size cannot account for the typicality effects documented in Chapter 16 because those experiments held category size constant. Longer RTs to verify that a penguin is a bird than a sparrow is a bird cannot be due to category size. Familiarity also cannot account for typicality (Rosch & Mervis, 1975). In our example, penguins and sparrows are about equally familiar and yet different RTs are found. Category size, familiarity, and typicality all play a role in processing. Consistent with the outcomes in several other domains of inquiry, behavior is influenced by several, rather than just a single, variable.

18
Learning and Thinking

Interaction of Processes

Learning Concepts

Prototype Learning
  Insofarasicansee
  Dot Patterns

Temporal Course of Learning
  Learning Curves

State-Dependent Learning
  The Learner's Mood
  Pollyanna Principle

Cognitive versus Affective Systems
  Double Dissociation Revisited
  Negative Evidence

Judgment and Decision Making
  Evaluation
  Value of Money
  Integration of Multiple Sources
    of Information
  Representativeness
  Availability
  Prior Odds
  Experience and Logic

Problem Solving
  Anagrams
  Heuristics versus Algorithms

Game Playing
  Skilled Players
  Short-Term Memory
  Knowledge and Memory

Learning to Read Lips

*. . . and it is no wonder that she [the soul] should be able to
call to remembrance all that she ever knew about virtue, and
about everything; for as all nature is akin, and the soul has
learned all things, there is no difficulty in her eliciting, or,
as men say, learning, out of a single recollection all the rest.*
Plato's Meno

Implicit throughout the book is the assumption that people are continually learning, and this learning process plays a factor in normal perceptual and cognitive functioning, as well as in experimental tasks. In our experiments subjects usually show a remarkable improvement in performance during the first few or even the first few hundred trials. In a pitch discrimination experiment subjects' identifications improve remarkably during the first 20- or 30-minute session, leveling off thereafter. In our studies we have eliminated the contribution of learning as a possible confounding by (1) practicing the subjects before the experiment proper so that performance is asymptotic during the trials of interest, or (2) randomizing all conditions within experimental sessions and among subjects so that, on the average, all experimental conditions are tested equally at all levels of learning. As a result, our studies are informative with respect to the study of perceptual and cognitive functioning for a relatively fixed learning level.

INTERACTION OF PROCESSES

Learning itself is, of course, an interest to the experimental psychologist. There is a fine line between a study of memory and study of learning since successful memory requires, at least, successful learning and learning any new action depends on memory. However, learning, as traditionally studied, appears to be a result of the interaction of a number of psychological processes rather than a distinct process itself, analogous to recognition or decision. In fact, learning typically results when we recombine many of the processes discussed throughout this book. Hence, we actually know more about learning and how to study learning than might be inferred from our disuse of the term. The verbal short-term memory studies provide a good case in point. If a subject correctly recognizes that an item was presented earlier in a previous list of items, we can say he has *learned* that it was presented earlier. Accordingly, a description of the learning process will include the same processes of perception and storage, retention and retrieval, and decision that were necessary to describe performance in the short-term memory task. Learning might be considered to be involved in more complex actions and skills in which behavior reflects much more than simply memory of previous experience.

LEARNING CONCEPTS

The concept of learning has been discussed here without defining it explicitly; we have relied on the fact that our interpretations of this word are sufficiently similar to make this dialogue worthwhile. In fact, the use of a word or concept in this way presents a significant challenge to the learning psychologist or the philosopher of knowledge. For example, how do we come to know "learning"—an abstract concept—having had contact with nothing more than a series of relatively unrelated concrete instances of the learning process? This problem was posed by Plato in the *Meno* and has yet to be explained adequately. His explanation was that the soul or mind has already been acquainted with abstract concepts from a previous reality, so that all present signs of learning are actually signs of anamnesis [recollections]. Plato solved the problem of learning by redefining it so that no explanation was necessary. Since we know everything there is to know, there is no need to describe how we come to know.

Aristotle rejected his mentor's solution and proposed, instead, that learning and knowledge are derived from experience with concrete particulars. Aristotle reformulated the problem so that the question to be answered was: How does experience with a sequence of learning acts lead us to the generic concept of learning? His solution was one of abstraction; we isolate out common elements of learning scenarios to derive what is critical to the learning process. Aristotle's common elements will not enable us to abstract enough information to define learning, mainly because perception is not a passive process but an active, constructive one. For example, we have discussed how the rules of English orthography are utilized to help make unambiguous a sequence of written letters. By constructing the relevant dimensions, we seem to be able to derive concepts from particulars. In philosophical terms, we arrive at universals on the basis of experience with particulars. This chapter will concern the rules by which one comes to learn a concept or schema as a function of experience with concrete particulars.

PROTOTYPE LEARNING

Plato was concerned with the acquisition of the concept of virtue. Since virtue is difficult to bring into the laboratory, however, recent experimenters have studied the learning of visual and auditory concepts that can be specified precisely. The task is to have subjects classify instances of prototypical patterns while varying the similarity between the prototype and the instance to be classified. Consider two prototype patterns, A and B; these patterns can be distorted to various degrees and presented to subjects for classification. The experimenter seeks to determine which stimulus attributes are critical for classification and, more importantly, how the subject comes to know these stimulus attributes.

Insofarasicansee

How does learning fit into our general information-processing model? Learning occurs when the subject imposes a transformation in the processing sequence that leads to more accurate performance on subsequent trials. Consider *insofarasicansee*, the sequence of letters presented one at a time to a subject who is to learn them in sequential order. This task could be relatively difficult, since the number of letters exceeds the span of immediate memory. If the observer learns, however, that the letter sequences spell a common and simple phrase, his learning rate should increase dramatically. In this case, calling on lexical memory structures facilitates learning. Whether or not the subject applies this rule, the sequence of processes is easily understood in terms of our information-processing model. In one case, the transfer from synthesized visual memory to generated abstract memory is in terms of letter names; in the other, the transfer is in terms of words. However, the question here is how the subject comes to know that the letters spell words; and when she does, how does she recognize the correct words?

One way to ensure that the reader will interpret the sequence of letters as words is to put blank spaces in the appropriate places. Here we have changed a structural aspect of the stimulus to obtain this effect. By varying the number of blank spaces in the sequence of letters, we should be able to systematically influence the probability that the subject will read the letters as words. Even with no blank spaces, however, a reader will have some probability of interpreting the letters as words. This probability could also be influenced by context variables; for example, the subject could be given the appropriate set by first presenting other letter sequences that spell words. However, the best index of performance the experimenter can get is a probability; we cannot predict exactly whether a particular person will see words or unrelated letters on a particular trial. This is no different from our probabilistic interpretations of detection, recognition, and retention discussed in detail throughout this book.

The learning of dot patterns and other conceptual categories falls within the realm of the influence of past experience on perception, memory, and learning. Bartlett (1932) developed the concept of a schema to describe how past experience has its influence. Essentially, we interpret new experiences in a framework of past experiences. Consider the problems faced by a dedicated baseball fan when he spends a year in Europe trying to follow soccer. New information now requires much more than a simple updating of what is already known and well-organized. Attneave (1957) used the concept of schema to explain how new instances of a category were learned and differentiated from each other and from old instances. Subjects were asked to learn to associate letter patterns with male names. The letter patterns were variations of a prototype pattern. Some subjects learned to reproduce the prototype pattern before the learning task. These subjects were better at learning the new letter patterns than a group of subjects who learned to reproduce an irrelevant nonsense shape. Attneave interpreted the results to mean that people learn some central tendency of a class of varying members and use this information to enhance learning of the members themselves. The schema aids the learning of how the members differ from each other in terms of which dimensions are relevant and the amount of variation along each dimension.

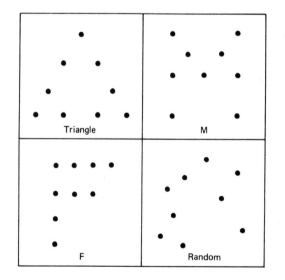

Figure 1. The four prototypical patterns used in the Posner, Goldsmith, and Welton (1967) study.

Dot Patterns

The discussion above implies that learning is critically dependent upon perception, which is critically dependent upon the structural aspects of the stimulus situation. One demonstration of this has been a series of experiments carried out by Posner and his colleagues in which they distorted dot patterns that were then categorized by college students. In the Posner, Goldsmith, and Welton (1967) study, subjects were required to classify visual dot patterns as an instance of either a triangle, the letter M, the letter F, or a specific random pattern. The instances presented to the subjects were distorted from their prototypical pattern (shown in Figure 1), so that classification was not easy. Four levels of distortion were employed in generating instances from the prototypical patterns. The instances corresponding to these 4 levels of distortion of the triangle are shown in Figure 2.

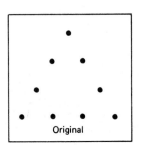

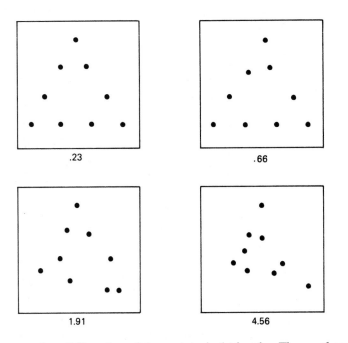

Figure 2. Four examples of distortion of the prototypical triangle. The numbers define the average number of squares each dot was moved for that level of distortion (after Posner, Goldsmith, & Welton, 1967).

Each prototypical dot pattern was represented on graph paper divided into squares. The dot would essentially fill one complete square. Each dot of the prototype would be moved according to a probabilistic schedule that differed for the different levels of distortion. The space was partitioned into 5 areas by defining a series of rings around the prototypical cell. The cell containing the prototypical dot was called 0, the 8 surrounding cells called 1, and the next 16 cells surrounding these 8 were called 2, and so on until 5 such areas were defined. For each level of distortion, the dot could move into any of these 5 areas with a certain probability. Once it entered an area, it was equally likely to enter any of the cells defined by this area. By varying the probabilities that a given dot can enter any of the 5 areas, the experimenter has direct control over the average distance each dot in the pattern will move. In one experiment (Experiment III, replication) Posner et al. (1967) chose 3 levels of distortion. Table 1 gives the average number of squares moved for each of the 3 levels of distortion.

Table 1. Three levels of distortion defined by the average distance (number of squares). Each dot was moved and the mean number of classification errors to a criterion of learning (after Posner, Goldsmith, & Welton, 1967).

Average Distance	Mean Number of Errors to Criterion
.23	4.6
1.91	12.2
4.56	71.1

In the experiment subjects were assigned to 1 of the 3 levels of distortion and presented instances of the 4 prototypes shown in Figure 1 generated from the appropriate distortion rule. The subject's task was to respond to each pattern by pushing 1 of 4 buttons. The task involved learning to hit the correct button to each pattern. After the response the subjects were given feedback on each trial, indicating the appropriate response for each pattern. Three different instances of each of the 4 prototypes were presented in a random order until the subject made 24 correct classifications in a row or completed 240 trials. The mean number of errors to criterion at each of the 31 levels of distortion is presented in Table 1. As can be seen, the difficulty of the classification task is a direct function of the level of distortion employed to generate the instances. To the extent a dot was moved from its prototypical location, performance was disrupted. This result is not surprising and can be located in the recognition stage of information processing. If an instance of a triangle is distorted so that it no longer looks like a triangle, it cannot be classified correctly on this basis. Subjects given instances which were highly distorted had to learn the appropriate response to each of the 12 instances individually, since they were not able to see them as members of a prototypical pattern class.

TEMPORAL COURSE OF LEARNING

Although these experiments tell us that structural aspects of the stimulus are critical in prototype learning, we still do not know how the observers come to know the concept. Throughout the history of psychology there have been two major theories of the learning process. One theory assumes that learning occurs in a gradual incremental fashion; the subject slowly builds up the relevant information required for the task. The incremental learning theory can be viewed as a multistate process in which the subject goes through many successive learning states. In each learning state the probability of a correct response is slightly higher than it was in the preceding learning state. The other theory is that the subject learns, or comes to know, in an all-or-none fashion. He tests out certain rules describing the situation and operates according to these rules or hypotheses until he settles on one that leads to accurate performance. The all-or-none learning theory is a two-state process. In the first state the subject knows very little and the probability of a correct response is near chance. In the second state the subject has solved the problem and the probability of a correct response is as high as is possible in the learning task. (The asymptotic probability may not be 1, since problems might not be capable of a perfect solution.)

Learning Curves

How do we test between these two theories of learning? The task seems easy enough. We devise an experimental task and plot out a learning curve—performance across successive learning trials. The incremental learning theory predicts that percentage of correct responses should increase gradually across learning trials, whereas the all-or-none theory predicts that learning should occur in a single step at some point in the training session. However, when we look at the responses of a given subject across trials, it is difficult to tell which theory gives a better description of performance. On each trial, performance is either correct or incorrect, and a trend in the data is not directly apparent. For this reason investigators have pooled the results over a number of subjects and have plotted group learning curves as shown in Figure 3. Here the curves plot the probability of a correct response on each trial derived from dividing the number of correct responses on each trial by the total number of subjects. These results invariably show incremental learning rather than all-or-none learning curves.

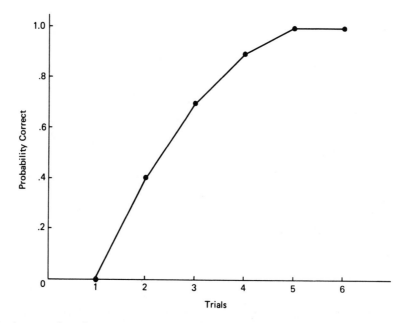

Figure 3. A group learning curve demonstrating gradual learning based on the all-or-none results in Table 2.

Unfortunately, the group learning curves say nothing about the learning of individual subjects. As pointed out by a number of investigators (e.g., Sidman, 1952), the individual subjects may actually have learned the problem in an all-or-none fashion, but by pooling the results this effect is washed out, giving a gradual learning curve. That is to say, pooling the results could give the incremental data shown in Figure 3, even if subjects learn in an all-or-none fashion on different trials. Table 2 is an example of the individual results of ten subjects who learned the problem in an all-or-none fashion but gave the pooled results of Figure 3. This demonstration convinces most investigators that individual subject analysis is necessary to distinguish between the all-or-none and incremental learning theories.

Table 2. When pooled, individual protocols which show all-or-none learning give the gradual incremental curve shown in Figure 3. The letters I and C refer to incorrect and correct responses, respectively, and P(C) is probability correct.

Subject	Trial Number					
	1	2	3	4	5	6
1	I	C	C	C	C	C
2	I	C	C	C	C	C
3	I	C	C	C	C	C
4	I	C	C	C	C	C
5	I	I	C	C	C	C
6	I	I	C	C	C	C
7	I	I	C	C	C	C
8	I	I	I	C	C	C
9	I	I	I	C	C	C
10	I	I	I	I	C	C
Group Average P(C)	0	.4	.7	.9	1.0	1.0

STATE-DEPENDENT LEARNING

An important fact in learning and memory is the role of participant's state during the original learning and later testing. Consider the question of whether marijuana influences the learning of a mathematical concept. Half of the subjects are taught the concept under the influence and half while straight. A week later, all of the subjects are asked to explain the concept. The results would probably show better recall for those subjects who learned the concept while straight. One cannot conclude that marijuana led to poorer learning, however, since the poor performance of these subjects may have been due to the mismatch between their states during learning and testing. To provide a proper assessment of the influence of marijuana, four groups of subjects are required as illustrated in Table 4.

The Learner's Mood

Gordon Bower and his colleagues (Bower, Monteiro, & Gilligan, 1978) studied the role of mood in memory for word lists. The question was whether an affective state such as happy or sad would function analogously to a physiological state in showing state dependency in learning. To induce the affective state, the authors used hypnosis. With this technique, a real and lasting affective state can be produced relatively quickly. In two initial experiments, happy or sad subjects memorized a list of unrelated words. The recall test was carried out with the subjects either in the same mood or the opposite mood. No state dependency was observed; subjects recalled equally well regardless of whether they were tested in the same or opposite mood. Evidently subjects were able to retrieve the words from memory even if they were in an altered mood. Learning a single list of words must have been a distinctive enough experience that the switch in mood was not important.

Good experimenters do not give up after a couple of failures. To demonstrate state-dependency learning, Bower et al. (1978) made the memory task more difficult. Subjects now learned a different list of words in each of the two moods. The test for recall for a given list was given when the subject was either in the same or opposite mood. Six groups of subjects were tested as illustrated in Table 5.

Learning to Read Lips

Recognizing visible speech in face-to-face communication without sound is called speechreading or lipreading. Walden, Prosek, Montgomery, Scherr, and Jones (1977) studied the visual recognition of consonants in 31 hearing-impaired adults. The subjects were tested on 20 consonant-vowel syllables. On any trial, one of the 20 syllables could be presented, and subjects identified the syllable. A total of 400 test trials was presented. Repeated observations were made to increase the reliability of the test. These subjects without any previous formal training appeared to discriminate among five categories of consonants. These categories that can be discriminated are usually called visemes, and are analogous to the concept phonemes. Phonemes describe the contrasts in speech that can be recognized auditorily (Chapter 19, p. 414). Table 3 gives the percentage of within-category identification responses for nine visemes before training. Based on a criterion of 75 percent identification responses from within the viseme category, the five viseme categories that could be discriminated were /ðθ, fv, pbm, ʃž, and w/.

After this initial test, the subjects were given systematic training in the recognition of the consonants. Training involved 14 one-hour sessions of intensive and individualized speechreading instruction, spread over a two-week period. Subjects made same-different judgments to pairs of syllables and identified single syllables with immediate feedback. After training, subjects were given the same recognition test given at the beginning of the study. Table 3 also gives the performance for the nine visemes after training. Replicating previous studies of training (e.g., Heider & Heider, 1940), the training succeeded in improving speechreading. The number of discriminable viseme categories increased from five to nine.

Table 3. Percentage of within category identification responses for nine viseme categories. Results are given before and after training (after Walden et al., 1977).

Viseme	Pretraining	Posttraining
θ, ð	90.1	99.4
f, v	92.2	97.5
ʃ, ž	71.9	94.5
s, z	34.9	79.2
p, b, m	90.6	99.3
t, d, n, k, g, j	57.3	97.1
w	74.8	92.9
r	36.1	88.6
l	72.6	93.4

Figure 4 gives the results for the three groups of subjects. Relative to the control groups, a mismatch between affective states reduces performance whereas a unique match between affective states improves performance. There was no overall difference in learning and memory due to the subject's mood. What is important is whether the mood in learning and recall match or mismatch. These positive results seem to indicate that emotional mood allowed the subject to distinguish the appropriate list for recall and thereby reduce the interfering effects of the other list. To state this finding in practical terms, if you are studying for two exams, learn the material in different mood states. And, of course, induce the appropriate mood state during each of the exams.

Table 4. The four groups of subjects needed to test the influence of marijuana on learning and memory along with the necessary comparisons to evaluate the drug's influence on learning, memory, and state dependency.

Group	Learning	Test
1	straight	straight
2	straight	high
3	high	straight
4	high	high

(Groups 1 & 2) vs. (Groups 3 & 4) = effect of marijuana on learning
(Groups 1 & 4) vs. (Groups 2 & 3) = effect of state-dependent learning
(Groups 2 & 4) vs. (Groups 1 & 3) = effect of marijuana on recall

Table 5. The design of the Bower et al. (1978) experiment.

Group	Learn List A	Learn List B	Test List A
Control	Happy Sad	Happy Sad	Happy Sad
Same State	Happy Sad	Sad Happy	Happy Sad
Different State	Happy Sad	Sad Happy	Sad Happy

The positive contribution of enhanced recall is fairly strong and has been replicated in several studies (Frijda, 1986). In a typical recall task, the subject must retrieve words from the test list, using whatever recall cues are available. It is reasonable that mood could function as a retrieval cue. Matching mood states in learning and recall would allow more accurate retrieval than mismatching mood states. The effect only occurs, however, when other factual retrieval cues are weak. Given some other retrieval information, the role of mood might have have less influence. For example, being told the actors in a story might facilitate your recall of the story independently of whether your current mood matches your mood during the initial learning. This explanation also implies that mood might have less influence when retrieval is not critical for accurate performance. We know that recall is dependent on retrieval cues whereas recognition is not. Thus, we would not expect subjects to show state-dependent learning in recognition tasks and, in fact, they do not (Bower & Cohen, 1982).

Mood-dependent memory is also apparent outside of the laboratory and in clinical settings (Frijda, 1986; Weingartner, Miller, & Murphy, 1977). Clark and Teasdale (1982), for example, found that clinical depression operated in a similar manner to experimentally-induced depression. Subjects were asked to keep track of emotional incidents and to record these in a diary (Bower, 1981). They recorded the specifics of each emotional incident along with a rating of intensity of a pleasant or unpleasant experience. After a week of recording, the diaries were collected. A week later, the subjects were hypnotized; a random half were put in a pleasant mood and the other half in an unpleasant mood. They were asked to recall the incidents recorded in their diaries. As you might predict by now, pleasant episodes were more likely to be recalled in a pleasant mood than in an unpleasant mood whereas the opposite was the case for the unpleasant episodes. The lesson to

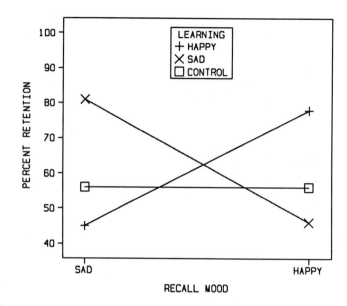

Figure 4. Percentage retention scores as a function of the match between learning mood and recall mood. The sloping lines refer to subjects who learned the two lists under different moods. The mood controls learned both lists under the same mood.

be learned here is not to think freely when you are unhappy. If you do, you are likely to recall unpleasant events which will in turn make you unhappier.

Pollyanna Principle

Another result witnessed by Bower and his colleagues was the Pollyanna principle (Matlin & Stang, 1978). Pollyanna was the child heroine in a movie by Walt Disney based on the book by Eleanor Porter. A happy and optimistic person is a Pollyanna and, interestingly, we are all Pollyannas to some degree. In general, people tend to seek out, record, and remember pleasant as opposed to unpleasant experiences. Matlin and Stang (1978) have documented the Pollyanna principle across a wide range of phenomena. Our psychological interpretation of the world is tinted by rose-colored glasses. We will not review the evidence presented by Matlin and Stang (1978) but simply mention one or two experiments illustrating the Pollyanna principle.

Cason (1932) used a paired-associate paradigm to test whether the learning and memory of words would differ as a function of the pleasantness of the words. Word length, frequency of occurrence, and syntactic class of the words was controlled. After presentation of the word pairs, subjects were given the stimulus word and asked to supply the response word. The results showed that performance accuracy was a positive function of the pleasantness of the words. Visual imagery usually plays an important role in paired-associate learning (Bower, 1970; Paivio, 1971) in that vivid imagery leads to much better memory. Given the Pollyanna principle, it is not surprising that Cason's subjects would have formed more vivid and powerful images with pleasant than with unpleasant words. Given these results, investigators carefully control for the affective value of their stimuli when investigating other dimensions of our experience.

COGNITIVE VERSUS AFFECTIVE SYSTEMS

Several recent experiments have attempted to demonstrate that stimulus exposure can modify the affective reaction to that stimulus without necessarily influencing cognitive recognition of the stimulus. Wilson (1975, 1979) used a dichotic listening procedure in which subjects shadowed a story presented to one ear while melodies were presented to the other ear. A recognition memory test after the shadowing revealed that these melodies were recognized at a chance level. However, a liking response showed that melodies heard previously were better liked than melodies not previously encountered. Kunst-Wilson and Zajonc (1980) exposed polygons for brief intervals in a tachistoscope. Subjects then made affective judgments indicating how much they liked each polygon, or made recognition memory judgments indicating whether or not they had seen the polygons previously. The liking response distinguished old from new stimuli much better than did the old-new recognition memory response. From these results, Zajonc (1980) concluded that the affective process is partly independent and separate from the cognitive process. That is, changes in affect might result without any change in a corresponding cognitive process.

Birnbaum and Mellers (1979a, 1979b) have taken issue with the conclusions reached by Zajonc and his colleagues (Moreland & Zajonc, 1979). Birnbaum and Mellers have shown that a single factor (which might be called affective, cognitive, or both) can be responsible for both the recognition memory and affective responses. This demonstration is an important one because it provides a caveat (cautionary note) for investigators who think that different results with different dependent variables necessarily imply different mediating processes. Although the proof given by Birnbaum and Mellers is somewhat sophisticated at mathematical and statistical levels, the argument can be explained at an intuitive level.

Assume that a single process, which we might call subjective recognition, is responsible for both recognition memory and liking judgments. Subjective recognition can be expected to be some function of exposure frequency. The recognition-memory liking judgments are in turn some function of subjective recognition, not exposure frequency. If recognition memory and liking judgments are different functions of subjective recognition, then different results might occur in the two tasks. If the liking judgment begins higher and grows faster with changes in subjective recognition than does the recognition memory judgment, liking judgments could change with exposure frequency even though recognition memory does not. Because there is no correct answer, the liking judgment might encourage the subject to be more informative in his or her response. The recognition memory task might encourage subjects to be less informative because they can be incorrect. Therefore, results such as those found by Moreland and Zajonc (1977) do not necessarily imply independent processes responsible for affective and cognitive judgments.

Double Dissociation Revisited

The argument of Zajonc (1980) rests on the same logic researchers have used in arguing for a distinction between episodic and semantic memory (Chapter 17). A study by Seamon, Brody, and Kauff (1983) is representative of studies contrasting affective and memory judgments, and finding a double dissociation. The test stimuli were 20 irregular polygons (Vanderplas & Garvin, 1959). During the study session, the shapes were presented one at a time in random order. Each shape was presented 5 times. The subjects were instructed to simply look at the shapes being presented. Each shape was presented for 5 msec and followed immediately by a masking stimulus made up of small random shapes. During the study session, subjects also shadowed (repeated back) a list of spoken words. The study session was followed by a test session. On each test trial, two polygons were presented: an old one that had been presented during the study session, and a new one. For the recognition judgment, the subjects were instructed to select the one they had seen before. For the affective (liking) judgment, the subjects were to select the one they liked the best.

Following the logic of a double dissociation (see Chapter 17), the goal is now to find an independent variable that influences the two types of judgments in opposite directions. Seamon et al. chose cerebral laterality. Results have indicated that there is some specialization in the processing of the two hemispheres of the brain (Beaton, 1986). Information presented to the left visual field is first transmitted to the right hemisphere before it is sent on to the left hemisphere. The analogous route is taken by information presented to the right visual field: the information is transmitted to the left hemisphere before it is sent on to the right. Many experiments have evaluated the processing of test stimuli as a function of the visual field of presentation. The logic is that any differences due to the visual field of presentation reflect the relative role of the two hemispheres in processing the information. Results showing that geometric forms are better recognized when they are presented to the left visual field have been interpreted in terms of the greater role of the right hemisphere in visual pattern recogniton. There is also some evidence that subjects discriminate affect more effectively if the stimulus is presented to the right visual field. Following the logic of the these studies, the results indicate that the left hemisphere plays a larger role than the right in affective judgments.

One independent variable that has the potential to show a double dissociation is, therefore, whether the polygons are presented to the right or left visual field. The question of interest is to what extent this variable interacts with the type of judgment (memory or affect). Seamon et al. (1983) had subjects study the test polygons and make affective and memory judgments in the manner described earlier, but now the polygons were originally presented to either the right or left visual field. Figure 5 gives the results in terms of the accuracy of the judgments as a function of whether the left or right hemisphere was primarily involved in processing the test polygons. Accuracy for the affective judgments means that subjects chose the old polygon from the test pair as the one they liked. As can be seen in the figure, a crossover interaction occurred. The affect judgments were better than memory judgments when the study presentation primarily engaged the left hemisphere. The opposite was the case for the polygons presented to the left visual field and primarily engaged the right hemisphere: the memory judgments were better than affect judgments.

Proponents of separate affective and cognitive systems would argue that these results cannot easily be explained by a single processing system. Zajonc's claim is that affective judgments result from an affective system whereas recognition memory judgments result from a cognitive system. One limitation in the dissociation method is that different results in two types of judgments do not necessarily imply that different systems are responsible. As argued by Birnbaum and Mellers (1979a, 1979b), the same memory system could mediate both types of judgments. A reasonable explanation of the differences in the results given different types of judgments is that different retrieval cues are used, and that some are more effective than others. For example, the liking judgment might be mediated by relative familiarity—with the more familiar polygon being better liked. On the other hand, the recognition memory judgment might be mediated by some memory that the subject experienced the polygon in the context of the current experiment. Exposures to the polygons might increase familiarity without increasing memory for having seen them in this specific context. For example, you might become familiar with someone's face at a party without remembering that you saw the face at that specific party.

Negative Evidence

Two recent results weaken Zajonc's claim of separate affective and cognitive systems. First, Bonnano and Stilling (1986) asked subjects to make both liking and familiarity judgments. There were no differences between these two types of judgments. According to Zajonc's logic, these judgments must be coming from the same system. Second, Mandler, Nakamura, and Van Zandt (1987) used Zajonc's logic to analyze other types of judgments. Subjects were given brief

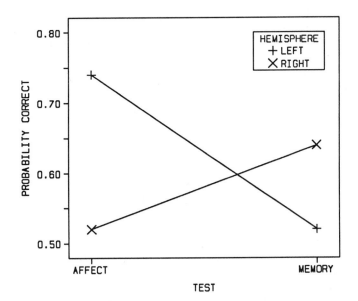

Figure 5. The probability of correct affect and memory judgments as a function of whether the left or right hemisphere was primarily involved in processing the test polygons. A correct affect judgment signifies that subjects chose the old polygon from the test pair as the one they liked (results from Seamon et al., 1983).

exposures of irregular octagons and were instructed to pay attention to the brief exposures and to say "yes" each time they saw a flash. Following this exposure phase, the subjects were tested with four kinds judgments. The test involved presentation of a pair of octagons—one which had been presented in the exposure phase and a new one. The *recognition* task required the subject to indicate which octagon he or she had seen previously. The *preference* task asked which shape they liked better. The *brightness* and *darkness* tasks required the subject to indicate which of the two shapes seemed brighter or darker, respectively.

Replicating previous results, Mandler et al. (1987) found better performance for the liking judgments than for the recognition memory judgments. Based on Zajonc's logic, the difference has to be explained by different systems. However, the brightness and darkness judgments were also better than the recognition memory judgments and were as good as the liking judgments. Using Zajonc's logic, these differences also require different systems; there must be a brightness/darkness system mediating these judgments. One can see that this logic can only lead to finding a plethora of mediating systems. Rather than postulating separate systems, it seems more parsimonious to interpret the results in the same manner as we did in the discussion of differences in semantic and episodic memory tasks. The final judgment of the subject is based on different cues in the different tasks; some of these cues are more effective than others.

In summary, differences in the two types of judgments can be explained in terms of retrieval differences. Affect judgments appear to be influenced by familiarity of the test polygon. Recognition memory, on the other hand, might be more dependent on the degree to which the subject retrieves epeisodic information associated with the test polygon. If these two judgments are viewed from the perspective of pattern recognition, it is reasonable that different sources of information might mediate the different judgments. In pattern recognition, for example, subjects might be asked how complex something is as opposed to how beautiful it is. We would not expect equivalent answers nor expect the answers to be influenced identically by other independent variables.

JUDGMENT AND DECISION MAKING

Human judgment is one of the most pervasive determinants of our existence. In almost every endeavor, we are faced with sources of evidence and we are called upon to evaluate and integrate the evidence and to make some appropriate decision. This sequence of events is not only frequent in our rather mundane decisions about restaurants, automobiles, clothes, and movies; it is also found in voting, interpersonal interaction, the jury process, and ethics. What is unique about judgment is the availability of normative or prescriptive principles based on probability theory and statistics. That is, optimal routines are available for evaluating and integrating information from two or more sources and many fields of social science, such as economics, take these normative routines as representative of human judgments. The question addressed by research in experimental psychology is *how* do humans, in fact, make judgments. We will find that the prescriptive theories of probability and statistics are not sufficient to describe human judgment. But human judgment is not chaos because it seems to follow orderly and, in some sense, reasonable procedures.

We saw in Chapters 10 through 13 that decision making is central to understanding performance in psychophysical tasks. Decision making has been studied in more cognitive domains such as asking subjects to choose among different gambles. Decision making represents an ideal domain for illuminating the role of prescriptive and descriptive theories in psychology. A prescriptive theory prescribes the ideal, whereas a descriptive theory describes the actual. A scientific question is whether a prescriptive theory is also descriptive. Any rational person would agree with the prescription that people should optimize the consequences of decision making. Decide in favor of the greatest value, all other things being equal. In terms of our distinction between prescriptive and descriptive theories, are people optimal decision makers?

Consider the typical decision-making situation in which a person is faced with choosing one of a number of alternative actions, given a number of sources of information. For example, the decision whether or not to marry involves evaluating the prospective partner, financial status, and career goals (besides a host of other considerations). All of these sources of information must be combined (integrated) to arrive at some overall measure of support for each possible decision. Finally, a decision must be made to pick one of the alternatives. A theory of decision making must describe each of these three processes: how each source of information is evaluated, how the sources are integrated, and how the choice is made among the alternatives.

Evaluation

The psychological value of a source of information is not easy to predict, because it has different values for different people. One person values intelligence more than appearance in the choice of a partner, whereas another gives more weight to appearance. Even the quantitative commodity money has varying psychological value for different individuals. A poor student and a successful businesswoman would probably assign different values to a gift of $50. To acknowledge the individual differences in the value of alternatives, we speak of their *utility* for a particular individual.

One prescriptive theory of decision making we consider is called subjective utility theory (Hogarth, 1987). People will always choose the alternative that optimizes their subjective utility. That is to say, if we know a person's subjective value of each alternative, we can predict that person's choice. This seems like nothing more than a truism, but in fact, subjective utility fails in many common decision-making situations. People in many cases tend to violate logical consistency in their choices in everyday life.

We will consider subjective utility theory in the context of risky decision making. In many cases, our decision involves taking a chance on some uncertain event. If we are invited to dinner, we might speculate on (evaluate) the quality of the dinner and conversation. To compare this alternative to some other, therefore, requires some estimated value of the dinner alternative. Chance is an important factor in the estimation. If we know that our potential host has a good reputation for high quality dinner parties, then there is a good chance of a high quality dinner and, therefore, justification for giving the dinner alternative high value.

When the outcomes are uncertain, subjective utility theory translates into expected utility theory. The rational decision maker should maximize the expected gains. In order to compute expected gains, the decision maker must compute both the probability of an alternative and its subjective utility. In the dinner invitation example, it is necessary to estimate the likelihood of a good dinner and the actual utility of the dinner. If the probabilities and utilities are represented numerically, it is possible to compute the expected utility in any given choice situation. Consider the case in which a good dinner is expected 5 times out of 10 or with a probability of .5. A poor dinner is expected half the time or with a probability of .5. The value of a good dinner is $10, whereas the value of a poor dinner is $1. The expected utility, EU, of this alternative is

$$EU = [P \text{ (Good Dinner) x Value of Good Dinner]}$$
$$+ [P \text{ (bad dinner) x Value of Bad Dinner]}$$
$$= .5 \text{ x } \$10 + .5 \text{ x } \$1$$
$$= \$5 + \$.50 = \$5.50$$

The utility of the dinner alternative over the long run is $5.50. This would be the utility of this alternative which would be compared to the utilities of other alternatives in the situation.

Now consider the situation in which a person has two dinner invitations: the invitation given above and one in which there is a certainty of a mediocre dinner with a value of $6. Faced with these alternatives, the person maximizing expected utility would always accept the second invitation since the expected utility of the certain but mediocre dinner is slightly greater. However, travelers don't always stop at chain restaurants, where the food is highly predictable but mediocre. They are willing to take a chance even though they are disappointed often enough. Therefore, expected utility theory may not capture what people actually do in risky decision-making situations.

This simple example illustrates a limitation of expected utility theory. The expected utility alone is assumed to predict decisions. The variability associated with an expected outcome should not influence the decision. In the universe of dinners, people prefer a small gamble over a sure thing even if the expected utility of the sure thing is somewhat greater. In the universe of money, we prefer the more predictable situation when the odds are in our favor. The economist Paul Samuelson gives an illuminating anecdote in this regard (Samuelson, 1963; Lopes, 1981). He offered a good gamble to a colleague: two to one odds on a single coin flip for $100. If heads, Samuelson would pay $200; if tails, the colleague would pay $100. The colleague refused because it would hurt to lose $100, even if the odds were in your favor. However, the colleague made a counteroffer: 100 flips of the same coin for $1 a flip. Just the foggiest notion of probability informs us that this latter gamble is a sure thing. One won't win as much as $200 but one won't lose either. With two to one odds, the colleague would have to win only 34 or more of the 100 flips to make money. Although the expected utility might be greater for Samuelson's original offer, we prefer the more predictable and safer course of action.

Value of Money

Consider a choice between a sure thing of winning $80 versus winning $100 with probability of .85 and winning nothing with probability of .15. The expected utility of the first alternative is $80 whereas the expected utility of the second is $85. Thus, subjects should choose the second alternative but they don't. Now consider a choice between a sure thing of losing $80 versus losing $100 with probability of .85 and losing nothing with probability of .15. The expected utility of the first alternative is -$80 whereas the expected utility of the second is -$85. Therefore, subjects should choose the first alternative, because in the long run it is less costly than the second alternative. Once again, subjects will tend to choose the "wrong" alternative by taking the gamble of losing $85.

In fact, a simple modification can explain these apparent violations of expected utility theory. Bernoulli (1738/1967) proposed that the subjective value of money is not equivalent to its objective value. A linear increase in money does not produce a linear increase in value. If a gift of $10 increases your happiness a certain amount, a gift of $20 falls short of doubling your increase in happiness. The subjective value of money is a decreasing function of its objective value (Kahneman & Tversky, 1982).

It turns out that the subjective value of money can explain the results that supposedly violated expected utility theory. Consider the choice between a sure thing of winning $80 versus winning $100 with probability of .85 and winning nothing with probability of .15. In terms of the subjective value of money, what must $80 and $100 be worth to a subject to explain choosing the sure thing (i.e., to have expected utility theory predict the choices that are made)? If the value of $80 is more than 85% of the value of $100, then the subject made the optimal choice. Assume that $100 dollars is worth just $70 to the subject. To predict the choice of the sure thing, the value of $80 must be greater than 85% of $70 or greater than $59.50. That is, if $80 is worth $60 and $100 is worth $70, then expected utility theory can predict the results. In this case, expected utility theory can be called subjective expected utility theory because the subjective value of money is taken into account.

Integration of Multiple Sources of Information

We have seen that subjects do not appear to evaluate information as prescribed by subjective utility theory. One reason is that apparently other sources of information besides the expected utility are entering into their decision. A fundamental problem is to understand how these multiple sources are combined (integrated) in order to achieve a final judgment. To address this question experimentally, people are given various sources of information and are asked to make some judgment such as a prediction of the most likely state of affairs. As an example, solve the following problem.

> Given four tosses of an unbiased coin, consider the odds of getting the sequence HHTH; the sequence TTTT; or the sequence THTH. Which sequence is most likely and which is least likely?

You may or may not be surprised to learn that these sequences are equally likely. Each of the sequences is unique and, therefore, has a probability of $(1/2)^4$. However, subjects estimate that THTH is more likely than TTTT (Kahneman & Tversky, 1973; Tversky & Kahneman, 1973). This error in judgment might reflect the contribution of other knowledge than simply the sequence probabilities. The subjects also know that the average number of heads in four tosses of a coin is two. This information can influence the decision as well as information about the likelihood of the two sequences. Information about the average would tend to make the sequence with two heads appear more likely than the sequence with four heads.

We tend not to use algorithms specified by the normative principles of probability and statistics in our decision making but we rely on heuristics. An algorithm can be considered a formal routine for solving some computational problem. A heuristic is more similar to a rule of thumb or simple decision rule which requires much less computation than an algorithm. As you might expect, heuristics are reasonable in some situations but lead to severe and systematic errors in others.

Representativeness

One heuristic that many people employ in prediction situations is representativeness (Kahneman & Tversky, 1973). A person will tend to predict an outcome that is most representative of the evidence. People see THTH as more representative of a sequence of four coin tosses than TTTT. Therefore, they will estimate the likelihood of the former sequence as greater than the latter. Kahneman and Tversky (1972) posed the following question:

> All families of six children in a city were surveyed. In 72 families the exact birth order of births of boys and girls was GBGBBG. What is your estimate of the number of families surveyed in which the exact order of births was BGBBBB?

As in our coin tossing example, the two birth sequences are equally likely. Over 80% of the subjects, however, judged the second sequence with five boys and one girl as less likely than the standard sequence. Evaluating the two sequences, the second seems less representative since it fails to reflect the equal proportion of boys and girls in the population. However, the relative proportion of boys and girls is not the only source of information contributing to representativeness. Apparent randomness is also important. People expect the birth sequence to be relatively random. Therefore, subjects judge the frequency of BBBGGG as less likely than the sequence GBBGBG.

The subjects in these experiments were undergraduates, not skilled scientists with knowledge of probability. But even sophisticated psychologists can be influenced by representativeness and hence misjudge the likelihood of an event. This research documents that people do not integrate the sources of information available to them in an optimal manner.

Availability

Another heuristic proposed by Tversky and Kahneman (1973) is that of availability. In their view, people estimate the frequency of a class of events, the likelihood of an event, or the co-occurrences of events by evaluating the ease with which the relevant mental operation to recall these events can be performed. Consider one of the judgments asked of Tversky and Kahneman's subjects.

> The frequency of appearance of letters in the English language was studied. A typical text was selected, and the relative frequency with which various letters of the alphabet appeared in the first and third positions in words was recorded. Words of less than three letters were excluded from the count. You will be given several letters of the alphabet, and you will be asked to judge whether these letters appear more often in the first or in the third position, and to estimate the ratio of the frequency with which they appear in these positions. Do this for the letters k, l, n, r, and v.

All of these letters tended to be judged as being more frequent in first than in the third position. The median ratio estimate for each of the letters was about 2:1. In actual fact, all of these letters are more frequent in the third position. According to the availability heuristic, a person answers the question by thinking of words that begin with the letter and of words that have the letter in third position. It is easier to think of words that start with a particular letter than of words that have that letter in third position. The judgment of frequency follows from the assessed availability of words in each of the two categories. Therefore, people mistakenly conclude that certain letters are more frequent in initial position since words beginning with these letters are easier to recall.

It is important to note that the authors did not use vowels in their test. Vowels tend to be more frequent in third than in initial position. Would subjects also mistakenly judge just the opposite? There are two reasons that they may not. First, people may realize that the typical letter patterning in English is consonants at the beginning and ending of words with vowels somewhere in the middle. In this case, they might judge vowels to be more frequent in third than in initial position. Secondly, we may be able to retrieve more words with vowels in third than in initial position. These possibilities make viable another interpretation of the original findings. Subjects may realize that words usually begin with consonants and, therefore, judge the particular consonants as more frequent in initial position. Subjects may have used this knowledge in making their judgment. Even if this alternative explanation is correct, however, availability seems to be an important heuristic in judgment.

Prior Odds

The concept of availability is also relevant to the weight people give direct experience as opposed to prior odds. Consider the following problem faced by Kahneman and Tversky's (1972) subjects.

> Consider two very large decks of cards, denoted A and B. In deck A, 5/6 of the cards are marked X, and 1/6 are marked O. In deck B, 1/6 of the cards are marked X, and 5/6 are marked O. One of the decks has been selected by chance, and 12 cards have been drawn at random from it, of which 8 are marked X and 4 are marked O. What do you think the probability is that the 12 cards were drawn from deck A, that is, from the deck in which most of the cards are marked X?

A second group of subjects was asked to solve the same problem when the population proportions 5/6 and 1/6 were changed to 2/3 and 1/3, respectively. The results showed no effect of the proportion of cards marked X. The true odds of the sample in the two versions of the task can be computed using Bayes theorem (Chapter 16). Using Bayes theorem, the true odds is the probability that the sample came from deck A divided by the sum of the probability that it came from deck A and the probability that it came from deck B. In this case, the odds that the sample came from deck A is .998 with a population proportion of 5/6 and .941 with a population proportion of 2/3. Other experiments of this type show that subjects are influenced by the actual number of X's and O's in the sample.

The results of experiments of this type reveal that people tend to weight the actual sample and tend to ignore the prior odds (Kahneman & Tversky, 1972). Thus, one of the sources of information is not contributing as much as it should to the judgment. This result is surprising when contrasted with how easily subjects are influenced by a priori probability in the signal-detection task (Chapter 12). If a signal is more likely to occur than noise, subjects report that a signal was presented more often. Increasing the likelihood of a signal influences both the hit rate and the false alarm rate.

People are not always oblivious to prior odds in decision-making situations, however. Imagine a subject faced with the following task (Leon & Anderson, 1974). There are two transparent plastic bags of white and red beads. There are 100 beads in each bag. In addition to seeing the bags, the subject sees the specified proportion of red and white beads written above each bag. For example, the subject might see 80/20 over the left bag and 20/80 over the right bag. The subject would then be told the composition of the sample which was drawn from one of the bags. The sample consisted of a number of red and white beads. The task is to guess which bag was sampled on that trial.

Figure 6 presents the mean likelihood of choosing one of the bags as a function of the composition of the sample and the specified proportion of red and white beads in the two bags. As can be seen in the figure, both the composition of the sample and the prior odds influenced the judgment. Subjects were more likely to choose the bag with the greater proportion of red beads as the number of red beads in the sample increased. In addition, the judgment was highly sensitive to the prior odds. Subjects were more likely to choose the bag with the best prior odds as the prior odds of this bag over the other bag increased. The interaction between the sample composition and prior odds reflects the fact that value of the sample depends on prior odds. If the bags contain an equal number of red and white beads, then any sample is completely uninformative. These results reveal that people do use prior odds in decision making.

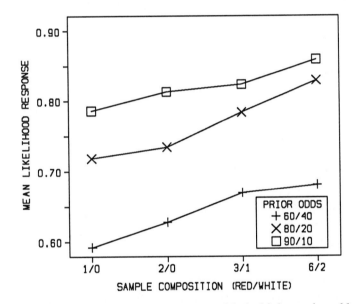

Figure 6. The mean likelihood of choosing the bag with the highest prior odds as a function of the prior odds of the two bags and the sample composition (number of red/white beads) drawn from the urn (results from Leon & Anderson, 1974).

A critical methodological difference between the two lines of research involves the use of between-subject versus within-subject designs (Birnbaum & Mellers, 1983). In the typical judgment task showing no effect of prior odds, a subject is given only one problem. In the signal-detection task and in the experiments of Leon and Anderson (1974), a subject is tested repeatedly with different levels of prior odds. When subjects are given repeated trials in the probability-judgment task and tested with different prior odds, effects of prior odds are found. It is clear that we cannot conclude that subjects use or do not use prior odds, but that we must specify the conditions under which this source of information is used.

For example, most people feel that there is a higher likelihood of being mugged in New York City than in San Francisco. In actual fact, the likelihood of any particular person being mugged in the two cities is not much different. However, New York has a much bigger population and the overall frequency of muggings is much greater there than in San Francisco. People call to mind the number of muggings they have heard about (or experienced) and do not weight these by prior odds.

Since the absolute number of muggings is dependent on population size, the town with a larger population is more likely to acquire a worse reputation. In this case, prior odds does not play as much of a role as it should. On the other hand, most people feel more likely to win a prize in a small local raffle than in a large state lottery. In this case, prior odds are psychologically real. As in the experimental studies, there is no easy generalization about the use of prior odds in real life. Its strong effects in signal detection (Chapter 12) and categorization (Chapter 16), however, reinforces the important role that prior odds plays in psychological processing.

Experience and Logic

People tend to reason from specific experiences and not from mathematical logic. Consider an experiment carried out by Hamill, Wilson, and Nisbett (1979). Subjects observed videotapes of an interview of a person alleged to be a guard at a state prison. Subjects were told that this guard was typical or atypical of guards at the prison. In a third condition, no information was given about typicality. The second independent variable was the nature of the interview; in one case, the guard was humane; in the other case, the guard was brutish. Subjects were then asked to rate how humane the prison guards were in that prison. The nature of the interview was the only determinant of the ratings; typicality information had no effect.

Given this research, one might conclude that people trust their senses and are skeptical of abstract, theoretical, or mathematical information. An exception to this conclusion is a seminal result from Asch (1951). He asked a subject to choose the longest of a set of lines, after observing the choices of a number of other subjects (actually confederates in collusion with the experimenter). The confederates picked a shorter line and the subject tended to agree with this choice. Social influence in the form of the opinions of colleagues encourages people to report a line that is *seen* as shorter as the longer line. The choices of the confederates might be viewed as another source of information that has an impact on the judgment. It would be interesting to provide information about prior odds in the form of social influence to evaluate whether this would enhance the effect of prior odds. For example, would a subject be influenced in line judgment in the same way if he or she were simply told that seven other students saw the shorter line as longer?

Our belief about likelihood is at least partially determined by heuristics such as availability or representativeness. The biases that may be introduced by these heuristics might be corrected in various ways. As an example, persons asked to judge the probability of a certain event such as divorce might adjust their estimates downward when they realize that they have recently observed a few divorces. Or faced with two sources of evidence, prior knowledge and immediate experience, people might remember the natural tendency to give more weight to the latter. Finally, faced with what seems to be an orderly set of events, it is wise to remember that these events could have resulted from a completely random process. Awareness of the heuristics used in human judgment is a first step towards correcting likely errors resulting from these heuristics.

PROBLEM SOLVING

We became acquainted with some aspects of problem solving in Chapter 5. We stated there that the scientific process was problem solving and we discussed a few properties of human problem solving. People form hypotheses about a state of affairs and seek to confirm these hypotheses in their generation and evaluation of new information. This confirmation bias can lead to illogical thinking and interpretations. Accordingly, the problem solver must be on guard for this bias and attempt to remain objective in the quest for a solution.

People are curious and problem solving will be central to human conduct, regardless of the electronic computer revolution. A computer serves as an extension of human memory, not as a substitute for analytical thought, judgment, and decision making. The computer's large memory allows for a fuller evaluation of the relevant facts which should better optimize what we learn from these facts. Rather than generalizing from a few incidents of accidents in the various methods of generation of electricity, we can perform an exhaustive analysis of the accident history of all forms of electricity generation. In this way, we can provide a more direct assessment of the advantages and disadvantages of hydroelectric versus nuclear power or some alternative means. The computer not only allows an analysis of the past, it can be programmed to predict the future. That is, we can generate highly probable states of affairs given certain courses of action. With this information, we as decision makers are better informed about the potential consequences of our actions.

What motivates people to spend endless hours seeking new knowledge or even rediscovering what is already known? To say that the consequences of such action are rewarding seems circular; in many cases, the rewards of discovery are never obtained. It is the process itself that is rewarding. Consider the recent fascination of millions of people with Rubik's cube. Rubik's cube is a large cube made up of a 3 x 3 x 3 matrix of connected cubes with each exposed side of a cube painted one of six colors. The cubes can be moved in a limited number of directions, and the goal is to align the cubes to give a solid color on each of the six sides of the large cube. From one perspective, what could be more frivolous than attempting to line up the cubes to produce solid sides of color? Try it for a few minutes. More likely than not, you will be seduced and you will find yourself devoting many hours to the problem. I know many practical and sensible people who have devoted hundreds of hours to this "worthless" project.

Anagrams

Consider the rather straightforward task of solving an anagram problem. A string of letters is presented and the goal is to rearrange the letters to form an English word. To get the feel for this type of task, try to solve the anagram *TERALBAY*.

When faced with such a task, we seem to try out various combinations of letters until a word is discovered. Find a clock that measures time in seconds and find a solution to the anagram *TARIL*. What word did you find and how long did it take? Previous research has shown that *TRAIL* is the easiest answer and takes about 7 seconds. The answer *TRIAL*, on the other hand, is more difficult with a solution time of about 4 minutes. The easier solution requires the transpositions of just the letters *A* and *R*, where *TRIAL* requires the rearrangement of three letters. We might expect that solutions requiring the rearrangement of even more letters would take even longer.

What other variables might be expected to influence the solution to anagram problems? Needless to say, easy access to a large vocabulary should be helpful. Anagrams are similar to the game of mystery word or hangman in which people must guess a word by guessing one letter at a time. If they are correct, the letter is indicated in the appropriate position in the mystery word. Consistent with this belief, there is evidence that people with more skill in retrieving and recalling words are better at solving anagrams (Mendelsohn, Griswold, & Anderson, 1966; Greeno, 1978). Other evidence for the importance of lexical retrieval comes from studies which show facilitation of anagram solutions when the solution words are primed sometime earlier. To prime a word, subjects read the solution words or read words associated with the solution words (Dominowski & Ekstrand, 1967).

Top-down or goal-directed processing might also be functional in anagram solutions. Familiar words are more easily discovered than unfamiliar words (Mayzner & Tresselt, 1966). Given an anagram like *letab*, the more frequent solution word *table* is usually discovered before the less frequent solution word *bleat*.

Knowledge of our orthography—rules of spelling—should also be important for a rapid solution to an anagram. It would be wasteful to consider letter combinations that don't occur in

English. For example, considering sequences beginning with *TL*, *RT*, or *RL* would be fruitless in solving *TARIL*. Readers know these are illegal sequences even though they haven't checked all the words that they know. Therefore, some sequences can be rejected before lexical retrieval is attempted. This makes for more efficient solution. Evidence for this component in anagram solution comes from a study by Ronning (1965), who found that anagrams with a larger number of permissible letter combinations are more difficult to solve. Anagrams with only a few permissible combinations are solved more easily (Ronning, 1965).

The frequency of occurrence of letter patterns also appears to be important for anagram solution. Words with frequent letter combinations are solved faster than words with infrequent letter combinations. Thus, *nacrh* is solved more quickly than *fekin*. (The solutions are *ranch* and *knife*, respectively.)

The anagram problem makes apparent some essential components of a problem solving situation. The subject begins with an initial knowledge state and seeks to arrive at a goal state by way of intermediate operations. The intermediate operations take the subject through a series of new knowledge states. (We refer to the stages involved in creative problem solving in Chapter 1.) The intermediate knowledge states in solving a problem can sometimes be revealed by an introspective protocol analysis (see Chapter 2). Here the subject talks out loud while she is solving the problem. Table 6 illustrates a subject's protocol in the solution of the anagram *TERALBAY*. As can be seen in this protocol, the intermediate states are critical to a solution in that the letter rearrangements can be considered as successive approximations to a solution. Given the limitations of short-term memory, having some of the letters in their correct positions is necessary to see a solution. Rearranging all of the letters from *TERALBAY* to *BETRAYAL* in one step is beyond the processing power of most individuals. (However, some people such as Dick Cavett are wizards at anagrams and other letter games such as pantomimes and may be able to leap to solutions without intermediate arrangements.)

Table 6. A subject's protocol for the solution of an anagram (from Cohen, 1971).

Response	Subject's Protocol
0. TERALBAY	"Hmmmmm!"
1. AALBERTY	"I thought they ought to be alphabetized."
2. RALBATEY	"Fooling around. No idea."
3. TEABLARY	"Still no idea."
4. TEARABLY	"Another variation."
5. RATEABLY	"The *ably* in TEARABLY suggested that the word might end in *ably*. Many words do."
6. YARTABLE	"Maybe the word ends in *able* which is similar to *ably*."
7. RAYTABLE	"I don't know. I'm hunting for a word ending in *able*."
8. TRAYABLE	"This isn't a word either."
9. LATRAYBE	"Maybe the word has something to do with *tray*."
10.	"I have it!" (Solution given in text.)

The findings of a "tip of the tongue" phenomenon (Chapter 17) offers an interpretation of the codes used in solving anagrams. Rearranging the letters of the anagram provides both orthographic (spelling) and phonological (speaking) codes for achieving word recognition. It is well known that regular and easy to pronounce anagrams require longer solution times than irregular and unpronounceable anagrams (Ekstrand & Dominowski, 1965). This result might mean that subjects waste time trying to achieve lexical access when the anagram is pronounceable. Figure 7 illustrates a process model of the anagram task. Given the anagram, the subject evaluates whether the spelling could be an English word. If the anagram passes this test, lexical access is attempted. Otherwise, the letters are rearranged and evaluated once again. If lexical access occurs, the spelling of the word is checked against the anagram for correctness. A correct spelling gives a solution word whereas an incorrect spelling sets the subject back to point zero. In terms of this model, a pronounceable anagram encourages the subject to attempt lexical access which leads to a longer solution time relative to an unpronounceable anagram.

Using a speech code can help achieve lexical access in the anagram task (Fink & Weisberg, 1981). Given an anagram, subjects were also given a bigram that was pronounced either correctly or incorrectly. As an example, prior to the presentation of the anagram *BLAOR* (*labor*) subjects saw the bigram *LA* and heard it pronounced as "lay." Another group of subjects heard *LA* pronounced as "lah." The subjects were told whether the pronunciation was correct or incorrect. Another group of subjects was given the bigram *LA* without any pronunciation whatsoever. The results revealed that the subjects given the correct pronunciation solved the anagram more quickly than either of the other two groups of subjects. The latter two groups took nearly identical times for solution. This result shows that a speech code can aid lexical access and decrease the anagram solution time.

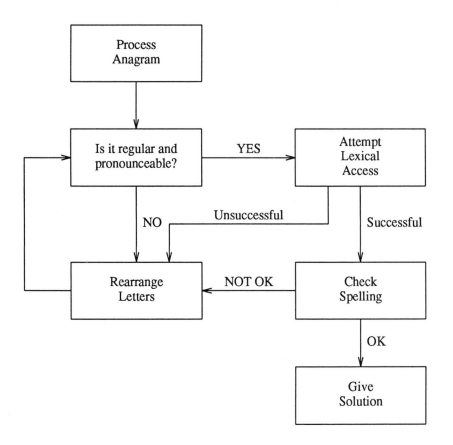

Figure 7. A process model of solving an anagram problem.

Although an anagram task might seem to be relatively artificial, it illustrates some basic principles of perception and cognitive processing (Mayer, 1983):

1. The fewer operations required, the less time needed to reach solution. (Given *taril*, *trail* requires only one change between *a* and *r*, which is easier than the two consecutive changes needed to find *trial*.)

2. Familiarity influences perception and memory. We more easily perceive, remember, and retrieve familiar relative to unfamiliar objects. (Given *letab*, *table* is easier to see than *bleat*.)

3. Psychological processing is intelligent in that people can terminate unproductive strategies for solution. Given a rearrangement of the letters of a test string that produces inadmissible letter strings, lexical access is *not* attempted, nor are other letters in the string rearranged. Given the anagram *taril* and the student tries *tlair*, he or she immediately changes the first letter or two without attempting lexical access or rearranging the final three letters. (Results show that anagrams that can only be arranged on a few admissible letter combinations are easier to solve.)

4. If the anagram is made somewhat meaningful, discovery of the solution word can be delayed. Experience is limited to a single, meaningful event at any moment. Seeing a meaningful anagram slows down the discovery of another meaningful arrangement of the letters. (Going from *cause* to *sauce* is more difficult than going from *erten* to *enter*.)

5. Processing is often guided by what we expect to experience. If subjects are given anagrams that all have food items as solutions, processing is speeded up relative to a complete set of solution words. (It is easier to solve *limk* if the subject knows that the solution is a food or drink than if the set of potential solutions is unconstrained.)

Heuristics versus Algorithms

In our discussion of solutions to anagrams, we have taken it for granted that people use heuristics to solve the problem. A heuristic strategy might be considered as a few rules of thumb that when applied will usually lead to a solution. However, sometimes heuristics will fail. Solutions are guaranteed if an algorithm is used. An algorithm is an exactly prescribed set of operations which will lead to a solution. One algorithmic solution to the anagram problem is to generate every possible sequence of letters and test each combination for its lexical status. This can be highly wasteful since we know many combinations are not possible words. In addition, a 5-letter anagram has 5 factorial or 5! = 5 x 4 x 3 x 2 x 1 = 120 unique letter combinations. Although inefficient, this algorithm guarantees a solution if the solution word is in the problem solver's lexicon. The heuristic method is unsystematic and may not lead to a solution because subjects may simply fail to try out the solution combination.

GAME PLAYING

We might expect that thinking and decision making are important processes in playing games such as chess, go, bridge, or othello. Although these processes are important, we find that perception and memory are equally central to complex skills such as game playing. A Dutch chess player, de Groot, performed a seminal set of studies of skilled and novice chess players. His initial hypothesis was that these two classes of players would have fundamentally different thought processes in playing the game. In fact, de Groot was unable to find any differences in the heuristics and algorithms utilized by the two classes of players. As an example, masters search through about the same number of possibilities as weaker players, and the depth of search (how many future moves are considered) is about the same for players of highly different skill levels. What de Groot was able to conclude was that masters don't do things all that differently, but simply come up with better moves than their weaker colleagues.

Skilled Players

Skill in chess is reflected in performance on a relatively simple task, memory for chess positions. De Groot's players viewed a chess position for 5 seconds and then reconstructed the position from memory. Masters could reconstruct the board almost perfectly, whereas the less-skilled players could recall only a few pieces. One apparent hypothesis is that skilled chess players have better memories than do less-skilled players. To test this idea, de Groot replicated the memory study, but now placed the pieces on the board randomly. If memory was responsible in the first study, then masters should show a similar advantage with random pieces. However, they did not. A critical attribute of chess masters appears to be their encoding and storage of meaningful chess positions. This result is analogous to the advantage of well-structured letter strings over poorly structured strings. Faced with a regular sequence of letters, a reader can encode it meaningfully. If the sequence is not regular, the sequence has to be encoded and remembered letter by letter. A nonreader would have equal difficulty with regular and irregular sequences. Weak chess players are still nonreaders (or early readers) using this analogy.

Given that chess positions can be interpreted in highly organized and meaningful ways by chess masters, it is of interest to discover the meaningful units or chunks that are used. Chase and Simon (1973) replicated the studies of de Groot and devised a way to evaluate the meaningful relationships used by chess players at different levels of playing skill. The central idea was that the players might be expected to reconstruct the chessboard in meaningful units. That is, all of the pieces of one unit (or chunk) would be placed before moving on to another chunk. The authors used both the memory task used by de Groot and a perception task, in which the test board remained in view during the player's reconstruction of an answer board. The authors hypothesized that the players in the perception task would encode a chunk or two and then reconstruct these pieces before encoding additional pieces. Therefore, successive glances from the test board to the answer board should reveal what chunks were being used. For the memory task, the authors believed that pieces within a chunk should be placed on the answer board relatively rapidly, whereas the time between placing the last piece from one chunk and the first piece from the next chunk should be relatively long. If I ask you to recall both your phone number and that of a close friend, the time between digits within each of the numbers would be very short, whereas the time between digits from the two different phone numbers would be relatively long.

Chase and Simon (1973) videotaped the reconstruction of the chess positions, and used the time between successive piece placements as the dependent variable. These time intervals between piece placements were used to evaluate the hypothesis that long pauses would correspond to boundaries between different chunks. Short pauses would indicate pieces belonging to the same chunk. The time between the placement of chess pieces, called the interpiece interval, was analyzed as a function of the pieces that were placed within or between glances in the perception task. The interpiece intervals were much shorter for within-glance than for between-glance placements. For the memory condition, the analysis is less straightforward because there is no external index of successive glances at the original test board. One question is whether the subjects appear to be performing the memory task in a similar manner as the perception task. One answer is provided in terms of a comparison between the interpiece intervals in the two conditions of the experiment. Very similar interpiece intervals were found in the two conditions, supporting the idea of similar performance in the perception and memory tasks.

The authors concluded that interpiece intervals greater than two seconds indicated a boundary between two chunks. Therefore, the chess relations within a chunk should be revealed by analyzing the combinations of pieces that were played. The authors defined the chess relations *attack, defense, same color, same piece,* and *proximity.* One interesting finding was that the three subjects of varying skill levels showed the same kinds and degrees of relatedness between successive pieces. Although beyond the scope of the present discussion, the results were informative about the relationships and structures that chess players perceive and utilize in playing chess.

We still don't know why skilled chess players show better memory for meaningful board positions than their less-skilled colleagues. Chase and Simon (1973) proposed that a master player has more pieces per chunk, but the same number of chunks as a weaker player, which is within the short-term memory span. However, their results showed that the master recalls both more pieces per chunks and a larger number of chunks. Given that the interpiece intervals cannot be expected to be direct indices of chunks, the authors are to be applauded for making headway in a difficult and murky problem.

Short-Term Memory

Chase and Simon's (1973) conclusion located one difference between skilled and unskilled chess players at the level of short-term memory. Recall that masters supposedly have a larger number of chunks and more pieces per chunk in short-term memory for a meaningful board position. However, two independent experimental tests provided negative evidence for this hypothesis. Charness (1976) reasoned that, if chunks are held in short-term memory, then rapid forgetting should be found with an interpolated task in the Peterson and Peterson paradigm (see Chapter 14). The author compared immediate recall of a board position with recall after a 30-second interval. Chess players either rehearsed, avoided rehearsal, shadowed random digits, performed a running addition task, or mentally rotated and copied abstracted symbols. Relative to the immediate recall and rehearsal conditions, the interpolated tasks produced only about 7% of interference. In addition, the various forms of interpolated activity did not differ in terms of the amount of interference with memory. If the board position was being held in short-term memory, we should have seen much greater forgetting with interpolated activity, and a large influence due to the nature of the interpolated activity.

Frey and Adesman (1976) found equally damaging evidence to the short-term memory explanation. They reasoned that, if a board position was held in short-term memory, then requiring a chess player to remember a second board position would be highly disruptive to memory for the first. The analogy here would be, given one new telephone number to remember, a person is immediately given a second number to remember. Chess positions were shown on 35 mm photographic slides. Either a single slide was presented, or two successive slides were presented. Each chess position was presented for 8 seconds. After presentation, subjects counted backwards by sevens for 3 or 30 seconds. At the beginning of recall, subjects were cued to recall just one of the board positions. This was done to eliminate output interference—recall of one position might interfere with the memory for the other position, whereas the experimental question was how much was remembered about each position at the end of the counting period.

The dependent variable was the number of pieces placed correctly in reconstruction of the board position. Table 7 shows that recall was better when only one position was presented than when the chess player was required to remember two positions. Also, recall was slightly better after 3 seconds than after 30 seconds of counting. What is striking, however, is the finding that chess players can remember many more pieces than indexed by recall of a single board position. Using the logic of Sperling (1960) in determining the number of items available, the subjects had about 20 pieces at recall when given two board positions to remember. That is, they were able to recall 10 pieces from whichever board position was cued for recall. Given that the chunk size, according to Chase and Simon's results, is only slightly larger than two pieces, the estimate of 20 pieces or 10 chunks far exceeds the capacity of short-term memory. These results and those of Charness (1976) provide strong evidence against a short-term memory explanation of a skilled chess player's accurate reconstruction of a chessboard. Similarly, children who are skilled chess players can remember more chess pieces than adult novices. We wouldn't want to say that the children have a larger short-term memory than adults.

Table 7. Number of pieces reconstructed correctly in the recall of a single chess position as a function of presentation condition and the direction of interpolated counting.

Presentation	Duration of Counting	
	3 seconds	30 seconds
1 board	13.1	11.6
2 boards	10.3	9.5

Knowledge and Memory

The good memory of a skilled chess player should not be too surprising. If a person recalls a 10- or 15-word sentence verbatim or even two such sentences, we are not overly impressed. Even more to the point, we don't analyze the results in terms of the number of distinct letters or sounds recalled. A skilled chess player's knowledge imposes higher-order meaning on a meaningful board position, and only this higher-order meaning has to be recalled. Chess players are not remembering particular pieces any more than is our subject remembering letters or sounds. The conclusion to be reached from this research is that highly skilled performance in games, or in other domains, involves the utilization of overlearned patterns in perception and memory. Just as the reader sees the meaning of "Jane went to the store to buy milk and eggs," and not the individual letters, the skilled chess player sees meaningful game positions and not individual pieces.

19

Understanding Speech

Sound

Sine Waves
 Amplitude
 Frequency
 Phase

Complex Sound Patterns
 Power Spectra

The Ear

Speech Sounds
 Voiced
 Voiceless
 Formants
 Vowel Sounds
 Consonant Sounds

Speech Perception

Perceptual Units in Speech
 Phonemes
 Consonant Recognition
 CV Syllables
 Recognition Masking

Categorical Perception
 Experimental Example
 Experimental Studies

Theories of Word Recognition
 Logogen Model
 Cohort Model
 TRACE Model
 Autonomous-Search Model

Linguistic Context
 Detecting Mispronunciations
 Limitations of Results
 Gating Task
 Integrating Sentential Context

Acoustic Features
Phonemes and Professor
 Backwards

. . . speech perception is a perceptual constancy; that is, that
it involves interpreting an acoustic object in terms of background
information that the hearer brings to the perceptual process.
J. A. Fodor, T. G. Bever, and M. F. Garrett (1974)

Speech perception and music appreciation are the most impressive demonstrations of auditory information processing. Consider the spoken sentence: "He was seen running from the scene of the obscene crime." By what rules do we process these sounds, so that we are able to discriminate not only the different sounds in the sentence, but also the three different meanings of one sound? In time experimenters hope to accumulate enough understanding of each of the simpler component processes of auditory perception to begin to describe the complex operations by which we perceive such a sentence.

SOUND

The stimulus that the auditory system processes is an atmospheric sound wave. The atmosphere is composed of small particles that are highly sensitive to the motion of the other particles around them. When one particle is displaced from its stable resting position, and thus moves closer to a neighboring particle, the two particles are said to be in a state of compression. In this state they repel each other. The second particle moves away, and its direction is the same as that of the original motion of the first particle. The first particle, however, is in the meantime compelled by this state of compression to reverse its direction and move back towards its original position.

At some point the two particles are farther away from each other than normal; a state of rarefaction now exists between them, and they are drawn back together. Thus, the motion of any particle influences its neighbor, and the motion induced in its neighbor influences the first particle in turn, so that the two oscillate in close relation to each other. Meanwhile, the motion of the second particle has set a third one to oscillating, which in turn affects a fourth, and so on until the motion of the air particles adjacent to the ear pushes the eardrum back and forth.

Consider the schematic diagram presented in Figure 1. As the prong of a vibrating tuning fork moves out from its resting position, it pushes a neighboring air particle ahead of it, and the return movement of the prong toward the center of the fork sets up a state of rarefaction that draws that particle back with it. The oscillation of the prong induces a corresponding oscillation in this neighboring air particle. Next to the neighboring particle, particle A, is particle B. As the outward moving prong drives A toward B, a point is reached at which A and B repel each other. A moves back, pushed by its reaction against B and drawn by the returning prong, while B moves outward, repelled by A. Eventually A and B are in a state of rarefaction and are attracted toward one another again; meanwhile the outward push of B has set in motion particle C. Gradually the original motion of the tuning fork prong is transmitted to one particle after another, until the particles adjacent to the ear receive it, and the eardrum is pushed back and forth in the same way.

The representation of such a periodic motion over time is a sine wave. Think of an oscillating particle as a pencil point resting on a sheet of paper. The paper is being drawn along at a constant rate in a direction perpendicular to the direction of particle movement. The particle will describe a continuous line in the form of a wave back and forth across the stable position of the particle. This is the sound wave pattern, a representation over time of the motion that is reproduced in particle after particle until it reaches the ear. Note that it is the movement pattern that flows from the sound source to the receptor, not the particles themselves. On the contrary, the particles simply oscillate around their original distance from the source (see Figure 1).

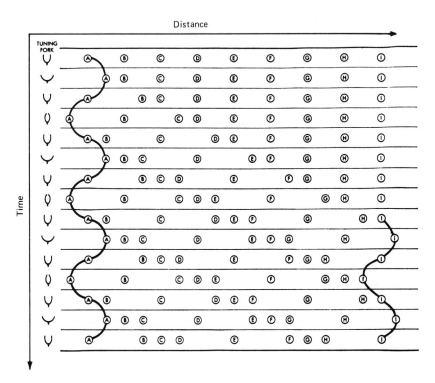

Figure 1. The propagation of a sine wave along the particles of the atmosphere (after Denes & Pinson, 1963).

The tuning fork prong is actually surrounded by adjacent air particles, so that each of these particles carries the message to its neighbors, and the sound radiates in concentric circles from the source. The speed at which the message is transmitted from particle to particle is the velocity of sound. The velocity is dependent on the atmospheric pressure; in our atmosphere at sea level, sound travels 1130 ft per second, or 770 miles an hour.

SINE WAVES

One way to think of a wave is to imagine a man running around a circle painted on the floor of a dark room. A light attached to the top of the man's head throws a small circle of light onto the wall behind him as he runs. Suppose that we place a roll of photographic paper horizontally on the floor next to the wall and have a student pull it upward at a constant rate. The paper is sensitive to light and dark so that it records the tracing of the light reflected by the man. As the man runs around the circle, the light reflected on the paper moves back and forth, and because the paper is moving upward, the light describes a wave upon it. The design recorded on the paper will be a sine wave pattern as shown in Figure 2. The amplitude of the sine wave, or the height of the wave's crest measured from the center, is equal to the radius of the circle. As we increase the radius of the circle we increase the amplitude of the sine wave. Analogously, the amplitude of an oscillating air particle varies according to the amount of energy expended in the oscillation. A sound source of great energy displaces air particles far from their resting position, and the amplitude of the sound wave is correspondingly large. A very faint sound stimulus displaces the air particles by only a small distance, and the amplitude of the sound wave is therefore very small.

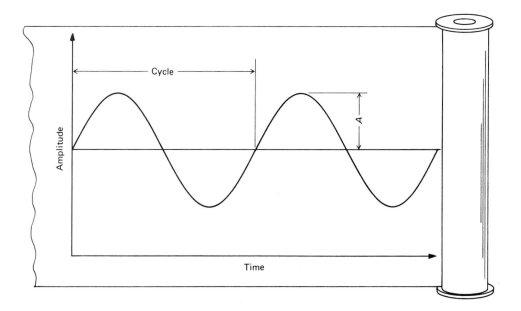

Figure 2. Sine wave pattern. The amplitude of the wave is given by A. The frequency is measured by the number of complete cycles per unit of time. The phase is the position in the wave cycle with respect to the beginning of the cycle.

Amplitude

The amplitude of a sound wave is given by its sound pressure, which is the amount of force acting over a unit area and is measured in dynes per square centimeter (dynes/cm^2). One dyne is the amount of force required to give a mass of 1 gram an acceleration of one cm/sec^2. (The computed sound pressure is actually the amount of pressure change in the oscillations of the air particles.) We can hear sounds within the range of roughly .0002 to 2000 dynes/cm^2. Since this scale contains a range on the order of a million units, a smaller, more useful scale has been devised. The measure used is a decibel (dB), which specifies the sound pressure of a sound stimulus relative to some reference sound pressure level. The amplitude in decibels of a sound stimulus is given by the equation

$$A = 20 \log_{10} \frac{P_1}{P_0}$$

where P_1 is the sound pressure of the sound stimulus and P_0 is the sound pressure of a reference sound pressure level, usually taken as .0002 dynes/cm^2. Using this measure, the range of audible sound can be expressed within the range of 140 dB. Every time the sound pressure is increased by a factor of 10, we add 20 dB. Changes in amplitude primarily affect the perceived loudness of the sound pattern. Speech is normally in the range of 60 to 80 dB.

Frequency

The second property by which the sound wave can be described is its frequency. If the man in the dark room runs very slowly—perhaps pondering how he got into this situation—he may complete a circuit only once a minute. If he then begins to run twice as fast, he will complete two full circuits in a minute and describe two wave cycles on the moving paper in the same space as had earlier been required for only one. The frequency of the sound wave then is equal to the number of complete cycles traced out by the running man per unit of time. It corresponds to a measure of the rate of oscillation of the air particles per unit of time.

The frequency of sine waves is measured in cycles per second, technically referred to as hertz (Hz) after the nineteenth-century German physicist. Sound patterns can usually be heard if they have sine waves in the range of 20 to 20,000 Hz. The psychological experience of pitch quality is primarily determined by the frequency of the wave. The musical note middle C is roughly 261 Hz, and A above middle C is 440 Hz. The musical scale is an octave scale; a note that is an octave higher than another note is twice its frequency. When a note is played on most musical instruments, sound pressure variations are also present at the frequencies that are some multiple of the frequency of the note. These frequencies are called harmonics of the fundamental note.

Phase

The final dimension of the scene of the man running around the circle is his position at any point in time. The position can be described independently of the amplitude and the frequency by specifying the number of degrees traversed from the beginning of a wave. Accordingly, position or phase is a measure of position in a wave and can vary between 0 and 360 degrees. A phase of 90 degrees corresponds to a point on the positive crest of a wave.

COMPLEX SOUND PATTERNS

The pure tones generated by a tuning fork are described by true sine waves, making their description very easy. However, most sound patterns are represented by much more complex waves. The French mathematician Fourier showed that any complex wave could be analyzed into component sine waves. By the method of Fourier analysis, then, one can both break down and rebuild complex waves into the sine waves whose amplitude and frequency can be specified precisely. Figure 3 shows a complex wave broken down into its component sine waves.

Power Spectra

Another method of representing a complex sound pattern is in terms of its power spectrum. The power spectrum plots the amplitude of the component waves on the ordinate as a function of their frequency on the abscissa. Figure 4 shows the power spectrum of a musical note of 261 Hz played by a violin. The power spectrum is not only a simpler method of representing complex sound patterns; it is also in a sense more accurate. We do not perceive sounds continuously, that is, we do not attach meaning to each small change in the continuous wave pattern. Rather, we perceive a set of discrete meaningful units such as musical notes or speech syllables. This means that the power spectrum of short sound patterns sometimes represents sound as we perceive it more accurately than does the continuous wave representation. Somehow the auditory system

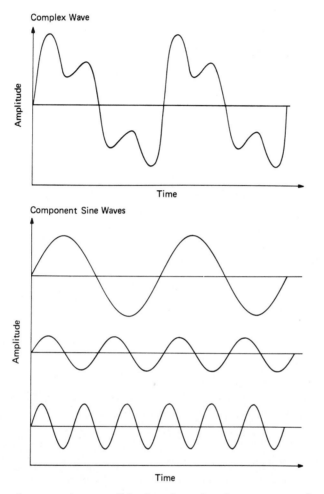

Figure 3. A complex wave (top panel) broken down into its component sine waves (bottom panel). Adding together the three component sine waves will give the complex wave.

preserves the sound pattern over some finite chunk of time and we perceive that segment of the sound pattern as a unitary whole, or a gestalt.

White noise, with which we are familiar as radio static, is a complex sound that has some interesting properties. When analyzed into its component sine waves, white noise will be found to have its energy distributed evenly throughout all the frequencies within its frequency spectrum. The wave shape and power spectrum of a white noise pattern is shown in the top panel of Figure 5. Other sounds such as the /sh/ sound in the bottom panel of the same figure usually have much of their energy concentrated within certain frequency ranges of the frequency spectrum.

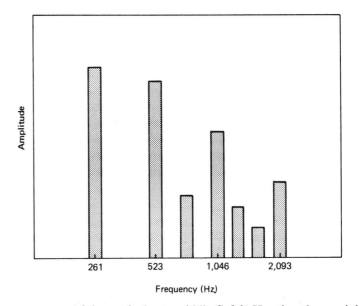

Figure 4. Power spectrum of the musical note middle C, 261 Hz, played on a violin.

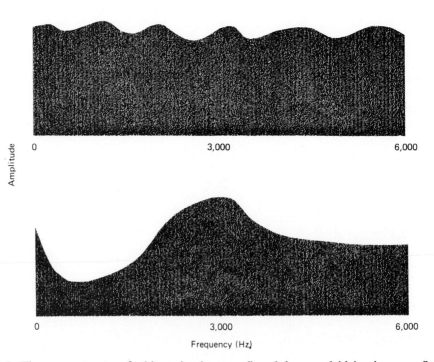

Figure 5. The power spectra of white noise (top panel) and the sound /sh/ as in *sugar* (bottom panel).

THE EAR

When the atmospheric pressure variations reach the potential listener, they pass through the auditory canal and set the eardrum into motion (see Figure 6). The auditory canal not only funnels the pressure vibrations but also amplifies certain sound waves because of its resonance properties. The phenomenon of resonance refers to one body being set into motion by the vibrations of another. One body resonates to the vibrations of another when they have the same natural frequency of vibration. For example, a tuning fork will resonate to the vibrations of another fork equal to it in frequency. The ear canal amplifies sound near its natural resonance, which lies between 3000 and 4000 Hz. In fact, we seem to be most sensitive to sounds within this frequency range.

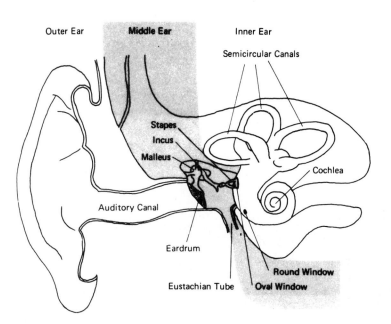

Figure 6. The ear.

The vibrations of the eardrum set into motion the three components of the middle ear that provide the mechanical linkage to the inner ear. The malleus is rigidly attached to the eardrum so that motions of the eardrum are carried to the incus and to the stapes which covers the entrance to the inner ear. The middle ear also amplifies the signal from the eardrum to the inner ear in two ways. First, the components of the middle ear function as a lever mechanism, which produces a greater force at the stapes than that applied at the malleus. Second, the total force of the stapes is applied over a much smaller area than the area at the eardrum. The amplification of the signal in the middle ear increases our sensitivity to pressure variations by roughly a factor of 1000.

The stapes carries the message to a bone opening of the inner ear called the oval window. Vibrations from the stapes set into motion the membrane of the oval window—the entrance into the cochlea—a cavity which resembles a snail's shell. The cochlea contains the basilar membrane with its attached hair cells. The vibrations of the oval window set the fluid in the cochlea into motion, producing wave motion in the basilar membrane. The vibration pattern along the membrane causes neural activity in the fibers connected to the hair cells on the membrane. The transformation of the mechanical vibrations into nerve impulses takes place here. These impulses then stimulate fibers of the auditory nerve which carries the message to the brain.

SPEECH SOUNDS

Humans make a variety of speech sounds, and these can be described by the phonetic symbols given in Table 1. For example, the vowel sound in *read* is referred to as i. The sounds of speech are a direct consequence of the manner in which the sound is produced by the human vocal apparatus. The speech organs, illustrated in Figure 7, are the lungs, the trachea, the vocal cords, the larynx, the pharnyx, the mouth, and nasal cavity. The sound pattern depends on three factors: 1) a source of energy, 2) a vibrating body, and 3) a resonator. The steady stream of air coming from the lungs and trachea when we exhale, provides the source of energy for speech sounds. This original stream of air is given its specific character during its passage past the vocal cords and through the resonating cavities of the vocal tract—the pharyngeal, oral, and nasal cavities.

Table 1. Table of phonetic symbols.

Phonetic Symbol	Key Word	Phonetic Symbol	Key Word
i	eve	d	day
I	it	k	key
ɛ	met	g	go
æ	at	h	he
a	father	f	for
ɔ	all	v	vote
ʊ	foot	θ	thin
u	boot	ð	then
3	word	s	see
ʌ	up	z	zoo
ə	about	ʃ	she
eI	say	ž	azure
aI	I	tʃ	church
ɔI	boy	dž	judge
aʊ	out	m	me
oʊ	go	n	no
Iu	new	ŋ	sing
p	pay	j	you
b	be	r	read
t	to	l	let
x	loch	w	we

Voiced

The vocal cords are two elastic folds of tissue controlled by movable cartilages in the back wall of the larynx. The opening between the two cords can be controlled by changing the position of the cartilages. In the voicing position, the vocal cords vibrate with the air stream as it flows past. The frequency of vibration is controlled by the size of the vocal folds and their degree of tension. The frequency of the vocal fold vibration determines what we perceive as the individual pitch

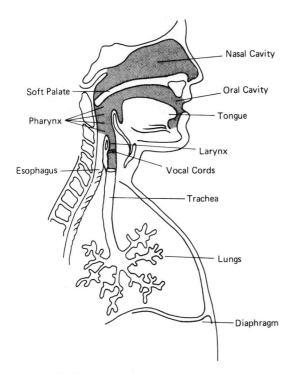

Figure 7. The human vocal organs.

quality of a speaker's voice. Generally, males have lower voices than females since the mass of the male vocal folds is usually larger than its female counterpart. Similarly, we have all noticed an increase in the pitch of a person's voice when he becomes excited. Excitement increases the tension of the vocal folds, which in turn increases their rate of vibration in the same way the tension of a guitar string determines its pitch quality.

Figure 8a shows the pressure variations in the breath stream caused by vibration of the vocal cords. The frequency of vibration varies between 60 and 350 Hz in normal speech. The wave shape in Figure 8a is called periodic because the pattern of pressure variations repeats itself over time. The pattern repeats itself at the rate of the vocal cord vibration. As mentioned earlier, a complex sound pattern such as the one in Figure 8a can be represented in terms of its power spectrum, which presents the frequencies and amplitudes of the component sine waves. (The power spectrum of the wave in Figure 8a is given in Figure 8b.) The largest frequency component corresponds to the rate of vibration of the vocal cords and is called the fundamental frequency. Frequencies of the other components are integer multiples of the fundamental frequency, called harmonics of the fundamental. The second harmonic is twice the fundamental frequency, the third is three times the fundamental, and so on. The amplitude of the harmonics decreases as the harmonics get large at the rate of 12 dB/octave. In this instance, the amplitude of the second harmonic is 12 dB less than the fundamental, the amplitude of the fourth harmonic is 24 dB less than the fundamental, the amplitude of the eighth harmonic is 36 dB less than the fundamental, and so on.

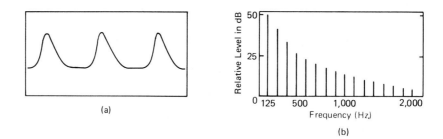

Figure 8. The pressure variations in the breath stream during a voiced sound and its power spectrum.

Voiceless

In a second position of the vocal cords, they do not vibrate with the air stream flowing past. In this case, speech sounds are produced by producing turbulence in the air stream during its passage through the vocal tract. For example, the sound /sh/ is produced by forcing the outgoing air stream at a high enough velocity through a constriction formed by the tongue and the roof of the mouth. The wave shape produced by the sound source when the vocal cords do not vibrate is aperiodic since no regular pattern exists in the sound wave. Because the wave shape is not periodic but is highly irregular, the waves contain all frequencies rather than just the harmonics of a given fundamental. All components have roughly equal intensity, defining the sound source as white noise comparable to radio static.

The wave shape of both voiced and voiceless sounds is modified by its passage through the throat, oral, and nasal cavities, which together make up the upper vocal tract. The vocal tract extends from the vocal cords to the lips, a distance of about 17 cm. As we see in Figure 7, the width of the tract is variable and can be changed by placement of the lips, jaw, tongue, and soft palate. The soft palate controls the passage of air through the nasal cavity, which is about 12 cm long. The vocal tract functions as a series of resonance chambers which respond differentially to sounds of different frequencies. Each resonator has a preferred or natural resonance frequency. Two different violins playing the same note will have different pitch qualities because the inevitable differences in the physical composition of the violins produce different natural resonances.

Formants

The amplitude of component frequencies which are equal to or near the natural frequency of the resonator is amplified (reinforced) whereas other frequencies are attenuated (dampened). The shape of the vocal tract, analogous to the shape of the violin, determines which frequencies will be reinforced or dampened. Hence, the final sound wave is uniquely determined by the shape of the vocal tract. These natural resonances of the vocal tract are called formants. Since the resonances change with changes in the shape of the vocal tract, each configuration of the vocal tract has its characteristic formants.

The sound source and its modification by the vocal tract can be approximated by a two-stage process. The sound which can be periodic or aperiodic passes through the vocal tract and is modified depending on its shape. These two components can be varied independently to produce different sounds. For a fixed sound source, we can change the speech sound by changing the configuration of the vocal tract. Conversely, for a fixed shape of the vocal tract, we can modify the speech sound by changing the sound source, for example, from periodic to aperiodic. The sounds /s/ as in *see* and /z/ as in *zoo* are articulated with very similar configurations of the vocal tract. However, the sound source in /s/ is aperiodic, whereas the sound source for /z/ is produced by vibrating the vocal cords. Figure 9 shows that the power spectra of the sounds are different. The fact that /s/ has some energy across the entire frequency spectrum gives its noise-like quality. The speech sound /z/, on the other hand, is much more tone-like, since most of the energy is concentrated at the formant frequencies.

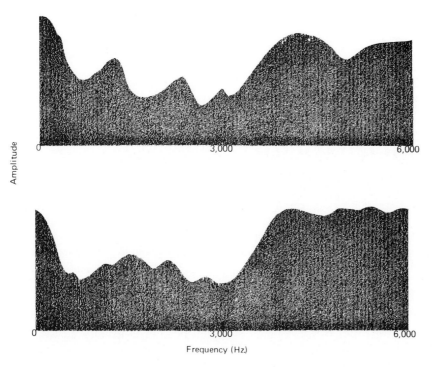

Figure 9. Power spectra of /z/ as in *zoo* (top panel) and /s/ as in *see* (bottom panel).

For voiced sounds produced with a periodic sound source, the overall shape of the power spectrum is a function of the configuration of the vocal tract and is relatively independent of changes in the frequency of vocal fold vibration. Figure 10 presents the wave patterns and power spectra of the vowel /ah/ pronounced with two different rates of vocal cord vibration (90 and 150 Hz). The vertical lines in the power spectra give the amplitude at the fundamental and harmonic frequencies. Connecting these lines, we get the same overall shape for both sounds. In this case, the formant frequencies indicated by the spectral peaks are the same under both frequencies of vibration. These peaks, of course, correspond to the natural resonances of the configuration of the vocal tract in producing the sound /ah/.

Vowel Sounds

The sounds of speech can be divided between the two classes of vowels and consonants. Vowels are spoken with a relatively fixed configuration of the vocal tract and the vocal folds are vibrated with the outgoing breath stream. The exact vowel sound is produced by the position of the

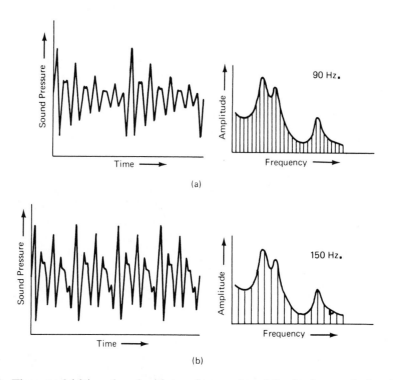

Figure 10. The sound /ah/ produced with two frequencies of the fundamental, showing that the power spectrum is relatively invariant with respect to changes in the fundamental (after Denes & Pinson, 1963).

tongue in the mouth. Tongue position is usually described according to the location of the tongue and the height of the highest part of the tongue. Tongue location is usually classified as in the front, central, or back part of the mouth. The highest point of the tongue can be in the high, middle, or low part of the mouth within each of these three regions. Figure 11 presents the configuration of the vocal tract during the articulation of some vowel sounds.

Because the shape of the vocal tract and the resulting vowel sound does not change much over time, it is convenient to represent the vowel sounds in terms of their respective power spectra. Figure 11 also presents the power spectra of the vowel sounds. The peaks of energy in the power spectra correspond to the formants of the vowel. That is to say, the frequencies of the natural resonances of the vocal tract are determined by the shape of the vocal tract. For vowels, the primary determinants of the first and second formants are the location and height of the tongue.

Consonant Sounds

Consonant sounds are more complex than vowels for a number of reasons. One reason is that, unlike vowels, a number of consonants cannot be spoken in isolation. For example, try to articulate the consonant /d/ as in *dog* without an accompanying vowel. In the articulation of /d/, we actually say a consonant-vowel syllable. The consonant must, therefore, be isolated out of the consonant-vowel syllable. The articulation of consonants can be described according to three attributes: the point of articulation, the manner of articulation, and whether or not the vocal cords are vibrated. The point of maximum closure in the vocal tract during articulation of a consonant is referred to as the point of articulation. The manner of articulation describes how the speech sound is produced.

Independent of the point of maximum closure and the manner of articulation, the vocal cords may or may not be vibrated during production of the speech sound.

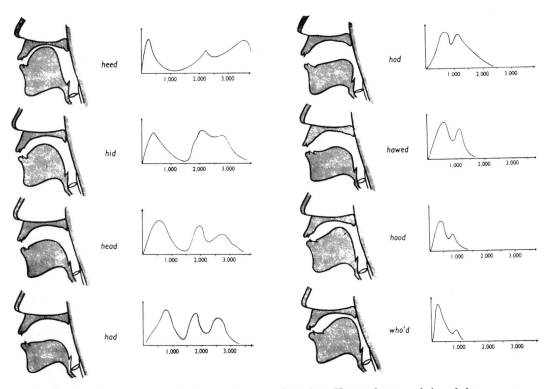

Figure 11. The positions of the vocal organs (based on X-ray photographs) and the spectra of the vowel sounds in the middle of the words *heed, hid, head, had, hod, hawed, hood,* and *who'd* (after Ladefoged, 1962).

The consonant sounds in English can be divided roughly into stops, fricatives, nasals, and glides. Stops, sometimes called plosive sounds, are produced by closing the vocal tract completely (usually with the lips or tongue), building air pressure up behind the closure, and then suddenly opening the closure. The stop consonants in English are /b, p, d, t, g/ and /k/. In fricative sounds, such as /s/ or /f/, the vocal tract is only partially closed at some point and the air forced through the constriction produces a unique fricative sound, depending on the point of constriction and whether the vocal folds are also vibrating. Nasal sounds such as /m/ and /n/ are produced when the breath stream is allowed to pass through the nasal cavity (by lowering the soft palate) as well as through the oral cavity. Finally, the glides are characterized by changing the point of articulation during their production. The sound source for the glides is accompanied by vocal cord vibration and the vocal tract is relatively open, giving the glides such as /l/ and /r/ vowel-like properties.

In representing consonant sounds or a series of speech sounds, the power spectrum is no longer sufficient since it loses temporal information. For sounds that change over time, or for a sequence of sounds, it would be convenient to represent the sound in a successive sequence of power spectra. This is accomplished by a sound spectrograph, specifically developed for the visual representation of speech sounds across time. A spectrogram plots the amplitude of each of the component frequencies over time. Time is represented on the horizontal axis and frequency is

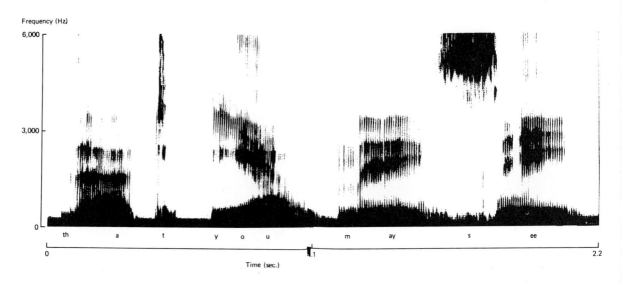

Figure 12. Sound spectrogram of the phrase, "That you may see." The phrase lasts roughly 2.2 sec—the standard duration of a spectrogram.

represented on the vertical axis. The amplitude is indexed by the relative blackness of the coordinate points. Figure 12 presents a spectrogram of the sound sequence from the popular example phrase, "That you may see." Although we hear a word boundary between "may" and "see," the spectrogram in Figure 12 shows that there is very little silence between the two words. In fact, there is more silence during the "at" portion of the word "that" than there is between the words "may" and "see."

The acoustical signal specifying a particular linguistic unit is also context sensitive: acoustic properties of a unit found in one context are significantly modified in another. Figure 13 shows spectrograms of the syllables /di/ (as in *deed*) and /du/ (as in *do*). The acoustic signal corresponding to the initial /d/ sound is significantly different in these two syllables. This example shows that perceptual recognition of the consonant /d/ must take into account the surrounding vowel context. The important properties of the /d/ sound differ as a function of the following vowel and an accurate recognition process must take into account the different vowel contexts.

SPEECH PERCEPTION

The noted psychologist George Miller (1981) observed that language and speech are a special gift. If speech is a gift, it is a recent gift. Only a quarter of a million years ago, our ancestors could not speak in the manner to which we are accustomed. Neanderthal man had a short neck, high larynx, and a small immobile throat. These physical characteristics precluded production of the vowels /i/ as in *heat*, /a/ as in *father*, and /u/ as in *boot*.

Language requires not only production, but also perception and understanding. Speech perception can be described as a pattern-recognition problem. Given some speech input, the perceiver must determine which message best describes the input. An auditory stimulus is transformed by the auditory receptor system and sets up a neurological code in a preperceptual auditory storage. This storage holds the information in a preperceptual form for roughly 250 msec,

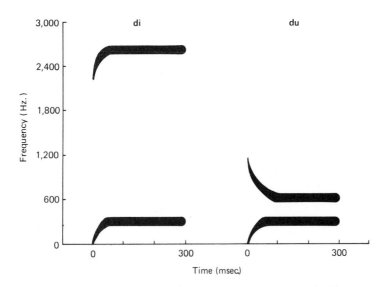

Figure 13. Spectrographic patterns that are heard as /di/ and /du/. The vowel /i/ is pronounced as the word *deed* and the vowel /u/ as in the word *do*.

during which time the recognition process must take place. The recognition process transforms the preperceptual image into a synthesized percept. One issue given this framework is, what are the patterns that are functional in the recognition of speech? These sound patterns are referred to as perceptual units.

PERCEPTUAL UNITS IN SPEECH

One reasonable assumption is that every perceptual unit in speech has a representation in long-term memory, which is called a prototype. The prototype contains a list of acoustic features that define the properties of the sound pattern as they would be represented in preperceptual auditory storage. As each sound pattern is presented, its corresponding acoustic features are held in preperceptual auditory storage. The recognition process operates to find the prototype in long-term memory which best describes the acoustic features in preperceptual auditory storage. The outcome of the recognition process is the transformation of the preperceptual auditory image of the sound stimulus into a synthesized percept held in synthesized auditory memory. Figure 14 presents a schematic diagram of the recognition process.

According to this model, preperceptual auditory storage can hold only one sound pattern at a time for a short temporal period. Recognition masking studies have shown that a second sound pattern can interfere with the recognition of an earlier pattern if the second is presented before the first is recognized (Chapter 15). Each perceptual unit in speech must occur within the temporal span of preperceptual auditory storage and must be recognized before the following one occurs for accurate speech processing to take place. Therefore, the sequence of perceptual units in speech must be recognized one after the other in a successive and linear fashion. Finally, each perceptual unit must have a relatively invariant acoustic signal so that it can be recognized reliably. If the sound pattern corresponding to a perceptual unit changes significantly within different speech contexts, recognition could not be reliable, since one set of acoustic features would not be sufficient

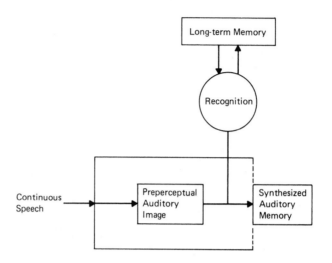

Figure 14. A schematic diagram illustrating the recognition process in speech transforming a preperceptual auditory image into synthesized auditory memory.

to characterize that perceptual unit. Perceptual units in speech as small as the phoneme or as large as the phrase have been proposed.

Phonemes

The first candidate we consider for the perceptual unit is the phoneme. Phonemes represent the smallest functional difference between the meaning of two speech sounds. Given the word *ten* we can change its meaning merely by changing the consonant /t/ to /d/. The two sounds form two different words when they are combined with *-en*; they are therefore different phonemes. On the other hand, sounds are said to be within the same phoneme class if substitution of one for the other does not change the meaning of the sound pattern. One example is the word *did*. The two *d*'s in the word are not the same acoustically and, if their sound patterns were extracted and interchanged with each other, the word would not sound the same. Yet they are not functionally different since interchanging them should still give the word *did*. In this case, they are called different allophones of the same phoneme. Thus, if the substitution of one minimal sound for another changes the meaning of the larger unit, then the two sounds are phonemes. If such substitution does not change the meaning of the larger unit, then the different sounds are allophones of the same phoneme class.

Consider the acoustic properties of vowel phonemes. Unlike some consonant phonemes, whose acoustic properties change over time, the wave shape of the vowel is considered to be steady-state or tone-like. The wave shape of the vowel repeats itself anywhere from 75 to 200 times per second. In normal speech, vowels last between 100 and 300 msec, and during this time the vowels maintain a fairly regular and unique pattern. It follows that, by our criteria, vowels could function as perceptual units in speech.

Acoustic Features

Determining the acoustic features utilized in speech perception is a relatively complicated affair because the speech signal is complex. One approach to the study of the acoustic features used in vowel perception follows the general procedures of multidimensional scaling (Chapter 12). The different vowels are characterized by having their peaks of energy, called formants, at different frequencies. Therefore, the acoustic features utilized in vowel perception could be the frequency location of their formants. The question is the extent to which each of the vowel formants contributes to vowel recognition, that is to say, which vowel formants are critical acoustic features in vowel recognition.

Klein, Plomp, and Pols (1970) had 50 people pronounce 12 different vowels in a b-vowel-t context. The test vowels were obtained by removing 100 msec segments of the steady-state vowel sound. In order to describe the physical properties of these vowels, the investigators measured the sound intensity across the audible frequency spectrum and determined the location of formant frequencies for each of the vowels. The next step was to obtain perceptual judgments of the vowels. Observers identified each of the 100 msec vowel segments as one of the 12 alternatives, getting 74% correct. The critical dependent variable in this test, however, is a measure of the confusion errors between vowel stimuli. To the extent that a listener confuses one vowel for another, it can be said that these vowels are perceptually similar. According to our analysis, this implies that similar vowels share or have in common a number of acoustic features.

Now the task was to determine if the location of the formant frequencies of the vowel stimuli could describe the perceptual confusions between the vowels. The results indicated that locations of the first two formants were critical for vowel perception. That is to say, two vowels were confused with each other to the extent that the first two formant frequencies of the vowels were similar. This study provides one example of how confusion errors in a recognition task can be utilized to determine what stimulus features are used in perception.

Consonant Recognition

Next let us consider consonant phonemes. Consonant sounds are more complicated than vowels and some of them do not seem to qualify as perceptual units. We have noted that a perceptual unit must have a relatively invariant sound pattern in different contexts. However, some consonant phonemes appear to have different sound patterns in different speech contexts. Figure 13 shows that the stop consonant phoneme /d/ has different acoustic representations in different vowel contexts. Since the steady-state portion corresponds to the vowel sounds, the first part, called the transition, must be responsible for the perception of the consonant /d/. As can be seen in the figure, the acoustic pattern corresponding to the /d/ sound differs significantly in the syllables. Hence, one set of acoustic features would not be sufficient to recognize the consonant /d/ in the different vowel contexts. Therefore, we must either modify our definition of a perceptual unit or eliminate the stop consonant phoneme as a candidate.

CV Syllables

There is another reason why the consonant phoneme /d/ cannot qualify as a perceptual unit. In the model perceptual units are recognized in a successive and linear fashion. Research has shown, however, that the consonant /d/ cannot be recognized before the vowel is also recognized. If the consonant were recognized before the vowel, then we should be able to decrease the duration of the vowel portion of the syllable so that only the consonant would be recognized. Experimentally, the duration of the vowel in the consonant-vowel syllable (CV) is gradually decreased and the subject is asked when she hears the stop consonant sound alone. The CV syllable is perceived as a complete syllable until the vowel is eliminated almost entirely (Liberman, Cooper,

Phonemes and Professor Backwards

All of us have participated in language games. One of the most popular is some form of pig Latin, in which words are modified before being spoken. People's potential for mastering this type of modified language was impressed upon my colleagues and me by a professor of philosophy who could speak backwards (Cowan, Leavitt, Massaro, & Kent, 1981). For obvious reasons, we refer to him as Professor Backwards. Upon discovery, it was obvious that Professor Backwards was performing a unique skill and it was necessary to determine exactly what it was that he was able to do. Although he had some idea of what he did, it was necessary to assess it objectively. Accordingly, the researchers evaluated his ability to speak backwards and forwards in a variety of situations. He was asked to repeat back (shadow) what someone else was saying, to read, and to give an extemporaneous dialogue, all in backwards speech. These vocalizations were then analyzed to determine the nature of the backwards speech and the manner in which it was spoken backwards.

Professor Backwards was asked to reverse about 250 words and a linguistic analysis was made of his reversed speech. One question of particular interest is the units that are reversed. Words might be reversed letter by letter, syllable by syllable, or simply the root and the affixes of a word might be reversed. In fact, Professor Backwards usually reversed the phonemes in a word. Consider the word *bet*. It contains the phonemes /b/, /ɛ/, and /t/. A reversal of the phonemes would produce the pseudoword *teb*. In many cases, a reversal word violated the manner in which phonemes are sequenced in English and the reversed speech sounds foreign. For example, the word *bold* was reversed *dlobe*; however, the phoneme sequence /dl/ does not occur in initial position in English.

It was also important to observe that Professor Backwards reversed the actual sounds of the words and not the letters that spelled the words. For example, the silent /s/ in *island* was not pronounced in his reversed speech. In addition, the same letters were pronounced differently when they represented different sounds (as in the soft *c* in *city* and the hard *c* in *cut*). Homographs were also pronounced as would be predicted from their spoken version and not their spelling.

The investigators were interested in whether Professor Backwards had exceptionally good perceptual or memory skills. He did not appear to be exceptional in basic skills such as sensitivity to hearing fine distinctions in sounds or an extraordinary memory. Also, it was of interest to determine if he could speak backwards as easily as forwards. He can not. It was found that backwards speaking took more processing capacity and effort and that he was slower and less accurate in backwards than in forwards speech. For example, it took him about 1/5 of a second longer to name a word or picture in backwards than in forwards speech. In summary, this skill might be viewed as the speaker having a second language, although a highly unique one, which is not as natural and well-learned as his native language.

Shankweiler, & Studdert-Kennedy, 1967). At that point, however, instead of the perception changing to the consonant /d/, a nonspeech whistle is heard. Liberman et al. show that the stop consonant /d/ cannot be perceived independently of perceiving a CV syllable. Therefore, it seems unlikely that the /d/ sound would be perceived before the vowel sound; it appears, rather, that the CV syllable is perceived as an indivisible whole or gestalt.

These arguments lead to the idea that the syllables function as perceptual units rather than containing two perceptual units each. One way to test this hypothesis is to employ the CV syllables in a recognition-masking task. Liberman et al., found that subjects could identify shortened versions of the CV syllables when most of the vowel portion is eliminated. Analogous to our interpretation of vowel perception, recognition of these shortened CV syllables also should take time. Therefore, a second syllable, if it follows the first soon enough, should interfere with perception of the first. Consider the three CV syllables /ba/, /da/, and /ga/ (/a/ pronounced as in *father*), which differ from each other only with respect to the consonant phoneme. Backward recognition masking, if found with these sounds, would demonstrate that the consonant sound is not recognized before the vowel occurs and also that the CV syllable requires time to be perceived.

Recognition Masking

There have been several experiments on the backward recognition masking of CV syllables (Massaro, 1974, 1975a; Pisoni, 1972). Newman and Spitzer (1987) employed the three CV syllables /ba/, /da/, and /ga/ as test items in the backward recognition masking task. These items were synthetic speech stimuli that lasted 40 msec; the first 20 msec of the item consisted of the CV transition and the last 20 msec corresponded to the steady-state vowel. The masking stimulus was the steady-state vowel /a/ presented for 40 msec. In one condition, the test and masking stimuli were presented to opposite ears, that is, dichotically. All other procedural details followed the prototypical recognition-masking experiment (see Chapter 15).

Figure 15 shows the percentage of correct recognitions for 8 observers as a function of the silent interval between the test and masking CVs. The results show that recognition of the consonant is not complete at the end of the CV transition, nor even at the end of the short vowel presentation. Rather, correct identification of the CV syllable requires perceptual processing after the stimulus presentation. These results support our hypothesis that the CV syllable must have functioned as a perceptual unit, because the syllable must have been stored in preperceptual auditory storage, and recognition involved a transformation of this preperceptual storage into a synthesized percept of a CV unit. The acoustic features necessary for recognition must, therefore, define the complete CV unit. An analogous argument can be made for VC syllables also functioning as perceptual units.

We must also ask whether perceptual units could be larger than vowels, CV, or VC syllables. Miller (1962) argued that the phrase of two or three words might function as a perceptual unit. According to our criteria for a perceptual unit, it must correspond to a prototype in long-term

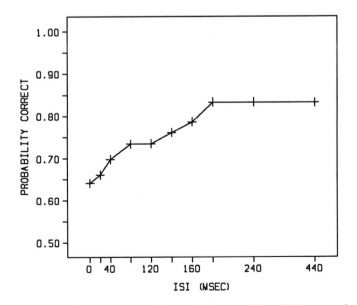

Figure 15. Probability of correct recognitions of the test CV syllables as a function of the duration of the silent intersyllable interval in a backward recognition-masking task (results of Newman & Spitzer, 1987).

memory which has a list of features describing the acoustic features in the preperceptual auditory image of that perceptual unit. Accordingly, preperceptual auditory storage must last on the order of one or two seconds to hold perceptual units of the size of a phrase. But the recognition-masking studies usually estimate the effective duration of preperceptual storage to be about 250 msec. Therefore, perceptual units must occur within this period, eliminating the phrase as the perceptual unit.

The recognition-masking paradigm developed to study the recognition of auditory sounds has provided a useful tool for determining the perceptual units in speech. If preperceptual auditory storage is limited to 250 msec, the perceptual units must occur within this short period. This time period agrees nicely with the durations of syllables in normal speech.

CATEGORICAL PERCEPTION

One persistent and popular belief is that speech is perceived categorically. Perception is said to be categorical if the subject can only make judgments about the name of a stimulus, not its particular sound quality. For example, the same speaker may repeat the same syllable a number of times. The acoustic patterns representing this syllable would differ from each other since a speaker cannot repeat the same sound exactly. A listener who perceives the sounds categorically would not be able to discriminate any difference in the particular sound quality of each repetition of the syllable. The same listener, on the other hand, would be able to recognize a difference between any of these sounds and another syllable spoken by the same speaker. In categorical perception, the listener can recognize differences when the syllables have different names but not when they have the same name. Upon examination of the stimuli, we may find that the acoustic differences were as large when the same syllable was repeated as were the acoustic differences between two different syllables. In this case, we say that discrimination is limited by identification; the observer only discriminates that two sounds differ if she identifies them as having different names.

Subjects certainly are not limited in this way in the processing of nonspeech. They are able to discriminate two tones as different even though they can not differentially label them. This is true for all sound dimensions: subjects can discriminate many more differences than they can identify successfully. This phenomenon, in fact, was one of the observations that convinced George Miller (1956) of the magical number 7 ± 2. Miller observed that although we can make many discriminations along a unidimensional stimulus continuum, we can identify accurately about 7 ± 2 of these stimuli. In this case, discrimination is not limited by identification, since subjects can discriminate differences along a stimulus continuum which they cannot identify absolutely.

Experimental Example

Going back to our hypothetical experiment in the penultimate paragraph, we could provide a set of stimuli by having a speaker repeat the syllables /bæ/ and /dæ/ three times each (the vowel is pronounced as in *hat*). These sounds are recorded and used in our experiment. We must determine whether the subject's discrimination of every pair of sounds is limited by identifying them as "different." Accordingly, we must determine how well she identifies the sounds and, also, how well she discriminates them.

In the first part of the experiment, we present one of the 6 stimuli on each trial and ask the observer to identify it as /bæ/ or /dæ/. We obtain a number of repeated observations by selecting the stimuli randomly from trial to trial for a sequence of many trials. The dependent measure is the percentage of times each stimulus is identified as one of the two alternatives. After this identification task, we present pairs of the stimuli in a discrimination task. On each trial, we present one stimulus followed by a second one and ask the observer to report whether the stimuli were the same or different in sound quality. We warn the subjects to respond on the basis of how the sounds sound, not on the basis of their names. If they notice any difference whatsoever between the two sounds, they should respond "different" even if the sounds have the same name. Also, we tell the subjects that, on 50% of the trials, the two sounds will be different.

In the the example experiment, we simply recorded the sounds from natural speech and did not have specific control over the physical differences in the stimuli. In real life, synthetic speech produced artificially is used to control exactly the stimulus properties. Also, the speech syllables are made to differ from each other along an acoustic dimension or continuum. For example, seven synthetic syllables could be made to change the sound gradually from one syllable into another, for example, from /bæ/ to /dæ/.

Experimental Studies

A number of early studies showed that some speech sounds appear to be perceived categorically. Eimas (1963) used a speech synthesizer to make 13 sounds that ranged from /bæ/ to /dæ/ to /gæ/. Figure 16 shows three of the sounds which are always heard as /bæ/, /dæ/, and /gæ/, respectively. The figure shows that the starting point of the second formant (F_2) transition is the only acoustic difference between the three sounds. Therefore, it was possible to make a sound between /bæ/ and /dæ/ by simply starting the F_2 transition at a point somewhere between the starting points of F_2 for these stimuli. Eimas, in fact, divided the range between the F_2 starting points of /bæ/ and /gæ/ into 11 equal steps, giving him 13 stimuli that differed only with respect to the starting frequency of the second formant. Observers first identified the stimuli as /b/, /d/, or /g/; they were then asked to discriminate them.

In Eimas' study, the subjects always heard the syllables in triads. Subjects were instructed to listen to a complete triad before making their three identification responses. For discrimination, Eimas employed an ABX task rather than a same-different comparison task. In the ABX task, subjects are presented with a sequence of three sounds, A, B, and X, and are asked to state whether the last sound, X, is equal to sound A or to sound B. Unfortunately, the ABX paradigm may encourage the verbal encoding of the stimuli A and B since it would be very difficult to remember their auditory sound quality. Therefore, subjects might simply be performing the ABX discrimination test as if it were an identification test, and we should not be surprised if subjects show poor discrimination of different syllables that have the same name.

Can within-category discriminations be made with stop consonants at all? If so, this would provide evidence that consonants are perceived continuously rather than categorically. Two straightforward demonstrations have shown that subjects can discriminate the auditory differences between stop consonants that are given the same name in identification.

Categorical perception means that if subjects give different stimuli the same label, they cannot discriminate differences among these stimuli. To test this, Barclay (1970) first had subjects identify stimuli along the /bæ/, /dæ/, and /gæ/ continuum. As in previous experiments, subjects were given the alternatives /bæ/, /dæ/, and /gæ/. The subjects consistently labeled three sets of the stimuli as /bæ/, /dæ/, and /gæ/, respectively. The next day, the subjects were brought back, were given a description of the stimuli, and were told that the /dæ/ stimuli lay between /bæ/ and /gæ/. The subjects were then given another identification test with the same stimuli, but were limited to the alternatives /bæ/ and /gæ/. If perception of /dæ/ were indeed categorical, the subjects should not have been able to respond differentially to the stimuli called /da/ on the previous day. We would, therefore, expect a random assignment of the responses /bæ/ and /gæ/ to the /dæ/ stimuli. However, the results indicated that the subjects did differentiate between the different /dæ/ stimuli.

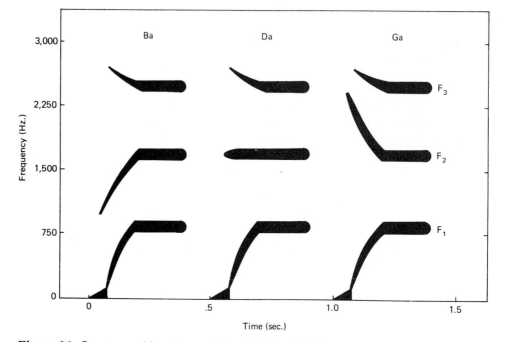

Figure 16. Spectrographic patterns of /bæ/, /dæ/, and /gæ/.

The /dæ/ stimuli near the /gæ/ boundary were more frequently called /gæ/, and the identification response, /bæ/, increased reliably as the /dæ/ stimuli approached the /bæ/ end of the stimulus continuum.

Pisoni and Lazarus (1974) showed that special training and a sensitive discrimination test can eliminate the categorical perception of stop consonants found in ABX tasks after the regular identification task. The special training involved presenting the stimuli in sequential order across the continuum and instructing subjects to listen carefully to the differences between the successive stimuli. The discrimination test involved presentation of two pairs of stimuli; one pair was always the same and one pair was always different. Subjects reported which of the two pairs was the same. These subjects, then, were trained to utilize information in synthesized auditory memory and were given a discrimination test that made it easy to do so. The subjects given the special training showed improved discrimination performance and no categorical perception. Discriminating between sounds that are usually given different names was not significantly better than discriminating between sounds that are usually given the same name.

There have been many demonstrations of continuous perception of speech since these initial studies (Massaro, 1987a; Repp, 1984). Without a doubt, the task of the speech perceiver is to categorize. The child must decide whether the adult said, *Get the ball* or *Get the doll*. However, the decision appears to be based on continuous information provided by the speech signal. As in other domains of categorization discussed in Chapter 16, speech recognition involves the evaluation and integration of continuous, not categorical, features. It is particularly important that the information is maintained in a noncategorical form because it can then be supplemented with other types of information. If the child had insufficient acoustic information to distinguish between *ball* and *doll*, a nod or hand gesture by the speaker toward one of the objects could help disambiguate the instruction. We now turn to the question of how spoken words are recognized.

THEORIES OF WORD RECOGNITION

Although there are several current theories of spoken-word recognition, they can be classified and described fairly easily. All theories begin with the acoustic signal and usually end with access to a word or phrase in the mental lexicon. Four models of word recognition will be discussed to highlight some important issues in understanding how words are recognized. We will review several important characteristics of the models to contrast and compare the models. Figure 17 gives a graphical presentation of these characteristics. One important question is whether word recognition is mediated or nonmediated. A second question is whether the perceiver has access to only categorical information in the word recognition process, or whether continuous information is available. A third consideration is whether information from the continuously-varying signal is used on-line at the lexical stage of processing, or whether there is some delay in initiating processing of the signal at the lexical stage. A fourth characteristic involves parallel versus serial access to the lexical representations in memory. The final characteristic we will consider is whether the word recognition process functions autonomously, or whether it is context-dependent.

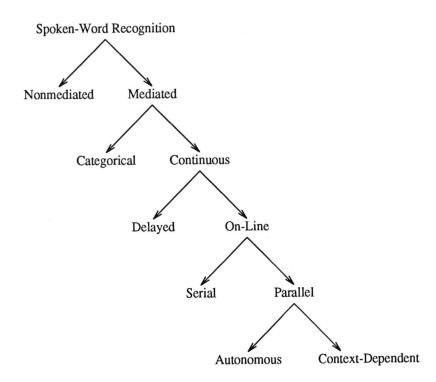

Figure 17. Tree of wisdom illustrating binary oppositions central to the differences among theories of spoken-word recognition.

Logogen Model

The logogen model described by Morton (1964, 1969) has had an important influence on how the field has described word recognition. Morton proposed that each word that an individual knows has a representation in long-term memory. To describe this representation, Morton used the term *logogen*—*logos*, meaning word, and *genus*, meaning birth. Each logogen has a resting level of activity, and this level of activity can be increased by stimulus events. Each logogen has a threshold—when the level of activation exceeds the threshold, the logogen fires. The threshold is a function of word frequency; more frequent words have lower thresholds and require less activation for firing. The firing of a logogen makes the corresponding word available as a response. Figure 18 gives a schematic diagram of the logogen model.

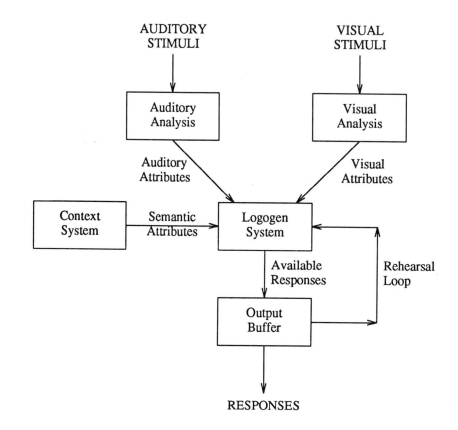

Figure 18. A schematic diagram of the logogen model. Recognition occurs when the activation in a logogen exceeds a critical level and the corresponding word becomes available as a response (adapted from Morton & Broadbent, 1967).

Morton's logogen model can be evaluated with respect to the five characteristics shown in Figure 17. The model is nonmediated because there is supposedly a direct mapping between the input and the logogen. That is, no provision has been made for smaller segments, such as phonemes or syllables, to mediate word recognition. The perceiver of language appears to have continuous information, given that the logogen can be activated to various degrees. On the other hand, one might interpret the theory as categorical because of the assumption of a threshold below which the logogen does not fire. Processing is on-line rather than delayed. With respect to the fourth issue, words are activated in parallel rather than serially. Finally, as can be seen in Figure 18, the logogen allows for the contribution of contextual information in word recognition. Contextual information activates logogens in the same way that information from the stimulus word itself activates logogens. The main limitation in the logogen model is its nonmediated nature. Thus, the model has difficulty explaining intermediate recognition of sublexical units (e.g., CV syllables) and how nonwords are recognized.

/ɛ/	/ɛl/	/ɛl ə /	/ɛl ə f/	/ɛl ə f ə /
aesthetic	elbow	elegiac	elephant	elephant
any	elder	elegy	elephantine	_____
.	eldest	element	_____	(1)
.	eleemosynary	elemental	(2)	
.	elegance	elementary		
ebony	elegiac	elephant		
ebullition	elegy	elephantine		
echelon	element	elevate		
.	elemental	elevation		
.	elementary	elevator		
economic	elephant	elocution		
ecstacy	elephantine	eloquent		
.	elevate	_____		
.	elevation	(12)		
element	.			
elephant	.			
elevate	.			
.	_____			
.	(28)			
entropy				
entry				
.				
.				
extraneous				
.				
_____				
(324)				

Figure 19. Illustration of how the word *elephant* is recognized, according to the cohort model (Marslen-Wilson, 1984). Phonemes are recognized categorically and on-line in a left-to-right fashion as they are spoken. All words inconsistent with the phoneme string are eliminated from the cohort. The number below each column represents the number of words remaining in the cohort set at that point in processing the spoken word. Note that the example is for British pronunciation in which the third vowel of *elephantine* is pronounced /æ/.

Cohort Model

A recent influential model of word recognition is the *cohort* model (Marslen-Wilson, 1984). According to this model, word recognition proceeds in a left-to-right fashion on-line with the sequential presentation of the information in a spoken word. The acoustic signal is recognized phoneme by phoneme from left to right during the word presentation. Each phoneme is recognized categorically. Word recognition occurs by way of the elimination of alternative word candidates (cohorts). Recognition of the first phoneme in the word eliminates all words that do not have that phoneme in initial position. Recognition of the second phoneme eliminates all of the remaining cohorts that do not have the second phoneme in second position. Recognition of phonemes and the elimination of alternative words continues in this fashion until only one word remains. It is at this point that the word is recognized. Figure 19 gives an example illustrating how the cohort model recognizes the word *elephant*.

The cohort model is easy to describe with respect to the five characteristics in Figure 17. The model is mediated, categorical, on-line, parallel, and contextually dependent to some extent. Word recognition is mediated by phoneme recognition, phonemes are recognized on-line categorically, words are accessed in parallel, and the word alternative finally recognized can be influenced by context. The primary evidence against the cohort model concerns the categorical recognition of phonemes. We have seen that phonemes are not perceptual units and the speech perception is not categorical.

TRACE Model

The TRACE model of speech perception (McClelland & Elman, 1986) is one of a class of models in which information processing occurs through excitatory and inhibitory interactions among a large number of simple processing units. These units are meant to represent the functional properties of neurons or neural networks. Three levels or sizes of units are used in TRACE: feature, phoneme, and word. Features activate phonemes which activate words, and activation of some units at a particular level inhibits other units at the same level. In addition, an important assumption of interactive-activation models is that activation of higher-order units activates their lower-order units; for example, activation of the /b/ phoneme would activate the features that are consistent with that phoneme.

With respect to the characteristics in Figure 17, the TRACE model is mediated, on-line, somewhat categorical, parallel, and context-dependent. Word recognition is mediated by feature and phoneme recognition. The input is processed on-line in TRACE, all words are activated by the input in parallel, and their activation is context-dependent. In principle, TRACE is continuous, but its assumption about interactive activation leads to categorical-like behavior at the sensory (featural) level. According to the TRACE model, a stimulus pattern is presented and activation of the corresponding features sends more excitation to some phoneme units than others. Given the assumption of feedback from the phoneme to the feature level, the activation of a particular phoneme feeds down and activates the features corresponding to that phoneme (McClelland & Elman, 1986, p. 47). This effect of feedback produces enhanced sensitivity around a category boundary, exactly as predicted by categorical perception. Evidence against phonemes as perceptual units and against categorical perception is, therefore, evidence against the TRACE model.

Autonomous-Search Model

A fourth model of word recognition is an autonomous-search model of word recognition (Forster, 1979, 1981, 1985). The model involves two stages—an initial access stage and a serial-search stage. This model was developed for the recognition of written words rather than for recognizing spoken words. However, advocates of the model have begun to apply its basic assumptions to spoken-word recognition (Bradley & Forster, 1987). For ease of presentation, we will present the model in terms of recognizing a written word.

The first stage in processing a written stimulus is in terms of recognizing the letters that make up a word. The abstract representation of this information serves as an access code to select some subset of the lexicon. The distinctive feature of this model is that words within this subset must be processed serially. The serial order of processing is determined by the frequency of occurrence of the words in the language. After making a match in the search stage of processing, a verification or post-search check is carried out against the full orthographic properties of the word. If a match is obtained at this stage, the relevant contents of the lexical entry are made available.

The autonomous-search model can be described with respect to the five characteristics in Figure 17. The model is mediated, categorical, on-line, serial, and contextually independent. Written word recognition is mediated by letter recognition, letters are recognized on-line categorically, final recognition of a word requires a serial search. All of this processing goes on without any influence from the context at other levels, such as the sentence level. The autonomous-search model appears to fail on, at least, two counts: categorical perception and contextually-independent processing. We have reviewed evidence for continuous perception and there is convincing evidence for the influence of context in word recognition (see section on Linguistic Context). Some progress has been made in this area, but it is beyond the scope of this book. The interested reader can continue the inquiry by following up on the relevant suggested readings.

LINGUISTIC CONTEXT

There is considerable debate concerning how informative the acoustic signal actually is (Blumstein & Stevens, 1979; Cole & Scott, 1974; Liberman, et al., 1967; Massaro, 1975b; Massaro & Oden, 1980). Even if the acoustic signal was sufficient for speech recognition under ideal conditions, however, few researchers would believe that the listener relies on only the acoustic signal. It is generally agreed that the listener normally achieves good recognition by supplementing the information from the acoustic signal with information generated through the utilization of linguistic context. A good deal of research has been directed at showing a positive contribution of linguistic context (Cole & Jakimik, 1978; Marslen-Wilson & Welsh, 1978; Pollack & Pickett, 1963).

Detecting Mispronunciations

Abstracting meaning is a joint function of the independent contributions of the perceptual and contextual information available. In one experiment, Cole (1973) asked subjects to push a button every time they heard a mispronunciation in a spoken rendering of Lewis Carroll's *Through the Looking Glass*. A mispronunciation involved changing a phoneme by 1, 2, or 4 distinctive features (for example, *confusion* mispronounced as *gunfusion*, *bunfusion*, and *sunfusion*, respectively). The probability of recognizing a mispronunciation increased from 30% to 75% with increases in the number of feature changes, which makes the contribution of the perceptual information passed on by the primary recognition process. The contribution of contextual information should work against the recognition of a mispronunciation since context would support a correct rendering of the mispronounced word. In support of this idea, all mispronunciations were correctly recognized when the syllables were isolated and removed from the passage.

Cole and Jakimik (1978) extended Cole's (1973) mispronunciation task to evaluate how higher-order contextual information can influence sentence processing. To the extent that a word is predicted by its preceding context, the listener should be faster at detecting a mispronunciation. This follows from the idea that the quickest way to detect a mispronunciation is to first determine what the intended word is and then notice a mismatch with what was said. Given the sentences, "He sat reading a *book/bill* until it was time to go home for his tea," mispronouncing the /b/ in *book* as /v/ should be detected faster than the same mispronunciation of *bill*. In fact, listeners were 150 msec faster detecting mispronunciations in highly predictable words than in unpredictable words.

In other experiments Cole and Jakimik (1978) demonstrated similar effects of logical implication. Consider the test sentence, "It was the middle of the next day before the killer was caught," with the /k/ in *killer* mispronounced as /g/. Detection of the mispronunciation should be faster when the text word is implied by the preceding sentence, "It was a stormy night when the phonetician was murdered," compared to the case in which the preceding sentence states that the phonetician merely died. Thematic organization also facilitated recognition of words in their stories. Given an ambiguous story, a disambiguating picture shortened reaction times to mispronunciations of thematically related words but not to mispronunciations of other words that were unrelated to the theme of the story.

Marslen-Wilson (1973) asked subjects to shadow (repeat back) prose as quickly as they heard it. Some individuals were able to shadow the speech at extremely close delays with lags of 250 msec, about the duration of a syllable or so. One might argue that the shadowing response was simply a sound to sound mapping without any higher order semantic-syntactic analyses. When subjects make errors in shadowing, however, the errors are syntactically and semantically appropriate given the preceding context. For example, given the sentence, "He had heard at the Brigade," some subjects repeated, "He had heard that the Brigade." The nature of the errors did not vary with their latency; the shadowing errors were always well-formed given the preceding context.

Limitations of Results

Perceivers have been shown to be efficient exploiters of different types of context to aid in speech perception. Only the autonomous-search model has difficulty in accounting for the contribution of context because it assumes that speech perception goes on without any help of context. Even this model is not necessarily eliminated by the context effects, however, because it can be claimed that the context effects that were observed occurred *after* speech perception. One might argue, for example, that the rapid shadowing errors observed by Marslen-Wilson (1973) occurred at the stage of speech production rather than speech perception. Analogous to research in other domains, it is essential to locate the stage of processing responsible for experimental findings. A new task has helped address this issue and, more importantly, the results can be used to reveal how stimulus information and context jointly contribute to word recognition.

Gating Task

The gating task (Grosjean, 1980, 1985) has been a recent method developed to assess speech perception and word recognition. As indicated by the name of the task, portions of the spoken message are eliminated or gated out. In a typical task with single words, only the first 50 msec or so of the word is presented. Successive presentations involve longer and longer portions of the word by increasing the duration of each successive presentation by 20 msec. Subjects attempt to name the word after each presentation. Warren and Marslen-Wilson (1987), for example, presented words such as *school* or *scoop*. Figure 20 shows that the probability of correct recognition of a test word increases as additional word information is presented in the gating task.

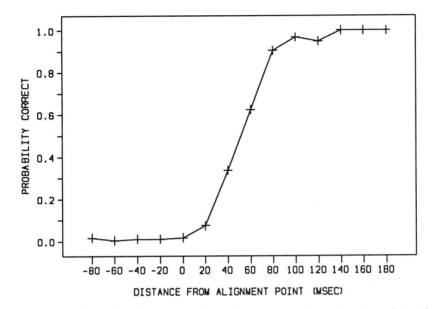

Figure 20. Probability of correct recognition of the test word as a function of the distance from the alignment point in the test word. The alignment point corresponds to a point near the onset of the final consonant of the word (results adapted from Warren & Marslen-Wilson, 1987).

The gating task appears to have promise for the investigation of speech perception and spoken language understanding. Investigators have worried about two features of the gating task that may limit its external validity. The first feature task is that subjects hear multiple presentations of the test word on a given trial. The standard procedure is to present increasingly larger fragments of the same word on a given trial. The subject responds after each presentation of the fragment. The repeated presentations of the fragment may enhance recognition of the test word relative to the case in which the subject obtains only a single presentation of an item. In visual form perception, for example, it has been shown that repeated tachistoscopic presentations of a test form lead to correct recognition, even though the duration is not increased as it is in the gating task (Uhlarik & Johnson, 1978). The same short presentation of a test form that does not produce correct recognition on its initial presentation can give correct recognition if it is repeated three or four times in the task. This improvement in performance occurs even though the duration of the test stimulus was not increased. These repeated looks at the stimulus can lead to improved performance relative to just a single look. Information from successive presentations can be utilized to improve performance and therefore multiple presentations lead to better performance than just a single presentation. Based on this result, performance in the gating task might reflect repeated presentations of the test word, in addition to the fact that the successive presentations increased in duration.

Cotton and Grosjean (1984) compared the standard multiple presentation format with the format in which subjects heard only a single fragment from each word in the task. Similar results were found in both conditions. Salasoo and Pisoni (1985) carried out a similar study and found that the average duration of the test word needed for correct identification was only 5 msec less in the task with multiple presentations on a trial than for a single presentation of the test word. Thus, using successive presentations in the gating task appears to be a valid method to increase the duration of the test word to assess its influence on recognition.

A second question concerning gating tasks has to do with how quickly subjects are required to respond in the task. It could be the case that subjects, given unlimited time to respond in the task, will perform differently from their performance in the on-line recognition of continuous speech. That is, the gating task might be treated as a conscious problem-solving task in which subjects are very deliberate in making their decision about what word was presented. This deliberation would not be possible in a typical situation involving continuous speech and, therefore, the results might be misleading. To assess performance under more realistic conditions, Tyler and Wessels (1985) employed a naming response in the gating task. Subjects were required to name the test word as quickly as possible on each trial. In addition, a given word was presented only once to a given subject. The results from this task were very similar to the standard gating test. The durations of the test words needed for correct recognition were roughly the same as that found in the standard gating task. Thus, the experiments exploring the external validity of the gating task have been very encouraging. The results appear to be generalizable to the on-line recognition of continuous speech.

Integrating Sentential Context

Tyler and Wessels (1983) used the gating paradigm to assess the contribution of various forms of sentential context to word recognition. Subjects heard a sentence followed by the beginning of the test word (with the rest of the word gated out). The word was increased in duration by adding small segments of the word until correct recognition was achieved. The sentence contexts varied in syntactic and semantic constraints. Some sentence contexts had minimal semantic constraints in that the target word was not predictable in a test given the sentence context and the first 100 msec of the target word. Performance in this condition can be compared to a control condition in which no sentential constraints were present. The experimental question is whether context contributes to recognition of the test word.

Figure 21 gives the probability of correct word recognition as a function the number of segments in the test word and the context condition. Both variables had a significant influence on performance. In addition, the interaction between the two variables reveals how word information and context jointly influence word recognition. Context influences performance most at intermediate levels of word information. The contribution of context is most apparent when there is some but not complete information about the test word. The lines in Figure 21 give the predictions of the fuzzy logical model of perception (FLMP) developed in Chapter 16. The FLMP describes word recognition in terms of the evaluation and integration of word information and sentential context followed by a decision based on the outcome. As can be seen in the figure, the model captures the exact form of the integration of the two sources of information.

A positive effect of sentence context in this situation is very impressive because it illustrates a true integration of word and context information. The probability of correct recognition is zero when context is given with minimum word information. Similarly, the probability of correct recognition is zero with 3 segments of the test word presented without context. That is, neither the context alone nor the limited word information permits word recognition; however, when presented jointly word recognition is very good. Thus, the strong effect of minimum semantic context illustrated in Figure 21 can be considered to reflect true integration of word and contextual sources of information.

The form of the interaction of stimulus information and context is relevant to the prediction of the cohort model. Marslen-Wilson (1987) assumes that some minimum cohort set must be established on the basis of stimulus information *before* context can have an influence. In terms of FLMP description, this assumption implies that the evaluation of context should change across different levels of gating. To test this hypothesis, another model was fit to the results. In this

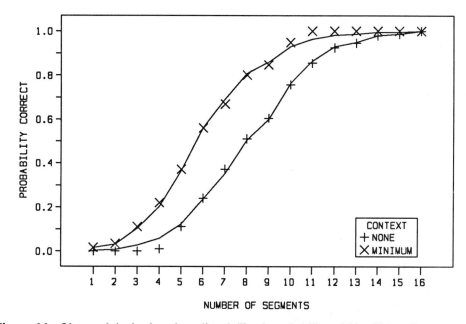

Figure 21. Observed (points) and predicted (lines) probability of identifying the test word correctly as a function of the sentential context and the number of segments of the test word. The minimum context refers to minimum semantic and weak syntactic constraints. The none context refers to no semantic and weak syntactic constraints (after Tyler & Wessels, 1983).

model, context was assumed to have an influence only after some minimum gating interval. Because it is not known what this minimum interval should be, an additional free parameter was estimated to converge on the interval that gave the best description of the observed results. This model did not improve the description of the results, weakening the claim that context has its influence only after some minimum stimulus information has been processed. This result is another instance of the general finding that there are no discrete points in psychological processing. The system does not seem to work one way at one point in time (i.e., no effect of context), and another way in another point in time (i.e., an effect of context).

Reading

Ethnography of Reading

Written Language

A Short History of Reading Research
  Tunnel Vision and Knowledge

Visual Information and Redundancy
  Orthographic Structure
  Measures of Orthographic Structure
  Perceptual versus Memory Contributions

Reicher Paradigm
  Two Models of Reicher Paradigm
  Redundancy at Response-Selection Stage
  Redundancy at Recognition Stage
  Words versus Rules

Phonological Mediation
  Experimental Tests

Theories of Word Recognition
  Logogen Model
  Cohort Model
  Activation-Verification Model
  Autonomous-Search Model
  Integrating Sentential Context
  Theoretical Analysis

Comprehension

_____

  Supraletter Features in Words

_____

The brain—our prior knowledge of the world—
contributes more information to reading than the
visual symbols on the printed page.
Frank Smith (1971)

A literate person faced with a written word is captured by it and seems to have no choice but to read it. Our phenomenal experience attests to this fact, as do experimental demonstrations of the Stroop (1935) effect. Take a set of colored pens or crayons and write a vertical list of color names. Write each color name with ink of a different color. For example, the word *red* is written in blue ink, the word *green* in red ink, and so on. Now read aloud the list of words from top to bottom. This task is not meant to insult your intelligence, but to serve as a reference for the next task. Name the colors of the words from top to bottom. Having the colors presented in written words corresponding to color names interferes with the naming of the colors. Although the reader's intention is to name the colors and ignore the words, it is not possible. Reading is such an overlearned skill, it is not easily put on hold.

Adult readers are clearly experts rather than novices in the reading domain of pattern recognition, in the same sense that experts are differentiated from novices in chess or radiography (Chapter 18; Lesgold, 1984). Expertise is acquired in reading in the same manner that it is acquired in other domains. A millionaire recently admitted that he was illiterate. What is impressive beyond his deception through school and college is his success in learning to read at the age of 48. For our purposes, it is important to note that his learning to read required 60 40-hour weeks of studying and sounding out words. This extended period of time on task might seem excessive, but probably is in the ballpark of time most of us have spent in learning to read.

ETHNOGRAPHY OF READING

Despite the onslaught of electronic media, reading remains central to our conduct. The average person reads about two hours a day. The distribution of reading times among adults is highly variable, however. Figure 1 plots a frequency distribution of reading times for a sample of five thousand readers (Sharon, 1973/74). About 15% of these literates read less than one-half hour per day. Less than 10% read more than four hours per day. In the primary grades one through three, about nine hours a week are devoted to reading. This drops to about six hours a week in the intermediate grades. As might be expected, the educated read more than the uneducated, and the young read more than the old. The most common kind of reading is newspaper reading; seven out of ten readers report spending an average of thirty-five minutes with a newspaper. The Bible is the most frequently read book. As every scholarly author believes, his or her book is least frequently read. Averages are not very illuminating, since people differ greatly in the amount of time they spend reading.

Some change in reading habits is also noticeable (Robinson, 1980). Young people are reading less, but those who do read are more committed. In one study, 85% of the youngsters who appeared in juvenile court were disabled readers (Kvaraceus, 1974). With more education, there is a shift from newspapers to magazines and books. There is also a well-known decline in literacy (Copperman, 1980). The upward trend in academic achievement reversed in the mid-sixties. Scores on the Scholastic Aptitude Test (SAT) also declined throughout the seventies. The verbal score declined about 4% per year; the math score declined about 2.5% a year. It seems also the case that

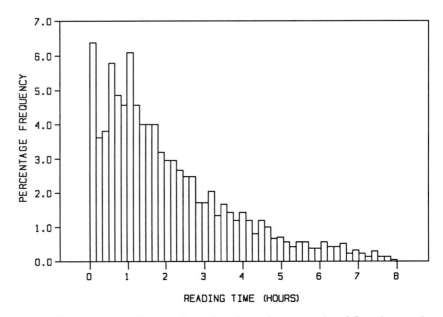

Figure 1. A frequency distribution of reading times for a sample of five thousand readers (after Sharon, 1973/74).

these declines cannot be attributed to an increased number of lower ability students taking the test. In addition to scholastic achievement, the quality of instruction may have declined. Public schools no longer require a prescribed curriculum for students and teachers. Encouragingly, the scores have shown consistent improvement in the eighties.

WRITTEN LANGUAGE

One of the earliest known uses of written language is the cuneiform writing of the Sumerians. Short, straight lines were impressed by a broad-based stylus. This writing system, like hieroglyphic writing, included word-signs or sound pictures, phonograms which expressed phonetic sounds, and determinatives (which was the context to eliminate ambiguities). Linear A and Linear B differed from earlier writing systems in that the written form was directly tied to the spoken form of writing. Linear B was a syllabary with open consonant-vowel syllables. A syllabary was also developed by the Japanese, who had difficulty using Chinese characters as the bases for their script. The alphabet was invented in about 1600 B.C., although its development is not well known. The unique feature of the alphabet was that each unique sound was denoted by only one symbol.

We can imagine that significant changes in reading occurred in parallel with the changes in writing. Unfortunately, we know even less about the historical development of reading and learning to read than we do about the history of writing. Written messages (especially those on clay tablets) remain to be found and studied; the historical readings of these messages do not. We might guess that most early reading was oral reading or at least was closely tied to speaking. St. Augustine was amazed by his mentor when he discovered St. Ambrose reading without moving his lips. In the future, we might expect to read even more, given the electronic communications revolution. Electronic mail is an important medium for communication, and we will be asked to read not just black letters on white paper but luminous dots on a TV screen.

A SHORT HISTORY OF READING RESEARCH

Reading research has had a short but lively history. Many of the issues being addressed today in research on reading were also studied during the early period of experimental psychology, shortly after the invention of the tachistoscope and Emile Javal's discovery of saccadic eye movements in the 1870s. Until then, it had been assumed that the eye moved continuously across the page, identifying each letter as it appeared. Now it was revealed that the eye moved in a series of discrete steps across the page. This finding generated the question of how much could be read in a single fixation between steps. James M. Cattell (1888), the first American to write a dissertation directed by Wundt, did a tachistoscopic study of letter, word, and phrase recognition showing that subjects could read out words, or even phrases and short sentences, from a display presented for so short a time that an eye movement was not possible.

In the 1890s, Erdmann and Dodge found that subjects could read words at distances too great to permit the identification of the component letters when they were presented alone. Since acuity breaks down with increasing distance, this is another experimental technique which can be used to obtain errors; it does not limit the amount of processing time but decreases the S/N (signal to noise) ratio. This method should produce the same qualitative results as a method which manipulates processing time to obtain errors. Erdmann and Dodge also found that subjects could read sentences at a distance too great to permit the recognition of the words presented alone.

Further insights into reading were provided by the work of Pillsbury, a disciple of Wundt, who in 1897 devised an experiment to test Wundt's theory of apperception. Wundt, influenced by the philosophy of Kant, argued that what one perceives is dependent upon a pre-existent structure of knowledge. Pillsbury's demonstration of apperception in reading involved presenting subjects with visually distorted words. For instance, the word *word* might be presented with a slash drawn through the *o*. Other stimulus words might simply be missing a letter. These displays were presented very briefly to subjects, who were then asked to report what they had seen. Subjects were able to identify the distorted words correctly, and sometimes they failed to perceive anything unusual in the display. The apperceptive process enabled them to perceive the words as accurately as if they were complete and undistorted.

A great deal of excitement in psychological and educational circles was generated by this work. The research results convinced many people that word recognition was not dependent upon the recognition of individual letters. Many educators, convinced that the basic unit of recognition in reading was not the letter—as had always been assumed— but the word and even the phrase, began to advocate the whole-word method of teaching. Thus began the controversies that have raged ever since around the proper method for teaching children to read. If skilled readers perceive entire words and phrases, it was reasoned, the method of teaching children spelling patterns and spelling-to-sound correspondences (phonics) could only interfere with their developing the optimal technique for deriving meaning from the text.

Psychologists meanwhile intensified their study of reading, convinced that it held the key to a great many crucial psychological issues. Edmund Huey wrote in 1908:

> . . . to completely analyze what we do when we read would almost be the acme of a psychologist's achievements, for it would be to describe very many of the most intricate workings of the human mind, as well as to unravel the tangled story of the most remarkable specific performance that civilization has learned in all its history.

In spite of such grand expectations, most of the work done on reading in this period concerned the measurements of eye movements. A great deal of time was spent on devising apparatus of varying degrees of ingenuity to record the flight of the eye from one fixation to the next.

In 1900, Wilhelm Wundt objected. To understand reading, he pointed out, one would have to understand far more than the duration of eye fixations and the speed of eye movements. Crucial psychological processes, such as attention and expectancy, were being ignored by the reading psychologists in their study of how the reader derives meaning from printed text. For instance, the reader brings to the reading task a variety of sources of knowledge. When reading, the skilled reader is able to predict the next word or words to some extent. This could result from either of two causes. (1) The information is available in the reader's peripheral vision; although focused on one point on the page, the reader can actually see words that occur further on in the text. (2) Knowledge enables the reader to guess at what is coming on the basis of what has already been read. It is possible, therefore, that reading efficiency is due not to an effect of the peripheral processing, but rather to the reader's ability to construct hypotheses about what lies ahead on the basis of what is already known.

Wundt's observations are highly relevant to the study of psychological processes in reading. It is important to know how much visual information is available to the reader at any moment and, secondly, to what extent readers utilize higher-order knowledge to impose meaning on the printed page. These two issues might be considered to be central to much of today's reading-related research (Gibson & Levin, 1975; Just & Carpenter, 1987).

Tunnel Vision and Knowledge

In reading, our eyes make short ballistic movements about four or five times a second. Each movement covers between four and eight characters. The movement time is very short and accounts for only about 10% of the time spent reading. We derive visual information only during the pauses between eye movements. Hold your fixation on the large dot in the center of the following sentence.

Pev au lbc kmrw dmr zfl jsrb wcm svf•uxrwa fc esrh br htc ozh wl hfuws cnvmhwp.

How many letters can you identify without moving your fixation? Now do the same for the next sentence.

Now is the time for all good men and•women to come to the aid of their country.

This one is easier, since it conforms to English writing, whereas the top sentence does not. However, not more than about four or five words can be seen in a given fixation. Letters and words outside of this range seem blurred or fuzzy.

The knowledge of the perceiver is critical in reading, since the sensory information available to the reader is imperfect. With respect to the visual system, the letters on a page are highly fuzzy. Readers utilize their knowledge of the content of the passage and their knowledge of the language to make the written word less fuzzy. There are many knowledge sources available to the reader such as the sentential constraints given by well-formed English sentences. Consider the passage, "the actress was praised for an outstanding ..." Most of you probably thought of the word *performance*. Consider an early experiment in psychology. Subjects were given 0, 4, or 8 words of a context sentence, and this was followed by a test word presented for a short duration in a tachistoscope. As might be expected, subjects were more accurate when the duration of the test word was increased. In addition, the context improved performance so that words were more likely to be recognized when more of the context sentence was present. Readers appear to utilize the sentential context to facilitate their perception of a test word when the visual information alone is insufficient. We now turn to a more detailed study of how the reader utilizes the visual information and knowledge in imposing meaning on written text.

Supraletter Features in Words

The early work on letter and word recognition led some researchers and educators to conclude that words are learned as patterns of unique shapes rather than as sequences of unique letters. If words have unique shapes, readers would learn words in terms of relatively gross properties which define their shape. We call these properties supraletter features since they supposedly are composed of multiletter patterns and even whole word patterns. This belief was responsible for the whole-word method of teaching reading.

As appealing as the concept of supraletter features might be, there is no evidence for this idea (Anderson & Dearborn, 1952; Gibson & Levin, 1975; Huey, 1968). One of the strongest arguments against the idea of supraletter features is the small potential contribution of supraletter features to reading. Overall word shape, for example, does not sufficiently differentiate among the words of a language. Groff (1975) examined the shapes of high-frequency words taken from schoolbook sources. The shape was defined by drawing a contour around the letters so that elephant would be elephant . Only 20% of the 283 words were represented by a unique shape. The author rightly concludes that the small number of words that can be represented by a unique shape precludes the utilization of this cue for accurate word recognition.

There is also experimental evidence against the idea of word recognition based on supraletter features. The role of supraletter features has been evaluated in a number of studies by determining whether mixing the type fonts of letters eliminates the tachistoscopic identification advantage of word over nonword letter strings. Adams (1979) studied the tachistoscopic recognition of words, pseudowords very high in orthographic structure, and nonwords very low in structure. The items were presented in a single type font or the items were constructed from a variety of fonts. Table 1 presents examples of the words, pseudowords, and nonwords in single and mixed type fonts. Performance was more accurate for words than pseudowords and poorest for nonwords. Most importantly, the size of the differences among the three types of items did not change when the letters of the items were presented in a variety of type fonts. If supraletter features or whole-word cues contribute to the perceptual advantage of well-structured strings, the advantage of the word and pseudoword strings should have been drastically attenuated in the mixed-case presentation.

Table 1. Words, pseudowords, and nonwords printed in mixed uppercase and lowercase.

Word	Pseudoword	Nonword
rEAd	tHaP	yIbv
bACk	SuCE	gTsI
wEak	BleT	MbIa

VISUAL INFORMATION AND REDUNDANCY

Wundt's criticism of the reading experimentalists of his time brought to light the crucial requirement of a valid study of reading: the separation of the effects of two different contributions to the process. The first contribution is that of the stimulus—the visual symbols on the page of text. The second is nonvisual information possessed by the sophisticated reader and stored in memory.

There are three sources of nonvisual information that can aid the reader in decoding the written message. These sources are the orthographic, syntactic, and semantic structures that exist in English prose. The orthographic constraints define the valid spelling patterns in English. We know that words are separated by blank spaces and must have at least one vowel. Syntactic rules establish the permissible sequences of different parts of speech. For example, "The boy down fell the hill" is grammatically incorrect. Finally, semantic rules allow the reader to predict the word or words that make sense in a given sentence context. "The hill fell down the boy" is syntactically correct but semantically anomalous. All of these rules allow us to agree on the missing word in "Please clean the dirt from your s---s before walking inside."

In terms of the information-processing approach, the visual stimulus is transformed by the visual system, and a list of features is recorded in preperceptual visual storage. Recognition, or the readout of this information, depends on the features of the information in preperceptual store and on the information possessed by the reader about the occurrences of spelling patterns in English. Figure 2 demonstrates how two identical visual patterns can be interpreted as different letters because of meaningful context. Thus, although the visual information available about the last letter of the first word is the same as the first letter of the second word, the contribution of what one knows about the valid spelling patterns in English text demands that they be interpreted as different letters. (This knowledge is sometimes referred to as redundancy, since it reduces the number of valid alternatives a particular visual configuration can possess.) In reading, we would expect that this knowledge of English spelling would enable us to extract meaning from a page of text without analyzing all the visual information present or to identify words even when some of the visual information is incomplete or fuzzy.

Figure 2. The same visual configuration can be interpreted as two different letters, depending on the meaningful context.

It should be stressed that knowledge of orthographic constraints involves more than simply a knowledge of the spelling of each word in our vocabulary. For example, we know that *cht* does not spell a word, not because the meaning of *cht* is unknown, but because we know that *cht* is an invalid spelling sequence for a three-letter word. To illustrate, consider the spelling configuration *cit*. Even though one may not have this word in his or her vocabulary, it would be incorrect to conclude that this configuration could not spell a word.

Given that the reader may utilize orthographic, syntactic, or semantic context, two interpretations emerge from the early experiments of Erdmann and Dodge, and Pillsbury. In the Erdmann and Dodge study, subjects were able to read words and sentences better than they could read isolated letters and words, respectively. One interpretation is that words are easier to read because they are easier to perceive. For example, words may have unique visual characteristics which make them easier to perceive than individual letters. The alternative interpretation is that subjects were able to guess correctly more often when the impoverished letters formed word sequences than when they did not. Consider the example in Figure 2. If the subject is presented the letter *c* at a very great distance, she may be unsure if it is a *c* or an *e* and may have to guess randomly between the two. On the other hand, if she is presented with cool, the *c* may be just as ambiguous visually, but if *ool* is interpreted as such, she can guess correctly with the word *cool*. In this case, the results would show better recognition for words than for isolated letters. We can also develop an analogous explanation for the result that sentences are better recognized than isolated words.

Similarly, we do not know why the subjects in the Pillsbury experiment were able to identify words when a letter was missing or distorted. It is possible that they actually perceived the intact word, and that they did not need each letter to be present and intact in order to perceive the word. On the other hand, it is possible that they did not perceive it as complete and intact, but that their knowledge of English spelling enabled them to make a good guess at the word after perception was complete. This interpretation weakens the relevance of these results to natural reading. Readers may not be able to utilize nonvisual information in rapid reading when their eyes move across the page at a rate of four or five fixations a second. However, given a short tachistoscopic exposure with a relatively long time to respond, the subject might be able to utilize nonvisual information. In this case, subjects need not perceive every letter before they can correctly identify the word.

Orthographic Structure

Orthographic structure refers to the fact that a written language, such as English, follows certain rules of spelling. These rules prohibit certain letter combinations and make some letters and combinations much more likely in certain positions of words than others. Readers might utilize these constraints in the written language in letter and word perception. Concern for orthographic structure in reading has occurred only recently.

One of the first studies of the utilization of orthographic constraints in reading was carried out by Miller, Bruner, and Postman (1954). These authors had subjects reproduce letter sequences flashed in a tachistoscope. The eight-letter strings corresponded to different approximations to English based on Shannon's (1948, 1951) algorithms. The authors found that performance improved with increases in the degree to which the letter strings approximated English. By correcting for the statistical redundancy in the strings, the amount of information transmitted (Chapter 1) was shown to be equal for the various approximations.

Measures of Orthographic Structure

Given that readers are sensitive to orthographic structure, an important question is the nature of a reader's knowledge about orthographic structure. It is possible to distinguish between two broad categories of orthographic structures: statistical redundancy and rule-governed regularity (Venezky & Massaro, 1987). The first category includes all descriptions derived solely from the frequency of letters and letter sequences in written texts. The second category includes all descriptions derived from the phonological constraints in English and scribal conventions for the sequences of letters in English words. Although these two descriptions are highly correlated in written English, it is possible to create letter strings that allow the descriptions to be orthogonally varied. Given these strings as test items, perceptual recognition tasks have been carried out to decide which general category seems to reflect the manner in which readers store and utilize knowledge of orthographic structure.

Massaro et al. (1980) contrasted specific statistical-redundancy descriptions with specific rule-governed descriptions by comparing letter strings that varied orthogonally with respect to these descriptions. The statistical redundancy measures were summed token single-letter frequency, bigram frequency, and log bigram frequency. The rule-governed regularity measures were various sets of rules based on phonological and scribal constraints. In a typical experiment, six-letter words and anagrams of these words were used as test items. The anagrams were selected to give letter strings which represented the four combinations formed by a factorial arrangement of high or low frequency and regular or irregular orthographic structure. In a series of experiments utilizing a target-search task, subjects were asked to indicate whether or not a target letter was present in these letter strings. Both accuracy and reaction-time measures indicated some psychological reality for both frequency and the regularity description of orthographic structure.

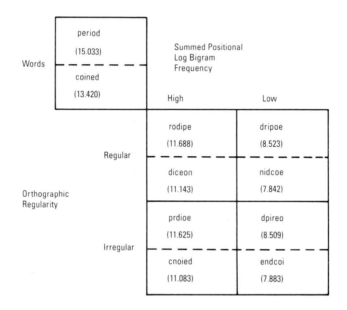

Figure 3. Examples of the words and anagrams used in the Massaro et al. (1981) task.

Consider an experiment carried out by Massaro et al. (1981). Some examples of the words and their respective anagrams are presented in Figure 3. *Period* has a high word frequency, while *coined* has a low word frequency. The letter string *rodipe* is a regular-high anagram of the word *period*, and *nidcoe* is a regular-low anagram of *coined*. The number in each cell gives the average summed-positional log bigram frequency for the items of that class. For example, the irregular-high anagrams of high-frequency words have an average count of 11.625. Forty high-frequency and 40 low-frequency words were selected along with four anagrams of each word. The anagrams were selected so that they formed a factorial arrangement of high and low summed-positional log bigram frequency crossed with regular and irregular orthographic structure.

These six-letter words and their anagrams were used as test stimuli in a target-search task. The test string was presented for a short duration, followed by a masking stimulus and the target letter. Subjects responded "yes" or "no" whether the target letter was present in the test string. There was an advantage of words over regular-high anagrams and an advantage of regular over irregular anagrams. There was also an advantage of high-frequency words over low-frequency words. Word frequency of the items from which the anagrams were derived did not have a significant effect on perceptual recognition of the anagrams. Post hoc correlations with performance accuracy on each of the test strings gave significant effects of position-sensitive log bigram frequency and regularity. The results of these studies provided evidence for the utilization of higher-order knowledge in the perceptual processing of letter strings. Lexical status, orthographic regularity, and frequency appear to be important components of the higher-order knowledge that is used.

Perceptual versus Memory Contributions

Although Miller et al. (1954) and, later, Eleanor Gibson and her colleagues (Gibson, Pick, Osser, & Hammond, 1962) found positive effects of orthographic structure in tachistoscopic tasks, the results do not necessarily implicate a perceptual effect. Memory is a critical component in the tachistoscopic task. In a similar vein, Baddeley (1964) questioned the perceptual contribution to the original psychological study of orthography carried out by Miller et al. (1954). Recall that the authors had subjects reproduce letter sequences, eight letters in length, corresponding to different approximations to English based on Shannon's (1948) algorithms. The displays were exposed for durations of 10 to 500 msec, and the number of letters reported increased with display duration. Also, performance was a systematic function of the order of approximation to English. By correcting for redundancy of the string, the amount of information transmitted was shown to be equivalent for the four different approximations.

Baddeley (1964) observed that performance in the task was unlikely to be a direct index of how well the letter sequences were perceived. Given that performance improved at a negatively accelerated function of log exposure duration, one or two hours would be required for correct report of all eight letters. Baddeley argued that Miller et al.'s results may have reflected differences in the memory for the sequences rather than differences in their perception. To test this idea, he presented the eight-letter sequences of Miller et al. at a duration that was sufficient for that subject to name each of the eight letters. Presentation times ranged between one and two seconds. The contribution of orthographic redundancy to performance in this task was essentially identical to that reported by Miller et al. (1954). Baddeley concluded that both interletter redundancy and exposure time allow a more effective coding and, therefore, better memory and recall of the letter sequence.

We have seen that, in addition to perception, post hoc guessing and memory are critical contributions to performance in tachistoscopic experiments. In order to assess how some variable influences perception, the experiments must account for both post hoc guessing and memory contributions to performance. This might be seen as an insurmountable obstacle, but some good solutions have been proposed. The most influential solution was invented by Gerald Reicher for his dissertation research at the University of Michigan in the late sixties. His goal was to control for both post hoc guessing and memory in the tachistoscopic report of letter strings.

REICHER PARADIGM

In Reicher's task, subjects saw a short display of letters in a tachistoscope. Reicher presented either single letters, words, or random letter strings (nonwords) for a short duration, followed by a masking stimulus (see Figure 4). For example, on one trial, the subject might be presented with the word WORD for a very brief time, followed immediately by a visual noise mask made up of overlapping X's and O's. The masking stimulus also contained a cue to report one of the four letters. When the task was to name the fourth letter in the word, two alternatives would be presented at the time of the cue, D and K. The subject would have to choose one of these alternatives. In this task, then, the subject must make a choice only on the basis of the information obtained from the visual display. Knowledge of the rules of English spelling will not help this decision: both alternatives D and K form words given the information WOR-. Of course, a different word was presented on each trial, and the subject did not know which letter position would be tested until the cue appeared.

Performance in this condition was compared with performance when the subject was presented with a single letter at any of the four serial positions defined by the word. For example, the subject could be presented with D alone and asked whether it was D or K.

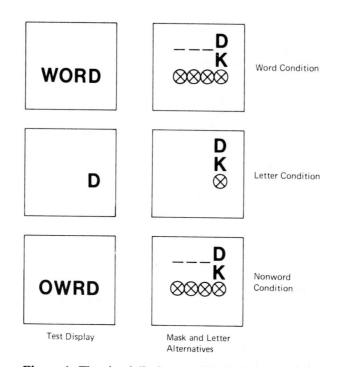

Figure 4. The visual displays used in the Reicher (1969) study.

The third condition allowed Reicher to compare word versus nonword recognition. On some trials, the subject was presented with a nonsense word that did not conform to the spelling rules of English: for example, OWRD or OWRK. This procedure appears to control for both post hoc guessing and memory in the task. To control for the contribution of English orthography, Reicher and Wheeler limited the subject to two response alternatives, both of which spelled words. Why does equating the number of valid response alternatives under the different conditions control for post hoc guessing? The answer to this question makes explicit the model the investigators employed. First of all, the model assumes two stages of processing between stimulus and response: recognition and response selection. The central feature of the model, however, is that it can be interpreted as the all-or-none guessing model traditionally employed in psychophysical tasks (see Chapter 10). The subject either correctly recognizes what was presented, or he does not: if he does not, he guesses at the response-selection stage. The two stages of processing assumed in this model—recognition and response selection—correspond directly to the sensory and decision stages in Chapter 11.

This model assumes that post hoc guessing can operate at the response-selection stage. If the subject does not know what was presented at the recognition stage, the knowledge of spelling of English can be used at the response-selection stage to enhance the accuracy of guesses. When a letter is presented in a word, rather than alone, the subject can reduce the population of valid alternatives and, hence, will be more likely to be correct. For example, if the subject has recognized WOR_ and is asked to report for the fourth letter, he can reduce the guessing set from 26 letters to five because only five letters spell a word given WOR_. Accordingly, the subject's guessing rate would go from 1/26 to 1/5, and performance based on guessing alone would be enhanced in the word, relative to the nonword or letter conditions. In order to control for different guessing probabilities, then, the subject is forced to guess from two alternatives in all conditions. This should set the probability of a correct guess at 1/2 in all conditions. Given this model and the precautions taken, any advantage observed in letter recognition performance in the word condition must be due to an increase in the amount of information transmitted by the recognition process.

What about memory differences in the three different conditions? By testing for just one letter in each display, Reicher reduced the memory load relative to the traditional full-report task. However, we might expect that slightly more forgetting would occur with nonwords than with words. Differences between these two displays, then, might be due to memory rather than perception. The single-letter displays provide a good check on the contribution of forgetting in the task. If anything, the memory load should be greater for the word than for the single-letter condition. Therefore, any advantage of words over single letters cannot be due to memory differences but must be due to differences in ease of recognition.

Performance in the task revealed a word advantage. Subjects picked the correct alternative 12% more often when faced with a word display than when tested with a single-letter display. The nonword display produced performance equivalent to the single-letter condition. This result shows that memory loss was not a significant contribution in this task as it was in the Miller et al. studies.

Reicher's results have been interpreted as a demonstration that the common perceptual unit in reading is the word. If experienced readers recognize text word-by-word, letter identification of D and K would be unusual and might take longer. The word was therefore more easily identified than the letter. The nonsense words are not perceptual units, making it necessary to recognize all of their individual letters. Given that perceptual units are available for the words WORK and WORD, but not the nonsense words OWRD and ORWK, recognition of the words should proceed faster than recognition of the nonsense words. To recognize the nonsense words, each of the component letters must be identified individually, which should take longer than single-word identification.

Reicher's findings have been replicated repeatedly (Johnston & McClelland, 1973; Wheeler, 1970) and the research has focused on the explanation of the findings. The results are inadequate as a demonstration that the perceptual unit is a word, because an alternative conclusion from the experiment is possible. In visual perception, as in any psychological behavior, there is a sequence of mental processes that exists between stimulus and response, and the experimenter's model of how these processes operate determines her interpretation of the results. The conclusion one reaches from Reicher's and Wheeler's results is, therefore, dependent upon the processing model assumed. When the Reicher paradigm is made explicit, it becomes clear that an alternative model is possible. The alternative model leads to a different interpretation of the experimental findings.

Two Models of Reicher Paradigm

We know that the visual pattern presented to the observer is transformed by the visual system and placed in preperceptual visual store. Recognition is the process by which the observer synthesizes a percept from this store. By this process, the information in preperceptual storage is analyzed and transformed into a percept, which is held in synthesized visual memory. In order to provide the experimenter with some measurable indication of the information that he has about the stimulus, the observer must make a response. This response is all that is available to the experimenter. The percept cannot be measured directly; for example, Pillsbury was not able to determine whether his subjects actually saw the configurations as words or made a good guess. The process of response selection intervenes between the percept which the experimenter wishes to study and the response which is observed. The effect of orthography, which Reicher and Wheeler took pains to eliminate from the response, could operate at either the recognition stage or at the response-selection stage.

Redundancy at Response-Selection Stage

According to the first alternative, orthography could operate at the response-selection stage. A formulation of this model in an information-processing model is shown in Figure 5. In the model, a light-wave pattern is held in preperceptual storage, and the recognition process operates on the information to find a match with a sign or signs in long-term memory. Reicher and Wheeler used a mask to terminate recognition before it was complete, so that errors would occur. The output of the recognition process produces some synthesized percept in synthesized visual memory. The synthesized percept is made available to the response-selection stage, which has access to the rules of English orthography. To control for redundancy on word trials, the subject is limited to two response alternatives that both spell words. Accordingly, since the knowledge of these rules should be superfluous, orthography should be eliminated as a contributing factor in the comparison between word and nonword recognition. Given this model and the Reicher paradigm, any advantage in word recognition must be due to the recognition process, which is dependent on the signs of perceptual units in long-term memory.

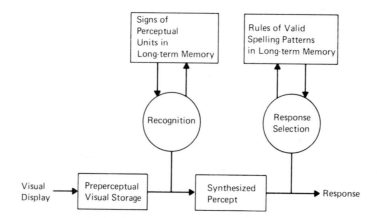

Figure 5. Model of visual recognition in which the knowledge of valid spelling patterns can be utilized only at the response-selection stage.

Redundancy at Recognition Stage

Figure 6 presents an alternative model which assumes that the effect of redundancy operates at the recognition stage, not at the response-selection stage of information processing. Accordingly, the subject can employ the rules of English orthography during the readout or synthesis of the preperceptual visual image. This model can describe Reicher's results even if it is assumed that the letter is the basic perceptual unit of analysis. Redundancy serves to enhance letter recognition when the letter is embedded in a valid spelling pattern, since it reduces the number of possibilities that can occur. This model assumes that the signs of perceptual units are letters and that, therefore, the visual features are defined with respect to letters. It should be pointed out that the assumption of letters as perceptual units does not require that each letter in a word be recognized in serial order. Letters can be recognized simultaneously (in parallel), and this must be the case if redundancy at recognition is responsible for the advantage of words over single letters. In a typical trial, because of the brief duration of the preperceptual visual image, the recognition process has only partial information about the letters in the display. However, the recognition process can utilize the rules of English orthography and synthesize a correct percept based on partial visual information.

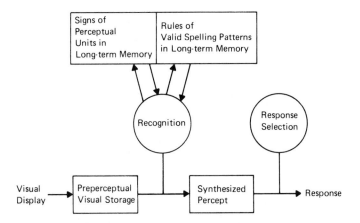

Figure 6. Model of visual recognition in which the knowledge of valid spelling patterns can be utilized at the recognition stage.

Consider a particular trial in which the word WORD is presented. Assume that the subject has some visual information about each letter. The visual features that were processed reduce the alternatives to V or W, C or O, R or P, and D or B in the four positions, respectively. However, if it is assumed that the letter configuration must spell a word, the reader could synthesize the word WORD since it is the only valid spelling pattern given this visual information in each of the serial positions. In the letter-alone case, or in the nonsense word, the recognition process could not use the spelling rules of English to reduce the number of alternatives for the tested letter. If the visual information limits the alternatives to D or B in the letter-alone case, the subject's synthesis or best guess will be correct only half the time. On half the trials, he sees a D; on half, he sees a B.

Recognition of the letters is complete at the time of test. When the subject is presented with the two response alternatives D and K in the word conditions, he selects the correct letter D since he saw WORD. In contrast, in the letter-alone case, on half the trials, he must guess randomly between the two alternatives D and K since he sees a B on half the trials. Accordingly, when we compare recognition of a letter embedded in a word to recognition of a letter alone in terms of the second model, we see that the letter-alone case would be more difficult. Given a few features in the letter condition, the recognition process must choose among all the letters in the alphabet that share features in common with the D presented. Thus, given the curvilinear component of the stimulus letter D, the letters C, O, Q, and P are also valid alternatives. These letters could be eliminated in the word condition since they do not form a word with the features from the other letters in the word. This analysis shows that the advantage of words over nonwords and single letters in the Reicher task does not necessarily indicate that words are recognized as unanalyzed wholes. Rather, information about how letters make up words supplements the visual information in the letters to give an advantage of words over nonwords and single letters.

Words versus Rules

There are two fundamentally different accounts of the word advantage. These two accounts parallel summary-description and exemplar-based accounts of categorization (Chapter 16). Similar to our conclusions with respect to these two alternatives, we might expect that both explanations are correct to some degree. The reader probably uses both rule-like knowledge and specific word knowledge in perceiving letters and words in reading. The traditional one that we have discussed is that the reader has rule-like information that makes a contribution to word recognition. These rules do not have to be consciously known or applied, and they do not have to be perfect. That is, a rule can still make a positive contribution to word recognition even if it provides only partial information. Analogous to the use of cues to depth or the use of top-down constraints in speech perception, several pieces of partial information can yield an unambiguous situation.

A more recent account of the word advantage dispenses with the idea of rules entirely, and explains the word advantage in terms of the contribution of the specific words in the reader's lexicon (Brooks, 1978; Glushko, 1979). The most complete model within this class is the interactive activation model. The model was designed to account for context effects in word perception (McClelland & Rumelhart, 1981) and was extended to account for other phenomena (Rumelhart & McClelland, 1982). The model postulates three levels of units: features, letters, and words. Features activate letters that are consistent with the features and inhibit letters that are inconsistent; letters activate consistent words and inhibit inconsistent words; and most importantly, words activate consistent letters. A letter is more accurately recognized in the context of a word than in context of random letters. Interactive activation explains this word advantage in terms of interactive activation from the word level to the letter level. Definitive tests between rule-based and word-based accounts of the word advantage have not been developed. A safe bet is that both rule-based and word-based information is brought to bear in reading.

PHONOLOGICAL MEDIATION

A very old question in reading-related research, one that is probably as old as reading itself, is whether the reader must translate print into some form of speech before meaning is accessed. This question can be formalized in terms of two different models in which speech mediation either does or does not occur in a derivation of meaning. Figure 7 presents a schematic diagram of both models. The top model assumes that phonological mediation must occur in order for the meaning of a message to be determined. In this model a letter string is presented, and the letters are identified by evaluating the visual information against feature lists of letters in long-term memory. The letters then are translated into a speech-like or a sound-like medium by the spelling-to-sound correspondences of the language. We call this kind of mediated word recognition phonological mediation. One example of a spelling-to-sound rule is that a medial vowel is usually pronounced as short unless it is followed by a consonant and a final *e*. Thus, we have *fin* and *fine* or *fat* and *fate*. The speech code derived from spelling-to-sound rules is then used to access the lexicon in order to recognize the meaning of the word. The critical assumption of this model is that lexical access is achieved only by way of a speech code.

The bottom model in Figure 7 assumes that a speech code becomes available only after lexical access is achieved. The letters are identified in the same way as in the speech mediation model. However, the meaning of the letter string is determined by utilizing a visual code to achieve lexical access. The important assumption in this model is that the reader has information about what letter sequences represent what words. In this model the speech code becomes available only after lexical access is achieved. Given these two formal models, one would expect that it would be relatively easy to distinguish between them.

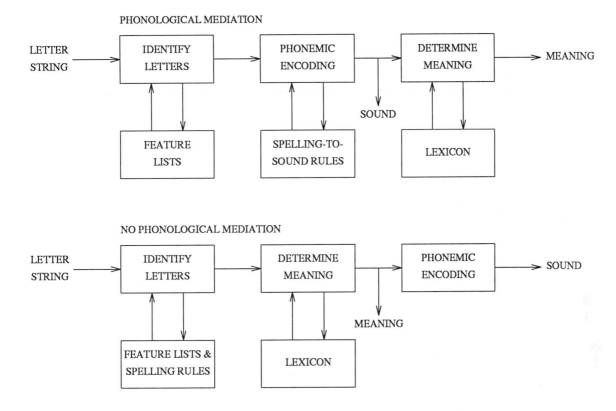

Figure 7. Two models of word recognition with and without phonological mediation.

Experimental Tests

Experiments have been done utilizing the time needed for lexical access in order to test between the models. Consider an experiment carried out by Gough and Cosky (1977). Subjects were asked to read aloud words that either obeyed or violated spelling-to-sound rules. One example of a word that violates a spelling-to-sound rule would be the word *give*; the vowel is not pronounced as long as it should be as, for example, in the word *hive*. If subjects recognize words via speech mediation and utilize spelling-to-sound rules to achieve the speech code, then recognition of the word *give* should take longer than recognition of the word *hive*. Utilizing spelling-to-sound rules, the reader would first interpret the letters *give* as [ga^{i}v] (rhymes with *hive*). Failing to achieve lexical access, a backup strategy would be initiated, and the short form of the vowel would be inserted, giving the correct pronunciation [gIv]. In this case, lexical access would be achieved on the second try. Given the word *hive*, recognition would occur directly from the speech code [haIv] produced by spelling-to-sound rules. The obvious hypothesis is that the pronunciation time for exception words, such as *give*, should be longer than the pronunciation time for regular words, such as *hive*. Gough and Cosky found that the pronunciation times for the exception words were in fact 27 msec longer than the pronunciation times for regular words. This result would seem to provide evidence for the speech mediation model.

Before these results can be interpreted as supporting the speech mediation model, however, it is necessary for the investigator to locate the differences in reaction time at the word-recognition stage of processing. The naming task requires a number of processing stages, and it is necessary to perform a stage analysis of the naming task. Naming a written pattern includes word-recognition and speech-production operations. In terms of this analysis, the RT between the onset of the written pattern and the onset of the spoken response is a composite of these two component times plus the times for other processes. It could be that lexical access time did not differ for exception and regular words but that the time for the subjects to program the naming response did differ. It could be that exception words are more difficult to pronounce once they are recognized and therefore require more time in the pronunciation task. One possible control would have been to present the words auditorily and see if naming times differ in this situation. If they do not, this result would provide some evidence that the original differences with visual presentation are due to differences in time to achieve lexical access.

Another test for differences between exception and regular words is a category judgment task. Subjects are asked to categorize the words, such as whether they are nouns or verbs. The differences in the times to complete the categorization task would not be confounded with response processes because the response of categorization is identical for the exception and regular words. Following this logic, Bias (cited by McCusker, Hillinger, & Bias, 1981) tested for differences between exception and regular words using animal/nonanimal judgments.

Even if lexical access is slower for exception than for regular words, phonological mediation may not be responsible. Differences between exception and regular words could be the result of differences in the times to process the letters of the words. There is good evidence that readers utilize orthographic structure to facilitate letter processing in word strings (see previous section). It could be that exception words have less orthographic structure than regular words, and letter recognition is therefore faster for regular than for exception words. Controlling for orthographic structure differences is difficult because an exact description of structure has not been validated.

We have distinguished between orthographic structure and spelling-to-sound regularity in our description of written language. It would be of interest to assess the contribution of each of these in reading written words. Also of interest is word frequency—perhaps the most potent variable in naming and lexical decision tasks. Waters and Seidenberg (1985) assessed the contributions of these three variables in both naming and lexical decision tasks. Very similar results were found in both tasks. It is important in tasks such as these to look at performance on each test item rather than just on a class of items. One procedure is to compute an average RT for each word pooled across subjects, and to correlate the variables of interest with the RTs to the individual words. When this type of analysis was carried out on the Waters and Seidenberg (1985) results, there were significant effects of all three variables (Venezky & Massaro, 1987). This outcome has several implications. First, there must be some truth to both of the routes to the lexicon illustrated in Figure 7. Second, there is no single source of information responsible for written-word recognition. Finally, readers appear to evaluate and integrate multiple sources of information in reading, as they do in speech perception.

THEORIES OF WORD RECOGNITION

Theories of visual-word recognition can be classified within the same scheme used for spoken-word recognition. For written words, the visual signal initiates a process that begins with the visual processing of the word and ends with access to a word or phrase in the mental lexicon. Three word recognition models will be discussed to highlight some important issues in understanding how written words are recognized. The same characteristics used to contrast and compare the models of spoken-word recognition will be used for written-word recognition. In fact, we will find that models of written-word recognition resemble analogous models of spoken-word recognition. One important question is whether word recognition is mediated or nonmediated. A second question is whether the perceiver has access to only categorical information in the word-recognition process, or whether continuous information is available. A third consideration is whether information from the continuously-varying signal is used on-line at the lexical stage of processing, or whether there is some delay in initiating processing of the signal at the lexical stage. A fourth characteristic involves parallel versus serial access to the lexical representations in memory. The final characteristic we will consider is whether the word-recognition process functions autonomously, or whether it is context-dependent. Figure 8 gives a graphical presentation of these characteristics.

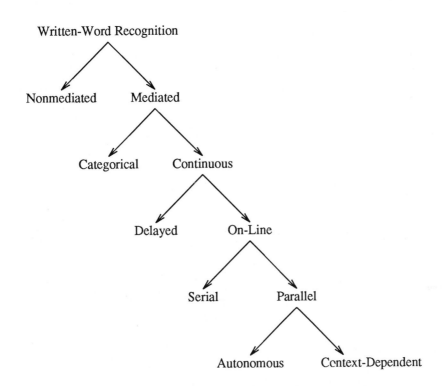

Figure 8. Tree of wisdom illustrating binary oppositions central to the differences among theories of written-word recognition.

Logogen Model

Morton's logogen model (Morton, 1964, 1969) described for spoken-word recognition has also played an important role in the theoretical analysis of visual-word recognition. It is important to understand that the logogens could be activated by both auditory and visual words. Given that either auditory or visual words activate logogens, the description and evaluation of the model given in Chapter 19 applies directly to written-word recognition. (It might be worthwhile to review the section on word recognition at this time.)

The logogen model makes a strong prediction that once a logogen is activated, the consequences of that activation are independent of how the logogen was activated. Either stimulus information or context can push a logogen over the threshold, and the stimulus information could be auditory or visual. Winnick and Daniel (1970) tested this assumption in a test of visual-word recognition. Subjects were first primed with visual words, pictures, or definitions of the words, and asked to name each word. These same words were presented sometime later in a tachistoscopic identification task. Later identification of a written word was facilitated more when the word was presented in written form rather than in a picture or by a definition. These results parallel those discussed in Chapter 17, showing that the visual form of a word can contribute to its later identification. Morton (1979) replicated and extended these results, and now has revised the logogen model to include separate input logogens corresponding to the modality of the linguistic input.

Cohort Model

The cohort model might be extended to account for reading words. The most natural extension would assume that written words are recognized letter by letter in a left-to-right manner. In fact, Gough (1972) proposed exactly such a model, and this serial model is favored by Just and Carpenter (1987). For all of these models, a written word is recognized serially letter by letter from left to right during the word presentation. In addition, each of the models assumes that each letter of a word is recognized categorically. For the cohort model, word recognition occurs by way of the elimination of alternative word candidates (cohorts). Recognition of the first letter in the word eliminates all words that do not have that letter in initial position. Recognition of the second letter eliminates all of the remaining cohorts that do not have the second letter in second position. Recognition of letters and the elimination of alternative words continues in this fashion until only one word remains. It is at this point that the word is recognized.

Activation-Verification Model

A third model of word recognition is an activation-verification model (Becker, 1976; Paap, Newsome, McDonald, & Schvaneveldt, 1982). The model has three operations: encoding, verification, and decision. Figure 9 presents a schematic representation of the activation-verification model. Encoding refers to the initial processing of the visual information that activates letters and words. Verification is responsible for achieving a conscious recognition or a single lexical entry. The verification process is a serial-comparison between information made available by encoding and the set of candidate words generated during encoding. For each comparison, the output is positive or negative. If the match exceeds some criterion, then a word is recognized. Otherwise, the next word candidate is compared. The search is, therefore, self-terminating (see Chapter 9). Both semantic context and word frequency are assumed to contribute to the processing. Context constrains the candidate set that is verified, and word frequency influences the order of verification of the words in the candidate set.

The activation-verification model can be described with respect to the five characteristics in Figure 8. The model is mediated, categorical, on-line, serial, and context-dependent. Written-word recognition is mediated by letter recognition, letters are recognized on-line categorically, final recognition of a word requires a serial search, and context can have an influence.

Autonomous-Search Model

An autonomous-search model of word recognition (Forster, 1979, 1981, 1985) is similar in many respects to the activation-verification model. Both models involve two stages—an initial access stage and a serial-search stage. In the autonomous-search model, the first stage in processing a written stimulus is in terms of recognizing the letters that make up a word. The abstract representation of this information serves as an access code to select some subset of the lexicon. The distinctive feature of this model is that words within this subset must be processed serially. The serial order of processing is determined by the frequency of occurrence of the words in the language. After making a match in the search stage of processing, a verification or post-search check is carried out against the full orthographic properties of the word. If a match is obtained at this stage, the relevant contents of the lexical entry are made available.

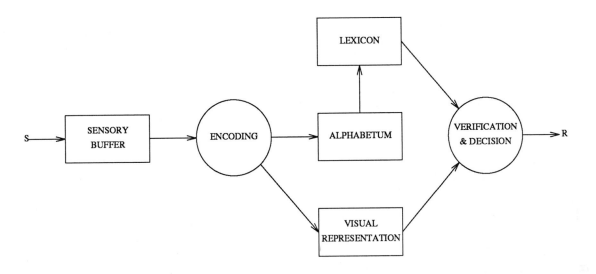

Figure 9. Illustration of the activation-verification model of written word recognition.

The autonomous-search model can be described with respect to the five characteristics in Figure 8. The model is mediated, categorical, on-line, serial, and is independent of context. Written-word recognition is mediated by letter recognition, letters are recognized on-line categorically, final recognition of a word requires a serial search. A critical feature of the autonomous-search model is that all of this processing occurs independently of context.

We limit the discussion to these four models because they differ from one another on the characteristics that we consider important to word recognition. Although these models have been studied and tested in a variety of tasks and domains, no difinitive tests among the models has been carried out. We know, however, much about the answers to the questions illustrated in Figure 8. We saw in Chapter 16 that readers have continuous information about written letters. Evidence presented in this chapter argues strongly in favor of letter information mediating word recognition; words are not recognized as unanalyzed wholes. Written words, as spoken words, are recognized on-line and alternative letter and word candidates appear to be accessed in parallel. With respect to the issue of context, we now discuss how sentential context and word information contribute to reading.

Integrating Sentential Context

Tulving, Mandler, and Baumal (1964) combined eight exposure durations with four sentential context lengths in a word-recognition task in which a tachistoscopic presentation of a word followed the reading of the sentence context. One of the 18 sentence contexts was "Her closest relative was appointed as her legal ..." The test word, which you may have guessed, was "guardian." Subjects read either the last 0, 2, 4, or 8 words of the context part of the sentence, and the test word was presented at either 20, 40, 60, 80, 100, 120, or 140 msec. Subjects were instructed to write down the test word and to guess if they were not sure of their answer. They were told that the context words might be helpful in recognition of the test word.

Figure 10 presents the percentage of correct responses as a function of the duration of the test word; context length is the curve parameter. The context with two words is not presented since it produced results roughly identical to the context with four words. As expected, performance improved with increases in word duration and with increase in sentential context. The contribution of

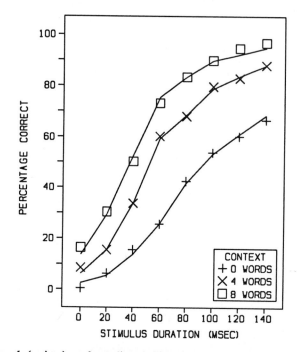

Figure 10. Observed (points) and predicted (lines) percentage correct identifications as a function of the stimulus duration of the test word and the number of context words (after Tulving et al., 1964).

sentential context was larger when the exposure duration was intermediate and performance was neither very poor nor very good. This result indicates that context is most effective when subjects have some but not relatively complete stimulus information about the test word.

Theoretical Analysis

Tulving et al. (1964) tested the assumption that the contribution of context is independent of the extraction of visual information from the word. These authors proposed that the independence assumption made the following prediction. Assume that f is the probability of recognition of a word presented without any context and c is the probability of recognizing the same word given only the context. If the visual information and context are processed independently, then p, the probability of recognizing the word, given both the stimulus presentation and context, should be

$$p = f + c - fc \tag{1}$$

which is the equation given by probability theory for describing the summation of two independent probability events. A straightforward interpretation of Equation 1 would assume that the duration of the stimulus can influence f and that the number of context words can influence c. Therefore, eight parameter values of f and four parameter values of c must be estimated before the model can be evaluated. The estimates of f were assumed to be the probabilities of a correct response at the 0-context condition. Similarly, the estimates of c were obtained from the response probabilities at the 0-exposure duration. To test the model, the authors compared the observed probabilities under the 21 other experimental conditions to those predicted by Equation 1, given the appropriate estimates of f and c. The observed recognition probabilities were in every case larger than that predicted by the independence equation. Therefore, the idea of independence of stimulus information and context was rejected.

The rejection of independence may have been premature. As Gough, Cosky, and Holly-Wilcox (1978) pointed out, the response probabilities at the 0-context or 0-duration conditions may not be valid estimates of c and f, respectively. All of the observed data should be used to make the parameter estimates. Tulving et al. did not have a computer to estimate the parameters by minimizing the deviations between the predicted and observed recognition probabilities. A more critical problem in the application of the model is the implicit assumption that c is zero when no context is presented. It is possible that the experience of the readers in the experiment allowed them to utilize some knowledge about the set of target words even in the 0-context condition. If this were the case, the model may also have failed for this reason.

It should also be stressed that the formulation of Tulving et al. is only one instance of an independence model. A critical, although implicit, component of their formulation is that recognition via context and stimulus is all-or-none. Context either allows recognition of a word or it does not; it does not allow the contribution of partial information about the word. This is also the case for stimulus information. This stands in sharp contrast to our idea of continuous information in the fuzzy logical model of perception (FLMP) developed in Chapter 16. Further, the Tulving et al. formulation makes the implicit assumption that false information is not possible, since there is no rule to apply if stimulus information triggers one alternative and context information another. In the FLMP, however, the reader has partial information from both context and the stimulus. The integration of these sources of partial information is analogous to the integration of the letter features making up G and Q (see Chapter 16).

In the framework of the FLMP, the reader has two sources of information about the test word; the visual information is indexed by Vi and the context by Cj. The reader evaluates both of these sources of information to arrive at the amount of support for a particular word alternative. The overall degree of support for the correct word can be indexed by $g(\text{correct word}: S_{ij})$, where S_{ij} is the stimulus condition corresponding to the ith level of visual information and the jth level of context. Combining the two sources of information would give

$$g(\text{correct word}: S_{ij}) = V_i \times C_j \tag{2}$$

In Equation 2, V_i is the visual information, and C_j is the sentential context information. Before the overall degree of support for the correct alternative can be used to indicate the likelihood of a correct response, the support for all other alternatives must be taken into account. For simplicity, it seems reasonable to assume that there is a relative trade-off between the correct and incorrect alternatives for each source of information. In this case, if V_i represents the degree of visual support for the correct alternative, $(1-V_i)$ would represent the degree of support for all incorrect alternatives. Similarly, $(1-C_j)$ would represent the degree of support for all incorrect alternatives given by sentential context. Therefore, the likelihood of a correct response should be equal to the support for the correct word relative to the total support for all alternatives

$$P(\text{correct}) = \frac{V_i C_j}{V_i C_j + (1-V_i)(1-C_j)} \tag{3}$$

In order to fit the model to the observed results, eight values of V_i and four values of C_j must be estimated as parameters in Equation 3. Figure 10 also presents the predictions of the model. The model provides a reasonably good description of the results.

The FLMP has been formalized within a successive stage model of information processing. Previously, context effects have been interpreted as evidence against stage models, since it appeared that information provided by a later stage modified processing of the earlier stage. However, contextual constraints made available by later stages simply function as additional sources of information at an earlier stage of processing. As an example, the context sentence in the Tulving et al. (1964) study contributes information that is combined with featural information in perceptual processing of the tachistoscopically presented test word. The contextual constraints were processed in the same successive stage fashion as was the test word. The outcome of this processing is made available to processing of the test word. This interpretation stands in marked contrast to views such as that of Neisser, who has argued against the idea of people adding information from memory to information in the stimulus to achieve a combined result (Neisser, 1976, p. 42). Neisser believes that the existing schema (context) determines what is picked up rather than simply adding to it. However, context does not override stimulus information, as we have shown in our analysis of a wide range of experimental studies.

The framework developed in the above analysis, and that in the previous chapter, has implications for extant views of the interaction of prior knowledge of context and perceptual processing. One popular distinction has been embedded in the issue of top-down versus bottom-up processing. This is a false distinction in the present framework. The influence of higher-order variables does not mean that processing is top-down. It simply means that higher-order constraints provide information to lower-order perceptual processes. Most importantly, lower-level processes are not somehow negated or modified in their operations by higher-level constraints. The operations of feature evaluation, prototype matching, and pattern classification proceed in the same manner regardless of the degree of higher-order constraints. In this sense, lower-level processing remains independent of higher-order constraints, although the outcome of these processes reflects exactly those constraints in addition to the featural information in the signal.

COMPREHENSION

Understanding printed text involves more than correctly recognizing letters, words, phrases, and sentences. The leap from recognition to comprehension requires certain cognitive prerequisites on the part of the reader. The text must be capable of activating the appropriate knowledge to effect understanding of the message. In some cases, reading occurs easily, but the message is not understood. Listening to a lecture on some issue in contemporary philosophy, for example, each of the words and phrases might make sense in isolation, but any general message would be missed by the uninitiated student. Bransford and Johnson (1972) read the following passage to a group of students:

> The procedure is actually quite simple. First, you arrange items into different groups. Of course, one pile may be sufficient depending on how much there is to do. If you have to go somewhere else due to lack of facilities that is the next step: otherwise, you are pretty well set. It is important not to overdo things. That is, it is better to do too few things at once than too many. In the short run this may not seem important but complications can easily arise. A mistake can be expensive as well. At first, the whole procedure will seem complicated. Soon, however, it will become just another facet of life. It is difficult to foresee any end to the necessity for this task in the immediate future, but then, one never can tell. After the procedure is completed one arranges the materials into different groups again. Then they can be put into their appropriate places. Eventually they will be used once more and the whole cycle will then have to be repeated. However, that is part of life. (Bransford, 1979, pp. 134-135)

These students, asked to rate the passage for comprehensibility, rated it as highly incomprehensible. In addition, their recall of the passage was very poor. Another group of subjects was given the theme "washing clothes" before the passage. These subjects rated the passage as very comprehensible and recalled much more than the no-context group. This experiment demonstrated that comprehension is critically dependent on activating the appropriate knowledge sources in the mind of the reader.

Comprehension criteria are flexible; one person's bewilderment is another's understanding. Bransford and Nitsch (1978) gave people the following passage:

> The man was worried. His car came to a halt and he was all alone. It was extremely dark and cold. The man took off his overcoat, rolled down the window, and got out of the car as quickly as possible. Then he used all his strength to move as fast as he could. He was relieved when he finally saw the lights of the city, even though they were far away. (Bransford, 1979, p. 196)

When asked if the passage made sense, most people said that it did. However, these people could not answer why the man took off his overcoat or rolled down the window. These actions make sense if the car is submerged in water but not otherwise. Therefore, people may feel that they know when, in fact, they do not or know only a little.

Reading, like speech perception, is a form of pattern recognition. Visual features of the text and context contribute to the perception and comprehension of the passage. The information-processing framework allows us to break down these complex activities into component parts and to gain a better understanding how each part works. Although we have only scratched the surface of two burgeoning areas of psychological inquiry, I hope the student has appreciated the value of the experimental method in taking seemingly intractable problems and opening them for objective analysis.

Suggested Readings

Psychology and the cognitive sciences are bursting at the seams. Each new year adds as many contributions as there were in the first century of psychology. The student must be prepared to build on previous accomplishments in the field; the primary charge is to determine the state of the art as efficiently as possible. The goal of the suggested readings is to make it easier to track down the literature; of course, the list of recommendations is only representative, not exhaustive. Important reference sources are encyclopedias of psychology (e.g., Corsini, 1987; Gregory & Zangwill, 1987) and dictionaries of psychological terms (Bruno, 1986; Reber, 1985).

Journals provide the most current coverage of experimental psychology. Articles relevant to the philosophy of science and such topics as the mind-body problem can sometimes be found in *American Psychologist; Psychological Review; Psychological Bulletin*; and *Cognition.*

Behavioral Research Methods, Instruments, & Computers presents papers dealing with the methodology, instrumentation, and computing involved in psychological inquiry. The scientist in the twentieth century is critically dependent on the most technologically advanced equipment. This journal gives the reader a good idea of the state of the art in the relevant technology. Research in psychophysics and perception can be found in *Journal of the Acoustical Society of America; Vision Research; Perception & Psychophysics; Journal of Experimental Psychology: Human Perception and Performance; Perception*; and *American Journal of Psychology.*

Articles on attention, auditory and visual information processing, memory, learning, and decision making are published in the same journals recommended for psychophysics and perception. They can also be found in *Journal of Experimental Psychology: Learning, Memory, and Cognition; Journal of Memory and Language; Cognitive Psychology; Cognitive Science; Memory & Cognition; Journal of Mathematical Psychology; Acta Psychologica; British Journal of Psychology; The Quarterly Journal of Experimental Psychology*; and *The European Journal of Cognitive Psychology.* Theoretical articles are more likely to be found in *Psychological Review,* whereas review articles are presented in *Psychological Bulletin; Annual Review of Psychology*; and *Journal of Experimental Psychology: General.* Articles of general interest to psychologists sometimes are published in *Science; Scientific American; The American Scientist*; and *Nature.*

A significantly greater proportion of research is being published in books. Book reviews can be found in *Contemporary Psychology* and the *American Journal of Psychology.*

The following suggested tutorials and advanced readings are organized in terms of the chapters in which they are discussed.

Chapter 1

Many of the questions raised in William James' (1890) two monumental volumes remain central to experimental psychology. Almost a century after they were written, the volumes make particularly good reading.

There has been a resurgence of interest in the mind-body problem within the cognitive sciences. In addition to philosophers, psychologists and neuroscientists have addressed the topic at some length (Flanagan, 1984). The ecletic set of readings on the mind-body problem (Blakemore & Greenfield, 1987) is engaging exploration of this persisting issue. Jackendoff (1987), a linguist, relates the computational level to the phenomenological level in his systematic development of a theory of consciousness. Searle (1987) has presented the most forceful arguments against the middle-computational level. LeDoux and Hirst (1986) present a series of papers that illustrate how cognitive psychologists and neuroscientists address the same phenomena. Pribram (1986) also blends the cognitive and neurological levels in his solution to the mind-body problem. Churchland (1986), a philosopher, presents an engaging review of neuroscience research and its implications for the mind-body problem.

Hadamard's (1954) eclectic treatment of the nature of discovery was influential in developing the stage analysis of discovery. Albert Einstein's reflections on the thought processes involved in the creation of the theory of relativity were the source for a chapter in Wertheimer's classic study (1945, reissued in 1959).

In a stimulating essay, Gregory (1987) has questioned whether the rejection of information theory was premature. Young (1987) attempts to describe the nature of information in terms of a physical phenomenon based on energy. Palmer and Kimchi (1986) articulate the information-processing paradigm in a thorough and comprehensible manner. I defend the use of the computer as a metaphor in psychological inquiry in Massaro (1986). Anderson (1985), Bourne, Dominowski, Loftus, and Healy (1986), Solso (1988), and Holyoak and Glass (1986) are recent second editions of well-accepted textbooks in cognitive psychology. A recent survey of cognitive science is by Johnson-Laird (1988). Bridgeman (1988) covers the fundamentals of the biology of behavior and mind. The chapters in Heuer and Sanders (1987) represent most of the major contemporary approaches to inquiry in experimental psychology.

Chapter 2

Some relevant sources for the history of experimental psychology are Boring (1950), Rancurello (1968), Hearnshaw (1987), and Wertheimer (1987). Hilgard (1987) has beautifully documented some of America's first hundred years of experimental psychology. His coverage will remain unique throughout the future of our discipline, not only because of its comprehensive treatment, but because the author actively participated in much of it. Buxton (1985), Baars (1986), Knapp and Robertson (1986), and Gardner (1985) are also valuable sources for the history and current state of affairs in the field. Other valuable glimpses of American history are recent publications of centennial celebrations of psychology within universities (e. g., Hulse & Green, 1986) and *festshrifts* for psycholgists (e. g., Hirst, 1988).

Richards (1987) describes the emergence of evolutionary theories of mind and behavior. A set of papers in the *Journal of Experimental Psychology: Learning, Memory, and Cognition* (Vol. 11, July, 1985) marks the centennial of the book reporting Ebbinghaus' seminal investigations of memory. Particularly noteworthy is the issue of the value of Ebbinghaus' contribution and the extent to which new endeavors negate or invalidate research within his paradigm (e.g., Kintsch, 1985; Slamecka, 1985). The centennial issue of the *American Journal of Psychology* (Vol. 100, Nos. 3-4, 1987) is an illuminating chronicle of classic papers, library exhibits, and commentary covering the journal's founding and history.

Lyons (1986) gives a pedagogical and valuable critique of introspection. Rescorla (1988) justifiably complains that classical conditioning is being inadequately explained in our psychology textbooks. The last 20 years have seen an infusion of information-processing concepts into the classical-conditioning paradigm. Even the simplest behavior has several stages of processing, and the different stages are being discovered by researchers in the study of conditioning. Conditioning is a form of learning that has important perceptual, memory, and response-selection processes. The discovery of these processes in conditioning makes it a much richer phenomenon than the typical textbook explanation.

Chapters 3-5

Giere (1984) is a basic and comprehensive testbook on understanding scientific reasoning. Both potential scientists and potential consumers of scientific findings should be well-versed in the fundamental concepts developed in his text. McCain and Segal (1973) introduce the student to the psychology of the scientist and his game of science, while Kuhn (1962), in an important work, covers the nature of scientific discovery.

Good textbooks on methods include Calfee (1985), Martin (1985), Snodgrass, Levy-Berger, and Haydon (1985), Shaughnessy and Zechmeister (1985), and Kantowitz, Roediger, and Elmes (1988). Bromley (1986) describes the use of the case-study method in psychology.

Applications of experimental psychology are emerging as quickly as the field is growing. A good introduction is a collection of scientists' reports to the U. S. Congress (Farley & Null, 1987).

Further reading on the psychology of the scientific process should begin with the references given in Chapter 5. Bechtel (1988) is a comprehensive overview of the philosophy of science. Additional sources are Berkson and Wettersten (1984) and Cummins (1983). Feyerabend (1975) offers a set of challenging criticisms of a coherent paradigm of scientific inquiry, such as the one given by falsification and strong inference. More recent contributions include Greenwald, Leippe, Pratkanis, and Baumgardner (1986).

Chapter 6

Krathwohl (1988) gives the facts on preparing a research proposal. Cleveland (1985) presents a systematic tutorial on the elements of graphing data—an important form of communication too often neglected and misused by scientists. Houghton and Willows (1987) present research on basic issues in the psychology of illustration. Houghton and Willows (1987) present instructional issues in the psychology of illustration.

Chapters 7-9

Additional papers on subtractive method are Brožek (1970) and Pieters (1983). Good reviews of early work using RTs are Theios (1973) and Teichner and Krebs (1974). Methods and theories of reaction times have increased in sophistication over the last decade. Most of the advances have emerged from the speed-accuracy method. Townsend (1984) gives a valuable overview on the use of reaction time as a dependent variable. Miller (1988) reviews and critiques evidence relevant to the question of discrete-stage models of human performance. Valuable, although highly technical, books and papers on RT include Luce (1986), Ratcliff (1988), and Meyer, Irwin, Osman, and Kounios (1988).

Keele (1986) and Annett (1983) give good overviews of motor control and motor learning.

Sternberg (1975) reviews the literature on visual and memory search. Shiffrin and Schneider (1977) extended the paradigm and models, and initiated work on controlled and automatic processing. The serial-exhaustive search model has not gone unchallenged (Ratcliff, 1978). Townsend and Ashby (1983) provide a pedagogical survey of results that can discriminate between serial and parallel processes. Schweickert (1978, 1983) has developed important generalizations of the additive-factor method

Chapters 10-13

Psychophysics continues to play an important role in psychological inquiry. Important readings include Falmagne (1985) and the chapters in the *Handbook of Perception and Human Performance* (Boff, Kaufman, & Thomas, 1986a). Birnbaum (1982) provides a pedagogical treatment of important issues in psychological measurement. Gescheider (1988) reviews recent work in psychophysical scaling attending particular problems and methodological issues confronting the field. A set of papers on the auditory processing of complex sounds can be found in Yost and Watson (1987). Ashby and Gott (1988) and Ashby and Perrin (1988) develop a model for recognition using a multidimensional-scaling framework.

Baird (1987) confronts the issues involving communication with other planets.

Chapter 14

The chapters in the *Handbook of Perception and Human Performance* (Boff, Kaufman, & Thomas, 1986b) provide a thorough coverage of most areas of perception, attention, memory, and learning. Gibson (1950, 1966, 1979) focuses on the structural information defining our visual world. For introductions to Gibson's work and to neo-Gibsonian viewpoints, see Cutting (1982) and Lombardo (1987). Marr's (1982) important contribution to the study of vision has had a large impact on the field. Gibson and Spelke (1983), McKenzie and Day (1987), and Aslin and Smith (1988) provide broad overviews of recent research in perceptual development.

Two engaging books on the psychology of art are Hagen (1986) and Kubovy (1986). Coren and Girgus (1978) is a good resource for entering the world of visual illusions. The study of illusory contours has become a cottage industry of its own, as witnessed by the edited volume of Petry and Meyer (1987). The experimental and theoretical approaches to the problem exemplify exactly those found in mainstream perception research.

Chapters 15 and 16

Attention has not gone unattended. The special issue of *Acta Psychologica* (1985) gives a series of papers representing advances in the field. Recent theoretical contributions include Allport (1987) and Neumann (1987).

The empirical and theoretical work has blossomed since Rosch's seminal studies of categorization. Mervis and Rosch (1981) and Smith and Medin (1981) provide an informative update on this work, as well as a converging framework for understanding categorization. Neisser's (1987) edited volume presents a broad spectrum of approaches to the problem. There has been a resurgence of interest in connectionist models of perception, categorization, and learning (McClelland & Rumelhart, 1986; Rumelhart & McClelland, 1986; Minsky & Papert, 1969). Lakoff's book on categorization is a rich study of the intersection of categorization and language. Boster's (1988) work is a recent valiant attempt at teasing apart the contribution of familiarity, typicality, and similarity in categorization. Sattath and Tversky (1987) discuss the relation between common and distinctive feature models of categorization.

The logic and psychological reality of fuzzy logic has been hotly debated (Oden, 1984b; Smith & Osherson, 1984; Zadeh, 1982).

Chapters 17 and 18

Gorfein and Hoffman (1987) have edited a good set of papers to celebrate Ebbinghaus' centennial. Richardson-Klavehn and Bjork (1988) capture the rapidly changing field of memory research and provide some coherence to what might appear to be unreconcilable approaches and findings. Klatzky (1984) provides an information processing perspective on memory and awareness. The pervading issue of perception without awareness is back in the mainstream of inquiry (Lazarus, 1982; Marcel, 1986a, 1986b, Weiner, 1986). There is substantial literature on the information processing of pictures and words, and how it might differ in these two domains (Jolicoeur, Gluck, & Kosslyn, 1984; Lupker & Katz, 1982). The research on imagery is also important (Anderson, 1978, Pylyshyn, 1984). The papers by McKoon, Ratcliff, and Dell (1986), Tulving (1986), Roediger (1984), and Ratcliff and McKoon (1986) are valuable discussions of both memory and methods of studying and describing the phenomenon. Dunn and Kirsner (1988) provide an informative critique of the use of dissociations in memory research, and describe a new method of reversed association.

The mood-congruity effect occurs when new information that is consistent with the subject's mood is better learned and remembered than information that is inconsistent with the subject's mood. In an interesting twist on state-dependent learning, Perrig and Perrig (1988) simply told subjects to behave *as if* they were depressed or happy. They found that indeed a mood-congruity effect occurred, even if subjects were simply instructed to have a particular mood rather than actually having the mood.

A textbook by Hogarth (1987) is a good introduction to problems in decision making. Gigerenzer and Murray (1987) describe how our statistical tools have influenced our theories of perception, memory, and decision making. Cherniak (1986) makes an engaging case for limitations in knowledge and understanding, which appear to be more consistent with what we know about human information processing. Petty and Cacioppo (1986) present an original study of communication and persuasion. Mayer (1983) remains one of the best treatments of problem solving.

Chapters 19 and 20

Fromkin and Rodman (1988) provide a thorough introduction to language. There is no good textbook on speech perception. However, there is a valuable tutorial paper by Jusczyk (1986), and more specialized papers in Perkell and Klatt (1986), Schouten (1987), and Harnad (1987). Klatt (in press) gives a pedagogical overview of current models of speech perception and how they fare against empirical results. Just and Carpenter (1987) present a comprehensive coverage of the psychology of reading, using an information-processing model as their framework. The selections in Coltheart (1987) are the most recent coverage of current research in the reading domain. Estes and Brunn (1987) provide evidence for the general interpretation of the word advantage developed here. Foss (1988) provides a comprehensive survey of research in experimental psycholinguistics. The readings in Allport, MacKay, Prinz, and Scheerer (1987) present a broad series of approaches to the study and description of language processing. Premack (1986) offers an instructive foray into the study of language in nonhuman animals.

References

Adams, M. J. (1979). Models of word recognition. *Cognitive Psychology, 11,* 133-176.

Allport, A. (1987). Selection for action: Some behavioral and neurophysiological considerations of attention and action. In H. Heuer & A. F. Sanders (Eds.), *Perspectives on perception and action.* Hillsdale, NJ: Lawrence Erlbaum.

Allport, A., MacKay, D. G., Prinz, W., & Scheerer, E. (Eds.). (1987). *Language perception and production: Relationships between listening, speaking, reading and writing.* London: Academic Press.

American Psychological Association. (1981). Ethical principles of psychologists (revised). *American Psychologist, 36,* 633-638.

American Psychological Association. (1983). *Publication manual of the American Psychological Association.* Washington, DC: American Psychological Association.

Anderson, I. H., & Dearborn, W. F. (1952). *The psychology of teaching reading.* New York: Ronald Press.

Anderson, J. R. (1978). Arguments concerning representations for mental imagery. *Psychological Review, 85,* 249-277.

Anderson, J. R. (1985). *Cognitive psychology and its implications.* New York: W. H. Freeman.

Anderson, N. H. (1970). Functional measurement and psychophysical judgment. *Psychological Review, 77,* 153-170.

Anderson, N. H. (1974). Algebraic models in perception. In E. C. Carterette & M. P. Friedman (Eds.), *Handbook of perception: Vol. II. Psychophysical judgment and measurement.* New York: Academic Press.

Anderson, N. H. (1981). *Foundations of information integration theory.* New York: Academic Press.

Anderson, N. H. (1982). *Methods of information integration theory.* New York: Academic Press.

Annett, J. (1983). Motor learning: A review. In H. Heuer, U. Kleinbeck, K. Schmidt (Eds.), *Motor behavior: Programming, control, and acquisition.* Heidelberg: Springer.

Armstrong, S. L., Gleitman, L. R., & Gleitman, H. (1983). What some concepts might not be. *Cognition, 13,* 263-308.

Asch, S. E. (1946). Forming impressions of personality. *Journal of Abnormal and Social Psychology, 41,* 258-290.

Asch, S. E. (1951). Effects of group pressure upon the modification and distortion of judgment. In H. Guetzkow (Ed.), *Groups, leadership, and men.* Pittsburgh: Carnegie.

Ashby, F. G., & Gott, R. E. (1988). Decision rules in the perception and categorization of multidimensional stimuli. *Journal of Experimental Psychology: Learning, Memory, and Cognition, 14,* 33-53.

Ashby, F. G., & Perrin, N. A. (1988). Toward a unified theory of similarity and recognition. *Psychological Review, 95,* 124-150.

Aslin, R. N., & Smith, L. B. (1988). Perceptual development. *Annual Review of Psychology, 39,* 435-473.

Attneave, F. (1957). Transfer of experience with a class schema to identification learning of patterns and shapes. *Journal of Experimental Psychology, 54,* 81-88.

Baars, B. J. (1986). *The cognitive revolution in psychology.* New York: Guilford Press.

Baddeley, A. D. (1964). Immediate memory and the "perception" of letter sequences. *Quarterly Journal of Experimental Psychology, 16,* 364-367.

Baddeley, A. D. (1978). The trouble with levels: A reexamination of Craik and Lockhart's framework for memory research. *Psychological Review, 85,* 139-152.

Bahrick, L. E., Walker, A. S., & Neisser, U. (1981). Selective looking by infants. *Cognitive Psychology, 13,* 377-390.

Baird, J. C. (1987). *The inner limits of outer space.* Hanover, NH: University Press of New England.

Ballard, J. G. (1974). The subliminal man. In H. A. Katz, P. Warrick, & M. H. Greenberg (Eds.), *Introductory psychology through science fiction.* Chicago: Rand McNally.

Barber, T. X. (1972). Suggested ("hypnotic behavior"): The trance paradigm versus an alternaive paradigm. In E. Fromm & R. E. Shor (Eds.), *Hypnosis: Research developments and perspectives* (pp. 115-182). Chicago: Aldine-Atherton.

Barber, T. X. (1976). *Pitfalls in human research: Ten pivotal points.* New York: Pergamon Press.

Barclay, J. R. (1970). Noncategorical perception of a voiced stop consonant: A replication. *Proceedings of the 78th Annual Convention of the American Psychological Association,* 9-10.

Bartlett, F. C. (1932). *Remembering: A study in experimental and social psychology.* Cambridge, MA: Harvard University Press.

Battig, W. F., & Montague, W. E. (1969). Category norms for verbal items in 56 categories: A replication and extension of the Connecticut norms. *Journal of Experimental Psychology, 80,* 1-46.

Beaton, A. (1986). *Left side, right side: A review of laterality research.* New Haven, CT: Yale University Press.

Bechtel, W. (1988). *Philosophy of science: An overview for cognitive science.* Hillsdale, NJ: Lawrence Erlbaum.

Beck, J., & Gibson, J. J. (1955). The relation of apparent shape to apparent slant in the perception of objects. *Journal of Experimental Psychology, 50,* 125-133.

Becker, C. A. (1976). Allocation of attention during visual word recognition. *Journal of Experimental Psychology: Human Perception and Performance, 2,* 556-566.

Becker, C. A., & Killion, T. H. (1977). Interaction of visual and cognitive effects in word recognition. *Journal of Experimental Psychology: Human Perception and Performance, 3,* 389-401.

Berkson, W., & Wettersten, J. (1984). *Learning from error: Karl Popper's psychology of learning*. La Salle, IL: Open Court.

Bernoulli, D. (1967). *Exposition of a new theory on the measurement of risk.* (L. Sommer, Trans.). Farnborough Hants, England: Gregg Press. (Original work published 1738)

Biederman, I. (1987). Recognition-by-components: A theory of human image understanding. *Psychological Review, 94,* 115-147.

Bieri, P. (1985, January). *What is the mind-body problem?* Lecture given at the Center for Interdisciplinary Research, University of Bielefeld, FDR.

Birnbaum, M. H. (1973). The devil rides again: Correlation as an index of fit. *Psychological Bulletin, 79,* 239-242.

Birnbaum, M. H. (1982). Controversies in psychological measurement. In B. Wegener (Ed.), *Social attitudes and psychophysical measurement* (pp. 401-485). Hillsdale, NJ: Lawrence Erlbaum.

Birnbaum, M. H., & Mellers, B. A. (1979a). One-mediator model of exposure effects is still viable. *Journal of Personality and Social Psychology, 37,* 1090-1096.

Birnbaum, M. H., & Mellers, B. A. (1979b). Stimulus recognition may mediate exposure effects. *Journal of Personality and Social Psychology, 37,* 391-394

Birnbaum M. H., & Mellers, B. A. (1983). Bayesian inference: Combining base rates with opinions of sources who vary in credibility. *Journal of Personality and Social Psychology, 45,* 792-804.

Blakemore, C., & Greenfield, S. (Eds.). (1987). *Mindwaves.* New York: Basil Blackwell.

Bland, D. E., & Perrott, D. R. (1978). Backward masking: Detection versus recognition. *Journal of the Acoustical Society of America, 63,* 1215-1220.

Blumenthal, A. L. (1979). The founding father we never knew. *Contemporary Psychology, 24,* 547-550.

Blumstein, S. E., & Stevens, K. N. (1979). Acoustic invariance in speech production: Evidence from measurements of the spectral characteristics of stop consonants. *Journal of the Acoustical Society of America, 66,* 1001-1017.

Boff, K. R., Kaufman, L., & Thomas, J. P. (1986a). *Handbook of perception and human performance: Vol. I. Sensory processes and perception.* New York: Wiley.

Boff, K. R., Kaufman, L., & Thomas, J. P. (1986b). *Handbook of perception and human performance: Vol. II. Cognitive processes and performance.* New York: Wiley.

Bonnano, G. A., & Stilling, N. A. (1986). Preference, familiarity, and recognition after repeated brief exposures to random geometric shapes. *American Journal of Psychology, 99,* 403-415.

Boring, E. G. (1942). *Sensation and perception in the history of experimental psychology.* New York: Appleton-Century.

Boring, E. G. (1943). The moon illusion. *American Journal of Physics, 11,* 55-60.

Boring, E. G., Langfeld, H. S., & Weld, H. P. (1939). *Introduction to psychology.* New York: Wiley.

Boster, J. S. (1988). Natural sources of internal category structure: Typicality, familiarity, and similarity of birds. *Memory & Cognition, l6,* 258-270.

Bourne, L. E., Dominowski, R. L., Loftus, E. F., & Healy, A. F. (1986). *Cognitive processes.* Englewood Cliffs, NJ: Prentice-Hall.

Bower, G. H. (1970). Imagery as a relational organizer in associative learning. *Journal of Verbal Learning and Verbal Behavior, 9,* 529-533.

Bower, G. H. (1981). Mood and memory. *American Psychologist, 36,* 129-148.

Bower, G. H., & Cohen, P. R. (1982). Emotional influences in memory and thinking: Data and theory. In M. S. Clark & S. T. Fiske (Eds.), *Affect and cognition.* Hillsdale, NJ: Lawrence Erlbaum.

Bower, G. H., Monteiro, K. P., & Gilligan, S. G. (1978). Emotional mood as a context for learning and recall. *Journal of Verbal Learning and Behavior, 17,* 573, 585.

Bradley, D. C., & Forster, K. I. (1987). In U. H. Frauenfelder & L. K. Tyler (Eds.), *Spoken word recognition* (pp. 103-134). Cambridge, MA: MIT Press.

Bransford, J. D. (1979). *Human cognition: Learning, understanding and remembering.* Belmont, CA: Wadsworth.

Bransford, J. D., & Johnson, M. K. (1972). Contextual prerequisites for understanding: Some investigations of comprehension and recall. *Journal of Verbal Learning and Verbal Behavior, 11,* 717-726.

Bransford, J. D., & Nitsch, K. E. (1978). Coming to understand things we could not previously understand. In J. F. Kavanagh & W. Strange (Eds.), *Speech and language in the laboratory, school, and clinic.* Cambridge, MA: MIT Press.

Bridgeman, B. (1988). *The biology of behavior and mind.* New York: Wiley.

Broadbent, D. E. (1954). The role of auditory localization and attention in memory span. *Journal of Experimental Psychology, 47,* 191-196.

Broadbent, D. E. (1958). *Perception and communication.* New York: Pergamon Press.

Broadbent, D. E. (1970). Stimulus set and response set: Two kinds of selective attention. In D. I. Mostofsky (Ed.), *Attention: Contemporary theory and analysis.* New York: Appleton-Century-Crofts.

Broadbent, D. E. (1971). *Decision and stress.* London: Academic Press.

Broadbent, D. E. (1982). Task combination and selective intake of information. *Acta Psychologica, 50,* 253-290.

Broadbent, D. E., & Gregory, M. (1962). Donders' B- and C-reactions and S-R compatibility. *Journal of Experimental Psychology, 263,* 575-578.

Broadbent, D. E., & Gregory, M. (1964). Stimulus set and response set: The alternation of attention. *Quarterly Journal of Experimental Psychology, 16,* 309-317.

Broadbent, D. E., & Gregory, M. (1965). On the interaction of S-R compatibility with other variables affecting reaction time. *British Journal of Psychology, 56,* 61-67.

Bromley, D. B. (1986). *The case-study method in psychology and related disciplines.* Great Britain: Wiley.

Brooks, L. (1978). Nonanalytic concept formation and memory for instances. In E. Rosch & B. B. Lloyd (Eds.), *Cognition and categorization* (pp. 169-211). Hillsdale, NJ: Lawrence Erlbaum.

Brown, R., & McNeill, D. (1966). The "tip of the tongue" phenomenon. *Journal of Verbal Learning and Verbal Behavior, 5,* 325-337.

Brožek, J. (1970). Contributions to the history of psychology: XII. Wayward history: F. C. Donders (1818-1889) and the timing of mental operations. *Psychological Reports, 226,* 563-569.

Bruner, J. S., Goodnow, J., & Austin, G. (1956). *A study of thinking.* New York: Wiley.

Bruner, J. S., & Potter, M. C. (1964). Interference in visual recognition. *Science, 144,* 424-425.

Bruno, F. J. (1986). *Dictionary of key words in psychology.* London: Routledge & Kegan Paul.

Bruno, N., & Cutting, J. E. (1988). Minimodularity and the perception of layout. *Journal of Experimental Psychology: General, 117,* 161-170.

Busemeyer, J. R., Dewey, G. I., & Medin, D. L. (1984). Evaluation of exemplar-based generalization and the abstraction of categorical information. *Journal of Experimental Psychology: Learning, Memory, and Cognition, 10,* 638-648.

Bush, R. R., Galanter, E., & Luce, R. D. (1963). Characterization and classification of choice experiments. In R. D. Luce, R. R. Bush, & E. Galanter (Eds.), *Handbook of mathematical psychology* (Vol. 1, pp. 77-102). New York: Wiley.

Buxton, C. E. (Ed.). (1985). *Points of view in the modern history of psychology.* Orlando: Academic Press.

Calfee, R. C. (1985). *Experimental methods in psychology.* New York: CBS College Publishing, Holt, Rinehart, and Winston.

California Achievement Tests. (1978). New York: McGraw-Hill.

Campbell, D. T. (1960). Blind variation and selective retention in creative thought as in other knowledge processes. *Psychological Review, 67,* 380-400.

Campbell, D. T. (1974). Evolutionary epistemology. In P. Schilpp (Ed.), *The Philosophy of Karl Popper.* La Salle, IL: Open Court.

Campbell, D. T. (1977). *Descriptive epistemology: Psychological, sociological, and evolutionary.* Preliminary draft of the William James Lectures, Harvard University, Cambridge, MA.

Carr, T. H. (1986). Perceiving visual language. In K. R. Boff, L. Kaufman, & J. P. Thomas (Eds.), *Handbook of perception and human performance: Vol. II. Cognitive processes and performance* (chapter 29). New York: Wiley.

Carterette, E. C., Friedman, M. P., & Wyman, M. J. (1966). Feedback and psychophysical variables in signal detection. *Journal of Acoustical Society of America, 39,* 1051-1055.

Cason, H. (1932). The learning and retention of pleasant and unpleasant activities. *Archives of Psychology, 21,* No. 134.

Cattell, J. M. (1888). The time it takes to think. *Popular Science Monthly, 32,* 488-491.

Caws, P. (1969). The structure of discovery. *Science, 166,* 1375-1380.

Chandler, J. P. (1969). Subroutine STEPIT - Finds local minima of a smooth function of several parameters. *Behavioral Science, 14,* 81-82.

Charness, N. (1976). Memory for chess positions: Resistance to interference. *Journal of Experimental Psychology: Human Learning and Memory, 2,* 345-375.

Chase, W. G., & Simon, H. A. (1973). Perception in chess. *Cognitive Psychology, 4,* 55-81.

Cherniak, C. (1986). *Minimal rationality.* Cambridge, MA: MIT Press.

Cherry, E. C. (1953). Some experiments on the recognition of speech, with one and with two ears. *Journal of the Acoustical Society of America, 25,* 975-979.

Cherry, E. C., & Taylor, W. K. (1954). Some further experiments on the recognition of speech with one and two ears. *Journal of the Acoustical Society of America, 26,* 554-559.

Christensen, L. B. (1988). *Experimental methodology.* Boston: Allyn & Bacon.

Churchland, P. S. (1986). *Neurophilosophy: Toward a unified science of the mind-brain.* Cambridge, MA: MIT Press.

Churchman, C. W. (1971). *The design of inquiring systems: Basic concepts of systems and orginazation.* New York: Basic Books.

Clapper, J. P., & Bower, G. H. (1988). *The impact of category knowledge on representing instances.* Paper presented at the Western Psychological Association, Burlingame, CA.

Clark, D. M., & Teasdale, J. D. (1982). Diurnal variation in clinical depression and accessibility of memories of positive and negative experiences. *Journal of Abnormal Psychology, 91,* 87-95.

Cleveland, W. S. (1985). *The elements of graphing data.* Monterey, CA: Wadsworth Advanced Books and Software.

Cohen, D. (1979). *J. B. Watson: The founder of behaviorism, a biography.* London: Routledge & Kegan Paul.

Cohen, J. (1971). *Thinking.* Chicago: Rand McNally.

Cole, R. A. (1973). Listening for mispronunciations: A measure of what we hear during speech. *Perception & Psychophysics, 13,* 153-156.

Cole, R. A., & Jakimik, J. (1978). Understanding speech: How words are heard. In G. Underwood (Ed.), *Strategies of information-processing.* London: Academic Press.

Cole, R. A., & Scott, B. (1974). Toward a theory of speech perception. *Psychological Review, 81,* 348-374.

Collins, A. M., & Quillian, M. R. (1969). Retrieval time from semantic memory. *Journal of Verbal Learning and Verbal Behavior, 8,* 240-247.

Coltheart, M. (Ed.). (1987). *Attention and performance XII: The psychology of reading.* London: Lawrence Erlbaum.

Conant, J. B. (1947). *On understanding science.* New Haven, CT: Yale University Press.

Conrad, C. E. H. (1972). Cognitive economy in semantic memory. *Journal of Experimental Psychology, 92,* 149-154.

Coombs, C. H. (1969). Unpublished lecture.

Copperman, P. (1980). The decline of literacy. *Journal of Communication, 30,* 113-122.

Corballis, M. C. (1975). Access to memory: An analysis of recognition times. In P. M. A. Rabbitt & S. Dornic (Eds.), *Attention and performance* (pp. 591-612). London: Academic Press.

Corbett, A., & Wickelgren, W. (1978). Semantic memory retrieval: Analysis by speed-accuracy trade-off functions. *Quarterly Journal of Experimental Psychology, 30,* 1-15.

Coren, S., & Girgus, J. S. (1978). *Seeing is deceiving: The psychology of visual illusions.* Hillsdale, NJ: Lawrence Erlbaum.

Coren, S., Porac, C., & Ward, L. M. (1984). *Sensation and perception.* Orlando: Academic Press.

Cornine, C. M., & Clifton, C. (1987). Interactive use of lexical information in speech perception. *Journal of Experimental Psychology: Human Perception and Performance, 13,* 291-299.

Cornsweet, T. N. (1962). The staircase-method in psychophysics. *American Journal of Psychology, 75,* 485-491.

Corsini, R. J. (Ed.). (1987). *Concise encyclopedia of psychology.* New York: Wiley.

Cotton, S., & Grosjean, F. (1984). The gating paradigm: A comparison of successive and individual presentation formats. *Perception & Psychophysics, 35,* 41-48.

Cowan, N., Leavitt, L. A., Massaro, D. W., & Kent, R. D. (1982). A fluent backward talker. *Journal of Speech and Hearing Research, 25,* 48-53.

Craik, F. I. M., & Lockhart, R. S. (1972). Levels of processing: A framework for memory research. *Journal of Verbal Learning and Verbal Behavior, 11,* 671-684.

Craik, F. I. M., & Tulving, E. (1975). Depth of processing and the retention of words in episodic memory. *Journal of Experimental Psychology: General, 104,* 268-294.

Crowder, R. G. (1982). The demise of short-term memory. *Acta Psychologica, 50,* 291-323.

Cummins, R. (1975). Functional analysis. *The Journal of Philosophy, 72,* 741-765.

Cummins, R. (1977). Programs in the explanation of behavior. *Philosophy of Science, 44,* 269-287.

Cummins, R. (1983). *The nature of psychological explanation.* Cambridge, MA: MIT Press.

Cutting, J. E. (1982). Two ecological perspectives: Gibson vs. Shaw and Turvey. *American Journal of Psychology, 95,* 199-222.

Dawkins, R. (1987). *The blind watchmaker.* New York: Norton.

de Groot, A. D. (1966). *Thought and choice in chess.* The Hague: Mouton.

Denes, P. B., & Pinson, E. N. (1963). *The speech chain.* Bell Telephones Laboratories.

Deutsch, J. A., & Deutsch, D. (1963). Attention: Some theoretical considerations. *Psychological Review, 70,* 80-90.

Deutsch, J. A., & Deutsch, D. (1967). Comments on "Selective attention: Perception or response?" and reply. *Quarterly Journal of Experimental Psychology, 19,* 362-363.

Doherty, M. E., Mynatt, C. R., Tweney, R. D., & Schiavo, M. D. (1979). Pseudodiagnosticity. *Acta Psychologica, 43,* 111-121.

Dominowski, R. L., & Ekstrand, B. R. (1967). Direct and associative priming in anagram solving. *Journal of Experimental Psychology, 74,* 84-86.

Donders, F. C. (1969). On the speed of mental processes. In W. G. Koster (Ed.), *Attention and performance II: Acta Psychologica, 30,* 412-431. (Original work published 1869)

Duncan, J. (1981). Directing attention in the visual field. *Perception & Psychophysics, 30,* 90-93.

Dunn, J. C., & Kirsner, K. (1988). Discovering functionally independent mental processes: The principle of reversed association. *Psychological Review, 95,* 91-101.

Ebbinghaus, H. (1964). *Memory: A contribution to experimental psychology.* New York: Dover. (Original work published 1885; translated 1913)

Egeth, H., Marcus, N., & Bevan, W. (1972). Target-set and response-set interaction: Implications for models of human information processing. *Science, 2176,* 1447-1448.

Eimas, P. D. (1963). The relation between identification and discrimination along speech and non-speech continua. *Language and Speech, 6,* 206-217.

Ekstrand, B. R., & Dominowski, R. L. (1965). Solving words as anagrams. *Psychonomic Science, 2,* 239-240.

Elio, R., & Anderson, J. R. (1981). The effects of category generalizations and instance similarity on schema abstraction. *Journal of Experimental Psychology: Human Learning and Memory, 7,* 397-418.

Ellis, A. W. (1979). Slips of the pen. *Visible Language, XIII,* 265-282.

Epstein, W. (1973). The process of "taking-into-account" in visual perception. *Perception, 2,* 267-285.

Epstein, W., & Hatfield, G. (1978). Functional equivalence of masking and cue reduction in perception of shape at a slant. *Perception & Psychophysics, 23,* 137-144.

Epstein, W., & Hatfield, G. (1978). The locus of masking shape-at-a-slant. *Perception & Psychophysics, 24,* 501-504.

Epstein, W., Hatfield, G., & Muise, G. (1977). Perceived shape at a slant as a function of processing time and processing load. *Journal of Experimental Psychology: Human Perception and Performance, 3,* 473-483.

Epstein, W., & Park, J. N. (1963). Shape constancy: Functional relationships and theoretical formulations. *Psychological Bulletin, 60,* 265-288.

Ericsson, K. A., & Simon, H. A. (1984). *Protocol analysis: Verbal reports as data.* Cambridge, MA: MIT Press.

Estes, W. K. (1986). Memory storage and retrieval processes in category learning. *Journal of Experimental Psychology: General, 115,* 155-174.

Estes, W. K., & Brunn, J. L. (1987). Discriminability and bias in the word-superiority effect. *Perception & Psychophysics, 42,* 411-422.

Evans, C. R., & Marsden, R. P. (1966). A study of the effect of perfect retinal stabilization on some well-known visual illusions using the after-image as a method of compensating for eye movements. *British Journal of Physiological Optics, 23,* 242-248.

Falmagne, J. (1985). *Elements of psychophysical theory.* New York: Oxford University Press.

Fantz, R. (1965). Visual perception from birth as shown by pattern selectivity. *Annals of the New York Academy of Sciences, 118,* 793-814.

Fantz, R. (1967). Visual perception and experience in early infancy: A look at the hidden side of behavior development. In H. Stevenson (Ed.), *Early behavior: Comparative and developmental approaches.* New York: Wiley.

Farley, F., & Null, C. H. (1987). *Using psychological science: Making the public case.* Washington, DC: The Federation of Behavioral, Psychological & Cognitive Sciences.

Fechner, G. T. (1966). *Elements of psychophysics* (Vol. 1.) (H. E. Adler, D. H. Howes, & E. G. Boring Eds. and Trans.). New York: Holt, Rinehart, & Winston. (Original work published 1860)

Feldman, J. A. (1985). Connectionist models and their applications: Introduction. *Cognitive Science, 9,* 1-2.

Feyerabend, P. K. (1975). *Against method.* London: NLB.

Fink, T. E., & Weisberg, R. W. (1981). The use of phonemic information to solve anagrams. *Memory & Cognition, 9,* 402-410.

Flanagan, O. J., Jr. (1984). *The science of the mind.* Cambridge, MA: MIT Press.

Fodor, J. (1968). *Psychological explanation: An introduction to the philosophy of psychology.* New York: Random House.

Fodor, J. (1975). *The language of thought.* New York: Crowell.

Fodor, J. (1981). The mind-body problem. *Scientific American, 244*(1), 114-123.

Fodor, J., Bever, T. G., & Garrett, M. F. (1974). *The psychology of language.* New York: McGraw-Hill.

Forster, K. I. (1979). Levels of processing and the structure of the language processor. In W. Cooper & E. Walker (Eds.), *Sentence processing: Psycholinguistic studies presented to Merrill Garrett* (pp. 27-86). Hillsdale, NJ: Lawrence Erlbaum.

Forster, K. I. (1981). Priming and the effects of sentence and lexical contexts on naming time: Evidence for autonomous lexical processing. *Quarterly Journal of Experimental Psychology, A,* 465-495.

Forster, K. I. (1985). Lexical acquisition and the modular lexicon. *Language and Cognitive Processes,* 87-108.

Foss, D. J. (1988). Experimental psycholinguistics. *Annual Review of Psychology, 39,* 301-348.

Freud, S. (1947). *Leonard da Vinci—A study in psychosexuality.* New York: Modern Library.

Freud, S. (1976). *The interpretation of dreams.* In J. Strachey (Ed. and Trans.), *The standard edition* (Vols. 4-5). New York: Norton. (Original work published 1900)

Frey, P. W., & Adesman, P. (1976). Recall memory for visually presented chess positions. *Memory & Cognition, 4,* 541-547.

Fried, L. S., & Holyoak, K. J. (1984). Induction of category distributions: A framework for classification learning. *Journal of Experimental Psychology: Learning, Memory, and Cognition, 10,* 234-257.

Frijda, N. H. (1986). *Studies in emotion and social interaction.* Cambridge, England: Cambridge University Press.

Fromkin, V. A. (Ed.). (1973). *Speech errors as linguistic evidence.* The Hague: Mouton.

Fromkin, V. A. (Ed.). (1980). *Errors of linguistic performance: Slips of the tongue, ear, pen, and hands.* New York: Academic Press.

Fromkin, V., & Rodman, R. (1988). *An introduction to language.* New York: Holt, Rinehart & Winston.

Gardner, H. (1985). *The mind's new science: A history of the cognitive revolution.* New York: Basic Books.

Geldard, F. A. (1953). *The human senses.* New York: Wiley.

Gengerelli, J. A. (1976). Graduate school reminiscences: Hull and Koffka. *American Psychologist, 31,* 685-688.

Gentner, D., & Grudin, J. (1985). The evolution of mental metaphors in psychology: A 90-year retrospective. *American Psychologist, 40,* 181-192.

Gescheider, G. A. (1988). Psychophysical scaling. *Annual Review of Psychology, 39,* 169-200.

Gibson, E. J., & Levin, H. (1975). *The psychology of reading.* Cambridge, MA: MIT Press.

Gibson, E. J., Osser, H., & Pick, A. D. (1963). A study of the development of grapheme-phoneme correspondences. *Journal of Verbal Learning and Verbal Behavior, 2,* 142-146.

Gibson, E. J., Pick, A. D., Osser, H., & Hammond, M. (1962). The role of grapheme-phoneme correspondence in the perception of words. *American Journal of Psychology, 75,* 554-570.

Gibson, E. J., & Spelke, E. S. (1983). The development of perception. P. H. Mussen (Gen. Ed.), *Handbook of child psychology, Vol. 3:* J. H. Flavell & E. M. Markman (Eds.) *Cognitive development.* New York: Wiley.

Gibson, J. J. (1950). *The perception of the visual world.* Boston: Houghton Mifflin.

Gibson, J. J. (1966). *The senses considered as perceptual systems.* Boston: Houghton Mifflin.

Gibson, J. J. (1979). *The ecological approach to visual perception.* Boston: Houghton Mifflin.

Giere, R. N. (1984). *Understanding scientific reasoning.* New York: CBS College Publishing.

Gigerenzer, G., & Murray, D. J. (1987). *Cognition as intuitive statistics.* Hillsdale, NJ: Lawrence Erlbaum.

Glass, A. L., & Holyoak, K. J. (1975). Alternative conceptions of semantic memory. *Cognition, 3,* 313-339.

Glass, A. L., & Holyoak, K. J. (1986). *Cognition.* New York: Random House.

Glushko, R. J. (1979). The organization and activation of orthographic knowledge in reading aloud. *Journal of Experimental Psychology: Human Perception and Performance, 5,* 674-691.

Goguen, J. A. (1969). The logic of inexact concepts. *Synthese, 19,* 325-373.

Goldmeier, E. (1936). Uber Ahnlichkeit bei gesehene Figuren. *Psychologica Forschung, 21,* 146-208.

Goldmeier, E. (1972). Similarity in visually perceived forms. *Psychological Issues, 8*(1, Monograph 29).

Goldstein, M., & Goldstein, I. F. (1978). *How we know: An exploration of the scientific process.* New York: Plenum Press.

Goodman, N. (1984). *Of mind and other matters.* Cambridge, MA: Harvard University Press.

Gorfein, D. S., & Hoffman, R. R. (1987). *Memory and learning: The Ebbinghaus centennial conference.* Hillsdale, NJ: Lawrence Erlbaum.

Gough, P. B. (1972). One second of reading. In J. F. Kavanagh & I. G. Mattingly (Eds.), *Language by eye and ear: The relationships between speech and reading.* Cambridge, MA: MIT Press.

Gough, P. B., & Cosky, M. J. (1977). One second of reading again. In N. J. Castellan, Jr., D. B. Pisoni, & G. R. Potts (Eds.), *Cognitive theory* (Vol. 2). Hillsdale, NJ: Lawrence Erlbaum.

Gough, P. B., Cosky, M. J., & Holly-Wilcox, P. (1978). *Words and contexts.* Paper presented at the National Reading Conference, St. Petersburg Beach, FL.

Graboi, D. (1971). Searching for targets: The effects of specific practice. *Perception & Psychophysics, 10,* 300-304.

Gray, J., & Wedderburn, A. (1960). Grouping strategies with simultaneous stimuli. *Quarterly Journal of Experimental Psychology, 12,* 180-184.

Green, D. M., & Swets, J. A. (1966). *Signal detection theory and psychophysics.* New York: Wiley.

Greeno, J. G. (1978). Notes on problem-solving abilities. In W. K. Estes (Ed.), *Handbook of learning and cognitive processes.* Hillsdale, NJ: Lawrence Erlbaum.

Greenwald, A. G., Leippe, M. R., Pratkanis, A. R., & Baumgardner, M. H. (1986). Under what conditions does theory obstruct research progress? *Psychological Review, 93,* 216-229.

Gregg, L. W., & Steinberg, E. R. (Eds.). (1980). *Cognitive processes in writing.* Hillsdale, NJ: Lawrence Erlbaum.

Gregory, R. L. (1963). Distortion of visual space as inappropriate constancy scaling. *Nature, 199,* 678-680.

Gregory, R. L. (1966). *Eye and Brain: The psychology of seeing.* New York: McGraw-Hill.

Gregory, R. L. (1968). Visual illusions. *Scientific American, 219*(5), 66-76.

Gregory, R. L. (1987). *Odd perceptions.* London: Methuen.

Gregory, R. L., & Zangwill, O. L. (Eds.). (1987). *The Oxford companion to the mind.* Oxford, England: Oxford University Press.

Groff, P. (1975). Research in brief: Shapes as cues to word recognition. *Visible Language, 9,* 67-71.

Grosjean, F. (1980). Spoken word recognition processes and the gating paradigm. *Perception & Psychophysics, 28,* 267-283.

Grosjean, F. (1985). The recognition of words after their acoustic offset: Evidence and implications. *Perception & Psychophysics, 38,* 299-310.

Haber, R. N. (1970, August). How we remember what we see. *Scientific American, 222,* 104-112.

Hadamard, J. (1954). *The psychology of invention in the mathematical field.* New York: Dover.

Hagen, M. A. (1986). *Varieties of realism.* New York: Cambridge University Press.

Hamill, R., Wilson, T. D., & Nisbett, R. E. (1980). Insensitivity to sample bias: Generalizing from atypical cases. *Journal of Personality and Social Psychology, 39,* 578-589.

Hampton, J. A. (1979). Polymorphous concepts in semantic memory. *Journal of Verbal Learning and Verbal Behavior, 18,* 441-461.

Harcum, E. R. (1967). Parallel functions of serial learning and tachistoscopic pattern perception. *Psychological Review, 74,* 51-62.

Harlow, H. F. (1953). Mice, monkeys, men, and motives. *Psychological Review, 60,* 23-32.

Harnad, S. (Ed.). (1987). *Categorical perception.* Cambridge, England: Cambridge University Press.

Hatfield, G., & Epstein, W. (1985). The status of the minimum principle in the theoretical analysis of visual perception. *Psychological Bulletin, 97,* 155-186.

Hayes, J. R., & Flower, L. S. (1980). Identifying the organization of writing processes. In L. W. Gregg & E. R. Steinberg (Eds.), *Cognitive processes in writing.* Hillsdale, NJ: Lawrence Erlbaum.

Hearnshaw, L. S. (1987). *The shaping of modern psychology: A historical introduction from dawn to present day.* London: Routledge & Kegan Paul.

Hearst, E. (Ed.). (1979). *The first century of experimental psychology.* Hillsdale, NJ: Lawrence Erlbaum.

Hecht, S. (1934). Vision II: The nature of the photoreceptor process. In C. Murchison (Ed.), *A handbook of general experimental psychology.* Worcester, MA: Clark University Press.

Hecht, S., Shlaer, S., & Pirenne, M. H. (1942). Energy, quanta, and vision. *Journal of General Physiology, 25,* 819-840.

Heider, F. K., & Heider, G. M. (1940). An experimental investigation of lipreading. *Psychological Monographs, 52,* 124-153.

Helmholtz, H. von (1962). *Treatise on physiological optics* (3rd ed.). (J. P. C. Southall, Ed. and Trans.). New York: Dover. (Original work published 1856-1866)

Helmholtz, H. von (1968). A series of lectures delivered in Frankfurt and Heidelberg. In R. M. Warren & R. P. Warren (Eds.), *Helmholtz on perception: Its physiology and development.* New York: Wiley. (Original work published 1867)

Henley, N. M. (1969). A psychological study of the semantics of animal terms. *Journal of Verbal Learning and Verbal Behavior, 8,* 176-184.

Heuer, H., & Sanders, A. F. (Eds.). (1987). *Perspectives on perception and action.* Hillsdale, NJ: Lawrence Erlbaum.

Hibbard, H. (1965). *Bernini.* Baltimore, MD: Penguin Books.

Hick, W. E. (1952). On the rate of gain of information. *Quarterly Journal of Experimental Psychology, 24,* 11-26.

Hilgard, E. R. (1987). *Psychology in America.* San Diego: Harcourt Brace Jovanovich.

Hinton, G. E., & Anderson, J. A. (1981). *Parallel models of associative memory.* Hillsdale, NJ: Lawrence Erlbaum.

Hintzman, D. L., & Ludlam, G. (1980). Differential forgetting of prototypes and old instances: Simulation by an exemplar-based classification model. *Memory & Cognition, 8,* 378-382.

Hirst, W. (Ed.). (1988). *The making of cognitive science: Essays in honor of George A. Miller.* Cambridge, England: Cambridge University Press.

Hochberg, J. (1971). Perception I: Color and shape. Perception II: Space and movement. In J. W. Kling & L. A. Riggs (Eds.), *Experimental psychology.* New York: Holt, Rinehart, & Winston.

Hofstadter, D. R. (1979). *Gödel, Escher, Bach.* New York: Basic Books.

Hogarth, R. M. (1987). *Judgement and choice.* New York: Wiley.

Holway, A. H., & Boring, E. G. (1941). Determinants of apparent visual size with distance variant. *American Journal of Psychology, 54,* 21-37.

Homa, D., Sterling, S., & Trepel, L. (1981). Limitations of exemplar-based generalization and the abstraction of categorical information. *Journal of Experimental Psychology: Human Learning and Memory, 7,* 418-439.

Houghton, H. A., & Willows, D. M. (1987). *The psychology of illustration: Instructional issues.* (Vol. 2). New York: Springer-Verlag

Hubel, D., & Wiesel, T. (1962). Receptive fields, binocular interaction and functional architecture in the cat's visual cortex. *Journal of Physiology, 160,* 106-154.

Huey, E. B. (1968). *The psychology and pedagogy of reading.* Cambridge, MA: MIT Press. (Original work published 1908)

Huff, D. (1954). *How to lie with statistics.* New York: Norton.

Hulse, S. H., & Green, B. F., Jr. (1986). *One hundred years of psychological research in America.* Baltimore: Johns Hopkins University Press.

Hunt, K. P., & Hodge, M. H. (1971). Category-item frequency and category-name meaningfulness (m'): Taxonomic norms for 84 categories. *Psychonomic Monograph Supplements, 4* (6, Whole No. 54).

Hurvich, L. M., & Jameson, D. (1979). Helmholtz's vision: Looking backward. *Contemporary Psychology, 24,* 901-904.

Jackendoff, R. (1987). *Consciousness and the computational mind.* Cambridge, MA: MIT Press.

Jacoby, L. L. (1983). Perceptual enhancement: Persistent effects of an experience. *Journal of Experimental Psychology: Learning, Memory, and Cognition, 9,* 21-38.

Jacoby, L. L., & Dallas, M. (1981). On the relationship between autobiographical memory and perceptual learning. *Journal of Experimental Psychology: General, 110,* 306-340.

Jacoby, L. L., & Kelley, C. M. (1987). Unconscious influences of memory for a prior event. *Personality and Social Psychology Bulletin, 13,* 314-336.

Jacoby, L. L., & Woloshyn, V. (1987). *Becoming famous without being recognized: Different effects of divided attention.* Unpublished manuscript.

James, W. (1950). *The principles of psychology.* New York: Dover. (Original work published 1890)

Johnson, M. K., & Hasher, L. (1987). Human learning and memory. *Annual Review of Psychology, 38,* 631-668.

Johnson-Laird, P. N. (1983). *Mental models.* Cambridge, MA: Harvard University Press.

Johnson-Laird, P. N. (1988). *The computer and the mind: An introduction to cognitive science.* Cambridge, MA: Harvard University Press.

Johnston, J. C., & McClelland, J. L. (1973). Visual factors in word perception. *Perception & Psychophysics, 14,* 365-370.

Jolicoeur, P., Gluck, M. A., & Kosslyn, S. M. (1984). Pictures and names: Making the connection. *Cognitive Psychology, 216,* 243-275.

Jones, G. V., & Langford, S. (1987). Phonological blocking in the tip of the tongue state. *Cognition, 28,* 113-123.

Jusczyk, P. W. (1986). Speech perception. In K. R. Boff, L. Kaufman, & J. P. Thomas (Eds.), *Handbook of perception and human performance: Vol. II. Cognitive processes and performance* (chapter 27). New York: Wiley.

Just, M. A., & Carpenter, P. A. (1987). *The psychology of reading and language comprehension.* Boston, MA: Allyn & Bacon.

Kahneman, D. (1973). *Attention and effort.* Englewood Cliffs, NJ: Prentice-Hall.

Kahneman, D. (1975). Effort, recognition, and recall in auditory attention. In P. M. A. Rabbitt & S. Dornic (Eds.), *Attention and performance V* (pp. 65-80). New York: Academic Press.

Kahneman, D., & Tversky, A. (1972). Subjective probability: A judgment of representativeness. *Cognitive Psychology, 3,* 430-454.

Kahneman, D., & Tversky, A. (1973). On the psychology of prediction. *Psychological Review, 80,* 237-251.

Kahneman, D., & Tversky, A. (1982). The psychology of preferences. *Scientific American, 246*(1), 160-173.

Kanizsa, G. (1969). Perception, past experience, and the impossible experiment. *Acta Psychologica, 31,* 66-69.

Kantowitz, B. H., Roediger, H. L., III, & Elmes, D. G. (1988). *Experimental psychology: Understanding psychological research.* St. Paul, MN: West Publishing Company.

Keele, S. W. (1986). Motor control. In K. R. Boff, L. Kaufmann, & J. P. Thomas (Eds.), *Handbook of perception and human performance: Vol. II. Cognitive processes and performance* (chapter 30). New York: Wiley.

Kelley, H. H. (1967). Attribution theory in social psychology. In D. Levine (Ed.), *Nebraska Symposium on Motivation* (Vol. 15, pp. 192-238). Lincoln, NE: University of Nebraska Press.

Kemler, D. G., & Smith, L. B. (1978). Assessing similarity and dimensional relations: Effects of integrality and separability on the discovery of complex concepts. *Journal of Experimental Psychology: General, 108,* 133-150.

Keesey, U. T. (1960). Effects of involuntary eye movements on visual acuity. *Journal of the Optical Society of America, 50,* 769-774.

Keppel, G., & Underwood, B. J. (1962). Proactive inhibition in short-term retention of single terms. *Journal of Verbal Learning and Verbal Behavior, 1,* 153-161.

Kintsch, W. (1985). Reflections on Ebbinghaus. *Journal of Experimental Psychology: Learning, Memory, and Cognition, 11,* 461-463.

Klapp, S. T., Hill, M. D., Tyler, J. G., Martin, Z. E., Jagacinski, R. J., & Jones, M. R. (1985). On marching to two different drummers: Perceptual aspects of the difficulties. *Journal of Experimental Psychology: Human Perception and Performance, 11,* 814-827.

Klatzky, R. L. (1984). *Memory and awareness: An information-processing perspective.* New York: W. H. Freeman.

Klatzky, R. L., Juola, J. F., & Atkinson, R. C. (1971). Test stimulus representation and experimental context effects in memory scanning. *Journal of Experimental Psychology, 87,* 281-288.

Klein, W., Plomp, R., & Pols, L. C. W. (1970). Vowel spectra, vowel spaces, and vowel identification. *Journal of the Acoustical Society of America, 48,* 999-1009.

Knapp, T. J., & Robertson, L. C. (Eds.). (1986). *Approaches to cognition: Contrasts and controversies.* Hillsdale, NJ: Lawrence Erlbaum.

Koffka, K. (1935). *Principles of Gestalt psychology.* New York: Harcourt Brace.

Kohler, W. (1929). *Gestalt psychology.* New York: Liveright.

Krathwohl, D. R. (1988). *How to prepare a research proposal: Guidelines for funding and dissertations in the social and behavioral sciences.* Syracuse, NY: Syracuse University Press.

Krech, D. (1955). Discussion: Theory and reductionism. *Psychological Review, 62,* 229-231.

Kristofferson, M. W. (1972a). Effects of practice on character-classification performance. *Canadian Journal of Psychology, 26,* 54-60.

Kristofferson, M. W. (1972b). Types and frequency of errors in visual search. *Perception & Psychophysics, 11,* 325-328.

Kristofferson, M. W. (1972c). When item recognition and visual search functions are similar. *Perception & Psychophysics, 12,* 379-384.

Kristofferson, M. W. (1975). On the interaction between memory scanning and response set. *Memory & Cognition, 23,* 102-106.

Kristofferson, M. W., Groen, M., & Kristofferson, A. B. (1973). When visual search functions look like item recognition functions. *Perception & Psychophysics, 14,* 186-192.

Kruskal, J. B., & Wish, M. (1978). *Multidimensional scaling.* Beverly Hills: Sage Publications.

Kubovy, M. (1986). *The psychology of perspective and Renaissance art.* New York: Cambridge University Press.

Kuhn, T. S. (1962). *The structure of scientific revolutions.* Chicago: University of Chicago Press.

Kunst-Wilson, W. R., & Zajonc, R. B. (1980). Affective discrimination of stimuli that cannot be recognized. *Science, 207,* 557-558.

Kvaraceus, W. (1974). *Reading: Failure and delinquency. Discipline in the classroom.* Washington, DC: National Education Association.

Labov, W. (1973). The boundaries of words and their meanings. In C. N. Baily & R. W. Shuy (Eds.), *New ways of analyzing variations in English* (Vol. 1, 340-373). Washington, DC: Georgetown University Press.

Ladefoged, P. (1962). *Elements of acoustic phonetics.* Chicago: University of Chicago Press.

Lakoff, G. (1987). *Women, fire, and dangerous things: What categories reveal about the mind.* Chicago: University of Chicago Press.

Landauer, T. K., & Freedman, J. L. (1968). Information retrieval from long-term memory. *Journal of Verbal Learning and Verbal Behavior, 7,* 291-295.

Landauer, T. K., & Meyer, D. E. (1972). Category size and semantic retrieval. *Journal of Verbal Learning and Verbal Behavior, 11,* 539-549.

Latane, B., & Darley, J. M. (1970). *The unresponsive bystander: Why doesn't he help?* New York: Appleton-Century-Crofts.

Lawson, E. A. (1966). Decisions concerning the rejected channel. *Journal of Experimental Psychology, 18,* 260-265.

Lazarus, R. (1982). Thoughts on the relations between emotion and cognition. *American Psychologist, 37,* 1019-1024.

LeDoux, J. E., & Hirst, W. (Eds.). (1986). *Mind and brain.* Cambridge, MA: Cambridge University Press.

Leibowitz, H. W., & Bourne, L. E., Jr. (1956). Time and intensity as determiners of perceived shape. *Journal of Experimental Psychology, 51,* 227-231.

Leon, M., & Anderson, N. H. (1974). A ratio rule from integration theory applied to inference judgments. *Journal of Experimental Psychology, 102,* 27-36.

Leonard, J. A. (1959). Tactual choice reactions: I. *Quarterly Journal of Experimental Psychology, 211,* 76-83.

Lesgold, A. M. (1984a). Acquiring expertise. In J. R. Anderson & S. M. Kosslyn (Eds.), *Tutorials in learning and memory* (pp. 31-60). New York: W. H. Freeman.

Lesgold, A. M. (1984b). Human skill in a computerized society: Complex skills and their acquisition. *Behavior Research Methods and Instrumentation, 16,* 79-87.

Levitt, H. (1971). Transformed up-down methods in psychoacoustics. *Journal of the Acoustical Society of America, 49,* 467-477.

Lewicki, P. (1986). *Nonconscious social information processing.* New York: Academic Press.

Liberman, A. M., Cooper, F. S., Shankweiler, D. P., & Studdert-Kennedy, M. (1967). Perception of the speech code. *Psychological Review, 74,* 431-461.

Linker, E., Moore, M. E., & Galanter, E. (1964). Taste thresholds, detection models, and disparate results. *Journal of Experimental Psychology, 67,* 59-66.

Loftus, G. R. (1978). On interpretation of interactions. *Memory & Cognition, 6,* 312-319.

Lombardo, T. J. (1987). *The reciprocity of perceiver and environment: The evolution of James J. Gibson's ecological psychology.* Hillsdale, NJ: Lawrence Erlbaum.

Longstreth, L. E., El-Zahhar, N., & Alcorn, M. B. (1985). Exceptions to Hick's Law: Explorations with a response duration measure. *Journal of Experimental Psychology: General, 114,* 417-434.

Lopes, L. L. (1981). Decision making in the short run. *Journal of Experimental Psychology: Human Learning and Memory, 7,* 377-385.

Lovie, A. D. (1983). Attention and behaviourism—fact and fiction. *British Journal of Psychology, 74,* 301-310.

Luce, R. D. (1959). *Individual choice behavior.* New York: Wiley.

Luce, R. D. (1963). A threshold theory for simple detection experiments. *Psychological Review, 70,* 61-79.

Luce, R. D. (1977). The choice axiom after twenty years. *Journal of Mathematical Psychology, 15,* 215-233.

Luce, R. D. (1986). *Response times: Their role in inferring elementary mental organization.* New York: Oxford University Press.

Lupker, S. J., & Katz, A. N. (1982). Can automatic picture processing influence word judgments? *Journal of Experimental Psychology: Learning, Memory, and Cognition, 28,* 418-434.

Lyons, W. (1986). *The disappearence of introspection.* Cambridge, MA: MIT Press.

MacKay, D. G. (1970). Spoonerisms and the structure of errors in the serial order of speech. *Neuropsychologia, 8,* 323-350.

MacKay, D. G. (1973a). Aspects of the theory of comprehension, memory, and attention. *Quarterly Journal of Experimental Psychology, 25,* 22-40.

MacKay, D. G. (1973b). Spoonerisms: The structure of errors in the serial order of speech. In V. Fromkin (Ed.), *Speech errors as linguistic evidence.* The Hague: Mouton.

MacKay, D. G. (1980). Psychology, prescriptive grammar, and the pronoun problem. *American Psychologist, 35,* 444-449.

MacKay, D. M. (1957). Moving images produced by regular stationary patterns. *Nature, 180,* 849-850.

Mandler, G., Nakamura, Y., & Shebo Van Zandt, B. J. (1987). Nonspecific effects of exposure on stimuli that cannot be recognized. *Journal of Experimental Psychology: Learning, Memory, and Cognition, 13,* 646-648.

Manicas, P. T., & Secord, P.F. (1983). Implication for psychology of the new philosophy of science. *American Psychologist, 38,* 399-413.

Marcel, A. J. (1983a). Conscious and unconscious perception: Experiments on visual masking and word recognition. *Cognitive Psychology, 15,* 197-237.

Marcel, A. J. (1983b). Conscious and unconscious perception: An approach to the relations between phenomenal experience and perceptual processes. *Cognitive Psychology, 15,* 238-300.

Marks, L. E. (1976). *Sensory processes: The new psychophysics.* New York: Academic Press.

Marr, D. (1982). *Vision.* San Francisco: W. H. Freeman.

Marslen-Wilson, W. D. (1973). Linguistic structure and speech shadowing at very short latencies. *Nature, 244,* 522-523.

Marslen-Wilson, W. D. (1984). Function and process in spoken word recognition: A tutorial review. In H. Bouma & D. G. Bouwhuis (Eds.), *Attention and performance X: Control of language processes* (pp. 125-150). Hillsdale, NJ: Lawrence Erlbaum.

Marslen-Wilson, W. D. (1987). Functional parallelism in spoken word recognition. In U. H. Frauenfelder & L. K. Tyler (Eds.), *Spoken word recognition* (pp. 71-102). Cambridge, MA: MIT Press.

Marslen-Wilson, W. D., & Welsh, A. (1978). Processing interactions and lexical access during word recognition in continuous speech. *Cognitive Psychology, 10,* 29-63.

Martin, D. W. (1985). *Doing psychology experiments.* Monterey, CA: Brooks/Cole.

Massaro, D. W. (1970). Perceptual processes and forgetting in memory tasks. *Psychological Review, 77,* 557-567.

Massaro, D. W. (1973). *Perception of rotated shapes revisited.* Unpublished manuscript.

Massaro, D. W. (1974). Perceptual units in speech recognition. *Journal of Experimental Psychology, 102,* 199-208.

Massaro, D. W. (1975a). *Experimental psychology and information processing.* Chicago: Rand McNally.

Massaro, D. W. (Ed.). (1975b). *Understanding language: An information processing analysis of speech perception, reading, and psycholinguistics.* New York: Academic Press.

Massaro, D. W. (1986). The computer as a metaphor for psychological inquiry: Considerations and recommendations. *Behavior Research Methods, Instruments, & Computers, 18,* 73-92.

Massaro, D. W. (1987a). Categorical partition: A fuzzy logical model of categorization behavior. In S. Harnad (Ed.), *Categorical perception.* Cambridge, England: Cambridge University Press.

Massaro, D. W. (1987b). *Speech perception by ear and eye: A paradigm for psychological inquiry.* Hillsdale, NJ: Lawrence Erlbaum.

Massaro, D. W., & Hary, J. M. (1986). Addressing issues in letter recognition. *Psychological Research, 48,* 123-132.

Massaro, D. W., & Hestand, J. (1983). Developmental relations between reading ability and knowledge of orthographic structure. *Contemporary Educational Psychology, 8,* 174-180.

Massaro, D. W., Jastrzembski, J. E., & Lucas, P. A. (1981). Frequency, orthographic regularity, and lexical status in letter and word perception. In G. H. Bower (Ed.), *The psychology of learning and motivation* (Vol. 15, pp. 163-200). New York: Academic Press.

Massaro, D. W., Jones, R. D., Lipscomb, C., & Scholz, R. (1978). Role of prior knowledge on naming and lexical decisions with good and poor stimulus information. *Journal of Experimental Psychology, 4,* 498-512.

Massaro, D. W., Neumann, O., & Sanders, A. F. (Eds.). (1985). Action attention and automaticity. *Acta Psychologica, 60.*

Massaro, D. W., & Oden, G. C. (1980). Speech perception: A framework for research and theory. In N. J. Lass (Ed.), *Speech and language: Advances in basic research and practice* (Vol. 3, pp. 129-165). New York: Academic Press.

Massaro, D. W., Taylor, G. A., Venezky, R. L., Jastrzembski, J. E., & Lucas, P. A. (1980). *Letter and word perception: Orthographic structure and visual processing in reading.* Amsterdam: North-Holland.

Matlin, M. W., & Stang, D. J. (1978). *The pollyanna principle.* Cambridge, MA: Schenkman.

Mayer, R. E. (1983). *Thinking, problem solving, cognition.* San Francisco: W. H. Freeman.

Mayzner, M. S., & Tresselt, M. E. (1966). Anagram solution times: A function of multiple-solution anagrams. *Journal of Experimental Psychology, 71,* 66-73.

McCain, G., & Segal, E. M. (1973). *The game of science.* Monterey, CA: Brooks/Cole.

McClelland, J. L. (1979). On the time relations of mental processes: An examination of systems of processes in cascade. *Psychological Review, 86,* 287-324.

McClelland, J. L., & Elman, J. L. (1986). The TRACE model of speech perception. *Cognitive Psychology, 18,* 1-86.

McClelland, J. L., & Rumelhart, D. E. (1981). An interactive activation model of context effects in letter perception: Part I. An account of basic findings. *Psychological Review, 88,* 375-407.

McClelland, J. L., & Rumelhart, D. E. (1985). Distributed memory and the representation of general and specific information. *Journal of Experimental Psychology: General, 104,* 159-188.

McClelland, J. L., & Rumelhart, D. E. (Eds.). (1986). *Parallel distributed processing: Vol. 2. Psychological and biological models.* Cambridge, MA: MIT press.

McCloskey, M. (1980). The stimulus familiarity problem in semantic memory research. *Journal of Verbal Learning and Verbal Behavior, 19,* 485-502.

McCloskey, M., & Glucksberg, S. (1978). Natural categories: Well defined or fuzzy sets? *Memory & Cognition, 6,* 462-472.

McCusker, L. X., Hillinger, M. L., & Bias, R. G. (1981). Phonological recoding and reading. *Psychological Bulletin, 89,* 217-245.

McKenzie, B. E., & Day, R. H. (Eds.). (1987). *Perceptual development in early infancy: Problems and issues.* Hillsdale, NJ: Lawrence Erlbaum.

McKoon, G., Ratcliff, R., & Dell, G. S. (1986). A critical evaluation of the semantic-episodic distinction. *Journal of Experimental Psychology: Learning, Memory, and Cognition, 12,* 295-306.

Medin, D. L., & Schaffer, M. M. (1978). Context theory of classification learning. *Psychological Review, 85,* 207-238.

Mehler, J., Morton, J., Jusczyk, P. W. (1984). On reducing language to biology. *Cognitive Neuropsychology, 1,* 83-116.

Mendelsohn, G. A., Griswold, B. B., & Anderson, M. L. (1966). Individual differences in anagram-solving ability. *Psychological Reports, 19,* 429-439.

Mervis, C. B., & Rosch, E. (1981). Categorization of natural objects. *Annual Review of Psychology, 32,* 89-115.

Meyer, D. E., Irwin, D. E., Osman, A. M., & Kounios, J. (1988). The dynamics of cognition and action: Mental processes inferred from speed-accuracy decomposition. *Psychological Review, 95,* 183-237.

Meyer, D. E., Schvaneveldt, R. W., & Ruddy, M. G. (1975). Loci of contextual effects of visual word recognition. In P. M. A. Rabbitt & S. Dornic (Eds.), *Attention and performance V.* New York: Academic Press.

Miller, A. I. (1986). *Imagery in scientific thought.* Cambridge, MA: MIT Press.

Miller, G. A. (1956). The magical number seven, plus or minus two: Some limits on our capacity for processing information. *Psychological Review, 63,* 81-97.

Miller, G. A. (1962). Decision units in the perception of speech. *Institute of Radio Engineers (IRE) Transactions on Information Theory, 8,* 81-83.

Miller, G. A. (1981). *Language and speech.* San Francisco: W. H. Freeman.

Miller, G. A., Bruner, J. S., & Postman, L. (1954). Familiarity of letter sequences and tachistoscopic identification. *Journal of General Psychology, 50,* 129-139.

Miller, J. (1982). Discrete versus continuous stage models of human information processing: In search of partial output. *Journal of Experimental Psychology: Human Perception and Performance, 28,* 273-296.

Miller, J. (1988). Discrete and continuous models of human information processing: Theoretical distinctions and empirical results. *Acta Psychologica, 67,* 191-257.

Millodot, M. (1968). Influence of accommodation on the viewing of an illusion. *Quarterly Journal of Experimental Psychology, 20,* 329-335.

Minsky, M. (1985). *The society of mind.* New York: Simon & Schuster.

Minsky, M., & Papert, S. (1969, 1988). *Perceptrons.* Cambridge, MA: MIT Press.

Mitroff, I. I. (1974). *The subjective side of science.* Amsterdam: Elsevier.

Mitroff, I. I., & Kilmann, R. H. (1978). *Methodological approaches to social science.* San Francisco: Jossey-Bass.

Moray, N. (1959). Attention in dichotic listening: Affective cues and the influence of instructions. *Quarterly Journal of Experimental Psychology, 11,* 56-60.

Moreland, R. L., & Zajonc, R. B. (1979). Exposure effects may not depend on stimulus recognition. *Journal of Personality and Social Psychology, 37,* 1085-1089.

Morton, J. (1964). A preliminary functional model for language behavior. *International Audiology, 3,* 216-225.

Morton, J. (1969). Interaction of information in word recognition. *Psychological Review, 76,* 165-178.

Morton, J. (1979). Facilitation in word recognition: Experiments causing change in the Logogen model. In P. A. Kolers, M. E. Wrolstad, & H. Bouma (Eds.), *Processing of visible language.* New York: Plenum Press.

Morton, J., & Broadbent, D. E. (1967). Passive versus active recognition models, or is your hommunculus really necessary? In W. Wathen-Dunn (Ed.), *Models for the perception of speech and visual form.* Cambridge, MA: MIT Press.

Motley, M. T. (1987, February). What I meant to say. *Psychology Today, 21,* 24-28.

Murphy, G., & Kovach, J. K. (1972). *Historical introduction to modern psychology.* San Diego: Harcourt Brace Jovanovich.

Mynatt, C. R., Doherty, M. E., & Tweney, R. D. (1977). Confirmation bias in a simulated research environment: An experimental study of scientific inference. *Quarterly Journal of Experimental Psychology, 29,* 85-95.

Mynatt, C. R., Doherty, M. E., & Tweney, R. D. (1978). Consequences of confirmation and disconfirmation in a simulated research environment. *Quarterly Journal of Experimental Psychology, 30,* 395-406.

Nachmias, J., & Steinman, R. M. (1963). Study of absolute visual detection by the rating scale method. *Journal of the Optical Society of America, 53,* 151-155.

Navon, D. (1984). Resources—A theoretical soup stone? *Psychological Review, 91,* 216-234.

Navon, D., & Gopher, D. (1979). On the economy of the human processing system. *Psychological Review, 86,* 214-255.

Neisser, U. (1963). Decision time without reaction time: Experiments in visual scanning. *American Journal of Psychology, 76,* 376-385.

Neisser, U. (1964). Visual search. *Scientific American, 210*(6), 94-102.

Neisser, U. (1967). *Cognitive psychology.* New York: Appleton-Century-Crofts.

Neisser, U. (1976). *Cognition and reality.* San Francisco: W. H. Freeman.

Neisser, U. (Ed.). (1987). *Concepts and conceptual development: Ecological and intellectual factors in categorization.* Cambridge, England: Cambridge University Press.

Neisser, U., & Becklen, R. (1975). Selective looking: Attending to visually specified events. *Cognitive Psychology, 7,* 480-494.

Neisser, U., Novick, R., & Lazar, R. (1963). Searching for ten targets simultaneously. *Perceptual and Motor Skills, 17,* 955-961.

Nelson, T. O. (1977). Repetition and depth of processing. *Journal of Verbal Learning and Verbal Behavior, 16,* 151-172.

Neumann, O. (1987). Beyond capacity: A functional view of attention. In H. Heuer & A. F. Sanders (Eds.), *Tutorials on perception and action.* Hillsdale, NJ: Lawrence Erlbaum.

Newell, A., & Simon, H. A. (1956). The logic theory machine. *Institute of Radio Engineers (IRE) Transactions on Information Theory, 2,* 61-79.

Newell, A., & Simon, H. A. (1972). *Human problem solving.* Englewood Cliffs, NJ: Prentice-Hall.

Newman, C. W., & Spitzer, J. B. (1987). Monotic and dichotic presentation of phonemic elements in a backward recognition-masking paradigm. *Psychological Research, 49,* 31-36.

Nickerson, R. S. (1965). Short-term memory for complex meaningful visual configurations: A demonstration of capacity. *Canadian Journal of Psychology, 19,* 155-160.

Nisbett, R. E., & Wilson, T. D. (1977). Telling more than we can know: Verbal reports on mental processes. *Psychological Review, 84,* 231-259.

Norman, D. A. (1968). Toward a theory of memory and attention. *Psychological Review, 75,* 522-536.

Norman, D. A. (1969). Memory while shadowing. *Quarterly Journal of Experimental Psychology, 21,* 85-93.

Norman, D. A. (1976). *Memory and attention: An introduction to human information processing.* New York: Wiley.

Norman, D. A. (1981). Categorization of action slips. *Psychological Review, 88,* 1-15.

Norman, D. A., & Bobrow, D. G. (1975). On data-limited and resource-limited processes. *Cognitive Psychology, 7,* 44-64.

Oden, G. C. (1979). A fuzzy logical model of letter identification. *Journal of Experimental Psychology: Human Perception and Performance, 5,* 336-352.

Oden, G. C. (1981). A fuzzy propositional model of concept structure and use: A case study in object identification. In G. W. Lasker (Ed.), *Applied systems and cybernetics* (Vol. VI, pp. 2890-2897). Elmsford, NY: Pergamon Press.

Oden, G. C. (1984a). Dependence, independence, and emergence of word features. *Journal of Experimental Psychology: Human Perception and Performance, 10,* 394-405.

Oden, G. C. (1984b). Everything is a good example of something, and other endorsements of the adequacy of a fuzzy theory of concepts. *Wisconsin Human Information Processing Program (WHIPP 21).* University of Wisconsin, Madison.

Oden, G. C., & Massaro, D. W. (1978). Integration of featural information in speech perception. *Psychological Review, 85,* 172-191.

Ogden, G. D., & Allusi, E .A. (1980). Stimulus-response compatibility effects in choice reactions and memory scanning. *Journal of Experimental Psychology: Human Learning and Memory, 6,* 430-438.

Oppenheimer, J. R. (1984). *Uncommon sense.* Boston: Birkhauser.

Owens, D. A. (1987). Oculomotor information and perception of three-dimensional space. In H. Heuer & A. F. Sanders (Eds.), *Perspectives on perception and action.* Hillsdale, NJ: Lawrence Erlbaum.

Paap, K. R., Newsome, S. L., McDonald, J. E., & Schvaneveldt, R. W. (1982). An activation-verification model for letter and word recognition: The word-superiority effect. *Psychological Review, 89,* 573-594.

Paivio, A. (1971). *Imagery and verbal processes.* New York: Holt, Rinehart, & Winston.

Palmer, S. E., & Kimchi, R. (1986). The information processing approach to cognition. In F. J. Knapp & L. C. Robertson (Eds.), *Approaches to cognition: Contrasts and controversies* (pp. 37-77). Hillsdale, NJ: Lawrence Erlbaum.

Pavlov, I. P. (1927). *Conditioned reflexes* (G. V. Anrep, Trans.). London: Oxford University Press.

Pelli, D. G. (1987, May). *The ideal psychometric procedure.* Paper presented at the annual meeting of the Association for Research in Vision and Ophthalmology, Sarasota, Florida.

Perfetti, C. A. (1985). *Reading ability.* New York: Oxford University Press.

Perrig, W. J., & Perrig, P. (1988). Mood and memory: Mood-congruity effects in absence of mood. *Memory & Cognition, 16,* 102-109.

Perkell, J. S., & Klatt, D. H. (Eds.). (1986). *Invariance and variability in speech processes.* Hillsdale, NJ: Lawrence Erlbaum.

Peterson, W. W., Birdsall, T. G., & Fox, W. C. (1954). The theory of signal detectability. *Transactions IRE Professional Group on Information Theory, 4,* 171-212.

Peterson, L. R., & Peterson, M. J. (1959). Short-term retention of individual verbal items. *Journal of Experimental Psychology, 58,* 193-198.

Petry, S., & Meyer, G. E. (1987). *The perception of illusory contours.* New York: Springer-Verlag.

Petty, R. E., & Cacioppo, J. T. (1986). *Communication and persuasion: Central and peripheral routes to attitude change.* New York: Springer-Verlag.

Piaget, J. (1970). Piaget's theory. P. H. Mussen (Gen. Ed.), *Handbook of child psychology,* Vol. 1: W. Kessen (Ed.) *History, theory, and methods.* New York: Wiley.

Pieters, J. P. M. (1983). Sternberg's additive factor method and underlying psychological processes: Some theoretical considerations. *Psychological Bulletin, 293,* 411-426.

Pillsbury, W. B. (1897). A study in apperception. *American Journal of Psychology, 8,* 315-393.

Pisoni, D. B. (1972). *Perceptual processing time for consonants and vowels.* Haskins Laboratories Status Report on Speech Research, SR 31/32, 83-92.

Pisoni, D. B., & Lazarus, J. H. (1974). Categorical and noncategorical modes of speech perception along the voicing continuum. *Journal of the Acoustical Society of America, 55,* 328-333.

Platt, J. R. (1962). *The excitement of science.* Boston: Houghton Mifflin.

Platt, J. R. (1964). Strong inference. *Science, 146,* 347-353.

Polanyi, M. (1966). *The tacit dimension.* New York: Doubleday.

Pollack, I., & Pickett, J. M. (1963). The intelligibility of excerpts from conversation. *Language and Speech, 6,* 165-171.

Popper, K. (1959). *The logic of scientific discovery.* New York: Basic Books.

Popper, K. R. (1976). *Unended quest.* London: Fontana/Collins.

Posner, M. I. (1978). *Chronometric explorations of mind.* Hillsdale, NJ: Lawrence Erlbaum.

Posner, M. I. (1980). Orienting of attention. *Quarterly Journal of Experimental Psychology, 32,* 3-25.

Posner, M. I., Goldsmith, R., & Welton, K. E. (1967). Perceived distance and the classification of distorted patterns. *Journal of Experimental Psychology, 73,* 28-38.

Posner, M. I., & Marin, O. S. M. (1985). *Attention and performance XI.* Hillsdale, NJ: Lawrence Erlbaum.

Postman, L. (1968). Hermann Ebbinghaus. *American Psychologist, 23,* 149-157.

Potter, M. C., & Levy, E. I. (1969). Recognition memory for a rapid sequence of pictures. *Journal of Experimental Psychology, 81,* 10-15.

Premack, D. (1986). *Gavagai! Or the future history of the animal language controversy.* Cambridge, MA: MIT Press.

Pribram, K. H. (1986). The cognitive revolution and mind/brain issues. *American Psychologist, 41,* 507-520.

Pylyshyn, Z. N. (1984). *Computation and cognition: Toward a foundation for cognitive science.* Cambridge, MA: MIT Press.

Quillian, M. R. (1968). Semantic memory. In M. Minsky (Ed.), *Semantic information processing.* Cambridge, MA: MIT Press.

Rancurello, A. C. (1968). *A study of Franz Brentano.* New York: Academic Press.

Raphael, B. (1976). *The thinking computer: Mind inside matter.* San Francisco: W. H. Freeman.

Ratcliff, R. (1978). A theory of memory retrieval. *Psychological Review, 85,* 59-108.

Ratcliff, R. (1988). Continuous versus discrete information processing: Modeling accumulation of partial information. *Psychological Review, 95,* 238-255.

Ratcliff, R., & McKoon, G. (1986). More on the distinction between episodic and semantic memories. *Journal of Experimental Psychology: Learning, Memory, and Cognition, 12,* 312-313.

Ratcliff, R., McKoon, G., & Verwoerd, M. (1988). *A bias interpretation in perceptual identification.* Unpublished manuscript.

Reason, J. T. (1979). Actions not as planned. In G. Underwood & R. Stevens (Eds.), *Aspects of Consciousness.* London: Academic Press.

Reber, A. S. (1985). *The Penguin dictionary of psychology.* New York: Penguin Books.

Reed, A. V. (1976). List length and the time-course of recognition in immediate memory. *Memory & Cognition, 4,* 16-30.

Reicher, G. M. (1969). Perceptual recognition as a function of meaningfulness of stimulus material. *Journal of Experimental Psychology, 81,* 275-281.

Repp, B. H. (1984). Categorical perception: Issues, methods, findings. In N. J. Lass (Ed.), *Speech and language: Advances in basic research and practice* (Vol. 10, pp. 243-335). New York: Academic Press.

Rescorla, R. A. (1988). Pavlovian conditioning: It's not what you think it is. *American Psychologist, 43,* 151-160.

Restle, F. (1970). Moon illusion explained on the basis of relative size. *Science, 167,* 1092-1096.

Richards, R. J. (1987). *Darwin and the emergence of evolutionary theories of mind and behavior.* Chicago: University of Chicago Press.

Richardson-Klavehn, A., & Bjork, R. A. (1988). Measures of memory. *Annual Review of Psychology, 39,* 475-543.

Rips, L. J., & Marcus, S. L. (1977). Supposition and the analysis of conditional sentences. In M. J. Just & P. A. Carpenter (Eds.), *Cognitive processes in comprehension.* Hillsdale, NJ: Lawrence Erlbaum.

Robinson, J. P. (1980). The changing reading habits of the American public. *Journal of Communication, 30,* 141-152.

Rock, I. (1983). *The logic of perception.* Cambridge, MA: MIT press.

Rock, I., (1985). Perception and knowledge. *Acta Psychologica, 59,* 3-22.

Rock, I., & Kaufman, L. (1962). The moon illusion, II. *Science, 136,* 1023-1031.

Rock, I., Shallo, J., & Schwartz, F. (1978). Pictorial depth and related constancy effects as a function of recognition. *Perception, 7,* 3-19.

Roediger, H. L. (1984). Does current evidence from dissociation experiments favor the episodic/semantic distinction? Commentary on E. Tulving Précis of Elements of episodic memory. *The Behavioral and Brain Sciences, 7,* 252-254.

Ronning, R. R. (1965). Anagram solution times: A function of the "ruleout" factor. *Journal of Experimental Psychology, 69,* 35-39.

Rosch, E. (1975a). Cognitive reference points. *Cognitive Psychology, 7,* 532-547.

Rosch, E. (1975b). Cognitive representations of semantic categories. *Journal of Experimental Psychology: General, 104,* 192-233.

Rosch, E. (1978). Principles of categorization. In E. Rosch & B. B. Lloyd (Eds.), *Cognition and categorization.* Hillsdale, NJ: Lawrence Erlbaum.

Rosch, E., & Mervis, C. B. (1975). Family resemblance studies in the internal structure of categories. *Cognitive Psychology, 7,* 573-605.

Rosenbaum, D. A. (1980). Human movement initiation: Specification of arm, direction, and extent. *Journal of Experimental Psychology: General, 109,* 444-474.

Rosenblatt, F. (1958). The perceptron: A probabilistic model for information storage and organization in the brain. *Psychological Review, 65,* 386-407.

Rosenthal, R. (1966). *Experimenter effects in behavioral research.* New York: Appleton-Century-Crofts.

Rosenthal, R. (1976). *Experimenter effects in behavioral research* (enlarged ed.). New York: Halsted Press.

Rosenthal, R., & Fode, K. L. (1963). Psychology of the scientist: V. Three experiments in experimenter bias. *Psychological Reports, 12,* 491-511.

Rosenzweig, S. (1987). The final tribute of E. G. Boring to G. T. Fechner. *American Psychologist, 42,* 787-790.

Rosinski, R. R., & Levine, N. P. (1976). Texture gradient effectiveness in the perception of surface slant. *Journal of Experimental Child Psychology, 22,* 261-271.

Rosinski, R. R., & Wheeler, K. E. (1972). Children's use of orthographic structure in word discrimination. *Psychonomic Science, 26,* 97-98.

Ross, H. E., & Ross, G. M. (1976). Did Ptolemy understand the moon illusion? *Perception, 5,* 377-385.

Rumelhart, D. E., & McClelland, J. L. (Eds.). (1986). *Parallel distributed processing: Vol. 1. Foundations.* Cambridge, MA: MIT Press.

Russell, P. N., Consedine, C. E., & Knight, R. G. (1980). Visual and memory search by process schizophrenics. *Journal of Abnormal Psychology, 89,* 109-114.

Sacks, O. (1987). *The man who mistook his wife for a hat and other clinical tales.* New York: Harper & Row.

Salasoo, A., & Pisoni, D. (1985). Interaction of knowledge sources in spoken word identification. *Journal of Memory and Cognition, 2,* 210-231.

Salthouse, T. A. (1981). Converging evidence for information-processing stages: A comparative-influence stage-analysis method. *Acta Psychologica, 247,* 39-61.

Samuelson, P. A. (1963). Risk and uncertainty: A fallacy of large numbers. *Scientia, 98,* 108-113.

Sanders, A. F. (1980). Stage analysis of reaction processes. In G. E. Stelmach & J. Requin (Eds.), *Tutorials in motor behavior* (pp. 331-354). Amsterdam: North Holland.

Sanford, A. J., Garrod, S., & Boyle, J. M. (1977). An independence of mechanisms in the origins of reading and classification-related semantic distance effects. *Memory & Cognition, 5,* 214-220.

Santee, J. L., & Egeth, H. E. (1982). Do reaction time and accuracy measure the same aspects of letter recognition? *Journal of Experimental Psychology: Human Perception and Performance, 8,* 489-501.

Sattath, S., & Tversky, A. (1987). On the relation between common and distinctive feature models. *Psychological Review, 94,* 16-22.

Schaeffer, B., & Wallace, R. (1970). The comparison of word meanings. *Journal of Experimental Psychology, 86,* 144-152.

Schaller, M. J. (1975). Chromatic vision in human infants: Conditioned operant fixation to "hues" of varying intensity. *Bulletin of the Psychonomic Society, 6,* 39-42.

Schaller, M. J., & Dziadosz, G. M. (1975). Individual differences in adult foveal visual asymmetries. *Journal of Experimental Psychology: Human Perception and Performance, 1,* 353-365.

Schneider, W., & Shiffrin, R. M. (1977). Controlled and automatic information processing: I. Detection, search, and attention. *Psychological Review, 84,* 1-66.

Schouten, M. E. H. (Ed.). (1987). *The psychophysics of speech perception.* Boston: Martinus Nijhoff.

Schweickert, R. (1978). A critical path generalization of the additive factor method: Analysis of a Stroop task. *Journal of Mathematical Psychology, 18,* 105-109.

Schweickert, R. (1983). Latent network theory: Scheduling of processes in sentence verification and the Stroop effect. *Journal of Experimental Psychology: Learning, Memory, and Cognition, 9,* 353-383.

Seamon, J. G., Brody, N., & Kauff, D. M. (1983). Affective discrimination of stimuli that are not recognized: Effects of shadowing, masking, and cerebral laterality. *Journal of Experimental Psychology: Learning, Memory, and Cognition, 9,* 544-555.

Searle, J. (1987). Minds and brains without programs. In C. Blakemore & S. Greenfield (Eds.), *Mindwaves.* New York: Basil Blackwell.

Selfridge, O. G. (1959). Pandemonium: A paradigm for learning. In *Mechanization of thought processes* (pp. 511-526). London: Her Majesty's Stationery Office.

Simon, H. A. (1969). *Sciences of the artificial.* Cambridge, MA: MIT Press.

Shannon, C. (1948). The mathematical theory of communication. *Bell System Technical Journal, 27,* 379-423, 623-658.

Shannon, C. E. (1951). Prediction and entropy of printed English. *Bell System Technical Journal, 30,* 50-64.

Shapiro, M. (1956). Leonardo and Freud—An art-historical study. *Journal of the History of Ideas, 17,* 147-178.

Shapiro, R. G., & Krueger, L. E. (1983). Effect of similarity of surround on target letter processing. *Journal of Experimental Psychology: Human Perception and Performance, 9,* 547-559

Sharon, A. T. (1973/74). What do adults read? *Reading Research Quarterly, IX,* 148-169.

Shaughnessy, J. J., & Zechmeister, E. B. (1985). *Research methods in psychology.* New York: Knopf.

Shepard, R. N. (1967). Recognition memory for words, sentences, and pictures. *Journal of Verbal Learning and Verbal Behavior, 6,* 156-163.

Shepp, B. E. (1983). The analyzability of multidimensional objects: Some constraints on perceived structure, the development of perceived structure, and attention. In T. J. Tighe & B. E. Shepp (Eds.), *Perception, cognition, and development: Interaction analyses* (pp. 39-75). Hillsdale, NJ: Lawrence Erlbaum.

Sidman, M. (1952). A note on functional relations obtained from group data. *Psychological Bulletin, 49,* 263-269.

Skinner, B. F. (1950). Are theories of learning necessary? *Psychological Review, 57,* 193-216.

Slamecka, N. J. (1985). Ebbinghaus: Some associations. *Journal of Experimental Psychology: Learning, Memory, and Cognition, 11,* 414-435.

Smith, E. E., & Medin, D. L. (1981). *Categories and concepts.* Cambridge, MA: Harvard University Press.

Smith, E. E., & Osherson, D. N. (1984). Conceptual combination with prototype concepts. *Cognitive Science, 8,* 337-361.

Smith, E. E., Shoben, E. J., & Rips, L. J. (1974). Structure and process in semantic memory: A featural model for semantic decisions. *Psychological Review, 81,* 214-241.

Smith, F. (1971) *Understanding reading.* New York: Holt, Rinehart, & Winston.

Smith, L. B., & Kemler, D. G. (1977). Developmental trends in free classification: Evidence for a new conceptualization of perceptual development. *Journal of Experimental Child Psychology, 24,* 279-298.

Smith, L. B., & Kemler, D. G. (1978). Levels of experienced dimensionality in children and adults. *Cognitive Psychology, 10,* 502-532.

Smith, M., & Wilson, E. A. (1953). A model of the auditory threshold and its application to the problem of the multiple observer. *Psychological Monograhs: General and Applied, 67* (9, Whole No. 359).

Snodgrass, J. G., Levy-Berger, G., & Haydon, M. (1985). *Human experimental psychology.* New York: Oxford University Press.

Solso, R. L. (1988). *Cognitive Psychology.* Boston: Allyn & Bacon.

Spelke, E. S. (1979). Perceiving bimodally specified events in infancy. *Developmental Psychology, 15,* 533-560.

Sperling, G. (1960). The information available in brief visual presentations. *Psychological Monographs, 74* (11, Whole No. 498).

Sperling, G. (1984). A unified theory of attention and signal detection. In R. Parasuraman & D. R. Davies (Eds.), *Varieties of attention.* New York: Academic Press.

Stanovich, K. E. (1986). Matthew effects in reading: Some consequences of individual differences in the acquisition of literacy. *Reading Research Quarterly, XXI,* 360-407.

Sternberg, S. (1966). High-speed scanning in human memory. *Science, 153,* 652-654.

Sternberg, S. (1967). Two operations in character recognition: Some evidence from reaction-time measurements. *Perception & Psychophysics, 2,* 45-53.

Sternberg, S. (1969a). Memory-scanning: Mental processes revealed by reaction-time experiments. *American Scientist, 57,* 421-457.

Sternberg, S. (1969b). The discovery of processing stages: Extensions of Donders' method. *Acta Psychologica, 30,* 276-315.

Sternberg, S. (1975). Memory scanning: New findings and current controversies. *Quarterly Journal of Experimental Psychology, 27,* 1-32.

Stevens, J. C., & Marks, L. E. (1971). Spatial summation and the dynamics of warmth sensation. *Perception & Psychophysics, 9,* 291-298.

Stevens, S. S. (1961). Is there a quantal threshold? In W. A. Rosenblith (Ed.), *Sensory communication.* New York: Technology Press and Wiley.

Stevens, S. S., & Warshofsky, F. (1965). *Sounds and hearing.* New York: Time Inc.

Stroop, J. R. (1935). Studies of interference in serial verbal reactions. *Journal of Experimental Psychology, 18,* 643-662.

Strunk, W., Jr., & White, E. B. (1972). *The elements of style.* New York: Macmillan.

Swets, J. A. (1961). Is there a sensory threshold? *Science, 134,* 168-177.

Swets, J. A., Tanner, W. P., & Birdsall, T. G. (1961). Decision processes in perception. *Psychological Review, 68,* 301-340.

Tanner, W. P., & Swets, J. A. (1954). A decision-making theory of visual detection. *Psychological Review, 61,* 401-409.

Taylor, D. A. (1976). Stage analysis of reaction time. *Psychological Bulletin, 83,* 161-191.

Taylor, M. M., & Creelman, C. D. (1967). Efficient estimates on probability functions. *Journal of the Acoustical Society of America, 41,* 782-787.

Teichner, W. H., & Krebs, M. J. (1974). Laws of visual choice reaction time. *Psychological Review, 281,* 75-98.

Teller, D. Y. (1979). The forced-choice preferential looking procedure: A psychophysical technique for use with human infants. *Infant Behavior and Development, 2,* 135-153.

Theios, J. (1973). Reaction-time measurements in the study of memory processes: Theory and data. In G. H. Bower (Ed.), *The psychology of learning and motivation* (Vol. 7). New York: Academic Press.

Theios, J., & Amrhein, P. C. (1985). *A theoretical analysis of the cognitive processing of pictures and words: Effects of stimulus size on reading, naming, and visual comparisons.* Unpublished manuscript.

Toulmin, S. (1972). *Human understanding* (Vol. I, General Introduction and Part I). Princeton, NJ: Princeton University Press.

Townsend, J. T. (1984). Uncovering mental processes with factorial experiments. *Journal of Mathematical Psychology, 28,* 363-400.

Townsend, J. T., & Ashby, F. G. (1983). *Stochastic modeling of elementary psychological processes.* London: Cambridge University Press.

Treisman, A. M. (1960). Contextual cues in selective listening. *Quarterly Journal of Experimental Psychology, 12,* 242-248.

Treisman, A. M. (1964). The effect of irrelevant material on the efficiency of selective listening. *American Journal of Psychology, 77,* 533-546.

Treisman, A. M. (1986). Properties, parts, and objects. In K. R. Boff, L. Kaufmann, & J. P. Thomas (Eds.), *Handbook of perception and human performance: Vol. II, Cognitive processes and performance* (chapter 35). New York: Wiley.

Treisman, A. M., & Geffen, G. (1967). Selective attention: Perception or response? *Quarterly Journal of Experimental Psychology, 19,* 1-17.

Treisman, A. M., & Gelade, G. (1980). Feature-integration theory of attention. *Cognitive Psychology, 12,* 97-136.

Tukey, J. W. (1984). *The collected works of John W. Tukey.* Monterey, CA: Wadsworth.

Tulving, E. (1972). Episodic and semantic memory. In E. Tulving & W. Donaldson (Eds.), *Organization and memory.* New York: Academic Press.

Tulving, E. (1985). How many memory systems are there? *American Psychologist, 40,* 385-398.

Tulving, E. (1986). What kind of a hypothesis is the distinction between episodic and semantic memory? *Journal of Experimental Psychology: Learning, Memory, and Cognition, 12*, 308-311.

Tulving, E., Mandler, G., & Baumal, R. (1964). Interaction of two sources of information in tachistoscopic word recognition. *Canadian Journal of Psychology, 18*, 62-71.

Tversky, A. (1977). Features of similarity. *Psychological Review, 84*, 327-352.

Tversky, A., & Kahneman, D. (1973). Availability: A heuristic for judging frequency and probability. *Cognitive Psychology, 5*, 207-232.

Tyler, L. K., & Wessels, J. (1983). Quantifying contextual contributions to word-recognition processes. *Perception & Psychophysics, 34*, 409-420.

Tyler, L. K., & Wessels, J. (1985). Is gating an on-line task? Evidence from naming latency data. *Perception & Psychophysics, 38*, 217-222.

Uhlarik, J., & Johnson, R. (1978). Development of form perception in repeated brief exposures to visual stimuli. In R. D. Pick & H. L. Pick, Jr. (Eds.), *Perception and experience.* New York: Plenum.

Underwood, B. J., & Schulz, R. W. (1960). *Meaningfulness and verbal learning.* New York: Academic Press, Lippincott.

Van der Heijden, A. H. C., & La Heij, W. (1982). The array size function in simple visual search tasks: A comparison between "go-no go" and "yes-no" tasks under conditions of high and low target-noise similarity. *Psychological Research, 44*, 355-368.

Van der Heijden, A. H. C., & La Heij, W. (1983). The array size function in simple visual search tasks: A comparison between a "go-no go" and a "detection" task under conditions of low target-noise similarity. *Psychological Research, 45*, 221-234.

Vanderplas, J. M., & Garvin, E. A. (1959). The association value of random shapes. *Journal of Experimental Psychology, 57*, 147-154.

Venezky, R. L., & Massaro, D. W. (1987). Orthographic structure and spelling-sound regularity in reading English words. In D. A. Allport, D. G. MacKay, W. Prinz, & E. Scheerer (Eds.), *Language perception and production: Shared mechanisms in listening, speaking, reading and writing.* London: Academic Press.

Wachtel, P. L. (1980). Investigation and its discontents: Some constraints on progress in psychological research. *American Psychologist, 35*, 399-408.

Waite, H., & Massaro, D. W. (1970). A test of Gregory's constancy-scaling explanation of the Müller-Lyer illusion. *Nature, 227*, 733-734.

Walden, B. E., Prosek, R., Montgomery, A., Scherr, C. K., & Jones, C. J. (1977). Effects of training on the visual recognition of consonants. *Journal of Speech and Hearing Research, 20*, 130-145.

Ward, T. B. (1980). Separable and integral responding by children and adults to the dimensions of length and density. *Child Development, 51*, 676-684.

Ward, T. B. (1983). Response tempo and separable-integral responding: Evidence for an integral-to-separable processing sequence in visual perception. *Journal of Experimental Psychology: Human Perception and Performance, 9*, 103-112.

Ward, T. B., Foley, C. M., & Cole, J. (1986). Classifying multidimensional stimuli: Stimulus, task, and observer factors. *Journal of Experimental Psychology: Human Perception and Performance, 12,* 211-225.

Warren, P., & Marslen-Wilson, W. D. (1987). Continuous uptake of acoustic cues in spoken word recognition. *Perception & Psychophysics, 41,* 262-275.

Wason, P. C. (1960). On the failure to eliminate hypotheses in a conceptual task. *Quarterly Journal of Experimental Psychology, 12,* 129-140.

Wason, P. C., & Johnson-Laird, P. N. (1972). *Psychology of reasoning: Structure and content.* Cambridge, MA: Harvard University Press.

Wason, P. C., & Shapiro, D. (1971). Natural and contrived experience in a reasoning problem. *Quarterly Journal of Experimental Psychology, 23,* 63-71.

Waters, G. S., & Seidenberg, M. S. (1985). Spelling-sound effects in reading: Time-course and decision criteria. *Memory & Cognition, 13,* 557-572.

Watson, A. B., & Pelli, D. G. (1983). Quest: A Bayesian adaptive psychometric method. *Perception & Psychophysics, 33,* 113-120.

Watson, J. B. (1913). Psychology as the behaviorist views it. *Psychological Review, 20,* 158-177.

Waugh, N. C., & Norman, D. A. (1965). Primary memory. *Psychological Review, 72,* 89-104.

Wegel, R. L. (1932). Physical data and physiology of excitation of the auditory nerve. *Annals of Otology, Rhinology, and Laryngology, 41,* 740-779.

Weimer, W. B. (1979). *Notes on the methodology of scientific research.* Hillsdale, NJ: Lawrence Erlbaum.

Weiner, B. (1986). *An attributional theory of motivation and emotion.* New York: Springer-Verlag.

Weingartner, H., Miller, H., & Murphy, D. L. (1977). Mood-state-dependent retrieval of verbal associations. *Journal of Abnormal Psychology, 86,* 276-284.

Wertheimer, M. (1987). *A brief history of psychology.* New York: CBS College Publishing.

Werner, H. (1957). *Comparative psychology of mental development.* New York: International Universities Press.

Wever, E. G. (1949). *Theory of hearing.* New York: Wiley.

Wheeler, D. D. (1970). Processes in word recognition. *Cognitive Psychology, 1,* 59-85.

Wickelgren, W. A. (1972). Trace resistance and decay of long-term memory. *Journal of Mathematical Psychology, 9,* 418-455.

Wickens, C. D. (1980). The structure of attentional resources. In R. S. Nickerson (Ed.), *Attention and performance VIII.* Hillsdale, NJ: Lawrence Erlbaum.

Wickens, C. D., Sandry, D. L., & Vidulich, M. (1983). Compatibility and resource competition between modalities of input, central processing, and output. *Human Factors, 25,* 227-248.

Wilkening, F., & Lange, K. (1987). When is children's perception holistic? Goals and styles in processing multidimensional stimuli. Unpublished paper. To appear in T. Globerson & T. Zelniker (Eds.), *Cognitive style and cognitive development.* Norwood, NJ: Ablex.

Willows, D. M., & Houghton, H. A. (1987). *The psychology of illustration: Basic research* (Vol. 1). New York: Springer-Verlag.

Wilson, W. R. (1975). *Unobtrusive induction of positive attitudes*. Unpublished doctoral dissertation.

Wilson, W. R. (1979). Feeling more than we can know: Exposure effects without learning. *Journal of Personality and Social Psychology, 37*, 811-821.

Winnick, W. A., & Daniel, S. A. (1970). Two kinds of response priming in tachistoscopic recognition. *Journal of Experimental Psychology, 84*, 74-81.

Winnick, W. A., & Rosen, B. E. (1966). Shape-slant relations under reduction conditions. *Perception & Psychophysics, 1*, 157-160.

Winston, P. H. (1977). *Artificial Intelligence*. Reading, MA: Addison-Wesley.

Wittgenstein, L. (1953). *Philosophical investigations* (G. E. M. Anscombe, Trans.). New York: Macmillan.

Woodworth, R. S. (1938). *Experimental psychology*. New York: Holt.

Young, P. (1987). *The nature of information*. New York: Praeger Publishers.

Yost, W. A., & Watson, C. S. (Eds.). (1987). *Auditory processing of complex sounds*. Hillsdale, NJ: Lawrence Erlbaum.

Zadeh, L. A. (1965). Fuzzy sets. *Information and Control, 8*, 338-353.

Zadeh, L. A. (1982). A note on prototype theory and fuzzy sets. *Cognition, 12*, 291-297.

Zadeh, L. A. (1984). Making computers think like people. *IEEE, 21*, 26-32.

Zajonc, R. B. (1980). Feeling and thinking: Preferences need no inferences. *American Psychologist, 35*, 151-175.

Figure Credits

Name Index

Page numbers in italics indicate names listed in references.

Adams, M. J., 435, *459*
Adesman, P., 396, *467*
Adler, H. E., *466*
Aguilonius, F., 270
Akorn, M. B., 22
Alcorn, M. B., *474*
Allport, A., 457-458, *459, 487*
Allusi, E .A., 164, *480*
Amrhein, P. C., 20, *486*
Anderson, I. H., 435, *459*
Anderson, J. A., 17, *470*
Anderson, J. R., 325, 333, 455, 458, *459, 466*
Anderson, N. H., 102, 122, 231-232, 244, 246-249, 388-389, *459*
Angell, J. R., 41
Annett, J., 456, *459*
Anrep, G. V., *480*
Anscombe, E. M., *489*
Aristotle, 6, 25, 36, 46, 320, 372
Armstrong, S. L., 322-323, *459*
Asch, S. E., 390, *459*
Ashby, F. G., 20, 457, *460, 486*
Aslin, R. N., 457, *460*
Atkinson, R. C., 106, 160, *472*
Attneave, F., 373, *460*
Austin, G., 320, *463*

Baars, B. J., 455, *460*
Bacon, F., 82
Bacon, R., 284
Baddeley, A. D., 349-350, 439, *460*
Bahrick, L. E., 306, *460*
Baily, C. N., *473*
Baird, J. C., 457, *460*
Baldwin, J. M., 41

Ballard, J. G., 193, *460*
Barber, T. X., 9, 90, *460*
Barclay, J. R., 419, *460*
Bartlett, F. C., 373, *460*
Battig, W. F., 179, 320, *460*
Baumal, R., 449, *487*
Baumgardner, M. H., 456, *469*
Bayes, T., 327-328, 388
Beaton, A., 382, *460*
Bechtel, W., 456, *460*
Beck, J., 274, 276, *460*
Becker, C. A., 321, 448, *460*
Becklen, R., 306, *479*
Beethoven, L. van, 5
Bell, A. M., 113, 122, *465, 484*
Berkeley, G., 8-9, 25, 71-72
Berkson, W., 456, *461*
Bernini, G., 29-30, *470*
Bernoulli, D., 386, *461*
Bessel, F. W., 132
Bevan, W., 164, *466*
Bever, T. G., 399, *467*
Bias, R. G., 86, 221-222, 446, *477*
Biederman, I., 318, *461*
Bieri, P., 15-16, *461*
Birdsall, T. G., 211, 226-229, *480, 486*
Birnbaum, M. H., 381-382, 389, 457, *461*
Bjork, R. A., 351, 458, *482*
Blakemore, C., 455, *461, 484*
Bland, D. E., 309, *461*
Blumenthal, A. L., 27, *461*
Blumstein, S. E., 425, *461*
Bobrow, D. G., 305, 307-308, *479*
Boff, K. R., 457, *461, 463, 472, 486*
Bonnano, G. A., 382, *461*

Boring, E. G., 27, 272-273, 275, 277, 286, 313, 455, *461, 466, 470, 483*
Borromini, F., 281
Boster, J. S., 457, *461*
Bouma, H., *475, 478*
Bourne, L. E., 277, 455, *462, 474*
Bouwhuis, D. G., *475*
Bower, G. H., 325, 377, 379-380, *462, 464, 476, 486*
Boyle, J. M., 321, *483*
Bradley, D. C., 425, *462*
Bransford, J. D., 452-453, *462*
Brentano, F., 27, 33, *481*
Bridgeman, B., 455, *462*
Broadbent, D. E., 291-297, 299-305, 307-308, 341, 344-345, 422, *462, 478*
Brody, N., 381, *484*
Bromley, D. B., 456, *462*
Brooks, L., 324, 444, *462*
Brown, R., 106, 169, 356-358, *463*
Broz, J., 456, *463*
Bruner, J. S., 83, 320, 437, *463, 477*
Brunn, J. L., 458, *466*
Bruno, F. J., 454, *463*
Bruno, N., 271, *463*
Busemeyer, J. R., 325, *463*
Bush, R. R., 316, *463*
Buxton, C. E., 455, *463*

Cacioppo, J. T., 458, *480*
Calfee, R. C., 456, *463*
Campbell, D. T., 13, 82, 114, *463*
Carpenter, P. A., 434, 448, 458, *472, 482*
Carr, T. H., 18, *463*
Carroll, L., 425
Carterette, E. C., 329, *459, 463*
Cason, H., 380, *463*
Castellan, N. J., *468*
Cattell, J. M., 42, 59, 139, 433, *463*
Cavett, D., 392
Caws, P., 45, *463*
Chandler, J. P., 209, 329, *463*
Charness, N., 396-397, *463*
Chase, W. G., 316, 395-397, *464*
Checkosky, S. F., 152
Cherniak, C., 458, *464*

Cherry, E. C., 296-297, *464*
Christensen, L. B., *464*
Churchill, W., 18
Churchland, P. S., 455, *464*
Churchman, C. W., 89, *464*
Clapper, J. P., 325, *464*
Clark, D. M, 379, *464,*
Clark, M. S., *462,*
Cleveland, W. S., 100, 456, *464*
Clifton, C., 223, *465*
Cohen, D., 34, *464*
Cohen, J., 392, *464*
Cohen, P. R., 379, *462*
Cohen, M. M., 108, 111, 115, 117, 122
Cole, J., 337, *488*
Cole, R. A., 425-426, *464*
Collins, A. M., 359-361, *464*
Coltheart, M., 458, *464*
Conant, J. B., 80, *464*
Conrad, C. E. H., 361-362, *464*
Consedine, C. E., 151, *483*
Coombs, C. H., 59, *464*
Cooper, F. S., 415, *467, 474*
Copperman, P., 431, *464*
Corballis, M. C., 165, *464*
Corbett, A., 178, *464*
Coren, S., 457, *464-465*
Cornine, C. M., 223, *465*
Cornsweet, T. N., 186, *465*
Corsini, R. J., 454, *465*
Cosky, M. J., 445, 451, *468-469*
Cotton, S., 427, *465*
Cowan, N., 416, *465*
Craik, F. I. M., 348-349, *460, 465*
Creelman, C. D., 186, *486*
Crowder, R. G., *465*
Crusoe, R., 260
Cummins, R., 18, 456, *465*
Cunningham, B., 263, 267
Cutting, J. E., 271, 457, *463, 465*

Dallas, M., *471*
Daniel, S. A., 447, *489*
Darley, J. M., 29, *473*
Darwin, C., 14, *482*
Davies, D. R., *485*

Dawkins, R., 19, *465*
Day, R. H., 151, 457, *477*
Dearborn, W. F., 435, *459*
Defoe, D., 260
Dell, G. S., 458, *477*
Denes, P. B., 400, 410, *465*
Descartes, R., 6-8, 11, 81, 268
Deutsch, D., 299, 302, *465*
Deutsch, J. A., 299, 302, *465*
Dewey, G. I., 325, *463*
Disney, W., 380
Dodge, R., 433, 436
Doherty, M. E., 86-87, *465, 478*
Dominowski, R. L., 391, 393, 455, *462, 465-466*
Donaldson, W., *486*
Donders, F. C., 36, 42, 129, 133-139, 141-142, 146-147, 149-150, 154, 163-165, 172, 176, 181, 309, *462-463, 465, 485*
Dornic, S., *464, 472, 477*
Duncan, J., 157, 197, 310, *465*
Dunn, J. C., 458, *465*
Dziadosz, G. M., 69-71, *483*

Ebbinghaus, H., 31-33, 357, 455, 458, *465, 468, 472, 481, 484*
Egeth, H. E., 164, 174-175, *466, 483*
Eimas, P. D., 419, *466*
Einstein, A., 154, 455
Ekstrand, B. R., 391, 393, *465-466*
El-Zahhar, N., 22, *474*
Elio, R., 325, *466*
Ellis, A. W., 46-47, *466*
Elman, J. L., 424, *476*
Elmes, D. G., 456, *472*
Epstein, W., 276-277, *466, 470*
Erdmann, B., 433, 436
Ericsson, K. A., 31, *466*
Escher, M. C., 77, *470*
Estes, W. K., 325, 328, 458, *466, 469*
Evans, C. R., 259, *466*

Falmagne, J., 457, *466*
Fantz, R., 72, *466*
Farley, F., 456, *466*

Fechner, G. T., 181-183, 185-189, 191-195, 197-199, 209, 223, 232, 236-241, *466, 483*
Feldman, J. A., 17, *467*
Feyerabend, P. K., 456, *467*
Fink, T. E., 393, *467*
Fiske, S. T., *462*
Flanagan, O. J., 455, *467*
Flavell, J. H., *468*
Flower, L. S., 93-94, *470*
Fode, K. L., 90, *483*
Fodor, J., 18, 399, *467*
Foley, C. M., 337, *488*
Forster, K. I., 424-425, 448, *462, 467*
Foss, D. J., 458, *467*
Fourier, C., 402
Fox, W. C., 211, *480*
Frauenfelder, U. H., *462, 475*
Freedman, J. L., 365, *473*
Freud, S., 6, 16, 27, 36-37, 193, *467, 484*
Frey, P. W., 396, *467*
Fried, L. S., 324-325, *467*
Friedman, M. P., 329, *459, 463*
Frijda, N. H., 379, *467*
Fromkin, V. A., 37, 46, 317, 458, *467, 475*
Fromm, E, *460*

Galanter, E., 228, 316, *463, 474*
Galileo, G., 25, 36, 59
Gardner, H., 25, 88, 455, *467*
Garrett, M. F., 399, *467*
Garrod, S., 321, *483*
Garvin, E. A., 381, *487*
Geffen, G., 301-303, 305, *486*
Gelade, G., 310-311, *486*
Geldard, F. A., 232, *467*
Gengerelli, J. A., 40, *468*
Gentner, D., 15, *468*
Gescheider, G. A., 457, *468*
Gibson, E. J., 48, 434-435, 439, 457, *468*
Gibson, J. J., 41, 274, 276, *460, 465, 468, 474*
Giere, R. N., 456, *468*
Gigerenzer, G., 458, *468*
Gilligan, S. G., 377, *462*
Girgus, J. S., 457, *464*
Glass, A. L., 337, 363, 425, 455, *468*

Gleitman, H., 322, *459*
Gleitman, L. R., 322, *459*
Globerson, T., *488*
Gluck, M. A., 458, *471*
Glucksberg, S., 329, *477*
Glushko, R. J., 444, *468*
Gogh, V. van, 284
Goguen, J. A., 327, *468*
Goldmeier, E., 39-40, *468*
Goldsmith, R., 314, 373-375, *481*
Goldstein, I. F., 37, *468*
Goldstein, M., 37, *468*
Goodman, N., 15, *468*
Goodnow, J., 320, *463*
Gopher, D., 307, *478*
Gorfein, D. S., 458, *468*
Gott, R. E., 457, *460*
Gough, P. B., 445, 448, 451, *468-469*
Graboi, D., 169-170, *469*
Gray, J., 294-295, *469*
Green, B. F., 455, *471*
Green, D. M., 228, *469*
Greenberg, M. H., *460*
Greenfield, S., 455, *461, 484*
Greeno, J. G., 391, *469*
Greenwald, A. G., 456, *469*
Gregg, L. W., 93, *461, 469-470*
Gregory, M., 295, 344-345, *462*
Gregory, R. L., 255, 260-261, 274, 286-287,
    454-455, *469, 487*
Griswold, B. B., 391, *477*
Groen, M., 169, *473*
Groff, P., 435, *469*
Groot, A. D., 394-395, *465*
Grosjean, F., 426-427, *465, 469*
Grudin, J., 15, *468*
Guetzkow, H., *459*

Haber, R. N., 357, *469*
Hadamard, J., 455, *469*
Hagen, M. A., 457, *469*
Hamill, R., 390, *469*
Hamlet, 341
Hammond, M., 48, 439, *468*
Hampton, J. A., 322, *469*
Harcum, E. R., 68, *469*

Harlow, H. F., 91, 106, *469*
Harnad, S., 458, *469, 476*
Harris, S., 83
Hary, J. M., 329, 332, *476*
Hasher, L., 351, *471*
Hatfield, G., 277, *466, 470*
Haydon, M., 456, *485*
Hayes, J. R., 93-94, *470*
Healy, A. F., 455, *462*
Hearnshaw, L. S., 455, *470*
Hearst, E., 59-60, *470*
Hecht, S., 51-55, *470*
Heider, F. K., 378, *470*
Heider, G. M., 378, *470*
Held, A., 279-280
Helmholtz, H. von, 133-134, 273-274, 276,
    470-471
Henley, N. M., 250-252, *470*
Heraclites, 313
Hestand, J., 48-49, *476*
Heuer, H., 455, *459, 470, 479-480*
Hibbard, H., 29, *470*
Hick, W. E., 22, *470, 474*
Hilgard, E. R., 41, 455, *470*
Hill, M. D., 307, *472*
Hillinger, M. L., 446, *477*
Hinton, G. E., 17, 333, *470*
Hintzman, D. L., 325, *470*
Hipparchus, 240
Hirsch, A., 133-134
Hirst, W., 455, *470, 474*
Hochberg, J., 274, *470*
Hodge, M. H., 179, *471*
Hoffman, R. R., 458, *468*
Hofstadter, D. R., 324, *470*
Hogarth, R. M., 280-281, 384, 458, *470*
Holender, 458
Holly-Wilcox, P., 451, *469*
Holway, A. H., 272-273, 275, 277, *470*
Holyoak, K. J., 324-325, 363, 455, *467-468*
Homa, D., 324, *471*
Houghton, H. A., 456, *468, 471, 480, 489*
Howes, D. H., *466*
Hubel, D., 317, *471*
Huey, E. B., 433, 435, *471*
Huff, D., 100, *471*

Hull, C. L., 40, *468*
Hulse, S. H., 455, *471*
Hume, D., 25, 79-80
Hunt, K. P., 179, *471*
Hurvich, L. M., 274, *471*

Irwin, D. E., 456, *477*

Jackendoff, R., 455, *471*
Jacoby, L. L., 353-355, *471*
Jagacinski, R. J., 307, *472*
Jakimik, J., 425-426, *464*
James, H., 6
James, W., 5-6, 8, 12, 26, 41, 59, 132, 169,
    260, 291, 293, 310-311, 337, 433, 454,
    463, 471, 474
Jameson, D., 274, *471*
Jastrzembski, J. E., 49, *476*
Javal, E., 433
Johnson, M. K., 351, 427, *462, 471*
Johnson, R., 452, *487*
Johnson, S., 8-9
Johnson-Laird, P. N., 84-86, 455, *471, 488*
Johnston, J. C., 441, *471*
Jolicoeur, P., 458, *471*
Jones, C. J., 378, *487*
Jones, G. V., 358, *471*
Jones, M. R., 307, *472*
Jones, R. D., 321, *476*
Juola, J. F., 160, *472*
Jurine, L., 57
Jusczyk, P. W., 15, 458, *472, 477*
Just, M. A., 6, 385, 397, 434, 448, 458, *472,
    482*

Kahneman, D., 305, 308, 386-388, *472, 487*
Kanizsa, G., 282, 284-285, *472*
Kant, I., 26, 433
Kantowitz, B. H., 456, *472*
Katz, A. N, 458, *460, 475*
Katz, H. A, 458, *460, 475*
Kauff, D. M., 381, *484*
Kaufman, L., 285-286, 289, 457, *461, 463,
    472, 482*
Kavanagh, J. F., *462, 468*
Keele, S. W., 456, *472*

Keesey, U. T., 257, *472*
Kelley, C. M, 354-355, *471*
Kelley, H. H, 89, *472*
Kemler, D. G., 337, *472, 485*
Kent, R. D., 416, *465*
Keppel, G., 343-344, *472*
Killion, T. H., 321, *460*
Kilmann, R. H., 88, *478*
Kimchi, R., 18, 455, *480*
Kinnebrook, D., 131-132
Kintsch, W., 455, *472*
Kirsner, K., 458, *465*
Klapp, S. T., 307, *472*
Klatt, D. H., 115, 122, 458, *480*
Klatzky, R. L., 160, 458, *472*
Klein, W., 169, 415, *473*
Kleinbeck, U., *459*
Kling, J. W., *470*
Knapp, T. J., 455, *473, 480*
Knight, R. G., 151, *483*
Koffka, K., 38, 40, 274, 276, *468, 473*
Kohler, W., 38, *473*
Kolers, P. A., *478*
Kosslyn, S. M., 458, *471, 474*
Kounios, J., 456, *477*
Kovach, J. K., 25, *478*
Krathwohl, D. R., 456, *473*
Krebs, M. J., 456, *486*
Krech, D., 15, *473*
Kristofferson, A. B., 169, *473*
Kristofferson, M. W., 165, 169, *473*
Krueger, L. E., 175, *484*
Kruskal, J. B., 249, *473*
Kubovy, M., 457, *473*
Kuhn, T. S., 154, 456, *473*
Kunst-Wilson, W. R., 381, *473*
Kvaraceus, W., 431, *473*

Labov, W., 334-335, *473*
Ladefoged, P., 411, *473*
La Heij, W., 165, *487*
Lakoff, G., 457, *473*
Landauer, T. K., 365, *473*
Lange, K., 337, 339, *488*
Langfeld, H. S., *461*
Langford, S., 358, *471*

Lasker, G. W., *479*
Lass, N. J., *476, 482*
Latane, B., 29, *473*
Lawson, E. A., 302-303, 305, *474*
Lazar, R., 166, *479*
Lazarus, J. H., 420, *480*
Lazarus, R., 458, *474*
LeDoux, J. E., 455, *474*
Leavitt, L. A., *465*
Leibniz, G. W., 7-8, 11, 27
Leibowitz, H. W., 277, *474*
Leippe, M. R., 456, *469*
Leon, M., 102, 388-389, *474*
Leonard, J. A., *467, 474*
Leonardo da Vinci, 37, *467, 484*
Lesgold, A. M., 316, 431, *474*
Levin, H., 434-435, *468*
Levine, N. P., 263, *472, 483*
Levitt, H., 186, 416, *474*
Levy, E. I., 357, *481*
Levy-Berger, G., 456, *485*
Lewicki, P., 16, *474*
Liberman, A. M., 257-258, 415-416, 425, *474*
Lichtenstein, R., 260-261
Lincoln, A, 203, *472*
Linker, E., 228, *474*
Linnaeus, 46
Lipscomb, C., 321, *476*
Lloyd, B. B., 342, *462, 482*
Locke, J., 25-26
Lockhart, R. S., 348, *460, 465*
Loftus, E. F., 70, 455, *462, 474*
Lombardo, T. J., 457, *474*
Longstreth, L. E., 22, *474*
Lopes, L. L., 385, *474*
Lovie, A. D., 291, *474*
Lucas, P. A., 49, *476*
Luce, R. D., 157, 197, 205, 316, 331, 333-
    334, 456, *463, 474*
Ludlam, G., 325, *470*
Lupker, S. J., 458, *475*
Lyons, W., 455, *475*

MacKay, D. G., 46, 98, 298, 458, *459, 475,*
    487
MacKay, D. M., 259, *475*

Magritte, R., 16
Mandler, G., 382-383, 449, *475, 487*
Manicas, P. T., 59, *475*
Marcel, A. J., 458, *475*
Marcus, N., 164, *466*
Marcus, S. L., 85, *482*
Marin, O. S. M., *481*
Markman, E. M., *468*
Marks, L. E., 241-242, *475, 485*
Marr, D., 457, *475*
Marsden, R. P., 259, *466*
Marslen-Wilson, W. D., 120, 122, 423-426,
    428, *475, 488*
Martin, D. W., 456, *475*
Martin, Z. E., 307, *472*
Maskelyne, N., 131-132
Massaro, D. W., 15, 20, 48-49, 108-123, 171,
    287-288, 321-322, 329-332, 346, 348,
    416-417, 420, 425, 437-438, 446, 455,
    465, 475-476, 479, 487
Matlin, M. W., 380, *476*
Mattingly, I. G., *468*
Mayer, R. E., 263, 394, 458, *476*
Mayzner, M. S., 391, *476*
McCain, G., 88, 456, *476*
McClelland, J. L., 153-154, 333, 424, 441,
    444, 457, *471, 476-477, 483*
McCloskey, M., 329, 367-369, *477*
McCusker, L. X., 446, *477*
McDonald, J. E., 448, *480*
McKenzie, B. E., 457, *477*
McKoon, G., 223, 355, 458, *477, 481*
McNeill, D., 356-358, *463*
Medin, D. L., 324-325, 457, *463, 477, 484*
Mehler, J., 15, *477*
Mellers, B. A., 381-382, 389, *461*
Mendelsohn, G. A., 391, *477*
Mervis, C. B., 320, 322, 369, 457, *477, 482*
Meyer, D. E., 321, 365, 456, *473, 477*
Meyer, G. E., 457, *480*
Miller, A. I., 98, *477*
Miller, G. A., 412, 417-418, 437, 439, 441,
    470, 477
Miller, H., 379, *488*
Miller, J., 154, 456, *477*
Millodot, M., 259-260, *478*

Minsky, M., 17, 59, 457, *478, 481*
Mitroff, I. I., 77, 87-88, *478*
Monet, C., 260-261
Montague, W. E., 179, 320, *460*
Monteiro, K. P., 377, *462*
Montgomery, A., 378, *487*
Moore, M. E., 228, *474*
Moray, N., 297, 302-303, *478*
Moreland, R. L., 381, *478*
Morton, J., 15, 422, 447-448, *477-478*
Mostofsky, P. I., *462*
Motley, M. T., 38, *478*
Muise, G., 277, *466*
Murphy, D. L., 379, *488*
Murphy, G., 25, *478,*
Murray, D. J., 458, *468*
Mussen, P. H., *468, 480*
Mynatt, C. R., 86-87, *465, 478*

Nachmias, J., 229, *478*
Nakamura, Y., 382, *475*
Navon, D., 307, *478*
Neisser, U., 59, 166-169, 304-306, 308, 452, 457, *460, 478-479*
Nelson, T. O., 15, 350, *479*
Neuman, A. E., 277
Neumann, O., 457, *476, 479*
Newell, A., 17, *479*
Newman, C. W., 417, *479*
Newsome, S. L., 448, *480*
Newton, I., 59, 154, 313
Nickerson, R. S., 357, *479, 488*
Nisbett, R. E., 29, 88, 390, *469, 479*
Nitsch, K. E., 453, *462*
Norman, D. A., 37, 46, 231, 244, 297-300, 305, 307-308, 345-348, *479, 488*
Novick, R., 166, *479*
Null, C. H., 456, *466*
Oden, G. C., 330-331, 334-336, 425, 458, *476, 479*
Ogden, G. D., 164, *480*
Oppenheimer, J. R., 82, *480*
Osherson, D. N., 458, *485*
Osman, A. M., 456, *477*
Osser, H., 48, 439, *468*
Othello, 82

Owens, D. A., 268, *480*

Paap, K. R., 448, *480*
Paivio, A., 357, 380, *480*
Palmer, S. E., 18, 455, *480*
Papert, S., 17, 457, *478*
Park, J. N., 276, *466*
Pavlov, I. P., 33, 34, *480*
Pelli, D. G., 186-187, *480, 488*
Perfetti, C. A., 18, *480*
Perkell, J. S., 458, *480*
Perrig, P., 458, *480*
Perrig, W. J., 458, *480*
Perrin, N. A., 457, *460*
Perrott, D. R., 309, *461*
Peterson, L. R., 342-343, 345, 396, *480*
Peterson, M. J., 342-343, 345, 396, *480*
Peterson, W. W., 211, *480*
Petry, S., 457, *480*
Petty, R. E., 458, *480*
Piaget, J., *480*
Pick, A. D., 48, 439, *468, 487*
Pickett, J. M., 425, *481*
Pieters, J. P. M., 456, *480*
Pillsbury, W. B., 433, 436-437, 441, *480*
Pinson, E. N., 400, 410, *465*
Pirenne, M. H., 51, 55, *470*
Pisoni, D. B., 417, 420, 427, *468, 480, 483*
Plato, 5-6, 11, 255, 371-372
Platt, J. R., 80-81, 91, *480-481*
Plomp, R., 415, *473*
Polanyi, M., 89, *481*
Pollack, I., 111, 425, *481*
Pols, L. C. W., 415, *473*
Popper, K. R., 79-81, *461, 463, 481*
Porac, C., *465*
Porter, E., 380
Posner, M. I., 310, 373-375, *481*
Postman, L., 31, 357, 437, *477, 481*
Potter, M. C., 83, 357, *463, 481*
Potts, G. R., *468*
Pratkanis, A. R., 456, *469*
Premack, D., 458, *481*
Pribram, K. H., 455, *481*
Prinz, W., 458, *459, 487*
Professor Backwards, 416

Professor Spooner, 46
Prosek, R., 378, *487*
Ptolemy, 284, *483*
Pylyshyn, Z. N., 458, *481*

Quillian, M. R., 359-361, *464, 481*

Rabbitt, P. M. A., *464, 477*
Rancurello, A. C., 27, 455, *481*
Raphael, B., 17, *481*
Ratcliff, R., 223, 355-356, 456-458, *477, 481*
Reason, J. T., 46, *481*
Reber, A. S., 454, *481*
Redi, F., 56
Reed, A. V., 176-177, *481*
Reicher, G. M., 439-443, *482*
Reid, T., 26, 273
Repp, B. H., 420, *482*
Requin, J., *483*
Rescorla, R. A., 455, *482*
Restle, F., 289, *482*
Richards, R. J., 455, *482*
Richardson-Klavehn, A., 458, *482*
Riggs, L. A., *470*
Riley, B., 263
Rips, L. J., 85, 364, *482, 485*
Robertson, L. C., 455, *473, 480*
Robinson, J. P., 260, 431, *482*
Rock, I., 274, 285-286, 289, 313-315, *482*
Rodman, R., 317, 458, *467*
Roediger, H. L., 456, 458, 472, *482*
Ronning, R. R., 392, *482*
Rosch, E., 314, 320, 322, 369, 457, *462, 477,
　　482*
Rosen, B. E., 276, *489*
Rosenbaum, D. A., 154, *482*
Rosenblatt, F., 17, *482*
Rosenblith, W. A., *485*
Rosenthal, R., 90, *482-483*
Rosenzweig, S., 182, *483*
Rosinski, R. R., 48, 263, *483*
Ross, G. M., 284, 359, *483*
Ross, H. E., 284, 359, *483*
Rubens, P. P., 266, 270
Ruddy, M. G., 321, *477*
Rumelhart, D. E., 333, 444, 457, *476-477, 483*

Russell, P. N., 151-152, *483*

Sacks, O., 313, *483*
St. Ambrose, 432
St. Anne, 37
St. Augustine, 46, 432
St. Theresa, 29-30
Salasoo, A., 427, *483*
Salthouse, T. A., 171, *483*
Samuelson, P. A., 385, *483*
Sanders, A. F., 154, 455, *459, 470, 476, 479-
　　480, 483*
Sandry, D. L., 307, *488*
Sanford, A. J., 321, *483*
Santee, J.L., 174-175, *483*
Sattath, S., 457, *483*
Schaeffer, B., 363, *483*
Schaffer, M. M., 324, *477*
Schaller, M. J., 69-71, 74-75, *483*
Scheerer, E., 458, *459, 487*
Scherr, C. K., 378, *487*
Schiavo, M. D., 87, *465*
Schilpp, P., *463*
Schmidt, K., *459*
Schneider, W., 167, 169, 310, 456, *484*
Scholz, R., 321, *476*
Schopenhauer, A., 27
Schouten, M. E. H., 458, *484*
Schulz, R. W., 32, 357, *487*
Schvaneveldt, R. W., 321, 448, *477, 480*
Schwartz, F., 313, *482*
Schweickert, R., 457, *484*
Scott, B., 425, *464*
Seamon, J. G., 381-383, *484*
Searle, J., 455, *484*
Secord, P.F., 59, *475*
Segal, E. M., 88, 456, *476*
Seidenberg, M. S., 114, 122, 446, *488*
Selfridge, O. G., 318, 331, *484*
Seurat, G., 260
Shallo, J., 313, *482*
Shankweiler, D. P., 416, *474*
Shannon, C. E., 20, 437, 439, *484*
Shapiro, D., 85, *488*
Shapiro, M., 37, *484,*
Shapiro, R. G., 175, *484,*

Sharon, A. T., 431-432, *484*
Shaughnessy, J. J., 456, *484*
Shaw, R., *465*
Shebo Van Zandt, B. J., *475*
Shepard, R. N., 357, *484*
Sheperd, J. C., 107
Shepp, B. E., 337, *484*
Shiffrin, R. M., 106, 167, 169, 310, 456, *484*
Shlaer, S., 51, 55, *470*
Shoben, E. J., 364, *485*
Shor, R. E., *460*
Shuy, R. W., *473*
Sidman, M., 376, *484*
Simon, H. A., 17, 31, 316, 395-397, *464, 466,*
    478-479, 484
Skinner, B. F., 25, 34, 36, *484*
Slamecka, N. J., 455, *484*
Smith, E. E., 363-365, 367-369, 457-458,
    484-485
Smith, F., 431, *485*
Smith, L. B., 337, 457 *460, 472, 485*
Smith, M., 191-192, 203-204, 207-209, *485*
Snodgrass, J. G., 456, *485*
Snow, J., 46
Solso, R. L., 303, 455, *485*
Sommer, L., *461*
Southall, J. C. C., *470*
Spallanzani, L., 56-57, 61, 87
Spelke, E. S., 306, 457, *468, 485*
Sperling, G., 61, 65-66, 310, 396, *485*
Spitzer, J. B., 417, *479*
Stang, D. J., 380, *476*
Stanovich, K. E., 18, *485*
Stefanski, R., 16
Steinberg, E. R., 93, *469-470*
Steinman, R. M., 229, *478*
Stelmach, G. E., *483*
Sterling, S., 324, *471*
Sternberg, S., 18, 141-142, 150, 152, 154,
    157-158, 160-167, 169, 176, 181, 245,
    351-352, 367, 456, *480, 485*
Stevens, J. C., 241, *485*
Stevens, K. N., 425, *461,*
Stevens, R., *481,*
Stevens, S. S., 56, 241, 243, *485*
Stevenson, H., *466*

Stilling, N. A., 382, *461*
Strachey, J., *467*
Stroop, J. R., 175, 431, *484-485*
Strunk, W., Jr., 93, 106, *486*
Studdert-Kennedy, M., 416, *474*
Swets, J. A., 211, 222, 226-229, *469, 486*

Tanner, W. P., 222, 226-229, *486*
Taylor, D. A., 152, *486*
Taylor, G. A., 49, *476*
Taylor, M. M., 186, *486*
Taylor, W. K., 297, *464*
Teasdale, J. D., 379, *464*
Teichner, W. H., 456, *486*
Teller, D. Y., 72-73, *486*
Theios, J., 20, 148, 150, 456, *486*
Thiebaud, W., 262, 264
Thomas, J. P., 26, 327, 457, *461, 463, 472*
Thorndike, E. L., 33, 42
Tighe, T. J., *484*
Titchener, E. B., 27, 38, 40
Toulmin, S., 154, *486*
Townsend, J. T., 20, 456-457, *486*
Treisman, A. M., 297, 301-305, 307-308,
    310-311, *486*
Trepel, L., 324, *471*
Tresselt, M. E., 391, *476*
Tschisch, von, 132-133
Tukey, J. W., 100-101, *486*
Tulving, E., 349, 351, 353, 449-451, 458, *465,*
    482, 486-487
Turvey, M. T., *465*
Tversky, A., 250, 386-388, 457, *472, 483, 487*
Tweney, R. D., 86-87, *465, 478*
Tyler, J. C., 307, *472,*
Tyler, L. K., 428-429, *462, 475, 487*

Uhlarik, J., 427, *487*
Underwood, B. J., 32, 343-344, 357, *472, 481,*
    487

Van der Heijden, A. H. C., 165, *487*
Vanderplas, J. M., 381, *487*
Vasarely, V., 262, 264, 266, 268, 279
Venezky, R. L., 49, 437, 446, *476, 487*
Verwoerd, M., 223, 355, *481*

Vidulich, M., 307, *488*

Wachtel, P. L., 88, *487*
Waite, H., 287-288, *487*
Walden, B. E., 378, *487*
Walker, A. S., 306, *460, 467*
Wallace, R., 363, *483*
Ward, L. M., *465,*
Ward, T. B., 337, *487-488*
Warren, P., 426-427, *470, 488*
Warrick, P., *460*
Warshofsky, F., 56, *485*
Wason, P. C., 84-86, *488*
Waters, G. S., 446, *488*
Watson, A. B., 33-34, 36, 38, 40, 186, 457, *464, 488-489*
Waugh, N. C., 345-348, *488*
Weber, E. H., 232, 235-239
Wedderburn, A., 294-295, *469*
Wegel, R. L., 185, *488*
Wegener, B., *461*
Weimer, W. B., 89, *488*
Weiner, B., 458, *488*
Weingartner, H., 379, *488*
Weisberg, R. W., 393, *467*
Weld, H. P, *461*
Welsh, A., 120, 122, 425, *475*
Welton, K. E., 373-375, *481*
Werner, H., 337, *488*
Wertheimer, M., 38, 455, *488*
Wessels, J., 428-429, *487*
Wettersten, J., 456, *461*
Wever, E. G., 185, *488*
Wheeler, D. D., 440-442, *488*
Wheeler, K. E., 48, *483,*
White, E. B., 93, 106, 255, 263, 403, *486*
Wickelgren, W. A., 178, 356, *464, 488*
Wickens, C. D., 307, *488*
Wiesel, T., 317, *471*
Wilkening, F., 337, 339, *488*
Willows, D. M., 456, *471, 489*
Wilson, E. A., 191-192, 203-204, 207-209, 381, 390, 427, *485,*
Wilson, T. D., 29, 88, 381, 390, *469, 479,*
Wilson, W. R., 381, 390, *489*
Winnick, W. A., 276, 447, *489*

Winston, P. H., 17-18, *463, 466-467, 470, 480, 485, 489*
Wish, M., 249, *473*
Wittgenstein, L., 323-324, *489*
Woloshyn, V., 354, *471*
Woodworth, R. S., 42, 141, 358, *489*
Wrolstad, M. E., *478*
Wundt, W., 26-27, 33, 38, 40-41, 60, 131, 139, 433-435
Wyman, M. J., 329, *463*

Yost, W. A., 457, *489*
Young, P., 431, 455, *489*

Zadeh, L. A., 327, 330, 458, *489*
Zajonc, R. B., 381-383, *473, 478, 489*
Zandt, B. J., 382, *475*
Zangwill, O. L., 454, *469*
Zechmeister, E. B., 456, *484*

Subject Index

A, B, and C tasks, 137-139
Abbreviations, 95, 97, 103-104
    and symbols, 103
Absolute threshold, 189, 234.
        See also Threshold
Abstract, 86, 91, 95, 106-107, 109
ABX task, 419
Accommodation, 258-260, 269
Accuracy, and RT methods compared, 171-175
Acoustic features, 413, 415, 417-418
Acquisition. *See* Learning
Activation-verification model, 448-449
Act psychology, 27
Acuity, 62-64, 67-68, 73, 258
Adaptive methods, 186-187
Additive effects, 144-146, 152, 245
Additive-factor method, 141-154, 161-164, 166, 176, 178, 310, 457
    versus subtractive method, 146-152
Afterimages, 259
Algorithms, 158, 169, 387, 394
    versus heuristics, 394
Allophones, 414
All-or-none learning, 376-377
Alpha blocking, 10-11
Alpha wave, 10-11
Ambiguity, and integrating cues, 269
Ambiguous figures, 28
American Psychological Association.
        See APA
Anagrams, 391-394
    reading of, 437-438
Analogy
    dice game, 212-214
    in science, 81-82
Analysis-by-synthesis, 304, 308

Analysis of variance, 97, 165
Analytic processing, 338
Anchors, 247
Animal space, 251-252
Anticipation errors, 135
APA (American Psychological Association), 93-95, 100, 103-105
    editorial style, 103-107
Apperception, 26-27, 433
A priori probability, 214-217, 222, 228-229, 328, 388-390. *See also* Prior odds
    and payoffs, 228
    of signal, 214
Artificial intelligence, 17, 82, 318
Association, 26, 31, 33, 113, 178-179, 341-343, 347, 349, 357, 458
Astrology, 46-47
Astronomy, 131-132
Attention, 9, 14, 25-27, 98, 169, 290-311, 341, 344, 351, 355, 383, 434, 454, 457
    attenuation, 303
    Broadbent model, 290-293
    Deutsch/Norman model, 299-300
    feature and conjunction search, 310-311
    in infants, 306
    Kahneman model, 305
    location of selective filter, 299-301
    Neisser model, 304
    Norman/Bobrow model, 305, 307
    precueing, 310
    and processing stages, 307-309, 311
    resources, 305, 307
    shadowing, 296-299
    split-span experiments, 293-296
    Treisman model, 303-304
    to unattended channel, 298
    in visual search, 310-311

Attenuation, 303
Attitude of the observer, 191-192
Auditory memory, 341
Auditory perception, 112, 120, 399.
     See also Hearing
Auditory presentation, 136
Author's name, and institutional affiliation, 95
Autonomous-search model, 424-426, 448-449
Availability, 384, 387-388, 390
Averaging, 118, 178

Backward recognition masking
     of shape perception, 276-277
     of speech perception, 417-418
     of tone perception, 308-309
Bar graph, 99, 105
Basilar membrane, 405
Bat navigation, 56, 87
Bayes theorem, 327-328, 388
Becoming famous overnight, 354
Behaviorism, 8, 33-36, 40-41, 91, 291
Between-subject designs, 69
Binary-choice task, 41
Binary digit, 21
Binocular disparity, 265-267
Biofeedback training, 9-11
Bit, 21
Blivet, 277-278
Blocking lexical access, 358
Box graph, 100-101
Boxology. *See also* Information processing
     science of, 18
Brain waves, 10-11, 141
British empiricism, 25, 31, 129, 181
Broadbent and Gregory study, 344
Broadbent model, 291-293
     tests of, 293-299, 301-303
Buffer, 291-294, 299, 422, 449

Cartesian interactionism, 6, 9
Cascade model, 153-155
Categorical perception, 418-421, 424-425
Categorization. *See* Recognition and
     categorization
Category size, 369
Causation, 7, 26, 45, 48, 51, 287

Ceiling effect, 70
Channels, 291-296, 302-304, 308, 341
Chartjunk, 100
Chess, 45, 82, 316-317, 394-397, 431
Choice of stimulus levels, 184
Choice RT task, 136, 146-147, 149
Classical conditioning, 35, 455
Classical psychophysical scaling, 232-233
Classical psychophysics, 181-182
Classical theory, 320
Clicks, 302
CMP. *See* Connectionist model of perception
Cochlea, 405
Cognitive economy, 360-361, 363
Cognitive systems, 382
     versus affective systems, 381-384
Cohort model, 423-424, 448
Competition, 323-324, 342, 345
     in science, 88
Complex cells, 318
Complex sound patterns, 402-403
Comprehension, 49-50, 98, 368-369, 452-453
Computer
     for experimental control, 90,
     as information-processing system, 13-15,
          17-18
Concept learning, 371-372
Concepts and categorization, 319-320, 322
Conceptual codes, 251
Conditional probability, 216
Conditioned response, 35
Conditioned stimulus, 35
Cones, 256
Confidence ratings, 228
Confirmation bias, 82-87, 390
Conflicting results, and distinguishing among
     stages, 345
Confounding, 61, 63-64, 70, 134, 297, 361,
     371
     of category size, 365-367, 369
     of co-occurrence, 361-362
     of familiarity, 367-368
     processes, 63
     of similarity, 363-365
     variables, 61, 63
Confusion matrix, 193-194, 201, 224

Conjunction, 199, 310-311, 330
    search, 310
Connectionist model of perception, 333-334
Consciousness, 8, 11-13, 16, 27, 31, 33-34,
    36, 41, 296
Consistent mapping, 171
Consonant recognition, 415
Consonant sounds, 410-411, 415
Constancy scaling, 284-289
Contemporary psychophysical methods, 185,
    187
Content-addressable search, 160-171
Continuous information, 117, 327, 420-421,
    447-452
Continuous perception, 420, 425
Contrast effect, 246-247
Control group, 56-57, 378
Controlling variables, 62-63
Control manipulations, importance of, 56
Convergence, 171, 260
Cornea, 255-256
Correct rejection, 192
Correlation, 7, 45, 47-50, 173, 228
    coefficient, 50
Counterbalancing, 73, 96, 151, 162, 176
Cover page, 95, 107
CR, 35
Creativity, 13-14
Criterion
    in activation-verification model, 448
    in multistate theory, 211-214
CS, 35
Cued recall, 352
Cues to depth, 235, 261-272, 314-315, 444
Cups and bowls, 334
CV syllables, 116, 415-417

d', 176-179, 222, 225-226, 229, 297-298,
    355-356, 364, 414
    calculation of, 218-221
Dark-adaptation, 52
Data analysis, 25, 39, 83, 88, 176, 178, 192,
    223-224
Data-limited task, 175
dB. *See* Decibel

Dear Aunt Jane task, 295
Debriefing, 96
Decay theory, 341-343, 345
Decibel, 237, 401
    description of, 237
Decision bias, 202, 206-207, 222-223
Decision criterion, 329
Decision process, 130, 197, 205, 348
Decision system, 195, 198-200, 205, 212-217,
    224, 229
Deductive reasoning, 79
Demons, 318, 331
Dependent variables, 33, 61, 95-96, 172, 381
    properties of, 60-61
Detecting mispronunciations, 425-426
Detection
    process, 129-131
    and recognition processes, 308-309
    thresholds for, 190
    time, 144, 146
Deutsch/Norman model, 299-300
    tests of, 301-303
Developmental issues, 68
Development of categorization, 337-339
Dice game, 212-214, 217-218, 219, 221, 224,
    228-229
Dichotic listening, 381
Dimensional processing, 337
Dimensions of science, 91
Discrimination, 73-74, 100, 146, 154-155,
    181, 223, 235-236, 355, 371, 418-420
Discussion section, 97
Dissimilarity ratings, of animals, 250-252
Dissociation method, 352-354, 381-383
Dominant hand, 143-144, 146
Dot chart, 100-101
Dot patterns, 373-375
Double-blind experiment, 72
Double dissociation, 352-353, 381-383
Dreams, 37
D task, 139
Dualism, 5
Dumbbell illusion, 286-287
Duration of mental processes, 128-139
Dynes, 237-238, 401
    description of, 237

Ear, structure of, 405-406
Ecological validity, 60
Editorial style, 103
Embodying, 12
Encoding distinctiveness, 350
English language, 387
Epiphenomenalism, 8-9, 11-12
Episodic memory, 351, 354, 359, 383
    priming of identification, 355
    versus semantic memory, 351-356
Ethics, 88, 384
Ethnography of reading, 431-432
Euclidean space, 250
Evaluation. *See also* Feature evaluation
    in judgment and decision making, 384-386
Evolution, 13
Exemplar-based representation, 324
Exemplar theory, 324
Exhaustive search, 158-159
Expected utility theory, 385-386
Experience, and logic, 390
Experimental control, 56
Experimental design, 13, 32, 61-62, 99, 135,
        182, 346
    and control, 60
Experimental method, 13, 25, 31, 47, 58-75,
        182, 192, 223, 335, 357
External validity, 428
Extrapolation, 66
Eye, structure of, 256
Eye movements, 66-67, 72, 257-260, 306
    accommodation, 258-260
    nystagmus, 257
    in reading, 434
    saccades, 257
    vergence, 260, 268-269

Factorial designs, 151, 244-246, 247, 271,
        329-330
False alarms, 12, 130, 208
Falsification, 20, 79-81, 88, 294, 456
Familiarity, 347, 352, 355, 367-369, 382-383,
        394, 457
Fan effect, 325
Feature analysis, 317-318
Feature and conjunction search, 310-311

Feature evaluation, 330-331
Feature generation, 322
Feature integration, 330-331
Features
    acoustic, 415
    semantic, 364-365
    visual, 277, 288
Feature search, 310
Fechner's model, 191, 236-239, 241. *See also*
        Threshold
Fechner's psychophysical methods, 182-183,
        185, 239
Feedback, 45, 90, 135, 172, 197, 214, 217,
        235, 268, 375, 378, 424
Figure-ground contrast, 62, 64, 257
Figures, 97-101, 104-105, 107,
        illusions in, 102-103
Filter, 291-294, 297, 299, 301, 303-304, 308
Fine-grained analyses, 175, 339
Fire alarm scenario, 130
FLMP. *See* Fuzzy logical model of perception
Floor effects, 186
Footnotes, 105, 107
Forced-choice
    in preferential looking, 72-73
    recognition, 352, 357
    two-alternative, 187
Forgetting, 32-33, 37, 68-69, 298, 341-348,
        356, 359, 396, 441
Formants, 115, 122, 408-409, 415, 419
    description of, 408
Fovea, 256
Foveal vision, 52
Free recall, 345-346, 348-349, 352
Freudian psychology, 36-38
Functional components, 19
Functionalism, 41-42
    and information processing, 41-43
Functional measurement, 231-232, 244-249,
        271
Functional relationship, 29, 33, 45, 51-56, 59,
        62, 65-66, 276
Fuzzy logic, 327, 330, 458
    description of, 327
Fuzzy logical model of perception, 330-333,
        334-337 428, 451-452
Fuzzy truth values, 330

Galilean view, 25
Game playing, 394-397
Gating task, 426-428
General two-state threshold theory, 205-209, 228
  empirical test of, 207-209, 226-229
Generated abstract memory, 372
Geometrical illusions, 286. *See also* Illusions
Gestalt psychology, 38-41
Gray and Wedderburn study, 294-295
Group learning curves, 376
Guessing, 21, 62-63, 65, 69, 73, 203, 222, 226, 228, 269, 391, 439-440

Hand dominance, 143-146
Harmonics, 402, 407-408
Headings, 103-105
Hearing, 57, 87, 121, 176, 183-185, 190, 198, 297, 314, 416
  of bats, 57
  range of, 185
Height in picture plane, 262
Hertz, 402
Heuristics, 387, 390, 394
  versus algorithms, 394
Hierarchical organization, 362
High threshold theory, 199-203, 205-206, 209, 226
  empirical test of, 203-205
Histograms, 99
Hits, 194
Holistic processing, 337-338
Homunculi, 6
Honesty, 69, 223
Horopter, 266-267, 270
Hypnosis, 9, 11, 377
Hypothesis generation, 78
  in reading, 434
Hypothesis testing, 45, 56-57, 79-81

Idealism, 8
Identification. *See* Recognition and categorization
Identification time, 142, 149
Illusions, 277-289, 457
  size-weight, 246-249

Illusory contours, 279, 457
Illusory weight judgments, 246
Immunization, 80
Impossible figures, 277
Impossible scenarios, 280-281
Incremental learning, 375-376
Independent manipulation, 61
Independent processes, 141, 381
Independent variables, properties of, 61
Individual differences, 33, 69, 174, 384
Inductive inference, 273-274, 276
Inductive reasoning, 79
Infants, 71-74, 91, 306
  perception in, 71-75
Inferences, 48, 153, 273
Information, 20-23
Information coming through unattended channel, 296
Information integration, 232
Information processing, properties of, 18-19
Information-processing model, 20
Insofarasicansee, 372-373
Instance generation, 320
Integrating sentential context, 428
Integration, 81, 122, 244, 307, 310, 326-329, 331-332, 338, 420, 428. *See also* Feature integration
  in judgment and decision making, 386
  of multiple sources of information, 386
Interaction
  in additive-factor method, 144-146
  of processes, 371
Interactionism, 6, 11-12
Interactive effects, 144-146, 153
Interference theory, 341-343, 346
Interpolation, 66, 131
Interposition, 262, 271, 314
Interval scale, 232, 244-245
Introspection, 9, 13, 16, 29-31, 33, 139, 193, 455
Introspective method, 26-27, 38, 354
  critique of, 29-31
Introspective reports, 33, 41, 138
Intuitive scientists, 89
Invariance hypothesis, 171, 269, 274-277
Isolating stages, 129

Judgment and decision making, 384-390
    availability, 387-388
    evaluation, 384-385
    experience and logic, 390
    integration, 386-387
    prior odds in, 388-390
    representativeness, 387
Just noticeable difference, 232-241, 243

Kahneman model, 305
Knowledge
    and memory, 397
    of orthographic structure, 436-444
    and perception, 28, 282-283

Language, 14, 18, 26, 49, 98, 108-109, 111-
    114, 122, 296-297, 307, 356, 398-453,
    457-458
Latency. See RT
Lateral interference, 175
Learner's mood, 377-380
Learning
    in cognitive versus affective systems, 381-
        384
    concepts, 371-372
    curves, 376-377
    dot patterns, 373-375
    interaction of processes in, 371
    prototype, 372-375
    to read, 431-432
    to read lips, 378
    state-dependent, 377-380
    temporal course of, 375-377
Learning and thinking, 370-397
Learning concepts, 371-372
Left hemisphere, 382
Letter memory, 344
Letter recognition, 61-66, 174-175, 329-333.
        See also Reading
    developmental issues, 68-69
    and memory, 67-68
    perceptual units in, 441-442
    perceptual versus memory contributions,
        439
    and report, 67-68
    and supraletter features, 435
Levels of inquiry, 15-17,

Levels of processing, 348-350
Light
    description of, 255-256
    physics of, 51, 55
Lighting and shadow, 262
Likelihood ratio, 216
Limited capacity channel, 291-293
Limited capacity processor, 291-294, 299-300
Linear function, 151, 164, 167, 203, 235, 238,
    243
Linear perspective, 262-263
Line drawing, 99
Linguistic context, 121, 425, 427, 429
Lipreading, 108-109, 112, 115-120, 123, 378
Logarithms, 21, 100, 234, 243
    description of, 234
Logogen model, 422-423, 447-448
Long-term memory, 93, 300, 356-357, 359,
    413, 442

Magnitude estimation, 241-244
Magnitude of sensation, 181, 209, 211, 239
Main effect, 70, 96-97
Malleus, 405
Manner of articulation, 410
Manuscript, 94-97, 107
    format, 94-95
Masking, 41, 111, 162, 277, 309, 355, 381,
    417
Materialism, 8-9, 11-12, 181
Measure of decision bias, 221-222
Measure of sensitivity, 197, 200, 202, 206,
    217, 221
Measurement, 31, 52, 56, 59, 104-105, 181,
    231, 234-235, 237-240, 349, 357, 366,
    457
Melodies, 38, 381
Memory, 340-369
    decay theory, 341
    direct versus indirect measures of, 351-352
    episodic versus semantic, 351-356
    interference theory, 342
    levels of processing, 348-350
    long-term, 356-359
    perceptual processing theory of, 347-348
    proactive interference, 343
    and processing capacity 344-345

Memory (*continued*)
    processing for a good memory, 350-351
    and report limitations, 67
    retroactive interference, 342
    stages of processing in, 345, 348
Memory search, 81, 151, 153, 157-166, 168-
        171, 176-177, 319, 325, 352, 369, 456
    revisited, 176
Memory strength, 347-348
Mental image, 13
Mental operations, 12-13, 16, 41-42
Mental processes, 12-13, 15-16, 33-34, 36-37,
        62, 129-131, 138
Mental processing, 11-12, 134
Metaphysics, 6-7, 181
Method of adjustment, 182, 184
Method of constant stimuli, 53-54, 182, 184,
        186, 203, 226
Method of limits, 182-184, 186, 285, 314
Method of magnitude estimation, 244
Method section, 96
Methods of psychological inquiry, 45-57
Middle ear, 405
Mind-body problem, 5-13, 16, 27, 181-182,
        454-455
    dualism, 6
    epiphenomenalism, 8
    idealism, 9-10
    interactionism, 6-7
    materialism, 8
    monism, 12
    parallelism, 7
Mispronunciations, 121, 425-426
Misses, 93, 192
Models, of the sensory system, 198-199
Modifications to keep the observer honest,
        188, 192-193, 195
Modus tollens, 85
Monism, 12
Moon illusion, 283-286
Moral responsibility, 91
Motion parallax, 264-265
Motivation, 40, 151, 173-174, 205, 333
    of observer, 194-195
Müller-Lyer illusion, 277-278, 286-288

Multidimensional scaling, 249-251, 253, 271,
        415
Multiple resource pools, 307
Multistate theory, 211-212, 217, 223, 226,
        228-229, 347, 355. *See also* Theory of
        signal detectability
    and confidence ratings, 228
    and psychometric functions, 226-227
    versus two-state theory, 226-229, 229

Naming and button-pushing tasks, 147-148
Naturalistic observation, 45-47, 59
Neanderthal man, 412
Neisser model, 304-305
Nerve conduction velocity, 133
Network representation, 360-361
Neural models, and metaphors, 15
Noise
    and normal distribution, 190
    in sensory system, 189-190
Nominal scale, 231
Nondominant hand, 143-146
Nonsense syllable, 31-33, 357
Nonspecific episode, 352
Normal curve. *See* Normal distribution
Normal distribution, 55, 189-190, 218-219,
        225
    and z scores, 217-221
Norman/Bobrow model, 305, 307
Nystagmus, 257, 259-260

Ogive curves, 190
Operant conditioning, 35, 74
Operations of mental processes, 140-155
Optical illusions, 277-289
    in figures, 102-103
Optimal performance, 316
Order effects, 147
Ordinal scale, 231-232
Orthographic structure, 437
    controlling for, 446
    measures of, 437-438
Oscilloscope, 10
Overlapping stages, 153. *See also* Cascade
        model

Panum's area, 267
Parallelism, 7-8, 11-12, 27
Parameters, 82, 115, 178, 206-207, 209, 247-248, 250, 313, 330, 332, 451
Parsimony, 38, 78
Pattern recognition, 307, 315-317, 325, 337, 354. *See also* Recognition and categorization
    feature analysis, 317-318
    template matching, 316-317
Payoffs, 130, 197-198, 214, 226, 228-229, 234-235
People as scientists, 84-85, 87
Perceiving letters, 61-65
Perception. *See also* Recognition and categorization
    and knowledge, 28, 260 282-283
    in reading, 441-444
Perceptual bias, 102, 356
    versus response bias, 222-223
Perceptual magnitude and discriminability, 235
Perceptual processing theory, 347
Perceptual processing time, for shape perception, 276-277
Perceptual reports, 39-42,
Perceptual units, 330, 413-418, 424
    in speech, 413-418
Performance slips, 46-47
Peripheral vision, 52
Perspective theory, 286-288
    test of, 287-288
Peterson and Peterson task, 342-343, 345
Phenomenological experience, 16-17, 228, 255, 277, 286, 296
Phonemes, 114, 317, 378, 414-416, 422-424
    description of, 414
    and professor backwards, 416
    table of, 406
Phonetic symbols, table of, 406
Phonological mediation, in reading, 444-446
Photopic vision, 52
Picture memory, 357
Pineal gland, 6
Placebo effects, 9, 11
Platonic dualism, 5
Poggendorf illusion, 277-278

Point of articulation, 411
Point of subjective equality, 233
Pointers and bells, 132-133
Pollyanna principle, 380
Ponzo illusion, 277-278
Population comparisons, 150-152
Potential pitfalls in research, 90-91
Power function, 243
Power spectra, 402-404, 407, 409-410
    description of, 402-404
Practice. *See also* Learning
    in RT tasks, 174
Pragnanz, 38
Precueing detection and recognition, 310
Preferential looking, 72-73
Preperceptual auditory image, 413-414, 418
Preperceptual auditory storage, 413, 418
Prescriptive theory, 384
Priming, 321-322, 352, 355-356
Prior entry, 291
Prior odds, 388-390. *See also* A priori probability
Proactive interference, 343
Probabilistic theory, 323
Probabilistic threshold, 191, 194, 200, 205
Probability and combining events, 199
Probability density, 190, 222
Probability distribution, 99, 189
Probe recall, 345, 351
Probe recognition, 345, 350
Problem solving, 94, 223, 225, 352, 390-394
Processing capacity, 91, 300-302, 304, 308-309, 344, 416
Processing for a good memory, 350-351
Processing well-defined concepts, 322-323
Professor backwards, 416
Projected shape, 276
Properties of dependent variables, 60
Properties of independent variables, 61
Properties of information processing, 19
Prototype learning, 372-375
Prototypes, 330-332, 337, 364, 372-375, 413, 417, 452
Proximity, 38, 250, 265, 396
Psychoanalysis, 37
Psychology of science, 82-83
Psychometric function, 73, 185, 226

Psychophysical methods, 130, 180-195, 232-235, 236
  adaptive procedures, 186-187
  and attitude of observer, 191-192
  category judgments, 240
  choice of stimulus levels, 184-185
  classical, 181-182
  contemporary, 185-188
  Fechner's, 182-185
  functional measurement, 231-232, 244-249
  for infants, 71-74
  magnitude estimation, 241-244
  modifications, 192-194
  and motivation of observer, 194-195
  multidimensional scaling, 249-251, 253, 271, 415
Psychophysical scaling, 232-236, 249, 457
  method of, 232
Psychophysical task. *See* Psychophysical methods
Psychophysics, 34, 73, 181-182, 198, 209, 241, 326, 454, 457
Publication and acceptance, 57

Quality of test stimulus, 162
Quantum theory, 256
Questioning assumptions, 139, 244, 295

Randomization, 61, 73, 96, 141, 173, 176
Rating judgments, 368
Ratio scale, 232, 238
Reaction time. *See* RT
Reading, 430-453
  comprehension in, 452-453
  ethnography of, 431-432
  history of, 432-434
  and knowledge of spelling, 48
  phonological mediation in, 444-446
  redundancy in, 435-437
  research, 50
Reading and writing research reports, 92-122
Receptive field, 318
Recognition and categorization. *See also* Pattern recognition
  binary oppositions in, 319
  classical theory, 320-323

Recognition and categorization (*continued*)
  and concepts, 319
  decision in, 328-329
  and development, 337-339
  evaluation in, 326-327
  exemplar theory, 324
  fuzzy view, 325-337
  holistic versus analytic, 337-339
  integration in, 327-328
  and knowledge, 314
  probabilistic theory, 323-324
  summary descriptions versus exemplars, 324-325
  tests of classical view, 320-321
Recognition and perception, 313-315
Recognition masking. *See* Backward recognition masking
Recognition time, 136, 139, 142, 159, 163
Redundancy, 98, 436, 438, 442
  at recognition stage, 442
  at response selection stage, 442
Reference citations in text, 105
Reference lists, 106
References, 94-95, 97, 105-107, 122, 456
Reflection, 26, 57, 61, 68
Rehearsal, 161, 300, 305, 342-343, 345, 350, 396, 422
Reicher paradigm, 439-444
  two models of, 441-443
Reinforcement, 74
Reliability, 61, 378
Replication, 64, 94, 375
Representativeness, 387, 390
Research reports, 92-126
  figures in, 98-103
  format of, 94-97
  sample paper, 108-126
Resource pools, 307
Response bias, 200, 203
  versus perceptual bias, 222-223
Response compatibility, 141-146
Response interference, 175
Response selection, 130-131, 134-139, 142, 146-148, 154-155, 157-158, 161, 164, 172, 174-175, 245
Response-selection time, 137
Results section, 96

Retention, 31-33, 342-346, 348, 350-351, 357, 359, 371, 373, 380
Retina, 54, 256-259, 265, 318
Retinal size match, 272
Retrieval, 31, 95, 177-179, 352, 354, 358, 371, 379, 382-383, 391-392
    from semantic memory, 177
Retrieval process, 33
Reversibility, 279-280
Right hemisphere, 382-383
ROC curve, 202-205, 207-208, 217-218, 228
Rods, 54-55, 256, 344
RT (reaction time), 105, 128-179 310, 325, 344, 352, 360, 362, 366-369, 392, 456
    and intensity of stimulus, 134
Running head, 107

Saccades, 257, 260. *See also* Saccadic eye movements
Saccadic eye movements, 66, 257, 259, 433
Sample research paper, 107-122, 125
Sampling, 65
Scales, 100, 102, 231-232, 285
    interval, 232
    nominal, 231
    ordinal, 231
    ratio, 232
Scaling psychological processes, 230-252
Scatterplot matrix, 100, 102
Schema, 372-373, 452
Science, dimensions of, 91
Scientific frameworks, 79
Scientific investigation, 77-83
Scientific method, 23, 33, 45, 89
Scientific process, 76-91
Scientists are people, 88-89, 91
Scotopic vision, 52
Seeing light, 51-56
    and dark adaptation, 52
    and development, 69-74
Selective attention, 299, 303-304, 306, 309-310. *See also* Attention
Selective filter, location of, 299-301
Self-terminating search, 160
Semantic features, 322, 363-364
Semantic features model, 363-369

Semantic memory, 26, 160, 352-354, 359, 361, 381. *See also* Episodic memory, versus semantic memory
Sensation, versus perception, 26
Sensation magnitude, 231, 236-237, 239, 241, 243
Sensitivity, measure of, 197, 200, 202, 206, 217, 221
Sensory and decision processes, 196-209
Sensory system, 16, 23, 55, 189, 191-192, 197-200, 205-207, 211-217, 221, 223-226, 228-229, 275-276, 330
Sensory threshold, 182-183, 197
Sentence verification, 321, 325, 367
Sentence verification task, 360-369
    and category size, 365-367, 369
    and co-occurrence, 361-362
    and familiarity, 367-368
    processes in, 63
    and similarity, 363-365
    and typicality, 369
Sentential context, 428-429, 434, 449-452
Serial search, 158-171, 425, 448-449
Seriation, 105
Sexist language, 98
Shadowing, 121, 296-299, 301-305, 381, 426
Shape constancy, 274-277
Short-term memory, 299, 342, 371, 396-397
Short-term store, 291-295
Signal detection, 134, 194, 207, 211-212, 214, 222-223, 228-229, 390
Signal detection task, 192-194, 199, 217, 228, 328
    data analysis, 224-226
    experimental method, 223-224
Signal detection theory. *See* Multistate theory
Signal-to-noise ratio, 111
Similarity, 38-39, 142, 167, 174-175, 250, 324, 337-338, 342, 358, 363-367, 372, 457
Simple RT task, 135
    versus choice RT task, 134-135
Simplicity of figure, 264
Sine waves, 400-403
Single-factor design, 61, 271
Size constancy, 272-273, 284, 286

Size illusion, 314-315
Size in picture plane, 262
Size of the memory set, 161
Size-weight illusion, 246-249
Skilled players, 395
Slips of the mind, 46-47
Slips of the pen, 46-47
Slips of the tongue, 37-38, 46-47
Soul, 5-7, 60, 181, 371
Sound, description of, 399-404
Sound discrimination, 236
Sound spectrogram, 412
Sound spectrograph, 411-412
Specific practice, 169
Speech, organs, 406-408
Speech perception, 108-123, 399, 412-429
    integrating sentential context in, 428-429
    perceptual units in, 413-418
Speech sounds, 113, 406-409, 411, 416, 419
    description of, 406-412
    voiced, 406, 408-409
    voiceless, 408
Speech synthesis, 115
Speed-accuracy trade-off method, 175-179
Spelling. See Orthographic structure
Spelling test, 48-50
Split-span experiments, 293-296
Spread of encoding, 350
Stabilized images, 258-260
Stages between stimulus and response, 197-198
Stages of processing, 13, 129-130
Staircase method, 186
Stars, 46, 48, 131-132, 240, 265, 325, 358
    and category judgments, 240
State-dependent learning, 377-380
Statistical significance, 67, 165
Statistics, 39, 67, 90, 97, 100, 384, 387
STEPIT, 329-330
Sternberg's modification, 141, 163
Sternberg task, 167
Stevens' power model, 241-244
Stimulus intensity, and RT, 134
Stimulus loudness and hand dominance, 143
Stimulus onset asynchrony, 277
Stimulus recognition, 136, 147

Stimulus-response compatibility, 171
Stimulus-response psychology, 34-35, 42
Stimulus set, 154-155, 184, 303
Stop consonants, 411, 419-420
Strong inference, 20, 80-81
Structuralism, 26-27, 29, 41
Structure and process, 359
Structure of semantic memory, 359-369
Studying mental processes, 5-23
Style in science, 91
Subject differences, 64
Subjective recognition, 381
Subjective utility theory, 384-386
Subliminal perception, 193
Subtractive method, 133-139, 146-147, 149,
    151, 163, 165, 176
    and additive-factor methods compared,
        146-151
    criticism of, 138
Surface texture, 263
Switching time, 294-295
Synthesized auditory memory, 420
Synthesized visual memory, 372
Synthetic speech, 112, 116, 417, 419

Tables, 96-97, 105, 107
Tachistoscope, 20, 61, 223, 321, 381, 433,
    439
Target episode, 351-353
Template matching, 316-317
Temporal course of learning, 375-377
Testing theories of attention, 290-311
Theories of word recognition
    in reading, 446-452
    in speech, 421-429
Theory and methods, history of, 26-43
Theory of signal detectability, 55, 210-229,
    328, 355. See also Multistate theory
    decision system, 213-214
    measure of decision bias, 221-222
    measure of sensitivity, 217-221
    sensory system, 211-214
Thinking. See Judgment and decision making;
    Problem solving; Game playing

Threshold, 13, 73, 116, 182-193, 197-209, 211-212, 226-229, 236-238, 422
  and attitude of observer, 191-192
  for detection, 190
  and motivation of observer, 194-195
  variability of, 189-190
Threshold theory, 205, 209, 226, 229
Tip of the tongue, 356, 392. *See also* TOT
Title, 94-95, 105-107, 241, 260
TOT (tip of the tongue), 357-359
Total impression theory, 289
TRACE model, 424
Transition matrices, 201-202, 212
Treisman model, 303-304
Two-alternative forced choice task, 187
Two-factor design, 61, 165, 174
Two levels of selection, 303-304, 308
Two-state theory, 206-207, 209, 228-229
  and confidence ratings, 228
  versus multistate theory, 226-229
  and psychometric functions, 226-227
Tunnel vision and knowledge, 434
Typicality, 320-321, 329, 369, 390, 457
  ratings, 320
Typing format, 107

UCR, 35
UCS, 35
Unattended channels, 303-304
Unconditioned response, 35
Unconditioned stimulus, 35
Unconfounding recognition and memory, 297
Unconscious, 14, 16, 36-37, 273-274
Understanding speech, 398-429
Utility. *See* Subjective utility theory

Validity, 14-15, 60-61, 86
Value of money, 386
Value of signal, 214
Variability, 55, 61, 165, 189, 191, 205, 235, 250, 329, 385
  of light, 55
  of subject, 55
  of the threshold, 189
Variations in memory search, 164, 171
Varied mapping, 170

Verbal learning and memory, 32-33, 357
Vergence, 260, 267-269
  angle of, 271
Verification, 84, 178, 294, 367-369, 425, 448-449
Virtue, 371-372
Vision, 12, 52, 73, 228, 274, 454, 457
Visual acuity, 64, 71-73, 257
Visual angle, 53, 272
Visual detection, 51-52, 222
Visual features, 277, 288
Visual imagery, 380
Visual memory, 347, 357
Visual perception, 12, 132, 254-289
Visual presentation, and RT, 135-136
Visual scanning, 166-167, 169
Visual sensory system, 260
Visual stimulus, 51, 69, 134, 257, 260-261
Vocal cords, 406-408, 410-411
Vowel sounds, 136, 409-411

Warmth sensation, measure of, 241-242
Weber's constant, 236, 238
Weber's law, 235-237, 239
Well-defined concepts, 323
White noise, 403-404, 408
Within-subject designs, 69, 389
Word fragment completion, 352
Word recognition, 42, 48, 122, 305, 421, 423-425, 428, 433, 435, 442-452
  binary contrasts in, 421, 446-447
  and linguistic context, 425-429, 449-453
Words versus rules, 444
Writing, 6, 46-47, 88, 93-95, 97-100, 107, 110, 112-113, 130, 266, 432, 434
  common glitches in, 99
  as problem solving, 93-94
Writing style, 97-98
Written language, 48, 82, 109, 114, 307, 432

Yes-no recognition, 349

A 9
B 0
C 1
D 2
E 3
F 4
G 5
H 6
I 7
J 8